最新
アメリカ英語表現辞典

Dictionary of Current American Spoken English Expressions

市橋敬三 著

大修館書店

はしがき

この辞典について

筆者は，次の2つの理由で長年この辞典を書きたいと思ってきた．

(1) 既刊の辞典は現代英語を反映していない

書店へ行くと，英語の辞典が多数並び，棚を埋めつくしている．しかし筆者の見るところでは，現代アメリカ英語でよく使われている意味・用法が正しく紹介されていないのが実情である．

ここで現代アメリカ英語といっているのは，アメリカの日常会話で広く使われていると共に，*New York Times*, *Washington Post*, *Newsweek* などの一流新聞・雑誌でも使われて確立している意味・用法のことである．

2つほど例をあげよう．

「どこの会社」「どこの銀行」「どこのテレビ局」「どこの店」「どこの国」「どこのチーム」というとき，次のように who で簡単に表すことができるのだが，これまでの多くの辞典ではこのことがわからない．（本書「どこの」の項参照）

彼女はどこの会社に勤めているのですか．
　Who does she work for?
どこの銀行がいちばん利息が高いですか．
　Who's offering the highest interest rate?
どこのテレビ局がいちばん視聴率が高いですか．
　Who has the highest TV viewer ratings?
東京ではどこの店でドイツ食品を売っていますか．
　Who sells German food in Tokyo?
世界でどこの国がいちばん人口が多いですか．
　Who has the largest population in the world?
どこのチームとどこのチームがやっているの．
　Who's playing who now?

次は，over である．over の意味の中で「比較して」「裏」「もう一度」の意味はたいていの辞典では紹介されていないか，きわめて軽視されている．「比較して」の意味では，例えば次のような場合に使われる．

　うちの売上げは昨年と比較して増えている．
　　Our sales're up over last year.

over のほか from（これも辞典にはほとんど出ていない），compared to, compared with がよく使われているが，辞典によく出ている in comparison with はあまり使われていない．（本書「(…と) 比較して」を参照）

(2) 既刊の辞典には誤りが多い

　筆者の見るところでは，辞書には誤りが多すぎる．英和辞典には，現代英語で使われていないのに《古語》《廃語》といった表示なしで大きく紹介されている語義・用例が多数あるし，和英辞典にはさらに問題が多い．こうした辞典を使うことは学習者にとって非常に時間の無駄であるばかりでなく，英語をわざわざ難しいものにしている．

　筆者は高校生のとき，単語は例文で覚えることを英語の先生に強く勧められ，辞書を引くたびに必ず例文を片っ端からひたすら音読し，算数の九九のようにすらすら出るまで覚えた．辞書の著者には全幅の信頼をおき，そこに出ている例文が実際には使われていないなどとは露ほども思ったことがなかった．

　しかし，後にアメリカに留学し，レポートを提出したところ，膨大な時間をかけて苦労して辞書で覚えた英語が現代英語でまったく使われていない古くさい英語だったり，Japanese English だったりということを指摘された．このときの挫折感，失望は長年たった今でも忘れられない．これからの英語学習者には，筆者のような挫折感を味わわせたくないと思っている．

　筆者が初めて留学してから何十年もたっている．この間，日本の社会は大きく変わった．特に 1990 年代に入ってからは，明治維新，敗戦に次ぐ転換期にあるとさえいえる．しかしながら，こと英語の辞典，特に和英辞典となると旧態依然である．もちろん，何も変わっていないというわけではなく，40 年前の辞典と比較すれば改良された点は多い．しかし，現代の用法をきちんと紹介していないことが多いという点で，まったく不十分である．

多くの辞典に共通する誤りの例をいくつかあげる．

時間を尋ねられて「ちょうど3時です」というとき，よく辞典に出ているのが
 It's just 3:00.
だが，これは使われていない．よく使われるのは
 It's exactly 3:00.
 It's 3:00 on the dot.
という言い方である．just は数字と共に使うと原則として only の意味であり，
 It's just 3:00.
は「まだ3時です」の意味になる．ただし，数字といっしょでなければ
 That's just [exactly] what I want. それは私がちょうど望んでいることです．
のように「ちょうど，まさに」の意味で広く使われている．（本辞典の「ちょうど」の項参照）

男女の交際の意味での「付き合う」では
 Tom's keeping company with Jane.
といった言い方がよく辞典に出ているが，使われていない．よく使うのは
 Tom and Jane're going together.
である．男女の交際でないときも，使われるのは辞典にしばしば出ている go around with...ではなく，hang around with..., associate with...などである．（本辞典の「付き合っている」参照）

「故障している」については，be out of order が辞典には必ずと言ってよいほどあがっているが，時計のような小さい物には be broken，車のような大きい物には be broken down などと言うのが普通である．be out of order は公衆電話のような公共物にしか使えない．また，「私の車はどこが故障しているのですか」には
 What's wrong with my car? や
 What's the problem with my car?
などが使われ，ある辞典に出ている
 What's broken with my car?
は使われていない．（本辞典の「故障している」「故障する」参照）

もうひとつ，最近の辞典も含めて，大部分の辞典で working conditions の訳語は「労働条件」となっている．しかし，これは「労働環境」とすべきものであり，「労働条件」は the terms of the job という．（本辞典「条件」の項参照）

多くの辞典の誤りの原因

辞典の誤りの原因はいろいろあるが，そのひとつは，話す英語を得意としている編者が少ないことである．文章英語にだけ権威である諸先生に辞書作りを委ねてきた時代，学閥で辞書を作っていた時代は遠くなったにもかかわらず，この点は進歩が見られない．

もうひとつは，インフォーマントの利用法の問題である．辞書作りにインフォーマントを多く利用するようになってきているのは近年大きく変わった点だが，その利用法には大いに問題があり，依然として不適切な用例が多い．一例をあげれば，

  I had my salary raised. 私は給料を上げてもらいました．

という文が多くの辞典に出ているが，これは用いられず，正しくは

  I got a raise.

である．

インフォーマントをただ参加させても，編者・執筆者の尋ねる姿勢次第で彼らの答えは大きく変わり，生きた英語の慣用事実を引き出せない．彼らの力を十分引き出すには，利用する側にも文章英語だけでなく，話す英語に対する深い知識が必要である．

インフォーマントの選択

インフォーマントの選択には，次のような配慮が必要である．

(1) 熟年層と若年層は不適切

熟年層（主に 55 歳以上）の人たちは，30〜40 年前にはよく使われていたが現在はあまり使われない表現を使おうとする傾向があり，インフォーマントとして不適切である．例えば，現在 60 代以上の女性は girl Friday（有能な秘書）とか little woman（妻）と呼ばれることを好むが，50 歳以下の世代の女性はこのように呼ばれると怒ることが多い．

逆に若年層（25 歳以下）も不適である．このことは日本の若年層の日本語力を考えればわかりやすいであろう．筆者の経験では，25 歳以下では，適切な用法についての知識が不足している．

(2) 日本語が流暢な米人は不適切

日本語に流暢な米人は，次の2つの理由でインフォーマントして適任でない．

第1に，筆者の経験では，日本語のよくできる人は日本人的な英語を話すはっきりした傾向が見られるからである．

第2に，日本語が流暢ということは日本に10年，15年と長く滞在している人が多い．これはつまり長くアメリカを不在にしていたことになり，現在アメリカでよく使われている英語の表現にうとくなってきているのが，筆者の調査では常だったからである．

例をあげておこう．「アパート（の建物）」について，以前は apartment house と apartment building が，多少違いがあるものの共によく使われていたが，1980年代始め以降は apartment house はあまり使われなくなった．（これはほとんどの辞典には注記がない．本書「アパート」参照）

supermarket は，以前ほどには使われなくなってきて，big grocery store に取って代わられてきている．（本書「店」の項の8参照）

(3) 学者は不適切

日本人は学者の意見をありがたがり，耳を傾ける習慣がある．しかし，筆者の経験では，日常的な英語のインフォーマントには学者は不適切である．彼らは文章にしか使われていない硬い表現を話し言葉の中に使うからである．

筆者がアメリカに留学して当時の辞書に多数の誤りや不適切な表現があることを知ってから何十年も経つ．以来，今後の学習者のために正しい英語がわかる辞書を作ることを筆者の使命とし，ひたすらこれを追求してきた．この長年の苦労の甲斐あって，日本の英語辞書史上初めてともいうべきユニークな辞典を出版できることになり，ほっとしている．

本書によって今までの誤った解説・訳語が一掃され，利用者の英語力が大いに向上するものと確信している．

筆者はすでに，第2弾を作る用意もしている．ぜひ読者の皆さんのご感想をお聞かせいただきたい．

この辞典が世に出るに際して，大修館書店編集第二部次長の飯塚利昭氏に示唆に富む助言をいただき，その他の点においてもいろいろお世話になった．また協力をいただいた桑田健氏をはじめとする日本アイアール株式会社辞書部のスタッフは，筆者が今まで知っている中で最高の編集力を発

揮された．共に，厚くお礼を申しあげたい．

　最後の最後になったが，この辞典の原稿を作成するのが可能になったのは，ボストン・アカデミーの教務部長　福原正子氏が休日を返上してまでの言葉では言い尽くせない献身的な仕事により，原稿の清書・校正その他いろいろな面で筆者を補佐してくれたおかげである．心から感謝を申しあげたい．

　　2003年2月25日

亡き母に贈る
市橋敬三

この辞典の記述について

本辞典の構成と使用頻度表示
　見出しは五十音順．**1，2**…で語義区分を行った（必要により下位区分として**a）b）**…を使用）．
　〈　　〉印で示した日本語の例文に対する英訳例を**ABC**…で掲げ，アメリカ英語における実際の使用頻度を次の記号で表示した．

　　　☆　　いちばんよく使われる
　　　◎　　非常によく使われる
　　　○　　よく使われる
　　　△　　時々使われる
　　　▽　　たまに使われる
　　　×　　使われない

　例文中の［　］内は直前の部分と交換可能，（　）内は省略可能であることを示す．

インフォーマント
　使用頻度は，別記の米国人インフォーマントに対する調査結果に基づいている．見解が割れるときは，同一項目について 50 名以上に意見をきいた．世代による差もあるので，インフォーマントは 30〜45 歳に限り，全員大卒以上で，南部以外の出身者である（「はしがき」の「インフォーマントの選択」の項参照）．

　従来の辞典では正しい英語か否かを問題にしているが，本辞典では実際にどのくらい広く使われているかという観点から調査した結果を示した．

卑語などについて
　性に関係する語句を用いた表現，呪いの表現，一部の敬虔なクリスチャンが抵抗を示す神を冒瀆する表現なども，必要に応じて収録した．これらは従来の辞典では十分な記述がないことが多かったが，本辞典では使用頻度の高いものはきちんと紹介した．これを知らないとコミュニケーションに支障をきたすからである．多くの場合，注をつけて注意を喚起した．

省略形

本辞典では，話し言葉で用いられる表現については，be動詞，have, 助動詞などの省略形を用いて表記した．

例：The police detective's got an eye on him. ('s ← has)

The stock market'll recover soon. ('ll ← will)

通常は，主語が人称代名詞でないときはこうした省略形では書かないが，本辞典では話し言葉の実際の姿を紹介するために省略形を用いている．

インフォーマント・リスト

Amy Bruni
Barbara Canover
Brian Nelson
Carol Taylor
Christine Morgenson
David Kirk
Elisabeth Malone
Gerald Gorman
Greg Baldwin
James Blair
Jean Norris
Joan Withers
Julia Bernstein
Karl Burns
Lisa Cramptor
Leslie Dale
Maria Brooke
Matt Belson
Nina Bergstein
Peter Byford
Robert Friedman
Sally Tilton
Susan Venable
William Smith

Andrew Hoge
Biance Martim
Carol Menkes
Cathy Adams
Cindy O'connor
Deborah Tyler
Eric Meller
Grace Malkin
Gregory Cohen
Jane Dao
Jean Power
Jon Kirk
Julia Yermakov
Kathy Preston
Lisa Merluzzi
Leslie Reno
Mary Langley
Mike Kurz
Paul Weber
Rebecca Roth
Robert Rutenberg
Sarah Wines
Tom Sanger
Ann Landler

Bill Edwards
Carol Simon
Chris Sanders
David Eckholm
Eileen Leduff
Frank Harrison
Greg Gordon
Howard Broad
Janice Adams
Jim Clarke
Jeffrey Russel
Justin Stout
Linda Kirk
Lisa Mitchell
Marcia Lavery
Mary Yermakov
Neal Brown
Paula Cowell
Richard Fisher
Rose Anderson
Stephen Glassman
Victoria Brooke
(全員米国人；前ページ「インフォーマント」の項参照)

本辞典の内容の一部または全部の無断転載は著作権法違反になります．転載される場合は，大修館書店あて許諾申請をお願いいたします．

〔あ〕

愛している
  1 《異性愛》
  a）現在の状態
  〈私は彼女を愛しています〉
    ◎ A I'm in love with her.
    ◎ B I love her.
      ❖(1) 辞典ではA, Bを同意語として紹介しているが，Aには「深く愛しています」の意味合いがある．Aは2人の初期の段階でよく使われる．つまり，Aは強くひきつけられるという意味が入っている「愛している」である．
      ❖(2) 分かりやすくするために次例を紹介しよう．We have to break up because I love you but I'm not in love with you anymore. (あなたのことは好きだけど，もうひきつけられるような魅力を感じないから，私たちは別れなければならないの)
  b）過去の状態
  〈私たちは高校生のとき，とても愛し合っていました〉
    ◎ A We were really in love with each other when we were in high school.
    ○ B We really loved each other when we were in high school.
    ▽ C We had a great love affair when we were in high school.
      ❖ Cの have a great love affair がどの辞典にも「浮気をしている」の意味で紹介されているが，今はこの意味では全く使われていない．しかし，19世紀，20世紀初めくらいの小説ではよく使われている．
  2 《親・兄弟・子供の愛》
  〈お父さん，私はお父さんを愛していますよ〉
    ☆　Dad, I love you.

(…の)間
  1 《浮沈のない期間の場合》
  〈彼女はこの3年間，管理職についています〉
    ◎ A She's been in management for the last three years.
    ○ B She's been in management over the last three years.
    △ C She's been in management during the last three years.
  2 《浮沈のある期間の場合》
  〈ドルはこの3年間，値上がりしてきました〉
    ◎ A The dollar's been getting stronger for [over] the last three years.
    ○ B The dollar's been getting stronger during [in] the last three years.
  3 《最上級が先行するとき》
  〈これは30年間で最高の積雪です〉
    ☆ A This is the heaviest snowfall in 30 years.
    ○ B This is the heaviest snowfall for 30 years.
    △ C This is the heaviest snowfall during 30 years.
    × D This is the heaviest snowfall over 30 years.
  4 《最上級＋主語＋現在完了の場合》
  〈これは10年間で最高の降水量です〉
    ◎ A This is the heaviest rainfall we've had in ten years.
    ○ B This is the heaviest rainfall we've had for ten years.

2　あいている

  5　《継続を表す否定の現在完了が先行する場合》
〈私はこの10年近くの間, ロシア料理を食べていません〉
      ◎　A　I haven't eaten Russian food in nearly ten years.
      ○　B　I haven't eaten Russian food for nearly ten years.
  6　《一定の期間を表す名詞を従えるとき》
〈私はクリスマス休暇の間, 両親の家にいます〉
      ◎　　　I'll be at my parents' home over [during, for] Christmas vacation.
  7　《季節を従えるとき》
〈うちのビジネスは冬の間は景気が悪いんです〉
      ◎　A　Our business is bad during the winter.
      ○　B　Our business is bad over [for, in] the winter.
  8　《長さを強調するとき》
〈この寒い天気が続いている間はハイキングに行けません〉
      ◎　A　As long as this cold weather lasts, we can't go hiking.
      ○　B　While this cold weather lasts, we can't go hiking.
      △　C　So long as this cold weather lasts, we can't go hiking.

空いている

  1　《アパート》
〈あのアパートはまだ空いていますか〉
      ◎　A　Is that apartment still available [open, vacant, empty]?
      ◎　B　Is that apartment still for rent?
      ◎　C　Is that apartment still listed?
      ◎　D　Isn't that apartment taken [rented] yet?
  2　《レストラン》
〈この席は空いていますか〉
      ◎　A　Is this seat taken [available, open, vacant]?
      ◎　B　Is somebody sitting here?
      ○　C　Is this seat empty?
  3　《トイレ》
〈トイレは空いていますか〉
      ☆　A　Is anyone in the bathroom?
      ☆　B　Is anyone using the bathroom?
      ○　C　Is the bathroom occupied [taken, vacant, empty]?
      ×　D　Is the bathroom open?
        ❖ A, B の anyone は anybody, someone, somebody に置き換えても, A, B と同様一番よく使われている.

相乗りする　→乗る 8

相反する

〈多くの黒人は黒人の医師に対して相反する複雑な感情を持っている〉
      ☆　A　Many black people have mixed feelings about black doctors.
      ◎　B　Many black people have ambivalent feelings about [toward] black doctors.
      ○　C　Many black people have ambivalence about [toward] black doctors.
      ○　D　Many black people're ambivalent about [toward] black doctors.
        ❖ ambivalent は教育レベルの低い人の間ではあまり使われていない.

会う

  1　《場所を明示するとき》
  a）肯定文

〈駅で会おう〉
- ◎ A Let's meet at the station.
- ○ B Let's see each other at the station.
- × C Let's see at the station.
  - ❖ see は常に see＋人の型，つまり他動詞として使われている．meet は他動詞だけでなく A のように自動詞，つまり名詞を従えなくてもよく使われている．

b) どこで落ち合うか相談するとき
〈どこで会いましょうか〉
- ◎ A Where will [should] we meet?
- △ B Where should we see each other?
- × C Where should we see?

2 《場所ではなく時間・日付・曜日などが明示されるとき》
〈来週いつか会いましょう〉
- ◎ A Let's get together [meet] sometime next week.
- ○ B Let's see each other sometime next week.

3 《「知り合う」の意味のとき》→知り合う

a) プロセスがない場合
〈お会いできて嬉しいです〉
- ◎ A I'm glad to meet you.
- ◎ B It's nice to meet you.

b) プロセスがある場合
〈どこでご主人とお会いになったのですか〉
- ◎ A Where did you get to know your husband?
- ○ B Where did you meet your husband?

4 《約束して会うとき》

a) 特別な準備が不要な場合
〈私は今晩彼らに会う予定です〉
- ◎ A I'm going to meet [see] them this evening.
- × B I'm going to meet with them this evening.
  - ❖ B が多くの辞典に出ているが使われていない．

b) 特別な準備が必要な場合
〈小泉首相はブッシュ大統領と3月4日に会います〉
- ◎ A Prime Minister Koizumi'll meet with President Bush on March 4th.
- ○ B Prime Minister Koizumi'll meet President Bush on March 4th.

〈私は生みの母親と20年振りに会うんです〉
- ◎ A I'm going to meet my biological mother for the first time in twenty years.
- ○ B I'm going to meet with my biological mother for the first time in twenty years.
  - ❖ブッシュ大統領と会うことや，生みの母親と20年振りに会うことは，精神面だけでなくいろいろの準備が不可欠である．このようなときは meet, meet with の両方が使われている．

5 《偶然会うとき》→偶然 1
〈私は先日混んだ電車の中でリンダに偶然会いました〉
- ◎ A I met [saw] Linda on a crowded train the other day.
- ◎ B I happened to meet [see] Linda on a crowded train the other day.
- ◎ C I ran [bumped] into Linda on a crowded train the other day.
- ◎ D I met Linda by chance on a crowded train the other day.

△ E I saw Linda by chance on a crowded train the other day.
△ F I ran across Linda on a crowded train the other day.

合う

《色などについて言う場合》

a) 対照的なもの

〈店員：その黄色いネクタイはあなたの黒いスーツによく合いますよ〉

Salesperson:
- ◎ A That yellow tie works well [looks good] with your black suit.
- ◎ B That yellow tie goes (well) with your black suit.
- ◎ C That yellow tie matches your black suit.
- ○ D That yellow tie complements your black suit.
- × E That yellow tie mixes (well) with [fits well on, harmonizes with] your black suit.

❖(1) E が辞典に出ているが使われていない．
❖(2) B の go with は他より少し弱い響きがある．

b) 同系統のもの

〈店員：そのブルーのドレスはあなたのブルーの帽子によく合いますよ〉

Salesperson:
- ◎ A That blue dress matches your blue hat.
- ◎ B That blue dress goes (well) with your blue hat.
- ◎ C That blue dress works well [looks good] with your blue hat.
- ◎ D That blue dress complements your blue hat.
- ▽ E That blue dress suits your blue hat.
- ▽ F That blue dress blends (well) with your blue hat.
- × G That blue dress mixes (well) [harmonizes] with your blue hat.
- × H That blue dress fits well on your blue hat.

❖(1) G, H が辞典に出ているが使われていない．
❖(2) D は友人同士などの会話では時々使われる程度．

赤字

1 《会社》

〈うちの会社は赤字なんです〉
- ☆ A Our company's in the red.
- ◎ B Our company's losing money.
- ○ C Our company bottom line's in the red.
- ○ D Our bottom line's in the red.
- × E Our company's in the deficit.

2 《国》

a) 貿易赤字

〈アメリカは巨額な貿易赤字をかかえている〉
- ◎ A America has a huge trade deficit.
- ○ B America has a huge trade imbalance.

b) 財政赤字

〈日本は莫大な財政赤字をかかえている〉
- ◎ Japan has a huge financial [fiscal] deficit.

3 《家庭》

〈私が失業して以来，うちの家計は赤字なんです〉
- ◎ A We haven't been able to make ends meet since I lost my job.
- △ B We've been in the red since I lost my job.
- △ C Our family budget's been in the red since I lost my job.

赤の他人
〈彼は私にとって赤の他人です〉
- ◎ A He's a total [complete] stranger to me.
- ▽ B He's a perfect [an utter, an entire] stranger to me.
- ❖ B が辞典に出ているがほとんど使われていない．

あがる
1 《売り上げ・輸出（入）額》
〈売り上げがあがった〉
- ◎ A Sales have been going up [increasing, rising, growing].
- ◎ B Sales have been on the rise.

2 《成績》
〈今学期の私の成績はあがりました〉
- ◎ A My grades've improved this semester.
- ◎ B My grades're better this semester.
- ◎ C I have better grades this semester.
- ◎ D I have improved my grades this semester.

3 《税金》
〈所得税は来年あがるだろう〉
- ◎ A Income tax'll go up [increase, rise] next year.
- ◎ B Income tax'll be raised [increased, hiked] next year.
- ◎ C Income tax'll be higher next year.

4 《気温》
〈気温が33度にあがった〉
- ◎ A The temperature's risen [gone up] to thirty-three degrees.
- ◎ B The temperature's climbed (up) to thirty-three degrees.
- ◎ C The temperature's soared to thirty-three degrees.
- ◎ D The temperature's skyrocketed to thirty-three degrees.
- ❖ A が一番弱く，次が B，次は C．一番強いのは D．

5 《階段》
〈階段を歩いてあがろう〉
- ◎ Let's go up [walk up, climb, take] the stairs.

6 《演壇》
〈彼は演壇にあがるときに，つまずいたんです〉
- ◎ He tripped while he was stepping [walking] onto [on] the platform.

7 《議題》
〈この問題は会議で議題にあがるでしょう〉
- ◎ This question'll be brought up [be addressed, come up] at the meeting.

8 《意識過剰》
a） 人に会ったとき
〈初めて私は彼女に会ったとき，あがってしまったんです〉
- ◎ A The first time I met her, I got nervous.
- ◎ B The first time I met her, I got [felt] self-conscious.

b） 聴衆を前にしたとき
〈初めてテレビに出たとき私はあがってしまいました〉
- ◎ A The first time I appeared on TV, I got [had] stage fright.
- ◎ B The first time I appeared on TV, I got nervous.
- ◎ C The first time I appeared on TV, I felt [got] self-conscious.

9 《費用がまかなえる》
〈800 ドルですべての旅費はあがるでしょう〉
- ☆ A $800'll cover all the traveling expenses.
- ◎ B $800'll take care of all the traveling expenses.
- ◎ C $800'll be enough to pay for all the traveling.

明るい

1 《性格》
〈彼は明るい人です〉
- ◎ A He's always happy [upbeat].
- ◎ B He's happy all the time.
- ○ C He's always cheerful.
- ○ D He's upbeat [cheerful].

2 《部屋》
〈この部屋は明るい〉
- ◎ A This room has good lighting.
- ◎ B This room is bright.
- ○ C This room is well-lit.
- × D This room is light.
  - ❖(1) D は辞典に出ているが使われていない．
  - ❖(2) A, B, C いずれも, 電気がついているときでも, ついていない昼間でも等しく使われている．

3 《専門分野》
〈彼は金融市場に明るいんです〉
- ◎ A He's very familiar with the money markets.
- ◎ B He knows a lot about the money markets.
- ◎ C He knows the money markets very well.
- ○ D He's well-informed about the money markets.
- △ E He's well-versed in the money markets.
- △ F He's in the know about the money markets.
- × G He has the money markets at his fingertips [fingers' ends].
  - ❖ G は辞典に出ているが使われていない．

4 《将来の見通し》
〈日本の経済の将来は明るい〉
- ◎ A Japan's economy has a bright future.
- △ B Japan's economy'll be better and better.

空地 →土地 5

明らかにする

〈彼女はその問題についての自分の立場を明らかにした〉
- ◎ A She clarified her position on that problem.
- ◎ B She stated her position clearly on that problem.
- ◎ C She made her position clear on that problem.
- ○ D She spelled out [defined, outlined] her position on that problem.
- △ E She articulated her position on that problem.
- × F She represented [delineated, designated] her position on that problem.
  - ❖(1) F が辞典に出ているが使われていない．
  - ❖(2) A は説明した後, 聞き手が分からなかったときのみに使われている．
  - ❖(3) B は初めて説明したときのみ使われている．
  - ❖(4) C〜E は初めて説明したか, A と同様であるかは不明．

あきらめる

〈私は 10 回司法試験に失敗してあきらめました〉
- ☆ A After I failed the bar ten times, I gave up.
- ◎ B After I failed the bar ten times, I gave up trying.
- ◎ C After I failed the bar ten times, I gave it up.
- ◎ D After I failed the bar ten times, I called it quits.
- ◎ E After I failed the bar ten times, I quit.
- ○ F After I failed the bar ten times, I threw in the towel.
- ○ G After I failed the bar ten times, I gave up my plan to be a lawyer.
- △ H After I failed the bar ten times, I abandoned my plan to be a lawyer.

あくせくしていない

〈彼は将来のことを気にかけていません。あくせくしていないんです〉
- ◎ A He doesn't care about his future. He's easy-going [laid-back].
- ○ B He doesn't care about his future. He's relaxed.

あごで使う

1 《相手に依頼するとき》

〈私をあごで使わないで下さい〉
- ◎   Don't boss [order] me around, please.

2 《一般的に述べるとき》

〈彼女は人をあごで使うんです〉
- ☆ A She bosses people around at work.
- ◎ B She's bossy at work.
- ◎ C She orders people around at work.

朝

〈朝早く私に電話しないで下さい〉
- ◎ A Please don't call me early in the morning.
- △ B Please don't call me in (the) early morning.

❖「夕方」「夜」も参照のこと。

足手まとい

〈私がどこへ行っても末の息子が付いてくるのです。彼は本当に足手まといなんです〉
- ◎ A No matter where I go, my youngest son follows me around. He's a real pain in the neck [ass, butt].
- ○ B No matter where I go, my youngest son follows me around. He's a real nuisance [drag, burden].

あそこにある

1 《単数のとき》

〈ビル：僕のコートはどこにあるのかな〉

Bill: Where's my coat?

〈トム：あそこにあるよ〉

Tom:
- ◎   There it is.

2 《複数のとき》

〈ビル：僕の手袋はどこにあるのかな〉

Bill: Where are my gloves?

〈トム：あそこにあるよ〉

Tom:
- ◎   There they are.

暖かい

〈このストーブは暖かい〉

- ◎ A This heater puts out [produces] a lot of heat.
- ◎ B This heater is warm.
- △ C This heater throws (out) a lot of heat.
  - ❖ A, C は熱を出す観点から述べた表現であるのに対し，B は熱を出す点には言及せず，自分に暖かいと言っているだけである．

頭がいい

1 《ホワイトカラー》
〈彼は非常に頭がいいんです〉
- ☆ A He's very intelligent.
- ◎ B He's very smart.
- ○ C He's very bright.
- △ D He's very clever.

2 《ブルーカラー》
〈彼は非常に頭がいいんです〉
- ☆ A He's very smart.
- ◎ B He's very intelligent.
- ○ C He's very bright.
- △ D He's very clever.

3 《子供（13 歳くらいまで）》
〈彼はとても頭がいいんです〉
- ☆ A He's very bright.
- ◎ B He's very smart.
- ○ C He's very intelligent.
- △ D He's very clever.

4 《「抜け目がない」の意味のとき》
〈彼は非常に頭がいいんです〉
- ◎ A He's very sly [clever].
- △ B He's very crafty.
  - ❖ sly, crafty の方が clever より「悪賢い」というニュアンスが強い．

頭がおかしい

1 《医師の治療を受けているとき》

a） 症状が重いとき
〈彼は頭がおかしいんです〉
- ☆ A He's insane.
- ◎ B He's gone off the deep end.
- ◎ C He's lost it.
- ◎ D He's a lunatic.
- ○ E He's off the deep end.
- △ F He's an insane person.
  - ❖ A, B, C, F は一番症状が重い．2 番目は E，3 番目は D．

b） 症状が軽いとき
〈彼は頭がおかしいんです〉
- ☆ A He's crazy [nuts].
- ◎ B He's lost his marbles.
- ○ C He isn't playing with a full deck.
- ○ D He's a lunatic.
- ○ E He's loony.
- △ F He's a madman.

2 《医学上でなく冗談で述べるとき》

〈彼は頭がおかしいよ〉
- ☆ A He's crazy [nuts].
- ◎ B He's lost his marbles.
- ○ C He's not playing with a full deck.
- ○ D He's a lunatic.

3 《「常識を欠いている」という意味のとき》
〈彼はこの株にお金を全部投資するとは頭がおかしい〉
- ☆ A He's crazy [nuts] to invest all his money in this stock.
- ◎ B He's out of his mind to invest all his money in this stock.
- ○ C He's insane to invest all his money in this stock.
- ○ D He's a nut to invest to all his money in this stock.
- ○ E He's fanatic about investing all his money in this stock.

頭にくる
〈彼は頭にくる〉
- ☆ A He drives me crazy.
- ◎ B He drives me up the wall.
- ◎ C He makes me crazy.
- ◎ D He makes [drives] me nuts.
- ○ E He drives me to drink.
- ○ F He makes me insane.

(…しか)頭にない
〈たいていのアメリカの会社は短期間で利益を上げることしか頭にないが，日本人は長期的な観点から考えている〉
- ◎ A Most American companies only think about short-range profits, but the Japanese have a long-range point of view.
- ○ B Most American companies only have [have only] short-range profits in mind, but the Japanese have a long-range point of view.

当たり
〈ピーター：君はいくつなんだい〉
Peter: How old are you?
〈スティーヴ：当ててごらん〉
Steve: Guess how old I am.
〈ピーター：41歳かい〉
Peter: Forty-one?
〈スティーヴ：当たり〉
Steve:
- ◎ A Bingo!
- ◎ B You hit the nail right on the head!
- ◎ C Bull's eye!

…あたりで
〈私は原宿のあたりでアパートを探しています〉
- ◎ A I'm looking for an apartment around Harajuku.
- ◎ B I'm looking for an apartment in the Harajuku area.
- ○ C I'm looking for an apartment in and around Harajuku.
  - ❖(1) A は会話だけでなく，文章でも B と同じように非常によく使われている．
  - ❖(2) around は建物などの外側の「まわりに」「周囲に」，また内側の「まわりに」「周囲に」の意味では辞典に出ている．しかし，建物，場所などの内側と外側の両方を意味する「周辺」「あたりで」の意味でも非常によく使わ

れているのに，辞典ではこの意味を紹介していない．

当たる
《日が重なる》
〈彼のリサイタルが私の卒業式に当たるんです〉
　◎ A　His recital falls on my graduation.
　△ B　His recital occurs [takes place, happens] on my graduation.

悪化する
1　《景気》
〈景気は悪化するでしょう〉
　◎ A　The economy'll go bad.
　◎ B　The economy'll go down.
　○ C　The economy'll drop.
　○ D　The economy'll fall.
　○ E　The economy'll get bad.
　△ F　The economy'll decline.
　❖ A, D, E のほうが B, C, F よりも悪化する程度は強い．

2　《失業》
〈失業は今秋悪化するでしょう〉
　◎ A　The unemployment'll be [get] worse this fall.
　○ B　The unemployment'll increase [rise, worsen, go up] this fall.
　○ C　The unemployment'll become worse this fall.
　× D　The unemployment'll be aggravated this fall.
　× E　The unemployment'll degenerate [deteriorate] this fall.

3　《失業率》
〈失業率はもっと悪化するでしょう〉
　◎ A　The unemployment rate'll get higher.
　◎ B　The unemployment rate'll go up more.
　○ C　The unemployment rate'll go up further.
　○ D　The unemployment rate'll rise further [more].
　△ E　The unemployment rate'll increase further.
　△ F　The unemployment rate'll be worse.
　△ G　The unemployment rate'll be [become] higher.

4　《患者の容態》
〈患者の容態が悪化したんです〉
　◎ A　The patient's taken a turn for the worse.
　◎ B　The patient's condition's become more serious.
　○ C　The patient's taken a bad turn.

5　《2つの国の関係》
〈アメリカと中国の関係は悪化するでしょう〉
　◎ A　The relationship between America and China'll be damaged [hurt].
　◎ B　The relationship between America and China'll get worse.
　○ C　The relationship between America and China'll be worse [stressed, strained, undermined].
　○ D　The relationship between America and China'll become worse.

6　《悪化させる》
〈それはアメリカと中国の関係を悪化させるであろう〉
　☆ A　That'll damage the relationship between America and China.
　☆ B　That'll hurt the relationship between America and China.
　◎ C　That'll stress [strain] the relationship between America and China.

    ◎ D That'll create friction between America and China.
    ○ E That'll aggravate the relationship between America and China.
 ❖ Aが一番強い響きがある．Bが2番目，C, Dが3番目，Eは4番目．
集まり
  1 《一般的な集まり》
  〈私は彼とビジネスの集まりで知り合ったんです〉
    ☆ A I met him at a business function.
    ◎ B I met him at a business gathering.
    ○ C I met him at a business get-together.
  2 《パーティー》
  〈私は彼とビジネスの集まり（パーティー）で知り合ったんです〉
    ◎ A I met him at a business social [party].
    ○ B I met him at a business affair.
  3 《教会での集まり》
  〈私は彼と教会の集まりで知り合ったんです〉
    ◎ A I met him at a church get-together [gathering].
    ○ B I met him at a church social.
…宛に
  〈東京貿易会社宛に小切手を切って下さい〉
    ◎ A Please make your check out to the Tokyo Trading Corporation.
    ○ B Please make your check payable to the Tokyo Trading Corporation.
    × C Please draw [make, make out, write, write out] your check in favor of the Tokyo Trading Corporation.
    × D Please draw [write, write out] your check to the Tokyo Trading Corporation.
 ❖ C, Dが多くの辞典に出ているが使われていない．
当てにする
  1 《目的語を従えるとき》
  〈彼を当てにすることはできませんよ〉
    ◎ A You can't depend [count, rely, fall back] on him.
    △ B You can't bank on him.
  2 《名詞を修飾するとき》
  〈私には当てにできる人がいないんです〉
    ◎ A I don't have anybody to depend [count, rely, fall back] on.
    △ B I don't have anybody to bank on.
  3 《不定詞を従えるとき》
  〈彼が融資してくれることを当てにできません〉
    ◎ A You can't depend [count, rely, fall back] on him to finance you.
    △ B You can't bank on him to finance you.
当てはまる
  〈あなたが言ったことは日本にも当てはまる〉
    ◎ A What you've said is the case with Japan too.
    ◎ B What you've said is true of [is applicable to] Japan too.
    ◎ C What you've said applies to [goes for] Japan too.
    ○ D What you've said holds true of Japan too.
    ○ E What you've said covers Japan too.
    ○ F What you've said is valid for Japan too.
(…の)後で
  1 《会話で名詞を従えるとき》

〈卒業式の後で私たちはパーティーを開きました〉
- ◎ A After the graduation, we had a party.
- △ B Following the graduation, we had a party.
- ▽ C Subsequent to the graduation, we had a party.

2 《会話で文を従えるとき》

〈レポートを書き終えた後で電話します〉
- ◎ A I'll call you after I finish my paper.
- ○ B I'll call you after finishing my paper.

3 《堅い文章で名詞を従えるとき》

〈大恐慌の後, 多くの会社が倒産した〉
- ◎ A After the Great Depression, many companies went into bankruptcy.
- ○ B Following [Subsequent to] the Great Depression, many companies went into bankruptcy.

4 《堅い文章で文を従えるとき》

〈弁護士と相談した後で, 彼は彼らを訴えることに決めた〉
- ☆ A After he talked to the lawyer, he decided to sue them.
- ☆ B After talking to the lawyer, he decided to sue them.
- ◎ C After he had talked to the lawyer, he decided to sue them.
- ○ D Having talked to the lawyer, he decided to sue them.

❖ D の完了分詞構文は, 会話ではほとんど使われていない.

後の祭り

〈後の祭りだ〉
- ☆ A The damage's (already) done.
- ◎ B It's too late to fix it.
- ○ C It's too late to change anything.
- × D The doctor after death.
- × E The day after the fair.

❖ D, E が辞典に出ているが使われていない.

アパート

1 《ビル全体》

〈彼は大きいアパートのビルを持っています〉
- ◎ A He owns a big apartment building.
- ◎ B He owns a big apartment complex.
- ◎ C He owns a big block of flats.
- ▽ D He owns a big apartment house.

❖(1) D はどの辞典にも出ているが, 使われてもまれ.
❖(2) B はプール, テニスコートのようなレクリエーションの設備がある 1 棟の apartment building, または数棟の apartment building のこと. C はイギリス英語. D は 1970 年代まではよく使われていた.

2 《ビルの中の一世帯》

〈彼らは美しいアパートに住んでいます〉
- ◎ They live in a beautiful apartment [flat].

❖ flat はイギリス英語.

あぶく銭を稼ぐ

〈彼は最近取引であぶく銭を稼いだんです〉
- ◎ A He made a quick [fast] buck on a deal recently.
- △ B He made easy [quick] money on a deal recently.

危ない

〈危ない. 車が来るよ〉

◎ A Watch [Look] out. A car's coming.
◎ B Be careful. A car's coming.
▽ C Take care. A car's coming.
× D Have an eye. A car's coming.
❖ D が辞典には出ているが使われていない．

虻蜂取らずになる
〈あなたは同時に2つのことをやろうとしている．虻蜂取らずになると思うよ〉

◎ A You're trying to achieve two things at the same time. I'm afraid you won't succeed at either of them.
◎ B You're trying to achieve two things at the same time. I'm afraid you'll end up losing both of them.
○ C You're trying to achieve two things at the same time. I'm afraid you can't get either of them.
○ D You're trying to achieve two things at the same time. I'm afraid you'll fail at both of them.

甘党
〈私は甘党なんです〉

◎ A I have a sweet tooth.
◎ B I like sweets.
○ C I like sweet stuff.

甘やかす
1 《動作として述べる場合》
〈息子さんを甘やかしちゃ駄目だよ．大人になって苦労しますよ〉

◎ A Don't spoil your son. He'll have a hard time when he grows up.
○ B Don't baby your son. He'll have a hard time when he grows up.
× C Don't pamper your son. He'll have a hard time when he grows up.
❖ 多くの辞典に C が「甘やかす」の意味で出ているが，使われていない．pamper が使われるのは次のようなニュアンスの時である．

2 《状態として述べる場合》
〈彼は甘やかされているから，私は彼と結婚したくないんです〉

◎ A I don't want to marry him because he's spoiled by his mother.
◎ B I don't want to marry him because he's a mama's boy.
○ C I don't want to marry him because he's pampered [babied] by his mother.
○ D I don't want to marry him because he's spoiled by his mama [mom].
△ E I don't want to marry him because he's pampered by his mama.

洗う
1 《身体》
〈パーティーへ行く前に身体を洗いたいんだ〉

☆ A I want to take a shower before I go to the party.
◎ B I want to freshen up [shower] before I go to the party.
○ C I want to freshen [clean] myself up before I go to the party.
× D I want to wash myself [my body] before I go to the party.
❖ D が辞典に出ているが使われていない．

2 《食器》
〈食器を洗ってくれますか〉

☆ A Will you do the dishes?
◎ B Will you wash the dishes?

3 《比喩的に》
a) 相手の会社を調べる
〈あなたは取引をする前にその会社を洗った方がいいですよ〉
- ◎ A You'd better check (out) [look into] the company before you make the deal.
- ○ B You'd better investigate [check into, look over] the company before you make the deal.

b) ある職業から足を洗う
〈私は不動産業から足を洗いたいんです〉
- ☆ A I want to get out of the real estate business.
- ◎ B I want to quit [back away from] the real estate business.
- ◎ C I want to make a break from the real estate business.
- ○ D I want to wash my hands of the real estate business.
- ○ E I want to bail out of the real estate business.

c) 暴力団から足を洗う
〈私は暴力団から足を洗いたいんです〉
- ☆ A I want to get out of my life as a part of the mob.
- ◎ B I want to make a break from my life as a part of the mob.
- ○ C I want to wash my hands of my life as a part of the mob.

アラカルト
〈うちのレストランは昼間はバイキングで、夜はアラカルトです〉
- ◎ Our restaurant has a buffet during the day and (a) menu service in the evening.

アル中 →中毒 3
アルツハイマー病 →病気 4

アルバイトをする
1 《他に定職を持っている人のとき》
〈彼はアルバイトで警備員をしています〉
- ☆ A He has another job [a second job] as a security guard.
- ◎ B He's working another job [a second job] as a security guard.
- ◎ C He works another job [a second job] as a security guard.
- ◎ D He has another job on the side as a security guard.
- ○ E He has a job on the side as a security guard.
- ○ F He's moonlighting as a security guard.
- △ G He moonlights as a security guard.
  - ❖ F, G は昼間に定職を持っている人が夜にアルバイトをするときの表現．夜に定職を持っている人が昼間にアルバイトをする場合には使われていない．

2 《主婦・学生が昼間にアルバイトをするとき》
〈母は私が大学に行けるようにアルバイトをしています〉
- ◎ A My mother works part time so I can go to college.
- ◎ B My mother's working part time so I can go to college.
- ◎ C My mother has a part time job so I can go to college.
- △ D My mother has a job part time so I can go to college.

合わない
1 《食物・飲み物》
〈コーヒーは私に合わないんです〉
- ◎ A Coffee doesn't agree with me.
- ○ B Coffee doesn't sit well with me.
- ○ C Coffee disagrees with me.

△　D　Coffee doesn't suit me.
　　　×　E　Coffee don't fit me.
　2　《気候》
〈インドネシアの気候は私に合わないんです〉
　　　◎　A　Indonesia's climate doesn't suit me.
　　　○　B　Indonesia's climate doesn't agree with me.
　　　△　C　Indonesia's climate doesn't fit me.
　3　《勘定》
〈勘定が合わないんです〉
　　　◎　A　The books don't balance (out).
　　　○　B　The books don't match (with each other).
　　　△　C　The books don't jive (with each other).
　　　△　D　The books don't mesh (with each other).
　　　△　E　The books don't agree (with each other).
　4　《商品と送り状》
〈商品が送り状と合いません〉
　　　◎　A　The merchandise doesn't match [agree with] the invoice.
　　　○　B　The merchandise doesn't jive with the invoice.
　　　▽　C　The merchandise doesn't square [mesh, tally] with the invoice.
　　　❖Cが辞典に出ているがまれ．
　5　《話の内容》
〈2人が言っていることは合わない〉
　　　◎　A　What they're saying is contradictory [conflicting].
　　　◎　B　What they're saying doesn't jive.
　　　○　C　What they're saying doesn't mesh.
　　　△　D　What they're saying doesn't match [agree].
　6　《血液》
〈彼の血液は私のと合わないんです〉
　　　◎　A　His blood isn't compatible with mine.
　　　×　B　His blood doesn't agree with mine.
　7　《色》
〈グリーンのブラウスは黒のスカートに合いません〉
　　　◎　　A green blouse doesn't work well [go well, go, look good] with a black skirt.
　　　❖詳細は「合う」の項を参照されたい．
　8　《性格》
〈私は彼と気が合わないんです〉
　　　◎　　I don't get along [click] with him.
　　　❖詳細は「気が合う」の項を参照されたい．

暗記する
　1　《行為を意味しているとき》
〈この本の文を全部暗記しなさい〉
　　　◎　A　Memorize all the sentences in this book.
　　　○　B　Learn all the sentences in this book by heart.
　　　○　C　Learn by heart all the sentences in this book.
　　　○　D　Commit to memory all the sentences in this book.
　　　×　E　Learn all the sentences in this book off by heart.
　　　❖Eはイギリスでは非常によく使われている．
　2　《朗読を意味するとき》

〈誰か3課を暗唱できますか〉
　　◎　Can someone recite Lesson 3?
　3　《状態を意味しているとき》
　〈私はこの本を暗記しています〉
　　◎　A　I know this book by heart.
　　△　B　I have this book down by heart.
　　×　C　I have this book by heart.
　　❖ C が辞典に出ているが使われていない．

安定した
〈彼には安定した収入がないんです〉
　　☆　A　He doesn't have a steady income.
　　○　B　He doesn't have a steady paycheck.
　　○　C　He doesn't have a stable income.
　　△　D　He doesn't have a stable paycheck.

案内する
　1　《話し手が案内するとき》
〈東京をご案内しましょうか〉
　　◎　A　Do you want me to show you around Tokyo?
　　◎　B　Do you want me to give you a tour around [of] Tokyo?
　　○　C　Do you want me to guide you around Tokyo?
　　×　D　Do you want me to guide you a trip of [around] Tokyo?
　2　《社員・友人・知人・家族などに案内させるとき》
〈秘書に東京をご案内させましょうか〉
　　◎　A　Do you want me to have my secretary show you around Tokyo?
　　◎　B　Do you want me to have my secretary give you a tour around [of] Tokyo?
　　◎　C　Do you want me to have my secretary arrange (for) a tour around [of] Tokyo?
　　◎　D　Do you want me to have my secretary line up a tour of Tokyo?
　　○　E　Do you want me to have my secretary line up a tour around Tokyo?
　　❖ C, D, E は文尾に for you を付けてもよく使われている．
　3　《観光ガイド・観光バスなどの手配を取ろうか否かを尋ねているとき》
〈東京をご案内しましょうか〉
　　◎　A　Do you want me to line up a tour around [of] Tokyo?
　　◎　B　Do you want me to arrange (for) a tour around [of] Tokyo?
　　◎　C　Do you want me to make arrangements for a tour around [of] Tokyo.
　　◎　D　Do you want me to set up a tour around [of] Tokyo?
　　○　E　Do you want me to hook up a tour around [of] Tokyo?
　　❖ A〜E まで文尾に for you を付けてもよく使われている．
　4　《強い助けを必要としている「案内をする」とき》
〈私は老人の男性を駅まで案内してあげました〉
　　◎　　I guided [helped] the old man to the station.
〈犬が主人を出口に案内したんです〉
　　◎　　The dog guided its master to the exit.

〔い〕

いい男 →美人 1
いい女 →美人 4
いい買物
  1 《普通に言うとき》
  〈営業マン：この車はいい買物ですよ〉
  Salesperson:
    ◎ A This car's a good buy.
    ◎ B This car's a good deal.
    ○ C This car's a (good) bargain.
    △ D This car's a good purchase.
      ❖「安い」という度合いの点ではCが一番. 2番目B, 3番目はA, D.
  2 《少し強調して言うとき》
  〈営業マン：この車はすごくいい買物ですよ〉
  Salesperson:
    ◎ A This car's a great deal [buy, bargain].
    ◎ B This car's a steal.
    ○ C This car's a real bargain.
  3 《非常に強調して言うとき》
  〈営業マン：この車はものすごくいい買物ですよ〉
  Salesperson:
    ◎ A This car's an incredible [a real] deal.
    ◎ B This car's a fantastic deal.
    ◎ C This car's a wonderful [terrific] deal.
    ◎ D This car's a great deal.
    ◎ E This car's an incredible bargain.
    ◎ F This car's a real bargain.
    ◎ G This car's a fantastic bargain.
    ◎ H This car's a wonderful [terrific] bargain.
    ◎ I This car's a great bargain.
    ◎ J This car's an incredible buy.
    ◎ K This car's a fantastic buy.
    ◎ L This car's a wonderful [terrific] buy.
    △ M This car's a dirt cheap.
      ❖(1) Mは話し手が客ならば非常によく使われている.
      ❖(2) 強さの点ではA, E, J, Mが1番, B, F, Kが2番, C, H, Lが3番, D, G, Iが4番.
      ❖(3)「ぎりぎりの値段」「お買い得だ」はそれぞれの項を参照.
いい加減にしなさい
  1 《強く述べるとき》
  〈あなたは私たちに少なくとも3時間文句を言っている. いい加減にしなさい〉
    ◎ A You've been complaining about us for at least 3 hours. I've had enough of it.
    ◎ B You've been complaining about us for at least 3 hours. I'm sick and tired with it.

◎ C You've been complaining about us for at least 3 hours. I'm fed up with it.

2 《少し弱く述べるとき》

〈あなたは私たちに少なくとも3時間文句を言っている。いい加減にしなさい〉

◎ A You've been complaining about us for at least 3 hours. Enough's enough.

◎ B You've been complaining about us for at least 3 hours. That's enough.

◎ C You've been complaining about us for at least 3 hours. I've heard enough.

いい線いっている

〈リンダ:彼はいくつだと思う〉

Linda: How old do you think he is?

〈メアリー:40歳〉

Mary: 40.

〈ビル:いい線いってるよ〉

Bill:

◎ A You almost got it.
◎ B You're very warm.
◎ C You're on the right track.
○ D You nearly got it.
○ E You're almost [nearly] there.

いい先生

1 《人柄》

〈彼女はいい先生です〉

◎ A She's a nice [friendly] teacher.
× B She's a good teacher.

2 《教え方》

〈彼女はいい先生です〉

◎ A She's a good teacher.
○ B She's a capable teacher.

いい天気

〈いいお天気ですね〉

◎ A It's a beautiful [nice] day, isn't it?
◎ B Nice day [weather], isn't it?
◎ C It's nice weather, isn't it?
○ D It's good weather, isn't it?
○ E It's a lovely day, isn't it?
○ F Good weather, isn't it?
× G It's a fine day, isn't it?

❖(1) E は女性の間で主として使われている。

❖(2) G はイギリスでは非常によく使われているが、アメリカでは全く使われていない。

言いなりになる

〈ジェーンの夫は彼女の言いなりになっている〉

◎ A Jane's husband's at her beck and call.
◎ B Jane has her husband in the palm of her hand.
◎ C Jane's got her husband wrapped around her little finger.
◎ D Jane has her husband eating out of her hand.

× E Jane's husband's tied to her apron strings.
　　　❖(1) E が多くの辞書に出ているが使われていない．
　　　❖(2) E は He's tied to her mother's apron strings.（彼はマザコンです）の意味ではよく使われている．
　詳細は「マザコン」の項を参照されたい．
言い分
　1　《言うべきこと》
　〈私の言い分を言わせて下さい〉
　　　◎ A Let me have my say.
　　　◎ B Let me state [plead] my case.
　　　× C Let me have [express, tell] my case.
　　　× D Let me say my say.
　　　❖ C, D が辞典に出ているが使われていない．
　2　《文句》
　〈私は言い分があります〉
　　　◎ A I have something to complain about.
　　　× B I have a crow to pluck [pull, pick] with.
　　　❖ B が辞典に出ているが使われていない．
言い訳をする
　〈あなたは自分のミスの言い訳をしているだけじゃないか〉
　　　☆ A You're just making excuses for your mistake.
　　　○ B You're just trying to rationalize [defend, justify] your mistake.
言う
　〈上司は私に時間までに出勤するように言いました〉
　　　◎ A The boss told me to get to work on time.
　　　○ B The boss said for me to get to work on time.
　　　△ C The boss said to me to get to work on time.
　　　❖ B は A, C より軟らかい響きがある．
家
　1　《所在地を述べるとき》
　〈私の家は原宿にあります〉
　　　◎ A My place is in Harajuku.
　　　◎ B My house is in Harajuku.
　　　○ C My home is in Harajuku.
　　　❖ B, C は一軒家．A はアパート，分譲マンション，一軒家のいずれであるかは不明．
　2　《家を購入しようとしているとき》
　〈私は横浜の周辺で家を買おうと思っています〉
　　　◎ A I'm thinking of buying a house [place] around Yokohama.
　　　○ B I'm thinking of buying a home around Yokohama.
　3　《家の中へ入ったことがあるとき》
　〈彼らは美しい家を持っています〉
　　　◎ A They have a beautiful home.
　　　△ B They have a beautiful house.
　　　❖ A は家の中へ入って家具，装飾などの美しさをよく知っているニュアンスがある．
　4　《家の中へ入ったことがないとき》
　〈彼らは美しい家を持っています〉
　　　◎ A They have a beautiful house.

× B They have a beautiful home.

5 《家族が庭または家のすぐそばで話しているとき》
〈お父さんは家にいます〉
- ◎ A Dad's in the house.
- × B Dad's at home.

6 《家から離れている所・会社などで話しているとき》
〈彼は家にいます〉
- ◎ A He's at home.
- ▽ B He's in the house.

7 《「家のまわり」と言うとき》
〈私は家のまわりを毎晩ジョギングします〉
- ◎ A I jog around the neighborhood every evening.
- ○ B I jog the neighborhood every evening.
- ▽ C I jog round the neighborhood every evening.
- × D I jog around the house every evening.
  - ❖ D は日本語につられて言いがちであろう．しかし，これでは家の中で「ジョギングする」という意味になるので使えない．

8 《家を出る》
a) 一般的にいう場合
〈今朝何時に家を出たのですか〉
- ◎   What time did you leave home [the house] this morning?

b) 「家出する」と言う場合
・理由に言及しないとき
〈娘は家出したんです〉
- ◎ A My daughter ran away (from home).
- △ B My daughter drifted away from home.
- ▽ C My daughter went away [flew] from home.

・理由に言及するとき
〈娘は父親と大げんかして家出したんです〉
- ◎ A My daughter ran away (from home) because she had a big fight with her father.
- ○ B My daughter left home because she had a big fight with her father.
- △ C My daughter left the house because she had a big fight with her father.
- △ D My daughter drifted away from home because she had a big fight with her father.
- × E My daughter ran away from the house because she had a big fight with her father.

9 《住居》
a) 一般の人の家
〈(電話で) こちらはジム・ブラウンの住居ですが〉
- ◎ A This is Jim Brown's residence.
- ○ B This is Jim Brown's house.
- △ C This is Jim Brown's home.
  - ❖ 辞典に residence＝「大邸宅」と紹介されているが，これはアメリカ英語のニュアンスを歪曲している．residence は house の改まった語である．したがって，小さなアパートに住んでいる人に電話してもよく耳にする語である．

b) 大学に問合せをしている人に対して

〈ビル：ここの一番安い授業料の資格は何なのですか〉
Bill: How do you qualify for the lowest tuition here?
〈受付係：あなたの住居の所在地がこの市の中でなければならないのです〉
Receptionist:
 ☆ A Your place of residence has to be within the city limits.
 ◎ B Your house [residence] has to be within the city limits.
 × C Your home has to be within the city limits.

c) 要人の家
〈大使の住居は大使館の隣にあります〉
 ◎ A The ambassador's residence [house] is next-to the embassy.
 △ B The ambassador's home is next-to the embassy.

10 《屋敷》
〈彼は大きな屋敷に住んでいます〉
 ◎ He lives in a large estate [mansion].
 ❖ estate は広大な土地と屋敷，mansion は屋敷だけを意味しているという違いがある．

11 《プレハブ》
a) 建築方法を言及しているとき
〈私はプレハブ住宅を買いたいんです〉
 ◎ A I want to buy a prefabricated house [home].
 △ B I want to buy a prefab house [home].
 △ C I want to buy a prefab.
 ❖(1) 建築業者の間では B, C は非常によく使われている．
 ❖(2) prefabricated house とは，ほとんどを工場で規格品として作り上げ，現場でそれらを組み立てて建てられる家を呼ぶ．

b) 家の形状から述べるとき
〈彼らはプレハブに住んでいます〉
 ◎ A They live in a tract house.
 ◎ B They live in tract housing.
 △ C They live in a tract home.
 ❖ A, B, C は同じ型の小さな家が立ち並んでいるときに使われている．これも prefabricated house かもしれないが，この表現はその点には言及していない．家の造りからブルーカラーが主たる入居者で，そのイメージでも定着している．

12 《移動住宅》
〈彼らは移動住宅に住んでいるんです〉
 ☆ A They live in a trailer.
 ◎ B They live in a mobile [trailer] home.
 × C They live in a mobile [trailer] house.
 × D They live in a house trailer.
 ❖ C, D が辞典に出ているが使われていない．

13 《高層アパート》
〈彼らは高層アパートに住んでいます〉
 ☆ A They live in a high-rise.
 ◎ B They live in a high-rise apartment (building).

家にいる
1 《命令文のとき》
〈電話をするまで家にいて下さい〉
 ◎ A Stay (at) home until I call you.

△ B Be (at) home until I call you.
2 《疑問文のとき》
〈昨夜家にいたのですか〉
　　☆ A Did you stay home last night?
　　☆ B Were you home last night?
　　◎ C Did you stay at home last night?
　　○ D Were you at home last night?
3 《否定文のとき》
〈私は昨夜家にいませんでした〉
　　☆ A I wasn't home last night.
　　◎ B I didn't stay home last night.
　　◎ C I wasn't at home last night.
　　○ D I didn't stay at home last night.
4 《話し手と聞き手が家のそば（例：庭）にいて現在の状態を述べるとき》
〈彼は家にいます〉
　　◎　　He's at [in] his house.
5 《話し手と聞き手が家から離れた所にいて現在の状態を述べるとき》
〈彼は家にいます〉
　　◎ A He's at home.
　　○ B He's staying (at) home.
6 《…の「家に泊る」と言うとき》
〈私はニューヨークを訪ねたときはおじさんの家に泊ります〉
　　☆ A I'm going to stay with my uncle when I visit New York.
　　◎ B I'm going to stay at my uncle's when I visit New York.
　　◎ C I'm going to stay at my uncle's house [home] when I visit New York.
　　○ D I'm going to stay at my uncle's place when I visit New York.

胃潰瘍　→病気 5
生かせる
〈邦雄：どんな仕事を探しているのですか〉
Kunio: What kind of job are you looking for?
〈次郎：英語を生かせる仕事に就きたいんです〉
Jiro:
　　◎ A I want to get a job where I can use my English.
　　◎ B I want to get a job where I can use my English abilities.
　　◎ C I want to get a job where I can use my knowledge of English.
　　× D I want to get a job where I can use English.

医科大学
1 《名前に言及しないとき》
〈私は医科大学へ行きたいんです〉
　　◎ A I want to go to a medical school.
　　△ B I want to go to a school of medicine.
　　× C I want to go to a medical college [university].
　　❖日本語につられてCを使わないこと．Bは名前と共に使う．
2 《名前に言及するとき》
〈彼はハーバード医科大学へ通っています〉
　　◎ A He goes to Harvard Medical School.
　　◎ B He goes to Medical School at Harvard.
　　△ C He goes to Harvard School of Medicine.

❖(1) C は卒業証書のような文章でよく使われている.
❖(2) 「大学」の項も参照のこと.

息
1 《呼吸・息遣い》
〈どうして息を切らしているのですか〉
  ◎ A Why are you out of breath?
  △ B Why are you breathless?
2 《比喩的に》
〈彼は有名とは言えないが、息が長い作家だ〉
  ◎ A Although he isn't widely known, he's been writing for a long time.
  ◎ B Although he isn't widely known, he's been a writer for a long time.
  × C Although he isn't widely known, he's a writer of long standing.
  ❖ C が辞典で口語表現として紹介されているが、話し言葉では使われていない.

意気投合する
〈私たちは会った瞬間、意気投合したんです〉
  ☆ A We hit it off from the moment we met.
  ◎ B We really clicked from the moment we met.
  ○ C We got [had] really good vibes from the moment we met.
  ○ D There was really good chemistry between us from the moment we met.

行く →…しに行く
1 《話し手と聞き手が一緒になるとき》
〈(電話で) 今私はあなたの事務所へ行くところです〉
  ◎ A I'm coming to your office now.
  × B I'm going to your office now.
2 《着くというニュアンスのとき》
〈新宿へ行くにはどう行ったら一番いいのですか〉
  ◎ A What's the best way to get to Shinjuku?
  ○ B What's the best way to go to Shinjuku?
  × C What's the best way to arrive [be] at Shinjuku?
3 《場所と時間が明示されているとき》
〈私は5時にそこへ行きます〉
  ◎ I'll be [get, go] there at 5:00.
  ❖ go には「着く」と「出発する」の2つの意味があり、どちらであるかは話の前後から判断する.
4 《文中に somewhere などの場所を示す語があるとき》
〈あなたはどこかへ行かなければならないのですか. 急いでいるみたいな口振りですね〉
  ◎ A Do you have to be somewhere? You sound like you're in a hurry.
  ○ B Do you have to go somewhere? You sound like you're in a hurry.
  △ C Do you have to get somewhere? You sound like you're in a hurry.
5 《相手の家, 相手が指定するレストランへ食事に招かれたとき》
〈ジェーン: 今晩食事に来られますか〉
Jane: Can you come to my place for dinner tonight?
〈リンダ: 喜んで. 退社したらすぐ行きます〉
Linda:
  ◎ A I'd love to. I'll be [come] over right after I get off work.
  ◎ B I'd love to. I'll be there right after I get off work.

△ C I'd love to. I'll come over to your house right after I get off work.
6 《相手の事務所へ立ち寄ることを求められたとき》
〈ビル：仕事が終わった後で立ち寄れますか〉
Bill: Can you stop by my office after you get off work?
〈トム：もちろん．5時頃行きます〉
Tom:
　　◎　　Sure. I'll be over [come over, be there] around 5 o'clock.
7 《手段を述べるとき》
a) 電車の場合
〈私は電車で会社に行きます〉
　　☆　A I take the train to (get to) work.
　　◎　B I go to work on the train.
　　◎　C I get to work by train.
　　◎　D I go to work by train.
　　◎　E I ride (on) the train to work.
　　◎　F I use the train to get to work.
　　△　G I commute to work by train.
　　▽　H I use the train to work.
　　　❖ Hは辞典に出ているがほとんど使われていない．Gは多少使われているが堅い響きがある．
b) 車の場合
〈私は車で会社に行きます〉
　　◎　A I take my car to work.
　　◎　B I drive to work.
　　○　C I go to work by car.
　　△　D I use my car to get to work.
c) 自転車の場合
〈私は毎朝自転車で駅まで行きます〉
　　☆　A I bike to the station every morning.
　　☆　B I ride my bike to the station every morning.
　　◎　C I take my bike to the station every morning.
　　◎　D I ride my bicycle to the station every morning.
　　○　E I take my bicycle to the station every morning.
　　○　F I bicycle to the station every morning.
　　△　G I go by bike [bicycle] to the station every morning.
8 《乗り物・交通機関が明示されるとき》
〈東京では地下鉄でどこへでも行かれます〉
　　◎　A In Tokyo the subway can get [take] you anywhere.
　　◎　B In Tokyo you can get anywhere by subway.
　　○　C In Tokyo the subway'll get [take] you anywhere.
　　△　D In Tokyo you can go anywhere by subway.

いく人かの
1 《多いという気持ちで述べるとき》
〈ビル：ジムには親友が大勢いるのですか〉
Bill: Does Jim have a lot of good friends?
〈ロン：うん，いく人かいるよ〉
Ron:
　　◎　A Yes, he has several.
　　▽　B Yes, he has a few.

▽ C Yes, he has some.
❖ several, a few, some は日本語の上では同じで「いく人かの」になる。しかし、これらの語には次のような違いがある。several は数が「多い」、a few は数が「少ない」というニュアンスを持った主観的な語であるのに対して、some は「多い」「少ない」のどちらのニュアンスもなく、客観的に述べるときに使われている。

2 《少ないという気持ちで述べるとき》
〈ビル：ジムには親友が大勢いるのですか〉
Bill: Does Jim have a lot of good friends?
〈ロン：いいえ、でもいく人かはいますよ〉
Ron:
  ◎ A No, but he has a few.
  ◎ B No, but he has some.
  × C No, but he has several.

いくらですか

1 《金額を示す語があるとき》
〈消費税はいくらですか〉
  ◎ A What's the sales tax?
  ◎ B How much's the sales tax?

2 《手付金》
a) アパート・テーラー・旅行代理店で
〈手付金はいくらですか〉
  ◎ A What's the deposit?
  ◎ B How much's the deposit?
   ❖アパートを探していて気に入った物件が見つかったとき、旅行代理店で団体旅行に参加するとき、テーラーで注文するときに支払う手付金のこと。

b) デパート・店などで予約完納時に引き渡す
〈手付金はいくらですか〉
  ◎ A What's the layaway charge?
  ◎ B How much's the layaway charge?
  ◎ C How much does it cost for layaway?
   ❖売らないで取って置いて欲しいときに支払う手付金のこと。

3 《弁護士・会計事務所などの謝礼》
〈謝礼はいくらですか〉
  ◎ A What's your fee?
  ◎ B How much do you charge me?
  ○ C How much's your fee?

4 《ホテルでの宿泊代》
〈シングルルームの1泊の料金はいくらですか〉
  ◎ A What's the rate for a single room per night?
  ◎ B How much's the rate for a single room per night?

5 《高速道路の料金》
〈料金（通行料）はいくらですか〉
  ◎ A What's the toll?
  ◎ B How much's the toll?

6 《家・土地・店・会社などの値段》
〈(不動産屋に尋ねて) あの家はいくらですか〉
  ◎ A What's the seller asking for that house?
  ◎ B What's the price for that house?

- ○ C How much's the seller asking for that house?
- ○ D How much's the price for that house?
- ○ E What're they asking for that house?
  - ❖売り主は1人でも they がよく使われている．決り文句のひとつ．
7 《新聞・雑誌などの購読料金》
〈購読料はいくらですか〉
- ◎ A What's the subscription cost?
- ◎ B How much's the subscription?
- ○ C What's the subscription rate?
8 《請求額が驚くほど高いとき》
〈この弁護士はいくら私に請求したと思う〉
- ◎ A What kind of money do you think this lawyer charged me?
- ◎ B What do you think this lawyer charged me?
- ◎ C How much money do you think this lawyer charged me?
- × D What sort of money do you think this lawyer charged me?

意見
1 《一般的に述べるとき》
〈私はあなたの意見に同意します〉
- ◎ A I agree with your opinion.
- ○ B I agree with your view.
- × C I agree with your version.
2 《話し手または聞き手が当事者のとき》
〈日本の経済がどうなるかについては，対立する意見がある〉
- ◎ A There are conflicting versions [opinions] of what'll happen to Japan's economy.
- ○ B There are conflicting views of what'll happen to Japan's economy.

〈コロンバイン高校の乱射事件についてあなたの意見は何ですか〉
- ◎ A What's your version [opinion] of shooting spree incident at Columbine High School?
- ○ B What's your view of shooting spree incident at Columbine High School?
  - ❖コロンバイン高校に関係のない人に尋ねるときはAの version は使われていない．

意向［意図］
1 《確認する》
〈私は彼の意向が理解できませんでした〉
- ◎ A I couldn't figure out what he wanted (to do).
- ◎ B I couldn't figure out what he was going to do.
- △ C I couldn't figure out his intentions [intention].
  - ❖日本語につられて C を使う人が多いであろう．しかし，英語では A, B の方がずっとよく使われている．
2 《はっきりさせる》
〈あなたは自分の意向をはっきりさせるべきです〉
- ◎ A You should make it clear what you want to do.
- ◎ B You should make it clear what you're going to do.
- ○ C You should make your intentions [intention] clear.
3 《尋ねる》
〈あなたはこれについて彼の意向を尋ねたのですか〉
- ☆ A Did you ask him what he wants to do with this?

- ◎ B Did you ask him what he's going to do with [for] this?
- ◎ C Did you ask him what he wants for this?
- △ D Did you ask his intentions [intention] for this?
- △ E Did you ask his intentions [intention] about this?
- × F Did you ask his intentions [intention] with this?
  - ❖意図＝intention と結びつけているせいか，D，E が多くの辞典に出ている．しかし，アメリカ人は A，B，C で表現することが多い．

いじくりまわす
1 《強い口調のとき》
〈私のカメラをいじくりまわさないで下さい〉
- ◎ A Don't fuck around with my camera, please.
- ◎ B Don't screw around with my camera, please.
- ◎ C Don't fool around with my camera, please.
  - ❖(1) A が一番強い調子，B，C の順で下がる．
  - ❖(2) A，B とも劣俗な表現なので気を使う人がいるときは使われていない．

2 《普通の口調のとき》
〈私のカメラをいじくりまわさないで下さい〉
- ◎ A Don't play (around) with my camera.
- ◎ B Don't mess (around) with my camera.
- ○ C Don't monkey (around) with my camera.
- △ D Don't fiddle (around) with my camera.
- △ E Don't toy (around) with my camera.

いじめる
1 《深刻に》
〈みんな彼の訛りをいじめたんです〉
- ◎ A Everybody picked on his accent.
- ◎ B Everybody picked on him about his accent.
- ○ C Everybody picked on him for his accent.
- △ D Everybody pestered him about his accent.

2 《軽い気持ちで》
〈みんな彼の訛りをいじめたんです〉
- ◎ A Everybody teased [bugged] him about his accent.
- ◎ B Everybody poked fun at [made fun of] his accent.
- △ C Everybody needled him about his accent.

医者
1 《眼科医》
〈彼は眼科医です〉
- ☆ A He's an eye specialist.
- ◎ B He's an eye doctor.
- △ C He's an ophthalmologist.
  - ❖ C は医学界では非常によく使われている．

2 《肛門医》
〈彼は肛門医です〉
- ◎ A He's a proctologist.
- △ B He's a butt doctor.
- △ C He's an end specialist.

3 《産婦人科医》
〈彼は産婦人科医です〉
- ◎   He's an obstetrician.

28　いしゃ

4　《耳鼻咽喉科》
〈彼は耳鼻咽喉科医です〉
- ◎　A　He's an ear, nose and throat specialist.
- ○　B　He's an ear, nose and throat doctor [man].
- △　C　He's an ENT doctor.

5　《小児科医》
〈彼は小児科医です〉
- ◎　A　He's a pediatrician.
- ◎　B　He's a children's doctor.
- ○　C　He's a kid's doctor.

6　《心臓専門医》
〈彼は心臓専門医です〉
- ☆　A　He's a heart specialist.
- ◎　B　He's a heart surgeon [doctor].
- ○　C　He's a cardiologist.

7　《整形外科医》
〈彼は整形外科医です〉
- ☆　A　He's a bone doctor.
- ◎　B　He's an orthopedic surgeon.
- ◎　C　He's an orthopedist.

8　《精神科医》
a）客観的に述べるとき
〈彼は精神科医です〉
- ◎　　　He's a psychiatrist.

b）少し否定的に述べるとき
〈彼は精神科医です〉
- ◎　A　He's shrink.
- ○　B　He's a headshrinker.
- ○　C　He's a head doctor.
  - ❖ Bが一番否定的な響きがある．Cが2番目，Aが3番目．

9　《精神病院》
a）客観的に述べるとき
〈彼は精神病院に入っているんです〉
- ◎　A　He's in a mental [psychiatric] hospital.
- ○　B　He's in a mental [psychiatric] institution.
- ○　C　He's in a mental home.
- ○　D　He's in an insane asylum.
- △　E　He's in a psychiatric home [asylum].

b）軽蔑的に述べるとき
〈彼は精神病院にいます〉
- ◎　A　He's in a loony bin.
- ○　B　He's in a mad house.
- ○　C　He's in a nut house.
- △　D　He's in a loony [funny] farm.
- ×　E　He's in a bughouse.
- ×　F　He's in a sanatorium for the insane.
  - ❖(1) Bは50歳以上の人の間では非常によく使われている．
  - ❖(2) E, Fは辞典に出ているが使われていない．

c）婉曲に述べるとき

〈彼は精神病院に入っているんです〉
- ◎ He's in a state hospital.
  - ❖ state hospital は 40 歳以上の人の間では非常によく使われているが，若年層の間では時々しか使われていない．

10 《内科医》
〈彼は内科医です〉
- ◎ A He's an internist.
- × B He's a physician.
  - ❖(1) B は英和・和英辞典で「内科医」と紹介されているが使われていない．
  - ❖(2) A の internist（内科医）はアメリカの医者，または医療関係者の間では非常によく使われている．しかし，一般の人々の間では全く使われていない．なぜなら，一般の人々は日常，内臓のどこかが悪いと感じたときは general practitioner（もしくは G.P.；一般総合医）の所へ行く．general practitioner は family practice（全科医療；約 55 %），Internal Medicine（内科医学；約 35 %），Osteopathy（整骨療法；約 10 %）で構成されている．internal medicine は general practitioner の中に組み込まれているために，一般の人々は internist という言葉を使う機会がないので，知らないのである．
  - ❖(3) general practitioner は文字が示す通り，軽い治療なら内科，外科，耳鼻科などを診る．
  - ❖(4) physician を英和辞典で引くと，どれも「内科医」という訳語がつけられ誤訳されている．これは英米の辞典，つまり英英辞典にでてくる physician の定義を明治時代に誤訳したのがいまだに誤解されたまま，踏襲されているためであることをここで強く指摘したい．参考までに，ここに定義を紹介しておく．one engaged in general medical practice, as distinguished from one specializing in surgery. 下線部分の surgery（外科）にひっかかって，外科の反対の内科，つまり内科医と誤訳したのであろう．
  - ❖(5) アメリカ人には internist とは intern（医学研修生）と同意語であると思っている人が多い．前記した理由で internist の存在を知らないからである．

11 《脳外科医》
〈彼は脳外科医です〉
- ☆ A He's a brain surgeon.
- ◎ B He's a brain specialist.
- ○ C He's a neurologist.
- △ D He's a brain doctor.

12 《皮膚科医》
〈彼は皮膚科医です〉
- ☆ A He's a skin doctor.
- ◎ B He's a dermatologist.
- ○ C He's a skin specialist.

13 《美容外科医》
a） 一般の人対象
〈彼は美容外科医です〉
- ◎ He's a plastic surgeon.

b） 金持ちの人対象
〈彼は美容外科医です〉
- ◎ He's a cosmetic surgeon.

14 《婦人科医》

〈彼は婦人科医です〉
- ◎ A He's a gynecologist.
- △ B He's a women's doctor.

15 《麻酔専門医》
〈彼は麻酔専門医です〉
- ◎ A He's an anesthesiologist.
- × B He's an anesthetist.
  - ❖ B が辞典に出ているが使われていない．

16 《やぶ医者》
〈彼はやぶ医者です〉
- ◎ A He's a quack.
- ◎ B He's a bad doctor.
- △ C He's an incompetent doctor.
- × D He's a quack [horse] doctor.
  - ❖(1) D が辞典に出ているが使われていない．
  - ❖(2) A は B よりずっと否定的ニュアンスが強い．

慰謝料
〈航空会社は事故で死んだ人たちの遺族に，慰謝料を支払った〉
- ◎ A The airline compensated the relatives of the victims of the accident.
- ▽ B The airline paid compensation money to the relatives of the victims of the accident.
- × C The airline paid consolation money to the relatives of the victims of the accident.

忙しい
1 《動詞を従えるとき》
〈私は司法試験の準備で忙しいんです〉
- ☆ A I'm busy getting ready for the bar.
- ▽ B I'm busy in getting ready for the bar.
- × C I'm busy to get ready for the bar.
  - ❖ B が辞典に出ているがまれ．

2 《名詞を従えるとき》
〈私は今仕事で忙しいんです〉
- ◎ A I'm busy working now.
- ○ B I'm busy with [at] my work now.
  - ❖ A は名詞を従えていないが，動詞がある限り，A の型が一番よく使われている．

3 《スケジュール》
〈私は今日1日中スケジュールが忙しいんです〉
- ☆ A I'm really booked all day today.
- ◎ B My schedule's really full all day today.
- ◎ C My schedule's really booked (up) all day today.
- ◎ D I'm really tied up all day today.
- ○ E I'm really booked up all day today.
- ○ F My time's really limited all day today.

4 《忙殺される》
〈私は仕事で忙しいんです〉
- ◎ A I'm swamped with (my) work.
- ◎ B I'm swamped at my job.
- ◎ C I'm snowed under with (my) work.

◎ D I'm up to my elbows with (my) work.
　　　◎ E I'm up to my elbows [neck] in work.
　　　◎ F I'm pressed with (my) work.
　　　◎ G I'm pressed at work.
　　　❖ A, B, Cが一番忙殺度が強いというニュアンスがある．D, Eが次に強い．
5　《殺人的な》
〈彼は殺人的なスケジュールなんです〉
　　　◎ A He's on a killer [very tight] schedule.
　　　▽ B He's on a killing schedule.
　　　❖ Bが辞典に出ているがまれ．
6　《てんてこ舞い》
〈今日はてんてこ舞いでした〉
　　　◎ A Today was hectic [crazy].
　　　◎ B Today was extremely busy.
　　　◎ C Today was awfully [terribly] busy.
　　　❖ てんてこ舞いの度合いでは，Aが一番強いというニュアンスがある．2番目はB, 3番目はC．
7　《手が離せない》
〈私は今，手が離せないんです〉
　　　◎ A I'm tied up at the moment.
　　　◎ B I can't get away right now.
　　　◎ C My hands're full right now.

急ぐ

1　《目的地に言及するとき》
〈私たちは急いで病院へ行きました〉
　　　◎ A We rushed [ran, flew, hurried] to the hospital.
　　　○ B We dashed to the hospital.
　　　△ C We made a dash to the hospital.
　　　× D We hurried up to the hospital.
　　　❖ Dのhurry up toは命令文以外では使われていない．
2　《命令文》
a）成人に普通に言うとき
〈急いで下さい〉
　　　☆ A Hurry up, please.
　　　◎ B Hurry, please.
　　　△ C Rush, please.
　　　△ D Be quick, please.
　　　△ E Speed it up, please.
　　　▽ F Make haste, please.
b）子供に言うとき
〈急いで〉
　　　◎ A Be quick.
　　　◎ B Speed it up.
　　　◎ C Hurry up.
　　　○ D Hurry.
　　　△ E Rush.
3　《急いで何かを持って来させるとき》
〈急いで携帯電話を持ってきて〉
　　　☆ A Hurry. Bring my cell phone.

いそぐ

- ◎ B Bring my cell phone quick.
- ○ C Hurry and bring my cell phone.
- ○ D Hurry up. Bring my cell phone.

4 《急いで何かをやらせるとき》
〈急いで仕事をやって下さい〉
- ◎ A Hurry with your work.
- ◎ B Finish your work in a hurry.
- ◎ C Hurry and finish your work.
- ◎ D Finish your work quick.
- ◎ E Finish your work quickly.
- ○ F Get through (with) your work in a hurry.
- ○ G Be done with your work in a hurry.
- △ H Rush your work.

5 《「促進する」という意味のとき》
〈私の就労ビザを急いでくれますか〉
- ◎ A Will you speed up [hurry] my work visa?
- ○ B Will you expedite my work visa?

6 《「急がなければならない」と述べるとき》
〈私は急がなければならないんです〉
- ☆ A I've got to hurry.
- ◎ B I've got to hurry up.
- ◎ C I've got to get out of here.
- ◎ D I've got to run.
- ◎ E I've got to get going.
- ○ F I've got to rush.
- ○ G I've got to get a move on.
- △ H I've got to fly.
- △ I I'm running out of time.
- △ J My time's running out.
- △ K I'm pressed for time.

7 《急いで帰る》
a) 単に「急いで帰る」と言うとき
〈私は急いで事務所へ帰らなければならないんです〉
- ◎ I've got to fly [race, dash, rush, hurry] back to the office.
  - ❖ fly が一番急いでいるニュアンスがあり race, dash, rush, hurry の順で急いでいるニュアンスは下がる．

b)「車で急いで帰る」と言うとき
〈彼は車で急いで事務所へ行きました〉
- ◎ A He drove to the office in a hurry.
- ◎ B He jumped in a car and flew [rushed, raced off] to the office.
- ◎ C He flew to the office.
- △ D He sped off to the office.
- △ E He drove like a bat out of hell to the office.
  - ❖ C は「歩いて行く」という意味もある．

8 《急いで連れて行く》
〈彼はひどいけがをしています．急いで彼を病院へ連れて行かなければなりません〉
- ◎ A He's badly hurt. We've got to rush [race, bring] him to the hospital.
- ◎ B He's badly hurt. We've got to get him to the hospital.

- ◎ C He's badly hurt. We've got to take him to the hospital immediately [right away, quickly, quick].
- × D He's badly hurt. We've got to dash him to the hospital.
  - ❖(1) D が辞典に出ているが使われていない．
  - ❖(2) A, B にも「すぐに」の意味が入っているが，C の take には入っていないので，immediately, right away, quickly, quick が必要である．
  - ❖(3) A, B にも immediately, right away, quickly, quick をつけて強調してもよく使われている．
  - ❖(4) B の get には「すぐ連れて行く」の意味を紹介している辞典はないが，実際にはよく使われている．

9 《急ぐ理由を尋ねるとき》
〈どうして急いでいるのですか〉
- ◎ A What's the rush [hurry]?
- ◎ B Why're you in a hurry [rush]?

10 《「急いでいません」と言うとき》
〈これは急いでいません〉
- ◎ A I can wait for this.
- ◎ B There's no hurry [rush] for this.
- ◎ C I'm not in a rush for this.
- ○ D I'm not in a hurry for this.
- △ E I'm not pressed for this.

11 《車を運転している人に》
a) 普通に言うとき
〈急いで〉
- ☆ A Step on it.
- ◎ B Step on the gas.
- ○ C Speed (it) up.
- ○ D Get a move on.
- ○ E Give it some gas.
- △ F Hit the gas.
- △ G Give it a gun.
- × H Put on [Increase] the speed.
  - ❖ H が辞典に出ているが使われていない．

b) 強く急がせたいとき
〈急いでよ〉
- ◎ A Gun it.
- ○ B Put the pedal to the metal.
- △ C Give it a lot of gas.

12 《「さっさとする」という意味のとき》
〈息子：お昼までにもう5本電話しなければならないんだ〉
Son: I've got to make another five phone calls by noon.
〈父親：それなら急いでかけなさい〉
Father:
- ◎ A Get started [busy] then.
- ◎ B Get on [to] it then.
- ◎ C Get going then.
- △ D Hop to it then.
- △ E Get with it then.
- △ F Step on it then.

❖ C は別の部屋へ行って電話するときと，A, B, D, E, F と同様に同じ部屋でかけるときの両方で使われている．
 13　《「すっ飛んで行く」と言うとき》
〈私は彼が入口へすっ飛んで行くのを見ました〉
　　　◎　　I saw him flying [racing, dashing, rushing, hurrying] to the door.
　　　❖flyが一番速度が速いニュアンスがあり，race, dash, rush, hurryの順で下がる．

痛い
 1　《頭痛》
 a）頭全体に痛みがあるとき
〈私は頭が痛いんです〉
　　　◎　A　I have a headache.
　　　◎　B　My head hurts.
　　　○　C　My head's hurting [aching].
　　　○　D　My head aches.
　　　△　E　My head's painful.
　　　×　F　My head's smarts.
　　　❖ F が辞典に出ているが現代アメリカ英語では使われていない
 b）頭全体に強い痛みがあるとき
〈私はすごく頭痛がするんです〉
　　　◎　A　I have a terrible headache.
　　　◎　B　I have a severe headache.
　　　◎　C　I have an awful headache.
　　　◎　D　I have a bad headache.
　　　◎　E　My head's really hurts.
　　　○　F　My head's really hurting.
　　　○　G　My head's really aches.
　　　△　H　My head's really aching.
　　　❖ B が一番強く，A, C の順で弱くなり，D, E, F は同じで A, C よりさらに弱くなる．G, H が一番弱い．
 c）頭の一点，または一部に痛みがあるとき
〈私は頭の後ろがすごく痛いんです〉
　　　☆　A　I have a terrible pain in the back of my head.
　　　◎　B　I have a lot of pain in the back of my head.
　　　◎　C　I have an awful [a sharp, a bad] pain in the back of my head.
　　　◎　D　The back of my head really hurts.
　　　◎　E　The back of my head's really hurting (me).
　　　◎　F　The back of my head hurts terribly [a lot, bad].
　　　○　G　The back of my head hurts badly.
　　　△　H　The back of my head hurts awfully.
　　　△　I　The back of my head's really painful.
　　　❖(1) A〜C は頭の内部が病気，または打撲で痛いとき．
　　　❖(2) D〜I は頭の内部か表面か不明だが，原因は A〜C と同じで病気，または打撲で痛いとき．
 d）がんがんする痛み
〈頭ががんがん痛むんです〉
　　　☆　A　My head's pounding.
　　　☆　B　I have a pounding headache.
　　　◎　C　I have a throbbing headache.

◎ D My head's throbbing.
○ E My head throbs.
△ F My head pounds.
× G My head's stinging.
❖ A, B の方が C, D より痛みが激しい．

2 《背中の痛み》
a) 背中全体のとき
〈私は背中が痛いんです〉
◎ A I have a backache.
◎ B My back hurts.
○ C My back aches.
○ D My back's hurting.

b) 背中の 1 ヵ所のとき
〈私は背中がひどく痛いんです〉
☆ A I have a terrible pain in my back.
◎ B I have a lot of pain in my back.
◎ C I have an awful [a sharp, a bad] pain in my back.
◎ D My back really hurts.
◎ E My back's hurting (me).
◎ F My back hurts a lot [terribly, bad].
○ G My back hurts badly.
△ H My back hurts awfully.
△ I My back's really painful.
❖ D, E, F, G, H は背中の一部にも全体にも使われている．

3 《歯痛》
a) 一般的に述べるとき
〈私は歯が痛いんです〉
☆ A I have a toothache.
◎ B My tooth hurts.
○ C My tooth aches.
○ D I have a pain in my tooth.
○ E My tooth's hurting.
△ F My tooth's painful for me.
❖ 2本以上の歯が痛くても teeth ではなく，tooth を使う．teeth を使うときは全部の歯が痛いときだけ．

b) 強い歯痛があるとき
〈私は歯がすごく痛いんです〉
☆ A My tooth really hurts.
◎ B My tooth really aches.
○ C I have a lot of pain in my tooth.
○ D I have a terrible [an awful, a bad] toothache.
○ E My tooth's really hurting.
○ F I have a terrible [an awful, a bad] pain in my tooth.
△ G I have a severe pain in my tooth.
△ H I have a severe toothache.
△ I My tooth's really aching.
△ J The tooth's really painful to me.

c) ずきんずきんする痛み
〈歯がずきんずきん痛むんです〉

- ◎ A My tooth's throbbing.
- ○ B I have a throbbing toothache.
- △ C My tooth's pounding.
- ▽ D I have a pounding toothache.

4 《目の痛み》

a ）一般的に述べるとき

〈目が痛いんです〉
- ◎ A My eyes hurt.
- ◎ B My eyes're sore.
- △ C My eyes ache.
- △ D My eyes're aching.
- △ E My eyes're painful to me.

b ）「ひりひりする」「ちくちくする」と述べたいとき

〈目がちくちくするんです〉
- ☆ A My eyes're really burning.
- ☆ B My eyes really burn.
- ◎ C My eyes're really stinging.
- ◎ D My eyes really sting.

5 《のどの痛み》

a ）一般的に述べるとき

〈私はのどが痛いんです〉
- ◎ A I have a scratchy throat.
- ◎ B My throat's scratchy.
- ◎ C I have a sore throat.
- ◎ D My throat's sore.
- ◎ E My throat's hurts.
- ◎ F My throat's hurting (me).
    - ❖ A, B は初期の痛み, C, D は A, B より悪化していてかなり痛い状態をいう. E, F はいずれの段階にも使える.

b ）ひどく痛みがあるとき

〈私はのどがとても痛いんです〉
- ◎ A I have a really [very] scratchy throat.
- ◎ B My throat's really [very] scratchy.
- ◎ C I have a really [very] sore throat.
- ◎ D My throat's really [very] sore.
- ◎ E My throat's really hurting (me).
- ◎ F My throat really hurts.
- ◎ G My throat's stinging.
- ○ H My throat really stings.
- ○ I I have a lot of pain in my throat.
- △ J My throat's really painful to me.
- ▽ K My throat's really burning.
- × L My throat smarts.
    - ❖(1) L は辞典に出ているが使われていない.
    - ❖(2) A, B は初期の痛み, C, D は A, B より悪化している状態をいう. E〜H はいかなる段階にも使われている.
    - ❖(3) I が一番悪化している響きがある.
    - ❖(4) のどは狭いので, 頭や背中のように全体, 一か所の痛みで表現を区別しない.

6 《おなか》
a） 全体に痛みがあるとき
〈私はおなかが痛いんです〉
- ◎ A I have a stomachache.
- ◎ B My stomach hurts.
- ○ C My stomach's hurting (me).
- △ D My stomach aches.
    - ❖辞典には stomach＝「胃」と紹介されているが，アメリカ人は胃，大腸，小腸のことを stomach と呼ぶ．ただし，医者が患者に話すときは large intestine（大腸），small intestine（小腸），colon（結腸）と明示化して病状を説明する．

b） 局部的にすごく痛みがあるとき
〈私はおなかがすごく痛いんです〉
- ◎ A I have a terrible [a lot of, an awful, a bad] pain in my stomach.
- ◎ B My stomach really hurts.
- ◎ C My stomach's really hurting (me).
- △ D My stomach really aches.
- △ E My stomach's really painful.

c） 強い腹痛があることを述べるとき
〈私はおなかがすごく痛いんです〉
- ◎ A I have a terrible [a severe, an awful, a bad] stomachache.
- ◎ B My stomach really hurts.
- ◎ C My stomach's really hurting.
- ○ D I have a lot of [an awful, a bad] pain in my stomach.
- △ E I have a terrible [a severe] pain in my stomach.
- △ F My stomach really aches.

7 《傷が痛いと述べる場合》
a） 一般的に述べるとき
〈傷が痛いんです〉
- ☆ A The cut hurts.
- ◎ B The cut's hurting (me).
- △ C The cut hurts me.
- △ D The cut's painful to me.
- ▽ E The cut smarts.
- × F The cut's smarting.
- × G The cut aches.

b） 非常に痛いとき
〈傷口がとても痛いんです〉
- ☆ A My cut really hurts.
- ◎ B My cut really burns [stings].
- ◎ C My cut's really stinging.
- ◎ D My cut's really hurting.
- ○ E My cut's really burning.
- △ F My cut's really painful to me.
- × G My cut really smarts.
    - ❖(1) G が多くの辞典に出ているが使われていない．
    - ❖(2) A，D は鈍痛，B，C，E，F はひりひりする痛み．

8 《くつがきつくて痛いとき》
〈このくつはきついから指が痛いんです〉

- ◎ A These shoes pinch my toes because they're tight.
- ◎ B These shoes're pinching my toes because they're tight.
- ○ C These shoes hurt my toes because they're tight.
- ○ D These shoes're hurting my toes because they're tight.
- × E These shoes pinch [hurt] me at my toes because they're tight.
- × F These shoes're pinching [hurting] me at my toes because they're tight.

❖辞典に E, F が出ているが使われていない．

9 《行為を述べるとき》

〈注射を打ってもらったんです．とても痛かったです〉
- ☆ A I got a shot. It really hurt.
- ◎ B I got a shot. It really stung.
- ◎ C I got a shot. I was in a lot of pain.
- ○ D I got a shot. It was really painful [stinging].
- ○ E I got a shot. It was a terrible [a lot of] pain.
- ○ F I got a shot. I had a terrible [a lot of] pain.
- △ G I got a shot. It was an awful pain.
- × H I got a shot. It really ached.

10 《薬のために痛くなるとき》

〈この薬は痛いでしょう〉
- ◎ A This medicine'll hurt [sting].
- ○ B This medicine'll ache.
- △ C This medicine'll be painful.
- △ D This medicine'll smart.

11 《痛くて叫ぶとき》

〈痛い！〉
- ◎ A Ouch!
- ◎ B Oh! That hurts.
- × C How it hurts!
- × D How it's hurting!

❖辞典に C, D が出ているが使われていない．

12 《「…すると痛いんです」と述べる場合》

〈息をすると痛いんです〉
- ☆ A It hurts to breathe.
- ☆ B It hurts when I breathe.
- ◎ C It hurts breathing.
- ○ D It's painful to breathe.
- ○ E It's painful when I breathe.
- ○ F It's painful breathing.
- ○ G Breathing hurts.
- △ H Breathing's painful.
- △ I To breathe hurts.
- △ J To breathe's painful.

13 《痛い理由を述べる場合》

a ） 場所を明示しないとき

〈目が煙で痛いんです〉
- ☆ A My eyes hurt [sting] from the smoke.
- ☆ B My eyes're hurting [stinging, burning] from the smoke.
- ◎ C My eyes burn from the smoke.

- ◎ D My eyes hurt [sting, burn] because of the smoke.
- ◎ E My eyes're hurting [stinging, burning] because of the smoke.
- × F My eyes hurt [sting, burn] with the smoke.
- × G My eyes're hurting [stinging, burning, aching] with the smoke.
- × H My eyes're aching from [because of] the smoke.
  - ❖辞典に F, G, つまり前置詞 with の用例が出ているが使われていない. with が使われるのは, 下の b) の例のように場所を明示しているときである.

b) 場所を明示しているとき

〈事務所の煙で目が痛いんです〉

- ☆ A My eyes hurt [sting] from the smoke in the office.
- ☆ B My eyes're hurting [stinging, burning] from the smoke in the office.
- ◎ C My eyes burn from the smoke in the office.
- ◎ D My eyes hurt [sting, burn] because of the smoke in the office.
- ◎ E My eyes're hurting [stinging, burning] because of the smoke in the office.
- △ F My eyes hurt [sting, burn] with the smoke in the office.
- △ G My eyes're hurting [stinging, burning] with the smoke in the office.

14 《比喩的に》

a) 損害を述べるとき

〈私は昨年株で約 3000 万円損したんです. 私にはとても痛かったです〉

- ◎ A I lost about thirty million yen in the stock market. It was really painful for [to] me.
- ◎ B I lost about thirty million yen in the stock market. It was really hard to take [bear].
- ◎ C I lost about thirty million yen in the stock market. It really hurt me.
- ◎ D I lost about thirty million yen in the stock market. It hurts me a lot.

b) 被害を述べるとき

〈私は以前株で痛い思いをしたんです〉

- ◎ A I lost my shirt in the stock market before.
- ◎ B I got burned [hurt] in the stock market before.
- △ C I lost my ass [butt] in the stock market before.

c) 聞き手の急所を突いたとき

〈あなたは彼の痛いところを突いたね〉

- ☆ A You hit his sore spot.
- ◎ B You hit him where it hurts [hurt].
- △ C You touched him on his sore spot.
- △ D You hit him where it counts.
- △ E You hit him in his wallet.
- ▽ F You hit him where it counted.
- × G You trampled [treaded] on his corns.

d) 良心が痛む

〈良心が痛むんです〉

- ◎ A I have a guilty conscience.
- ◎ B My conscience bothers me.
- ○ C My conscience is bothering [bugging] me.
- ○ D My conscience bugs me.
- × E I have [feel] a pang of conscience.

一か八か
 1 《結果を恐れずにやるとき》
〈一か八かで東大を受けてみよう〉
- ◎ A No matter what happens, I'll try for Tokyo University.
- × B It's all or nothing. I'll try for Tokyo University.
  - ❖(1) 辞典に B が紹介されているが使われていない.
  - ❖(2) B の It's all or nothing. とは「ある場面でこれが最後のチャンス, このチャンスを逃したらもう道がない」というときにのみ使われている (→ 2).「一か八かで東大を受けてみよう」にはこのニュアンスがない. したがって使えないのである.

 2 《「これが最後のチャンス」を意味しているとき》
〈ジム：ガソリンの計器を見てくれよ. 足りるかね〉
Jim: Look at the gas gauge. Do we have enough gas to make it?
〈ダン：そう願いたいね. とにかく一か八かだ. この辺にはガソリンスタンドはないからね〉
Dan:
- ◎ I hope so. Anyway it's all or nothing now because there isn't a gas station around here.

1 日中 →…中 5
位置について, 用意, ドン
〈位置について, 用意, ドン〉
- ☆ A On your mark, get set, go.
- ◎ B Ready, set, go.
- ○ C Get ready, get set, go.

1 年中 →…中 7
1 年生
 1 《大学生》
〈彼女は 1 年生です〉
- ◎ A She's a freshman.
- × B She's a freshwoman [freshgirl].
  - ❖(1)「2 年生」は sophomore,「3 年生」は junior,「4 年生」は senior.
  - ❖(2) 女性でも freshwoman ではなく freshman である.

 2 《高校生》
〈彼女は 1 年生です〉
- ◎ A She's a freshman.
- ◎ B She's in the 9th grade.
  - ❖アメリカの中学校 (junior high) は① 6〜8 年, ② 7〜8 年, ③ 7〜9 年の 3 つがある. しかし, ①が圧倒的に多い. したがって, B は高校 (senior high) の 1 年生となる.

 3 《中学生》
〈彼女は 1 年生です〉
- ◎ A She's in the 7th grade.
- × B She's a freshman.

 4 《小学生》
〈彼女は 1 年生です〉
- ◎ A She's in the first grade.
- × B She's in the first year.

 5 《ビジネス》
〈彼はこのビジネスは 1 年生なんです〉

◎ A He's new to this business.
○ B He's a newcomer to [in] this business.
○ C He's a beginner in this business.
△ D He's a newbie to [in] this business.
△ E He's a greenhorn in this business.

一番重要だ
〈競争はビジネスで一番重要です〉
☆ A Competition is the name of the game in business.
○ B Competition is the most important thing in business.
○ C Competition counts the most in business.
△ D Competition matters the most in business.

一面のニュース
〈クリントンのスキャンダルは一面のニュースになった〉
☆ A The Clinton's scandal made the front page.
◎ B The Clinton's scandal hit the front page.
◎ C The Clinton's scandal made headlines.
◎ D The Clinton's scandal was on the front page.
○ E The Clinton's scandal was printed on the front page.
○ F The Clinton's scandal appeared on the front page.

一文無し
〈私は一文無しです〉
☆ A I'm flat broke.
◎ B I haven't got a dime [red cent].
○ C I don't have a dollar to my name.
△ D I'm penniless.
△ E I don't even have two nickels to rub together.
▽ F I'm stone-broke.
× G I'm stony-broke.
× H I'm dead beat.

一流の
1 《大学の場合》
〈彼は一流の大学を卒業しました〉
◎ A He graduated from a first-rate [top-notch, top-rate, top-ranking] university.
○ B He graduated from a leading [first-class] university.

2 《会社の場合》
〈XYZ は一流の会社です〉
◎ A XYZ is a leading [first-rate, top-notch, top-ranking] company.
○ B XYZ is a top-rate [first-class] company.

3 《デパートの場合》
〈高島屋は一流のデパートです〉
◎ A Takashimaya is a leading [first-class, top-notch, first-rate] department store.
△ B Takashimaya is a top-ranking [top-rate] department store.
❖「三流の」の項も参照のこと.

いつか
1 《夢を述べるとき》
〈私はいつか歌手になりたいんです〉
◎ A I want to be a singer someday.

- ○ B I want to be a singer one day.
- × C I want to be a singer sometime.

2 《時を明示しないで「いつか」と述べるとき》
〈いつか会いましょう〉
- ◎ A Let's get together sometime.
- ○ B Let's get together someday.
- △ C Let's get together one day.

3 《時を明示して「いつか」と述べるとき》
〈来週いつか会いましょう〉
- ◎ Let's get together sometime [someday, one day] next week.

一階

1 《「一階に」と言うとき》
〈彼の事務所は一階にあります〉
- ☆ A His office is on the first floor.
- ◎ B His office is on the ground floor.
- ○ C His office is on the ground level.
- △ D His office is on the street floor [level].
  - ❖(1) B はどの辞典もイギリス英語として紹介しているが，アメリカでも非常によく使われている．
  - ❖(2) C, D は辞典には出ていないが使われている．

2 《「一階上」と言うとき》
〈彼の事務所は一階上にあります〉
- ☆ A His office is the next floor up.
- ◎ B His office is one floor up.
- ◎ C His office is right above [over] us.
- ◎ D His office is just above [over] us.
- ○ E His office is directly above [over] us.
- △ F His office is immediately above [over] us.
- △ G His office is one flight up.
  - ❖ G は高層ビルがある大都市ほどよく使われている．高層ビルがない小さい町ではあまり使われていない．

3 《「一階下」と言うとき》
〈彼の事務所は一階下にあります〉
- ☆ A His office is the next floor down.
- ◎ B His office is one floor down.
- ◎ C His office is right below [under] us.
- ◎ D His office is just below [under] us.
- ○ E His office is directly below [under] us.
- △ F His office is immediately below [under] us.
- △ G His office is one flight down.
  - ❖ G は高層ビルがある大都市ほどよく使われている．高層ビルがない小さい町ではあまり使われていない．

いつから

1 《非批判的に尋ねるとき》
〈いつから日本にいらっしゃるのですか〉
- ◎ A How long've you been in Japan?
- ▽ B Since when've you been in Japan?

2 《批判的に尋ねるとき》
〈(父親から息子へ) いつからマリファナを吸っているんだ〉

◎ A Since when've you been smoking pot?
▽ B How long've you been smoking pot?
3 《驚きの気持ちで尋ねるとき》
〈ダイエットしているんですって．いつから〉
◎ A You're on a diet? Since when?
▽ B You're on a diet? How long?

一行
〈日本の政治家の一行が来月英国を訪問します〉
◎ A A group of Japanese politicians're going to visit Great Britain next month.
△ B A party of Japanese politicians're going to visit Great Britain next month.
❖テレビ，新聞などでは B は非常によく使われている．

いっしょくたにする
〈あなたが知っている他の日本の男性と私を，いっしょくたにしないでください〉
◎ A Please don't lump me in with all the other Japanese guys you know.
◎ B Please don't lump me together with all the other Japanese guys you know.
◎ C Please don't lump me with all the other Japanese guys you know.

一触即発
〈中東は一触即発ですね〉
☆ A The Middle East's touchy.
◎ B The Middle East's in an explosive situation.
○ C The Middle East's in a volatile situation.
△ D The Middle East's in a touch and go situation.
△ E The Middle East's in a hair-trigger situation.
× F The Middle East's a situation of dynamite.
❖(1) F が辞典に出ているが使われていない．
❖(2) C は新聞では非常によく使われている．

一緒に
1 《傘を使うとき》
〈一緒の傘に入りましょう〉
◎ A Let's share the umbrella.
○ B Let's use the umbrella together.
2 《どこかへ行く（来る）と述べるとき》
a）一般的に
〈今晩一緒に行ってもいいですか〉
◎ A Can I go with you tonight?
× B Can I accompany you tonight?
❖ B が辞典に出ているが使われていない．
b）強く述べるとき
〈私はそこへ彼と一緒に行ったんです〉
◎ A I went there along with him.
○ B I went there together with him.
c）子供が親に
〈一緒に行ってもいい〉
◎ Can I tag along [go] with you?
3 《歌うとき》
〈一緒に歌いましょう〉

◎ A Let's sing together.
△ B Let's sing in chorus [in unison, in one voice].

4 《手をつないで歩くとき》
〈2人は手をつないで一緒に歩いていました〉
◎ A They were walking along holding hands.
○ B They were walking hand in hand together.

5 《「一緒に苦労する」と述べるとき》
〈私たちはその頃一緒に苦労しました〉
◎ A We shared the bad times back then.
△ B We shared the hardships [hardship] back then.

6 《「力を合わせて」の意味のとき》
〈一緒に努力しましょう〉
☆ A Let's combine our efforts.
◎ B Let's pool [join] our efforts.
○ C Let's unite our efforts.
△ D Let's share our efforts.
△ E Let's put our efforts together.

7 《写真を撮ってもらうとき》
〈一緒に写真を撮ってもらいましょう〉
◎ A Let's have a picture taken (all) together.
○ B Let's have a picture take all in a group.

8 《「ひとまとめに」の意味のとき》
〈勘定は全部月末に一緒にお支払いします〉
☆ A I'll pay all the bills all together at the end of the month.
◎ B I'll pay all the bills in one [a] lump sum at the end of the month.
○ C I'll pay all the bills at one time at the end of the month.
○ D I'll pay all the bills in a [one] lump at the end of the month.
○ E I'll pay all the bills in one gross at the end of the month.

一線を画す

1 《2つの選択肢がある場合》
〈私は日本人は欧米人に対して親切すぎると思う。親切にすることと，過度に親切にすることとの間に一線を画さなければならない〉
◎ I think most Japanese people are overly kind to Europeans and Americans. We should draw the line [make a distinction, note the difference] between being polite and being overly kind.

2 《選択肢がない場合》
〈学生たちに親しみやすくすることは悪いことではない．しかしながら，それには限界がある．一線を画さなければならない〉
◎ A Nothing is wrong with being friendly to your students. But there's a limit to that. You have to draw the line.
× B Nothing is wrong with being friendly to your students. But there's a limit to that. You have to make a distinction [note the difference].

いったい

1 《Where と共に述べるとき》
a) 強く怒りの気持ちを表すとき
〈いったい彼はどこへ行ったんだ〉
◎ A Where (in) the hell've they gone?
◎ B Where the fuck've they gone?

- ○ C Jesus Christ, where've they gone?
- ○ D Jesus, where've they gone?
- ○ E Christ, where've they gone?
- △ F Where in hell've they gone?
- △ G Where the devil've they gone?
- × H Where in the nation've they gone?
- × I Where the deuce've they gone?
- × J Where the blazes've they gone?
- × K In the name of God [Christ, Jesus, heaven, goodness, common sense, devil], where've they gone?
    - ❖(1) H～K が辞典に出ているが使われていない．
    - ❖(2) 怒りの気持ちは B が一番強い．C が2番目，A, D, E, F, G が3番目．
    - ❖(3) B は性行為を意味する表現．したがって男性の方がよく使うが，女性同士の間でも非常によく使われている．
    - ❖(4) 信仰心の厚いキリスト教徒は A, C, D, E, F を使わない．アメリカ人の約85％はキリスト教徒でどこかの教会に所属しているが，敬虔な信者はきわめて少ない．

b) あまり怒りの気持ちを出さないとき

〈いったい彼らはどこへ行ったんですか〉

- ◎ A Where on earth've they gone?
- ◎ B Where in the world've they gone?
- ◎ C Where (in) the heck've they gone?
- △ D Where in heck've they gone?
    - ❖ C, D は hell の弱形で，1980 年代まではかなり怒りの気持ちが強かったが，今はもうそのような響きはない．

2 《When と共に述べる場合》

a) 未来形

・強く怒りの気持ちを表すとき

〈いったいいつになったら雨はやむんだ〉

- ◎ A When (in) the hell's it going to stop raining?
- ◎ B When the fuck's it going to stop raining?
- ○ C Jesus (Christ), when's it going to stop raining?
- ○ D Christ, when's it going to stop raining?
- △ E When in hell's it going to stop raining?
- △ F When in the devil's it going to stop raining?
- × G When in the nation's it going to stop raining?
- × H When the deuce's it going to stop raining?
- × I When the blazes is it going to stop raining?
- × J In the name of God [Christ, Jesus, heaven, goodness, common sense, devil], when's it going to stop raining?

・あまり怒りの気持ちを出さない

〈いったいいつになったら雨はやむんだろう〉

- ◎ A When's it ever going to stop raining?
- ◎ B When on earth's it ever going to stop raining?
- ◎ C When in the world's it ever going to stop raining?
- ◎ D When (in) the heck's it ever going to stop raining?
- △ E When in heck's it ever going to stop raining?

b) 過去形

・強く怒りの気持ちを表すとき
〈あなたはいったいいつ彼らの住宅ローンの連帯保証をしたのよ〉
- ◎ A When (in) the hell did you cosign for their home loan?
- ◎ B When the fuck did you cosign for their home loan?
- ○ C Jesus Christ, when did you cosign for their home loan?
- ○ D Jesus, when did you cosign for their home loan?
- △ E When (in) the heck did you cosign for their home loan?

・あまり怒りの気持ちを出さないとき
〈あなたはいったいいつ彼らの住宅ローンの連帯保証をしたの〉
- ◎ A When on earth did you cosign for their home loan?
- ◎ B When in the world did you cosign for their home loan?

3 《Why と共に述べる場合》

a）強く怒りの気持ちで述べるとき
〈いったいなぜ私が首になるのか〉
- ◎ A Why (in) the hell should I be fired?
- ◎ B Why (in) the hell would I be fired?
- ◎ C Why the fuck should [would] I be fired?
- ◎ D Why (in) the hell am I going to be fired?
- ◎ E Why the fuck am I going to be fired?
- ○ F Jesus (Christ), why am I going to be fired?
- ○ G Christ, why am I going to be fired?
- △ H Why in hell am I going to be fired?
- △ I Why the devil am I going to be fired?
- × J Why in the nation am I going to be fired?
- × K Why the deuce [blaze] am I going to be fired?
- × L In the name of God [Christ, Jesus, heaven, goodness, common sense, devil], why am I going to be fired?

❖(1) 怒りの気持ちは C, E が一番強い. A, B, D, F～I はだいたい同じで 2 番目.
❖(2) J, K, L が辞典に出ているが使われていない.

b）あまり怒りの気持ちを出さないとき
〈いったいなぜ私が首になるのですか〉
- ◎ A Why on earth am I going to be fired?
- ◎ B Why in the world am I going to be fired?
- ◎ C Why the hell am I going to be fired?
- ◎ D Why in the heck am I going to be fired?
- △ E Why in heck am I going to be fired?

4 《What と共に述べるとき》

a）強く怒りの気持ちを表すとき
〈1日中いったい何をしていたんだい〉
- ◎ A What (in) the hell've you been doing all day?
- ◎ B What the fuck've you been doing all day?
- ○ C Jesus (Christ), what've you been doing all day?
- ○ D Christ, what've you been doing all day?
- △ E What in hell've you been doing all day?

b）あまり怒りの気持ちを出さないとき
〈1日中いったい何をしていたのですか〉
- ◎ A What on earth've you been doing all day?
- ◎ B What in the world've you been doing all day?

◎ C　What the heck've you been doing all day?
　　　○ D　What (in) the heck've you been doing all day?
　5　《Who と共に述べるとき》
　a) 強く怒りの気持ちを表すとき
　〈いったいお前は自分をどこの誰だと思っているんだ〉
　　　◎ A　Who (in) the hell do you think you are?
　　　◎ B　Who the fuck do you think you are?
　　　○ C　Jesus (Christ), who do you think you are?
　　　○ D　Christ, who do you think you are?
　　　△ E　Who in hell do you think you are?
　b) 怒りの気持ちを表さないで述べるとき
　〈いったいあなたは自分を誰だと思っているのですか〉
　　　◎ A　Who on earth do you think you are?
　　　◎ B　Who in the world do you think you are?
　　　◎ C　Who (in) the heck do you think you are?
　　　△ D　Who in heck do you think you are?
　6　《How と共に述べるとき》
　a) 強く怒りの気持ちを表すとき
　〈いったいこのガラクタの車にいくら払ったんだい〉
　　　◎ A　How (in) the hell much did you pay for this piece of shit?
　　　◎ B　How the fuck much did you pay for this piece of shit?
　　　○ C　Jesus (Christ), how much did you pay for this piece of shit?
　　　○ D　Christ, how much did you pay for this piece of shit?
　　　△ E　How in hell much did you pay for this piece of shit?
　　　△ F　How the devil much did you pay for this piece of shit?
　　　△ G　How much (in) the hell did you pay for this piece of shit?
　　　△ H　How much the fuck did you pay for this piece of shit?
　b) あまり怒りの気持ちを表さないとき
　〈いったいこのポンコツにいくら払ったんですか〉
　　　◎ A　How on earth much did you pay for this pile of crap?
　　　◎ B　How in the world much did you pay for this pile of crap?
　　　◎ C　How (in) the heck much did you pay for this pile of crap?
　　　△ D　How in heck much did you pay for this pile of crap?
　　　△ E　How much on earth did you pay for this pile of crap?
　　　△ F　How much in the world did you pay for this pile of crap?
　　　△ G　How much (in) the heck did you pay for this pile of crap?

一杯にする

　1　《コーヒーカップなどのとき》
　〈カップを一杯にして下さい〉
　　　☆ A　Fill up the cup, please.
　　　◎ B　Fill the cup up, please.
　　　○ C　Fill the cup, please.
　2　《部屋を家具などで》
　〈部屋をたくさんの家具で一杯にしないで下さい〉
　　　◎ A　Don't fill the room with a lot of furniture.
　　　◎ B　Don't clutter the room (up) with a lot of furniture.
　3　《「一杯である」と状態を述べるとき》
　〈キャビネットは書類で一杯です〉
　　　◎ A　The cabinet's cluttered (up) with documents.

○ B The cabinet's full of documents.
❖ A はキャビネットの中が乱雑であるという響きがある．

一発で
1 《試験・クイズの場合》
〈彼は一発で運転免許証を取ったんです〉
☆ A He got his driver's license on the first try.
◎ B He got his driver's license on his first try.
○ C He got his driver's license the [his] first try.
○ D He got his driver's license the [his] first time.
× E He got his driver's license on the [his] first time.

2 《交渉の場合》
〈彼は一発で契約にサインしました〉
◎ He signed the contract after his first negotiation.

一匹狼
1 《一般的に述べるとき》
〈彼は一匹狼です〉
◎ A He's a maverick.
× B He's a lone wolf.
× C He's a loner.
❖(1) B, C が辞典に出ているが使われていない．
❖(2) C は「他人と付き合うのが好きではない」「親しい友人はいない」という意味ではよく使われている．

2 《政治家》
〈彼は一匹狼の政治家です〉
◎ A He's a maverick as a politician.
× B He's a lone wolf politician.
× C He's a lone wolf as a politician.
❖ B, C が辞典に出ているが使われていない．

一方的に
〈組合は一方的に話し合いを中止しました〉
◎ A The union canceled the talks unilaterally.
× B The union canceled the talks one-sidedly.
❖ B が辞典に出ているが使われていない．

いつまで
1 《滞在期間の予定を尋ねるとき》
〈いつまで日本にいらっしゃるのですか〉
◎ A How long're you going to be in Japan?
▽ B Until when're you going to be in Japan?
▽ C Until what day're you going to be in Japan?
❖ B, C は誤りではないがほとんど使われていない．

2 《雑誌などの購読期間を尋ねるとき》
〈いつまで購読期間がありますか〉
◎ A How long is your subscription good for?
◎ B When will your subscription run out?
○ C How long does your subscription last?
× D Until when is your subscription good?
❖ 日本語にとらわれて D のように言いがちであるが，使われていない．

3 《切符などの有効期間を尋ねるとき》
〈いつまでこの切符は有効ですか〉

◎ A How long is this ticket good (for)?
○ B How long is this ticket going to be good (for)?
○ C When does this ticket run out?
▽ D Until when is this ticket good?
▽ E Until what day is this ticket good?
 ❖ D, E は日本語につられた英語で，誤りとは言えないまでもほとんど使われていない．

移転する
 1 《人が主語で事務所・工場が「移転する」と述べるとき》
〈うちはシカゴに移転するんです〉
  ☆ A We're going to relocate to Chicago.
  ◎ B We're going to move into Chicago.
  ○ C We're going to move to [relocate into] Chicago.
 2 《人が主語で家が「移転する」と述べるとき》
〈私たちはシカゴに移転するんです〉
  ◎ A We're going to move to Chicago.
  △ B We're going to move into Chicago.
  ▽ C We're going to relocate to Chicago.
  × D We're going to relocate into Chicago.
 3 《事務所・工場が主語で「移転する」と述べるとき》
〈うちの本社はシカゴに移転するんです〉
  ☆ A Our office's going to move to Chicago.
  ◎ B Our office's going to move into [relocate to] Chicago.
  ○ C Our office's going to relocate [transfer] into Chicago.
  △ D Our office's going to transfer to Chicago.
 4 《事務所を「移転させる」の意味のとき》
〈うちは事務所をシカゴに移転させるんです〉
  ☆ A We're going to move our office to Chicago.
  ◎ B We're going to relocate our office to Chicago.
  ○ C We're going to move our office into Chicago.
  △ D We're going to relocate our office into Chicago.

移動住宅 →家 12

委任状
〈あなたの委任状なしでは私は行動を起こせません〉
  ◎ A I can't start working without your power of attorney.
  ▽ B I can't start working without your letter [warrant] of attorney.
  ▽ C I can't start working without your letter of proxy.
 ❖ B, C が辞典に出ているがほとんど使われていない．

祈っていて下さい
〈ブライアン：どこへ行くの〉
Brian: Where are you headed?
〈チャールズ：就職の面接に行くんだよ〉
Charles: I'm going for a job interview.
〈ブライアン：採用してもらえる自信があるのかい〉
Brian: Are you sure you'll get it?
〈チャールズ：いや，ないよ．祈っていてくれよ〉
Charles:
  ◎ A No, I'm not sure. Wish me luck.
  ◎ B No, I'm not sure. Keep your fingers crossed.

違反

1 《契約》

〈あなたがやっていることは契約違反だ〉

- ◎ A What you're doing is a violation of the contract.
- ◎ B What you're doing is a breach of contract.
- × C What you're doing is a breach of the contract.
  - ❖ breach of contract は決り文句で，contract に the はつかない．

2 《スピード違反》

〈彼はスピード違反で捕まったんです〉

- ☆ A He got busted for speeding.
- ◎ B He got busted for going [driving] too fast.
- ◎ C He got a speeding ticket.
- ◎ D He got a ticket for speeding.

今

1 《「ちょうど今」の意味のとき》

〈私は今忙しいんです〉

- ☆ A I'm busy right now.
- ◎ B I'm busy at this [the] moment.
- ○ C I'm busy at this time.
- △ D I'm busy at the present time.
- ▽ E I'm busy at (the) present.
- ▽ F I'm busy just now.

2 《「すぐに」の意味のとき》

〈今払って下さい〉

- ☆ A Pay me right now.
- ◎ B Pay me right away.
- ○ C Pay me immediately.
- ○ D Pay me at once.
- × E Pay me right down.
  - ❖ E を紹介している辞典があるが使われていない．

意味

1 《「よい意味で」というとき》

a)「使われている」というとき

〈この語はよい意味で使われています〉

- ☆ A This is used in the positive sense of the word.
- ◎ B This is used in the [a] positive sense.
- ○ C This is used in the good sense of the word.
- △ D This is used in a good sense.

b)「年上に見える」というとき

〈あなたはよい意味で年上に見えます〉

- ◎ A You look older than you are. I mean that in a good way.
- ○ B You look older than you are in a positive sense.
- △ C You look older than you are in the positive sense (of the word).
- × D You look older than you are in a [the] good sense.
- × E You look older than you are in the good sense of the word.

2 《「単語の意味」のとき》

〈あなたはこの単語の意味を知っていますか〉

- ◎ A Do you know the meaning of this word?
- ▽ B Do you know the sense of this word?

いれば 51

3 《「…する意味がない」と述べるとき》
〈彼を説得する意味がありません〉
- ◎ A There's no point (in) persuading him.
- ◎ B There's no use (in) persuading him.
- ◎ C It's (of) no use persuading him.
- ◎ D It's useless [pointless] to persuade him.
- ◎ E It's no good persuading him.

違約金 →罰金 3

いやな顔をする
〈上司は今朝私が会ったとき，いやな顔をしました〉
- ☆ A My boss gave me a dirty look when I saw him this morning.
- ◎ B My boss frowned (at me) when I saw him this morning.
- △ C My boss grimaced (at me) when I saw him this morning.
- △ D My boss scowled at me when I saw him this morning.
- × E My boss scowled on me when I saw him this morning.
- × F My boss made grimaces [a grimace] when I saw him this morning.
- × G My boss mopped and mowed when I saw him this morning.
- × H My boss made a wry face [mouth] when I saw him this morning.
- × I My boss made a sour mouth when I saw him this morning.
- × J My boss knitted his brows when I saw him this morning.
- × K My boss bent his eyebrows when I saw him this morning.
- × L My boss screwed his face into wrinkles when I saw him this morning.
- × M My boss puckered up his face when I saw him this morning.
- × N My boss pulled [drew, made] a long face when I saw him this morning.

❖ E～N が辞典に出ているが使われていない．

入れ歯

1 《総入れ歯》
〈私の歯は総入れ歯です〉
- ◎ A I have dentures.
- ◎ B All of my teeth're false.
- ○ C I have a full set of false teeth.
- ○ D I'm wearing a full set of false teeth.
- ○ E I wear a full set of false teeth.
- × F I have a full set of artificial teeth.

❖ F は辞典に出ているが使われていない．

2 《総入れ歯・部分的入れ歯の両方の意味》
〈私は入れ歯なんです〉
- ☆ A I have false teeth.
- ◎ B I wear false teeth.
- ○ C I'm wearing false teeth.
- × D I have artificial teeth.

❖ D は辞典に出ているが使われていない．

3 《入れ歯を入れる》
a）1本のとき
〈私は入れ歯を入れてもらうんです〉
- ◎ A I'm going to get [have] a false tooth put in.
- ○ B I'm going to get [have] a false tooth placed.

   × C I'm going to get a false tooth inserted.
   × D I'm going to get an artificial tooth.
 b）1本から2，3本のとき
〈私は入れ歯を入れてもらうんです〉
   ◎ A I'm going to get [have] a bridge put in.
   ○ B I'm going to get [have] a bridge placed.
 c）総入れ歯のとき
〈私は総入れ歯を入れてもらうんです〉
   ☆ A I'm going to get dentures.
   ◎ B I'm going to get a full set of false teeth put in.
   ○ C I'm going to get a full set of false teeth.
   △ D I'm going to have a full set of false teeth.
   △ E I'm going to have dentures.
   × F I'm going to get a full set of artificial teeth.
   ❖ F は辞典に出ているが使われていない．

入れる

 1 《部屋・建物へ招き入れる》
〈彼らを私の事務所へ入れて下さい〉
   ◎ A Please let them in [into] my office.
   ◎ B Please show them into my office.
   △ C Please show them in my office.
   △ D Please usher them into my office.
   × E Please admit them in [into] my office.
   × F Please allow them in [into] my office.
   ❖ E, F が辞典に出ているが使われていない．
 2 《車を車庫に入れる》
〈車を車庫に入れましょうか〉
   ◎ A Do you want me to put your car in the garage?
   ◎ B Do you want me to pull [drive] your car into the garage?
   ○ C Do you want me to put your car into the garage?
   × D Do you want me to run your car into the garage?
   ❖ D が辞典に出ているが使われていない．
 3 《箱に入れる》
〈箱に全部入れて下さい〉
   ☆ A Put everything in the box.
   ◎ B Put everything into the box.
   ○ C Place everything into [in] the box.
 4 《スーツケースに入れる》
〈これらをスーツケースに入れましょうか〉
   ◎ Do you want me to pack [put] these in your suitcase?
 5 《空気を部屋に入れる》
〈新鮮な空気を入れて下さい〉
   ☆ A Let some fresh air in.
   ◎ B Let some fresh air in here.
   ◎ C Let the fresh air in.
   ○ D Get some fresh air in here.
 6 《データを入力する》
〈この文を5行目と6行目の間に入れて下さい〉
   ◎ A Put this sentence between the fifth and sixth lines.

○ B Insert this sentence between the fifth and sixth lines.
7 《ミルクなどを飲物に入れる》
〈ミルクをコーヒーに入れましょうか〉
  ◎ A Do you want me to put milk in your coffee?
  △ B Do you want me to put milk into your coffee?
8 《会社に入れる》
〈うちの会社は不法滞在外国人は入れません〉
  ◎ A Our company doesn't hire illegal aliens.
  ○ B Our company doesn't employ illegal aliens.
  × C Our company doesn't take (on) illegal aliens.
    ❖ C が辞典に出ているが使われていない．
9 《学校に入れる》
〈私は息子をカトリックの学校へ入れるつもりです〉
  ◎ A I'm going to send my son to a Catholic school.
  ○ B I'm going to put my son in [into] a Catholic school.
10 《自動販売機などにお金を入れる》
〈料金差し入れ口に 10 ドル札を入れなさい〉
  ◎   Put [Place, Insert] a ten-dollar bill in the slot.
11 《(予約・スケジュールなどを) 無理に入れる》
〈(歯医者などで) 何とか(予約を)入れていただけませんか〉
  ◎ A Will you squeeze [fit] me in?
  ○ B Will you slip me in?
12 《検査のために中に入れる》
〈医師：胃に内視鏡を入れなければなりません〉
Doctor:
  ◎   I have to insert [put] an endoscopic tube into your stomach.
13 《コーヒーをいれる》
〈コーヒーをいれましょうか〉
  ◎ A Do you want me to make (some) coffee?
  ◎ B Do you want me to fix some coffee?
  ○ C Do you want me to fix coffee?
14 《助言をいれる》
〈彼はあなたの助言をいれるでしょう〉
  ◎   He'll take [follow] your advice.
異論のある
〈妊娠中絶は今日でさえアメリカでは異論のある問題である〉
  ◎ A Abortion's a hot issue in America even today.
  ○ B Abortion's a controversial issue in America even today.
  △ C Abortion's a highly debated issue in America even today.
  × D Abortion's a highly debatable issue in America even today.
    ❖ D は「疑わしい」の意味ではよく使われている．It's debatable whether he's guilty or not.（彼が有罪であるかどうかは疑わしい）
印刷会社 →会社 10
印刷工場 →工場 9
印象
1 《「良い [悪い] 印象を与える」と言うとき》
〈彼は私に好印象を与えました〉
  ☆ A He made a good impression on me.
  ◎ B He left me with a good impression.

- ◎ C He gave me a good impression.
- ○ D He made a favorable impression on me.
- × E He had a good impression on me.
- × F He exercised a favorable impression on me.
- ❖ E, F が辞典に出ているが使われていない．

2 《that節を従えるとき》
〈彼は正直だという印象を私に与えました〉
- ☆ A He gave me the impression that he was honest.
- ◎ B He left me with the impression that he was honest.
- ○ C He impressed me that he was honest.

3 《asを従えるとき》
〈彼は正直だという印象を私に与えました〉
- ☆ A He impressed [struck] me as being an honest man.
- ◎ B He impressed [struck] me as being honest.
- ○ C He impressed [struck] me as honest.

4 《どんな印象を得たかを尋ねるとき》
〈彼はどんな印象でしたか〉
- ☆ A What was your impression of him?
- ◎ B What impression did he give you?
- ◎ C What kind of impression did you get from him?
- ○ D What kind of impression did he give you?
- ○ E What impression did you get from him?
- ○ F How did he strike you?
- △ G What kind of impression did he leave you with?
- × H How did he impress you?

〔う〕

上の階の
〈上の階のコーヒーショップへ行こう〉
- ◎ A Let's go to the coffee shop upstairs.
- ◎ B Let's go upstairs to the coffee shop.
- ○ C Let's go to the coffee shop above us.
- ○ D Let's go to the coffee shop on the upper level.
- △ E Let's go to the coffee shop over us.
- ▽ F Let's go to the upstairs coffee shop.

上をいく
《負かす》
〈XYZ会社は今年の売上げではHHH会社の上をいくだろう〉
- ☆ A XYZ Company'll top HHH Company sales-wise this year.
- ☆ B XYZ Company'll beat HHH Company sales-wise this year.
- ◎ C XYZ Company'll outdo [exceed, outperform, surpass] HHH Company sales-wise this year.
- ○ D XYZ Company'll outshine [get ahead of] HHH Company sales-wise this year.
- × E XYZ Company'll outstrip [outmatch, excel] HHH Company sales-wise this year.

❖ E が辞典に出ているが使われていない．

うかがう
《承る》
〈(デパート・会社・事務所などで) ご用件をうかがっておりますか〉
- ◎ A Is anyone helping you?
- ◎ B Are you being helped?
- ○ C Is anyone taking care of you?
- ○ D Are you being taken care of?
- △ E Is anyone waiting on you?
- △ F Are you being waited on?
- ▽ G Is anyone attending to you?
- ▽ H Are you being attended to?

❖コーヒーショップなどでは E, F はよく使われている．

請け合う
〈彼女が無罪であることは私が請け合います〉
- ◎ A I (can) guarantee that she's innocent.
- ◎ B I (can) give you my word that she's innocent.
- ○ C I (can) assure you that she's innocent.
- ○ D I (can) give you my guarantee that she's innocent.
- ○ E I (can) assure you of her innocence.
- △ F I (can) vouch that she's innocent.
- △ G I vouch for her innocence.

❖請け合う度合いは can がついている方が強い．

受け入れる
1 《人》
〈今日でさえユダヤ人はアメリカの社会の多くの分野で受け入れられていない〉
- ◎ Even today Jewish people aren't accepted in many areas in American society.

2 《要求》
〈会社は組合の要求を受け入れました〉
- ◎ A The management granted the union's demands.
- ◎ B The management agreed to the union's demands.
- ◎ C The management went along with the union's demands.
- ◎ D The management accepted the union's demands.

❖A, B, C はいずれも喜んで受け入れられたニュアンスがあり，B が一番強く，C が2番目，A が3番目．

3 《条件》
〈私はそれを受け入れます→私はそれでいいです〉
- ◎ A I can live with that.
- ○ B I can tolerate that.

❖A, B ともに「嫌だけれども受け入れます」というニュアンスがある．

受け売りをする
〈彼はマクルーハンの受け売りをしているにすぎない〉
- ◎ A He's just repeating [mouthing] McLuhan.
- △ B He's just rehashing McLuhan.
- × C He's mouthing secondhand information from McLuhan.

❖C が辞典に出ているが使われていない．

受けやすい
〈有名人は批判を受けやすい〉

- ◎ A Famous people're subject [vulnerable] to criticism.
- ◎ B Famous people're likely [liable] to get criticized.
- ○ C Famous people're susceptible to criticism.
    - ❖ A, C は複数形の criticisms よりも使用頻度が高い．

うける
〈この新しい歌は中年の人たちにうけるでしょう〉
- ◎ A This new song'll appeal to middle-aged people.
- ◎ B This new song'll go over well with middle-aged people.
- ◎ C This new song'll catch on with middle-aged people.
- ◎ D This new song'll be a hit with middle-aged people.
- ▽ E This new song'll make a hit [an appeal] with middle-aged people.
- ▽ F This new song'll catch the fancy of middle-aged people.
- ▽ G This new song'll enjoy the popularity of middle-aged people.
    - ❖うける程度は D が一番強い．A が2番，C が3番，B が4番．

動く
〈この時計は動かないよ〉
- ◎ A This watch doesn't work [run].
- × B This watch doesn't move.

後ろ(に)
1 《後ろから1，2列目の場合》
〈私の席は講堂の後ろです〉
- ◎ A My seat is at the back of the auditorium.
- ◎ B My seat is in the back of the auditorium.
    - ❖ A は後ろから1，2列目．B は後ろから1〜5列目くらいまでを指す．

2 《一番後ろの場合》
〈あなたの席は一番後ろです〉
- ◎ A Your seat is in the last [back] row.
- ◎ B Your seat is in the very back.

3 《建物の後ろ》→裏 1

薄くする
〈スープが辛すぎるので薄くしよう〉
- ◎ A The soup is too salty. Let's make it weaker.
- ◎ B The soup is too salty. Let's weaken [dilute] it.
- ◎ C The soup is too salty. Let's water it down.

うそ
1 《うそをつく》
〈彼は私にうそをついたんです〉
- ◎ A He lied to me.
- ○ B He told me a lie.
- △ C He told me a fib.
    - ❖ C は 10 歳以下の子供が使う言葉．しかし，時々大人も使う．

2 《真っ赤なうそ》
〈彼女はよく真っ赤なうそをつくんです〉
- ◎ A She often tells flat-out [total, absolute, complete] lies.
- ○ B She often tells out and out lies.
- ○ C She often tells downright lies.
- △ D She often tells glaring lies.
- × E She often tells arrant [dead, all-out] lies.
    - ❖ E が辞典に出ているが使われていない．

3 《しらじらしいうそ》
〈彼女はよくしらじらしいうそをつくんです〉
- ○ A She often tells blatant [obvious, bold-faced] lies.
- × B She often tells brazen-faced [bare-faced] lies.
- ❖ B が辞典に出ているが使われていない．

4 《サバを読む》
〈彼女は2歳サバを読んだ〉
- ◎ A She lied about her age by two years.
- ▽ B She fudged on her age by two years.

疑っている

1 《(そうであると肯定的に) 疑っている》
〈私は彼が有罪だと疑っています＝私は彼が有罪だと思う〉
- ☆ A I think he's guilty.
- ◎ B I suspect he's guilty.
- ◎ C I assume he's guilty.
- ○ D I suppose he's guilty.
- △ E I figure he's guilty.
- △ F I'm suspicious he's guilty.
- △ G I presume he's guilty.
    - ❖疑っている度合いは，A は約 90 %，B, F は 70〜80 %，C は約 80 %，D は約 30 %，E は 60 %，G は約 95 %

2 《(そうでないと否定的に) 疑っている》
〈私は彼が有罪であることに疑いを持っている＝私は彼が有罪でないと思う〉
- ☆ A I don't think he's guilty.
- ☆ B I doubt he's guilty.
- ◎ C I doubt if he's guilty.
- ○ D I doubt whether he's guilty.
- ○ E I assume he isn't guilty.
- ○ F I'm doubtful he's guilty.
- △ G I'm doubtful if he's guilty.
- △ H I'm doubtful of [about] his guilt.
- △ I I'm skeptical of [about] his guilt.
- △ J I'm suspicious of his guilt.
- △ K I figure he isn't guilty.
- △ L I suppose he isn't guilty.
- △ M His guilt's questionable.
- △ N His guilt's debatable.
- △ O His guilt's in question.
- △ P His guilt's in doubt.
- △ Q Whether he's guilty or not is questionable [debatable].
- △ R Whether he's guilty or not is doubtful.
- △ S It's questionable [debatable] whether he's guilty or not.
- △ T It's doubtful whether he's guilty or not.
    - ❖(1) Q〜T は堅い文章では非常によく使われている．
    - ❖(2) A は他人の言ったことに対する主観的な応答．E は人から聞いたことを当然であると信じているというニュアンスがある．M は自分で導き出した判断を述べている．N は自分が述べていることの真偽はどちらでもかまわないという響きが強い．それ以外，B, C, D, F〜J, O〜T は多少なりとも調査をしたうえでの客観的な意見というニュアンスがある．

❖(3) 疑っている度合いは，A は約 90 %，B, E, F, J は約 80 %，C, D, G, H, I, P は約 70 %，K, M, R, T は約 60 %，N, O, Q, S は約 50 %，L は約 30 %．
❖(4) 辞典では B は A と等しく，B は C, D とは違うように解説されているが，これは B, C, D のニュアンスを歪曲している．これらの違いは(3)で明示した話者の疑いの強さの違いである．

打ち上げる
《衛星などを打ち上げる》
〈私たちは通信衛星を打ち上げる予定です〉
  ◎ A We're planning to launch [put up] a communication satellite.
  △ B We're planning to set off a communication satellite.

訴える
1 《訴えることのみを述べるとき》
〈私は訴えます〉
  ☆ A I'm going to sue.
  ◎ B I'm going to bring a suit [lawsuit].
  ◎ C I'm going to file a suit [lawsuit].
  ◎ D I'm going to take legal steps.
  ○ E I'm going to start litigation.
  △ F I'm going to take legal action.
  ▽ G I'm going to take a legal action.
  ▽ H I'm going to file an action.
  ▽ I I'm going to file legal steps [proceedings].
    ❖ G, H, I を紹介している辞典があるが使われてもまれ．

2 《訴える人と理由も述べるとき》
〈私は彼を名誉毀損で訴えるつもりです〉
  ☆ A I'm going to sue him for libel.
  ☆ B I'm going to take him to court for libel.
  ◎ C I'm going to bring a suit [lawsuit] against him for libel.
  ◎ D I'm going to file a suit [lawsuit] against him for libel.
  ◎ E I'm going to take legal steps against him for libel.
  ○ F I'm going to start litigation against him for libel.
  △ G I'm going to take legal action against him for libel.
  ▽ H I'm going to take a legal action against him for libel.
  ▽ I I'm going to file an action against him for libel.
  ▽ J I'm going to file legal steps [proceedings] against him for libel.
  ▽ K I'm going to take [have] the law on him for libel.

3 《集団訴訟》
〈私たちは差別を理由に XYZ 会社に対して集団訴訟を起す予定です〉
  ◎ A We're going to bring [file, take] a class action suit against XYZ Company for discrimination.
  ◎ B We're going to bring a class action (lawsuit) against XYZ Company for discrimination.
  ◎ C We're going to file a class lawsuit against XYZ Company for discrimination.
  ○ D We're going to take a class lawsuit against XYZ Company for discrimination.

うっとりさせられる
〈一番上の階のレストランからの景色にはうっとりさせられました〉

- ◎ A The view from the restaurant on the top floor was charming.
- ◎ B The view from the restaurant on the top floor was pleasant.
- ◎ C The view from the restaurant on the top floor was pleasing.
- ◎ D The view from the restaurant on the top floor was pretty.
- ◎ E The view from the restaurant on the top floor was lovely.
- ◎ F The view from the restaurant on the top floor was beautiful.
- ◎ G The view from the restaurant on the top floor was fascinating [captivating].
  - ❖「うっとりさせられる」の度合いは G が一番強い．次は F, E, D, A, B, C の順で弱くなる．

うぬぼれる
1 《動作を表す》
〈そんなことをしたら彼をうぬぼれさせるだけですよ〉
  - ◎ A That'll only give him a big head.
  - ◎ B That'll only go to his head.
  - ◎ C That'll only make him get a big head.
  - △ D That'll only make him big-headed [conceited].

2 《状態を表す》
〈彼はうぬぼれている〉
  - ◎ A He's cocky [conceited].
  - ◎ B He's stuck on himself.
  - ◎ C He has a bighead.
  - ○ D He's bigheaded.
  - △ E He has a swelled head.

うのみにする
〈彼が言うことをうのみにしては駄目ですよ〉
  - ☆ A Don't take what he says at face value.
  - ☆ B Take what he says with a grain of salt.
  - ◎ C Don't believe what he says at face value.
  - △ D Don't swallow what he says.
  - × E Don't gulp what he says.
    - ❖辞典に E が出ているが使われていない．

乳母車
〈私は乳母車を買わなくてはならないんです〉
  - ◎ A I have to buy a (baby) stroller.
  - △ B I have to buy a baby buggy.

うまくいかない
1 《失敗に終わったことを述べるとき》
〈組合との交渉はうまくいかなかった〉
  - ◎ A The talks with the union didn't work out.
  - ◎ B The talks with the union broke down.
  - ◎ C The talks with the union failed.
  - ◎ D The talks with the union didn't turn out well.
  - ◎ E The talks with the union didn't succeed.
  - ○ F The talks with the union didn't go well.
  - ○ G The talks with the union bombed.

2 《まだ続行中のことを述べるとき》
〈組合との交渉はうまくいかなかった〉
  - ◎ A The talks with the union didn't go well.

- ◎ B The talks with the union didn't go smoothly.
- ◎ C The talks with the union collapsed.
- △ D The talks with the union bombed.
  - ❖(1) A には次のニュアンスがある．a) 交渉が失敗した (=didn't work out)．b) 交渉は終わったが，譲歩したために当初予想していた通りにはうまくいかなかった．c) 交渉は続行中．
  - ❖(2) B には交渉の過程でうまくいかなかったというニュアンスもある．

生まれ

1 《金持ちの生まれであることを一般的に述べるとき》

〈彼は金持ちの生まれなんです〉

- ◎ A He was born rich.
- ◎ B He was born into money.
- ○ C He was born into wealth.
- △ D He was born with a silver spoon in his mouth.
- △ E He was born to wealth.

2 《「金持ちの家庭の出である」ことに焦点をあてて述べるとき》

〈彼は金持ちの家の生まれです〉

- ◎ A He comes from a rich [wealthy] family.
- ◎ B He comes from a family with (a lot of) money.
- ○ C He comes from a well-to-do family.
- ○ D He comes from a family with deep pockets.

3 《金持ちであることを，生まれた地域から述べるとき》

〈彼は裕福な地域の生まれです〉

- ◎ A He was born in a rich [wealthy, high-class] neighborhood.
- ○ B He was born in a well-to-do [an expensive, an upscale] neighborhood.

4 《貧しい生まれであることを一般的に述べるとき》

〈彼は貧しい生まれです〉

- ◎ A He was born into poverty.
- △ B He was born poor.
- × C He was born to poverty.

5 《「貧しい家庭の出である」ことに焦点をあてて述べるとき》

〈彼は貧しい家庭の生まれです〉

- ◎ A He's from a family with no [without] money.
- ◎ B He comes from a family with no [without] money.
- ◎ C He's from a poor family.
- ◎ D He comes from a poor family.

6 《貧しいことを，生まれた地域から述べるとき》

〈彼は貧しい地域 [貧民街] の生まれです〉

- ◎ A He was born in a bad [tough, rough] neighborhood.
- ◎ B He was born on the bad [wrong] side of town.
- ◎ C He's from the wrong side of town.
- ◎ D He comes from the bad [wrong] side of town.
- ○ E He was born on the bad [wrong] side of the city.
- ○ F He's from the wrong side of the city.
- ○ G He comes from the bad [wrong] side of the city.

海

〈彼の別荘は海に面しています〉

- ◎ A His second house looks out over the ocean.

○ B His second house looks out over the sea.
❖イギリスではBの方がAよりよく使われている．

生みの母　→母 2

埋め立て
〈政府は東京湾の埋め立てをしている〉
◎ A There's a government land-fill project in Tokyo Bay.
△ B The government's recovering [reclaiming] land from Tokyo Bay.
× C The government's reclaiming a tract [foreshore] from Tokyo Bay.
❖Cは辞典に出ているが使われていない．

裏
1 《建物の場合》
〈シカゴ銀行の裏に駐車場があります〉
◎ A There's a parking lot behind Chicago Bank.
◎ B There's a parking lot in the back of Chicago Bank.
○ C There's a parking lot at the back of Chicago Bank.
△ D There's a parking lot at [in] the rear of Chicago Bank.

2 《封筒の場合》
〈封筒の裏に必ず名前と住所を書いて下さい〉
☆ A Be sure to write your name and address on the back of the envelope.
◎ B Be sure to write your name and address on the other side of the envelope.
○ C Be sure to write your name and address on the opposite side of the envelope.

裏書きする
1 《個人が裏書きする場合》
〈この小切手に裏書きしてくれますか〉
◎ A Will you endorse this check?
◎ B Will you sign the back of this check?
○ C Will you sign over the back of this check?
△ D Will you sign on the back of this check
× E Will you underwrite this check?

2 《保険会社が裏書きする場合》
〈シカゴ保険会社がABC会社が売った車の保険証書を裏書きします〉
◎ A Chicago Insurance Company'll underwrite the auto insurance policies sold by ABC Company.
× B Chicago Insurance Company'll undertake the auto insurance policies sold by ABC Company.
× C Chicago Insurance Company'll cosign for [on] the auto insurance policies sold by ABC Company.

裏切る
1 《友人間の場合》
〈私はジムが私たちを裏切ったことを許せない〉
☆ A I can't forgive Jim for betraying [double-crossing] us.
◎ B I can't forgive Jim for selling out on us.
○ C I can't forgive Jim for going back on us.
△ D I can't forgive Jim for selling us down the river.
△ E I can't forgive Jim for turning traitor.
❖Eはusが不要．

2 《夫婦間の場合》

〈何度も私を裏切ったから私は主人と離婚するんです〉
- ◎ I'm going to divorce my husband because he cheated [fooled around] on me several times.

浦島太郎
〈私は10年振りに日本へ帰ってきたとき，浦島太郎になったような気がしました〉
- ◎ A When I came back to Japan for the first time in ten years, I felt like everything had changed completely.
- △ B When I came back to Japan for the first time in ten years, I felt like I was Rip Van Winkle.

裏づける
〈あなたは主張を事実で裏づけなければなりません〉
- ☆ A You have to support [back up] your argument with facts.
- ◎ B You have to back [substantiate] your argument with facts.
- ○ C You have to validate [verify, solidify] your argument with facts.

うらやましい
1 《主語が1人称のとき》
〈私はあなたがうらやましいです〉
- ◎ A I envy you.
- ◎ B I'm jealous of you.
- ○ C I'm envious of you.

2 《主語が3人称のとき》
〈彼女はあなたの成功をうらやましがっています〉
- ◎ A She envies your success.
- ◎ B She's envious of your success.
- × C She's jealous of your success.
  - ❖Cは「ねたんでいる」の意味なら非常によく使われている．

売り出す
1 《新製品を発表するというニュアンスのとき》
〈フォードは今年の9月新しい車を売り出します〉
- ◎ Ford'll release [introduce, launch, come out with, bring out] a new car this September.
  - ❖従来の車を改良して新しい型の車を「売り出す」というときに使われている．

2 《消費者をあっと驚かせる従来にない新製品を発表して売り出すというニュアンスのとき》
〈フォードは水で走る車を売り出します〉
- ◎ A Ford'll reveal [unveil] a new car that runs on water.
- × B Ford'll disclose a new car that runs on water.

3 《新製品を市場に出すというニュアンスのとき》
〈フォードは今年の9月新しい車を売り出します〉
- ◎ A Ford'll market a new car this September.
- ◎ B Ford'll put [place] a new car on the market this September.
- ◎ C Ford'll put up this car for sale this September.
- ◎ D Ford'll put this car up for sale this September.
- ◎ E Ford'll offer [place] this car on the market this September.
- ◎ F Ford'll put this car on sale this September.
  - ❖Aは売り出すための「広告を大々的にする」というニュアンスがあるのに対して，Bは「売る準備ができている」というニュアンスが強い．C，D，Eは新しい車にも古い車にも使われている点に注意．またFは値下げして売

るというときに使われている.
 4 《どこの国の市場で売り出すかを明示するとき》
〈この新製品はドイツの市場で来週売り出されます〉
   ◎ A This new product'll be on the German market next week.
   ◎ B This new product'll be on the market in Germany next week.
   ◎ C This new product'll be sold in Germany next week.
   ◎ D This new product'll be sold on the German market next week.
 5 《国中の店で売り出されるとニュアンスのとき》
〈この新製品は来週, 国中で売り出されます〉
   ◎ A This new product'll be in stores all over the country next week.
   ◎ B This new product'll be sold all over the country next week.
   ◎ C This new product'll be on the market all over the country next week.
   ❖そのときの話の前後で, all over the country はアメリカ, 日本, 中国, 英国などどこの国の意味でもよく使われる.

売りに出す
 1 《売りに出すものが主語のとき》
〈この家はまもなく売りに出されるでしょう〉
   ◎ A This house'll be (placed) on the market soon.
   ◎ B This house'll be (put up) for sale soon.
 2 《売りに出すものが目的語のとき》
〈XYZ会社はまもなく工場を売りに出すでしょう〉
   ◎ A XYZ Company'll sell its factory soon.
   ◎ B XYZ Company'll put its factory up for sale soon.
   ◎ C XYZ Company'll put its factory on the market soon.

うるう年
〈うるう年は何年ごとにあるのですか〉
   ◎ A How often does a leap year come around?
   ◎ B How often does leap year come around?
   × C How often does the leap year come around?

うれしい
 1 《同僚に言うとき》
〈トム：君は働き者だってみんなが言っているよ〉
Tom: Everybody's saying you're a hard worker.
〈ジム：うれしいよ〉
Jim:
   ◎ A I'm glad [happy] to hear that.
   ◎ B That's nice to hear.
   ◎ C It's nice [good] to hear that.
   ○ D That makes me happy.
   ○ E Nice to hear that.
   △ F Good to hear that.
 2 《同僚の場合で強調して言うとき》
〈とてもうれしいよ〉
   ◎ A It's great to hear that.
   ◎ B I'm really happy to hear that.
   ○ C I'm very happy to hear that.
   ○ D I'm thrilled to hear that.
   △ E It's terrific to hear that.
 3 《上司からほめられたとき》

〈上司:君は働き者だね〉
Boss: You're a hard worker.
〈社員:うれしいです〉
- ◎ A Thank you very much.
- △ B It's nice to hear that.
- △ C That makes me happy.
- ▽ D I'm glad to hear that.

4 《紹介されたとき》
a) かしこまって挨拶する場合
〈お目にかかれて非常にうれしく思っています〉
- ◎ A I'm very glad to meet you.
- ◎ B I'm delighted to meet you.
  - ❖ B の be delighted は,それだけで「非常にうれしく思っている」という意味なので,A のように very で強調することはできない.

b) かしこまらない挨拶をする場合
〈お知り合いになれてとてもうれしいです〉
- ◎ A I'm really glad to meet you.
- ◎ B It's so [really] nice to meet you.

c) くだけた挨拶をする場合
〈お会いできてうれしいです〉
- ◎ A Nice [Glad, Happy] to meet you.
- △ B Good to meet you.

5 《(パーティーなどで) 紹介された人と別れるとき》
a) 一般的に述べる場合
〈お目にかかれてうれしかったです〉
- ◎ A It was nice meeting you.
- ○ B It was nice to meet you.
- ○ C It was good meeting you.
- ○ D It was good to meet you.

b) 強調して述べる場合
〈お目にかかれてとてもうれしかったです〉
- ☆ A It was really great meeting you.
- ◎ B It was terrific [fantastic, incredible] meeting you.
  - ❖ great は一番意味が弱いので,強調するために really great とする.

c) 話ができて楽しかったことを強調する場合
〈お話できてうれしかったです〉
- ☆ A It was nice talking to you.
- ◎ B It was good [great, terrific] talking to you.
- ○ C It was nice [good, great, terrific] to talk to you.
  - ❖(1) terrific が一番強く,great, good, nice の順で弱くなる.
  - ❖(2) フィーリングの合う異性に会い,話がとてもはずんで「ものすごくうれしかった」と述べたければ,incredible とか really great, really terrific と強調することができる.

売れそうな

1 《消費者が言う場合》
〈この商品は売れそうだ〉
- ◎ A This product [item] looks like it's going to sell well.
- ◎ B This product [item] has a lot of potential.
- ◎ C This product [item] has the potential to sell well.

- ◎ D This product [item] has what it takes to sell well.
- △ E This merchandise looks like it's going to sell well.
- △ F This merchandise has a lot of potential.
- △ G This merchandise has the potential to sell well.
- △ H This merchandise has what it takes to sell well.

2 《業界人・ビジネスマンが言う場合》
〈この商品は売れそうだ〉
- ◎ A This is a highly marketable product [item].
- ◎ B This product [item] looks like it's going to sell well.
- ◎ C This product [item] has a lot of potential.
- ◎ D This product [item] has the potential to sell well.
- ○ E This product [item] has what it takes to sell well.
- ○ F This merchandise looks like it's going to sell well.
- ○ G This merchandise has a lot of potential.
- ○ H This merchandise has the potential to sell well.
- ○ I This merchandise has what it takes to sell well.
- ○ J This is highly marketable merchandise.
- × K This is a highly saleable product [item].
- × L This is highly saleable merchandise.

❖(1) K, Lが辞典に出ているが使われていない.
❖(2) item は時計のような小さいものに使われている.
❖(3) 辞典では merchandise を集合名詞としてのみ紹介しているが, 現代アメリカ英語では product の意味でよく使われている.

浮気する

1 《非難の気持ちが強いとき》
〈彼女は浮気しているんです〉
- ◎ A She's fucking [She fucks] around on her husband.
- ◎ B She's fucking [She fucks] around behind her husband's back.
- ◎ C She's screwing [She screws] around on her husband.
- ◎ D She's screwing [She screws] around behind her husband's back.
- ◎ E She's cheating [She cheats] behind her husband's back.
- ◎ F She's cheating [She cheats] on her husband.
- ◎ G She's cheating [She cheats] around on her husband.
- ◎ H She's messing [She messes] around on her husband.
- ◎ I She's messing [She messes] around behind her husband's back.
- ◎ J She's sleeping [She sleeps] around on her husband.
- ◎ K She's sleeping [She sleeps] around behind her husband's back.
- △ L She's sneaking [She sneaks] around behind her husband's back.
- △ M She's two-timing [She two-times] her husband.
- △ N She's two-timing [She two-times] on her husband.
- △ O She's two-timing [She two-times] behind her husband's back.
- × P She's having a love affair.

❖(1) 批判している気持ちは A, B が1番, C, D が2番, E, F, G, M, N, O が3番, H～L はほぼ同じで4番.
❖(2) A, B は女性が男性に述べるときは, 使用頻度は◎から○に下がるが, 女性同士が強く批判している気持ちで述べるときは非常によく使われる.
❖(3) P が多くの辞典に出ているがこの意味では全く使われていない.「愛している」の意味では時々使われている. We had a love affair when we were in high school. We were in love when we were in high school. (私たち

は高校生のとき愛し合っていた). 詳細は「愛している」の項を参照された
い.
2 《非難の気持ちが軽いとき》
〈彼女は浮気しているのよ〉
- ◎ A She fools [She's fooling] around.
- ◎ B She fools [She's fooling] around on her husband.
- ◎ C She fools [She's fooling] around behind her husband's back.

3 《客観的に述べるとき》
〈彼女は浮気しているのよ〉
- ◎ A She's having an affair.
- ◎ B She's having an affair on her husband.
- ○ C She has an affair on her husband.
- ○ D She has a man in side.

4 《少しうらやましい気持ちで述べるとき》
〈彼女は浮気しているのよ〉
- ◎ A She gets [She's getting] around.
- ◎ B She gets [She's getting] around on her husband.
- ◎ C She gets [She's getting] around behind her husband's back.
- ◎ D She gets [She's getting] a little on the side.

5 《浮気している相手の数が多いことを述べるとき》
〈彼女は大勢の男性と浮気しているんです〉
- ☆ A She's fooling [She fools] around with a lot of guys.
- ◎ B She's sleeping [She sleeps] around with a lot of guys.
- ◎ C She's messing [She messes] around with a lot of guys.
- ◎ D She's cheating [She cheats] around with a lot of guys.
- ◎ E She's fucking [She fucks] around with a lot of guys.
- ◎ F She's having affairs with a lot of guys.
- ◎ G She's getting [playing] around with a lot of guys.
- ◎ H She's fooling [She fools] around a lot.
- ◎ I She's sleeping [She sleeps] around a lot.
- ◎ J She's messing [She messes] around a lot.
- ◎ K She's cheating [She cheats] around a lot.
- ◎ L She's fucking [She fucks] around a lot.
- ◎ M She's having a lot of affairs.
- ◎ N She's getting [She gets] around a lot.
- ◎ O She's playing [She plays] around a lot.
- ○ P She's screwing [She screws] around with a lot of guys.
   ❖ H〜Oは, 浮気をしている人数が多いということだけでなく, 同じ人だが
   「頻度が高い」という意味でもよく使われている.

6 《頻繁に浮気をしていることを述べるとき》
〈彼女はしょっちゅう浮気しているんです〉
- ◎ A She's really fooling [She really fools] around.
- ◎ B She's really getting [She really gets] around.
- ◎ C She's really messing [She really messes] around.
- ◎ D She's really sleeping [She really sleeps] around.
- ◎ E She's really screwing [She really screws] around.
- ◎ F She's really fucking [She really fucks] around.
- ○ G She's fooling [She fools] around a lot.
- ○ H She's getting [She gets] around a lot.

- ○ I She's messing [She messes] around a lot.
- ○ J She's sleeping [She sleeps] around a lot.
- ○ K She's screwing [She screws] around a lot.
- ○ L She's fucking [She fucks] around a lot.
  - ❖ G〜L は「浮気している人数が多い」の意味にもよく使われている．

7 《「妻には男がいるんです」と述べるとき》
〈妻には男がいるんです〉
- ◎ A My wife is seeing another man.
- ○ B My wife has another man (on the side).
- ○ C My wife is seeing another man on the side.
- × D My wife has a man.

うわの空

1 《何か他のことを考えているとき》
〈彼はうわの空なのよ〉
- ◎ A His mind's somewhere else now.
- ◎ B His mind's on other things now.
- ○ C He's in another world now.
  - ❖ C は A, B より強く，表現が示している通り，現在起きていることから完全にしゃ断されているニュアンスがある．

2 《空想にふけっているとき》
〈彼女をそっとしておいてあげて．かわいい男の子に会ったのよ．彼女，彼のことでうわの空なんだから〉
- ◎ A Don't bother her. She met an adorable boy and she's daydreaming about him.
- ◎ B Don't bother her. She met an adorable boy and she's spacing about him.
  - ❖(1) A は若者，特に 10 代の人の間では時々にしか使われていない．B は 30 歳以下の人の間では非常によく使われているが，40 代以上の人の間ではあまり使われていない．
  - ❖(2) 何かそれまでに起きた出来事について，または誰か会った人のことを忘れられないで「空想にふける」，その結果として「うわの空である」というときに使う．

3 《いろいろなことに気をとられて忘れっぽくなっているとき》
〈彼はいろいろなことが頭にあるので，うわの空なのです〉
- ◎ A He's absent-minded because he has so many things on his mind.
- ◎ B He's forgetful because he has so many things on his mind.

うわべだけ

〈彼は紳士のように見えるがうわべだけです〉
- ☆ A He seems to be a gentleman but it's just a facade [front].
- ○ B He seems to be a gentleman but it's just a cover.
- △ C He seems to be a gentleman but it's just an appearance.
- △ D He seems to be a gentleman but it's just superficial.
- × E He seems to be a gentleman but it's just surface [looks].
- × F He seems to be a gentleman but it's just the front [frontage].
  - ❖ E, F が辞典に出ているが使われていない．

うんざりしている

〈私は彼にうんざりしている〉
- ◎ A I'm sick and tired of him.
- ◎ B I'm fed up with him.

- ◎ C I've had it with him.
- ◎ D I've had enough of him.
- ◎ E He turns me off.
  - ❖上の表現は目的語が人でも物でも使われている．Here we go again! This is the fifth time this washing machine has broken down. I've had it with this thing.（また始まった．これでこの洗濯機が壊れたのは5度目だよ．うんざりだ）．

運送会社 →会社 33
運送屋 →店 41
運転資金
〈運転資金が十分にないんです〉
- ◎ A We don't have enough working capital.
- × B We don't have enough running capital.

運動
1 《運動する（動詞）》
〈あなたは毎日運動しなければなりませんよ〉
- ☆ A You have to exercise [work out] every day.
- ◎ B You have to get some [your] exercise every day.
- ○ C You have to do exercises every day.
- ○ D You have to do some exercises [exercising] every day.
- ▽ E You have to get some exercising every day.
- × F You have to take some exercise [exercising] every day.
- × G You have to take bodily exercise every day.
  - ❖(1) F, G が辞典に出ているが使われていない．
  - ❖(2) 運動器具を使って運動する場合も使わない場合もA〜Eまで使用頻度に違いはない．

2 《運動させる（動詞）》
〈あなたは犬に毎日運動させなければなりません〉
- ◎ A You have to exercise your dog every day.
- × B You have to work out your dog every day.

3 《スポーツ（名詞）》
〈水泳はいい運動です〉
- ◎ A Swimming's good exercise.
- △ B Swimming's a good exercise.

4 《目的を達成するための運動》
a） 権利獲得
〈彼は市民権運動で有名になったんです〉
- ◎ A He became famous because of the civil rights movement.
- × B He became famous because of the civil rights campaign.

b） 反対・推奨
〈私たちは禁煙運動を推進しなければならないんです〉
- ◎ A We have to promote a campaign against smoking.
- × B We have to promote a movement against smoking.

c） 基金
〈彼は基金集めの運動で忙しいんです〉
- ◎ A He's busy with a fund-raising campaign.
- ◎ B He's busy with a fund-raising drive.
  - ❖Bの方がAより小規模のニュアンスがある．

d） 遊説

〈彼は市長の遊説運動で忙しいんです〉
- ◎ A He's busy with the Mayor's election campaign.
- × B He's busy with the Mayor's election movement.

e) 撲滅
〈私たちは麻薬撲滅運動に非常に興味を持っています〉
- ◎ A We're very interested in anti-drug crusade.
- × B We're very interested in anti-drug movement.

f) 陳情
〈私は陳情運動には興味がありません〉
- ◎ A I'm not interested in lobbying.
- ○ B I'm not interested in lobbying operations.

〔え〕

映画化する
〈私たちはこの本を映画化する予定です〉
- ◎ A We're going to make a movie of this book.
- ○ B We're going to bring this book to the screen.
- × C We're going to screen [picturize] this book.
  - ❖ C が辞典に出ているが使われていない．

映画館
〈角を曲がった所に映画館があります〉
- ◎ A There's a movie theater around the corner.
- × B There's a movie house around the corner.
- × C There's a motion picture theater around the corner.
- × D There's a picture theater [hall] around the corner.
  - ❖ B, C, D が辞典に出ているが使われていない．

永久に
1 《誇張して述べるとき》
〈私は永久にあなたを愛しています〉
- ☆ A I'll love you forever.
- ◎ B I'll love you always.
- ○ C I'll love you eternally.
- × D I'll love you permanently [for good].

2 《前に同様の試みに失敗して「今度こそ」と述べるとき》
〈私は彼と別れることができなかったんですが，今度は永久に別れます〉
- ◎ A I couldn't break up with him but this time I'll break up with him for good.
- ○ B I couldn't break up with him but this time I'll break up with him permanently.
- △ C I couldn't break up with him but this time I'll break up with him forever.

3 《live, stay とともに使うとき》
〈私は東京に永住したいんです〉
- ☆ A I want to live in Tokyo permanently.
- ◎ B I want to live in Tokyo forever.
- ○ C I want to live in Tokyo for good.

4 《任命・異動のとき》
〈ブラウン氏は永久にニューヨーク勤務に任命された〉
- ◎ A Mr. Brown was assigned to New York permanently [for good].
- △ B Mr. Brown was assigned to New York forever.

5 《子供っぽい話し方をするとき》
〈娘：お母さん，明日の夜のパーティーに赤いドレスを借りてもいいかしら〉
Daughter: Mom, can I borrow your red dress for the party tomorrow night?
〈母：ええ，ずっと持っていていいわよ〉
Mother:
- ◎ A Yes. You can have it for keeps.
- × B Yes. You can have it forever [for good, permanently].
    - ❖ B には子供っぽい響きはない．

6 《堅い文章英語のとき》
〈厚生年金受給者殿： 貴殿は学士号を習得したので，貴殿への学生手当はこれにより永久に停止になることをここに通知します〉
- ◎ Dear Social Security Recipient: This is to inform you that since you have now obtained your Bachelor's Degree, your student benefits are hereby discontinued permanently.

営業部　→…部 1
営業部長　→地位 13
営業マン　→職業 40

影響を及ぼす

1 《悪影響を与えるとき》
〈この大雪は野菜の値段に悪影響を及ぼすでしょう〉
- ☆ A This heavy snow's going to drive up the price of vegetables.
- ◎ B This heavy snow's going to make the price of vegetables go up.
- ◎ C This heavy snow's going to force the price of vegetables to go up.
- ◎ D This heavy snow's going to raise [increase] the price of vegetables.
- ○ E This heavy snow's going to affect the price of vegetables.
- △ F This heavy snow's going to have a negative [a bad, an adverse] effect on the price of vegetables.
- △ G This heavy snow's going to have a negative influence on the price of vegetables.
- △ H This heavy snow's going to have a negative [bad] impact on the price of vegetables.
- △ I This heavy snow's going to affect the price of vegetables adversely.
- △ J This heavy snow's going to negatively [adversely] affect the price of vegetables.
- ▽ K This heavy snow's going to negatively [adversely] influence the price of vegetables.
- × L This heavy snow's going to exercise a bad [an adverse] influence [impact, effect] on the price of vegetables.
    - ❖(1) 辞典には L が出ているが全く使われていない．
    - ❖(2) E, F, G は堅い文章，テレビ・ラジオのニュース英語ではよく使われている．

2 《いい影響を与えるとき》
〈この雨は野菜の値段にいい影響を与えるでしょう〉
- ◎ A This rain'll have a positive impact [effect] on the price of vegetables.

えいきょうを 71

- ○ B This rain'll positively affect [influence, effect] the price of vegetables.
- ○ C This rain'll influence [affect] the price of vegetables positively.
- ○ D This rain'll have a good impact [effect, influence] on the price of vegetables.
- △ E This rain'll have a favorable impact [effect, influence] on the price of vegetables.
- △ F This rain'll influence the price of vegetables favorably.
- × G This rain'll influence the price of vegetables well.

3 《「人の性質が人に影響を与えた」と言いたいとき》
〈父のアル中が私の人生に大きな影響を与えました〉

- ◎ A My father's alcoholism really affected [impacted, influenced] my life.
- ◎ B My father's alcoholism had a great affect on my life.
- ◎ C My father's alcoholism had a great [a lot of, a real] impact on my life.
- ◎ D My father's alcoholism had a great [a lot of, a real] influence on my life.
- ◎ E My father's alcoholism had a great [a lot of, a real] effect on my life.
- ◎ F My father's alcoholism really had an affect [impact, influence] on my life.
- ○ G My father's alcoholism affected [impacted, influenced] my life a lot.
- △ H My father's alcoholism affected [impacted, influenced] my life a great deal.
- × I My father's alcoholism exercised a great deal of [a lot of] affect [impact, influence, effect] on my life.

❖ I が辞典に出ているが使われていない。

4 《「ものすごい影響を及ぼす」と言いたいとき》
〈新しい税制度は経済にものすごい影響を与えるでしょう〉

- ☆ A The new tax system'll have a major [dramatic] impact on the economy.
- ◎ B The new tax system'll dramatically [drastically] influence the economy.
- ◎ C The new tax system'll have a major influence on the economy.
- ◎ D The new tax system'll dramatically [drastically] affect the economy.
- ◎ E The new tax system'll influence [affect] the economy dramatically.
- ◎ F The new tax system'll have a tremendous effect [impact] on the economy.
- ○ G The new tax system'll have a drastic [an incredible, a fantastic, a tremendous] influence on the economy.
- ○ H The new tax system'll have an incredible [a fantastic] impact on the economy.
- ○ I The new tax system'll have an incredible [a fantastic] effect on the economy.
- ○ J The new tax system'll incredibly [fantastically] influence the economy.

- K The new tax system'll incredibly [fantastically] affect the economy.
- L The new tax system'll incredibly [fantastically] impact the economy.

栄養士 →職業 28

えこひいきする

〈彼は彼らをえこひいきしているんです〉

- ☆ A He favors them.
- ☆ B He is partial to them.
- ☆ C He shows favoritism to them.
- ◎ D He shows partiality to them.
- ◎ E He is partial towards them.
- ◎ F He has a soft spot for them.
- ○ G He has a preference for them.
- ○ H He has a bias towards them.
- ▽ I He has a bias to [for] them.
- ▽ J He is predisposed towards [to] them.

❖ I, J が辞典に出ているがあまり使われていない．

エステ →店 34

MRI の検査を受ける →検査 1

えり好みする →好みがうるさい

演技

1 《特定の演技を述べる場合》

〈私は彼の映画を見ましたが，彼の演技は下手でした〉

- ◎ A I saw his movie but his performance was bad.
- ○ B I saw his movie but his acting was bad.

2 《一般的に述べる場合》

〈彼は演技が上手です〉

- ◎ A He's a great [good] actor.
- ○ B His acting is great [good].

❖ great の方がほめている度合いが強い．

援助する →力になってくれる

エンストする

〈私の車は空港へ行く途中でエンストしてしまったんです〉

- ☆ A My car died (on me) on the way to the airport.
- ☆ B My car stalled on the way to the airport.
- ◎ C My car quit [stopped] running on the way to the airport.
- ◎ D My car quit on me on the way to the airport.
- ○ E My car quit [stopped] working on the way to the airport.
- ○ F My car quit on the way to the airport.

演説をする

1 《一般の人の非厳粛な演説》

〈彼は公害について演説しました〉

- ☆ A He gave a speech on pollution.
- ◎ B He gave a talk [made a speech, spoke] on pollution.
- ○ C He delivered a speech on pollution.
- × D He made an address on pollution.

2 《辞任・就任のような厳粛な演説》

〈大統領は昨日国民に辞任演説をしました〉

- ☆ A The President gave his farewell speech to the nation yesterday.

◎ B The President made his farewell speech to his nation yesterday.
　　○ C The President delivered his farewell speech to his nation yesterday.
　　○ D The President gave [made, delivered] his farewell address to his nation yesterday.
　　○ E The President addressed the nation for the last time yesterday.

〔お〕

追い越す
1　《先行している相手の前に出ること》
a）話し手・聞き手が車を運転している場合
〈あのトラックを追い越そう〉
　　◎ A Let's pass that truck.
　　○ B Let's get in front of that truck.
　　○ C Let's get ahead of that truck.
　　△ D Let's overtake that truck.
　　× E Let's outstrip [outdistance, outpace] that truck.
　　❖辞典に E が出ているが使われていない。多くの辞典には D のみを出しているが、時々使われる程度。
b）話し手・聞き手が走っている場合
〈あのトラックを追い越そう〉
　　◎ A Let's pass that truck.
　　○ B Let's get ahead of that truck.
　　○ C Let's outrun that truck.
　　○ D Let's shoot ahead of that truck.
　　△ E Let's get in front of that truck.
2　《技術・成績などで上回ること》
〈うちはエンジンの技術においてフォードを追い越さなければならない〉
　　◎ A We have to get ahead of Ford in engine technology.
　　◎ B We have to outthink [beat, top] Ford in engine technology.
　　○ C We have to surpass [outdo] Ford in engine technology.
　　△ D We have to pass (up) Ford in engine technology.

おいしい
1　《一般的に言う場合》
a）原級で述べるとき
〈このアイスクリームはとてもおいしい〉
　　☆ A This ice cream is very good.
　　◎ B This ice cream is (very) delicious.
b）比較級で述べるとき
〈中国料理ほどおいしいものはない〉
　　◎ A Nothing's better than Chinese food.
　　○ B Nothing's more delicious than Chinese food.
2　《幼児に向かって言う場合》
〈お母さん：トミー，ケーキを食べなさい．おいしいわよ〉
Mom:
　　◎ A Tommy, have some cake. It's yummy.
　　○ B Tommy, have some cake. It's good.

▽ C Tommy, have some cake. It's delicious.

お医者さんごっこをする
〈彼らはお医者さんごっこをしています〉
- ◎ A They're playing doctor.
- ○ B They're playing hospital.
- × C They're playing doctors [hospitals].

追いつく
1 《学科の場合》
〈私はフランス語でクラスに追いつかなければならないんです〉
- ◎ A I've got to catch up to [with] my class in French.
- × B I've got to get [come] up with my class in French.
  - ❖ B は辞典に出ているが使われていない．

2 《技術の場合》
〈うちの会社はライバル会社にガソリンの燃費で追いつかなければならない〉
- ◎ Our company has to catch up to [with] our competitors in gas mileage.

3 《仕事の場合》
〈私は仕事に追いつかなければならないんです〉
- ◎ I've got to catch up on [with] my work.

4 《走っている人・車の場合》
〈彼らに追いつこう〉
- ◎ Let's catch up to [with] them.

置いていく
〈このオーバーをクリーニング屋へ置いていってくれますか〉
- ◎ A Will you drop this coat off at the cleaners?
- ◎ B Will you take this coat to the cleaners?
- ○ C Will you drop off this coat at the cleaners?

置いている
1 《店を主語にして言うとき》
〈あの店はドイツ食品を置いています〉
- ☆ A That store has [sells] German food.
- ◎ B That store carries German food.
- ○ C That store stocks German food.
- ○ D That store has German food in stock.

2 《社員 (They) を主語にして言うとき》
〈あの店はドイツ食品を置いています〉
- ☆ A They have [sell] German food at that store.
- ◎ B They carry German food at that store.
- ○ C They stock German food at that store.
- ○ D They have German food in stock at that store.

置いてくる →忘れる 4

追いまわす
〈彼がどこへ行っても，レポーターたちは彼を追いまわしているんです〉
- ◎ A No matter where he goes, reporters're hounding [following, trailing, pursuing] him.
- ◎ B No matter where he goes, reporters're chasing him.
- ◎ C No matter where he goes, reporters're tailing him.
- ◎ D No matter where he goes, reporters're stalking him.
- △ E No matter where he goes, reporters're shadowing [going after] him.

❖ C は車で，D は徒歩で追いまわすという響きがある．A, E は車，徒歩のいずれにも使われている．B は両者が走っている，または早足であるとのニュアンスがある．

追う
〈私には流行を追う余裕はありません〉
◎ A I can't afford to keep up with [follow, take up] the latest fashion.
× B I can't afford to run after the latest fashion.
❖ B は辞典に出ているが使われていない．

応援する
1 《新聞・テレビなどにより心の中で応援するとき》
〈私はジャイアンツを応援しています〉
◎ A I root for the Giants.
◎ B I'm rooting [cheering] for the Giants.
△ C I cheer for the Giants.
❖ C は辞典に出ているが時々使われる程度．

2 《野球場などで声を出して応援するとき》
〈彼らはジャイアンツを応援していて騒々しかった〉
◎ A They were noisily rooting [cheering, shouting, yelling] for the Giants.
× B They were noisily giving a yell for the Giants.
❖ B は辞典に出ているが使われていない．

3 《野球場などで声を出さないで応援するとき》
〈ホームチームを応援しよう〉
◎ Let's root [cheer] for the home team.

押収される
〈彼の財産は国税庁に押収されました〉
☆ A His property was seized by the IRS.
◎ B His property was taken (over) by the IRS.
○ C His property was confiscated by the IRS.

往復する
〈私は毎日支店と本店の間を少なくとも 10 回往復しています〉
◎ A I make at least ten trips between the branch and the head office every day.
◎ B I travel between the branch and the head office at least ten times every day.

大売り出しをやる
〈ウールワースで大売り出しをやっている〉
◎ A They're having a sale at Woolworth's.
○ B They're holding a sale at Woolworth's.
▽ C They're holding a bargain sale at Woolworth's.
❖ C は辞典に出ているがまれ．

大きい
1 《計ったサイズを意味するとき》
〈私に大きいコーラを下さい〉
◎ A Give me a large coke.
× B Give me a big coke.

2 《主観的にサイズに言及するとき》
〈私は大都市が好きです〉
◎ A I like big cities.

△ B I like large cities.
　　　❖ A の big は主観的に，つまり感情を込めて述べるとき，B の large は客観的に述べるときのように使い分けられている．
 3 《長さに言及するとき》
〈今日，松井は大きいホームランを打った〉
　　　◎ A Today Matsui hit a long home run.
　　　× B Today Matsui hit a big [large] home run.
 4 《major しか使えない語》
a) surgery
〈父は先週大きな手術を受けたんですよ〉
　　　◎ A My father underwent major surgery last week.
　　　× B My father underwent big [large] surgery last week.
b) reform
〈この会社は大きな改革が必要です〉
　　　◎ A This company needs a major reform.
　　　× B This company needs a big [large] reform.
 5 《major と big の両方が使える語》
a) intersection
〈大きな交差点に出るまでずっと歩いて下さい〉
　　　◎ A Keep walking until you get to a major intersection.
　　　○ B Keep walking until you get to a big intersection.
　　　△ C Keep walking until you get to a large intersection.
b) change
〈日本の社会は大きな変化を受けています〉
　　　◎ A Japanese society's undergoing major [big] changes.
　　　× B Japanese society's undergoing large changes.
c) impact
〈これは日本に大きな影響を及ぼすであろう〉
　　　◎ A This'll have a major [big] impact on Japan.
　　　△ B This'll have a large impact on Japan.
d) problem
〈これが彼の性格の大きな問題なのです〉
　　　◎ A This is his major [big] problem with his personality.
　　　× B This is his large problem with his personality.
e) stumbling block
〈あなたの態度が就職に大きな障害となっているんです〉
　　　◎ A Your attitude's the major [big] stumbling block to your getting a job.
　　　× B Your attitude's the large stumbling block to your getting a job.

大騒ぎする
〈そんなささいなことで大騒ぎするな〉
　　　☆ A Don't make a big deal [a fuss] about such a small matter.
　　　☆ B Don't get bent out of shape about such a small matter.
　　　◎ C Don't make a big production about such a small matter.
　　　◎ D Don't make a great deal to do about such a small matter.
　　　△ E Don't make a big show [a racket] about such a small matter.
　　　△ F Don't put up a fuss about such a small matter.
　　　× G Don't whoop it up about such a small matter.
　　　× H Don't raise the roof [the devil] about such a small matter.

おおめにみる　77

- × I Don't kick up a racket about such a small matter.
- × J Don't make a great uproar [a tumult, rumpus] about such a small matter.
  - ❖ G〜Jが辞典に出ているが使われていない．

オーダーメイド
〈これはオーダーメイドのスーツです〉
- ☆ A This is a custom-made suit.
- ◎ B This is a tailor-made suit.
- × C This is an order-made [a custom] suit.

オーバーね
〈あなたはオーバーね〉
- ☆ A You're exaggerating.
- ◎ B You're overstating.
- ○ C You're making an exaggeration.

OB

1 《男性》
〈彼はハーバード大学のOB（卒業生）です〉
- ◎ A He's a graduate of Harvard.
- ○ B He's an alumni of Harvard.
- △ C He's an alumnus of Harvard.
  - ❖ Cが正しい英語．しかし，アメリカ人はCが正しいと知りつつもBの方をよく使っている．

2 《女性》
〈彼女はハーバード大学のOBです〉
- ◎ A She's a graduate of Harvard.
- ○ B She's an alumni of Harvard.
- △ C She's an alumna of Harvard.

3 《複数の人を指している場合》
〈慶応のOBは実業界で非常に有力な人が多い〉
- ◎ A Many graduates of Keio University are very influential in the business world.
- ○ B Many alumni of Keio University are very influential in the business world.
- × C Many alumnus of Keio University are very influential in the business world.
  - ❖ Cは辞典に出ているが使われていない．

4 《特定の学閥を指している場合》
〈あの会社では慶応のOBが非常に有力なんです〉
- ◎ 　The old boy network of Keio University is very influential in that company.

5 《スポーツで》
〈ジャイアンツのOBは長嶋の作戦に批判的なものが多かった〉
- ◎ A Many former players for the Giants were critical of Nagashima's strategy.
- ○ B Many ex-players for the Giants were critical of Nagashima's strategy.
- ○ C Many old [past] players for the Giants were critical of Nagashima's strategy.

大目に見る
〈彼は私のミスを大目に見てくれました〉

◎ A He let my mistake go.
◎ B He overlooked my mistake.
◎ C He pretended not to see my mistake.
◎ D He ignored [glossed over] my mistake.
◎ E He let my mistake slide.
○ F He closed his eyes to my mistake.
△ G He passed over my mistake.
× H He shut his eyes to my mistake.
× I He winked at [passed up] my mistake.
❖(1) H, I が辞典に出ているが使われていない.
❖(2) B, G は「見落とす」の意味でも使われている.

多めに見る
1 《費用》

〈あなたが必要と思う費用より2割多めに見た方がいいですよ〉

☆ A You'd better add 20% more to the cost of what you think you need.
◎ B You'd better estimate an additional 20% more to the cost of what you think you need.
◎ C You'd better figure an extra 20% more to the cost of what you think you need.
○ D You'd better figure an additional 20% more to the cost of what you think you need.
❖ A〜D いずれも more はなくても非常によく使われている. B, C, D は more があると意味上重複になるが, よく使われている.

2 《時間》

〈横浜へ車で行くときは20分多めに見た方がいいよ〉

☆ A When you drive to Yokohama, you'd better allow an extra 20 minutes.
◎ B When you drive to Yokohama, you'd better figure an extra [additional] 20 minutes.
◎ C When you drive to Yokohama, you'd better add an extra 20 minutes.
○ D When you drive to Yokohama, you'd better give yourself a 20 minutes leeway.
△ E When you drive to Yokohama, you'd better give yourself a 20 minutes headstart.

大文字で書く → 字 4

大物
1 《実業界・政界の場合》

a) 現在の状態

〈彼は映画産業界で大物です〉

◎ A He's a big shot [a bigwig] in the movie industry.
○ B He's a big gun in the movie industry.
○ C He's an important figure in the movie industry.
× D He's a big pot [a big swell, a big bug, a big wheel, a big noise] in the movie industry.
❖(1) D が辞典に出ているが使われていない.
❖(2) C は堅い響きがある.

b) 未来の予想

〈彼は将来映画産業界の大物になるでしょう〉

◎ A He'll be a big shot [a bigwig, an important person] in the movie

industry in the future.
- ◎ B He'll be somebody [something] in the movie industry in the future.
- ○ C He'll be a big gun [an important figure] in the movie industry in the future.
- △ D He'll be a somebody in the movie industry in the future.

2 《スポーツ界の場合》
〈彼は野球界の大物の一人です〉
- ◎   He's one of baseball's greats [star players, superstars, stars].
- ❖「小物」の項も参照のこと．

お買い得だ
〈これはあれよりお買い得です〉
- ☆ A This is a better deal than that.
- ◎ B This is a better buy than that.
- ○ C This is a better bargain than that.
- ○ D This is more of a bargain than that.
- ○ E This is better for your money than that.
- ○ F This is more economical than that.
- △ G This is a better deal for your money than that.
- △ H This is more money-saving than that.
    - ❖詳細は「安い」の項を参照のこと．

お菓子屋　→店 11

起きている
1 《ベッドから起きている》
〈私は毎朝6時頃に起きています〉
- ◎ A Every morning I'm up around 6:00.
- ○ B Every morning I'm awake around 6:00.
- × C Every morning I'm stirring [astir] around 6:00.
    - ❖Cが辞典に出ているが使われていない．

2 《目は覚めているがベッドの中にいるとき》
〈私は毎朝6時頃に起きています〉
- ◎ A Every morning I'm awake around 6:00.
- △ B Every morning I'm up around 6:00.

置き忘れる　→忘れる 4

置く
〈彼は本をドンと机の上に置いた〉
- ◎ A He slammed his books (down) on the desk.
- ◎ B He slammed his books onto the desk.
- ◎ C He threw his books (down) on the desk.

奥様
1 《丁重に言うとき（学生が教授の奥さんのことを言うとき，教会の牧師に奥さんのことを言うとき，社長に奥さんのことを言うとき）》
 a）アメリカの場合
- ❖your wife，または Mrs. Smith のように呼ばれている．日本語の感覚から言うと your wife は失礼な感じがあるが，アメリカでは失礼に当たらない．しかし，Mrs. Smith の方が少し丁重になる．

 b）イギリスの場合
- ❖your wife も使えるが，Mrs. Smith の方がよく使われている．

2 《金持ちのお屋敷で》
〈執事：奥様，だんな様にお電話いたしましょうか〉

Butler:
 ◎　Madam, shall I call Mr. Rockefeller?

〈ロックフェラー夫人：はい，お願いします．この時間までは事務所にいるはずですよ〉

Mrs. Rockefeller: Yes, please. He should be at the office by this time.

3　《学生が教授に話すとき》

〈学生：奥様が車にはねられたそうですね．大丈夫なのですか〉

Student:
 ◎　I heard Mrs. Smith was hit by a car. Is she alright?

〈教授：ありがとう．今病院にいるんだけれど，数日でよくなるでしょう〉

Professor: Right now she's in the hospital, but she'll be alright in a few days. Thank you for asking.

億万長者

〈彼は億万長者です〉
- ◎　A　He's a billionaire.
- ◎　B　He's a multimillionaire.
  - ❖ A の方が B より金持ちである．

送る

1　《人をある場所へ送り届ける》

a) 自分で車で送るとき

〈私は駅まであなたを車でお送ります〉
- ◎　A　I'll drive [take] you to the station.
- ◎　B　I'll give you a ride [lift] to the station.
- ◎　C　I'll drop you off at the station.
- ×　D　I'll send you to the station.
  - ❖(1) A, B は話し手の I が聞き手の you をわざわざ駅まで車で送り届ける場合と，駅が話し手にとって通り道である場合のどちらの状況でも使える．
  - ❖(2) C は A, B と違って，駅が話し手にとって通り道である可能性が約 80 % である．

b) 一般的な状況のとき

〈家まで送り届けますよ〉
- ◎　A　I'll drive you home.
- ◎　B　I'll take you home.
- ◎　C　I'll give you a ride [lift] home.

c) 困難な状況にあるとき

〈心配しないで．家まで送り届けるよ〉
- ◎　Don't worry. I'll get you (back) home.
  - ❖深夜で電車，バスがないとか，車が故障してしまったような場面．

d) 部下のような人に送らせるとき

〈誰かに空港まで車で送らせます〉
- ◎　I'll have [arrange for] somebody to drive you to the airport.

e) 送ってきてもらったとき

〈彼が私をここまで車で送ってきてくれたんです〉
- ◎　A　He dropped me off here.
- ◎　B　He brought me.
- ◎　C　He drove me here.
- ◎　D　He gave me a ride here.
- ○　E　He gave me a lift here.
- △　F　He brought me here by car.

f) 歩いて入り口・門・駅まで送るとき
・友人などのとき
〈玄関までお送りしましょう〉
  ◎ A I'll walk you to the door.
  ○ B I'll see you to the door.
〈駅までお送りします〉
  ◎ A I'll walk you to the station.
  ○ B I'll see you to the station.
  ❖歩いて行ける距離のときは，see より walk の方が使われている．ただし，see は上のような場面では改まった響きになることに注意．
・VIP のとき
〈私たちは退任する社長を送別会の後，入り口までお送りしました〉
  ◎ We saw [walked] the retiring President to the door after the farewell party.
  ❖「see one to+場所」は非常にかしこまった状況のときにしか使えない．

2 《物を送る》
a) 発送する
〈販売員：金曜日までにご注文の品をお送りいたします〉
Salesperson:
  ◎ We'll ship [send, dispatch] your order by Friday.
  ❖主語がビジネスピープルでなければ，dispatch は時々使われる程度．

b) 飛行機・トラック・船で
〈(母が息子に) 重いものは後で全部飛行機で送ってあげるわよ〉
  ◎ A I'll send all the heavy stuff by plane later.
  ○ B I'll ship all the heavy stuff by plane later.
  ❖ship は飛行機，トラック，汽車のいずれにも使える．

c) 請求書を
〈後でこの請求書を送ってくれますか〉
  ◎ A Will you bill me for this later?
  ◎ B Will you send me the bill for this later?
  ▽ C Will you forward me the bill for this later?
  × D Will you send in [submit] the bill for this later?
  ❖ D が辞典に出ているが使われていない．

3 《2人称のyouを支店・外国などへ送るとき》
〈君をニューヨーク支店へ送る予定です〉
  ◎ A We're going to send [transfer] you to the New York branch.
  △ B We're going to dispatch you to the New York branch.
〈国務長官と話をしてもらうために君をワシントン D.C.へ送ります〉
  ◎ A I'll send you to Washington D.C. to talk to the Secretary of State.
  ◎ B I'll have you go to Washington D.C. to talk to the Secretary of State.

4 《3人称の人を送るとき》
a) 人を送るとき
〈もし非常に忙しいのなら，もう3人送りますよ〉
  ◎ If you're very busy, I'll send three more people.
〈うちは 50 の会社に約 2000 人の人を送っています〉
  ◎ A We're sending about 2,000 people to 50 companies.
  △ B We're dispatching about 2,000 people to 50 companies.

b) 軍隊を派遣するとき
〈アメリカ政府は平和を維持するためにそこへ軍隊を送るであろう〉

◎ Uncle Sam'll send [deploy] its troops there to maintain peace.

c) スポーツで選手団を送るとき

〈中国は強力な選手団をオリンピックに送ります〉

◎ A China's got some good athletes going to the Olympics.
◎ B China'll be well represented in the Olympics.
◎ C China'll send their top athletes to the Olympics.

d) 議員を国会へ送るとき

〈各州は2人の上院議員を送っています〉

◎ A Each state sends two people to the Senate.
◎ B Each state has two senators.
◎ C There are two senators for each state.
◎ D Each state's represented by two senators.

5 《教師が学習態度が悪い学生を家に送り返すとき》

〈先生:君たち2人,後ろでふざけるのをやめないと家に送り返すぞ〉

Teacher:

◎ If you two don't stop fooling around back there, I'll send you home.

❖(1) 「send+2人称の you to...」の型を使えるのは,次の条件が満たされているときに限る.(イ)主語が権限を持っているとき(上司と部下はその一例).(ロ)小中学校の先生が生徒に言うとき.

❖(2) 「send+3人称」は(1)のような制限なしに使える.

遅れる

1 《コンサート・会合などのように動かないものに》

a) 最初の部分に遅れたとき

〈私はコンサートに遅れてしまったんです〉

◎ A I was late for the concert.
◎ B I didn't get to the concert on time.
◎ C I didn't make (it to) the concert.
◎ D I wasn't on time for the concert.
◎ E I didn't get to the hall in [on] time for the concert.
○ F I didn't get to the concert in time.
○ G I didn't make it for the concert.
△ H I wasn't in time for the concert.

❖ F はコンサートの始めから終わりまで見そこなったという場合と,最初の部分だけ遅れてしまった場合の両方に等しくよく使われているが,H の型はコンサートの最初の部分という一部に間に合わなかっただけでなく,主として始めから終わりまで見そこなったときには非常によく使われている. b)も参照のこと.

b) まったく見ることが(または出席)できなかったとき

〈私はコンサートに遅れてしまったんです〉

☆ A I missed the concert.
◎ B I didn't make (it to) the concert.
◎ C I didn't get to the concert in time.
○ D I didn't make it for the concert.
× E I didn't make it on the concert.

2 《飛行機・電車のような動くものに》

〈私は飛行機に乗り遅れたんです〉

☆ A I missed the flight.
◎ B I didn't make [catch] the flight.
◎ C I was late for the flight.

- ○ D I wasn't on [in] time for the flight.
- ○ E I didn't get to the airport on [in] time.
- ○ F I didn't get to the plane on time.
- ○ G I didn't get to the flight on time.
- ○ H I didn't make it for [on] the flight.
- △ I I didn't make it to the flight.
- △ J I didn't get to the plane [flight] in time.

3 《時計が》

a) 遅れている事実を述べるとき

〈私の時計は5分遅れています〉

- ☆ A My watch's five minutes slow.
- ◎ B My watch's five minutes behind.
- ○ C My watch's five minutes late.

b) 遅れている分数を尋ねるとき

〈あなたの時計は何分遅れているのですか〉

- ☆ A How slow's your watch?
- ◎ B How many minutes slow's your watch?
- ◎ C How many minutes behind's your watch?
- ○ D How many minutes is your watch slow [behind]?
- △ E How late's your watch?
- △ F How many minutes late's your watch?
- △ G How many minutes is your watch late?

4 《数学・英語などの科目の進度が》

a) クラスメートと比較して遅れている事実を述べるとき

〈彼は数学においてクラスに遅れをとっています〉

- ◎ He's (lagging) behind his class in math.

b) クラスメートと比較して以前より落伍してきていることを述べるとき

〈彼は数学でクラスに遅れてしまっているんです〉

- ◎ A He's falling behind his class in math.
- ◎ B He isn't keeping up with his class in math.
- ○ C He's dropping behind his class in math.

   ❖ A, B, C いずれも，数学において彼は以前は他のクラスメートより進んでいた，または同じレベルであったという響きがある．

c) 生まれつき能力がなくて遅れていると述べるとき

〈彼は数学が遅れているんです〉

- ◎ A He's slow at [in] math.
- ◎ B He's bad at math.
- ◎ C He doesn't do well at math.
- ◎ D He isn't doing well at math.
- ○ E He's doing bad at math.

5 《毎月支払う家賃（ローン，食費）などの支払いが》

a) 単に遅れていると述べるとき

〈彼は家賃が遅れているんです〉

- ◎ A He's behind on [with, in] his rent.
- ◎ B He's late with his rent.
- ○ C He's late in (paying) his rent.
- △ D He's overdue with [in] his rent.

b) 遅れている日数，月数を述べるとき

・人を主語にして述べる場合

〈彼は家賃が2ヵ月遅れているんです〉
- ◎ A He's two months behind on [with, in] his rent.
- ◎ B He's two months late with his rent.
- ○ C He's two months late in (paying) his rent.
- △ D He's two months overdue with [in] his rent.

・家賃（ローン，会費）を主語にして述べるとき

〈彼の家賃は2ヵ月遅れています〉
- ◎ A His rent's two months late [overdue].
- ○ B His rent's two months behind.
- △ C His rent's two months slow.

6 《交通機関（電車，飛行機，バスなど）が》

a) 予定の時刻に遅れていることを述べるとき

〈10時の便は事故のため遅れています〉
- ◎ A The 10:00 flight's late [delayed, behind] because of the accident.
- ○ B The 10:00 flight's overdue because of the accident.

b) 遅れている時間数を述べるとき

〈10時の便は事故のため2時間遅れています〉
- ☆ A The 10:00 flight's two hours late because of the accident.
- ◎ B The 10:00 flight's two hours behind (the schedule) because of the accident.
- ◎ C The 10:00 flight's behind (the schedule) by two hours because of the accident.
- ◎ D The 10:00 flight's delayed [overdue] by two hours because of the accident.
- ○ E The 10:00 flight's late by two hours because of the accident.
- ○ F The 10:00 flight's two hours overdue because of the accident.
- ▽ G The 10:00 flight's two hours delayed because of the accident.

7 《他の会社（国，人）と比較して》

a) 遅れている事実を述べるとき

〈この会社はエンジンにおいてホンダに遅れています〉
- ◎ A This company's behind Honda in its engine.
- ◎ B This company's lagging behind Honda in its engine.
  - ❖ A と B は現在の状態だけに言及している点では同じであるが，B は批判しているとの響きがある．

b) 以前より落伍してきているということを述べるとき

〈この会社はエンジンにおいてホンダに遅れてしまっている〉
- ◎ A This company's falling behind Honda in its engine.
- ◎ B This company isn't keeping up with Honda in its engine.
- ○ C This company's dropping behind Honda in its engine.
  - ❖ A, B, C いずれも以前はエンジンにおいてホンダより進んでいた，または同じレベルであったという響きがある．

起こす

1 《目を覚まさせる》

a) 家庭の場合

〈6時に起こして下さい〉
- ◎ A Wake me (up) at 6:00.
- × B Awake me (up) at 6:00.
  - ❖ B が辞典に出ているが使われていない．

b) ホテルなどの場合

〈明日の朝7時に起こして下さい〉
- ◎ A Can you give me a wake-up call at 7:00 tomorrow morning?
- ◎ B Can I get [have] a wake-up call at 7:00 tomorrow morning?
- ○ C I'd like a wake-up call at 7:00 tomorrow morning.

2 《引き起こす》

a）主語に責任があると述べるとき

〈彼は事故を起こしたんです〉
- ◎ A He caused a car accident.
- ◎ B He got into [in] a car accident.
  - ❖ A は100％責任があるとき，B は約65％．したがって，B は A と違って，話者は断言していないことになる．

b）誰に責任があるかを明示しないとき

〈彼は事故を起こしたんです〉
- ◎ A He had a car accident.
- ◎ B He was in a car accident.
- ◎ C He got [was] involved in a car accident.
- × D He met with a car accident.

怒っている

1 《気分を害している》

〈彼女は私に気分を害しているんです〉
- ◎ A She's upset with me.
- ◎ B She isn't happy with me.

2 《むっとしている》

〈彼は私が遅れたのでむっとしていました〉
- ◎ A He was offended [put out] because I was late.
- ◎ B He was miffed [upset] because I was late.
- ○ C He was displeased because I was late.
  - ❖ A は B, C より強い響きがある．

3 《普通に怒っているとき》

a）人に対して

〈彼女はあなたのことを怒っています〉
- ◎ A She's upset with you.
- ◎ B She's angry [mad] at you.
- ◎ C She's ticked off at you.
- ○ D She's angry with you.
- ○ E She's upset about you.
  - ❖ B, C, D はほぼ同じで，A, E よりずっと強い怒り．

b）振舞い・事態などに対して

〈彼女はあなたの振舞いに怒っています〉
- ☆ A She's upset with your behavior.
- ◎ B She's angry with [about, at] your behavior.
- ◎ C She's mad about your behavior.
- ◎ D She's ticked off about your behavior.
- ◎ E She's upset at [about] your behavior.
- ○ F She's mad at your behavior.
- ○ G She's ticked off at [with] your behavior.
- △ H She's mad with your behavior.

4 《強く怒っているとき》

a）人に対して

〈彼女はあなたのことをすごく怒っています〉
- ◎ A She's pissed-off at you.
- ◎ B She's furious with [at] you.
- ◎ C She's peeved at you.
- ○ D She's pissed-off [peeved] with you.
- △ E She's irate at [with] you.
  - ❖(1) E は少し改まった響きがある.
  - ❖(2) A～E のいずれも怒りの度合いは同じ程度に強い.

b）振舞い・事態などに対して

〈彼女はあなたの振舞いにすごく怒っています〉
- ☆ A She's pissed-off at your behavior.
- ◎ B She's furious at [with] your behavior.
- ◎ C She's pissed-off about your behavior.
- ○ D She's irate at [about] your behavior.
- △ E She's peeved about [at, with] your behavior.

5 《「かっと怒る」と述べるとき》

〈彼が何を言っても，かっと怒っては駄目ですよ〉
- ◎ A No matter what he says, don't lose your temper.
- ○ B No matter what he says, don't blow your top [cool].
- ○ C No matter what he says, don't explode.
- × D No matter what he says, don't fly into a rage [fury].
- × E No matter what he says, don't get [fly, fall] into a passion.
- × F No matter what he says, don't burn up.
- × G No matter what he says, don't flame out.
- × H No matter what he says, don't get into a way.

6 《「ふくれている」と述べるとき》

a）13 歳くらいまでの子供の場合

〈娘は私がおもちゃを買わなかったのでふくれていました〉
- ◎ A My daughter was sulking because I didn't buy her a toy.
- ○ B My daughter was pouting because I didn't buy her a toy.
- ▽ C My daughter was sullen [cross] because I didn't buy her a toy.
- ▽ D My daughter was in the pouts because I didn't buy her a toy.
- ▽ E My daughter was looking sulky because I didn't buy her a toy.
- × F My daughter was pulling a sulky face because I didn't buy her a toy.
- × G My daughter was wearing a sulky face because I didn't buy her a toy.
- × H My daughter was putting on a sullen look because I didn't buy her a toy.
- × I My daughter was fretting because I didn't buy her a toy.
- × J My daughter was getting sulky because I didn't buy her a toy.
- × K My daughter was in the sulks because I didn't buy her a toy.
- × L My daughter was making grimaces [a wry, a mouth] because I didn't buy her a toy.
  - ❖(1) F～L が辞典に出ているが使われていない.
  - ❖(2) A は 13 歳くらいまでの女の子に特によく使われている.

b）成人の場合

〈息子は私が住宅ローンの連帯保証人にならなかったのでふくれていた〉
- ◎ A My son was sulking because I didn't cosign for his home loan.
- ○ B My son was pouting because I didn't cosign for his home loan.
- ▽ C My son was sullen because I didn't cosign for his home loan.

▽ D My son was in the pouts [sulks] because I didn't cosign for his home loan.

怒らせる
1 《一般的に述べるとき》
〈彼を怒らせないで下さい〉
- ◎ A Don't make him upset.
- ◎ B Don't upset him.
- ◎ C Don't make him angry [mad].
- ◎ D Don't tick him off.
- ○ E Don't get him upset [angry, mad].
- ○ F Don't get his goat.
- △ G Don't make [get] him ticked off.
- × H Don't put his back up.
- × I Don't stir him to anger.
- × J Don't drive him into passion.
- × K Don't rub him against the grain.
- × L Don't put him in a ruffle.
  - ❖(1) 辞書に H～L が出ているが使われていない.
  - ❖(2) F は老人の間では非常によく使われている. 30 歳以下は若くなるにつれて使用頻度は下がる. 35 歳～50 歳くらいの人の間ではよく使われている.
  - ❖(3) 怒っている度合いは A, B, F が一番弱い. あとの C, D, E, G はほぼ同じで, どれが強いかは個人差が非常にある.

2 《強く怒らせると述べるとき》
〈彼を怒らせないで下さい〉
- ◎ A Don't piss him off.
- ◎ B Don't make him furious.
- ◎ C Don't make [get] him pissed-off.
- ○ D Don't get him irate.
- △ E Don't make him irate.
- △ F Don't make him peeved.

起こる
〈このトラブルは誤解から起こったのです〉
- ☆ A This trouble happened from a misunderstanding.
- ◎ B This trouble occurred [came about] from a misunderstanding.
- ◎ C This trouble was caused by a misunderstanding.
- △ D This trouble arose from a misunderstanding.
  - ❖ D は堅い表現であるが, 会話でもよく使われている.

怒る →怒っている

おごる
〈もし私の仕事を手伝ってくれれば昼食をおごりますよ〉
- ◎ A If you help me with my work, I'll buy you lunch.
- ◎ B If you help me with my work, I'll treat you to lunch.
- ◎ C If you help me with my work, lunch'll be on me.
- ◎ D If you help me with my work, lunch'll be on my treat.
- × E If you help me with my work, I'll set you up to lunch.
- × F If you help me with my work, I'll get you a lunch.
- × G If you help me with my work, I'll stand [give] you lunch.
  - ❖ E, F, G が辞典に出ているが使われていない.

お先に
〈お先に〉
- ◎ A After you.
- ◎ B Go ahead.
- △ C Go first.
- ❖ C は子供に対しては非常によく使われている．

押し上げる
1 《景気》
〈この新しい減税は景気を押し上げるだろう〉
- ◎ A This new tax reduction'll stimulate [boost] the economy.
- ◎ B This new tax reduction'll give the economy a lift.
- ◎ C This new tax reduction'll help the economy improve.
- ○ D This new tax reduction'll bolster [lift] the economy.
- △ E This new tax reduction'll encourage [raise, build up] the economy.

2 《箱を棚に》
〈この箱を一番上の棚に押し上げて下さい〉
- ◎ A Take this box and put it on the top shelf.
- ◎ B Put this box on the top shelf.
- ○ C Lift this box and put it on the top shelf.
- △ D Place this box and put it on the top shelf.

教えている
1 《大学》
a）大学名を明示しないで述べるとき
〈彼は大学で教えているんです〉
- ☆ A He's a college professor.
- ◎ B He's teaching at a college.
- ◎ C He's a professor at a college.
- ◎ D He teaches at a college [university].
- ○ E He teaches in a college [university].
- ○ F He's on the faculty of a college.
- △ G He's a faculty member of a college.
- △ H He's a college faculty member.

❖(1) 大学の学園の中で「彼は教授です」と述べるときは以下のように言う．
- ☆ A He's a professor.
- ◎ B He's on the faculty.
- ○ C He's a member of the faculty.
- ○ D He's a faculty member.

❖(2) faculty には学校の事務職員，また学生も入ると書いてある辞典があるが，これはアメリカ英語の慣用事実を歪曲している．

b）大学名を明示して述べるとき
〈彼はスタンフォードで教えているんです〉
- ☆ A He's a professor at Stanford.
- ☆ B He's on the faculty at Stanford.
- ◎ C He's a member of the faculty at Stanford.
- ◎ D He's on the faculty of Stanford.
- ○ E He's a faculty member of Stanford.
- ○ F He's a member of the faculty of Stanford.

2 《高校・中学・小学校》
a）高校名を明示しないで述べるとき

〈彼は高校で教えているんです〉
- ☆ A He's a high school teacher.
- ◎ B He's a teacher at a high school.
- ◎ C He's teaching at a high school.
- ◎ D He teaches at a high school.
- ○ E He's on the faculty of a high school.
- △ F He's a faculty member of a high school.
- ▽ G He's a high school faculty member.

b) 高校名を明示して述べるとき

〈彼は XYZ 高校で教えているんです〉
- ☆ A He's a teacher at XYZ High School.
- ☆ B He teaches at XYZ High School.
- ☆ C He's teaching at XYZ High School.
- ◎ D He's on the faculty of [at] XYZ High School.
- ○ E He's a faculty member of XYZ High School.
- △ F He's a member of the faculty of XYZ High School.

押し込む

1 《乗客を電車に》

〈駅員たちは乗客を電車に押し込んでいました〉
- ◎ A The station employees were squeezing people onto [into] the train.
- ◎ B The station employees were cramming people onto [into] the train.
- ◎ C The station employees were packing people onto [into] the train.
- ◎ D The station employees were pushing people onto [into] the train.
- ○ E The station employees were stuffing people onto [into] the train.
- ○ F The station employees were crowding people onto [into] the train.
  - ❖ A, B, C が一番押し込んでいる程度が強い響きがある．E, F が 2 番目，D が一番弱い．

2 《食物を口に》

〈彼は口に食物を押し込んでいました〉
- ◎ A He was stuffing food into his mouth.
- ○ B He was stuffing food in his mouth.
- ○ C He was cramming food into [in] his mouth.

3 《物をカバンに》

〈全部カバンに押し込んでくれますか〉
- ☆ A Will you squeeze [cram, stuff] everything into the bag?
- ◎ B Will you squeeze [cram, stuff] everything in the bag?
- ○ C Will you jam everything into [in] the bag?

汚染されている

1 《空気》

〈この辺の空気は汚染されています〉
- ◎ A The air around here's smoggy.
- ◎ B The air around here's polluted.
- △ C The air around here's contaminated.
- △ D The air around here's sooty.
  - ❖(1) D が一番強い．C が 2 番目，B, A の順で弱くなる．
  - ❖(2) C は堅い文章英語では非常によく使われている．

2 《川・湖など》

〈この川は汚染されている〉
- ☆ A This river's polluted.

- ◎ B This river's dirty [filthy].
- △ C This river's contaminated.
- ▽ D This river's tainted.
- ❖ C はテレビ，新聞などでは一番よく使われている．

3 《食べ物》

〈この魚は汚染されている〉
- ◎ A This fish's contaminated.
- × B This fish's polluted.

遅い

〈彼は仕事が遅いんです〉
- ◎ A He gets very little done.
- ◎ B He doesn't get much done.
- ◎ C He isn't very productive.
- ◎ D He isn't productive.
- ◎ E He gets little done.
- ◎ F He doesn't get a lot done.
- ◎ G He's a slow worker.
- ❖ D, E は語調が少し弱い．

遅くとも

〈遅くとも4時までには電話します〉
- ◎ A I'll call you no later than 4 o'clock.
- ◎ B I'll call you by 4 o'clock at the latest.
- △ C I'll call you not later than 4 o'clock.
- △ D I'll call you by 4 o'clock at latest.
- ❖ B, D には by が必要であるが，A, C には付けられない．たとえ by がなくても，意味上は A～D のいずれも同じである．

おたふく風邪 →病気 6

落ち着いた

1 《顔・態度を述べるとき》

〈彼女は落ち着いているようだった〉
- ☆ A She looked relaxed.
- ◎ B She looked calm.
- ○ C She looked at ease.
- ○ D She looked cool and collected.
- △ E She looked composed.
- ▽ F She looked tranquil.

2 《気持ちが休まるという意味のとき》

〈私は彼女と一緒にいると落ち着かないんです〉
- ◎ A I can't feel relaxed [comfortable, at home] with her.
- ○ B I can't feel at ease with her.

落ち着く

1 《為替のレート》

〈為替のレートはまもなく落ち着くでしょう〉
- ◎ A The exchange rate'll stabilize [be stabilized] soon.
- ○ B The exchange rate'll be [get, become] stable soon.
- ○ C The exchange rate'll settle down soon.

2 《相手が急いであわてているとき》

〈落ち着きなさい〉
- ◎ A Take it easy.

- ◎ B Hold your horses.
- ◎ C Calm down.
- ◎ D Keep your shirt on.
- ○ E Settle down.
- △ F Calm yourself.

3 《相手が泣いたり，感情的になったりしているとき》

〈落ち着きなさい〉
- ☆ A Take it easy.
- ☆ B Take a deep breath.
- ☆ C Calm down.
- ☆ D Settle down.
- ◎ E Pull yourself together.
- ◎ F Get a hold of yourself.
- ○ G Get a grip.
- ○ H Don't let it go to you.
- △ I Don't get [be] excited.
- △ J Calm yourself.

❖強さの点ではGが一番強く，A, B, D, E, F, Hが2番，Iが3番，C, Jが4番．

夫を尻に敷く

〈彼女は夫を尻に敷いています〉
- ◎ A She's the man of the house.
- ◎ B She wears the pants in the family.
- ○ C She's the boss in the family.
- ○ D She rules the house.
- × E She wears the pants at home.

❖Aは主語がSheでもthe manを使う．

おととい

〈(話している日が日曜日) 彼はおとといの午後ここへ来ました〉
- ◎ A He came here on Friday afternoon.
- △ B He came here in the afternoon two days ago.
- △ C He came here two afternoons ago.
- × D He came here the afternoon before yesterday.

❖「おとといの午後」に相当する英語はない．今日が日曜日であればFriday afternoonのように具体的に曜日で述べる．

おととし

〈(話している年が2003年) 彼はおととしの3月にサンフランシスコに引っ越して来ました〉
- ◎ A He moved to San Francisco in March, 2001.
- ◎ B He moved to San Francisco the March before last.
- ○ C He moved to San Francisco in March, the year before last.
- ○ D He moved to San Francisco March before last.

驚く

1 《一般的に》

〈私は彼の横柄な態度に驚いています〉
- ◎ A I'm surprised by his arrogant attitude.
- ○ B I'm amazed by his arrogant attitude.
- △ C I'm astonished [astounded] by his arrogant attitude.

2 《感心して驚くとき》

〈私は彼の流暢なフランス語に驚いた〉
- ◎ A I was amazed [surprised] by his fluent French.
- △ B I was astonished [astounded] by his fluent French.

3 《よいことで非常に驚くとき》

〈ベルが1876年に電話を発明したとき,人々はきっと驚いたことでしょう〉
- ◎ A People must've been amazed [astounded] when Bell invented the telephone in 1876.
- △ B People must've been astonished [surprised] when Bell invented the telephone in 1876.

4 《信じられないようなことを聞いて驚くとき》

〈驚いたね〉
- ◎ A Now I've heard everything.
- ◎ B Now I've heard it all.
- ○ C That's really surprising.
- ○ D That really surprises me.
- △ E That's really amazing.
- △ F That really amazes me.
    - ❖ 20カ国語を流暢に話せるというような感心させられることを聞いたときには,E,Fは非常によく使われている.

5 《信じられないようなもの・人を見て驚くとき》

〈ビル:よお,あそこを見ろよ.自分の目が信じられないよ.あの女性は裸だよ.驚いたね〉

Bill: Hey, look over there! I don't believe my eyes. That girl's naked.
- ◎ A Now I've seen everything.
- ◎ B Now I've seen it all.
- ○ C That's really surprising.
- ○ D That really surprises me.
- △ E That's really amazing.
- △ F That really amazes me.

おなかがぺこぺこ

〈おなかがぺこぺこなんです〉
- ◎ A I could eat a horse.
- ◎ B I could eat a horse, I'm so hungry.
- ◎ C I'm awfully hungry.
- ◎ D I'm starved [starving].
- ○ E I'm famished.
    - ❖ 空腹度はA,Bが一番強く,Eが2番目,Dが3番目,Cが一番弱い.

お願い

1 《呼びかけ》

〈(長電話しているビルにむかって)母親:お願い,ビル.大切な電話を待っているのよ〉

Mother:
- ◎ A Do me a favor, Bill. I'm expecting an important phone call.
- ◎ B Please, Bill. I'm expecting an important phone call.
- ◎ C Listen, Bill. I'm expecting an important phone call.
- ◎ D Come on, Bill. I'm expecting an important phone call.
    - ❖ A,B,Cは主として初めて呼びかけるとき,Dは初めて,または2度目以上のときのどちらにも等しく使われている.

2 《頼み事をするとき》

a）非常に丁重に話すとき
〈お願いがあるのですが〉
- ☆ A May I ask you a favor?
- ◎ B Could you do me a favor?
- ◎ C Could I ask you a favor?
- △ D May I ask a favor of you?
    - ❖(1) 丁重さは D が 1 番，A は 2 番，B，C はほぼ同じで 3 番．
    - ❖(2) D は丁寧な表現のためか辞典や英文法書によく出ているが，堅い表現なのでそれほど使われていない．

b）少し丁重に話すとき
〈お願いがあるのですが〉
- ◎ Could [Would] you do me a favor?

c）気軽に話すとき
〈ちょっとお願いがあるんだけど〉
- ◎ Can you do me a (little) favor?

お久し振りです →久し振り 2
お一人様ですか →ひとりで 4
オフィス街 →…街 4
おめでとう

1 《結婚披露宴で新婦に対して》
〈招待された客：おめでとうございます〉
Invited Guest:
- ◎ A Congratulations!
- ○ B Best wishes.
    - ❖(1) 結婚する女性に対して A を使ってはならないといろいろな本に書いてあるが，今はそういう区別は不要である．今も B は使われているが，A の方が圧倒的に使われている．Congratulations! を女性に使ってはならないと過去に書かれていた理由は，努力をして獲得したという響きがあるからである．しかし，ウーマンリブの運動の影響もあって物の見方が変わり，今では Congratulations! が圧倒的に使われている．
    - ❖(2) 新郎に対してはいつも Congratulations! が使われている．

2 《かしこまった間柄の場合》
〈スミス氏：ブラウンさん，社長に昇格になったそうですね．おめでとうございます〉
Mr. Smith:
- ◎ A Mr. Brown, I heard you've been promoted to president. Congratulations!
- △ B Mr. Brown, I heard you've been promoted to president. Good for you!
    - ❖どちらを使うかは 2 人の間柄による．ファーストネームではなく，Mr. Brown と呼びかけるのは，日本と違ってアメリカでは非常にかしこまった間柄である．したがって，A の Congratulations! がこの場面ではぴったりする．

3 《第三者に言う場合》
〈高橋夫人：お嬢様はご卒業してから何をなさるのですか〉
Mrs. Takahashi: What is your daughter going to do after she graduates?
〈田中夫人：銀行に就職いたしました〉
Mrs. Tanaka: She got a job at a bank.
〈高橋夫人：あら，そうですか．おめでとうございます〉
Mrs. Takahashi:

◎ A Oh, really? Good for her!
○ B Oh, really? Congratulations!

4 《親しい間柄（クラスメートなど）の場合》
〈ジム：ハーバードに入ったよ〉
Jim: I've been accepted by Harvard.
〈リンダ：おめでとう〉
Linda:
  ◎ A Good for you!
  ○ B Congratulations!

5 《皮肉をこめて言う場合》
〈ジム：数学の試験で A を取ったよ〉
Jim: I got an A on my math exam.
〈トム：おめでとう．何が欲しいんだい，金メダルか〉
Tom:
  ◎　 Good for you. What do you want, a gold medal?

6 《おめでとうを言える主なお祝いの日》
〈新年おめでとう〉
  ☆ A Happy New Year!
  ◎ B Have a Happy New Year!
  ○ C Happy New Year to you!
  △ D A Happy New Year to you!
  ▽ E A Happy New Year!

〈バレンタインデーおめでとう〉
  ☆ A Happy Valentine's Day!
  ◎ B Have a Happy Valentine's Day!
  ○ C Happy Valentine's Day to you!
  △ D A Happy Valentine's Day to you!
  ▽ E A Happy Valentine's Day!

〈復活祭おめでとう〉
  ☆ A Happy Easter!
  ◎ B Have a Happy Easter!
  ○ C Happy Easter to you!
  △ D A Happy Easter to you!
  ▽ E A Happy Easter!

〈感謝祭おめでとう〉
  ☆ A Happy Thanksgiving Day!
  ◎ B Have a Happy Thanksgiving Day!
  ○ C Happy Thanksgiving Day to you!
  △ D A Happy Thanksgiving Day to you!
  ▽ E A Happy Thanksgiving!

〈誕生日おめでとう〉
  ◎ A Happy birthday!
  ◎ B Have a happy birthday!
  ○ C Happy birthday to you!
  △ D A happy birthday to you!
  ▽ E A happy birthday!

思いきった
〈私たちはいくつか思いきった対策を取らなければならない〉
  ☆ A We have to take some drastic measures.

◎ B We have to take some extreme [radical] measures.
   ○ C We have to take some bold measures.
思い詰めている
1 《ミス・失敗などを》
〈彼はミスを思い詰めているんです〉
   ◎ A He's obsessed with his mistake.
   ○ B He's hung up on his mistake.
   ○ C He's preoccupied with his mistake.
   △ D He's wrapped up [caught up] in his mistake.
   △ E He's lost in his mistake.
   △ F He's absorbed [fixated] in his mistake.
   ❖思い詰めている度合いはAが一番強い．B, Dが2番，Eが3番，C, Fが4番目．
2 《恋している人を》
〈彼は彼女のことを思い詰めているんです〉
   ◎ A He's obsessed [infatuated] with her.
   ○ B He's hung up on her.
   △ C He's preoccupied with her.
   △ D He's overcome by her.
思いとどまらせる
〈私は彼がそこへ行かないように思いとどまらせました〉
   ◎ A I persuaded [convinced] him not to go there.
   ◎ B I talked him out of going there.
   × C I dissuaded him out of going there.
   ❖Cが辞書に出ているが使われていない．
思う
1 《希望しているとき》
〈明朝までに雨がやむと思います〉
   ☆ A I hope it'll stop raining by tomorrow morning.
   ◎ B Hopefully it'll stop raining by tomorrow morning.
   ◎ C I'm hoping it'll stop raining by tomorrow morning.
   △ D I'm hopeful it'll stop raining by tomorrow morning.
   ❖Cは「しばらく考えてきた」という響きがある．A, B, Dは現在の気持ちだけを述べている．
2 《希望していないとき》
〈明日は雨が降ると思う〉
   ◎ A I'm afraid it'll rain tomorrow.
   △ B I fear it'll rain tomorrow.
3 《客観的に述べているとき》
〈明日は雨が降ると思う〉
   ◎ A I think it'll rain tomorrow.
   ○ B I suppose [guess] it'll rain tomorrow.
   ○ C I suspect [figure] it'll rain tomorrow.
   ○ D I have no doubt it'll rain tomorrow.
   △ E I assume it'll rain tomorrow.
   △ F I'm supposing [guessing] it'll rain tomorrow.
   △ G I don't doubt it'll rain tomorrow.
   △ H I'm figuring it'll rain tomorrow.
   △ I I'm assuming it'll rain tomorrow.

❖ A, D, G が一番強く確信している響きがある．C, H が2番目，E, I が3番目，B, F が4番目．

4 《自分の気持ちを述べるとき》

a）不満があるとき

〈彼が課長に昇進すると私は思うんだ〉

☆ A I suppose he'll be promoted to manager.
◎ B I guess [think] he'll be promoted to manager.
○ C I assume he'll be promoted to manager.

❖ B, C はいずれも沈んだ口調で発音する．

b）不満がないとき

〈彼は課長に昇進すると思う〉

◎ A I suppose [think] he'll be promoted to manager.
△ B I figure he'll be promoted to manager.

5 《推測するとき》

〈ジム：アメリカは近い将来イラクを攻撃すると思いますか〉

Jim: Do you think the United State'll attack Iraq in the near future?

〈ビル：そう思うね〉

Bill:

◎ A I think [guess, suppose] so.
○ B I assume so.
× C I figure so.

6 《「…しないと思う」と言うとき》

〈ビル：あなたは彼が私たちを支持しないと思いますか〉

Bill: Don't you think he'll support us?

〈ジム：はい，しないと思います〉

Jim:

☆ A I don't think so.
☆ B I don't think he will.
◎ C I doubt he will.
◎ D I doubt it.
◎ E I suppose he won't.
○ F I doubt if he will.
○ G I think [suppose, guess] not.
○ H I think [assume, figure] he won't.
○ I I don't suppose he will.
○ J I'm doubtful of it.
○ K I'm assuming he won't.
△ L I suspect [assume] not.
△ M I suspect [guess] he won't.
△ N I'm doubtful about it.
△ O I'm figuring he won't.
▽ P I don't assume he will.
▽ Q I'm supposing he won't.
▽ R I figure not.

7 《文中に数字があるとき》

〈このビルを取り壊すには10万ドル以上かかると私は思う〉

☆ A I think it'll cost more than $100,000 to demolish this building.
◎ B I figure it'll cost more than $100,000 to demolish this building.
○ C I guess [assume] it'll cost more than $100,000 to demolish this

        building.
    △ D I suppose it'll cost more than $100,000 to demolish this building.
 8 《意見を尋ねるとき》
〈景気は間もなくよくなるでしょう．どう思いますか〉
    ◎ A I think the economy'll pick up soon. What do you say?
    ◎ B I think the economy'll pick up soon. What's your opinion?
    ◎ C I think the economy'll pick up soon. What do you think about that?
    ○ D I think the economy'll pick up soon. How do you feel about that?
    × E I think the economy'll pick up soon. How do you think about that?
 9 《思っている》
〈ジム：私は大学へ行きたいんだ〉
Jim: I want to go to college.
〈トム：どこの大学へ行こうと思っているんだい〉
Tom:
    ◎ A Which one do you have in mind?
    ◎ B Which one are you thinking of going to?

お持ち帰り →持ち帰り

おりる
 1 《テレビなどの番組から》
〈あのテレビタレントはスキャンダルに関与した疑いがもたれているために番組からおりた〉
    ◎ A That TV personality quit [left] the program because he's suspected of being involved with the scandal.
    ○ B That TV personality got out of the program because he's suspected of being involved with the scandal.
    △ C That TV personality stepped down from the program because he's suspected of being involved with the scandal.
 2 《高い地位から》
〈私は明日会長の職からおります〉
    ◎ A I'm resigning [stepping down from] the chairmanship tomorrow.
    ○ B I'm quitting [leaving] the chairmanship tomorrow.
 3 《山から》
〈私たちは昼前に富士山をおり始めた〉
    ◎ A We started to climb down Mt. Fuji before noon.
    ○ B We started to go [come] down Mt. Fuji before noon.
 4 《船・飛行機から》
〈どこで彼は飛行機を降りたのですか〉
    ◎ A Where did he get off the plane?
    ○ B Where did he get out of the plane?
    ▽ C Where did he disembark the plane?
    × D Where did he leave the plane?
    ❖ C は乗務員・航空会社の社員の間では非常によく使われている．
 5 《タクシーから》
〈今朝私は彼が駅の正面でタクシーから降りるのを見ました〉
    ☆ A This morning I saw him get [getting] out of a cab in front of the station.
    ◎ B This morning I saw him leave [leaving] a cab in front of the station.
 6 《銀行ローンが》

〈家のローンがついにおりた〉
- ◎ Our house loan finally came [went] through.

7 《ビザが》

〈依頼人：いつ就労ビザはおりると思いますか〉

Client:
- ◎ When do you think the working visa will come [go] through?

8 《許可が》

〈秘書：いつお客様にこの招待状をお送りしましょうか〉

Secretary: When do you want me to send these invitations to our customers?

〈支配人：幹部から許可がおりしだい〉

Manager:
- ◎ As soon as we get the green light from upstairs.

卸売り

〈私は生地の卸売りをする会社に勤めています〉
- ◎ A I work for a fabric distributor.
- ◎ B I work for a fabric wholesale company.
- ◎ C I work for a fabric wholesale store.

❖(1) いずれも「卸売り会社，問屋」の意味だが，次のような違いがある．英和，和英辞典のいずれも「卸売り会社，問屋」＝wholesale store とのみ考えている印象を受ける．しかし，米国の wholesale store [company] は，小売り業者（retailer）に品物を卸す「卸売り業者」であると同時に，しばしば一般の消費者への販売もしていて，一般人にはこのイメージが強い．したがって，この面からいえば，wholesale store [company] は「量販店」にあたる．distributor は１つのメーカーの製品を専門に扱う会社であり，例えば Sony distributor といえば「ソニー製品のみを扱う販売会社，販売代理店」である．

❖(2) 関連のある語として supplier がある．これは，複数のメーカーの製品を，小売店や個人消費者へではなく，学校・病院・レストランなどへ売る「納入業者」をさすことが多い．

下ろす

〈私は銀行から 500 ドル下ろさなければならないんです〉
- ☆ A I have to get $500 from [out of] the bank.
- ◎ B I have to take $500 from [out of] the bank.
- ○ C I have to withdraw $500 from [out of] the bank.
- ○ D I have to draw $500 from the bank.
- △ E I have to draw $500 out of the bank.

降ろす

1 《タクシー》

〈角で降ろしてくれますか〉
- ◎ A Will you drop me off at the corner?
- ◎ B Will you let me off at the corner?
- ○ C Will you let me out at the corner?

2 《自家用車》

〈角で降ろしてくれますか〉
- ☆ A Will you drop me off at the corner?
- ◎ B Will you let me off at the corner?
- ◎ C Will you let me out at the corner?

3 《バス》

〈次の停留所で降ろしてくれますか〉

☆ A Will you let me off at the next stop?
◎ B Will you let me out at the next stop?
▽ C Will you drop me off at the next stop?

負わせる
1 《責任》
〈彼は私に責任を負わせようとしている〉
☆ A He's trying to push the responsibility on me.
◎ B He's trying to push the responsibility onto [to] me.
◎ C He's trying to shift the responsibility onto [on] me.
◎ D He's trying to pass the responsibility onto [on] me.
○ E He's trying to shift the responsibility to me.
○ F He's trying to pass the responsibility to me.
○ G He's trying to pass the buck on me.
△ H He's trying to pass the buck onto [to] me.

2 《罪》
〈彼は私に罪を負わせようとしている〉
◎ A He's trying to blame me for his crime.
◎ B He's trying to blame his crime on me.
◎ C He's trying to accuse me of his crime.
○ D He's trying to pin his crime on me.

終わり
〈リンダ：私はあなたにうんざりなの．これで終わりよ〉
◎ A I'm fed up with you. This is it.
◎ B I'm fed up with you. I'm through.
◎ C I'm fed up with you. We're through.
◎ D I'm fed up with you. We're finished.
○ E I'm fed up with you. This is the end.

❖「終わる」10 も参照のこと．

終わる
1 《長期のプロジェクト・一日の仕事・今やっていること》
a）終わったか否かを尋ねるとき
〈仕事は終わりましたか〉
◎ A Did you finish your work?
◎ B Is your work done [finished]?
◎ C Are you done [through] with your work?
◎ D Did you get your work done?
○ E Did you wrap up [complete] your work?
○ F Did you wrap your work up?
○ G Did you finish with your work?

❖ F, G は長期間のプロジェクトにも使われているが使用頻度は高くない．

b）終わる時間を尋ねるとき
〈あなたは何時に仕事が終わるのですか〉
◎ A What time do you get off (work)?
◎ B How late do you work?
◎ C What time are you done at work?
○ D What time are you through with work?

❖ A は毎日の終業時間を尋ねているのに対して，B, C, D は特定の曜日，たとえば「今日は何時に仕事が終わるのですか」の意味でもよく使われている．

2 《数名または大勢の人が出席している会議・パーティー・学校・卒業式・その他の各種の式》
〈会議は2時に終わります〉
- ◎ A The meeting'll be over [through, finished, wrapped up] at 2:00.
- ◎ B The meeting'll finish [wrap up] at 2:00.
- ○ C The meeting'll break up [let out] at 2:00.
- △ D The meeting'll get out [get through, be out] at 2:00.

3 《(会議など) 長引いていたものが終わる》
〈ナンシー：疲れちゃったわ．もうすぐ終わると思う．帰りたいわ〉
Nancy:
- ◎ I'm tired. Do you think it's almost over? I want to go home.

〈ジョン：もうすぐ終わるはずだよ．たぶんあと10分か15分だろう〉
John:
- ◎ They should be winding up soon. Maybe in another 10 or 15 minutes.

4 《長期間続いたもののとき》
〈ヴェトナム戦争は長い戦いの後に終わりました〉
- ◎ A The Vietnam War came to an end [a close] after a long battle.
- ◎ B The Vietnam War was over after a long battle.
- ◎ C The Vietnam War ended after a long battle.
- × D The Vietnam War was through after a long battle.
- × E The Vietnam War was wrapped up [finished, ended] after a long battle.

5 《政治生命》
〈彼の政治生命は終わった〉
- ◎ A His political life is through [over, finished].
- ◎ B His political life has finished.
- ◎ C His political life is history.
- △ D His political life is a thing of the past.
  - ❖ D はテレビ，ラジオのニュースなどではよく使われている．

6 《成功または失敗に終わると言うとき》
〈うちの改革は成功に終わった〉
- ☆ A Our reform resulted in success.
- ◎ B Our reform ended in success.
- ○ C Our reform finished in success.

7 《学校の授業》
a) 小学生・中学生・高校生の場合
〈今日は学校は何時に終わるの〉
- ◎ A What time is school over [out] today?
- ◎ B What time does school get [let] out today?
- ◎ C What time does school end [finish] today?

b) 大学生の場合
〈今日は何時に講義は終わるの〉
- ◎ A What time does your last class end [finish] today?
- ◎ B What time does your last class let [get] out today?
- ◎ C What time is your last class over [out] today?
- ◎ D How late will you be in class today?

8 《銀行などのカウンターで》
〈銀行の窓口係：全部終わりましたか〉

Teller:
- ☆ A Is everything done?
- ◎ B Is everything taken care of?
- ○ C Is everything finished?

9 《ビジネス・友人・結婚・恋愛などの関係》
〈私たちの関係は終わった〉
- ◎ A Our relationship's history.
- ◎ B Our relationship's over.
- ◎ C We're through [finished].
- ◎ D We're history.

10 《男女の関係》
〈私たちは終わったんです〉
- ◎ A It's over (between us).
- ◎ C We're history.
- ◎ D We're through [finished].
- ○ F Our love's history.
- ○ G Our love has ended.
- △ H Our love has finished.
- △ I Our love's over.

11 《支払い》
〈車の支払いが終わったら，新しいソファーを買いましょう〉
- ◎ A After we get our car paid off [for], let's buy a new sofa.
- ◎ B After we pay off our car, let's buy a new sofa.
- ◎ C After we finish paying for our car, let's buy a new sofa.

カーテン
  1 《高級品》
  〈カーテンを閉めて下さい〉
    ◎　Pull [Draw, Close] the drapes, please.
  2 《普通の品質》
  〈カーテンを閉めて下さい〉
    ◎　Pull [Draw, Close] the curtains, please.

…階
  1 《建物の外面から見て述べるとき》
  〈郵便局は 80 階建てのビルの裏にあります〉
    ◎ A　The post office is behind a 80-story building.
    × B　The post office is behind a 80-storey building.
    × C　The post office is behind a 80-storied building.
      ❖イギリス英語では B が使われている．
  2 《建物の床を意識して述べるとき》
  〈うちの事務所は 12 階にあります〉
    ◎　Our office is on the 12th floor.
  3 《階数を尋ねるとき》
  〈このビルは何階建てですか〉
    ◎ A　How many floors does this building have?
    ◎ B　How many floors are there in this building?
    ○ C　How many stories does this building have?
    ○ D　How many stories are there in this building?
    ○ E　How tall is this building?
    ▽ F　How many stories high is this building?
      ❖F は辞典に出ているがまれに使われる程度．
  4 《所在の階に言及するとき》
  〈マイク：男性の手洗いはどこにありますか〉
  Mike: Where's the men's room?
  〈トム：3 階にあります〉
  Tom:
    ◎ A　It's three floors up.
    ◎ B　It's three flights up.
    ◎ C　It's on the third floor.
    × D　It's three stories [stairs, staircases] up.
      ❖(1) A はエレベーターで上がって行くことを話者は心に描いて述べている．B は歩いて上がって行くことを意味している．C は歩いて上がっていくとか，エレベーターで上がっていくことには触れていないで，ただ 3 階にあるということだけに言及している．
      ❖(2) B はニューヨーク，シカゴのような高層ビルがある大都市で非常によく使われているが，小さい都市ではあまり使われていない．

…回
  1 《可算名詞があるとき》
  〈私は 2 回交通事故を起したことがあるんです〉

◎ A I've had two car accidents.
× B I've had car accidents twice.

〈私は昨日3回本社へ行きました〉
◎ A I made three trips to the head office yesterday.
◎ B I went to the head office three times yesterday.
× C I made trips to the head office three times yesterday.

2 《可算名詞がないとき》
〈私はホワイトハウスに5回入ったことがある〉
◎ A I've been in the White House five times.
○ B I've been in the White House on five occasions.
○ C I've been in the White House five separate times.

…界
〈彼は実業界で重要な人物です〉
☆ A He's an important figure in the business community.
◎ B He's an important figure in the business world.
○ C He's an important figure in the business circles.
▽ D He's an important figure in the business circle.

…街
1 《住宅街》
〈彼らは高級住宅街に住んでいます〉
◎ A They live in a rich neighborhood [area].
△ B They live in a rich residential neighborhood [area].
× C They live in a rich residential district.

2 《官庁街》
〈霞が関は官庁街で有名です〉
◎ A Kasumigaseki's well-known for its government office district.
△ B Kasumigaseki's well-known for its government office area.

3 《電気街》
〈秋葉原は電気街で有名です〉
◎ A Akihabara's well-known for its appliance and electronics district.
△ B Akihabara's well-known for its appliance and electronics area.

4 《ビジネス街》
〈丸の内はビジネス街で有名です〉
◎ A Marunouchi's well-known for its business district.
△ B Marunouchi's well-known for its business area.
❖日本語で「オフィス街」と言うが，英語では office district [area] とは言わない。

5 《歓楽街》
a) 肯定的に述べるとき
〈歌舞伎町は歓楽街で有名なんです〉
◎ A Kabukicho's well-known for its entertainment district.
△ B Kabukicho's well-known for its entertainment area.
× C Kabukicho's well-known for its entertainment neighborhood.

b) 否定的に述べるとき
〈歌舞伎町は歓楽街で有名です〉
◎ A Kabukicho's well-known for its sleazy area.
△ B Kabukicho's well-known for its sleazy neighborhood.
× C Kabukicho's well-known for its sleazy district.

c) 客観的に述べるとき

〈歌舞伎町は歓楽街で有名です〉
- ◎ A Kabukicho's well-known for its red-light district.
- △ B Kabukicho's well-known for its red-light area.
- × C Kabukicho's well-known for its red-light neighborhood.

6 《繁華街》
〈彼のレストランはシカゴの繁華街にあります〉
- ☆ A His restaurant's downtown in Chicago.
- ◎ B His restaurant's in downtown Chicago.
- ○ C His restaurant's in the downtown area of Chicago.
  - ❖ downtown は A では副詞，B，C では形容詞として使われている．名詞としての downtown の訳が辞典に紹介されているが，使われていない．

海岸
〈海岸へ行こう〉
- ◎ Let's go to the beach [shore].

〈私は海岸で夏を過したいと思っています〉
- ◎ I want to spend the summer at the beach [shore].
  - ❖ beach は「浜辺」，shore は波打ち際で「海岸」「湖岸」「河岸」．ただし，アメリカの東部の人が休暇で海岸に行くとき，shore と beach は同じ意味で使われていることに注意．

階級
1 《出身を言及するとき》
a）上流階級
〈彼は上流階級の出身です〉
- ◎ A He comes from a family with (a lot of) money.
- ◎ B He comes from a rich [wealthy] family.
- ◎ C He comes from the upper class.
- ◎ D He comes from an upper class family.
- ◎ E He comes from a family with old money.
- △ F He comes from a lot of money.
  - ❖(1) E は数代続いている名門という響きがある．A～D はその点は不明．
  - ❖(2) アメリカ・イギリスは日本と違って「階級社会」である．アメリカはビジネス上での成功による階級移動が可能な階級社会であるのに対して，イギリスは移動が不可能な生まれながらの階級社会．

b）中流の上の階級
〈彼は中流の上の階級の出身なんです〉
- ☆ A He comes from the upper-middle class.
- ◎ B He comes from the upper-middle income class [crowd].
- ◎ C He comes from upper-middle class people.
- ○ D He comes from the upper-middle income bracket.
- △ E He comes from the upper-middle income segment [group].

c）中流階級
〈彼は中流階級の出身です〉
- ◎ A He comes from a middle income family.
- ◎ B He comes from a middle-class family.
- ◎ C He comes from a middle class.
- ○ D He comes from an average income family.
- △ E He comes from the middle class.

d）中流の下の階級
〈彼は中流の下の階級の出身なんです〉

- ◎ A He comes from the lower-middle class.
- ○ B He comes from the lower-middle income bracket [group].
- ○ C He comes from lower-income people.
- △ D He comes from the lower-middle income segment [class].

2 《出世話をするとき》
〈彼は今では億万長者ですが下層階級の出身なんです〉
- ◎ A Now he's a billionaire but he came from the bad side of town.
- ◎ B Now he's a billionaire but he came from the wrong side of tracks.
- ◎ C Now he's a billionaire but he came from a bad part of town.
- ◎ D Now he's a billionaire but he came from the inner city.
- ○ E Now he's a billionaire but he came from the other side of the tracks.

3 《「ロミオとジュリエット」のような恋愛話のとき》
〈彼女は富豪の家庭の出身なのですが下層階級の人に恋してしまったんです〉
- ◎ A She comes from a very wealthy family but she fell in love with a guy who comes from the bad side of town.
- ◎ B She comes from a very wealthy family but she fell in love with a guy who comes from a bad part of town.
- ◎ C She comes from a very wealthy family but she fell in love with a guy who comes from the wrong side of the tracks.
- ◎ D She comes from a very wealthy family but she fell in love with a guy who comes from the inner city.
- ○ E She comes from a very wealthy family but she fell in love with a guy who comes from the other side of the tracks.

4 《犯罪者の出身に言及するとき》
〈犯人は下層階級の出身だったから人生でチャンスがなかったんです〉
- ◎ A The criminal never got a chance in life because he came from a bad part of town.
- ◎ B The criminal never got a chance in life because he came from the bad side of town.
- ◎ C The criminal never got a chance in life because he came from the wrong side of the tracks.
- ◎ D The criminal never got a chance in life because he came from the inner city.
- ○ E The criminal never got a chance in life because he came from the other side of the tracks.

5 《政治家の人気・支持に言及するとき》
a) 上流階級
〈この候補者は上流階級に非常に人気があるんです〉
- ☆ A This candidate's very popular with the upper class.
- ◎ B This candidate's very popular with (the) people with a lot of money.
- ◎ C This candidate's very popular with rich [wealthy] people.
- ◎ D This candidate's very popular with high income families.
- ◎ E This candidate's very popular with rich [wealthy] families.
- ○ F This candidate's very popular with the upper class bracket.
- △ G This candidate's very popular with the upper class segment.

b) 中流階級
〈この候補者は中流階級に非常に人気がある〉
- ☆ A This candidate's very popular with the middle class.
- ◎ B This candidate's very popular with the middle income bracket.

- ◎ C This candidate's very popular with middle income people [families].
- ○ D This candidate's very popular with the middle income class [group].
- △ E This candidate's very popular with the middle income segment.

c) 貧民階級

・客観的に述べるとき

〈この候補者は貧民階級に非常に人気があるんです〉

- ◎ A This candidate's very popular with the lower income class [bracket].
- ◎ B This candidate's very popular with low income families.
- ◎ C This candidate's very popular with poor people.
- ◎ D This candidate's very popular with lower class people.

・上流・中流階級の人が軽蔑して述べるとき

〈この候補者は貧民階級に非常に人気がある〉

- ◎ A This candidate's very popular with the little people.
- ◎ B This candidate's very popular with the lower classes.

d) 知識階級

〈この候補者は知識階級に非常に人気があるんです〉

- ◎ A This candidate's very popular with intellectuals.
- ○ B This candidate's very popular with the intellectual crowd.
- ○ C This candidate's very popular with intellectual people.
- △ D This candidate's very popular with the intellectual group [segment, bracket, class].
- ▽ E This candidate's very popular with the eggheads [the highbrows].
- ▽ F This candidate's very popular with the intelligentsia.
- × G This candidate's very popular with the intellects.
  - ❖(1) G は辞典に出ているが使われていない.
  - ❖(2) F は知識人の間では使われているが普通の大卒者でも知らない.

e) 非知識階級

〈この候補者は非知識階級に非常に人気があるんです〉

- ☆ A This candidate's very popular with anti-intellectuals.
- ◎ B This candidate's very popular with anti-intellectual people.
- ○ C This candidate's very popular with the anti-intellectual class.
- △ D This candidate's very popular with the anti-intellectual group [segment, bracket].
- ▽ E This candidate's very popular with low-brows.

海軍 →軍隊 4

解決する

1 《夫婦・友人・親子など身近な人との問題》

a) 深刻な問題

〈私は夫とのこの問題を解決しなければならないんです〉

- ☆ A I have to work on this problem with my husband.
- ◎ B I have to work out this problem with my husband.
- ◎ C I have to work this problem out with my husband.
- ◎ D I have to resolve this problem with my husband.
- ◎ E I have to settle this problem with my husband.
- ○ F I have to solve this problem with my husband.
  - ❖ D が一番深刻度が強い.

b）非深刻な問題
〈私は夫とのこの問題を解決しなければならないんです〉
- ◎ A I have to take care of this problem with my husband.
- ◎ B I have to fix this problem with my husband.
- ○ C I have to settle [solve, figure out, clear up] this problem with my husband.
- △ D I have to iron out this problem with my husband.

2 《外国・取引先など改まった関係との問題》

a）深刻な問題
〈アメリカとのこの貿易問題を解決しなければならない〉
- ◎ A We have to resolve [work out, work on, settle] this trade issue with America.
- ○ B We have to solve this trade issue with America.
- △ C We have to bring this trade issue to a settlement with America.

b）非深刻な問題
〈アメリカとのこの貿易問題を解決しなければならない〉
- ◎ A We have to settle [solve, work on] this trade issue with America.
- ○ B We have to iron out [fix, clear up] this trade issue with America.

3 《未解決の》
〈私たちはこの問題を未解決のままにしておけません〉
- ◎ A We can't leave this problem pending [undecided, unsettled].
- ◎ B We can't leave this problem up in the air.
- ◎ C We can't leave this problem indefinitely.
- ○ D We can't leave this problem unresolved.

外国

1 《ある国を中心にして言うとき》
〈ほとんどのアメリカ人は外国に興味がありません〉
- ◎ A Most Americans aren't interested in the rest of the world.
- ○ B Most Americans aren't interested in foreign countries.
- × C Most Americans aren't interested in overseas countries.

2 《go か travel と共に言うとき》
〈私はいつか外国に行きたいと思っています〉
- ◎ A I want to go overseas someday.
- ○ B I want to go abroad someday.
- × C I want to go oversea someday.
- × D I want to go to foreign countries someday.
- × E I want to go to the rest of the world someday.

3 《visit と共に言うとき》
〈私はいつか外国を訪ねてみたいと思っています〉
- ◎ A I want to visit other countries someday.
- ◎ B I want to visit the rest of the world someday.
- ○ C I want to visit foreign countries someday.

4 《see と共に言うとき》
〈私はいつか外国を見たいと思っています〉
- ◎ A I want to see the rest of the world someday.
- ◎ B I want to see other countries someday.
- ○ C I want to see foreign countries someday.

5 《study と共に言うとき》
〈私は外国のことを勉強したいんです〉

- ☆ A I want to study about other countries.
- ◎ B I want to study about foreign countries.
- ○ C I want to study about the rest of the world.
- ▽ D I want to study about overseas countries.

外国語学校 →各種学校 1
解雇される →首になる
概算の →見積り 2
概して
〈概してこの辺は安全です〉
- ☆ A On the whole this neighborhood's safe.
- ◎ B Generally this neighborhood's safe.
- ◎ C For the most part this neighborhood's safe.
- ◎ D By and large this neighborhood's safe.
- ○ E In general this neighborhood's safe.
- ○ F As a general rule this neighborhood's safe.
- ○ G Altogether this neighborhood's safe.

買い占める
1 《市場全体のとき》
〈誰かが石油市場を買い占めているに違いない〉
- ◎ A Somebody must be cornering the oil market.
- △ B Somebody must be cornering the oil supply.
- × C Somebody must be making [establishing] a corner in oil.
   ❖ C は辞典に出ているが使われていない．

2 《買い占める行為を述べるとき》
〈誰かがうちの株を買い占めているに違いない〉
- ◎ A Somebody must be buying up our stock [stocks, shares].
- ◎ B Somebody must be buying all our stock [stocks, shares].

会社
1 《小さい会社のとき》
〈私は新宿に小さい会社を持っています〉
- ◎ A I have a business in Shinjuku.
- ◎ B I have a small company in Shinjuku.
- ◎ C I have a small business in Shinjuku.
   ❖ 日本語で「会社」と言うとホワイトカラーの会社を連想する人が多いであろう．しかし，A，B はレストラン，コンビニ，弁護士事務所，会計事務所，その他ありとあらゆるものに使える．

2 《ホワイトカラー・ブルーカラーの職種を問わないとき》
〈彼女は大きな会社に勤めています〉
- ◎　 She works for a big business [company].
   ❖ company は業種，大小に関係なく類語の中で一番よく使われている．

3 《ホワイトカラーの会社であるとき》
〈彼女は大きな会社に勤めています〉
- ◎　 She works for a big firm.
   ❖ firm はブルーカラーの会社には使われていない．

4 《法人組織になっている会社を明示するとき》
〈彼女は大手の会社に勤めています〉
- ◎　 She works for a major corporation.
   ❖ company, firm, business, house, outfit いずれも「会社」の意味で広く使われているが，法人組織になっているか否かについては言及されていな

5 《友人同士またはくだけた調子で述べるとき》
〈彼女は大きな会社に勤めています〉
　　◎　She works for a big outfit.
6 《場所として述べるとき》
〈私は彼と会社で知り合ったんです〉
　　◎　A　I met him at work.
　　◎　B　I met him at the office.
　　◎　C　I met him on the job.
　　×　D　I met him at the company.
　　❖詳細は「職場で」を参照のこと．
7 《形容詞的に使われるとき》
a) 会社の規則
〈会社の規則に従わなければなりません〉
　　◎　A　You have to follow the company rules [regulations].
　　◎　B　You have to follow the company's rules [regulations].
b) 会社のレストラン
〈私は普通，会社のレストランで昼食を食べます〉
　　◎　A　I usually eat lunch at the company restaurant.
　　△　B　I usually eat lunch at the company's restaurant.
c) 会社の重役
〈うちのお客様は会社の重役の方がほとんどです〉
　　◎　A　Most of our customers are corporate executives.
　　○　B　Most of our customers are corporate directors.
　　△　C　Most of our customers are company executives [directors].
　　❖ C は辞典に出ているが時々使われる程度．
8 《出版・投資・貿易会社のとき》
〈彼女は出版社に勤めています〉
　　☆　A　She works for a publishing company.
　　◎　B　She works for a publishing house.
　　△　C　She works for a publishing firm [business].
9 《証券会社》
a) 小さい会社
〈私は証券会社に勤めています〉
　　◎　A　I work for a stock broker.
　　◎　B　I work at a stock broker's office.
b) 大きな会社
〈私は証券会社に勤めています〉
　　◎　A　I work for a (stock) brokerage firm.
　　◎　B　I work for a stock broker.
　　○　C　I work for a securities firm.
　　○　D　I work for a stock brokerage company [house].
10 《印刷会社》
a) 中規模のとき
〈彼女は印刷会社に勤めています〉
　　◎　A　She works for a printing company.
　　◎　B　She works for a printer's.
　　○　C　She works for a printing shop.
　　△　D　She works for a printing firm.

b）小規模のとき
〈彼女は印刷会社に勤めています〉
- ☆ A She works for a printshop.
- ◎ B She works for a printing shop.
- ○ C She works for a printer's.
- × D She works for a printing office.
  ❖多くの辞典に D が紹介されているが，規模に関係なく使われていない．

c）大きな会社のとき
〈彼女は印刷会社に勤めています〉
- ☆ A She works for a printing company.
- ◎ B She works for a printing firm.
- ○ C She works for a printer's.

11 《化学会社》
〈彼女は化学会社に勤めています〉
- ◎ A She works for a chemical company.
- △ B She works for a chemical industry company.

12 《カメラのメーカー》
〈彼女はカメラのメーカーに勤めています〉
- ☆ A She works for a camera company.
- ◎ B She works for a camera manufacturer.
- × C She works for a camera maker.

13 《ガラス会社》
〈彼女はガラス会社で働いています〉
- ☆ A She works for a glass company.
- ◎ B She works for a glass manufacturer.
- ○ C She works for a glass maker.
- ○ D She works for a glass manufacturing company.

14 《金属会社》
〈彼女は金属会社に勤めています〉
- ◎ A She works for a metal company.
- ◎ B She works for a metal manufacturing company.

15 《軽[重]金属会社》
〈彼女は軽[重]金属会社に勤めています〉
- × A She works for a light metal company.
- × B She works for a heavy metal company.
  ❖辞典に A，B が出ているが，アメリカでは軽金属会社 (light metal company)，重金属会社 (heavy metal company) という表現は一切使われていない．

16 《化粧品会社》
〈彼女は化粧品会社に勤めています〉
- ☆ A She works for a cosmetics company.
- ◎ B She works for a cosmetic [make-up] company.

17 《航空会社》
a）漠然と述べるとき
〈彼女は大手の航空会社に勤めています〉
- ◎ A She works for a major airline.
- ○ B She works for a major airline company.
- × C She works for a major airways [airlines].

b）会社名として述べるとき

⟨彼女は英国航空に勤めています⟩
- ◎ She works for the British Airways.
- ❖ airline, airways のどちらを使うかは各々の会社によって異なる．

18 《工務店》
⟨彼女は工務店で働いています⟩
- ☆ A She works for a general contractor.
- ◎ B She works for a contractor.
- ○ C She works for a general construction company.

19 《自動車会社》
⟨彼女は自動車会社に勤めています⟩
- ☆ A She works for a car company.
- ◎ B She works for a car manufacturer.
- ○ C She works for a car [an auto] maker.
- ○ D She works for an auto [an automobile] manufacturer.
- △ E She works for an automobile maker.
- △ F She works for an automobile [an auto] company.

20 《自動車部品会社》
⟨彼女は自動車部品会社に勤めています⟩
- ☆ A She works for an auto parts company.
- ◎ B She works for an auto parts manufacturer.
- ○ C She works for an auto parts maker.

21 《事務機器製造会社》
⟨彼女は事務機器製造会社に勤めています⟩
- ☆ A She works for an office supply manufacturing company.
- ◎ B She works for an office supply manufacturer.
- ○ C She works for an office supply maker.
- × D She works for an office supply producing [production] company.
  - ❖ D が辞典に出ているが使われていない．

22 《製薬会社》
⟨彼女は製薬会社に勤めています⟩
- ◎ A She works for a drug company.
- △ B She works for a pharmaceutical company.

23 《繊維会社》
⟨彼女は繊維会社に勤めています⟩
- ◎ A She works for a textile company.
- △ B She works for a cloth company.

24 《造船会社》
⟨彼女は造船会社に勤めています⟩
- ◎ A She works for a shipbuilder.
- ◎ B She works for a shipbuilding company.
  - ❖(1) A は会社が大きくても小さくても使える．
  - ❖(2) B は小さい会社にはあまり使われていない．

25 《タクシー会社》
⟨彼女はタクシー会社で働いています⟩
- ◎ A She works for a cab company.
- ○ B She works for a taxi company.

26 《通信社》
⟨彼女は通信社に勤めています⟩
- ◎ A She works for a news service.

△ B She works for a news organization.
27 《鉄道会社》
〈彼女は鉄道会社に勤めています〉
◎ A She works for a railroad company.
× B She works for a railway company.
28 《電気会社》
〈彼女は電気会社に勤めています〉
◎ She works for an appliance company.
29 《電子会社》
〈彼女は電子会社に勤めています〉
◎ She works for an electronics company.
30 《電力会社》
〈彼女は電力会社に勤めています〉
◎ A She works for a power company.
◎ B She works for an electric company.
○ C She works for an energy company.
○ D She works for an electric power company.
31 《乳製品会社》
〈彼女は乳製品会社に勤めています〉
◎ A She works for a dairy company.
△ B She works for a dairy product company.
32 《輸送会社》
〈彼女はフランスの輸送会社に勤めています〉
◎ A She works for a French shipping company.
◎ B She works for a French transport company.
○ C She works for a French transportation company.
❖(1) A, B は国内、海外の両方.
❖(2) A は船だけと考えやすいが，船だけでなく飛行機，トラック，電車による輸送会社にも広く使われている．
❖(3) C は本来，乗客のための「運輸会社」であるが，アメリカ人の間で広く誤用されている．
33 《運送会社》
〈彼女は運送会社に勤めています〉
◎ A She works for a mover.
◎ B She works for a moving company.

改宗する
〈彼はカトリックに改宗する予定です〉
◎ A He's going to convert to Catholicism.
△ B He's going to be [get] converted to Catholicism.
△ C He's going to turn [go over to] Catholic.

外出中
1 《過去のことを述べるとき》
〈私が外出中に誰か電話してきましたか〉
☆ A Did somebody call me while I was gone?
◎ B Did somebody call me while I was out?
△ C Did somebody call me while I was away?
❖ A は事務所，自宅の両方に等しくよく使われている．B は自宅にもよく使われているが，事務所のほうがより広く使われている．C は事務所と自宅の両方に使われている．

2 《現在外出中のとき》
〈彼は今外出中です〉
- ◎ A He's out now.
- × B He's gone now.

解消する
〈彼女はビルとの婚約を解消したんです〉
- ☆ A She broke off the engagement with Bill.
- ◎ B She broke her [the] engagement with Bill.

外食する
〈昼食は外食しましょう〉
- ◎ A Let's have [eat] lunch out.
- ◎ B Let's eat lunch outside.
  - ❖ Aはレストランで食べること，Bは自分で作った昼食を外で食べることを意味している．

改善する
1 《一般的に述べるとき》
〈会社は労働環境を改善することを約束しました〉
- ◎ A The management promised to improve the working conditions.
- ○ B The management promised to make the working conditions better.
- △ C The management promised to upgrade the working conditions.

2 《「徹底的に」と述べるとき》
〈会社は労働環境を徹底的に改善することを約束しました〉
- ◎ A The management promised to improve the working conditions 110%.
- ○ B The management promised to completely [totally] improve the working conditions.
- ○ C The management promised to make complete improvements on the working conditions.
- ○ D The management promised to completely upgrade the working conditions.

改装する
1 《大規模のとき》
〈店を改装しているところなんです〉
- ◎ We're having our store renovated [remodeled].
  - ❖店内を広くするため壁などを取り払うような改装．

2 《小規模のとき》
〈店を改装しているところなんです〉
- ◎ We're having our store fixed up.
  - ❖ペンキなどを塗り替えたり，壁紙を取り替えたりするような改装．

3 《店の正面だけのとき》
〈店を改装しているところなんです〉
- ◎ A We're giving our store a face-lift.
- ○ B We're improving our storefront's appearance.

会長 →地位 9

開通する
〈東西線は5月1日に三鷹と国立間が開通します〉
- ☆ A The Tozai Line'll start running between Mitaka and Kunitachi as of May 1st.
- ◎ B The Tozai Line'll begin running between Mitaka and Kunitachi as

of May 1st.
- ◎ C The Tozai Line'll start (its) service between Mitaka and Kunitachi as of May 1st.
- ○ D The Tozai Line'll begin (its) service between Mitaka and Kunitachi as of May 1st.
- △ E The Tozai Line'll go into operation between Mitaka and Kunitachi as of May 1st.
- △ F The Tozai Line'll be open for service between Mitaka and Kunitachi as of May 1st.

書いてある

《新聞に》

〈リンダ：今年の夏は暑くなるのよ〉

Linda: This summer's going to be hot.

〈ジェーン：そのように新聞に書いてあるわね〉

Jane:
- ☆ A That's what the papers say.
- ◎ B The papers say so.
- ○ C So the papers say.
  - ❖ C は多くの英文法書で大きく紹介しているが，皮肉な響きがある．

改訂版 →…版 1

快適な

1 《快適な（住み心地のいい）》

〈彼らは快適な家に住んでいます〉
- ☆ A They live in a nice home.
- ◎ B They live in a comfortable [comfy] home.
- △ C They live in a pleasant [delightful] home.
- × D They live in an agreeable home.

2 《快適に（心配ごとがない）》

〈彼らは快適に暮らしています〉
- ◎ A They're living comfortably.
- ○ B They're living worry-free.
- ○ C They're living a worry-free life.
- △ D They're living free from worry.
- △ E They're living at ease.
- ▽ F They're living at their ease.

買い手市場 →市場（しじょう）5

回転がいい

〈うちのレストランは回転がいい〉
- ☆ A Our restaurant gets customers in and out really fast.
- ◎ B Our restaurant gets customers in and out very fast.
- ◎ C Our restaurant gets customers in and out really quick [quickly].
- ○ D Our restaurant has customers in and out really fast.
- △ E Our restaurant has customers in and out very fast.
- △ F Our restaurant has customers in and out really quick [quickly].
- △ G Our restaurant has a high turnover rate of its customers.
- × H Our restaurant has a high turnover rate.
  - ❖ H が辞典に出ているがこの意味では使われていない．「従業員の定着率が悪い」という意味でならよく使われている．

かいふくする 115

開店記念日
〈今日はうちの店の開店記念日です〉
    ☆ A This is our store's anniversary.
    ◎ B This is the anniversary of our store.
    ○ C This is the anniversary of our store's (grand) opening.

開店する
1 《盛大な開店行事をするとき》
〈新しいメイシーはいつ開店するんだい〉
    ☆ A When'll the new Macy's be open?
    ◎ B When's the new Macy's opening?
    ◎ C When'll the new Macy's open?
    ○ D When'll the new Macy's be open for business?
    ○ E When'll the new Macy's start business?
    ○ F When's the new Macy's grand opening?
2 《盛大な開店行事をしないとき》
〈あのレストランはいつ開店するんだい〉
    ☆ A When'll that restaurant be open?
    ◎ B When's that restaurant opening?
    ○ C When'll that restaurant be open for business?
    ○ D When'll that restaurant open?
    ○ E When'll that restaurant start business?
3 《新聞の広告・店先の垂幕・張り紙》
〈近日開店〉
    ◎   Grand Opening Soon!
4 《日常の「開店する」》
〈メイシーは毎日何時に開店するのですか〉
    ◎ A What time does Macy's open every day?
    ○ B What time does Macy's start business every day?

解任される →首になる
開発部 →…部 2
回復する
1 《景気》
〈秋までに景気は回復するでしょう〉
    ☆ A I hope the economy'll pick up by the fall.
    ☆ B I hope the economy'll get better by the fall.
    ◎ C I hope the economy'll improve by the fall.
    ○ D I hope the economy'll be better by the fall.
    ○ E I hope the economy'll recover by the fall.
    △ F I hope the economy'll look up by the fall.
    × G I hope the economy'll look [turn] upward by the fall.
2 《消費》
〈まもなく消費は回復すると思います〉
    ☆ A I hope spending'll pick up soon.
    ◎ B I hope spending'll go up [increase] soon.
    ○ C I hope spending'll improve soon.
    △ D I hope spending'll rise soon.
    △ E I hope spending'll be up soon.
    × F I hope spending'll look up soon.
3 《天気》

〈日曜までに天気は回復するでしょう〉
- ◎ A The weather'll get [be] better by Sunday.
- ◎ B The weather'll improve by Sunday.
- △ C The weather'll become better by Sunday.

4 《健康》

〈まもなく彼は健康を回復するでしょう〉
- ◎ A I hope he'll recover soon.
- ◎ B I hope he'll get better soon.
- ○ C I hope he'll be OK soon.
- ○ D I hope he'll get well soon.
- △ E I hope he'll be well soon.

解放する

1 《人質を》

a) 人質を取っている犯人を主語にして述べるとき

〈彼らは人質を全員解放しました〉
- ☆ A They let all the hostages go.
- ◎ B They released all the hostages.
- ○ C They set all the hostages free.

b) 人質に取られている人たちを主語にして述べるとき

〈すべての人質は即刻解放されるべきである〉
- ◎ A All the hostages should be released [freed] immediately.
- ◎ B All the hostages should be set free immediately.
- ◎ C All the hostages should be let go immediately.
- × D All the hostages should be set at liberty immediately.
- × E All the hostages should be let loose immediately.

  ❖ D, E は辞典に出ているが使われていない.

2 《奴隷の状態から》

a) 解放した人を主語にして述べるとき

〈エイブラハム・リンカーンはアメリカの黒人を奴隷から解放した〉
- ◎ A Abraham Lincoln liberated [emancipated, freed] American blacks from slavery.
- △ B Abraham Lincoln set American blacks free from slavery.

b) 解放された人を主語にして述べるとき

〈南部の黒人はリンカーンによって解放された〉
- ☆ A The Southern blacks were emancipated by Lincoln.
- ◎ B The Southern blacks were freed by Lincoln.
- ○ C The Southern blacks were set free by Lincoln.

3 《洗脳されている状態から》

〈私たちは彼らをあのカルトの教えの洗脳から解放しなければならない〉
- ◎ A We have to liberate them from being brainwashed with the teachings of that cult.
- ○ B We have to free them from being brainwashed with the teachings of that cult.
- △ C We have to set them free from being brainwashed with the teachings of that cult.
- × D We have to set them at free from being brainwashed with the teachings of that cult.

  ❖ D は辞典に出ているが使われていない

4 《宗教上の迫害から》

〈ピューリタンは宗教上の迫害から解放されるためにアメリカへ渡った〉
- ☆ A Puritans went to America to be free of religious persecution.
- ◎ B Puritans went to America to be liberated from religious persecution.
- △ C Puritans went to America to be released from religious persecution.

5 《心配から》
〈彼は私を心配ごとから解放してくれました〉
- ◎ A He relieved me of my anxiety.
- ○ B He set me free from my anxiety.
- ○ C He freed [released] me from my anxiety.
- △ D He liberated me from my anxiety.
- ❖ D は辞典に出ているが時々使われる程度.

買物 →いい買物

解約する

1 《保険の場合》
〈私は生命保険を解約しなければならないんです〉
- ◎ A I have to cash in my life insurance.
- ◎ B I have to cancel my life insurance.
- × C I have to dissolve [surrender, rescind, annul] my life insurance.
- ❖(1) C は辞典に出ているが使われていない.
- ❖(2) A は現金が戻ってくる、B は現金は戻ってこないという違いがある.

2 《契約書の場合》
〈私はできれば契約を解約したいのですが〉
- ◎ A I'd like to cancel the contract if possible.
- △ B I'd like to dissolve the contract if possible.
- × C I'd like to annul [rescind, surrender] the contract if possible.
- ❖ C は辞典に出ているが使われていない.

改良する
〈うちの製品の質を改良しなければならない〉
- ☆ A We have to improve the quality of our products.
- ◎ B We have to work on the quality of our products.
- ○ C We have to upgrade the quality of our products.
- △ D We have to better [raise] the quality of our products.

換える

1 《「change+複数名詞」「change+one's+単数名詞」が共によく使われるとき》
a) 専攻
〈どうして専攻を換えたのですか〉
- ◎ A Why did you change majors?
- ◎ B Why did you change your major?

b) 銀行
〈どうして銀行を換えたのですか〉
- ◎ A Why did you change banks?
- ◎ B Why did you change your bank?

c) 美容院
〈どうして美容院を換えたのですか〉
- ◎ A Why did you change beauty shops?
- ◎ B Why did you change your beauty shop?

d) 秘書など
・要求が厳しく、満足できなくて次々に換えるが、その理由に言及しないで事実だけを述べるとき

〈社長に気をつけなさい．彼は秘書に対して厳しくて次々に換えることで有名なのよ〉
- ◎ Be careful with the boss. He's notorious for going through secretaries.

・要求が厳しく満足できなくて次々に換え，その理由を説明するとき

〈彼は秘書たちの仕事に決して満足しないので，しょっちゅう換えているんです〉
- ◎ He's always changing [going through] secretaries because he's never satisfied with their work.
    - ❖ 1の型で使われる類例：change chauffeurs (運転手を換える), change copy machines (コピー機を換える), change hotels (ホテルを換える), change suppliers (仕入れ先を換える).

2 《「change+複数名詞」はよく使われているが，「change+one's+単数名詞」が使われていないとき》

a) 飛行機

〈どこで飛行機を乗り換えたのですか〉
- ◎ A Where did you change planes?
- × B Where did you change your plane?

b) 電車

〈どこで電車を乗り換えたのですか〉
- ◎ A Where did you change trains?
- × B Where did you change your train?

c) 転職

・一般的に言う場合

〈いつ職を換えたのですか〉
- ◎ A When did you change jobs?
- △ B When did you change your job?

・「転々とする」というニュアンスがある場合

〈彼は転々と職を換えたんです〉
- ☆ A He changed jobs often.
- ◎ B He changed jobs one after another.
- ◎ C He bounced from job to job.
- ○ D He jumped from job to job.
- ○ E He changed his job often.
    - ❖ 2の型で使われる類例：change cars (車を換える), change maids (メイドさんを換える), change CPAs (会計士を換える).

帰る

1 《家庭に帰ってくるとき》

〈彼が帰ってきたらすぐに電話させます〉
- ☆ A As soon as he comes home [back], I'll have him call you.
- ☆ B As soon as he gets home [back], I'll have him call you.
- ◎ C As soon as he walks in, I'll have him call you.
- ◎ D As soon as he walks through the door, I'll have him call you.
- ○ E As soon as he returns (home), I'll have him call you.
- × F As soon as he returns back, I'll have him call you.
    - ❖ F は辞典に出ているが使われていない．

2 《予定の時間より遅く帰宅したとき》

〈何時に帰って来たの〉
- ◎ What time did you get in?
    - ❖深夜勤務で早朝の帰宅，早朝勤務で午後1，2時の帰宅，昼間勤務で夜の帰宅，いずれの場合でも予定の帰宅時間より遅ければ非常によく使われてい

る.
3 《家庭以外で話し手のいる所（例：会社）へ帰ってくるとき》
〈彼が帰ってきたらすぐに電話させます〉
- ◎ A As soon as he comes [gets] back, I'll have him call you.
- ◎ B As soon as he walks in, I'll have him call you.
- ◎ C As soon as he walks through the door, I'll have him call you.
- ◎ D As soon as he gets in, I'll have him call you.
- ○ E As soon as he returns, I'll have him call you.
  - ❖「帰ってきたらすぐ」という響きの強さの点では C が一番強く，B, D の順で下がり，A, E は 4 番目．

4 《退社時間を尋ねるとき》
〈何時に帰るの〉
- ◎ A What time're you leaving [going home]?
- ◎ B What time're you going to leave [go home]?

5 《今いる所（会社，学校，その他用事をしている所）を出て家に帰ろうと述べるとき》
〈帰ろう〉
- ◎ A Let's go home.
- ◎ B Let's get out of here.
- × C Let's go back.
- × D Let's return (home).

6 《夫婦または家族の者と買物をして帰るとき》
〈帰りましょう〉
- ◎ A Let's go home.
- ◎ B Let's go back home.
- × C Let's go [get, be] back.
- × D Let's return.
- × E Let's be home.

7 《母国に帰ると述べるとき》
〈私たちは今年のクリスマスに 10 年振りでアメリカへ帰るんです〉
- ◎ A We're planning to go back home to America for the first time in ten years this Christmas.
- ○ B We're planning to go back to America for the first time in ten years this Christmas.
  - ❖ A には郷愁的なニュアンスがあるが B にはない．

8 《郷里に帰ると述べるとき》
〈私は今年のクリスマスに郷里に帰る予定です〉
- ◎ A I'm planning to go (back) home this Christmas.
- △ B I'm planning to go back to my parents' home this Christmas.

9 《帰っている状態》
〈彼は 6 時までには帰っているでしょう〉
- ◎ He'll be back [home] by 6:00.

10 《帰る時間に焦点があるとき》
〈私は 3 時までに事務所に帰らなければならないんです〉
- ◎ A I've got to get [go] back to the office by 3 o'clock.
- ◎ B I've got to be back at the office by 3 o'clock.
- ○ C I've got to return to the office by 3 o'clock.

11 《帰ってしまってもういない状態のとき》
〈セールスマン：社長に会えますか〉

Salesman: May I see the boss?
〈秘書：申し訳ありませんが，今日はもう帰りました〉
Secretary:
◎　　I'm sorry, he's gone for the day.

12 《文章で》
a）帰って来るの例
〈サッチャー首相は今日，日本から帰国した．午後2時30分にヒースロー空港に着き全閣僚に出迎えられた〉
◎　　Prime Minister Thatcher returned home from Japan today. She arrived at Heathrow Airport at 2:30 p.m. and was met by the entire cabinet.

b）帰って行くの例
〈ブレア首相は昨日イギリスに帰国した．彼は午前10時30分に成田空港を出発した〉
◎　　Prime Minister Blair returned home to England yesterday. He left Narita Airport at 10:30 a.m.
　❖ return は帰って行く（go back）と帰って来る（come back）の両方の意味で使われている．この表現は文章英語．会話でもよく使われているが，少し改まった響きがある．

13 《交通機関に言及するとき》
a）徒歩
〈歩いて帰るのですか〉
◎　A　Are you going to walk back?
○　B　Are you going to go back on foot?

b）タクシー
〈タクシーで帰るのですか〉
◎　A　Are you going to take a cab back?
○　B　Are you going to go back by cab?

c）地下鉄
〈地下鉄で帰るのですか〉
☆　A　Are you going to take the subway back?
◎　B　Are you going to go back on the subway?
○　C　Are you going to go back by subway?

d）飛行機
・一般的に
〈飛行機で帰るのですか〉
◎　A　Are you going to fly back?
◎　B　Are you going to take a plane back?
○　C　Are you going to go back by plane?

・飛行機会社を明示するとき
〈日航で帰るのですか〉
☆　A　Are you going to take JAL back?
◎　B　Are you going to fly back on JAL?
○　C　Are you going to go back on JAL?
△　D　Are you going to go [fly] back by JAL?

化学会社　→会社 11

…がかった
《色について言う場合》
a）colorをともなって
〈ボブ：ビルは何色なんだい〉

Bob: What color is the building?
〈トム：言いにくいんだけど，まあピンクがかった色だね〉
Tom:
◎   It's hard to describe; it's kind of a pinkish color.
b) colorをともなわずに
〈もう少しピンクがかった口紅をつけるといいでしょう〉
◎ A It might be better for you to use a pinker shade of lipstick.
◎ B It might be better for you to use lipstick that's a little more pink.

かかる

1 《鍵の場合》
〈鍵がかからないんです〉
◎ A The lock doesn't work.
○ B The lock doesn't catch.

2 《エンジンの場合》
〈エンジンがかからないんです〉
◎ A I can't get the engine to start [work, run].
○ B I can't get the engine to go.
▽ C I can't get the engine to drive.

3 《わなの場合》
〈彼は彼女のわなにかかったんです〉
◎ A He fell into her trap.
◎ B He played into her hands.
○ C He was trapped by her.

4 《負担の場合》
a) 負担する人を述べるとき
〈費用は全部私にかかってきます〉
◎ A I'll have to bear all the expenses.
△ B All the expenses'll fall on me.
b) いくらかかるかを尋ねるとき
〈この車を修理するのにどのくらいかかりますか〉
◎ A How much will it cost me to have this car fixed?
○ B How much will the repairs on this car cost me?
○ C How much will you charge me to fix this car?

5 《依存の場合》
〈決定はあなたにかかっています〉
◎ A The decision is up to you.
◎ B The decision depends on [rests with] you.
○ C The decision hangs on you.
△ D The decision turns on you.

6 《時間の場合》
〈この仕事は時間がかかる〉
☆ A This is time-consuming work.
◎ B This work takes (up) a lot of time.
◎ C This work demands a lot of time.
○ D This work requires a lot of time.

〈車で横浜までどのくらいかかるのですか〉
◎ A How long does the drive to Yokohama take?
◎ B How long does it take to drive to Yokohama?
○ C How long does it take to get to Yokohama by car?

かぎ屋 →店 38
確実だ
〈彼が課長に昇進することは確実です〉
- ◎ A He'll definitely be promoted to manager.
- ◎ B I'm positive (that) he'll be promoted to manager.
- ◎ C I'm certain (that) he'll be promoted to manager.
- ◎ D I'm sure (that) he'll be promoted to manager.
- ◎ E He's a shoo-in for manager.
    - ❖ Aが一番確実なニュアンスがあり，B，Cが2番目，D，Eがほぼ同じで3番目．

各種学校
1 《外国語学校》
〈この近くに外国語学校がありますか〉
- ◎ A Is there a foreign language school near here?
- ○ B Is there a language school near here?

2 《歌手養成所》
〈新宿に歌手養成所がありますか〉
- ☆ A Is there a voice training school in Shinjuku?
- ◎ B Is there a singing school in Shinjuku?
- ○ C Is there a voice school in Shinjuku?
- ○ D Is there a singers' training school in Shinjuku?
- △ E Is there a singers' school in Shinjuku?

3 《看護学校》
a) 大学などの付属の学校
〈図書館の近くに看護学校があります〉
- ◎   There's a school of nursing near the library.

b) 付属ではない独立した学校
〈図書館の近くに看護学校があります〉
- ◎ A There's a nursing school near the library.
- ○ B There's a nurses' (training) school near the library.

4 《自動車教習所》
〈中野に自動車教習所がありますか〉
- ◎ A Is there a driving school in Nakano?
- △ B Is there a drivers' school in Nakano?

5 《コンピュータ学校》
〈中野にコンピュータ学校がありますか〉
- ◎ A Is there a computer school in Nakano?
- ◎ B Is there a computer training school in Nakano?

6 《写真学校》
〈中野に写真学校がありますか〉
- ◎ A Is there a school of photography in Nakano?
- ○ B Is there a photography school in Nakano?
- △ C Is there a photographers' (training) school in Nakano?

7 《職業(訓練)学校》
〈この近くに職業(訓練)学校がありますか〉
- ◎ A Is there a vocational [vocation] school near here?
- △ B Is there a trade school near here?

8 《ダンス学校》
a) プロになる人向け

〈この近くにダンス学校がありますか〉
- ◎ A Is there a dancing academy [school] near here?
- △ B Is there a dancers' training school near here?
- × C Is there a dancers' school near here?

b) 一般の人向け
〈この近くにダンス教室がありますか〉
- ◎ A Is there a dancing school near here?
- △ B Is there a dancers' (training) school near here?

9 《調理師学校》
〈中野に調理師学校がありますか〉
- ☆ A Is there a culinary institute in Nakano?
- ◎ B Is there a culinary [cooking] school in Nakano?
- △ C Is there a culinary college in Nakano?
- ▽ D Is there a cooks' training school in Nakano?

10 《デザイナー学校》
〈この近くにデザイナー学校がありますか〉
- ◎ A Is there a design school near here?
- ○ B Is there a design academy near here?
- ○ C Is there a designers' school near here?
- △ D Is there a designing school near here?
- △ E Is there a designers' training school near here?

11 《俳優養成所》
〈六本木に俳優養成所がありますか〉
- ◎ A Is there an acting school in Roppongi?
- △ B Is there a drama school in Roppongi?
- △ C Is there an actors' (training) school in Roppongi?

12 《パイロット養成所》
〈立川にパイロット養成所がありますか〉
- ☆ A Is there a flight school in Tachikawa?
- ◎ B Is there a flying school in Tachikawa?
- ○ C Is there a pilots' training school in Tachikawa?
- △ D Is there a pilots' school in Tachikawa?

13 《ろう学校》
〈図書館の近くにろう学校があります〉
- ☆ A There's a school for the deaf near the library.
- ◎ B There's a school for the hearing impaired near the library.
- ○ C There's a school for deaf people near the library.
- △ D There's a deaf people's school near the library.

…学生

1 《大学生》
〈私は大学生のとき一生懸命勉強しませんでした〉
- ☆ A I didn't study hard in college.
- ◎ B I didn't study hard when I was in college.
- ◎ C I didn't study hard when I was a college student.
- △ D I didn't study hard in my college days.
- △ E I didn't study hard at college.
  - ❖ D は話し手がだいぶ昔のことを話しているという響きがある．

2 《高校生》
〈私は高校生のとき一生懸命勉強しなかったんです〉

- ☆ A I didn't study hard in high school.
- ◎ B I didn't study hard when I was in high school.
- ◎ C I didn't study hard when I was a high school student.
- △ D I didn't study hard in my high school days.
- △ E I didn't study hard when I was a high schooler.
- ▽ F I didn't study hard in senior high (school).

3 《中学生》

〈私は中学生のとき一生懸命勉強しませんでした〉

- ☆ A I didn't study hard in junior high.
- ◎ B I didn't study hard when I was in junior high.
- ○ C I didn't study hard when I was in junior high school.
- ○ D I didn't study hard when I was a junior high school student.

4 《小学生》

〈私は小学生のとき一生懸命勉強しませんでした〉

- ◎ A I didn't study hard in elementary [grade] school.
- ◎ B I didn't study hard when I was in elementary [grade] school.
- ◎ C I didn't study hard when I was an elementary [a grade] school student.
- × D I didn't study hard in primary school.

5 《幼稚園生のとき》

〈私は幼稚園生のときわんぱくだったんです〉

- ◎ A I was always in trouble when I was in kindergarden.
- ○ B I was always in trouble when I was a kindergardener.
- ○ C I was always in trouble in kindergarden.
    - ❖ kindergarten が正しいとされているが，実際には kindergarden の方が普通使われている．

拡大する

〈うちの会社はシカゴで営業を拡大する予定です〉

- ◎ A Our company's going to expand its market [business, operations] in Chicago.
- ○ B Our company's going to expand its operation in Chicago.
    - ❖ in はすでにある営業を「拡大する」の意味．in Chicago を into Chicago または to Chicago にすると新規に「進出する」の意味になる．

確認する

1 《意図》

〈私は彼の意図を確認できなかったんです〉

- ◎ A I couldn't figure out what he wanted.
- △ B I couldn't find out what he wanted.
- △ C I couldn't make sure of what he wanted.
- △ D I couldn't figure out his intention.
- × E I couldn't confirm [check (out)] what he wanted.
- × F I couldn't confirm his intentions.
    - ❖ E, F が辞典に出ているが使われていない．

2 《ホテル・飛行機などの予約》

〈私たちの予約を確認してくれますか〉

- ◎ A Will you check [double-check, check on, confirm] our reservations?
- ◎ B Will you check [find out] if they have our reservations?
- ○ C Will you see if they have our reservations?

かくにんする 125

- ○ D Will you make sure they have our reservations?
- ○ E Will you find out about our reservations?
- △ F Will you make sure of our reservations?

3 《聞き手が相手の言ったことを理解しているか否かを確認するとき》
〈おっしゃられたことを確認させて下さい〉

- ☆ A Let me see if I understand you.
- ◎ B Let me get this straight.
- ◎ C Let me see if I get [got] this straight.
- ◎ D Let me see if I understand what you're telling [saying to] me.
- ◎ E Let me see if I understand what you told [said to] me.
- ◎ F Let me make sure (that) I understand you.
- ◎ G Let me make sure I get [got] this straight.
- △ H Let me confirm I understand you.
- △ I Let me see if I get you.
- △ J Let me check [find out] if I understand you.

4 《不在を確認するとき》

a) 初めて確認するとき
〈彼が事務所にいるかどうか確認してくれますか〉

- ☆ A Will you see if he's at the office?
- ◎ B Will you check [find out] if he's at the office?
- ◎ C Will you make sure he's at the office?
- ○ D Will you confirm he's at the office?
- △ E Will you check out if he's at the office?
- × F Will you check [find] out (that) he's at the office?
- × G Will you find he's at the office?
  - ❖(1) if の代わりに whether も使われているが使用頻度は下がる．
  - ❖(2) C の make sure, D の confirm は正しくは「再確認する」という意味である．しかし，アメリカ人の間では初めて確認する場合の「確認する」の意味でも非常によく使われている．

b) 再度確認するとき
〈彼が事務所にいるかどうか確認してくれますか〉

- ☆ A Will you double-check (if) he's at the office?
- ☆ B Will you make sure he's at the office?
- ◎ C Will you check [see] again if he's at the office?
- ◎ D Will you find [check] out if he's at the office?
- ◎ E Will you check again that he's at the office?
- ◎ F Will you see once more if he's at the office?
- ◎ G Will you make sure again that he's at the office?
- ◎ H Will you find out again if he's at the office?
- ○ I Will you see again that he's at the office?
- ○ J Will you see once again if he's at the office?
- ○ K Will you check out (once) again [once more] if he's at the office?
- ○ L Will you find out once again he's at the office?
- ○ M Will you confirm (that) he's at the office?
- ○ N Will you confirm again he's at the office?
- △ O Will you confirm once again [once more] he's at the office?
- △ P Will you reconfirm he's at the office?
  - ❖ B の make sure, M の confirm は「再確認する」という意味の「確認する」で使うのが正しい．しかし，現代アメリカ英語では初めて確認するとき

の「確認する」にも非常によく使われている．したがって，これらの語は again, once again, once more をしたがえた G, N, O もよく使われている．

5 《サイン・証拠などが本物であることを確認するとき》
a) 初めて確認するとき
〈あなたはサインが本物であるか否かを確認した方がいいよ〉
- ◎ A You'd better check [see] that the signature's real.
- ◎ B You'd better find out [see, check] if the signature's real.
- ○ C You'd better confirm [verify] that the signature's real.

b) 再度確認するとき
〈サインが本物であるかどうか確認した方がいいよ〉
- ☆ A You'd better double-check that [if] the signature's real.
- ☆ B You'd better make sure that the signature's real.
- ◎ C You'd better check again [confirm, verify] that the signature's real.
- ○ D You'd better check once again [once more] that the signature's real.
- ○ E You'd better confirm again that the signature's real.
- ○ F You'd better confirm once again [once more] that the signature's real.
- ○ G You'd better verify again [once more] that the signature's real.
- △ H You'd better check [confirm, verify] over again that the signature's real.
- △ I You'd better verify once again that the signature's real.

6 《医師・警察・検死官などが確認するとき》
a) 初めて確認するとき
〈私たちは死因を確認しなければならない〉
- ◎ A We have to find out [figure out, ascertain, check, verify] the cause of death.
- ○ B We have to confirm [check out] the cause of death.
- △ C We have to make sure [certain] of the cause of death.

b) 再度確認するとき
〈私たちは死因を確認しなければならない〉
- ◎ A We have to confirm the cause of death (again).
- ○ B We have to confirm the cause of death once again [once more].
- ○ C We have to confirm the cause of death over again.
- ○ D We have to make sure of the cause of death (again).
- ○ E We have to make sure of the cause of death once again [once more].
- ○ F We have to make sure of the cause of death over again.
- ○ G We have to double-check the cause of death.
- ○ H We have to make certain of the cause of death (again).
- ○ I We have to make certain of the cause of death once again [once more].
- ○ J We have to make certain of the cause of death over again.
- △ K We have to ascertain [verify] the cause of death again.

7 《一般の人が調査などにより初めて確認するとき》
〈私たちは彼の死因を確認しなければならない〉
- ☆ A We have to make sure how he died.
- ◎ B We have to find out [figure out] how he died.
- ◎ C We have to make sure what caused his death.

学部長 →地位 21
家具屋 →店 16
駆け落ちする
　1　《1人または2人ともが結婚しているとき》
　〈彼女は結婚している男性と駆け落ちしたんです〉
　　　◎　A　She ran off with a married man.
　　　○　B　She ran away with a married man.
　2　《2人とも独身のとき》
　〈彼女は彼と駆け落ちしたんです〉
　　　◎　A　She eloped with him.
　　　△　B　She ran away with him.
　　❖多くの辞典でAを1人または2人ともが結婚している場合の用例として出しているが，その意味では使われていない．elopeは2人とも独身で，親に結婚を反対されて「駆け落ちする」の意味でのみ使われる．

影が薄くなる
　〈彼は有名な経済学者なのですが，高名な父親の存在のために影が薄くなってしまっています〉
　　　◎　A　He's a famous economist but his prominent father's presence overshadows him.
　　　◎　B　He's a famous economist but he's overshadowed by his prominent father's presence.
　　　○　C　He's a famous economist but his prominent father's presence outshines him.
　　　○　D　He's a famous economist but his prominent father's presence steals the spotlight from him.

かけひきをする
　1　《誰にでも使える》
　〈彼は私たちにかけひきしようとしているんです〉
　　　◎　　He's trying to play games with us.
　2　《友人と話すとき》
　〈彼は私たちにかけひきしようとしているんです〉
　　　☆　A　He's trying to screw with us.
　　　◎　B　He's trying to screw us around.
　　　◎　C　He's trying to mess (around) with us.
　　　◎　D　He's trying to pull one over us.
　　　○　E　He's trying to screw around with us.
　3　《話し手がすごく怒っているとき》
　〈彼は私たちにかけひきしようとしているんです〉
　　　◎　　He's trying to fuck (around) with us.
　　❖性行為表現であるため，気を使う必要がない場面でしか使えない．

かける
　1　《音楽》
　〈音楽をかけましょうか〉
　　　◎　A　Can I put some music for you?

◎ B Can I play some music for you?
❖ A, B ともCD, ステレオに使われているが, B は楽器にも使われている.
 2 《エンジン》
〈エンジンをかけて下さい〉
◎ A Start [Turn on] the engine.
× B Switch [Flip] the engine.

重なる
〈今年はクリスマスが日曜日と重なります〉
◎ A This year Christmas falls on Sunday.
◎ B This year Christmas is on Sunday.
○ C This year Christmas comes on Sunday.

菓子屋　→店 11
過小評価する　→評価する 2

貸す
 1 《非貴重品》
〈消しゴムを貸してくれますか〉
◎ A Will you let me use [borrow] the eraser?
◎ B Will you lend [loan] me the eraser?
 2 《貴重品》
〈スティーブは車を貸してくれた〉
◎ A Steve loaned [lent] me his car.
◎ B Steve let me borrow [use] his car.
 3 《貸す期間が明示されているとき》
〈スティーブは車を週末の間貸してくれた〉
◎ A Steve loaned [lent] me his car for the weekend.
◎ B Steve let me borrow [use] his car for the weekend.
◎ C Steve let me have his car for the weekend.
○ D Steve gave me his car for the weekend.
 4 《貸す目的が明示されているとき》
〈彼女はカクテルドレスをパーティーのために貸してくれた〉
◎ A She loaned [lent] me her cocktail dress for the party.
◎ B She let me borrow [use] her cocktail dress for the party.
○ C She let me have her cocktail dress for the party.
○ D She gave me her cocktail dress for the party.
 5 《貸して [借りて] いる状態》
〈このタイプはいつまで借りていられるのですか〉
◎ A How long can I keep [use, borrow] this typewriter?
○ B How long can I have this typewriter?
○ C How long will you let me borrow [use] this typewriter?
○ D How long will you loan me this typewriter?
△ F How long can you loan me this typewriter?
△ G How long will you lend me this typewriter?
△ H How long will you let me have this typewriter?
❖以上の「貸す」の各種表現は, イギリスで loan が使用されていないことを除けば, 英米で使用の慣用に違いは認められていない. 違いがあれば各個人の好みの問題である.
 6 《賃貸しする》→賃貸しする
a）事務所・店舗・事務機など
〈うちはこの事務所を1ヶ月1000ドルでお貸しできます〉

☆ A We can lease [rent] this office space for $1,000 a month.
◎ B We can rent out this office space for $1,000 a month.
○ C We can lease out this office space for $1,000 a month.
× D We can let this office space for $1,000 a month.
× E We can let out this office space for $1,000 a month.
❖ イギリスでは E はよく使われている．また，B, D も非常によく使われている．

b) 家・アパート
〈私はこの家を1ヶ月1000ドルで貸したいんです〉
◎ A I want to rent out this house for $1,000 a month.
○ B I want to rent [lease] this house for $1,000 a month.
△ C I want to lease out this house for $1,000 a month.

7 《又貸しする》
〈私はこのアパートを又貸ししたいんです〉
☆ A I want to sublease this apartment.
◎ B I want to sublet this apartment.
△ C I want to sublease [sublet] out this apartment.
× D I want to subrent (out) this apartment.

風邪

1 《風邪をひいている》

a) 主語が単数のとき
〈彼は今風邪をひいています〉
◎   He has a cold now.

b) 主語が単数で2回以上のとき
〈彼はよく風邪をひいています〉
◎ A He always has a cold.
▽ B He always has colds.

c) 主語が複数のとき
〈彼女たちは風邪をひいています〉
◎ A They have colds.
△ B They have a cold.

d) 鼻風邪
〈彼は鼻風邪をひいているんです〉
◎ A He has a head cold.
△ B He has a cold in the head.
× C He has a cold on the head.
× D He has a cold in the nose.
❖ C, D が辞典に出ているが使われていない．

e) 軽い風邪
〈彼は軽い風邪をひいているんです〉
◎ A He has a mild cold.
○ B He has a slight cold.

f) ひどい風邪
〈彼はひどい風邪をひいているんです〉
◎ A He has a bad [nasty] cold.
○ B He has a miserable cold.

g) しつこいせき風邪
〈彼はしつこいせき風邪をひいているんです〉
◎ A He has a cough that (just) won't go away.

◯ B He has a stubborn [persistent] cough.
　2 《風邪をひき直す》
　〈彼は風邪をひき直したんです〉
　　　◎ A He caught another cold.
　　　◯ B He caught a cold again.
　　　× C He caught cold again.
　　　× D He caught a fresh cold.
　　　❖ C, D が多くの辞典に出ているが使われていない.
　3 《風邪をひく》
　〈風邪をひかないで下さい〉
　　　☆ A Don't catch a cold.
　　　◎ B Don't come down with a cold.
　　　◯ C Don't get a cold.
　　　◯ D Don't catch cold.
　　　× E Don't contract [take] a cold.
　　　❖ E は辞典に出ているが使われていない.
　4 《風邪をひきやすい》
　〈彼は風邪をひきやすいんです〉
　　　☆ A He catches colds easily.
　　　◎ B He catches a cold easily.
　　　◎ C He's likely to catch colds.
　　　◎ D He's prone [subject, susceptible] to catching colds.
　　　◯ E He's likely [prone] to catch a cold.
　　　◯ F He's susceptible [prone, subject] to catching a cold.
　　　◯ G He's susceptible to colds.

風が強い
〈今日は風が強いです〉
　　　◎ A It's windy today.
　　　◎ B The wind's blowing hard today.
　　　◯ C It's blowing hard today.

ガソリンを食う　→燃費 3

かたい
　1 《肉の場合》
　〈この肉はかたい〉
　　　◎　　This meat is tough.
　2 《レタスの場合》
　〈このレタスはかたい〉
　　　◎ A This lettuce is crisp [crispy].
　　　◯ B This lettuce is hard.
　3 《ドアの場合》
　〈このドアはかたくて開かない〉
　　　◎ A The door sticks and doesn't budge.
　　　◎ B The door gets stuck.
　4 《女性の貞操に言及する場合》
　〈彼女はかたい女だよ〉
　　　◎ A She isn't loose [promiscuous].
　　　× B She's virtuous.
　　　❖ B は口語では使われていない.
　5 《頭の良さに言及する場合》

〈彼は頭がかたいんだ．私が教えることは理解するんだけど，それを別の問題に応用できないんだよ〉
- ◎ A He's slow. He understands what I teach him, but he can't apply it to another question.
- ◎ B He isn't smart [bright]. He understands what I teach him, but he can't apply it to another question.

6 《商売の堅実性に言及する場合》

〈食料品店はかたい商売だ〉
- ◎ A A grocery store is a safe business.
- ○ B A grocery store is a solid [sound] business.

7 《雑誌・新聞の報道などに言及する場合》

〈タイムはかたい読み物だ〉
- ◎ *Time*'s a magazine known for hard reporting.

過大評価する →評価する 1

ガタがきている

1 《車》

〈この車はガタがきている〉
- ◎ A This car's falling apart.
- ○ B This car's running on a wing and a prayer.
- ○ C This car's dying.
- △ D This car's on its last leg.
- ❖ C, D は A, B よりひどい状態のときに使われている．

2 《人間》

〈彼はガタがきている〉
- ☆ A He's breaking down.
- ◎ B He's falling apart.
- ◎ C He's losing his mind.
- ❖ B は肉体，精神の両方に等しく使われているが，A と C は精神上にしか使われていない．

かたくなる

1 《食物》

〈それは今食べた方がいいよ．さもないとかたくなるから〉
- ☆ A You'd better eat it now, or it'll get hard.
- ◎ B You'd better eat it now, or it'll become hard.
- ◎ C You'd better eat it now, or it'll harden.
- ○ D You'd better eat it now, or it'll turn solid.
- ▽ E You'd better eat it now, or it'll get [become] solid.
- ❖ E は辞典に出ているがまれにしか使われていない．

2 《緊張する》

a) 硬直して動けなかった気持ちを述べるとき

〈私は大勢の聴衆の前に立ったとき，かたくなってしまったんです〉
- ◎ A When I stood in front of the large audience, I froze.
- ◎ B When I stood in front of the large audience, I was petrified [frozen].
- ○ C When I stood in front of the large audience, I was paralyzed.

b) どきどきして怖かった気持ちを述べるとき

〈私は大勢の聴衆の前に立って，かたくなってしまったんです〉
- ☆ A When I stood in front of the large audience, I was terrified.
- ◎ B When I stood in front of the large audience, I was [got] scared.
- ◎ C When I stood in front of the large audience, it was scary for me.

- ○ D When I stood in front of the large audience, it was scary to me.
- ○ E When I stood in front of the large audience, I was [got] afraid.
- △ F When I stood in front of the large audience, I got terrified.
- △ G When I stood in front of the large audience, I was frightened.

3 《確実にする》

〈この証拠で彼の有罪はかたくなるでしょう〉

- ☆ A This evidence'll prove his guilt.
- ◎ B This evidence'll guarantee [confirm] his guilt.
- ○ C This evidence'll assure [substantiate, insure] his guilt.
- △ D This evidence'll verify [nail down, solidify] his guilt.

かたずをのんで

〈私たちはかたずをのんで試合をじっと見ていました〉

- ◎ A We watched the game on the edge of our seats.
- ○ B We watched the game on pins and needles.
- △ C We watched the game holding our breath.
- △ D We watched the game with bated breath.
- △ E We watched the game on the edge of our chairs.
- △ F We watched the game in breathless [thrilling] suspense.
- ▽ G We watched the game with breathless attention [interest].
- ▽ H We watched the game with strained attention.
- ▽ I We watched the game breathlessly.
- ▽ J We watched the game catching my breath.
- ▽ K We watched the game in breathless excitement.

❖辞典に G〜K が紹介されているがほとんど使われていない．

かち合う

〈月曜日は予定がかち合うんです〉

- ◎ A I have a conflict on Monday.
- ◎ B I have a previous appointment on Monday.
- ○ C I have a previous engagement on Monday.
- ○ D My appointment on Monday conflicts with our meeting.
- △ E Monday conflicts with my appointment.

❖C は社会的地位の高い人の間で使われている．

価値観

1 《民主主義・自由のような普遍的・根本的・伝統的価値観》

〈彼らの価値観は私たちのと違う〉

- ◎ A Their values're different from ours.
- ◎ B Their sense of values're different from ours.

2 《個人の価値観》

〈彼の価値観は私のと違います〉

- ◎ A His sense of values're different from mine.
- × B His values're different from mine.

勝つ

1 《裁判》

〈彼は裁判に勝つでしょう〉

- ◎ A He'll win the case [lawsuit, suit].
- × B He'll win the trial.

2 《困難》

〈彼女は直面しているすべての困難に打ち勝つでしょう〉

- ☆ A She'll overcome all the difficulties she's facing.

- ◎ B She'll rise above all the difficulties she's facing.
- ○ C She'll get over all the difficulties she's facing.
- △ D She'll triumph over [conquer] all the difficulties she's facing.
  - ❖ D は堅い響きがあるので文章ではよく使われている.

3 《誘惑》

〈あなたはすべての誘惑に勝たなければならない〉
- ◎ A You have to overcome [resist] all the temptations.
- △ B You have to get over all the temptations.
- ▽ C You have to beat all the temptations.

4 《競技》

a）競走

〈彼女は 100 メートル競走でライバルに勝つでしょう〉
- ◎ A She'll beat [outrun] her rivals in the 100 meter-dash.
- ◎ B She'll do better than her rivals in the 100 meter-dash.
- ◎ C She'll run faster than her rivals in the 100 meter-dash.
- ○ D She'll outdo her rivals in the 100 meter-dash.
- × E She'll outdistance her rivals in the 100 meter-dash.
  - ❖ E は辞典に出ているが使われていない.

b）競泳

〈彼女は 100 メートルのレースですべてのライバルに勝つでしょう〉
- ◎ A She'll beat [outswim] all her rivals in the 100 meter race.
- ◎ B She'll do better than all her rivals in the 100 meter race.
- ◎ C She'll swim faster than all her rivals in the 100 meter race.
- ○ D She'll outdo all her rivals in the 100 meter race.

c）テニス・ゴルフのような個人スポーツ

〈テニスでは彼に勝てる人はいない〉
- ☆ A No one can beat him in tennis.
- ○ B No one can outplay [surpass, outdo] him in tennis.
- ○ C No one can do [play] better than him in tennis.

d）野球・フットボールのような団体スポーツ

〈早稲田が慶応に勝った〉
- ◎ A Waseda beat Keio.
- △ B Waseda defeated Keio.
- △ C Waseda got the better of Keio.
- × D Waseda carried the day over Keio.
  - ❖(1) D は辞典に出ているが使われていない.
  - ❖(2) 新聞・テレビなどのスポーツキャスターの間では B, C はよく使われている.

がっかりさせる →がっかりだ

がっかりだ

1 《努力したとき》

〈私はまた司法試験に失敗したのでがっかりしているんです〉
- ☆ A I'm discouraged because I've failed the bar exam again.
- ◎ B I'm disappointed because I've failed the bar exam again.
- △ C I'm disheartened because I've failed the bar exam again.
  - ❖ A は努力して失敗し, もう続けられないというニュアンス. B, C は失敗してがっかりしたという失望の気持ちを述べているにすぎず, 続けられないという響きはない.「がっくりしている」の項も参照のこと.

2 《努力を伴わないとき》

a）成人の友人間の場合
〈ジェーン：パーティーに行けないんです〉
Jane: I can't come to the party.
〈ビル：がっかりだな〉
Bill:
- ◎ A I'm sorry to hear that.
- ◎ B That's too bad.
- ◎ C That's a shame.
- ○ D I'm disappointed.
- ○ E That's disappointing.
- △ F That's a pity.
- ▽ G That's regretful.
  ❖ F, G はお年寄りの間，特に年配の女性の間ではよく使われている．

b）友人，親子の間の場合
〈父親：雨が降り出した．ピクニックは延期だ〉
Father: It's started to rain. The picnic's off.
〈息子：がっかりだな〉
Son:
- ◎ A That's great [terrific].
- ◎ B That's a bummer [drag].
- ◎ C That's too bad.
- △ D Oh, boy.
- △ E That's a letdown.
- △ F That's letting me down.
  ❖ A〜F いずれも下降調で述べる．Aを上昇調で言うと「それはすばらしい」の意味になる．

3 《がっかりさせる》
a）親から子供へ
〈がっかりさせないでね〉
- ◎ A Don't let me down.
- ◎ B Don't leave me hanging.
- ◎ C Don't let me be disappointed.
- ○ D Don't disappoint me.
- △ E Don't make me disappointed.

b）友人
〈がっかりさせないでくれよ〉
- ◎ A Don't leave me hanging.
- ◎ B Don't let me down.
- ◎ C Don't disappoint me.
- △ D Don't make me disappointed.
- ▽ E Don't get me disappointed.

c）ビジネス上の会話で
〈がっかりさせないで下さい〉
- ☆ A Please don't disappoint me.
- ◎ B Please don't let me down.
- ○ C Please don't leave me hanging.
- △ D Please don't make me disappointed.
- △ E Please don't let me be disappointed.
- △ F Please don't fail me.

活気づける
〈政府は景気を活気づけるために，税金を下げるべきです〉
- ▽ G Please don't get me disappointed.
- ◎ The government should lower taxes to jump-start [stimulate, boost] the economy.

がっくりしている
〈彼は司法試験にまた落ちてがっくりしているんです〉
- ☆ A He failed the bar again. He's depressed.
- ◎ B He failed the bar again. He's down in the dumps.
- ○ C He failed the bar again. He's downhearted.
- ○ D He failed the bar again. He's down in the mouth.
- ○ E He failed the bar again. He's feeling blue.
- ○ F He failed the bar again. He's feeling discouraged.
  - ❖ Aが一番強い．Fが2番目，以下BCDEの順．「がっかりだ」の項も参照のこと．

かっけ →病気 7

かっこいい
1 《鼻・口など》
〈彼女の鼻はかっこいい〉
- ☆ A She has a nice nose.
- ◎ B She has a pretty nose.
- ◎ C She has a beautiful nose.
- ○ D She has a lovely nose.
- △ E She has a sleek nose.
- × F She has a shapely nose.
  - ❖(1) 辞典にFが出ているが使われていない．
  - ❖(2) 強さの点ではCが1番，D，Eが2番，Bが3番，Aが4番．

2 《車》
〈彼はすごくかっこいい車を持っている〉
- ☆ A He has a hot car.
- ◎ B He has a great [an awesome, an amazing, a cool, a beautiful] car.
- ◎ C He has a really nice [sweet] car.
- ○ D He has a fantastic [an incredible, a slick, a sleek] car.
- ○ E He has a really pretty car.
- × F He has a groovy [swinging, smart, street, nifty] car.
  - ❖ 辞典にFが出ているが使われていない．

3 《帽子・ハンドバッグなど》
〈彼女はすごくかっこいい帽子を持っています〉
- ◎ A She has a really nice hat.
- ◎ B She has a great [terrific, beautiful] hat.
- ○ C She has a fantastic [an awesome, a cool, an incredible, an amazing] hat.
- ○ D She has a really pretty hat.

学校
1 《小中高生》
〈彼女は今学校にいます〉
- ◎ A She's at school now.
- ○ B She's in school now.

2 《自宅通学の大学生》

〈母：彼女は今学校（大学）にいます〉

Mother:
- ☆ A She's at [in] school now.
- ◎ B She's in class now.
- ○ C She's at class now.
- △ D She's at college now.
- × E She's in college now.

3 《自宅を出て寮に入っている大学生》

〈母：彼女は学校（大学）にいます〉

Mother:
- ☆ A She's away at college.
- ☆ B She's away at school.
- ◎ C She's at college.
- ○ D She's in school.
- △ E She's away in college.

4 《教師または学校の職員》

〈彼女は今学校にいます〉
- ◎ A She's at school now.
- × B She's in school now.

5 《「学校の近くに」と言うとき》

a) 通学している学生

〈彼女は学校の近くに住んでいます〉
- ◎ A She lives near the school.
- ◎ B She lives near school.
  - ❖ 英文法書には，学校を建物と見なしているときは B は使われていないと書かれているが，これは現代英語の慣用に反する．

b) 一般の人

〈彼女は学校の近くに住んでいます〉
- ◎ A She lives near the school.
- ◎ B She lives near school.

6 《父兄が学校に行くとき》

〈私は息子の先生と話すために学校へ行かなければならないんです〉
- ◎ A I have to go to the school to talk to my son's teacher.
- ◎ B I have to go to school to talk to my son's teacher.

7 《学生・教師・職員以外の人》

〈彼は天井の修理のために学校にいます〉
- ◎ A He's at the school fixing the ceilings.
- × B He's at school fixing the ceilings.
- × C He's in (the) school fixing the ceilings.
  - ❖ 「各種学校」の項も参照のこと．

かっこうのいい →かっこいい

合併する

〈XYZ 銀行は来年 ABC 銀行と合併します〉
- ◎ A XYZ Bank'll merge with ABC Bank next year.
- ○ B XYZ Bank'll be combined with ABC Bank next year.
- △ C XYZ Bank'll join [combine, unite] with ABC Bank next year.
- × D XYZ Bank'll amalgamate with ABC Bank next year.
  - ❖ D が多くの辞典に出ているが使われていない．

仮定する
〈彼女が正しいと仮定しよう〉
- ◎ A Let's assume [suppose] she's right.
- ○ B Let's presume she's right.
- × C Let's put the case she's right.
- × D Let's presuppose [postulate] she's right.
- ❖ C, D は辞典に出ているが使われていない.

悲しそうな顔
〈彼女は今朝とても悲しそうな顔をしていた〉
- ◎ A She had such a sad look on her face this morning.
- ◎ B She looked very sad this morning.
- ○ C She had such a long face this morning.
- △ D She was wearing such a long face this morning.

金物屋 →店 27

必ずしも…でない

1 《時・時間を示す語があるとき》

〈私は日曜日必ずしも家にいるわけではありません〉
- ◎ A I'm not always at home on Sundays.
- ○ B I'm not necessarily at home on Sundays.

〈私は昼間必ずしも事務所にいるわけではありません〉
- ◎ A I'm not always at the office in the daytime.
- ○ B I'm not necessarily at the office in the daytime.

2 《時・時間を示す語がないとき》

〈美しい女性が必ずしも幸せではない〉
- ◎ Beautiful women aren't necessarily [always] happy.

〈彼が言っていることが必ずしも正しいわけではありません〉
- ◎ What he says isn't necessarily [always] right.

必ず (…する)

1 《会話の場合（肯定文）》

〈彼は必ず来ます〉
- ☆ A I'm sure he'll come.
- ◎ B I'm positive he'll come.
- ◎ C He'll come for sure.
- ◎ D I'm sure about his [him] coming.
- ◎ E He's sure to come.
- ○ F It's a sure bet [thing] he'll come.
- ○ G I don't doubt he'll come.
- ○ H I'm certain he'll come.
- ○ I He's bound to come.
- ○ J He's certain to come.
- ○ K It's certain he'll come.
- △ L I'm sure of his [him] coming.
- △ M I'm certain of his [him] coming.
- △ N I'm certain about his [him] coming.
- △ O I'm positive of his [him] coming.
- △ P He'll come for certain.
- △ Q He'll surely [certainly] come.
- △ R Surely [Certainly] he'll come.
- △ S I'm positive about his [him] coming.

❖(1) 話者の確信度は B, O, S が一番強い．G, H, J, K, M, N, P, R が 2番，A, C, D, E, F, I, L, Q が 3番．
❖(2) certain, certainly, bound は会話でも使われているが，少し堅い響きがある．

2 《堅い会話，または文章英語の場合（肯定文）》
〈来春までに経済は必ず回復します〉
☆ A We're certain the economy will pick up by next spring.
☆ B It's certain that the economy will pick up by next spring.
○ C The economy will pick up by next spring for certain.
○ D We're certain of the economy's picking up by next spring.
△ E The economy will certainly pick up by next spring.
△ F Certainly the economy will pick up by next spring.

3 《主節と従節の主語が同一の場合（肯定文）》
〈私はこのビジネスに必ず成功してみせます〉
☆ A I'm sure I'll succeed in this business.
☆ B I'm positive I'll succeed in this business.
◎ C I'm sure to succeed in this business.
◎ D I'm certain to succeed in this business.
◎ E I'm bound to succeed in this business.
◎ F I'm certain I'll succeed in this business.
○ G I'm sure [certain, positive] that I'll succeed in this business.
○ H I'm sure [certain, positive] about succeeding in this business.
○ I I'm positive of succeeding in this business.
△ J I'm sure [certain] of succeeding in this business.
❖多くの辞典は C, D を不可として紹介しているが，これは現代アメリカ英語の慣用を著しく歪曲していることを，ここで強く指摘したい．

4 《疑問文の場合》
〈彼は必ず来ますか〉
☆ A Are you sure he'll come?
◎ B Are you certain [positive] he'll come?
◎ C Will he come for sure?
○ D Will he come for certain?
△ E Is he sure [certain, bound] to come?
△ F Will he surely [certainly] come?
△ G Will he come surely [certainly]?

5 《命令文の場合》
〈必ず今晩私に電話して下さい〉
☆ A Make sure you call me tonight.
◎ B Don't forget to call me tonight.
◎ C Be sure to call me tonight.
○ D Remember [Make sure] to call me tonight.
△ E Be certain to call me tonight.
× F Don't fail to call me tonight.
❖F は辞書などに出ているが使われていない．

6 《習慣的内容》
〈彼は週に1度必ず私に電話してきます〉
◎ A He never fails to call me once a week.
◎ B He calls me once a week without a fail.
○ C He calls me once a week for sure.

かなり

1 《技能》

〈彼女はかなり上手にフランス語を話します〉

- ◎ A She speaks French pretty well.
- ○ B She speaks French quite well.
- ○ C She speaks French rather well.
- ○ D She speaks French fairly well.

❖上手さの点では B が1番, C, A, D の順で下がる.

2 《収入》

〈彼はかなりいい収入があります〉

- ◎ A He has a pretty good income.
- ◎ B He has a fairly good income.
- ○ C He has a comfortable income.
- △ D He has a sizable [handsome, respectable] income.
- △ E He has a considerable income.
- ▽ F He has a rather good income.

❖A が一番収入が多いという響きがある. C, E は2番, D, F は3番, 一番少ないのは B.

3 《回数》

〈彼女はかなりしばしばテレビに出演しています〉

- ◎ A She's on TV quite often.
- ◎ B She's on TV quite a lot.
- ○ C She's on TV pretty [fairly] often.
- ▽ D She's on TV rather often.

可能性

1 《「…する可能性」と述べるとき》

〈彼女は回復する可能性が高い〉

- ☆ A She has a strong chance of recovery.
- ◎ B She has a strong possibility of recovery.
- ○ C She has a strong probability of recovery.
- △ D She has a strong likelihood of recovery.
- △ E She has a strong prospect of recovery.

❖確率の点では D が一番高く, 2番目は A, C, 3番目は B, E.

2 《「そういう可能性」と述べるとき》

〈そういう可能性はあるのですか〉

- ◎ A Is that a possibility?
- × B Is there such a possibility?

❖日本語につられて B を使いがちであろうが, A を使うのが正しい.

株

1 《株数》

〈私はあの会社の株を5万株持っています〉

- ◎ A I have fifty thousand shares in that company.
- × B I have fifty thousand stocks [interests] in that company.

2 《株を持っている会社の数に言及するとき》

〈私は3つの会社の株に投資しています〉

- ◎ A I'm investing in three different stocks.
- × B I'm investing in three different shares [interests].

3 《漠然とある会社の株に言及するとき》

〈私はこの会社の株を持っています〉

- ◎ A I hold an interest in this company.
- ◎ B I have shares [stock] in this company.
- ○ C I hold shares [stock] in this company.
- ○ D I have an interest in this company.
- × E I have stocks [a stock] in this company.
  - ❖ D は「興味がある」の意味でも使われている．しかし，「興味がある」の意味では be interested in の方がよく使われている．

4 《優良株》

〈これは優良株です〉

- ☆ A This is a blue chip stock.
- ◎ B This is a blue chip.
- △ C This is a high-grade [high-quality] stock.
- × D This is a gilt-edged stock.
  - ❖ D が辞典に出ているが使われていない．

5 《非上場株》

〈この株は非上場株です〉

- ☆ A This stock isn't listed.
- ◎ B This stock isn't public.
- ○ C This is an unlisted stock.

カフスボタン →ボタン 6

我慢する

1 《人の態度・事態》

〈私はもう彼の横柄さに我慢ができません〉

- ◎ A I can't stand [tolerate, put up with, live with] his arrogance anymore.
- △ B I can't bear [stomach] his arrogance anymore.
  - ❖ live with は一番語調が弱い．

2 《動詞を従えるとき》

〈私は彼と一緒に働くことにもう我慢できません〉

- ☆ A I can't stand working with him anymore.
- ◎ B I can't put up with working with him anymore.
- ○ C I can't stomach [bear, tolerate] working with him anymore.
- × D I can't live with working with him anymore.
  - ❖ A, C ともに不定詞を従えることはない．

雷を落とす →叱られる 3

髪の毛が長い

〈彼女の髪の毛は長い〉

- ◎ A She has long hair.
- △ B Her hair's long.
- ▽ C She wears her hair long.
  - ❖(1) C が辞典に出ているがまれ．
  - ❖(2)「彼女の目は大きい」「彼女の脚は長い」のように身体の一部を述べるときは，いつも have を使って She has big eyes. (Her eyes are big.ではない)，She has long legs. (Her legs are long.ではない) とする方が使用頻度が高い．

カメラマン →職業 26

…から

1 《時の表現の前》

a) 時間

〈パーティーは6時から始まります〉
    ☆ A The party starts at 6:00.
    ◎ B The party is from 6:00 on.
    × C The party starts from 6:00 (on).

b) 入学などの受付日
〈願書は3月4日から受付けます〉
    ◎ A Applications will be accepted starting [beginning] March 4th.
    ◎ B Applications will be accepted as of [on] March 4th.

c) 法律の施行日
〈この法律は5月1日から施行されます〉
    ◎ This law will be effective as of [on] May 1st.

2 《動詞が start のとき》

a) start 以下が数の多い課やページなどを従えるとき
〈10課から始めましょう〉
    ◎ A Let's start with Lesson 10.
    ○ B Let's start from Lesson 10.

〈55ページから始めましょう〉
    ◎ A Let's start with Page 55.
    ○ B Let's start from Page 55.

b) start 以下が単一のこと，または名詞を従えるとき
〈日本を発つ前にやることがたくさんある．車を売ることから始めよう〉
    ◎ A We have a lot to do before we leave Japan. Let's start with selling the car.
    × B We have a lot to do before we leave Japan. Let's start from selling the car.

〈数学とフランス語の期末試験の勉強をしなければならない．数学から始めよう〉
    ◎ A We have to study for our math and French finals. Let's start with math.
    × B We have to study for our math and French finals. Let's start from math.

3 《落下するとき》

a) 馬
〈彼は馬から落ちたんです〉
    ◎ A He fell off his horse.
    △ B He fell from his horse.

b) 橋
〈彼は橋から落ちたんです〉
    ◎ A He fell off the bridge.
    △ B He fell from [over] the bridge.

c) がけ
〈彼はがけから落ちたんです〉
    ☆ A He fell over the cliff.
    ◎ B He fell off the cliff.
    ○ C He fell from the cliff.

d) 木
〈彼は木から落ちたんです〉
    ◎ A He fell out of the tree.
    △ B He fell from the tree.
    × C He fell off the tree.

e）電車
〈彼は電車から落ちたんです〉
- ◎ A He fell off the train.
- △ B He fell from the train.
- × C He fell over the train.

4 《金額》

〈客：スーツを作ってもらうのにいくらかかりますか〉
Customer: How much does it cost to have a suit made?
〈テーラー：500ドルからあります〉
Tailor:
- ◎ A It starts at [from] $500.
- ◎ B It costs $500 and up.
- ◎ C The low end is $500 and up.
- ◎ D Prices start at $500.
- ○ E The range starts at $500.

辛い

1 《味》

a）料理

〈朝鮮料理は辛いです〉
- ◎ Korean food's hot [spicy].

b）チーズ

〈私は辛いチーズが好きです〉
- ◎ A I like sharp cheese.
- ○ B I like tangy cheese.
- △ C I like spicy cheese.

c）ドレッシング

〈私は辛いドレッシングが好きです〉
- ☆ A I like tangy dressing.
- ◎ B I like spicy dressing.
- × C I like sharp dressing.
    - ❖ C が辞典に出ているが使われていない．

d）ワイン

〈私は辛いワインが好きです〉
- ◎ A I like dry wine.
- × B I like spicy [hot] wine.

e）塩辛い

〈塩辛い食べ物は避けておきなさい〉
- ◎ A Stay away from salty food.
- ○ B Stay away from food with a lot of salt.

2 《教師の答案・レポートの採点》

〈今度の先生は点が辛い〉
- ☆ A Our new teacher's demanding in grading.
- ◎ B Our new teacher's strict in grading.
- ○ C Our new teacher's severe in grading.
- × D Our new teacher's severe in marking.
    - ❖辞典に D が出ているが使われていない．

ガラス工場　→工場 10

体

1 《文字通り体を意味しているとき》

a）体の中
〈血は体中を循環しています〉
- ◎ A Blood circulates through［around］the body.
- ○ B Blood circulates through［around］the system.

b）売春
〈彼女は体を売って生活しているんです〉
- ☆ A She's making a living selling her body.
- ◎ B She's making a living through selling her body.
- ○ C She's making a living through selling herself.
- △ D She's making a living selling herself.

c）洗う
〈私は背中が痛いんです．だから体が洗えないんです〉
- ◎ A I have a backache, so I can't wash myself.
- × B I have a backache, so I can't wash my body.

d）酷使・頑張り
〈私は家族を養うために体を張っているんです〉
- ◎ A I'm killing myself to support my family.
- ○ B I'm sacrificing myself to support my family.
- ○ C I'm supporting my family at the expense of my health.
- × D I'm supporting my family at the sacrifice of my health.
- ❖ D が辞典に出ているが使われていない．

2 《健康》

a）何かが体に良い・悪いと述べるとき
〈野菜は体にいいですよ〉
- ☆ A Vegetables're good for your health.
- ◎ B Vegetables're good for one's health.
- ○ C Vegetables're good for our health.
- △ D Vegetables're good for the health.

b）注意を求めるとき
〈体に気をつけて下さい〉
- ☆ A Take care of yourself.
- ◎ B Take care of your health.
- △ C Be careful of your health.
- × D Take care of your body.
- × E Be careful of your body.

c）取り柄・財産であることを述べるとき
〈体が丈夫なのが私の唯一の取り柄です〉
- ◎ A Good health's my only asset.
- ○ B Being healthy's my only asset.

3 《反射的になるまでの意味の「体で」》
〈体で覚えるまで練習しなさい〉
- ☆ A Practice makes perfect.
- ◎ B You have to practice until it's second nature.
- ◎ C You have to practice until it comes naturally.
- ○ D You have to practice until you can do it automatically.

借りがある
〈彼は私が批判されたとき支持してくれたんです．だから私は彼に借りがあるんです〉
- ◎ A He was supportive of me when I was criticized, so I owe him.
- △ B He was supportive of me when I was criticized, so I'm indebted［in

debt] to him.

借りる

1 《移動できないものを借りるとき》
〈手洗いを借りてもいいですか〉
- ◎ A Can I use the bathroom?
- × B Can I borrow the bathroom?
- × C Can I have the use of the bathroom?
    - ❖ C は辞典に出ているが使われていない．

2 《移動できるものを借りるとき》
〈傘を借りてもいいですか〉
- ◎ Can I use [borrow] your umbrella?

3 《借りる時を明示しているとき》
〈お父さん，今晩車を借りてもいいですか〉
- ☆ A Dad, can I borrow your car, tonight?
- ◎ B Dad, can I use [take] your car, tonight?
- ○ C Dad, can I have your car, tonight?

4 《借りている期間を尋ねるとき》
〈いつまでこのカメラを借りられますか〉
- ◎ How long can I keep [have, borrow, use] this camera?

5 《図書館で本を借りるとき》
〈1度に何冊借りられるのですか〉
- ◎ A How many books can I check [take] out at a time?
- △ B How many books can I borrow at a time?

6 《お金を借りるとき》
a）友人から
〈給料日まで500ドル借りられますか〉
- ☆ A Can I borrow $500 until payday?
- ◎ B Can I get [have] a loan of $500 until payday?
- ○ C Can I have [get] $500 until payday?

b）友人以外の人から
〈給料日まで500ドルお借りできますか〉
- ☆ A Can I borrow $500 until payday?
- ○ B Can I get [have] a loan of $500 until payday?

c）銀行から
〈私はXYZ銀行からお金を借りているんです〉
- ☆ A I owe XYZ Bank.
- ○ B I'm in debt to XYZ Bank.
- ○ C I have a debt with [to] XYZ Bank.

d）金額を明示して述べるとき
〈私はXYZ銀行から5000万円借りているんです〉
- ◎ A I owe XYZ Bank ¥50,000,000.
- △ B I owe ¥50,000,000 to XYZ Bank.
- △ C I have a ¥50,000,000 debt with XYZ Bank.
- △ D I have ¥50,000,000 in debt to XYZ Bank.

7 《有料で借りるとき》
a）短期間（数時間から数日間）借りるとき
〈車を借りよう〉
- ◎ A Let's rent a car.
- ◎ B Let's hire a car.

かわりをする　145

　❖ A はアメリカ英語，B はイギリス英語で共に非常によく使われている．
b) 数年借りるとき
〈私はこのアパートを 1 ヶ月 700 ドルで借りています〉
　　◎ A I'm renting this apartment for $700 a month.
　　◎ B I rent this apartment for $700 a month.
c) 長年借りるとき
〈私はこの事務所を 1 ヶ月 800 ドルで借りています〉
　　◎ A I'm leasing this office space for $800 a month.
　　◎ B I lease this office space for $800 a month.
8 《レンタカーを借りるとき》
〈小型の車を 2 日間お借りできますか〉
　　☆ A Can I rent a small car for two days?
　　◎ B Can I have a small car for two days?
　　◎ C I'd like to have a small car for two days.
　　◎ D I'd like a small car for two days.

カルテ
1 《病院で医師と話している》
〈患者：カルテを見せてもらえますか〉
Patient:
　　◎ A Can I see my chart?
　　○ B Can I see my medical chart?
　　× C Can I see my clinical chart?
　　❖ C は辞典に出ているが使われていない．
2 《幼時からのかかりつけの医師と話している》
〈患者：カルテを見せてもらえますか〉
Patient:
　　◎ A Can I see my medical records?
　　△ B Can I see my (medical) charts?

画廊　→店 40

可愛い
1 《子供》
〈2 人には可愛い娘がいるんです〉
　　☆ A They have a cute little girl.
　　◎ B They have an adorable girl.
　　◎ C They have a pretty little girl.
　　○ D They have a pretty little thing.
　　❖(1) 可愛さの点では B が 1 番，C, D が 2 番，A が 3 番．
　　❖(2) B, D は 5, 6 歳，A, C は 8 歳くらいまでの子供に使われている．
2 《動物》
〈彼女は可愛い犬を飼っています〉
　　☆ A She has a cute dog.
　　◎ B She has an adorable dog.
　　○ C She has a beautiful dog.
　　△ D She has a pretty dog.
　　× E She has a good-looking dog.

代わりをする
1 《シフト制で働いているとき》
〈今度の金曜日シフトを代わってくれる〉
　　◎ A Can you change [switch] shifts with me this Friday?

- ○ B Can you swap shifts with me this Friday?
- ○ C Can you take my shift this Friday?

2 《非シフト制で働いているとき》

〈今度の金曜日代わってくれる〉

- ◎ A Can you fill in for me this Friday?
- ◎ B Can you work [cover] for me this Friday?
- ○ C Can you sub for me this Friday?

3 《教師として働いているとき》

〈今週の金曜日，甥の披露宴に行かなければならないんです．私の代わりをしてくれますか〉

- ◎ A I have to go to my nephew's wedding reception this Friday. Can you substitute [sub, cover, work, fill in] for me?
- ◎ B I have to go to my nephew's wedding reception this Friday. Can you take my class?

替わる

1 《政権》

〈アメリカはまもなく政権が替わります〉

- ◎ A America's going to get a new administration soon.
- ◎ B America's going to have a new president soon.
- ○ C America's going to have a new tenant in the White House soon.
- ○ D America's going to have a new administration soon.
- ○ E America's going to have a changing of the guard soon.

2 《経営陣》

〈うちの会社はまもなく経営陣が替わるんです〉

- ☆ A Our company's going to be under new management soon.
- ◎ B Our company's going to get new management soon.
- ○ C Our company's going to have new management soon.
- ○ D Our company's going to have a new administration soon.
- △ E Our company's going to have a changing of the guard soon.

3 《持主》

〈このアパートはまもなく持主が替わります〉

- ☆ A This apartment building's going to change hands soon.
- ☆ B The ownership of this apartment building's going to change soon.
- ○ C This apartment building's going to change ownership soon.
- ○ D This apartment building's going to get [have] a new owner soon.
- ○ E This apartment building's going to be under new ownership soon.

眼科医　→医者 1

考え方

1 《物の見方》

〈私の考え方はあなたのとは違います〉

- ◎ A My way of thinking's different from yours.
- ○ B My mindset's different from yours.

2 《人生に対する考え方》

〈私の人生に対する考え方は変わりました〉

- ◎　My outlook [philosophy, perspective] on life's changed.

3 《事態に対する見方》

〈事態に対する私の考え方はあなたとは違います〉

- ◎ A I don't see the situation the way you do.
- ○ B I don't see the situation in the same light [perspective] as you.

○ C I don't see the situation from the same perspective [viewpoint] as you.
　　　○ D I don't see the situation from the same point of view as you.

考える
1 《頭に浮べる》
a) 色・曜日・大学・型など考える対象を尋ねて
〈何色を考えているのですか〉
　　　◎ A What color do you have in mind?
　　　○ B What color are you thinking about [of]?
b) 漠然と尋ねるとき
〈何を考えているのですか〉
　　　◎ A What's on your mind?
　　　◎ B What're you thinking about?
2 《A を B と「みなす」》
〈私たちは彼を保守的と考えています〉
　　　☆ A We think he's conservative.
　　　◎ B We see him as being conservative.
　　　◎ C We consider him to be conservative.
　　　○ D We think of him as being conservative.
　　　△ E We consider him conservative.
　　　△ F We regard him as (being) conservative.
　　　▽ G We look upon [at] him as conservative.
　　　▽ H We eye him as conservative.
　　❖ G, H が辞典に出ているがまれ．

関係
1 《国と国の関係》
〈中国とアメリカの関係は将来悪化するだろう〉
　　　◎ A The relationship between China and America'll deteriorate in the future.
　　　◎ B The relationships between China and America'll deteriorate in the future.
　　　◎ C The relations between China and America'll deteriorate in the future.
　　❖ B は 2 つ以上の分野を頭に置いているとき，C は分野の数に関係なくいつも複数形で使う．
2 《人と人との関係》
〈彼らはあなたと私の関係をこわそうとしている〉
　　　◎ A They're trying to break the relationship between you and me.
　　　△ B They're trying to break the relations between you and me.
　　　× C They're trying to break the relationships between you and me.
3 《スキャンダル・プロジェクトなどに関与している》
〈彼はこのスキャンダルに関係があるようだ〉
　　　☆ A He seems to be involved with this scandal.
　　　◎ B He seems to be mixed up in this scandal.
　　　◎ C He seems to have something to do with this scandal.
　　　◎ D He seems to have a connection with [to] this scandal.
　　　◎ E He seems to be connected with this scandal.
　　　○ F He seems to be mixed up with this scandal.
　　　△ G He seems to be a party with [in] this scandal.

△ H He seems to be implicated with this scandal.
　4　《男と女の関係》
〈2人は関係があるようだね〉
　　　☆ A They seem to be sleeping together.
　　　◎ B They seem to be intimate.
　　　◎ C They seem to have a physical [sexual] relationship.
　　　○ D They seem to be going all the way.
　　　○ E They seem to have an intimate relationship.
　　　○ F They seem to have physical relationships.
　　　△ G They seem to be deeply involved.

歓迎会
〈明日今度の社長であるブラウン氏の歓迎会をやるんです〉
　　　◎　　Tomorrow we're going to have a welcome [welcoming] party for Mr. Brown, the new president.

関係する　→関係
観光ガイド　→職業 2
肝硬変　→病気 8
看護学校　→各種学校 3
監査部　→…部 3

感じのいい
　1　《普通に言う場合》
〈彼女は感じのいい人です〉
　　　◎ A She has a likable personality.
　　　◎ B She has a nice personality.
　　　○ C She has a pleasant personality.
　　　△ D She has a pleasing personality.
　　　❖感じのよい程度はDが一番強く，A, Cが2番目，Bは3番目で一番弱い.
　2　《強調して言う場合》
〈彼の人柄はとても感じがいい〉
　　　◎ A He has a charming personality.
　　　◎ B He has a very likable personality.
　　　○ C He has a very sweet personality.
　　　△ D He has a very pleasing [pleasant] personality.
　　　△ E He has an engaging personality.
　　　△ F He has a very winning personality.
　　　❖(1) A～Eは男性，女性，年齢に関係なく使われている．Fは40歳以上の人の間で使われている．
　　　❖(2) 日本語で「チャーミングな」は，若い女性の顔が「可愛い」と言いたいときに使われているが，英語のcharmingは男女・年齢に関係なく，容姿ではなく人柄が「感じがいい」と言うときに使われている．

患者
　1　《発生した人数のことに言及するとき》
　a）場所が主語のとき
〈昨日，東京で20人の腸チフス患者が出ました〉
　　　☆ A Yesterday Tokyo had 20 people with typhoid fever.
　　　◎ B Yesterday 20 people came down with typhoid fever in Tokyo.
　　　◎ C Yesterday Tokyo had 20 cases of typhoid fever.
　　　▽ D Yesterday Tokyo had 20 instances of typhoid fever.
　　　❖(1) A, C, DのhadはgotとしてもOじ．

❖(2) D は新聞・テレビのニュースなどではよく使われている．
　b) 病院が主語のとき
〈この病院には腸チフスの患者が 20 人います〉
　　◎ A This hospital has 20 typhoid patients.
　　◎ B This hospital has 20 people with typhoid.
　　◎ C This hospital's treating 20 people with typhoid.
　2 《経営上から患者が大勢いることに言及するとき》
　a) 医師が主語のとき
〈この医者は患者が多いです〉
　　☆ A This doctor has a lot of patients.
　　◎ B This doctor has a large practice.
　　○ C This doctor has a big practice.
　b) 病院が主語のとき
〈あの病院は患者が多いです〉
　　◎ A That hospital has a lot of patients.
　　× B That hospital has a large practice.

感謝する
　1 《普通に述べるとき》
〈ご親切ありがとうございます〉
　　◎　　Thank you very much for your kindness.
　2 《改まった調子で述べるとき》
〈ご親切本当に感謝いたします〉
　　☆ A I sincerely appreciate your kindness.
　　◎ B I'm very thankful for your kindness.
　　○ C I'm very grateful to you for your kindness.
　　△ D Much obliged.
　　△ E I'm much obliged.
　　❖ D, E は南部ではよく使われている．
　3 《少しくだけた調子で述べるとき》
〈本当にありがとう〉
　　☆ A Thanks a lot.
　　◎ B Thanks so much.
　　○ C Thanks a million.
　　○ D Thanks a bunch.
　　○ E Many thanks.
　　△ F Thanks a great deal.
　　× G A thousand [million] thanks.
　　× H Thanks awfully.
　　❖(1) G, H が辞典に出ているが使われていない．
　　❖(2) C が一番感謝の度合いが強い．A が 2 番，D が 3 番，B が 4 番，E, F が 5 番．
　4 《感謝の理由に言及するとき》
　a)「…してくれてありがとう」と述べるとき
〈お電話ありがとう〉
　　◎　　Thank you for calling.
　b) してくれたすべてのことにお礼を述べるとき
〈いろいろありがとう〉
　　☆ A Thank you for everything.
　　◎ B Thank you for everything you've done for me.

◎ C Thank you for all the things you've done for me.
○ D Thank you for all you've done for me.
○ E Thank you for all the stuff you've done for me.

5 《レストランなどでウエイターなどに軽く感謝するとき》
〈どうも〉
  ◎ A Thank you.
  ◎ B Thanks.
  ❖ A は you を強調して述べる．

6 《強く感謝の気持ちを表すとき》
〈お礼の申しようがありません〉
  ◎ A I can't thank you enough.
  ○ B I can't thank you too much.
  ❖ A の方が B よりも感謝の気持ちは強い．

勘定

1 《バーで》
〈勘定を持ってきてくれますか〉
  ☆ A Will you bring me the tab?
  ◎ B Will you bring me the check [bill]?

2 《レストランで》
〈勘定を持ってきてくれますか〉
  ◎ A Will you bring me the check [bill]?
  × B Will you bring me the tab?

肝心な

1 《肝心な試合》
〈ジャイアンツは勝てば首位にたてた肝心な試合を落としたんです〉
  ◎ A The Giants lost the key game that'd have put them in first place.
  ◎ B The Giants lost the crucial game that'd have put them in first place.
  ◎ C The Giants lost the critical [decisive] game that'd have put them in first place.
  ◎ D The Giants lost the important game that'd have put them in first place.
  ○ E The Giants lost the determining [essential] game that'd have put them in first place.
  △ F The Giants lost the vital game that'd have put them in first place.
  △ G The Giants lost the indispensable game that'd have put them in first place.
  ❖ 重要さの点では C, E が一番強い．2番目は A, G, 3番目は B, F, 4番目は D．

2 《肝心なとき》
〈彼は肝心なときに病気になったんです〉
  ◎ A He got ill at a critical point.
  ○ B He got ill at a decisive [a crucial, an important] point.

3 《肝心な点》
〈それが肝心な点です〉
  ☆ A That's the main point.
  ◎ B That's the (important) point.
  ○ C That's the vital point.
  ○ D That's the name of the game.
  ▽ E That's the be-all and end-all.

▽ F That's the essential point.

関税 →税金 5

完全に

1 《ヒーターを消すとき》
〈ヒーターを完全に消してください〉
◎ A Turn the heater all the way off.
△ B Turn the heater off completely.

2 《窓を開けるとき》
〈窓を完全に開けて下さい〉
◎ A Open the windows all the way.
△ B Open the windows completely.

3 《同意するとき》
〈私は完全にあなたに同意します〉
◎ A I agree with you completely.
◎ B I totally [absolutely] agree with you.
◎ C I agree with you a hundred and ten percent.
○ D I agree with you totally.
○ E I agree with you without any doubt.

4 《間違っているとき》
〈あなたは完全に間違っていますよ〉
☆ A You're completely [totally] wrong.
◎ B You're absolutely wrong.
○ C You're entirely wrong.

官庁街 →…街 2
かん詰工場 →工場 8
館内電話 →電話 8

乾杯する

〈彼の成功に乾杯しよう〉
◎ A Let's make a toast to his success.
◎ B Let's drink to his success.
○ C Let's drink a toast to his success.
○ D Let's toast his success.
△ E Let's give a toast to his success.
△ F Let's toast to his success.
❖ A, B, C, E, F は成功する前，または成功した後の両方に使える．しかし，D は成功した後にしか使えない．

看板

1 《掲示》
〈店には看板が出ていますか〉
◎ A Does the store have a sign?
◎ B Is there a sign on the store?
◎ C Does the store have a sign up?
× D Is there a signboard on the store?
❖(1) D は辞典に出ているが使われていない．
❖(2) C は臨時に出しているという響きがある．

2 《比喩的に》
〈彼女は店の看板です〉
◎ A She attracts customers.
△ B She draws people to the store.

×　C　She draws to the store.

看病する

1　《いろいろなことをして看病したとき》

〈私は1晩中病気の母を看病しました〉

◎　I nursed [tended to, cared for, took care of] my sick mother all night.

2　《じっと見守って看病したとき》

〈私は1晩中病気の母を看病しました〉

◎　I watched over [sat up with] my sick mother all night.

幹部

1　《市役所・県庁など》

〈彼は市役所の幹部です〉

◎　A　He's a senior [high-ranking] city official.
◎　B　He has a senior [high-ranking] city job.
◎　C　He has a senior [high-ranking] city position.
◎　D　He has a high-ranking job [position] at city hall.

2　《政党・労組など》

〈彼は共和党の幹部です〉

◎　A　He's a senior [high-ranking] executive of the Republican Party.
◎　B　He's a senior [high-ranking] executive for the Republican Party.
◎　C　He's an executive member for the Republican Party.
○　D　He's an executive member of the Republican Party.
○　E　He's an executive officer of [for] the Republican Party.

歓楽街　→…街　5
管理職　→地位　3
管理人　→職業　15

官僚

1　《単に官僚と述べるとき》

〈彼は財務省の官僚です〉

◎　A　He's a Treasury Department official.
◎　B　He's an official at the Treasury Department.
◎　C　He has a position at the Treasury Department.
◎　D　He has a Treasury Department position.

❖A, Bの方がC, Dより地位が高いという響きがある.

2　《高級官僚と述べるとき》

a）所属官庁名を言及しないとき

〈彼は高級官僚です〉

◎　A　He's a top-ranking [high-ranking, senior] government official.
◎　B　He has a top-ranking [high-ranking] government position [job].
△　C　He has a senior government position [job].
×　D　He's a high-ranking bureaucrat.

❖(1) 日本語の「高級官僚」に相当する英語はA〜Dである.

❖(2) どの辞典にもDのbureaucratに「官僚」の訳語が出ている. しかし, 日本語の「官僚」には否定的なニュアンスはあまりないのに対し, 英語のbureaucratには以下の例のようにいつも否定的な響きがあり, 政治家・ロビイストにも広く使われている.

・That senator's a typical Washington bureaucrat.（あの上院議員は典型的なワシントンの官僚政治家なんです）

・I lost my passport in France, so I went to the American Consulate.

But a guy I talked to first didn't help me. He was such a bureaucrat. I got so angry. I was really sick and tired of him. I finally spoke with the top guy in the section. He was able to help me. (私はフランスでパスポートをなくしたんです。それでアメリカ領事館へ行きました。でも、私が最初に相談した男の人は助けてくれなかったんです。彼はすごく官僚的でした。私は腹が立ち、彼に本当にうんざりしました。ついに私はその課の一番上の人と相談したんです。彼は力になってくれました)

❖(3) A, B, C いずれも中央政府,地方政府の両方に広く使われている.

b) 所属官庁名を明示するとき

〈彼は財務省の高級官僚です〉

- ◎ A He's a top-ranking [high-ranking, senior] official at [in, with] the Treasury Department.
- ◎ B He has a top-ranking [high-ranking] position at [in, with] the Treasury Department.
- ○ C He has a senior position at [in, with] the Treasury Department.
- △ D He has a senior job at [in, with] the Treasury Department.

3 《下級官僚》

〈彼は下級官僚です〉

- ☆ A He's a low-ranking [minor] government official.
- ◎ B He's a low-level government official.
- ○ C He's a low-ranking official.
- △ D He's a minor-level official.

❖ A〜D はいずれも中央政府の意味でも地方政府の意味でも使われている. はっきりさせたいときは He's a Treasury Department official. と明示する必要がある.

緩和する

1 《外国人の入国制限》

〈政府は外国人の入国制限を緩和すべきである〉

- ☆ A The government should ease its restrictions on immigration.
- ◎ B The government should relax [let up on] its restrictions on immigration.
- ○ C The government should soften [loosen, go easy on] its restrictions on immigration.

2 《産業界への規制》

〈政府が銀行の多くの規制を緩和しなければ景気は回復しないでしょう〉

- ☆ A Unless the government eases up a lot of the regulations on banking, the economy won't pick up.
- ◎ B Unless the government eases up [relaxes, loosens, lets up on] a lot of the banking regulations, the economy won't pick up.
- ◎ C Unless the government eases up [relaxes, lets up on] the banking regulations in many ways, the economy won't pick up.
- ○ D Unless the government relaxes [loosens, lets up on, cuts down on] a lot of the regulations on banking, the economy won't pick up.
- ○ E Unless the government loosens [cuts down on] the banking regulations in many ways, the economy won't pick up.
- ○ F Unless the government cuts down on a lot of the banking regulations, the economy won't pick up.

3 《交通渋滞》

a) 場所を明示しないで言うとき

〈この新しい高速道路で交通渋滞は緩和されるでしょう〉
- ◎ A This new highway'll ease traffic.
- ◎ B This new highway'll reduce [decrease] the amount of traffic (jams).
- ◎ C This new highway'll reduce the number of traffic (jams).
- ○ D This new highway'll ease [relieve] the traffic.

b）場所を明示して言うとき

〈この新しい高速道路で東京の中心街の交通渋滞は緩和されるでしょう〉
- ◎ A This new highway'll ease the traffic in downtown Tokyo.
- ◎ B This new highway'll reduce [decrease] the amount of the traffic (jams) in downtown Tokyo.
- ◎ C This new highway'll reduce the number of the traffic (jams) in downtown Tokyo.
- ○ D This new highway'll ease the traffic jams in downtown Tokyo.
- ○ E This new highway'll relieve the traffic in downtown Tokyo.

〔き〕

気 →気が合う，気に障る，気のせいだ，気をつける，気をもませる

聞いてもらえない

〈昇給してくれるように頼んだんだけど，社長に聞いてもらえなかった〉
- ◎ A I asked for a raise but the boss ignored me.
- ◎ B I asked for a raise but the boss didn't listen to me.
- △ C I asked for a raise but the boss didn't pay attention to me.
- ▽ D I asked for a raise but the boss turned a deaf ear to me.

議員

1 《国会議員》

a）アメリカ

・上院議員

〈彼は上院議員です〉
- ☆ A He's a senator.
- ◎ B He's in the Senate.
- ◎ C He's a member of the Senate.
- △ D He's in Congress.
- ▽ E He's a member of Congress.

・下院議員

〈彼女は下院議員です〉
- ◎ A She's a member of Congress.
- ◎ B She's a Congresswoman.
- ○ C She's a member of the House.
- △ D She's in Congress.
- △ E She's a member of the House of Representatives.
- △ F She's a Congressman.
- × G She's a Congressperson.

b）日本

・衆議院議員

〈彼は衆議院議員です〉
- ☆ A He's a Congressman.

- ◎ B He's in Congress.
- ◎ C He's a member of Congress.
- ◎ D He's a member of the House (of Representatives).
- × E He's a Diet member.
- × F He's a member of the Diet.
    - ❖ E, F がどの辞典にも出ているが，英米では全く使われていない．したがって，「食餌療法をしている一員」という意味に誤解される．

・参議院議員

〈彼は参議院議員です〉

- ☆ A He's a Congressman.
- ◎ B He's in Congress.
- ◎ C He's a member of Congress.
- × D He's a member of the House of Councilors.
- × E He's a member of the Diet.
- × F He's a Diet member.
    - ❖(1) E, F が辞典に出ているが使われていない．
    - ❖(2) D は英米いずれでも使われていないが「食餌療法をしている一員」の意味になる E, F と違って誤解はされない．

2　《市会議員》

〈私は市会議員です〉

- ◎ A I'm on the city council.
- ◎ B I'm a city council member.
- ◎ C I'm a member of the city council.
- ▽ D I'm on the city assembly.
- ▽ E I'm on the municipal council [assembly].
- ▽ F I'm a municipal council member.
- ▽ G I'm a city [municipal] assembly member.
- ▽ H I'm a member of the city assembly.
- ▽ I I'm member of the municipal council.
    - ❖ D～I が辞典に出ているがあまり使われていない．

3　《町会議員》

〈彼は町会議員です〉

- ◎ A He's a member of the town council.
- ○ B He's on the town council.
- △ C He's a town council member.

気が合う

1　《恋人同士》

a) 初めて会ったとき

〈私たちは初めて会ったときとても気が合ったんです〉

- ◎ 　We really clicked [hit it off] the first time we met.

b) しばらく交際して

〈私たちはとても気が合うんです〉

- ◎ A He's really my soul-mate.
- ◎ B There's really good chemistry between us.
- ◎ C We have really good chemistry.
- ○ D We really click.
- ○ E He and I really click.
- ○ F We're like two peas in a pod.
- × G He's really my kindred spirit.

156 きかくぶ

　　❖ G が多くの辞典に出ているが使われていない．
　2 《女性同士》
　〈彼女と私は（私たちは）とても気が合うんです〉
　　　◎ A She and I really click.
　　　◎ B I really click with her.
　　　◎ C We really click.
　　　○ D We really get along.
　　　○ E I really get along with her.
　3 《男性同士》
　〈私たちは（私と彼は）とても気が合うんです〉
　　　◎ A We really get along.
　　　○ B We really click.
　　　○ C I really get along with him.

企画部　→…部 4
聞き覚えがない
　〈その名前は聞き覚えがありません〉
　　　◎ A That name doesn't ring a bell.
　　　◎ B That name doesn't sound familiar.
　　　◎ C That name doesn't click.
聞き違える
　〈あなたは私が言ったことを聞き違えたんだと思います〉
　　　◎ A I think you heard me wrong.
　　　○ B I think you misheard me.
　　❖辞典には B が出ているが，A の方が非常によく使われている．
企業
　1 《一般的に述べるとき》
　〈私は大きな企業に勤めたいんです〉
　　　☆ A I want to get a job at a big company.
　　　◎ B I want to get a job at a big business [firm].
　　　× C I want to get a job at a big enterprise.
　　❖ C が辞書に出ているが使われていない．
　2 《大企業・小企業を並列または併記してなくとも，念頭に置いて述べるとき》
　〈共和党は大企業の間で支持者が多い〉
　　　◎ A The Republican Party has a lot of supporters among big business.
　　　○ B The Republican Party has a lot of supporters among big businesses [companies].
　　❖英和・和英辞典はどれも「企業」には判で押したように enterprise を大きく紹介している．また，日本の英字新聞も enterprise を乱用している．しかし，口語英語では enterprise は全く使われておらず，文章英語でもまれに使われる程度．

効く
　1 《一般的に述べるとき》
　〈薬剤師：この薬はあなたの風邪に効くでしょう〉
　Pharmacist:
　　　◎ A This medicine'll work for [on] your cold.
　　　◎ B This medicine'll do the trick for your cold.
　　　◎ C This medicine'll help your cold.
　　　◎ D This medicine'll be good for your cold.
　　　○ E This medicine'll be effective for [on] your cold.

- △ F This medicine'll have an effect on your cold.
- × G This medicine'll have an effect for your cold.
- × H This medicine'll take effect on [for] your cold.
- × I This medicine'll be efficacious for your cold.
- ❖ G, H, I が辞典に出ているが使われていない．

2 《時間に言及するとき》

〈この薬を飲みなさい．30分かそこらしたら効きますよ〉

- ◎ A Take this medicine. It'll kick in, in half an hour or so.
- ◎ B Take this medicine. It'll take effect [do the trick, work] in half an hour or so.
- ◎ C Take this medicine. It'll be good in half an hour or so.
- ○ D Take this medicine. It'll have an effect on in half an hour or so.
- ○ E Take this medicine. It'll be effective in half an hour or so.
- △ F Take this medicine. It'll do its thing in half an hour or so.

聞く・聴く

1 《耳にする》

〈ビル：ブラウン教授は重病なんだよ〉

Bill: Professor Brown's very ill.

〈ジム：そのように聞いています〉

Jim:

- ◎ A That's what I understand [heard].
- ◎ B That's what they say [told me].
- ◎ C Yes, I heard that.
- ◎ D So I heard.
- ◎ E So they [people] say.
- ○ F So rumor has it.
- ○ G So it's said.
- ○ H So I understand.
- × I Yes, I heard so.

2 《聞き入れる》

〈あなたは彼の助言を聴いたほうがいいよ〉

- ☆ A You'd better take his advice.
- ◎ B You'd better follow his advice.
- ○ C You'd better listen to his advice.

器具

1 《医療器具》

〈私は医療器具の会社に勤めています〉

- ☆ A I work for a medical supply company.
- ◎ B I work for a medical supplies company.
- ○ C I work for a medical instrument [equipment] company.
  - ❖ C の instrument は注射器，聴診器などの小さいものを，equipment はレントゲン，入院用のベッドのような大きいものをいう．A, B の supply, supplies は大小に関係なく医療器具すべてを含んで使われている．

2 《運動器具》

〈あのジムにはたくさんの運動器具があります〉

- ◎ That gym has a lot of exercise machines [equipment].

3 《農機具》

〈うちは農機具を作っています〉

- ☆ A We're making farming equipment.

- ○ B We're making farming [farm] machines.
- ○ C We're making farming [farm] machinery.
- ○ D We're making farming [farm] tools.
- × E We're making farm appliances.
  - ❖ A は大きい機具，B，C は大小どちらにも使える．D は「シャベル」のような小さいもの．

4 《電気器具》

〈うちは電気器具を作っています〉

- ☆ A We're making appliances.
- ◎ B We're making electric instruments.
- ◎ C We're making electric equipment.
- ○ D We're making electric appliances.
- ○ E We're making electric devices.
- × F We're making electric apparatuses [outfits].
  - ❖(1) 辞典に F が出ているが使われていない．
  - ❖(2) A は洗濯機，冷蔵庫など比較的大きいもの，B は電動歯ブラシのような小さいもの，C は変圧器のように大きいもの，D はアイロン，トースターのような小さいものをいう．E は大小どちらの道具にも使われている．

危険な

1 《場所のとき》

〈今私たちのいる所は危険な場所だから油断しないで下さい〉

- ☆ A We're in a bad neighborhood, so be alert.
- ◎ B We're in a tough [rough] neighborhood, so be alert.
- ◎ C We're on the bad side of town [the city], so be alert.
- ◎ D We're on the wrong side of town [the city], so be alert.
- ◎ E We're in a bad part of town [the city], so be alert.
- ○ F We're in the bad side of the city, so be alert.
- △ G We're in the wrong side of the city, so be alert.
  - ❖ 厳密には危険な地域が複数あるときは定冠詞の the ではなく不定冠詞の a が正しい．しかし，この区別は守られていない．

2 《都市・町・地域のとき》

〈ニューヨークは危険な都市です〉

- ◎ New York's a dangerous [tough, rough] city.

3 《提案・助言・意見》

〈あなたの提案は私たちにとって危険です〉

- ◎ A Your proposal's dangerous for [to] us.
- ▽ B Your proposal's hazardous for [to] us.
- × C Your proposal's perilous for [to] us.

4 《人》

〈彼は危険な人です〉

- ◎ He's a dangerous [scary] guy.

5 《病状》

〈彼の容態は危険なんです〉

- ◎ A He's in critical condition.
- × B He's in dangerous condition.

生地

1 《具体的な生地に言及しているとき》

〈ドレスの色は好きですが，生地がよくないですね〉

- ◎ A I like the color of the dress but the fabric's no good.

◎ B I like the color of the dress but the material's no good.

2 《具体的な生地に言及していないとき》

〈(デパートで) 生地売場はどこですか〉

◎ A Where's the fabric department?
× B Where's the material department?

〈この辺に生地屋がありますか〉

◎ A Is there a fabric store near here?
× B Is there a material store near here?

期日までに

〈教授：みなさんは期日までにレポートを提出しなければいけません〉

Professor:

◎ A You've got to hand in your paper on time.
◎ B You've got to hand in your paper on the due date.
△ C You've got to hand in your paper by the designated date.
▽ D You've got to hand in your paper by the appointed date.

❖ D が辞典に出ているがまれ.

技術部　→…部 5

基準

〈アメリカの民主主義の基準は日本での基準と違う〉

◎　The criteria [standards] for democracy in the United States're different than in Japan.

傷つく

1 《精神》

〈彼女は傷つきやすいんです〉

◎ A She gets her feelings hurt easily.
◎ B Her feelings get hurt easily.
◎ C Her feelings're easily hurt.
◎ D She's very sensitive.
◎ E She gets hurt easily.

2 《肉体》

〈彼女はけがしやすいんです〉

◎ A She gets hurt easily.
◎ B She bruises easily.

3 《家具》

〈高級な家具は傷つきやすいんです〉

◎ A Expensive furniture's easy to scratch.
○ B Expensive furniture scratches easily.
○ C Expensive furniture gets scratched easily.
× D Expensive furniture gets scratches easily.

4 《果物》

〈桃は傷つきやすいんです〉

◎ A Peaches're easy to bruise.
◎ B Peaches get bruised easily.
○ C Peaches bruise easily.
○ D Peaches get bruises easily.
△ E Peaches're easy to get bruised.

5 《瀬戸物》

〈高級な瀬戸物は傷つきやすいんです〉

◎ A Expensive china breaks easily.

- ○ B Expensive china's easy to crack.
- ○ C Expensive china cracks easily.
- ○ D Expensive china gets cracked [cracks] easily.
- △ E Expensive china's easy to get cracked [cracks].

6 《評判》

a) reputationが主語のとき

〈彼の評判はこのスキャンダルで傷つくでしょう〉

- ☆ A His reputation'll be hurt by this scandal.
- ◎ B His reputation'll be destroyed [ruined] by this scandal.
- ◎ C His reputation'll be damaged [tarnished] by this scandal.
- ○ D His reputation'll be spoiled [harmed] by this scandal.
- △ E His reputation'll be injured by this scandal.

❖強さの度合いは destroyed が1番, ruined と C が2番, A, D, E が3番.

b) 人が主語のとき

〈彼はこのスキャンダルで傷つくでしょう〉

- ☆ A He'll be hurt by this scandal.
- ◎ B He'll be disgraced by this scandal.
- ◎ C He'll be destroyed by this scandal.
- ○ D He'll be harmed by this scandal.
- △ E He'll be damaged by this scandal.

❖C が一番強い, B が2番, E が3番, D が4番, A が一番弱い.

7 《「傷ついている」状態を述べるとき》

a) 精神的に

〈彼はとても気持ちが傷ついているんです〉

- ☆ A He's very hurt.
- ◎ B He's deeply hurt.
- ○ C He's very wounded.
- ○ D He's deeply wounded.

❖D が一番ひどく傷ついている. C, B, A の順で弱くなる.

b) 家具

〈この新しいテーブルは配達されたときに傷がついていました〉

- ◎ A This new table was scratched when it was delivered.
- ◎ B This new table had a scratch on it when it was delivered.
- ◎ C This new table was damaged when it was delivered.

❖C の be damaged はテーブルの脚などが「折れている」という意味でもよく使われている.

c) 瀬戸物

〈この花びんは傷ついています〉

- ◎ A This flower vase's cracked.
- ◎ B This flower vase has a crack.
- ◎ C There's a crack in this vase.

❖A は単にひびが入っているということで, どのような割れ方かは問わない. B, C は一筋の割れ目ができているというニュアンス.

d) 果物

〈この桃は傷ついている〉

- ◎ A This peach's bruised.
- × B This peach's scratched [hurt].

帰省客

1 《単に「帰省する人」と言うとき》

〈空港は休暇の帰省客でごった返していました〉
- ◎ A The airport was jampacked with people returning from their vacation.
- △ B The airport was jampacked with returning vacationers.

2 《乗物の「乗客」の意味を言うとき》

〈空港は帰省客でごった返していた〉
- ◎ A The airport was jammed with returning passengers.
- ○ B The airport was jammed with homeward-bound passengers.

規制を撤廃する

1 《業種を限定せず一般的に述べるとき》

〈政府が多くの規制を撤廃しなければ景気は上向かないでしょう〉
- ☆ A Unless the government gets rid of regulations, the economy won't pick up.
- ◎ B Unless the government drops [throws out] regulations, the economy won't pick up.
- ○ C Unless the government does away with [removes] regulations, the economy won't pick up.
- △ D Unless the government throws away [tosses out, scraps] regulations, the economy won't pick up.

2 《特定の業界を述べるとき》

〈政府が銀行業の多くの規制を撤廃しなければ景気は上向かないでしょう〉
- ☆ A Unless the government gets rid of a lot of the regulations on banking, the economy won't pick up.
- ◎ B Unless the government removes [throws out] a lot of the regulations on banking, the economy won't pick up.
- ○ C Unless the government does away with a lot of the regulations on banking, the economy won't pick up.
- ○ D Unless the government delegulates banking, the economy won't pick up.
- △ E Unless the government throws away [tosses out, scraps] a lot of the regulations on banking, the economy won't pick up.

気絶する

〈彼女は息子さんが交通事故で死んだと聞いたとき，気絶してしまったんです〉
- ◎ A She passed out when she heard that her son had been killed in a car accident.
- ◎ B She fainted when she heard that her son had been killed in a car accident.
- × C She fainted away [went faint, swooned] when she heard that her son had been killed in a car accident.
- × D She went off in a faint when she heard that her son had been killed in a car accident.
- × E She suffered a failing faint when she heard that her son had been killed in a car accident.
- × F She was attacked with faintness when she heard that her son had been killed in a car accident.
- × G She fell [went off] into a swoon when she heard that her son had been killed in a car accident.

❖辞典に C〜G が出ているが使われていない．

偽造だ
〈この署名は偽造だ〉
- ☆ A This signature's a forgery.
- ◎ B This signature's forged.
- ○ C This signature's a fraud [a phoney, a phony].
- ○ D This signature's phoney [phony, bogus].
- △ E This signature's a fake.
- △ F This signature's fake.

❖詳細は「にせもの」の項を参照されたい.

期待する
1 《一般的に述べるとき》
〈私はあなたに大いに期待しています〉
- ☆ A I expect a lot from you.
- ◎ B I'm expecting a lot [a great deal] from you.
- ◎ C I expect a great deal from you.
- ○ D I expect a lot [a great deal] of you.

2 《改まった言い方で述べるとき》
〈私はあなたに大いに期待しています〉
- ◎ A I have high expectation of you.
- ○ B I have high expectation from you.
- △ C I have a high expectation of you.
- × D I have a high expectation from you.

生粋の
〈彼は生粋のニューヨーク人です〉
- ◎ A He's a born and bred New Yorker.
- ◎ B He's a New Yorker through and through.
- ◎ C He's a New Yorker to the core.
- ◎ D He's a hundred percent New Yorker.
- ◎ E He's a native New Yorker.
- ▽ F He's a pure [dyed-in-the-wool] New Yorker.
- ▽ G He's a through and through New Yorker.
- ▽ H He's an every inch New Yorker.
- ▽ I He's a New Yorker to the backbone.

❖(1) F～I が辞典に出ているがほとんど使われていない.
❖(2) B, C, D はニューヨーク生まれであるだけでなく典型的なニューヨーク人であるというニュアンスであるのに対して, A, E には典型的なニューヨーク人であるというニュアンスはない.

きっと…である
1 《状態動詞を従えるとき》
〈彼女はきっと私たちのことを怒っているでしょう〉
- ☆ A She has to be mad at us.
- ☆ B She's got to be mad at us.
- ☆ C She must be mad at us.
- ☆ D I'm sure she's mad at us.
- ☆ E I'm positive she's mad at us.
- ◎ F I'm certain she's mad at us.
- ◎ G I bet she's mad at us.
- ◎ H I bet you she's mad at us.
- ◎ I I'll bet [I'll betcha, I betcha] she's mad at us.

◎ J It's a sure thing [bet] she's mad at us.
◎ K It's certain she's mad at us.
❖(1) F, K は改まった響きがある．I は非常にくだけた響きがある．
❖(2) A, E が一番断定の度合いが強い．2 番目は B, F, K, 3 番目は C, D.
❖(3) I の I'll betcha..., I betcha... は中年以上の人の間では非常によく使われているが，若年になるにつれて使用頻度数は下がる．

2 《動作動詞を従えるとき》
〈きっと彼女は彼と別れるでしょう〉
☆ A I'm positive she'll break up with him.
☆ B She's sure to break up with him.
☆ C I'm sure she'll break up with him.
☆ D She's bound to break up with him.
☆ E It's a sure thing [bet] she'll break up with him.
◎ F I'm certain she'll break up with him.
◎ G She's certain to break up with him.
◎ H I bet [I'll bet, I betcha, I'll betcha] she'll break up with him.
❖ F, G には改まった響きがある．H には非常にくだけた響きがある．

着ている

1 《過去を表す》
a) 過去の習慣的内容
〈その当時アメリカ人は地味な服を着ていました〉
◎ A In those days Americans wore conservative clothes.
△ B In those days Americans were wearing conservative clothes.
▽ C In those days Americans had on conservative clothes.

b) 過去の習慣的内容を表す文で every day があるとき
〈当時彼女は毎日同じドレスを着ていました〉
◎ A She wore the same dress every day back then.
○ B She had on the same dress every day back then.
△ C She was wearing the same dress every day back then.

c) 過去の一定の期間の間
〈私は山で道に迷ったとき，同じ服を 1 ヵ月着ていました〉
☆ A When I got lost in the mountains, I wore the same dress for a month.
◎ B When I got lost in the mountains, I had the same dress on for a month.
◎ C When I got lost in the mountains, I had on the same dress for a month.
○ D When I got lost in the mountains, I was wearing the same dress for a month.

d) 過去の一時的状況
〈彼はパーティーでブルーのスーツを着ていました〉
◎ A He was wearing a blue suit at the party.
◎ B He had a blue suit on at the party.
◎ C He wore a blue suit at the party.
◎ D He was (dressed) in a blue suit at the party.

e) 動作を述べているとき
〈彼の部屋へ行ったとき，彼は服を着ているところでした〉
◎ A When I went to his room, he was getting dressed.
◎ B When I went to his room, he was putting on his clothes.

2 《現在》
a) 状態として「着ている」と述べるとき
〈素敵なドレスを着ていますね〉
    ◎ A That's a nice dress you're wearing.
    ◎ B That's a nice dress you have on.
    ▽ C That's a nice dress you're (dressed) in.
b) 名詞を修飾しているとき
〈グリーンのスーツを着ている男性をご存知ですか〉
    ◎ A Do you know the guy who's wearing the green suit?
    ◎ B Do you know the guy who has the green suit on?
    ◎ C Do you know the guy who's (dressed) in the green suit?
    ◎ D Do you know the guy (dressed) in the green suit?
    ◎ E Do you know the guy with the green suit (on)?
    ◎ F Do you know the guy wearing the green suit?
    × G Do you know the guy having the green suit on?
      ❖ G の having on は現在分詞形では使われていない．
c) 習慣的に「着ている」ことを述べるとき
〈一般的に言ってアメリカ人は日本人より派手な服を着ています〉
    ◎ A Generally speaking the Americans wear flashier clothes than the Japanese.
    ○ B Generally speaking the Americans are wearing flashier clothes than the Japanese.
    × C Generally speaking the Americans have on flashier clothes than the Japanese.
d) always, usuallyが文中にあるとき
〈彼はいつもブルーのスーツを着ています〉
    ◎ A He always wears a blue suit.
    ○ B He's always wearing a blue suit.
    ○ C He always has a blue suit on.
e) often, sometimesが文中にあるとき
〈私の母はしばしば赤いドレスを着ている〉
    ☆ A My mother often wears a red dress.
    ◎ B My mother often has a red dress on.
    ○ C My mother often has on a red dress.
    △ D My mother is often wearing a red dress.
f) no matter whereが文中にあるとき
〈彼はどこへ行くにも同じブルーのスーツを着ています〉
    ◎ A No matter where he goes, he wears the same blue suit.
    △ B No matter where he goes, he has the same blue suit on.
    ▽ C No matter where he goes, he's wearing the same blue suit.
g) wheneverが文中にあるとき
〈彼女はパーティーに行くときはいつも赤いドレスを着ています〉
    ◎ A Whenever she goes to a party, she wears a red dress.
    △ B Whenever she goes to a party, she has a red dress on.
    ▽ C Whenever she goes to a party, she's wearing a red dress.

気取っている
〈彼女は気取っている〉
    ☆ A She's a snob.
    ☆ B She's stuck-up.

◎　C　She's snobbish [snooty].
　　　○　D　She's snobby [uppity].
　　　○　E　She thinks she's all that.
　　　△　F　She has her nose in the air.
　　　×　G　She's affected.
　　　×　H　She's uppish [high-hatted, supercilious].
　　　❖ A は30歳以上，B, E は25歳以下の人の間でよく使われている．F, G は堅い文章英語ではよく使われている．

気に障る
〈彼の横柄な態度は本当に気に障るんです〉
　　　☆　A　His arrogant attitude's really getting on my nerves.
　　　☆　B　His arrogant attitude's really getting to me.
　　　☆　C　His arrogant attitude's really bugging [bothering] me.
　　　◎　D　His arrogant attitude's really annoying me.
　　　△　E　His arrogant attitude's really getting under my skin.
　　　△　F　His arrogant attitude's really disturbing me.
　　　❖ 気に障る程度は D が一番強く，E が2番，A が3番，B, C, F はほぼ同じで一番弱い．

記入する
1　《たくさん書く欄があるとき》
〈応募者：今日の新聞に載っていた仕事のことで来ました〉
Applicant: I've come about the job in today's paper.
〈受付係：この申込書に記入して，どうぞお座り下さい．スミスさんがすぐ参ります〉
Receptionist:
　　　◎　　Fill out this application and have a seat please. Mr. Smith will be right with you.

2　《書き込むことが少ないとき》
〈(旅行代理店で) お客：この余白には何を書いたらよいのですか〉
Customer: What should I write in this space?
〈切符のエージェント：そこには行き先を記入して下さい〉
Ticket Agent:
　　　◎　　Fill in the destination there.

気のせいだ
〈ジム：誰かがあなたを呼んだよ〉
Jim: Someone called you.
〈ボブ：私には聞こえなかったよ．気のせいでしょう〉
Bob:
　　　◎　A　I didn't hear anyone. You must be hearing things.
　　　○　B　I didn't hear anyone. You must be dreaming it all up.
　　　○　C　I didn't hear anyone. It must have been a figment of your imagination.
　　　○　D　I didn't hear anyone. It must have been your imagination.
　　　❖ A, B は状態と見なした表現．C, D は相手の行動を完了と見なした表現．

寄付する
1　《金額に言及しないとき》
〈私は孤児院に寄付しようと思っています〉
　　　◎　A　I'm thinking of contributing [donating] to the orphanage.
　　　◎　B　I'm thinking of making a contribution [donation, gift] to the orphanage.

- ○ C I'm thinking of making a contribution [donation] for the orphanage.
- ▽ D I'm thinking of making a contribution [donation] toward the orphanage.
  ❖辞典に D が出ているがほとんど使われていない．

2 《金額に言及するとき》

〈私は孤児院に 1 千万円寄付しようと思っています〉

- ◎ A I'm going to contribute [donate] ten million yen to the orphanage.
- ◎ B I'm going to make a contribution [a donation] of ten million yen to [for] the orphanage.

3 《少額の寄付をするとき》

〈孤児たちにクリスマスのプレゼントをするために 20 ドル寄付しよう〉

- ◎ A Let's chip [pitch] in $20 to buy some Christmas presents for the orphans.
- ○ B Let's kick [toss] in $20 to buy some Christmas presents for the orphans.
- ○ C Let's donate [contribute in] $20 to buy some Christmas presents for the orphans.
- ○ D Let's make a donation of $20 to buy some Christmas presents for the orphans.

気分を害している →怒っている 1

期末試験 →試験 7

決まる

1 《不動産》

〈(不動産屋で) 客：あの事務所はもう決まりましたか〉

Customer:
- ☆ A Is that office space taken [rented] yet?
- ◎ B Is that office space leased yet?
- ◎ C Is that office space still for rent?
- ◎ D Is that office space still available [open]?
- ○ E Is that office space occupied [leased out, rented out] yet?
- ○ F Is that office space still for lease?
- ○ G Is that office space still listed?

2 《仕事》

〈応募者：ジャパンタイムズで広告を拝見しましたが，仕事はもう決まりましたか〉

Applicant:
- ◎ A I saw your ad in *the Japan Times*. Is the job still available [open]?
- ◎ B I saw your ad in *the Japan Times*. Is the job taken?
- △ C I saw your ad in *the Japan Times*. Have you hired somebody yet?

決める

1 《買う品物を選んだとき》

〈私はこの車に決めました〉

- ◎ A I'll take this car.
- ◎ B I want (to buy) this car.
- ◎ C I've made up my mind about this car.
- ○ D I've decided on this car.
- ○ E I'll buy [get] this car.
- ○ F I've chosen this car.
- △ G I'll choose this car.

- × H I'll decided on this car.
- × I I'll make up my mind about this car.
  - ❖ Cは「買わないことに決めた」の意味でもよく使われている．どちらであるかは会話の前後で判断する．

2 《結婚披露宴・開店・取引などの日取りのとき》
〈私たちは日取りを決めなければならない〉
- ◎ We have to set [decide on, choose] the [a] date.

3 《土地の境界線》
〈私たちの土地の境界線を決めましょう〉
- ◎ Let's establish [define, determine, lay down, settle, decide on] the boundary line between our lots.

4 《出発日》
a) 友人同士で
〈出発の日は決まったの〉
- ◎ A When're you leaving?
- ◎ B Have you decided when you're leaving?
- × C Have you decided on your departure?

b) 旅行代理店で
〈ご出発はお決まりですか〉
- ☆ A When would you like me to book your departure?
- ◎ B When would you like me to book your departure for?
- ◎ C When would you like me to schedule your departure?
- ◎ D When would you like me to schedule you for your departure?
- ○ E When would you like me to book you for your departure?

5 《レストランの注文》
a) 高級レストラン
〈お決まりですか〉
- ☆ A May I take your order?
- ◎ B Are you ready to order?
- ◎ C Have you decided?
- ○ D Have you made up your mind?
- △ E Are you ready?
- △ F Have you decided yet?
- △ G Have you made up your mind yet?

b) コーヒーショップ・ダイナーなど
〈お決まりですか〉
- ◎ A Can I take your order?
- ◎ B Are you ready (to order)?
- ◎ C Have you decided yet?
- △ D Have you made up your mind yet?
- × E May I take your order?

疑問である

1 《無生物が主語の場合》
〈彼が正直であるということは疑問である〉
- ☆ A His honesty's questionable.
- ◎ B His honesty's debatable.
- ○ C His honesty's in question [in doubt].
- ▽ D His honesty's doubtful.
- × E His honesty's skeptical.

2 《人が主語の場合》
〈彼が正直であるということは私には疑問である〉
- ☆ A I'm not sure if he's honest.
- ◎ B I'm not sure of [about] his honesty.
- ◎ C I doubt if he's honest.
- ○ D I'm doubtful if he's honest.
- ○ E I'm doubtful of [about] his honesty.
- ○ F I'm not positive about his honesty.
- △ G I'm positive if he's honest or not.
- △ H I'm not positive of his honesty.
- △ I I'm skeptical about [of] his honesty.
- △ J I'm not certain of [about] his honesty.
- ▽ K I'm dubious of [about] his honesty.
- × L I'm questionable [debatable] about his honesty.

3 《仮主語で述べる場合》
〈彼が正直であるかどうかは疑問である〉
- ◎ A It's doubtful whether he's honest.
- ◎ B It's questionable whether he's honest.
- ○ C It's debatable whether he's honest.
- ○ D It isn't clear whether he's honest.
- ○ E It's unclear whether [if] he's honest.
- △ F It isn't certain whether he's honest.
- △ G It's up in the air whether he's honest.
- △ H It's doubtful [questionable] if he's honest.
- ▽ I It's disputable whether he's honest.
- × J It isn't sure whether he's honest.

4 《whether節を主語にして現在の内容を述べる場合》
〈彼が正直であるか否かは疑問である〉
- ☆ A Whether he's honest or not isn't clear.
- ◎ B Whether he's honest or not is unclear [doubtful, questionable, debatable].
- ○ C Whether he's honest or not is up in the air.
- △ D Whether he's honest or not is open [subject] to question.
- △ E Whether he's honest or not is disputable [in dispute].

5 《whether節を主語にして未来の内容を述べる場合》
〈彼が成功するかどうかは疑問です〉
- ☆ A Whether he'll succeed or not isn't clear.
- ◎ B Whether he'll succeed or not is unclear [questionable].
- ◎ C Whether he'll succeed or not is up in the air.
- ○ D Whether he'll succeed or not is in question.
- ○ E Whether he'll succeed or not is subject to discussion.
- △ F Whether he'll succeed or not is in doubt [in dispute].
- △ G Whether he'll succeed or not is doubtful [disputable].

客

1 《招いた客》

a) 1人のとき

〈(電話で) 今話せないんだ. お客がいるんだよ〉
- ◎ A I can't talk to you now, I have company.
- ◎ B I can't talk to you now, I have a guest.

❖(1) A で a company とすると「会社」の意味になる．
❖(2) A の company はくだけた語で，1人か数名かは不明．
b）大勢のとき
〈今，大勢お客がいるんです〉
◎ A I have a lot of company now.
◎ B I have a lot of guests now.
❖A で a lot of companies とすると「多くの会社」の意味になる．
2 《法律事務所・会計事務所・銀行・不動産》
〈この不動産会社はお客が多い〉
◎ A This real estate agency has a lot of clients.
◎ B This real estate agency has a large clientele.
◎ C This real estate agency has a lot of customers.
❖A，B は常連で，しかも土地を買うような大口の重要なお客，C は普通1回だけのアパートを借りるような小口のお客．
3 《証券会社・広告代理店・銀行》
〈彼はうちの重要なお客です〉
◎ A He's our important client.
○ B He's our important account.
○ C He's our important customer.
❖重要な（important）がなければ C も非常によく使われている．
4 《常連客》
〈このレストランは常連客が多いんです〉
◎ A This restaurant has a lot of regular [repeat] customers.
◎ B This restaurant has a lot of regulars [repeaters].

逆
〈事態は逆なのかもしれない〉
◎ A The situation could be the other way around.
◎ B The situation could be reversed.
▽ C The situation could be the opposite.
❖C は辞典に出ているが使われてもまれ．

客観的に
〈客観的に話しましょう〉
◎ A Let's talk more objectively.
◎ B Let's talk without being [getting] emotional.
◎ C Let's talk without letting our emotions get in the way.
❖「主観的に」の項も参照のこと．

級
1 《初級》
〈私はドイツ語の初級コースを受講しています〉
☆ A I'm taking a German class for beginners.
◎ B I'm taking a German course for beginners.
◎ C I'm taking a beginners' class [course] in German.
◎ D I'm taking a beginning course in German.
◎ E I'm taking a beginning class in German.
○ F I'm taking a beginner's German course [class].
○ G I'm taking a beginning German course [class].
△ H I'm taking a German class for beginning student.
2 《中級》
〈私はドイツ語の中級コースを受講しています〉

☆ A I'm taking an intermediate German course [class].
◎ B I'm taking an intermediate course [class] in German.
△ C I'm taking a German course [class] for intermediate students.
× D I'm taking a German class for intermediate level.

3 《上級》
〈私はドイツ語の上級コースを受講しています〉
☆ A I'm taking an advanced German course [class].
◎ B I'm taking an advanced course [class] in German.
△ C I'm taking a German course [class] for advanced students.
× D I'm taking a German class for advanced level.

休暇 →休み 4
休憩する →休み 1
休日 →休み 2
吸収する
〈XYZ会社がHIJ会社を吸収するだろう〉
◎ XYZ Company'll absorb [buy out, swallow up] HIJ Company.

急落する →下がる 7
給料
1 《給料が安いと言うとき》
a) 友人間で話すとき
〈ダン：仕事を辞めようと思っているんだ〉
Dan: I'm going to quit my job.
〈ビル：どうして〉
Bill: How come?
〈ダン：給料が安いんだ〉
Dan:
◎ A It doesn't pay well (enough).
◎ B The pay's bad.
○ C They pay me peanuts [chickenfeed].
○ D The pay's peanuts [chickenfeed].

b) 就職の面接で
〈面接者：どうしてこの前の仕事を辞めたのですか〉
Interviewer: I was wondering why you quit your last job.
〈被面接者：給料が安かったんです〉
Interviewee:
◎ A It didn't pay well (enough).
○ B The pay was poor [bad].

2 《給料がいいと言うとき》
〈私は給料のいい仕事を探しています〉
◎ A I'm looking for a good-paying [well-paying] job.
△ B I'm looking for a well-paid job.

教育者
1 《会話で述べるとき》
〈私の父は教育者です〉
◎ A My father's a teacher.
△ B My father's an educator.
❖辞典にはBが出ているが時々使われる程度.

2 《歴史上の人物を述べる場合》
〈教授：アリストテレスは哲学者であったばかりでなく有名な教育者でもあった．彼

の学生の 1 人を言えますか〉
Professor:
- ☆ A Aristotle was not only a professor, but a famous teacher too. Can you name one of his students?
- ◎ B Aristotle was not only a professor, but a famous educator too. Can you name one of his students?

強化する

1 《スタッフ・輸送力などの場合》
〈会社は営業スタッフを強化するだろう〉
- ◎ A The company'll beef up [build up, increase] its sales staff.
- ○ B The company'll enhance [strengthen, bolster] its sales staff.
- △ C The company'll step up its sales staff.
    ❖ C が辞典に出ているが使用頻度は高くない．

2 《他国との関係の場合》
〈日本はフランスとの関係を強化すべきである〉
- ◎ A Japan should strengthen [build up, beef up] its relations with France.
- ○ B Japan should solidify its relations with France.

3 《取締りの場合》
〈政府はすべての麻薬の取締りを強化すべきである〉
- ◎ A The government should tighten its control over all drugs.
- ○ B The government should beef up [increase] its control over all drugs.

4 《軍隊の場合》
〈アメリカは太平洋艦隊を強化するだろう〉
- ☆ A The United States'll strengthen [enhance] its Pacific fleet.
- ☆ B The United States'll build up [beef up] its Pacific fleet.
- ◎ C The United States'll reinforce its Pacific fleet.
- ◎ D The United States'll bolster its Pacific fleet.
- △ E The United States'll augment its Pacific fleet.
    ❖ A は長期的なニュアンスがある．B, D は長期，短期の両方に使われている．C, E は短期間で他の地域からアメリカ軍を，または同盟国の軍を展開して強化するという意味に使われている．

行儀よくする

1 《子供に注意するとき》
〈今日お客様が来たら行儀よくしなさい〉
- ◎ A Behave yourself when we have company today.
- ○ B Behave when we have company today.
- × C Behave well when we have company today.

2 《成人（45 歳くらいまで）の女性が述べるとき》
〈私は有名なので行儀よくしなければならないんです〉
- ☆ A Since I'm famous, I have to be a good role model.
- ◎ B Since I'm famous, I have to behave myself.
- ◎ C Since I'm famous, I have to be careful of what I do.
- ○ D Since I'm famous, I have to behave [watch myself].
- △ E Since I'm famous, I have to cover my ass [butt].
- △ F Since I'm famous, I have to watch my P's and Q's.
- × G Since I'm famous, I have to behave well.

3 《成人（45 歳くらいまで）の男性が述べるとき》

〈私は有名なので行儀よくしなければならないんです〉
- ☆ A Since I'm famous, I have to be a good role model.
- ◎ B Since I'm famous, I have to cover my ass.
- ◎ C Since I'm famous, I have to be careful of what I do.
- △ D Since I'm famous, I have to watch [behave] myself.
- △ E Since I'm famous, I have to behave.
- △ F Since I'm famous, I have to cover my butt.
- △ G Since I'm famous, I have to watch my P's and Q's.
- × H Since I'm famous, I have to behave well.

4 《中年以上の女性が述べるとき》

〈私は有名なので行儀よくしなければならないんです〉
- ☆ A Since I'm famous, I have to be a good role model.
- ◎ B Since I'm famous, I have to mind [watch] my P's and Q's.
- ◎ C Since I'm famous, I have to be careful of what I do.
- ◎ D Since I'm famous, I have to watch [behave] myself.
- ○ E Since I'm famous, I have to behave.
- △ F Since I'm famous, I have to cover my ass [butt].

5 《中年以上の男性が述べるとき》

〈私は有名なので行儀よくしなければならないんです〉
- ☆ A Since I'm famous, I have to be a good role model.
- ◎ B Since I'm famous, I have to cover my ass.
- ◎ C Since I'm famous, I have to be careful of what I do.
- ◎ D Since I'm famous, I have to mind [watch] my P's and Q's.
- ◎ E Since I'm famous, I have to watch myself.
- ○ F Since I'm famous, I have to behave (myself).
- △ G Since I'm famous, I have to cover my butt.

行事

〈これはうちの会社の恒例行事のひとつです〉
- ◎　This is one of our company's annual affairs [events, functions].

教授　→地位 20

今日中に

〈今日中に私に連絡して下さい〉
- ◎ A Get in touch with me by tonight.
- ◎ B Get in touch with me by the end of the day.
- ○ C Get in touch with me before the day's through.
- × D Get in touch with me within (the course of) the day.

❖ D が辞典に出ているが使われていない．

狂信的な

〈彼らは新興宗教の狂信的な信者なんです〉
- ◎ A They're fanatics about the new religion.
- ◎ B They're fanatical about the new religion.
- ○ C They're fanatic about the new religion.

教頭　→地位 19

共同出資する

1 《小規模》

〈私たちはこのレストランを開くのに共同出資したんです〉
- ◎ A We went in together to open this restaurant.
- ◎ B We combined our money to open this restaurant.
- ○ C We pooled our money to open this restaurant.

2 《大規模》
〈これらの2つの自動車会社は，電気自動車を開発するために共同出資しました〉
- ☆ A These two auto companies went in together to develop an electric car.
- ◎ B These two auto companies pooled their resources to develop an electric car.
- ○ C These two auto companies combined their resources to develop an electric car.
- ○ D These two auto companies put their resources together to develop an electric car.
- ○ E These two auto companies collaborated to develop an electric car.
- ❖ E は堅い文章英語では非常によく使われている．

競売

1 《競売にかけられると述べるとき》
〈このアパートは競売にかけられるでしょう〉
- ◎ A This apartment building'll be sold at auction.
- ◎ B This apartment building'll be auctioned (off).
- ○ C This apartment building'll be put up for auction.
- ○ D This apartment building'll be put on the auction block.
- △ E This apartment building'll be put up to auction.
- × F This apartment building'll be (put) on the block.
- ❖ F は辞典に出ているが使われていない．

2 《競売で買った［売った］と述べるとき》
〈私はこの絵を競売で買ったんです〉
- ◎ A I bought this picture at an auction.
- △ B I bought this picture in an auction.
- △ C I bought this picture at a sale by auction.
- × D I bought this picture at [in] a public sale.
- × E I bought this picture at [in] an auction sale.
- × F I bought this picture at a sale at auction.
- ❖ D, E, F が辞典に出ているが使われていない

協力する

1 《ビジネス上の改まった間柄》
〈私たちはプロジェクトを遂行したいんです．ご協力してくれますか〉
- ☆ A We want to do our project. Will you help us with it?
- ◎ B We want to do our project. Will you work on it with us?
- ◎ C We want to do our project. Will you work with us on it?
- ○ D We want to do our project. Will you help us on it?
- ○ E We want to do our project. Will you cooperate with it?
- ○ F We want to do our project. Will you collaborate [team up] with us on it?
- △ G We want to do our project. Will you cooperate [pull together] with us on it?

2 《友人間で》
〈申し訳ないけど君の計画に協力できないんだよ〉
- ◎ A I'm sorry I can't help you with your plan.
- ○ B I'm sorry I can't help with your plan.
- ○ C I'm sorry I can't work (with you) on your plan.
- △ D I'm sorry I can't help you on your plan.

△　E　I'm sorry I can't team up with your plan.
×　F　I'm sorry I can't cooperate with (you on) your plan.
❖ F がくだけた会話文の内容で辞典に出ているが使われていない．

許可
〈我々は会社から許可をもらわなければならない〉
　　◎　A　We have to get the [a] go-ahead from the management.
　　◎　B　We have to get the [a] green light from the management.
　　○　C　We have to get permission [authorization] from the management.

きらきら輝く
1　《クリスマスツリー》
〈クリスマスツリーが電気できらきら輝いているのを見ました〉
　　☆　A　I saw a Christmas tree twinkling with lights.
　　◎　B　I saw a Christmas tree sparkling [shining] with lights.
　　△　C　I saw a Christmas tree glittering with lights.
　　▽　D　I saw a Christmas tree glimmering with lights.
2　《ネオンサイン》
〈ネオンサインが彼の店の正面全体にきらきら輝いていました〉
　　◎　A　Neon signs were glowing all over his storefront.
　　○　B　Neon signs were shining all over his storefront.
　　△　C　Neon signs were glittering [sparkling] all over his storefront.
　　▽　D　Neon signs were glimmering [twinkling] all over his storefront.

切らないでおく　→電話　5

ぎりぎり
1　《値段》
〈店員：これがぎりぎりの値段です〉
Salesperson:
　　☆　A　This is the best deal we could give you.
　　☆　B　This is the best price we could give you.
　　◎　C　This is the lowest price we could give you.
　　◎　D　This is our bottom price we could give you.
　　○　E　This is the bottom price we could give you.
2　《時間・締切日》
〈ぎりぎりで10時の飛行機に間に合いました〉
　　☆　A　I almost missed the 10:00 flight.
　　◎　B　I caught the 10:00 flight at the last minute.
　　◎　C　I just [barely] caught the 10:00 flight.
　　◎　D　I just about missed the 10:00 flight.
　　○　E　I narrowly caught the 10:00 flight.
　　○　F　I nearly [all but, practically] missed the 10:00 flight.
　　○　G　I came close to missing the 10:00 flight.
　　△　H　I came near to missing the 10:00 flight.

義理の両親　→母　4

着る
1　《動作》
〈外出するときはコートを着なさい〉
　　◎　　Put on your coat when you go out.
2　《着ている状態も含めて「着る」と述べるとき》
a)「着る」ことだけを述べるとき
〈このスーツは小さすぎて私には着られません〉

◎ A This suit's too small for me to wear.
　　○ B This suit's too small for me to put on.
 b) 着ていく目標を述べるとき
〈私はパーティーへ着ていくような服が全然ないんです〉
　　◎ A I don't have anything to wear to the party.
　　× B I don't have anything to put on to the party.
　　❖「着ている」の項も参照のこと．

切れる
 1 《賃貸契約》
〈賃貸契約はこの7月に切れるんです〉
　　◎ A The lease'll run out [expire] this July.
　　◎ B The lease'll be up this July.
　　○ C The lease'll end this July.
　　△ D The lease'll finish [terminate, come to an end] this July.
　　▽ E The lease'll be over this July.
　　▽ F The lease'll be history this July.
　　❖ E, F が辞典に出ているがこの文脈では使われてもまれである．
 2 《忍耐》
〈彼はたぶんすぐ忍耐が切れるでしょう〉
　　◎ A He'll probably run out of patience soon.
　　◎ B He'll probably be out of patience soon.
　　◎ C He'll probably lose his patience soon.
　　△ D His patience'll probably be running out soon.
 3 《生地》
〈この生地はすぐすり切れるでしょう〉
　　◎ A This fabric'll be worn out soon.
　　◎ B This fabric'll wear out soon.
　　× C This fabric'll wear soon.
　　× D This fabric'll become threadbare [seedy] soon.
　　❖ C, D が辞典に出ているが全く使われていない．
 4 《商品の在庫》
〈これは今在庫を切らしています〉
　　◎ A We're out of stock on this now.
　　◎ B We don't have this in our store now.
　　◎ C This is out of stock now.
　　○ D We're out of this now.
　　○ E We're all sold out on this now.
　　△ F This isn't in our store now.
 5 《電気のヒューズ》
〈ヒューズがたぶん切れるでしょう〉
　　◎ A The fuse'll probably be blown.
　　○ B The fuse'll probably be out.
　　○ C The fuse'll probably be popped.
　　× D The fuse'll probably be gone [down].
　　❖辞典に D が出ているが使われていない．

きれる
 1 《秘書》
〈私の秘書は非常にきれます〉
　　◎ A My secretary's very competent.

- ◎ B My secretary's very capable.
- ◎ C My secretary's very efficient.
- ◎ D My secretary's really on the ball.
- ○ E My secretary has it all together.
- ○ F My secretary's really sharp.
  - ❖ A の competent は「資格がある」という意味が原義なので、「きれる」といってもその度合いは一番弱い。B は一般的な意味での「きれる」であるのに対して，C は「能率がいい」というニュアンスがある．D, E, F は問題の対処の仕方，仕事上のあらゆる面に通じているというニュアンスがある．

2 《社長》

〈うちの社長は非常にきれます〉

- ◎ A Our boss has it all together.
- ◎ B Our boss is really on the top.
- ◎ C Our boss is really sharp.
- ○ D Our boss is very efficient [capable].
- × E Our boss is very competent.

気をつける

1 《足元》

〈足元に気をつけなさい〉

- ◎ A Watch your step.
- ○ B Watch where you're going.

2 《言葉使い》

〈言葉使いに気をつけなさい〉

- ☆ A Watch how you speak.
- ◎ B Watch your language [mouth, tongue].
- ◎ C Watch how you're speaking.
- ○ D Watch how you're talking.
- ○ E Watch how you talk.

3 《体重》

〈太らないように気をつけなさい〉

- ◎ Watch your waistline [weight].

4 《風邪》

〈風邪をひかないように気をつけなさい〉

- ◎ A Be careful not to catch a cold.
- △ B Take care not to catch a cold.
- × C Watch not to catch a cold.

5 《後方》

〈後ろに気をつけて．トラックが来るわよ〉

- ◎ A Watch [Look] out behind you. A truck's coming.
- ○ B Watch your back [behind]. A truck's coming.
- × C Be careful of your back. A truck's coming.
- × D Take care of your back. A truck's coming.

6 《比喩的に》

〈気をつけなさいよ．彼女はあなたの無知につけ込むかもしれませんから〉

- ◎ A Look [Watch] out. She may take advantage of your ignorance.
- ◎ B Be careful. She may take advantage of your ignorance.
- ◎ C Watch your back. She may take advantage of your ignorance.
- ○ D Watch [Look] out for yourself. She may take advantage of your ignorance.

ぎんこう 177

    △ E Watch your behind. She may take advantage of your ignorance.

気をもませる
〈ビル：いつ私たちは結婚できるのかい〉
Bill: When can we get married?
〈リンダ：分からないわ〉
Linda: I don't know.
〈ビル：気をもませないでくれよ〉
Bill:
    ☆ A Please don't keep me hanging.
    ☆ B Please don't keep me in suspense.
    ◎ C Please don't keep me guessing.
    ○ D Please don't keep me in limbo.
    △ E Please don't keep me on pins and needles.
    △ F Please don't keep me on the edge of my seat.
    × G Please don't keep me holding my breath.
    × H Please don't keep me breathless.
    × I Please don't keep me catching my breath.
    ❖(1) G, H, I が辞典に出ているが使われていない．
    ❖(2) A が1番強い響きがあり，B, C, D の順で下がる．

金鉱
〈中国は将来日本にとって金鉱となるでしょう〉
    ☆ A China'll be a real gold mine for Japan in the future.
    ◎ B China'll be a money-maker for Japan in the future.
    ○ C China'll make Japan rich in the future.
    ❖ 「ドル箱」の項も参照のこと．

銀行
1 《銀行通帳》
a) アメリカ
〈私は途中で銀行通帳を落してしまったんです〉
    ◎ A I lost my checkbook on the way.
    × B I lost my passbook [bank book, deposit book] on the way.
    ❖ B をアメリカ英語として出している辞典があるが使われていない．
b) 日本
〈私は途中で銀行通帳を落してしまったんです〉
    ◎ A I lost my checkbook on the way.
    ◎ B I lost my bank book on the way.
    ○ C I lost my bankbook on the way.
    × D I lost my passbook on the way.
    ❖ A は当座預金，B, C は普通預金．

2 《銀行口座》
〈私はフロリダ銀行に口座があります〉
    ◎ A I have an account at Florida Bank.
    ○ B I have an account with Florida Bank.
    ▽ C I have an account in Florida Bank.

3 《自動現金預入払出機》
〈あの銀行は自動現金預入払出機がないんです〉
    ☆ A That bank doesn't have an ATM.
    ◎ B That bank doesn't have an ATM machine.
    ◎ C That bank doesn't have any ATM machines.

- ○ D That bank doesn't have a cash machine.
- ○ E That bank doesn't have any cash machines.

銀行家 →職業 10

禁止される

1 《人が主語のとき》

〈就労ビザのない外国人はわが国では働くことが禁止されている〉

- ☆ A Foreigners without papers aren't allowed to work in this country.
- ◎ B Foreigners without papers aren't permitted to work in this country.
- ○ C Foreigners without papers are prohibited [banned] from working in this country.
- ○ D Foreigners without papers are barred from working in this country.
- ○ E Foreigners without papers are forbidden to work in this country.

❖テレビ，新聞などでは B，D が非常によく使われている．

2 《物が主語のとき》

〈銃はわが国では禁止されています〉

- ◎ A Guns are banned [prohibited] in this country.
- ◎ B Guns aren't allowed [permitted] in this country.
- ○ C Guns are forbidden [barred] in this country.

3 《行為が主語のとき》

〈21歳以下の飲酒はアメリカでは禁止されています〉

- ☆ A Drinking under the age of 21 isn't allowed in America.
- ◎ B Drinking under the age of 21 is illegal in America.
- ◎ C Drinking under the age of 21 isn't legal in America.
- ◎ D Drinking under the age of 21 goes against the law in America.
- ◎ E Drinking under the age of 21 is prohibited in America.
- ○ F Drinking under the age of 21 isn't permitted in America.
- ○ G Drinking under the age of 21 is forbidden in America.
- ▽ H Drinking under the age of 21 is barred [banned] in America.
- ▽ I Drinking under the age of 21 isn't lawful in America.

近所

1 《所有格を使えないとき》

〈近所にいらしたらどうぞお立ち寄りください〉

- ◎ A Please stop by when you're in the neighborhood.
- △ B Please stop by when you come to the neighborhood.
- ▽ C Please stop by when you come to my neighborhood.
- × D Please stop by when you're in my neighborhood.

❖(1) neighborhood は動作動詞があるときは所有格と共にはあまり使われていない．

❖(2) neighborhood は動作動詞がなくても動作が意味されているときは所有格と共に使うことができない．したがって，D ではなく A を使う．

2 《所有格を使えるとき》

〈彼らの住んでいる近所は安全で美しいです〉

- ◎ Their neighborhood's safe and beautiful.

琴線に触れる

〈彼のスピーチは私の琴線に触れました〉

- ◎ A His speech touched [struck] a cord with me.
- ◎ B His speech hit home with me.
- ◎ C His speech moved [affected] me.

金属会社 →会社

緊張している
〈彼はまもなくテレビに出演するので緊張しているんです〉
- ◎ A He's nervous about being on TV soon.
- ◎ B He's stressed out about being on TV soon.
- ◎ C He's wound out about being on TV soon.
  - ❖ A, B の方が C より緊張の程度が強いという響きがある．

勤務
1 《時間帯》
〈私は A朝の/B昼の/C午後の/D夜の/E昼夜の/F深夜の 勤務で働いています〉
- ◎ A I work the morning shift.
- ◎ B I work the day shift.
- ◎ C I work the afternoon shift.
- ◎ D I work the night shift.
- ◎ E I work the day and night shift.
- ◎ F I work the graveyard shift.
  - ❖(1) I work on the...のように on を付けた表現は A～F いずれも時々使われる程度．
  - ❖(2) A～F いずれも始業時間が2つ以上あれば a morning shift のように the ではなく a をつけた形も使われている．これは会社のシステムによる．

2 《体系》
〈私は Aフレックス勤務で/Bフレックスで/C1日置きに2部交替勤務で/D半夜勤で/E分割勤務で 働いています〉
- ◎ A I work a flex shift.
- ◎ B I work flex time.
- ◎ C I work a double shift every other day.
- ◎ D I work a swing shift.
- ◎ E I work a split shift.
  - ❖(1) A～E いずれも勤務時間が2つ以上ある．したがって数えられるので the ではなく a を使う．ただし，B は a は不要である．
  - ❖(2) C は普通16時間勤務になる．
  - ❖(3) D は午後3時頃から真夜中までの勤務になる．
  - ❖(4) E は午前，午後のように勤務時間を2つ以上に分ける就労システム．

金融政策
1 《普通に「金融政策」と言うとき》
〈私はグリーンスパンの金融政策には同意しません〉
- ◎ A I don't agree with Greenspan's monetary policy.
- ◎ B I don't agree to Greenspan's monetary policy.
  - ❖ A は一般の人，B は政府関係者．詳細は「同意する」の項を参照されたい．

2 《「緩和政策を取る」と言うとき》
a) 公定歩合で言及するとき
〈政府はまもなく金融緩和政策を取るでしょう〉
- ☆ A The government'll lower the bank rate soon.
- ◎ B The government'll drop the bank rate soon.
- ○ C The government'll decrease [reduce] the bank rate soon.

b) 政策で言及するとき
〈政府はたぶんまもなく金融緩和政策を取るだろう〉
- ☆ A The government'll probably relax [ease] the money supply soon.
- ◎ B The government'll probably ease the [its] monetary policy soon.
- ○ C The government'll probably adopt a cheap money policy soon.

- ◯ D The government'll probably adopt a credit relaxation policy soon.
- ▽ E The government'll probably take an easy money policy soon.
  - ❖ E は金融政策者の間では時々使われている.
- 3 《「引き締め政策を取る」と言うとき》
- 〈政府はまもなく金融引き締め政策を取るでしょう〉
  - ☆ A The government'll raise its bank rate soon.
  - ◎ B The government'll increase its bank rate soon.
  - ◯ C The government'll hike its bank rate soon.
  - △ D The government'll hike up its bank rate soon.
  - ▽ E The government'll take a tight money policy soon.
  - ❖ E は金融政策者の間では時々使われている.

〔く〕

空気を入れ替える
〈お客が帰ったら部屋の空気を入れ替えてくれますか〉
- ◎ A Will you air out the room (well) after the guest have left?
- ◯ B Will you air the room well after the guest have left?
- × C Will you refresh [fan, ventilate] the room after the guest have left?
  - ❖ C が辞典に出ているが使われていない.

空軍 →軍隊 3

偶然
1 《偶然会う》
〈私は駅へ行く途中でジムに偶然会いました〉
- ☆ A I ran into Jim on the way to the station.
- ☆ B I bumped into Jim on the way to the station.
- ◎ C I met Jim on the way to the station.
- ◎ D I saw Jim on the way to the station.
- ◯ E I happened to meet Jim on the way to the station.
- ◯ F I met Jim by accident [chance] on the way to the station.
- ◯ G I ran across Jim on the way to the station.
- △ H I saw Jim by accident [chance] on the way to the station.
- △ I I crossed paths with Jim on the way to the station.
- × J I chanced to meet Jim on the way to the station.
  - ❖(1) J が辞典に出ているが使われていない.
  - ❖(2) C の met は偶然会って「話をした」という響きがある. しかし, D の saw には「話をした」というニュアンスはない.
  - ❖(3) C の met, D の saw は「約束をして会った」という意味でもよく使われている. どちらの意味であるかは会話の前後関係で決まる.

2 《偶然見つける》
a) 重要でないもののとき
〈部屋を掃除していたとき, 私は忘れていた古い教科書を何冊か偶然見つけました〉
- ◎ A While I was cleaning my room, I came across [ran across, found] some old textbooks I'd forgotten.
- ◯ B While I was cleaning my room, I stumbled upon some old textbooks I'd forgotten.
- △ C While I was cleaning my room, I happened upon some old text-

books I'd forgotten.
b）ドラマチックな場面のとき
〈私は山の中をハイキングしていたとき，偶然空き地で熊に出くわしたんです〉
- ◎ A When I was hiking up the mountain, I came upon [across] a bear in a clearing.
- ◎ B When I was hiking up the mountain, I ran into [across] a bear in a clearing.
- ◎ C When I was hiking up the mountain, I met up with a bear in a clearing.
- ○ D When I was hiking up the mountain, I encountered [stumbled upon] a bear in a clearing.
- △ E When I was hiking up the mountain, I happened upon [bumped into] a bear in a clearing.
- × F When I was hiking up the mountain, I hit upon [came against] a bear in a clearing.

❖ F が辞典に出ているが使われていない．

空前の →史上最高の

クーラー

1 《機械に言及する場合》
〈あなたの事務所にはクーラーが付いていますか〉
- ◎ A Does your office have air-conditioning?
- ◎ B Does your office have an air-conditioner?
- ○ C Does your office have air?

2 《稼動に言及する場合》
〈クーラーを切っておいてください〉
- ☆ A Please keep the air off.
- ◎ B Please keep the air-conditioning off.
- ○ C Please keep the air-conditioner off.

くぎ付けになる

1 《テレビなどに夢中になる》
〈野球の試合が非常に面白かったので，昨夜はテレビにくぎ付けになってしまったんです〉
- ◎ A The baseball game was so exciting I was glued to the TV last night.
- ○ B The baseball game was so exciting I couldn't take my eyes off the TV last night.
- × C The baseball game was so exciting I was transfixed to the TV last night.

❖ C は辞典に出ているが使われていない．

2 《恐ろしくて動けない》
〈庭で蛇を見たとたん，私はその場にくぎ付けになってしまいました〉
- ◎ A The minute I saw a snake in the yard, I froze.
- ◎ B The minute I saw a snake in the yard, I was petrified.
- ◎ C The minute I saw a snake in the yard, I couldn't move.
- ○ D The minute I saw a snake in the yard, I was frozen (stiff).

3 《仕事などに時間を取られる》
〈先週私は仕事にくぎ付けでした〉
- ◎ A I was tied up with my work last week.
- ◎ B I was tied with work last week.
- ○ C I was glued to my work last week.

- ○ D I was tied down with work last week.
- △ E I was glued to work last week.
- △ F I was tied down with my work last week.

4 《為替などが動かない》

〈為替のレートが先月からくぎ付けになっています〉
- ◎ The exchange rate hasn't changed since last month.

くぎを打つ

1 《箱の場合》

〈箱にくぎを打ってください〉
- ◎ A Nail the box shut.
- ○ B Nail the box closed.
- ○ C Nail the box up.
- △ D Nail up the box.

2 《ふたの場合》

〈ふたにくぎを打ってください〉
- ☆ A Nail the lid down.
- ◎ B Nail down the lid.
- ◎ C Nail the lid.
- × D Nail up the lid.

くじ

1 《宝くじのとき》

〈私は宝くじで1千万円当たったんです〉
- ◎ A I won ¥10,000,000 in the lottery.
- × B I won ¥10,000,000 in the raffle.

2 《景品が当たるくじのとき》

〈私はくじで景品が当たったんです〉
- ◎ A I won a prize in the raffle.
- △ B I won a prize in the lottery.

ぐずぐずする

〈彼は何をぐずぐずしているんだろう〉
- ◎ A What's making him late?
- ○ B What's holding him up?
- △ C What's preventing him from coming?

崩れる

1 《天気》

〈この晴天は来週崩れます〉
- ☆ A This good weather'll end next week.
- ◎ B This good weather won't last until next week.
- ○ C This good weather won't stay until next week.
- △ D This good weather won't hold until next week.
- × E This good weather won't break until next week.

  ❖ Eが辞典に出ているが使われていない．ただし，「悪天候がよくなる」の意味なら次のように使われている．This bad weather'll break soon.（この悪天候はまもなくよくなるでしょう）

2 《天井》

〈天井が崩れたんです〉
- ☆ A The ceiling's fallen down.
- ◎ B The ceiling's collapsed.
- ○ C The ceiling's fallen [caved] in.

        △ D The ceiling's given in.
   3 《塀》
   〈塀が崩れたんです〉
        ◎ A The wall's fallen apart [collapsed].
        ○ B The wall's broken [crumbled].

癖
   1 《癖がある》
   〈彼は人と話しているとき, すごくまばたきする癖がある〉
        ☆ A He has a habit of blinking a lot when he's talking to somebody.
        △ B He has the habit [a way] of blinking a lot when he's talking to somebody.
        △ C He's in the habit of blinking a lot when he's talking to somebody.
   2 《癖を直す》→直す 2

口車に乗る
〈彼の口車に乗らないよう気を付けなさい〉
        ☆ A Be careful. He's a smooth talker.
        ◎ B Be careful. Don't let him sweet-talk you.
        ◎ C Be careful of his fast [smooth] talk.
        ○ D Be careful. Don't let him pull a snow job on you.

口コミで
〈私は口コミで御社を知りました〉
        ◎ A I learned about your company by word of mouth.
        × B I learned about your company on word of mouth.

口先だけ
〈彼は口先だけです〉
        ◎ A He's all talk and no action.
        ◎ B He's all talk.
        ○ C He's just a talker.

口では言えない
〈掲示板に自分の番号を見つけたとき, どんなにうれしかったか口では言えません〉
        ◎   I can't tell you how happy I was when I saw my number on the bulletin board.

口やかましい
〈おばあちゃんは食事の作法に口やかましいんです〉
        ☆ A My grandma's particular about table manners.
        ◎ B My grandma's picky about table manners.
        ○ C My grandma's fussy about table manners.
        △ D My grandma's fastidious about table manners.

くどい
   1 《同類の語を使った表現のとき》
   〈"his acting as an actor's great"という言い方はくどい〉
        ◎ A That his acting as an actor's great is repetitious [repetitive, redundant].
        ▽ B That his acting as an actor's great is superfluous [excessive].
        ❖ B は辞典に出ているがまれ.
   2 《料理の味がしつこいとき》
   〈この味付けはくどすぎる〉
        ◎   This seasoning's too heavy.
   3 《同じことを何度も言われたとき》

〈ビル：約束の日に必ずお金を返してくれよ〉
Bill: Be sure to pay the money back on time.
〈トム：くどいぞ〉
Tom:
- ◎ A I heard this (all) before.
- ◎ B I heard this already.
- ○ C You've already said that.
- × D You're repeating.
  - ❖ D が辞典に出ているが使われていない．

国中に →…中に 1, 2

首になる

1 《社員に落度があったとき》
〈彼は首になったんです〉
- ◎ A He was fired.
- × B He got the grand bounce.
  - ❖ B が辞典に出ているが使われていない．

2 《社員に全く責任がなく会社の都合でリストラされたとき》
〈彼は首になったんです〉
- ◎ A He was [got] laid off.
- ○ B He was dismissed.
  - ❖ B は20％くらい社員に責任があるという響きもある．

3 《社員に責任があったときと会社の都合でリストラされたとき》
〈彼は首になったんです〉
- ○ A He was axed.
- ○ B He got a [his] pink slip.
- ○ C He got his walking papers.
- △ D He was sacked [booted out].
- △ E He got the boot.

4 《「ひまを出された」「ひまを出す」と婉曲に述べるとき》
〈私はひまを出されたんです〉
- ☆ A They let me go.
- ◎ B I was let go.

5 《「解任される」と述べるとき》
〈社長は解任されるだろう〉
- ◎ A The president'll be relieved [removed, dismissed] of his post.
- △ B The president'll be discharged of his post.
  - ❖ B は軍人にはよく使われる．

くやしい

〈失敗したときどんなにくやしかったか，口では言えません〉
- ◎ A I can't tell you how frustrated [upset] I was at my failure.
- × B I can't tell you how chagrined [vexatious] I was at my failure.
  - ❖ 多くの辞典に B が紹介されているが使われていない．

クリーニング屋 →店 12

来る

1 《一般的に述べるとき》
〈今日の午後私の事務所に来られますか〉
- ◎ Can you come (over) to my office this afternoon?

2 《「着く」という意味のとき》
〈明朝何時にここへ来られますか〉

◎ A How early can you get here tomorrow morning?
○ B How early can you come here tomorrow morning?

3 《「現れる」という意味のとき》
〈私たちは7時まで待っていたのですが彼女は来ませんでした〉
◎ A We waited until 7 o'clock but she didn't show up.
○ B We waited until 7 o'clock but she didn't show [turn up, appear, come].

4 《特別な日などが「めぐってくる」という意味のとき》
〈クリスマスはじきにやって来ます〉
◎ A Christmas'll come soon.
◎ B Christmas is almost here.

5 《来る必要, 不必要を述べるとき》
〈確認のため明日, 私に電話して下さい. 来る必要がないかもしれません〉
◎ A Please call me tomorrow to double-check. You might not have to come again.
◎ B Please call me tomorrow to double-check. You might not have to make another trip.

6 《「原因である」という意味のとき》
〈彼の胃潰瘍はストレスから来ているんです〉
☆ A His ulcer is caused by stress.
◎ B His ulcer is due to stress.
◎ C His ulcer comes from stress.
○ D His ulcer is traced back to stress.
△ E His ulcer is traced to stress.

苦しい

1 《生活》
〈彼らは生活が苦しいんです〉
◎ A They're hurting [hard up] for money.
◎ B They're in trouble financially.
◎ C They're financially in trouble.
◎ D They're in financial trouble.
◎ E They're having a hard time financially [money-wise].
◎ F They're pressed for money.
○ G They're hurting [hard up] for cash.
○ H They're financially pressed.
○ I They're on the edge financially.

2 《財政》
〈うちの会社は財政が苦しいんです〉
☆ A Our company's hurting for money.
☆ B Our company's having a financial problem.
◎ C Our company's having a hard time financially [money-wise].
◎ D Our company's in trouble financially.
○ E Our company's hard up [pressed] for money.
○ F Our company's on the edge financially [money-wise].
△ G Our company's hurting [hard up] for cash.

3 《家計の収支》
〈うちは家計のやりくりが苦しいんです〉
◎ A We're having a hard [tough] time making ends meet.
◎ B We're having trouble making ends meet.

◎ C It's tough for us to make ends meet.
△ D We're having difficulty [a difficult time] making ends meet.

来る日も来る日も
〈私は来る日も来る日も彼を病院に見舞いました〉
◎ A I visited him in the hospital every day.
○ B I visited him in the hospital day after day.
❖辞典ではBのみを紹介しているが，Aの方が非常によく使われている．

苦労する
1 《苦労した事実だけを述べるとき》
a) …することに苦労する
〈ビル：彼の事務所は見つかったかい〉
Bill: Did you find his office?
〈ジム：うん，でもすごく苦労したよ〉
Jim:
◎ A Yes, but I had a really hard time.
◎ B Yes, but I had a lot of trouble.
◎ C Yes, but it was really tough.
◎ D Yes, but it was very hard.
○ E Yes, but I went through a lot.
○ F Yes, but it was very difficult.

b) 集合的に考えた苦労
〈私は人生でいろいろ苦労をしました〉
◎ A I've suffered a lot of hardships [troubles] in my life.
◎ B I've endured a lot of hardships [troubles] in my life.
◎ C I've undergone a lot of hardships [troubles] in my life.
◎ D I've lived through a lot of hardships [troubles] in my life.
◎ E I've gone through a lot of hardships [troubles] in my life.
◎ F I've experienced a lot of hardships [troubles] in my life.
◎ G I've met with a lot of hardships [troubles] in my life.
❖苦労の度合いはA, Bが一番強い．C, D, Eが次に強く，F, Gが一番弱い．

2 《苦労した内容を述べるとき》
〈彼を説得するのにとても苦労しました〉
◎ A I had a really hard time persuading him.
◎ B I had a lot of trouble persuading him.
◎ C It was really tough [hard] to persuade him.
◎ E I went through a lot to persuade him.
○ F I had a lot of difficulty persuading him.
○ G It was very difficult to persuade him.

クロとする
〈警察にはブラウンをクロとする証拠が全部揃っているんだと思う．さもなければ逮捕しなかったよ〉
◎ I think they've got all the evidence they need to convict Brown, or they wouldn't have arrested him.
❖「クロとする」とは「有罪を証明する」ということだから，convictがぴったり．

詳しい
1 《専門的知識を持っているという意味での「詳しい」》
a) 普通に述べるとき

〈彼は金融市場に詳しいんです〉
- ◎ A He's knowledgeable about the money markets.
- ◎ B He's well-informed about [of] the money markets.
- ◎ C He's familiar with the money markets.
- ◎ D He's well-versed [quite at home] in the money markets.
- △ E He's well-acquainted [thoroughly acquainted] with the money markets.
- △ F He has a thorough knowledge of the money markets.
- × G He's well-posted in the money markets.
- × H He's conversant with the money markets.
- × I He has the money markets at his fingers' ends.
- × J He has the money markets at his fingertips.
  - ❖(1) 辞典に G〜J が出ているが実際には使われていない．
  - ❖(2) J は辞典に「精通している」で紹介されているが，この意味では使われていない．しかし，「情報を容易に得られる」という意味ではよく使われている．

b）非常に詳しいと述べるとき
〈彼は金融市場に非常に詳しいんです〉
- ◎ A He knows the money markets really well.
- ◎ B He's really [very] familiar with the money markets.
- ◎ C He knows everything with the money markets.
- ◎ D He knows a lot about the money markets.
- ◎ E He really knows about the money markets.
- ◎ F He knows all there's to know about the money markets.
- ○ G He knows a lot of stuff about the money markets.
- ○ H He's really knowledgeable about [on] the money markets.
- △ I He's really well-informed about the money markets.
- △ J He's really well-versed in the money markets.
- △ K He's knowledgeable of the money markets.
- △ L He knows the money markets like the back of his hand.

2 《名詞の前で使う「詳しい」》
〈私はもっと詳しい情報が必要なんです〉
- ☆ A I need more in-depth [detailed] information.
- ◎ B I need more precise [specific] information.
- ○ C I need more explicit [exact] information.

軍隊

1 《一般的に述べるとき》
〈彼は軍隊にいます〉
- ☆ A He's in the military.
- ◎ B He's in the service.
- ◎ C He's in the armed forces.
- ○ D He's in the armed services.
- △ E He's in (the) military service.
- ▽ F He's in military services.

2 《陸軍》
〈彼は陸軍にいます〉
- ☆ A He's in the Army.
- ◎ B He's serving in the Army.
- ○ C He's an Army man.

- ○ D He's a G.I.
- △ E He's a member of the Army.

3 《空軍》

〈彼女は空軍にいます〉
- ◎ A She's in the Air Force.
- ○ B She's a fly boy.
- ▽ C She's in the Air Service [the flying corps].
  - ❖ B は女性でも fly girl とは言わない．また年令に関係なく使われている．

4 《海軍》

〈彼は海軍にいます〉
- ◎ A He's in the Navy.
- ▽ B He's in the Navy service.
- ▽ C He's in the Naval forces [services].
- ▽ D He's in the armed sea force.
  - ❖ B, C, D が辞典に出ているが使われてもまれ．

〔け〕

経営者

1 《オーナーを指す場合》

〈彼がこのホテルの経営者なんだ〉
- ◎ A He owns this hotel.
- ◎ B He's the owner of this hotel.
- ○ C This hotel belongs to him.

2 《経営だけに言及する場合》

〈彼がこのホテルの経営者なんだ〉
- ◎ A He's managing this hotel.
- ◎ B He's running this hotel.
  - ❖(1) A, B とも，ホテルを所有しているオーナーなのか，雇われて経営をしているのかには言及していない．経営していることのみに言及している．
  - ❖(2) be running は小さいビジネスに用いる傾向がある．したがって，オーナーであるときは，「経営している」という事実だけに言及する場合でも，He's running this hotel. を使うことが多い．

経営修士号

〈私は3年前に経営修士号を取りました〉
- ◎ A I got my M.B.A. three years ago.
- ○ B I got an M.B.A. three years ago.
  - ❖ 博士号，修士号，学士号，運転免許などすべて A の型のほうがずっとよく使われている．

計画性

1 《計画性がある》

a ）普通に述べるとき

〈彼は計画性がある〉
- ☆ A He plans for the future.
- ◎ B He's planning for the future.
- ○ C He has a good plan for the future.
- ○ D He looks towards the future.

△ E He's future-oriented [future-minded].
 b) 強調するとき
〈彼は非常に計画性がある〉
　　　☆ A He really plans for the future.
　　　◎ B He's really planning for the future.
　　　○ C He has a really good plan for the future.
　　　○ D He really looks towards the future.
　　　△ E He's really future-oriented [future-minded].
 2 《計画性がない》
 a) 普通に述べるとき
〈彼は計画性がないんです〉
　　　◎ A He has no plan for the future.
　　　◎ B He doesn't have any plan for the future.
　　　◎ C He doesn't plan for the future.
　　　○ D He isn't planning for the future.
　　　△ E He isn't future-oriented future-minded].
 b) 強調して述べるとき
〈彼には全然計画性がないんです〉
　　　☆ A He has no plan for the future at all.
　　　◎ B He doesn't plan for the future at all.
　　　◎ C He doesn't have any plan [plans] for the future at all.
　　　○ D He isn't planning for the future at all.
　　　○ E He doesn't looks towards the future at all.
　　　△ F He has no plan for the future whatsoever.
　　　△ G He doesn't plan for [looks towards] the future whatsoever.
　　　△ H He isn't planning for the future whatsoever.

景気
 1 《一国全体の景気》
〈景気が悪いので政府はたぶん税金を下げるだろう〉
　　　◎ A The economy's very bad, so the government's probably going to lower taxes.
　　　○ B Business is very bad, so the government's probably going to lower taxes.
　　　△ C Things're very bad, so the government's probably going to lower taxes.
　　　× D Times're very bad, so the government's probably going to lower taxes.
 2 《ある一地域・一産業の景気》
〈今, ニューヨークの景気は悪い〉
　　　☆ A Now times in New York're very bad.
　　　◎ B Now things [business] in New York're very bad.
　　　△ C Now the economy in New York're very bad.
 3 《相手の景気を尋ねるとき》
 a) 友人に対して
〈景気はどう〉
　　　◎ A How's everything?
　　　○ B How goes it?
　　　○ C How's the world treating you?
　　　△ D How's your business?

- △ E How're things making out?
- × F How's the world using you?
  - ❖ F が辞典に出ているが使われていない．
- b）改まった話し方をする必要のある人に対して
- 〈景気はいかがですか〉
  - ◎ A How's everything?
  - ◎ B How's (your) business?
  - ○ C How's the world treating you?
  - △ D How goes it?
  - △ E How're things making out?
  - × F How's the world using you?
    - ❖ F が辞典に出ているが使われていない．

経験する

1 《同情を示すとき》

〈リンダ：離婚するんです．人生で難しい時なんです〉

Linda: I'm getting a divorce. It's a difficult time in my life.

〈リズ：分かるわ．私も経験しましたから〉

Liz:
- ◎ A I know. I've been down that road before.
- ◎ B I know. I've been there (before).
- ◎ C I know. I've been in your shoes.
- ○ D I know. I've gone through that.

2 《客観的に述べるとき》

〈私も同じことを経験しました〉
- ◎ A I've experienced the same thing.
- ◎ B I've experienced that.
  - ❖ A, B とも事実を客観的に述べる言い方で，同情を示してはいない．

警告する

1 《「…について警告する」と述べるとき》

〈彼は私たち全員に麻薬の危険について警告した〉
- ◎ A He warned us all against [of] the danger of the drugs.
- ○ B He alerted us all to the danger of the drugs.
- ○ C He cautioned us all against the danger of the drugs.

2 《「…するよう警告する」と述べるとき》

〈消防署は私たち全員に避難する準備をするように警告した〉
- ◎ A The fire station warned [alerted] us all to prepare to evacuate.
- ◎ B The fire station put us all on the alert to prepare to evacuate.
- ○ C The fire station gave us all a warning to prepare to evacuate.
- △ D The fire station cautioned us all to prepare to evacuate.

経済的に →力になってくれる 2

警察

〈警察は行方不明の男性を探しています〉
- ◎ A The police're searching for the missing man.
- ◎ B Police're searching for the missing man.

計算

〈彼は計算が得意です〉
- ◎ A He's good at figures [calculations, arithmetic, mathematics].
- ○ B He's good at calculating.
  - ❖「数字に強い」の項も参照のこと．

刑事 →職業 7
形跡
〈事務所には強盗に入られた形跡がある〉
- ☆ A The office shows evidence of being broken into.
- ◎ B The office shows signs of being broken into.
- ○ C The office shows traces [indications] of being broken into.
- △ D The office shows clues [marks] of being broken into.

携帯電話 →電話 7
警備員 →職業 17
軽蔑する
1 《怒りの気持ちが入っているとき》
〈彼は彼らを軽蔑しています〉
- ◎ A He despises them.
- ◎ B He really hates them.
  - ❖(1) despise＝look down on としている辞典があるが，両者はイコールではない．
  - ❖(2) A の方が B より強い響きがある．したがって，ニュアンスを近づけるために really が必要になってくる．

2 《怒りの気持ちがないとき》
〈彼は彼らを軽蔑しているんです〉
- ☆ A He looks down on them.
- ☆ B He doesn't think much of them.
- ◎ C He has a low opinion on them.
- ○ D He doesn't think highly [a lot] of them.
- ○ E He thinks nothing [little] of them.
- ○ F He's turning up his nose at them.
- △ G He holds them in low regard.
- △ H He has [feels] contempt for them.
- × I He slights [disdains, scorns] them.
- × J He holds them in contempt [scorn, low repute].
- × K He thinks meanly [lightly, scorn] of them.
- × L He holds them cheap.
- × M He is treading them under foot.
- × N He is scorning at them.
- × O He brings them into contempt.
- × P He has [feels] a contempt for them.
- × Q He has [feels] scorn for them.
  - ❖ I～Q は辞典に出ているが，会話はもちろん，堅い文章英語でも現在は使われていない．

契約
1 《ビジネス》
a) 書面に書いたもの
〈彼は契約を守るでしょう〉
- ◎ He'll honor the contract.

b) 口頭のもの
〈彼は口頭の契約を破ったんです〉
- ◎ He broke our verbal agreement.

2 《賃貸借契約》
〈家主は契約を更新しないでしょう〉

◎　The landlord won't renew the lease.

契約違反　→違反　1

経理　→職業　13

経理部　→…部　6

けがをする

1 《事故のとき》

〈彼は昨日車の事故でけがをしたんです〉

☆　A　He got hurt in a car crash yesterday.
☆　B　He was hurt in a car crash yesterday.
◎　C　He got injured in a car crash yesterday.
◎　D　He was injured in a car crash yesterday.
○　E　He was wounded in a car crash yesterday.
△　F　He got wounded in a car crash yesterday.

❖テレビ，新聞などのニュース英語では B, D, E が非常によく使われている．

2 《凶器が使われたとき》

〈彼は強盗にナイフで刺されてけがをしたんです〉

☆　A　He was hurt by a robber with a knife.
☆　B　He got hurt by a robber with a knife.
◎　C　He was wounded by a robber with a knife.
◎　D　He got wounded by a robber with a knife.
△　E　He was injured by a robber with a knife.
△　F　He got injured by a robber with a knife.

❖(1)　テレビ，新聞などのニュース英語では C, E が一番よく使われている．

❖(2)　辞典には①be wounded は故意に，②be hurt, ③be injured は非故意に「けがをさせられた」ときに使い分けられていると出ているが，これらは英語の慣用事実を歪曲している．①②③のいずれを使うかは話し手の主観による．

He was ① wounded［② hurt, ③ injured］because his wife stabbed him with a knife.（彼は妻がナイフで刺したからけがをしたんです）

出血の量が多かったと話し手が思えば①，多くなかったという気持ちで述べるときは②．③は②の改まった表現．血を見ることに慣れていない人，感受性の強い人は，出血の量が少なくても①を使う．

3 《重傷を負ったとき》

〈彼は強盗にナイフで重傷を負わされたんです〉

☆　A　He was badly [seriously] hurt by a robber with a knife.
☆　B　He got badly hurt by a robber with a knife.
◎　C　He got seriously hurt by a robber with a knife.
◎　D　He was badly [seriously] wounded by a robber with a knife.
◎　E　He got badly [seriously] wounded by a robber with a knife.
△　F　He was badly [seriously] injured by a robber with a knife.
△　G　He got badly [seriously] injured by a robber with a knife.

4 《話し手の不注意のとき》

〈私はナイフでけがをしたんです〉

◎　A　I hurt myself with a knife.
○　B　I wounded myself with a knife.
△　C　I injured myself with a knife.

景色

1 《周囲全体の景色》

〈彼の家の周囲の景色は美しい〉
- ◎ A The scenery [landscape] around his house is beautiful.
- ○ B The view around his house is beautiful.
  - ❖ A の scenery は一国, 一都市, 一町, 一地域という広い範囲の「景色」に使うと, 多くの慣用・類語辞典で解説しているが, これは scenery が実際に使われている姿を歪曲している. 上記の例文の「彼の家の周辺」のような, 狭い範囲にもよく使われている. つまり, 太陽が沈みかかっているというような一場面の景色でなければ, 面積の大小に関係なく使われている.

2 《一国の広い景色》
〈アメリカの景色は美しい〉
- ◎ A The scenery in America is beautiful.
- ▽ B The landscape [view] in America is beautiful.

3 《一地域の広い景色》
〈車でサンフランシスコへ行くとき, 高速道路の両側に美しい景色が楽しめます〉
- ◎ A You can enjoy the beautiful scenery [landscape] on both sides of the expressway when you drive to San Francisco.
- ○ B You can enjoy the beautiful view on both sides of the expressway when you drive to San Francisco.

4 《一目で見渡せる景色》
〈セントヘレンズ山の噴火は周囲の景色を永久に変えてしまった〉
- ◎ A The Mount St. Helens volcanic eruption forever changed the surrounding landscape.
- ○ B The Mount St. Helens volcanic eruption forever changed the surrounding scenery [view].

〈アリゾナの砂漠の景色は, 見ると驚くほど美しいです〉
- ☆ A The desert landscape in Arizona is stunning to look at.
- ◎ B The desert scenery in Arizona is stunning to look at.
- ○ C The desert view in Arizona is stunning to look at.

5 《目で見たそのままの光景という意味の景色》
〈私は太陽が沈むところを見ました. それは非常に美しい景色でした〉
- ◎ A I saw the sun setting. It was a very beautiful sight.
- ○ B I saw the sun setting. It was a very beautiful scene.

6 《風景というニュアンスのひとつの景色》
〈彼女は海の美しい景色を描きました〉
- ◎ A She painted a beautiful scene of the ocean.
- ○ B She painted a beautiful landscape of the ocean.

7 《個々の景色》
〈サンフランシスコには美しい景色がたくさんある〉
- ◎ A There are a lot of beautiful places [areas, spots] in San Francisco.
- ○ B There are a lot of beautiful views in San Francisco.

8 《眺めとしての景色》
〈一番上の階のレストランからサンフランシスコ湾の美しい景色が見られます〉
- ◎ A There's a beautiful view of San Francisco Bay from the restaurant on the top floor.
- ◎ B You can get a beautiful view of San Francisco Bay from the restaurant on the top floor.
- × C You can see a beautiful area [spot, place] of San Francisco Bay from the restaurant on the top floor.

下旬
〈彼らは5月の下旬に日本に来ました〉
- ☆ A They came to Japan in late May.
- ◎ B They came to Japan late in May.
- ○ C They came to Japan at the end of May.
- × D They came to Japan in the end of May.
- ❖「初旬」「中旬」の項も参照のこと．

血圧
1 《血圧の高さを聞くとき》
a) 一般的に聞くとき
〈血圧はどのくらいあるのですか〉
- ☆ A What's your blood pressure?
- ◎ B What's your blood pressure level?

b) 血圧が高い人に聞くとき
〈血圧はどのくらいあるのですか〉
- ☆ A How high's your blood pressure?
- ◎ B How high's your blood pressure level?
- ◎ C What's your blood pressure (level)?

2 《血圧を下げると述べるとき》
〈医師：あなたは血圧を下げなければなりませんよ〉
Doctor:
- ☆ A You have to lower your blood pressure.
- ◎ B You have to lower your blood pressure level.
- ◎ C You have to bring down your blood pressure (level).
- ◎ D You have to get your blood pressure (level) down.
- ○ E You have to reduce your blood pressure (level).

3 《高血圧だと述べたいとき》
〈彼女は高血圧なんです〉
- ◎ A She has high blood pressure.
- ○ B She has hypertension.
- ○ C Her blood pressure's high.

4 《低血圧だと述べたいとき》
〈彼女は低血圧なんです〉
- ◎ A She has low blood pressure.
- ○ B She has hypotension.
- ○ C Her blood pressure's low.

結婚
1 《結婚式そのものを述べるとき》
a) 結婚式が話題になっていないとき
〈結婚の日取りを決めよう〉
- ◎ A Let's set the date for our wedding.
- × B Let's set the date for our marriage.
- ❖ Bは辞典に出ているが使われていない．

b) 結婚式が話題になっているとき
〈結婚式は何時に始まるのですか〉
- ◎ A When does the wedding begin?
- ◎ B When does the service begin?
- ○ C When does the wedding ceremony begin?
- ▽ D When does the wedding service begin?

❖ D が辞典に出ているがまれにしか使われていない．
　2 《結婚生活を述べるとき》
　〈2人の結婚はうまくいかないと私は思う〉
　　　◎ A I'm afraid their marriage won't work out.
　　　× B I'm afraid their wedding won't work out.
　　　❖ B は「2人の結婚式はうまくいかないと私は思う」という意味でならよく使われている．

結婚記念日
　1 《一般的に述べるとき》
　〈今日は私たちの結婚記念日です〉
　　　◎ A This is our (wedding) anniversary.
　　　◎ B Today is our (wedding) anniversary.
　　　× C Today is our marriage anniversary.
　　　❖ C が辞典に出ているが使われていない．
　2 《結婚何周年と述べるとき》
　〈今日は私たちの結婚5周年の記念日です〉
　　　◎ A This is the [our] fifth anniversary.
　　　◎ B This is the fifth anniversary of our wedding [marriage].

結婚式
　1 《式のとき》
　〈結婚式の日を決めましょう〉
　　　◎ A Let's set the date for our wedding.
　　　△ B Let's set the date for our wedding ceremony.
　　　× C Let's set the date for our wedding service.
　　　× D Let's set the date for our marriage ceremony [service].
　　　❖ C, D が辞典に出ているが使われていない．
　2 《披露宴のとき》
　〈彼は披露宴に招待してくれました〉
　　　◎ A He invited me to his wedding reception.
　　　× B He invited me to his wedding party.
　　　❖(1) B が日本の英字紙によく出ているが使われていない．
　　　❖(2) wedding party は，「新郎，新婦，新郎の付添人 (the best man), 新婦の付添人 (maid of honor), ときには新郎・新婦の両親も含めた人たち」の意味ではよく使われている．

結婚紹介所
　〈私は結婚紹介所で彼と知り合ったんです〉
　　　◎ A I met him through a dating service.
　　　○ B I met him through a match-making service.
　　　○ C I met him through a dating agency.
　　　× D I met him through a matrimonial agency [center].
　　　❖(1) D が辞典に出ているが全く使われていない．
　　　❖(2) A の dating service は辞典に「デート斡旋所」「デートクラブ」の訳で紹介されているが，この訳は次の2つの理由でニュアンスを歪めている．(イ) service は「奉仕」が原義．したがって，「非営利的」「利用者のために一生懸命やります」というニュアンスを伝えたいときに使われている．(ロ) 日本語の「デート斡旋所」「デートクラブ」は，独身者のみを対象にしたものではない．しかし，dating service は独身の男女を対象にしている．

結婚する
　1 《結婚する相手を述べるとき》

〈彼女は小説家と結婚するんです〉
- ◎ A She's going to marry a novelist.
- △ B She's going to get married to a novelist.

2 《結婚する相手を述べないとき》

〈いつ結婚するんですか〉
- ☆ A When're you going to get married?
- ◎ B When're you going to be married?
- △ C When're you going to marry [get hitched]?
- ▽ D When're you going to wed?

❖ C, D が辞典に出ているが, D はまれ, C は時々使われている程度.

結婚指輪

〈彼女はパーティーで結婚指輪をしていませんでした〉
- ◎ A She wasn't wearing her wedding ring at the party.
- ▽ B She wasn't wearing her marriage ring at the party.

❖ B が辞典に出ているが, まれにしか使われていない.

決裂する

〈交渉は決裂した〉
- ◎ A The negotiations broke down [failed].
- ○ B The negotiations fell through [collapsed].
- △ C The negotiations fell by the wayside.
- △ D The negotiations faltered [flopped].
- △ E The negotiations went up in smoke.

下痢 →病気 9

けれども

〈彼はキャデラックに乗っているけれども, その日暮らしなんです〉
- ◎ A Even though he drives a Cadillac, he lives from paycheck to paycheck.
- ◎ B He drives a Cadillac, but he lives from paycheck to paycheck.
- ○ C Although he drives a Cadillac, he lives from paycheck to paycheck.
- △ D He drives a Cadillac and yet he lives from paycheck to paycheck.
- △ E Though he drives a Cadillac, he lives from paycheck to paycheck.

❖(1) 多くの辞典には口語英語では D が使われると書いてあるが, あまり使われていない.

❖(2) A を紹介していない辞典が多いが, 一番よく使われている.

権威

〈彼はこの分野の権威です〉
- ◎ A He's an expert in this field.
- ◎ B He's an authority in this field.
- ◎ C He's a specialist in this field.

❖ A が一番強い響きがあり, B, C の順で下がる.

原因である

1 《全面的な原因として述べるとき》

a) 原因が主語のとき

〈金融引き締め政策が不況の原因なのです〉
- ◎ A The tight money policy's causing the recession.
- ◎ B The tight money policy's the cause of the recession.
- ◎ C The tight money policy's responsible for the recession.
- ○ D The tight money policy's bringing about [on] the recession.
- △ E The tight money policy's giving rise to the recession.

b) 結果が主語のとき

〈この不況は金融引き締め政策が原因なのです〉
- ◎ A This recession has resulted from the tight money policy.
- ◎ B This recession has been caused by the tight money policy.
- ○ C This recession has occurred [come about] because of the tight money policy.
- ○ D This recession has been due to the tight money policy.
- △ E This recession has arisen from the tight money policy.

2 《「一因である」と述べるとき》

a) 原因が主語のとき

〈強い円がこの不況の原因なのです〉
- ◎ A The yen strength is contributing [adding] to this recession.
- ◎ B The yen strength is partially responsible for this recession.
- ◎ C The yen strength is partially causing this recession.
- △ D The yen strength is partially bringing on [about] this recession.

b) 結果が主語のとき

〈この不況は強い円が原因なのです〉
- ◎ A This recession is caused partially by the yen strength.
- ◎ B This recession is resulting partially from the yen strength.
- ◎ C This recession is partially due to the yen strength.
- ○ D This recession is arising partially from the yen strength.

牽引力

〈新しい税制度は景気を刺激する牽引力となるでしょう〉
- ◎ A The new tax system'll be the driving force [the key] to stimulating economy.
- ○ B The new tax system'll be the spark [the catalyst] to stimulating economy.

元気が出る

〈このコーヒーを飲みなさい．元気が出ますよ〉
- ◎ A Drink this coffee. It'll get you going.
- ◎ B Drink this coffee. It'll perk [wake] you up.
- ◎ C Drink this coffee. It'll give you a lift [boost].
- ○ D Drink this coffee. It'll pep you up.
- △ E Drink this coffee. It'll give you a jolt.
- △ F Drink this coffee. It'll refresh you.
- × G Drink this coffee. It'll refresh yourself.

  ❖ G が辞典に出ているが使われていない．

言及する

〈大統領は貿易不均衡について言及した〉
- ◎ A The President touched on [mentioned, referred to, commented on] the trade imbalance.
- ○ B The President made mention of the trade imbalance.
- ○ C The President noted the trade imbalance.

  ❖ B, C は少し堅い響きがある．

権限

〈彼にはこれを解決する権限はありません〉
- ◎　He doesn't have the authority [the power] to settle this.

健康診断

1 《普通の健康診断》

〈私は明日健康診断を受けるんです〉
- ◎ A I'm going in for a checkup tomorrow.
- ◎ B I'm going to have a checkup tomorrow.
- ○ C I'm going to get a checkup tomorrow.
- △ D I'm going to get a physical examination tomorrow.
- ▽ E I'm going to get a medical checkup [examination] tomorrow.
- × F I'm going to get a health checkup tomorrow.
- × G I'm going to undergo a checkup tomorrow.
- × H I'm going to undergo a medical checkup [examination] tomorrow.
- × I I'm going to undergo a physical examination tomorrow.
- ❖ F〜I が辞典に出ているが使われていない．

2 《人間ドックのような精密な健康診断》
〈私は明日精密な健康診断を受けるんです〉
- ☆ A I'm going to have a physical tomorrow.
- ◎ B I'm going to get a physical tomorrow.
- ○ C I'm going to have a complete physical [checkup] tomorrow.
- △ D I'm going to get a complete physical [checkup] tomorrow.

現行犯で
〈彼はXYZ銀行強盗の現行犯で捕まったんです〉
- ☆ A He was caught red-handed robbing XYZ Bank.
- ☆ B He was caught trying to rob XYZ Bank.
- ◎ C He was caught while robbing [trying to rob] XYZ Bank.
- ○ D He was caught red-handed trying to rob XYZ Bank.
- ○ E He was caught in the act of robbing XYZ Bank.
- △ F He was caught (red-handed) attempting to rob XYZ Bank.
- × G He was caught in the very act of robbing XYZ Bank.

検査
1 《MRIの検査を受ける》
a) 一般的に述べるとき
〈私は明日MRIの検査を受けるんです〉
- ◎ A I'm going to get an MRI tomorrow.
- ○ B I'm going to have an MRI tomorrow.
- ○ C I'm going to get [have] an MRI done tomorrow.

b) 検査の場所を明示するとき
〈明日，私はMRIで頭を検査してもらうんです〉
- ◎ I'm going to have [get] my head examined with an MRI tomorrow.

2 《内視鏡検査》
〈私は内視鏡の検査を受けるんです〉
- ◎ A I'm going to have an endoscopy.
- ○ B I'm going to have an endoscopic exam.
- △ C I'm going to have an endoscopy exam.
- ❖ C が辞典に出ているがあまり使われていない．

3 《尿の検査》
〈私は尿の検査をしてもらうつもりです〉
- ☆ A I'm going to have my urine tested.
- ◎ B I'm going to have my urine check.
- △ C I'm going to have my urine looked at [examined].

4 《酒気検査》
〈私は高速道路で酒気検査をさせられたんです〉

◎ A I got a breath test on the highway.
○ B I got breathalyzed on the highway.

5 《レントゲン検査》
〈私は明日胃のレントゲン検査をするんです〉

◎ A I'm going to have my stomach X-rayed tomorrow.
○ B I'm going to have an X-ray done on my stomach tomorrow.

検死官 →職業 34

現実的

〈もっと現実的になってください〉

◎ Be more realistic [practical], please.

現実を直視する

〈あなたは現実を直視しなければならないんです〉

☆ A You have to face reality.
◎ B You have to face the facts.
○ C You have to face up to (the) reality.
△ D You have to see [look at] (the) reality.
× E You have to face the music.
❖ E がある辞典に出ているが使われていない．しかし，「報いを甘んじて受け入れる，（自分が招いた事態に対して）罰を受け入れる」の意味ではよく使われている．

現代の

1 《歴史を述べるとき》
〈私は現代のアメリカ史に興味があるのです〉

◎ A I'm interested in modern American history.
◎ B I'm interested in contemporary American history.
◎ C I'm interested in current American history.
○ D I'm interested in present-day American history.
△ E I'm interested in today's American history.
❖ A は第二次大戦以降をさす．B は A の意味で時々使われることもあるが，1980 年代の意味で非常によく使われている．C は過去数年，D は 1990 年頃以降，E は 2001 年以降を意味している．

2 《考え方》
〈彼の考え方は現代的だ〉

◎ A His way of thinking's modern.
○ B His way of thinking's contemporary.
△ C His way of thinking's current.
▽ D His way of thinking's present-day.
❖ 考え方で A～D が使われると，歴史上の年代とは関係なく過去数年から現在に至るまでの意味になる．

3 《言語》
〈私はイギリス英語の古典には興味がありません．現代のイギリス英語に興味があるのです〉

◎ A I'm not interested in classical British English. I'm interested in modern [today's] British English.
○ B I'm not interested in classical British English. I'm interested in current [present-day] British English.
△ C I'm not interested in classical British English. I'm interested in contemporary British English.

言質を取られる
〈彼らに今晩会ったとき，言質を取られるなよ〉
- ◎ A When you see them tonight, don't commit yourself.
- ◎ B When you see them tonight, don't make any commitments.
- ◎ C When you see them tonight, don't tie yourself down.
- ▽ D When you see them tonight, don't bind yourself down.

兼任する
1 《人が主語のとき》
〈彼は首相と外相を兼任しています〉
- ☆ A He's acting as the Prime Minister and the Foreign Minister.
- ◎ B He's serving [doubling] as the Prime Minister and the Foreign Minister.
- ○ C He's performing [working] as the Prime Minister and the Foreign Minister.

2 《地位を示す語が主語のとき》
〈首相が外相を兼任しています〉
- ◎ A The Prime Minister is acting concurrently as the Foreign Minister.
- ◎ B The Prime Minister holds the post pf the Foreign Minister.
- ◎ C The Prime Minister doubles as the Foreign Minister.
- ○ D The Prime Minister serves [is serving] concurrently as the Foreign Minister.

〔こ〕

…個
1 《石けん》
〈石けんを2個下さい〉
- ◎ A Give me two bars of soap.
- × B Give me two cakes of soap.
  - ❖ Aは辞典，英文法書で紹介されていないが非常によく使われている．Bは辞典，英文法書に出ているが使われていない．

2 《石炭》
〈石炭を私に2個持ってきて下さい〉
- ◎ Please bring me two lumps of coal.

ご案内します →案内する

コイン投げ
〈コイン投げで決めよう．表か裏か〉
- ◎ A Let's toss. Heads or tails?
- ◎ B Let's flip a coin. Heads or tails?
  - ❖ アメリカでは二者択一の選択を迫られた場合コインを投げ，その裏表を当てて是非を決めることがある．日本人がジャンケンで順番を決めたりするようなもの．

コインランドリー →店 13

…号
1 《雑誌の最新号》
〈7月号を読みましたか〉
- ◎ A Did you read the July issue?

× B Did you read the July number?
　2　《雑誌の以前の号》
　〈ビル：何を読んでいるの〉
　Bill: What're you reading?
　〈リンダ：タイムのバックナンバーを読んでいるのよ〉
　Linda:
　　　◎ A I'm reading a back issue of Time.
　　　× B I'm reading a back number of Time.
　　　❖ B が和英辞典に出ているが使われていない．

行為
1　《1回の行為》
〈それは不法行為でした〉
　　　◎　　That was an illegal act.
2　《2回以上の行為》
〈彼は慈善的行為のために表彰されました〉
　　　◎ A He was awarded for his charitable acts.
　　　○ B He was awarded for his charitable actions.

こういうふうに
〈こういうふうにビジネスは日本で行われています〉
　　　◎ A This is the way [how] business's done in Japan.
　　　◎ B Business's done in Japan in this way.
　　　❖ This is...を強調したいときは A, Business を強調したいときは B を使う．

後遺症
〈彼は交通事故の後遺症に苦しんでいるんです〉
　　　◎　　He's been suffering from aftereffects of the car accident.

合意する　→同意する

公営住宅
〈彼は公営住宅に住んでいます〉
　　　◎ A He lives in a government-built apartment complex.
　　　◎ B He lives in an apartment complex built by the government.
　　　◎ C He lives in a (housing) project.
　　　◎ D He lives in a council house.
　　　❖(1) A, B は日本，C はアメリカ，D はイギリスの団地に相当する表現．
　　　❖(2) アメリカの project は，収入が少ない，または収入が全然ない主として黒人，ヒスパニック系の人々に対して，政府が犯罪防止の一環として建てたものであるにもかかわらず，犯罪率は以前と同じように高く，アメリカ人は暗いイメージを抱いている．一方，日本とイギリスの「団地」には，こういうイメージは何もない．それどころか明るいムードがある．日本の公営団地とアメリカの project の違いはそのほかにもいくつもあり，似ても似つかぬものである．したがって，アメリカ人に日本の団地に住んでいるという意味で，I live in a (housing) project. などと言ったら，非常に誤ったイメージをいだかせることになる．

甲乙つけがたい
〈ジム：ハーバードとイエールではどちらのほうがいいんですか〉
Jim: Which's better, Harvard or Yale?
〈ビル：甲乙つけがたいです〉
Bill:
　　　◎ A It's toss-up.
　　　◎ B They're neck and neck.

- ◎ C They're about the same.
- ◎ D They're equal.

豪華な

1 《アパート》

a） 建物全体ではなく一世帯一世帯，つまり apartment building ではなく apartment の豪華さに言及するとき

〈彼らは豪華なアパートに住んでいます〉
- ◎ A They're living in a luxurious apartment.
- ◎ B They're living in a gorgeous apartment.
- △ C They're living in a posh apartment.
- △ D They're living in a swanky apartment.
  - ❖(1) B はアパート全体にも使える．したがって，豪華に装飾したのはテナント・家主のどちらかは不明．
  - ❖(2) D はアメリカ南部，または南部に近い所で使われている．

b） アパート全体，また共同で使用するロビー，エレベーター，プール，テニスコートなどの豪華さに言及するとき

〈彼らは豪華なアパートに住んでいる〉
- ◎ A They're living in a luxury apartment (building).
- ○ B They're living in a swanky [posh] apartment building.

c） 大きさ・眺めがすばらしいというニュアンスのとき

〈彼らは豪華なアパートに住んでいます〉
- ◎ A They're living in a deluxe apartment.
- ○ B They're living in a deluxe apartment building.

2 《比較の気持ちがあるとき》

a） 旧版，または他の辞典と比較して述べるとき

〈新しい辞典はハードカバーで豪華版です〉
- ◎ A The new dictionary's a deluxe edition with a hard cover.
- × B The new dictionary's a gorgeous [luxurious, luxury] edition with a hard cover.

b） 最初考えていた予算と比較して述べるとき

〈私は約1万5千ドルの車を買うのに使うつもりだったのですが，セールスマンにこの豪華モデルを買うように説得されて2万ドル使う羽目になってしまったんです〉
- ◎ I was going to spend $15,000 for a car but the salesman talked me into the deluxe model. I ended up spending $20,000.

3 《「素敵な」とか「すばらしい」というニュアンスのとき》

〈課長に昇進したら豪華な夕食をごちそうしますよ〉
- ◎ A If you're promoted to manager, I'll buy you a nice dinner.
- ○ B If you're promoted to manager, I'll buy you a terrific [big] dinner.
- △ C If you're promoted to manager, I'll buy you a gorgeous dinner.

4 《「高級な」というニュアンスのとき》

〈もし課長に昇進したら豪華なレストランへ招待しますよ〉
- ◎ A If you're promoted to manager, I'll invite you to a fancy [five-star] restaurant.
- ○ B If you're promoted to manager, I'll invite you to a top-notch restaurant.

好奇心が強い

1 《肯定的意味のとき》

〈私の5歳の息子は何事につけ好奇心がとても強いんです〉
- ☆ A My five-year-old son wants to know about everything.

- ◎ B My five-year-old son is really curious about everything.
- △ C My five-year-old son is very inquisitive about everything.
  - ❖ C は堅い文章ではよく使われている。
2 《否定的意味のとき》
〈私の新しい隣人はとても好奇心が強いんです。私にすごくいろいろなことを尋ねるんです〉
- ☆ A My new neighbors're really nosey. They ask me too many questions.
- ◎ B My new neighbors're really curious. They ask me too many questions.
- △ C My new neighbors're really snoopy. They ask me too many questions.

高級な
1 《住宅街》
a) 2人称・人称が主語のとき
〈彼らは高級住宅街に住んでいます〉
- ◎ A They live in a wealthy [a rich, a high-class, an upscale, an exclusive] neighborhood.
- ○ B They live in an expensive neighborhood.
- △ C They live in a ritzy [a classy, a swanky, a top-notch] neighborhood.
- ▽ D They live in a posh [a luxurious] neighborhood.
  - ❖ C の swanky はアメリカの南部で使われている。

b) 1人称が主語のとき
〈(不動産屋で) 私たちは高級住宅街で家を探しています〉
- ◎ A We're looking for a house in an upscale [an exclusive, a nice, a good] neighborhood.
- ◎ B We're looking for a house in a nice [a good] area.
- △ C We're looking for a house in a classy [a high-class] neighborhood.
- × D We're looking for a house in a wealthy [a rich, an expensive] neighborhood.

2 《ビジネス街》
〈銀座は高級なビジネス街です〉
- ◎ A Ginza's a high-class [an upscale, a prestigious, an exclusive] business district.
- ○ B Ginza's a wealthy business district.
- △ C Ginza's a top-notch [a classy, a ritzy] business district.
- ▽ D Ginza's a posh business district.

3 《レストラン》
〈たまには高級レストランで食事をしましょう〉
- ☆ A Let's have dinner at a fancy restaurant for a change.
- ◎ B Let's have dinner at a five-star restaurant for a change.
- ○ C Let's have dinner at a high-class [a ritzy, a classy, a top-notch, a fine] restaurant for a change.
- △ D Let's have dinner at an exclusive restaurant for a change.
- × E Let's have dinner at a quality [high-quality] restaurant for a change.
  - ❖ B の five-star, C の top-notch が高級さの点では1番。

4 《車》
a) 車の外面を述べている

〈彼は高級車に乗っています〉
- ◎ A He drives an expensive [a luxury, a fancy] car.
- ○ B He drives a classy [a prestigious] car.
- △ C He drives an upscale [an exclusive, a high-priced] car.
- × D He drives a luxurious [high-class] car.
- × E He drives a high-class automobile.
  - ❖ D, E が辞典に出ているが使われていない．

b）車の中で述べているとき

〈これは高級車ですね〉
- ◎ A This is a luxurious car.
- ○ B This is a classy car.

5 《コーヒー》

〈この店は高級なコーヒーしか売っていません〉
- ◎ A This store only sells gourmet [top-quality] coffee.
- ◎ B This store only sells expensive coffee.
- ○ C This store only sells high-quality [fancy] coffee.
- △ D This store only sells fine coffee.
- × E This store only sells first-rate [superior] coffee.
  - ❖ B の expensive coffee とは「値段が高いコーヒー」が原義．高級なコーヒーは値段が高いので，B の expensive coffee は「高級なコーヒー」の意味で非常によく使われている．

6 《ワイン》

〈彼は高級なワインしか飲みません〉
- ◎ A He only drinks expensive [fine] wine.
- ○ B He only drinks high-quality [top-quality] wine.
- ○ C He only drinks vintage wine.
- △ D He only drinks high-priced [superior] wine.
- × E He only drinks aged wine.
  - ❖(1) C はワインを飲まない人の間では全く使われていない．
  - ❖(2) E が辞典に出ているが使われていない．

公共料金

〈公共料金は家賃に含まれています〉
- ◎ A The utilities're included in the rent.
- × B The public utility charges're included in the rent.
- × C The public utility rates're included in the rent.
- × D The fees for public services're included in the rent.
  - ❖ 辞典に B, C, D が出ているが使われていない．

航空会社 →会社 17

合計する

〈パーティーで使ったお金を全部合計してごらんなさい〉
- ◎ A Add up all the money you spent for the party.
- ○ B Total [Total up, Sum up, Add together] all the money you spent for the party.

高血圧 →血圧 3

貢献する

〈彼は日本のフランス語教育に大きく貢献した〉
- ☆ A He worked hard for French education in Japan.
- ☆ B He did a lot for French education in Japan.
- ◎ C He made a great contribution to French education in Japan.

こうこくする 205

- ◎ D He greatly contributed to French education in Japan.
- ◎ E He did a great deal for French education in Japan.
- ○ F He went a long way toward promoting French education in Japan.
- △ G He did very much for French education in Japan.
  - ❖(1) C, D は A, B, E, F, G より大きく貢献したというニュアンスがある．
  - ❖(2) C, D, E, G は文章だけでなく口語でも使われているが，堅い響きがある．A, B は非常に口語的な表現．

高校生 →…学生 2

広告する

1 《テレビ・ラジオ》

a) 数種類の広告をするとき

〈うちはテレビに広告を出す予定です〉

- ☆ A We're going to advertise on TV.
- ◎ B We're going to put [run] ads on TV.
- ○ C We're going to place ads on TV.
- ○ D We're going to buy air time on TV.
- ○ E We're going to buy time slots on TV.
- △ F We're going to buy time spots on TV.
- △ G We're going to buy some TV time.
- △ H We're going to buy TV time slots.
- △ I We're going to buy time [spots] on TV.
- △ J We're going to buy TV (time) spots.
  - ❖ D〜J は広告業界の人との話では非常によく使われている．

b) 1種類の広告を何回も出すとき

〈うちはテレビに広告を出す予定です〉

- ☆ A We're going to put an ad on TV.
- ◎ B We're going to run an ad on TV.
- ◎ C We're going to buy ad time on TV.
- ◎ D We're going to advertise on TV.
- ○ E We're going to buy advertising spot on TV.
- ○ F We're going to buy time spots on TV.
- ○ G We're going to buy air time on TV.
- ○ H We're going to place an ad on TV.
- △ I We're going to buy a TV spot [slot].
- △ J We're going to buy a TV time spot [slot].
- △ K We're going to put [run] ads on TV.
- △ L We're going to buy advertising spots on TV.
- △ M We're going to buy TV spots [slots].
- △ N We're going to buy TV time spots [slots].

2 《新聞・雑誌》

a) 数種類の広告を出すとき

〈うちは新聞と雑誌に広告を出す予定です〉

- ☆ A We're going to run ads in the papers and the magazines.
- ◎ B We're going to put [place] ads in the papers and the magazines.
- ◎ C We're going to advertise in the papers and the magazines.
- ◎ D We're going to buy ad space in the papers and the magazines.
- ◎ E We're going to buy some space in the papers and the magazines.
- ○ F We're going to buy advertising space in the papers and the magazines.

○ G　We're going to buy space [spots] in the papers and the magazines.
　　　○ H　We're going to buy some spots in the papers and the magazines.
　b）1種類の広告を出すとき
〈うちは新聞と雑誌に広告を出す予定です〉
　　　☆ A　We're going to run an ad [ads] in the papers and the magazines.
　　　◎ B　We're going to advertise in the papers and the magazines.
　　　◎ C　We're going to put an ad [ads] in the papers and the magazines.
　　　◎ D　We're going to place an ad [ads] in the papers and the magazines.
　　　◎ E　We're going to buy some space in the papers and the magazines.
　　　○ F　We're going to buy space [a spot, spots] in the papers and the magazines.
　　　○ G　We're going to buy advertising space in the papers and the magazines.
　3　《誇大広告》
〈これは誇大広告です〉
　　　◎ A　This is an exaggerated claim.
　　　▽ B　This is an exaggerated advertisement.
講師　→地位 22
公衆電話　→電話 6
工場
　1　《自動車工場》
〈彼は自動車工場で働いています〉
　　　◎ A　He works at an auto [a car] plant.
　　　○ B　He works at an auto [a car] factory.
　　　❖ plant は factory より機械が最新式というニュアンスがある．
　2　《自動車組立て工場》
〈彼は自動車組立て工場で働いています〉
　　　◎ A　He works at an auto assembly plant [factory].
　　　△ B　He works at an auto assembly facility.
　　　△ C　He works at a car assembly plant [facility].
　3　《鉄鋼工場》
〈彼は鉄鋼工場で働いています〉
　　　◎ A　He works at a steel mill.
　　　○ B　He works at a steel plant [factory].
　　　❖ B はアメリカの地域によって使用頻度は大きく異なる．A は地域に関係なく非常によく使われている．
　4　《製粉工場》
〈彼は製粉工場で働いています〉
　　　◎ A　He works at a flour mill.
　　　▽ B　He works at a flour factory [plant].
　　　× C　He works at a flour facility.
　5　《製紙工場》
〈彼は製紙工場で働いています〉
　　　◎ A　He works at a paper mill.
　　　○ B　He works at a paper factory.
　　　× C　He works at a paper facility.
　6　《繊維工場》
〈彼は繊維工場で働いています〉
　　　☆ A　He works at a textile mill.

- ◎ B He works at a textile factory.
   - ○ C He works at a textile plant.
   - × D He works at a textile facility.
7 《びん詰工場》
〈彼はびん詰工場で働いています〉
   - ◎ A He works at a bottling plant.
   - ○ B He works at a bottling factory.
   - △ C He works at a bottling facility.
8 《缶詰工場》
〈彼は缶詰工場で働いています〉
   - ◎ A He works at a cannery.
   - ○ B He works at a canning factory.
   - △ C He works at a canned food factory.
   - ▽ D He works at a canning plant.
   - ▽ E He works at canned food plant.
9 《印刷工場》
a）新聞・本・雑誌
〈彼は印刷工場で働いています〉
   - ☆ A He works at a printing press.
   - ◎ B He works at a printer's.
   - ○ C He works at a printing (press) company.
   - × D He works at a printing shop.
b）チラシ
〈彼は印刷工場で働いています〉
   - ◎ A He works at a printing [print] shop.
   - ○ B He works at a printing company.
   - △ C He works at a printing house.
10 《ガラス工場》
〈彼はガラス工場で働いています〉
   - ◎ A He works at a glass factory.
   - ▽ B He works at a glassworks.
   - ▽ C He works at a glass house.
   - × D He works at a glass foundry [plant].
   ❖ D が辞典に出ているが使われていない.

向上

1 《地位の向上》
〈私は今後女性の地位の向上のために働きたいんです〉
   - ◎ A I want to work for the advancement [improvement] of the status of woman from now on.
   - △ B I want to work for the elevation [raising] of the status of woman from now on.
2 《相互理解の向上》
〈私は今後日米の異文化理解の向上のために働きたいんです〉
   - ◎ A I want to work for the advancement [promotion, improvement] of intercultural understanding between America and Japan from now on.
   - ○ B I want to work for the betterment of intercultural understanding between America and Japan from now on.
   - △ C I want to work for the elevation [raising] of intercultural under-

standing between America and Japan from now on.

向上させる

〈私は今後婦人の地位を向上させるために働きたいんです〉
- ☆ A I want to work to advance [improve] the status of woman from now on.
- ◎ B I want to work to raise the status of woman from now on.
- ○ C I want to work to elevate the status of woman from now on.

興信所

1 《企業の成績を調べる》

〈彼女は興信所に勤めています〉
- ◎ A She works for a corporate performance-rating agency.
- ○ B She works for a business performance-rating agency.
- × C She works for a commercial [mercantile] agency.
  - ❖ C が辞典に出ているが使われていない．

2 《個人のクレジットカードの支払いを調べる》

〈彼女は興信所に勤めています〉
- ◎ She works for a credit-rating [credit] agency.

3 《個人の素行調査機関》

〈彼女は興信所に勤めています〉
- ◎ A She works for a private detective agency.
- ◎ B She works for a PI.

香水

1 《女性》

〈彼女はいつも香水をつけています〉
- ◎ A She's always wearing perfume.
- ○ B She's always wearing Cologne.
- × C She's always wearing eau de Cologne.

2 《男性》

〈彼はいつも香水をつけています〉
- ◎ A He's always wearing Cologne.
- × B He's always wearing perfume [eau de Cologne].

高性能の

〈これは高性能のステレオなんです〉
- ◎ A This is a high-end stereo.
- ○ B This is a high-quality stereo.
- △ C This is a high-powered stereo.
- × D This is a high-efficient stereo.

高層アパート →家 13

高速道路 →道 4

公定歩合

〈アメリカの中央銀行はまもなく公定歩合を上げるでしょう〉
- ☆ A The FED'll raise the bank rate soon.
- ◎ B The FED'll raise the official bank rate soon.
- ○ C The FED'll raise the official discount rate soon.

行動

1 《途切れない一連の行動》

〈行動するときがきた〉
- ◎ A The time has come for action.
- ▽ B The time has come for actions.

〈政府は行動を起こすのがずうっと遅いんです〉
- ◎ A The Government has been slow in taking action.
- ▽ B The Government has been slow in taking actions.

2 《途切れる一連の行動》

〈行動から判断して，リンダは幸せのようだ〉
- ◎ A Judging from her actions, Linda seems to be happy.
- ▽ B Judging from her action, Linda seems to be happy.

〈あなたの行動はあなたの言葉と矛盾している〉
- ◎ A Your actions contradict your words.
- △ B Your action contradicts your words.

〈彼は自分の行動を正当化しようとしている〉
- ◎ A He's trying to justify his actions.
- △ B He's trying to justify his action.

3 《「行動力のある人」と言うとき》

〈彼は行動力のある人です〉
- ◎ A He's a man of action.
- ◎ B He makes things happen.
- ◎ C He gets things done.
- ○ D He's a doer.
  - ❖ほめている強さはAが一番強く，B, C, Dの順で下がる．

高騰する

〈地価が高騰しています〉
- ◎ A Land prices're skyrocketing.
- ◎ B Land prices're going through the roof.
- ◎ C Land prices're soaring [shooting up].
- ◎ D Land prices're going up [increasing, rising] very fast.
- ○ E Land prices're going up [increasing, rising] very rapidly.
- △ F Land prices're zooming [running up].
  - ❖高騰の率はA, Bが一番高く，Cはほぼ同じで2番．D, E, Fはほぼ同じで3番．

強盗に入られる

1 《週末・休暇中》

〈私の事務所は強盗に入られたんです〉
- ◎ A My office was broken into.
- ○ B My office was robbed.
  - ❖Aは鍵，窓などを壊して侵入したことを意味する．

2 《夜中》

〈私の事務所は昨夜強盗に入られたんです〉
- ◎ A My office was broken into last night.
- ○ B My office was burglarized [robbed] last night.
- × C My office was burgled last night.
  - ❖Cが辞典に出ているが使われていない．

3 《昼間社員がいるとき》

〈私の事務所は強盗に入られたんです〉
- ◎ A My office was robbed.
- × B My office was broken into.

口頭の

1 《契約》

〈私たちは口頭契約をしたんです〉

◎　A　We made a verbal agreement.
　　　△　B　We made an oral agreement.
　2　《試験》
〈私は口頭試験に自信がないんです〉
　　　◎　A　I'm not confident of the oral test.
　　　△　B　I'm not confident of the verbal test.
購読する
〈あなたはどこの新聞を購読しているのですか〉
　　　◎　A　What paper do you get?
　　　○　B　What paper do you subscribe to?
　　　△　C　What paper do you take?
　　　×　D　What paper do you take in?
　　　　❖ Dは辞典にイギリス英語として出ているが，イギリスでも使われていない．
　　　　　Bはイギリスでは雑誌の購読にしか使われていない．

公認会計士　→職業　4
公認されている
〈あの大学は公認されていない〉
　　　◎　A　That college isn't accredited.
　　　×　B　That college isn't officially recognized [approved].
　　　×　C　That college isn't registered.
　　　×　D　That college isn't authorized.
　　　　❖(1)　和英辞典にはA〜Dが「公認されている」の訳語として出ているが，A しか使われていない．
　　　　❖(2)　イギリス英語ではDはまれ，B, Cはよく使われている．

後任になる
　1　《公の地位についている人の後任》
〈小泉氏が森首相の後任になった〉
　　　◎　A　Mr. Koizumi succeeded [replaced] Prime Minister Mori.
　　　◎　B　Mr. Koizumi took the place of Prime Minister Mori.
　　　◎　C　Mr. Koizumi took over the Prime Ministership from Mr. Mori.
　　　○　D　Mr. Koizumi followed [came after] Mr. Mori as (the) Prime Minister.
　　　△　E　Mr. Koizumi succeeded to the position of the Prime Ministership from [after] Mr. Mori.
　2　《公でない地位の人の後任》
〈彼の後任を見つけるのは難しい〉
　　　◎　A　We're having trouble finding someone to replace him.
　　　◎　B　We're having trouble finding someone to take his place.

購買部　→…部　7
購買力がある
　1　《現在のことを述べるとき》
〈円は外国でとても購買力がある〉
　　　◎　A　The yen has a lot of buying power abroad.
　　　○　B　The yen has a lot of purchasing power abroad.
　2　《過去と比較して述べるとき》
〈円は昔よりも購買力がある〉
　　　◎　A　The yen buys more than it used to be.
　　　◎　B　The yen is worth more than it used to be.
　　　◎　C　The yen has more buying power than it used to be.

- ○ D The yen has more purchasing power than it used to be.

校風

〈早稲田と慶応の校風は全然違う〉
- ◎ A The traditions and atmosphere of Waseda and Keio are completely different.
- ◎ B The traditions at Waseda and Keio are completely different.
- × C The school characteristics of Waseda and Keio are completely different.
    - ❖ C を「校風」の適訳として紹介している辞典があるが，この言い方は全く使われていない．

合法的な →法律で認められている 3
広報部 →…部 8
公民権 →市民権 3
公務員

1 《国家公務員》

a) 日本の場合

〈私は公務員です〉
- ◎ A I work for the Japanese Government.
- ◎ B I'm a Japanese Government employee.
- ◎ C I have a job in the Japanese Government.
- ◎ D I'm a Japanese Government worker.
- ○ E I have a position in the Japanese Government.
- ○ F I'm an employee for [of] the Japanese Government.
- ○ G I work for the government.
- ○ H I'm employed by the Japanese Government.
- ○ I I'm a civil servant.
- ○ J I'm an employee in the Japanese Government.
- × K I'm a public servant.
- × L I'm a government official.
- × M I'm a government officer.
    - ❖(1) K, L, M が多くの辞典に「国家公務員」として紹介されているが，この意味では使われていない．しかし，K の public servant は選挙で選ばれた国会議員，知事，市長，町長などに普通に使われている．したがって，public servant に相当する日本語はない．L の government official は政府の「官僚」，state government, county government の「幹部」の意味でなら非常によく使われている．M の government officer も L の government official の意味では使われているが，L の方が M よりもよく使われている．
    - ❖(2) I の civil servant は多くの辞典に「国家公務員」と紹介されているが，国家だけでなく県庁，市役所，町役場の「公務員」の意味でよく使われている．
    - ❖(3) B の government employee, D の government worker は高い地位にいる「公務員」として数冊の辞典に紹介されているが，英語のニュアンスを歪曲している．B は地位の高低に関係なく使われている．D は地位が非常に低い場合にのみよく使われている．
    - ❖(4) A, C は辞典に出ていないが，地位に関係なく非常によく使われている．
    - ❖(5) E は地位が高いという響きがある．
    - ❖(6) H は D ほどではないが地位が低いときに使われている．
    - ❖(7) G は政府，県庁，市役所，町・村役場，区役所の「公務員」の意味でよ

く使われている．

❖(8) アメリカ政府以外の国はすべて日本と同じ表現を使う．

b) アメリカの場合
・アメリカ人がアメリカ人に話すとき
〈私は公務員です〉

- ◎ A I work for the Federal Government.
- ◎ B I'm a Federal Government employee.
- ◎ C I have a job in the (Federal) Government.
- ◎ D I'm employed by the Federal Government.
- ◎ E I'm an employee of the Federal Government.
- ○ F I'm an employee for the Federal Government.
- ○ G I work at the Federal Government.
- ○ H I'm on the Federal Government payroll.

・アメリカ人が外国で話すとき
〈私は国家公務員です〉

- ◎ A I work for the (American) Government.
- ○ B I work for Uncle Sam.
- ○ C I have a job in the Government.
- ○ D I'm employed by the American Government.
- ○ E I'm an American Government employee.
- △ F I'm an employee of [for] the American Government.
- × G I work for the Federal Government.
- × H I'm a Federal Government employee.

2 《県庁》
〈私は公務員です〉

- ☆ A I work for the County (Hall).
- ◎ B I work for the County Government.
- ◎ C I work at [in] County Hall.
- ◎ D I'm an employee at [of] County Hall.
- ◎ E I'm an employee of the County Government.
- ◎ F I'm a County (Government) employee.
- × G I work for the Prefecture.

❖(1) 日本の辞典では「県」＝prefecture と出ている．しかし，アメリカでは全く使われていない．したがって，奇妙に聞こえる．county が日本の県に相当する．

❖(2) 話し手が働いている county（県）以外で話すときは，I work for a county. と the ではなく a を使う．

❖(3) county は小文字も等しくよく使われている．

3 《市役所》
〈私は公務員です〉

- ☆ A I work for (the) City Hall.
- ◎ B I work at (the) City Hall.
- ◎ C I work for the City.
- ◎ D I'm an employee at (the) city hall.
- ◎ E I work in (the) city hall.
- ◎ F I'm a city hall employee.
- ◎ G I'm a city (government) employee.
- ◎ H I work for the city government.
- ◎ I I'm employee by city hall.

- △ J I work for the municipal government.
- ▽ K I'm a city office employee.
  - ❖(1) city hall は大文字, 小文字共によく使われている.
  - ❖(2) city hall は全体でいくつかの city office から成り立っている. しかし, 一般の会話では city office は city hall の意味でよく使われている.
  - ❖(3) J の municipal government は「町役場」の意味でもよく使われている.

高名な →有名な 4
肛門医 →医者 2
合理化する
1 《経費の削減を意味するとき》
〈うちは合理化しなければならないんです〉
- ◎ A We have to streamline our operations.
- × B We have to rationalize our operations.
  - ❖(1) 和英辞典には B が紹介されているが, 全く使われていない. A は辞典に出ていないが, 非常によく使われている.
  - ❖(2) どの英和辞典も rationalize に「合理化する」の意味を出しているが, この語は「正当化する」の意味でしか使われていない.「正当化する」の項を参照のこと.
  - ❖(3) A の streamline は, 人件費, 制作費, 運搬費など, ありとあらゆる可能な費用の削減を意味している. したがって人員の解雇も含まれている.

2 《改良を意味するとき》
〈うちは合理化しなければならないんです〉
- ◎　　We have to improve [work on] our operations.

考慮に入れる
〈私たちは彼の未経験を考慮に入れなければならない〉
- ◎ A We have to take his inexperience into account.
- ◎ B We have to consider his inexperience.
- ○ C We have to take his inexperience into consideration..
- ○ D We have to make allowance(s) for his inexperience.
- ○ E We have to keep his inexperience in mind.
- △ F We have to bear his inexperience in mind.
- ▽ G We have to keep [bear] his inexperience in view.
  - ❖辞典に G が出ているがあまり使われていない.

誤解する
〈私が言っていることを誤解しないで下さい〉
- ☆ A Don't get me wrong.
- ◎ B Don't misunderstand me.
- ◎ C Don't get the wrong idea.
- ○ D Don't misinterpret what I'm saying.

小型版 →…版 2
国債 →債券 1
国産品
1 《アメリカ英語》
〈私たちはもっと国産品を使うようにすべきだ〉
- ☆ A We should try to use more domestic products.
- ◎ B We should try to use more domestic goods [merchandise].
- ◎ C We should try to use more domestically-produced goods [merchandise].

- ○ D We should try to use more domestically-made products [goods, merchandise].
- △ E We should try to use more domestic stuff.
- △ F We should try to use more domestically-produced stuff.

2 《イギリス英語》

〈私たちはもっと国産品を使うようにすべきだ〉

- ◎ A We should try to use more home-produced goods.
- ○ B We should try to use more domestically-produced articles.
- ○ C We should try to use more homemade articles.
- ○ D We should try to use more home-produced articles.
- △ E We should try to use more domestic products [goods].

国税庁

〈私は国税庁に勤めています〉

- ◎ A I work for the IRS.
- △ B I work for the Internal Revenue Service.
- × C I work for the National Tax (Administration) Agency.

❖(1) 堅い文章では B はよく使われている.

❖(2) A, B の使用を勧めたい. 日本の辞典では C を紹介しているが, アメリカでは使われていないので不自然に聞こえるからである. いずれにしろ, 日本の「国税庁」と同じ仕事をしている機関は A, B である. 多くの英和辞典で A, B を「内国税収入庁」という訳語を出しているのは不適切であり, the IRS の役目を知らないことを証明していることになる.

国民

1 《1人》

a) 非王制の国 (共和制, 軍事・警察国家の国民)

〈私はアメリカの国民として誇りを持っています〉

- ◎ A I have pride as an American citizen.
- × B I have pride as an American national.

b) 王制の国

・イギリス

〈私はイギリスの国民として誇りを持っています〉

- ◎ A I have pride as a British citizen.
- ○ B I have pride as a British subject.

❖イギリス国民でも君主制に反対の人は B は使わない.

・日本

〈私は日本の国民として誇りを持っています〉

- ◎ A I have pride as a Japanese citizen.
- × B I have pride as a Japanese subject.

❖タイ, オランダ, ノルウェー, サウジアラビアでは subject は時々使われる.

2 《普通名詞としての複数の国民》

a) ひとつの国民

〈日本人は勤勉な国民である〉

- ◎ A The Japanese are an industrious people.
- × B The Japanese are an industrious nation.

❖この意味のときは a+形容詞+people, つまり普通名詞としての a people である.

b) 普通名詞としての複数の国の国民

〈アジア人は勤勉な国民である〉

- ◎ A The Asians are industrious people.
- ▽ B The Asians are industrious peoples.
- × C The Asians are industrious nations.
  - ❖文法的には B が正しいがまれにしか使われていない．ただし，歴史書のような文章では使われている．

3 《集合名詞としての国民》

〈国民はイスラム教徒のテロリストたちに怒り狂っている〉

- ◎ A The country's furious about the Islamic terrorists.
- ◎ B The nation's furious about the Islamic terrorists.
- ◎ C The people're furious about the Islamic terrorists.
  - ❖A, B は国家も含まれた「国民」である．C には「国家」は含まれていない．

4 《外国の国民》

a) 治外法権の地域

〈横田空軍基地には大勢日本の国民が働いている〉

- ☆ A There are a lot of Japanese nationals working on Yokota Air Base.
- ◎ B There are a lot of Japanese people working on Yokota Air Base.
- ○ C There are a lot of Japanese citizens working on Yokota Air Base.
  - ❖横田基地は日本の領土であるが，治外法権の地域になっているので，たとえ日本人でも外国にいる国民とみなす．

b) 非治外法権の地域

〈東京には大勢のドイツ国民がいる〉

- ☆ A There are a lot of German people in Tokyo.
- ◎ B There are a lot of German citizens in Tokyo.
- ○ C There are a lot of German nations in Tokyo.

国立の

1 《大学の場合》

〈私は国立大学に勤務しています〉

- ◎ A I work for a government-run university.
- ○ B I work for a government university.
- △ C I work for a government-managed university.
- △ D I work for a national university.
- × E I work for a state university.
  - ❖(1) E が辞典に出ているが使われていない．
  - ❖(2) アメリカには国立大学はない．したがって，A, B, C いずれも使われていない．しかし，アメリカ人がアメリカ以外の国の国立大学を述べるときには，A が一番自然に聞こえる．
  - ❖(3) state university とは「州立大学」の意味ではよく使われる．state には「国家」の意味があるが，welfare state（福祉国家），police state（警察国家），the secretary of state（国務長官）のように名詞として使われており，形容詞として「国家の」の意味で使われることはない．
  - ❖(4) D の national には「国立の」の意味がある．しかし，アメリカの西海岸では私立大学が「○○ National University」という名称を 30 年ほど前から使っている．

2 《大学以外の場合》

- ❖national を使う．national park（国立公園），national library（国立図書館），national theater（国立劇場），National Public Radio (NPR)（国立公共ラジオ放送教会），National Security Agency (NSA)（国家安全保障局），national monument（国有記念物），National Science Foundation（全米科学財団）など．

心の準備をする →準備する 6

心を鬼にする

〈田中君が首になるのは忍びないが，もし我々が利益を上げようと思うならば心を鬼にしなければなるまい〉

- ◎ A It's too bad about Mr. Tanaka's getting fired, but we have to be tough if we're going to make a profit.
- △ B It's too bad about Mr. Tanaka's getting fired, but we have to be tough-minded if we're going to make a profit.
- × C It's too bad about Mr. Tanaka's getting fired, but we have to harden our hearts if we're going to make a profit.

   ❖ C が辞典に出ているが使われていない．

50 歩 100 歩です

〈50 歩 100 歩です〉

- ◎ A That's six of one and half a dozen of the other.
- ◎ B There's little difference between the two.
- ◎ C There isn't much difference between the two.

故障原因

〈私はまだエンジンの故障原因が見つけられないんです〉

- ☆ A I still can't find the engine problem.
- ◎ B I still can't find the engine trouble.
- ◎ C I still can't find the problem with [in] the engine.
- ○ D I still can't find the trouble with [in] the engine.
- △ E I still can't find the cause of engine problem.

故障している

1 《腕時計のような小さい物の場合》

〈私の時計は故障しています〉

- ◎ A My watch's broken.
- ◎ B My watch isn't working.
- ◎ C My watch's stopped.
- ◎ D My watch's screwed [fucked] up.
- × E My watch's out of order.
- × F My watch's broken down.
- × G My watch's on the blink [fritz].
- × H My watch's out.

   ❖ E～H が多くの辞典や参考書で紹介されているが誤用．D については 4 の注を参照のこと．

2 《車のような大きい物の場合》

〈私の車は故障しているんです〉

- ◎ A My car's broken down.
- ◎ B My car's fucked [screwed] up.
- ○ C My car's broken.
- ○ D My car's out of commission.
- ○ E My car's on the blink [fritz].
- × F My car's out of order.
- × G My car's out.

   ❖ 辞典などに F, G が出ているが使われていない．B については 4 の注を参照のこと．

3 《空調の場合》

〈空調は故障しています〉
- ◎ A The air-conditioning's broken.
- ◎ B The air-conditioning's out.
- ◎ C The air-conditioning's screwed [fucked] up.
- ○ E The air-conditioning's broken down.
- ○ F The air-conditioning's out of order [commission].
- ○ G The air-conditioning's on the blink [fritz].
    - ❖ Cについては4の注を参照のこと．

4 《腹を立てている場合》

〈このテレビは故障している〉
- ◎ A This TV's screwed up.
- ◎ B This TV's fucked up.
    - ❖(1) Aの screw up, Bの fuck up は本来, 性行為を意味する表現なので卑俗である．しかし, 使用頻度は高い．何かが故障してその事態に腹を立てているときは, その人の職業, 社会的地位にかかわりなくよく使われている．もちろん, その場所に見知らぬ人でなく, 親しい人がいる場面でしか使われない．
    - ❖(2) BのほうがAより腹を立てている度合いが強い．

5 《ユーモラスに述べる場合》

〈ビリー：こんな車は見たことがない．まだ走るんですか〉
Billy: I've never seen a car like this before. Does it still run?
〈博物館の案内係：実際, 1957年から故障しているんです〉
Museum Tour Guide:
- ◎　　Actually, it's been out of commission since 1957.

〈マイク：トムはどうしたんだい．腕を三角巾でつっているぞ〉
Mike: What happened to Tom? His arm's in a sling.
〈テッド：たいしたことはないんだよ．フットボールをしているときに腕を折ったんだよ．2週間ばかり故障しているだけだよ〉
- ◎　　Nothing serious. He broke it playing football. He'll be out of commission for about two weeks.
    - ❖上例に示したように機械だけでなく「人」にも使われている．

6 《荒っぽい言い方で述べる場合》

〈このワープロは故障していやがる〉
- ◎ A This word processor's fucked [screwed] up.
- ◎ B This word processor's busted.
    - ❖Aについては4の注を参照のこと．

7 《文中にnothing, anything, problemがあるとき》

a) 故障しているか否かを尋ねるとき

〈私の時計はどこか故障しているのですか〉
- ☆ A Is there anything wrong with my watch?
- ◎ B Is anything wrong with my watch?
- ○ C Is there anything the matter with my watch?
- ○ D Is there a problem with my watch?

b) what（どこが）を使って故障している箇所を尋ねるとき

〈あなたの車はどこが故障しているのですか〉
- ◎ A What's wrong with your car?
- ◎ B What's the problem with your car?
- ○ C What's the matter with your car?
- △ D What's the trouble with your car?

❖ B は腕時計のような小さいものについて述べるときは，使用頻度は○になる．

c) 「どこも故障していない」と述べるとき
〈あなたの時計はどこも故障していません〉
- ☆ A There's nothing wrong with your watch.
- ◎ B There isn't anything wrong with your watch.
- ◎ C Nothing's wrong with your watch.
- ◎ D Your watch doesn't have any problems.
- ○ E There's no problem with your watch.
- ○ F Your watch doesn't have anything wrong.
- ○ G Your watch has no problems [problem].
- ○ H Your watch has nothing wrong with it.
- △ I Your watch doesn't have a problem.

故障する

1 《エンジンが故障して完全に動かなくなったとき》
〈私の車は市役所の近くで故障したんです〉
- ◎ A My car broke down near City Hall.
- ◎ B My car died [quit] on me near City Hall.
- ◎ C My car gave out (on me) near City Hall.
- ◎ D My car stopped [quit] running near City Hall.
- ○ E My car stopped [quit] working near City Hall.
- ○ F My car died near City Hall.
- △ G My car stopped [quit] running on me near City Hall.
- △ H My car stopped [quit] working on me near City Hall.
- × I My car quit near City Hall.

❖ D～H は個人の好みで使用頻度は異なる．

2 《一部分の故障で動いていたとき》
〈車は市役所の近くで故障したんです〉
- ◎ A My car developed trouble [a problem] near City Hall.
- ◎ B My car started to have trouble [a problem] near City Hall.
- ◎ C My car had trouble [a problem] near City Hall.

3 《経験として尋ねる》
a) 車などのような大きい物のとき
〈あなたの車は故障したことがあるのですか〉
- ◎ A Have you ever had any problems [a problem] with your car?
- ◎ B Have you ever had (any) trouble with your car?
- ◎ C Has your car ever broken down?
- ◎ D Has your car ever died (on you)?
- ◎ E Has your car ever had a breakdown?
- ○ F Has your car ever quit on you?
- ○ G Has your car ever quit running?
- △ H Has your car ever quit running on you?
- △ I Has your car ever stopped running (on you)?
- △ J Has your car ever quit working (on you)?
- △ K Has your car ever stopped working (on you)?

❖腕時計のような小さい物には down が不要．Has your watch broken?（あなたの腕時計は故障したのですか）．

b) コンピュータのとき
〈あなたのコンピュータは故障したことがあるのですか〉

- ◎ A Have you ever had any problems [a problem] with your computer?
- ◎ B Have you ever had (any) trouble with your computer?
- ◎ C Has your computer ever crashed?
- ◎ D Has your computer ever broke down [locked up, died]?
- ○ E Has your computer ever frozen (on you)?
- ○ F Has your computer ever shut down (on you)?
- ○ G Has your computer ever had a breakdown?
- ○ H Has your computer ever died on you?
- △ I Has your computer ever stopped [quit] working?
- △ J Has your computer ever quit on you?
- △ K Has your computer ever broken?
- ❖ C は故障の程度が最悪であるという響きがある.

4 《Something, Anything, Nothing, Whatが主語のとき》
〈あなたの車はどこが故障したのですか〉
- ◎ A What went wrong with your car?
- ○ B What broke down on your car?

〈この車はどこか故障しているんでしょう〉
- ◎ A There must be something wrong with this car.
- ◎ B Something must be wrong with this car.

〈あなたの時計はどこも故障していません〉
- ◎ A There's nothing wrong with your watch.
- ◎ B Nothing's wrong with your watch.

小銭入れ
〈彼は私の誕生日に小銭入れをプレゼントしてくれました〉
- ◎ A He gave me a change purse for my birthday.
- ○ B He gave me a coin purse [bag] for my birthday.

こちこちになる　→かたくなる 2

ごちゃごちゃにする
〈机の上の書類をごちゃごちゃにしないで下さい〉
- ◎　Don't mess up [make a mess of, rearrange] the papers on the desk.

誇張する
〈彼は何でも誇張する癖があるんです〉
- ☆ A He has a habit of exaggerating.
- ◎ B He has a habit of stretching the truth.
- ○ C He has a habit of overstating everything.
- ○ D He has a habit of making a mountain out of a molehill.
- △ E He has a habit of laying [spreading] it on thick.

国家
1 《政治機構に言及しているとき》
〈北朝鮮は軍事国家である〉
- ◎ A North Korea's a military state.
- ▽ B North Korea's a military nation [country].
  ❖次のような語は政治機構に言及しているので, nation ではなく state を使う. police state (警察国家), welfare state (福祉国家), feudal state (封建国家), agrarian state (農業国家), totalitarian state (全体主義国家), socialist state (社会主義国家), capitalist state (資本主義国家), free state (自由国家), pluralistic state (複数国家).

2 《政治機構に言及していないとき》
〈アメリカの黒人の中には合衆国内に自分たちの国家を作ろうとしたものがいた〉

- ◎ Some black Americans tried to create a nation [country] for them within the United States.

3 《「政府」「国民」「国」の3つの意味を持って使われるとき》

〈ドイツは第2次大戦の後2つの国に分割された〉
- ◎ Germany was divided into two nations [countries] after World War II.
- ❖ nation は，①政府 ②国民 ③国の3つが意味されているが，①の政府の意味が約70％というニュアンスを持っている．country も，①国民 ②国 ③政府の3つが意味されているが，政府のニュアンスは一番弱い．

国会議事堂

1 《日本》

〈国会議事堂はどこにあるのですか〉
- ☆ A Where's the Capitol Building?
- ◎ B Where's the Capitol?
- ▽ C Where's the Building of the Capitol?
- × D Where's the Diet Building?
- ❖ どの辞典にも日本の国会議事堂を述べるときはDを使うと出ているが，次の理由で強く反対する．①筆者は在日アメリカ人が初めて the Diet Building と聞いたとき，「食餌療法をするビル」のことだと思ったと異口同音に言っているのを聞いているからである．②筆者はニューヨークタイムズ，ワシントンポスト，ロスアンゼルスタイムズ，ニューズウィーク，タイムなどで日本の国会議事堂のことに言及しているとき，A, B を使っているのを見たことはあるが，D を見たことがないからである．

2 《アメリカ》

〈国会議事堂はホワイトハウスから遠くありません〉
- ☆ A The Capitol Building isn't far from the White House.
- ◎ B The Capitol isn't far from the White House.
- ◎ C Capitol Hill isn't far from the White House.
- △ D The Hill isn't far from the White House.

3 《国会》

a）日本

〈法案は国会で審議されています〉
- ☆ A The bill's being debated in Congress.
- ◎ B The bill's being debated in the Congress.
- × C The bill's being debated in the Diet.

b）アメリカ

〈法案は国会で審議されています〉
- ☆ A The bill's being debated in Congress.
- ◎ B The bill's being debated on Capitol Hill.
- ○ C The bill's being debated in the Congress [the Capitol].
- ○ D The bill's being debated on the Hill.
- △ E The bill's being debated in the Capitol Building.

国家公務員 →公務員 1

ごったがえす →混んでいる 7

ごてごてした

1 《一点に言及するとき》

〈柄のシャツに柄の入ったネクタイをすれば，ごてごてしてしまいます〉
- ◎ A If you wear a patterned tie with a patterned shirt, it looks too busy [much].

- ◎ B A patterned tie with a patterned shirt is too busy [much].
 2 《色とりどりの洋服を着ているとき》
〈あなたの洋服はごてごてしてしまいます〉
- ◎ A Your outfit's too busy [much].
- ○ B Your outfit has too many colors.

子供
 1 《集合的に述べるとき》
〈彼には子供さんが大勢います〉
- ◎   He has a large family.
   - ❖ He has a large family.は①「子供さんが大勢います」と②「身内（または親族、家族）が大勢います」の2つの意味があるが、普通は①の意味で使われている。
 2 《1人1人を頭に置いて述べるとき》
〈彼には大勢子供がいます〉
- ◎ A He has a lot of kids.
- ○ B He has a lot of children.
   - ❖A, Bには「騒々しい」というニュアンスがあるが、上記の He has a large family.にはない。
 3 《堅い文章の中で述べるとき》
〈コーヒーは子供にはよくありません〉
- ◎ A Coffee isn't good for children.
- ○ B Coffee isn't good for kids.

断る
 1 《招待》
 a）友人
〈彼らは私たちの招待を断ってきたんです〉
- ☆ A They turned down our invitation.
- ◎ B They didn't accept our invitation.
- ○ C They passed up our invitation.
 b）ビジネス上、または改まった関係の人
〈彼らは私たちの招待を断ってきたんです〉
- ◎ A They didn't accept our invitation.
- ○ B They declined [passed up] our invitation.
- △ C They turned down our invitation.
 2 《デートの誘い》
〈私が彼女をデートに誘ったのですが断られたんです〉
- ◎ A I asked her out for a date, but she turned me down.
- △ B I asked her out for a date, but she declined [passed it up].
- △ C I asked her out for a date, but she gave me the cold shoulder.
- × D I asked her out for a date, but she passed me up.
- × E I asked her out for a date, but she declined it.
 3 《会社が組合の要求を》
 a）不可能、および望まないとして断ったことを述べるとき
〈会社は組合の要求を断ったんです〉
- ◎ A The management didn't accept the union's demands.
- ◎ B The management rejected the union's demands.
- ○ C The management refused the union's demands.
 b）不可能だとして断ったことのみを述べるとき
〈会社は組合の要求を断ったんです〉

◎ A The management turned down the union's demands.
△ B The management declined the union's demands.
4 《きっぱりと断る》
〈私たちは彼の要請をきっぱりと断りました〉
◎ A We flatly [definitely, positively, outright, point-blank] refused his request.
▽ B We decidedly [decisively] refused his request.
❖(1) B が辞典に出ているが，使われてもまれ．
❖(2) A は We refused his request flatly. のように，副詞を文尾に置いてもよく使われている．
5 《動詞を従えるとき》
〈私は彼らの住宅ローンの連帯保証をすることを断ったんです〉
◎ A I refused to cosign their home loan.
○ B I refused cosigning their home loan.
○ C I turned down cosigning their home loan.
△ D I turned down to cosign their home loan.
△ E I rejected [declined] cosigning their home loan.
× F I declined to cosign their home loan.

…後に
1 《未来》
〈彼女は1週間後に帰るでしょう〉
◎ A She'll be back in a week.
△ B She'll be back after a week.
× C She'll be back a week later.
❖(1) A の in は時の経過を意味する．また，この in には within，つまり「以内」というニュアンスも込められている．したがって，多少あいまいさがあって，6日〜8日くらいの幅があるときに使われている．
❖(2) B の after が未来時制で使われると，1週間後およびそれ以降であれば，2週間後でも1ヶ月後でも使える．したがって，意味があいまいになるので使用頻度が低い．after は in と違って within のニュアンスは全くない．
2 《過去》
〈彼は1週間後に帰って来た〉
◎　He came back in [after] a week.
3 《過去の文が先行しているとき》
〈彼は入院して1週間後に亡くなられたんです〉
☆ A He was hospitalized and passed away a week later.
◎ B He was hospitalized and passed away after a week.
○ C He was hospitalized and passed away in a week.

この先
1 《ビルの中で》
〈東京保険はこの先です〉
☆ A Tokyo Insurance is down the hall.
◎ B Tokyo Insurance is down the hallway.
○ C Tokyo Insurance is up the hall.
△ D Tokyo Insurance is up the hallway.
△ E Tokyo Insurance is down the corridor.
△ F Tokyo Insurance is up ahead.
△ G Tokyo Insurance is further (up) ahead.
2 《通りの数ブロック先》

⟨郵便局はこの先です⟩
- ☆ A The post office's down the street [road].
- ◎ B The post office's up the street [road].
- ◎ C The post office's further (up) ahead.
- ◎ D The post office's up ahead.

3 《同じブロックのとき》
a) ブロックが大きいとき
⟨東京保険はこの先です⟩
- ☆ A Tokyo Insurance is down the block [street, road].
- ◎ B Tokyo Insurance is up the block [street, road].

b) ブロックが小さいとき
⟨東京保険はこの先です⟩
- ☆ A Tokyo Insurance is down the block.
- ◎ B Tokyo Insurance is up the block.

4 《この少し先》
⟨市役所はこの少し先です⟩
- ☆ A The City Hall's just down the street.
- ☆ B The City Hall's a little ways down the street.
- ◎ C The City Hall's just up the street.
- ◎ D The City Hall's a little ways up the street.

5 《このずっと先》
⟨市役所はこのずっと先です⟩
- ◎ A The City Hall's a long way(s) down the street.
- ◎ B The City Hall's way down the street.
- ○ C The City Hall's a long way(s) up the street.
- ○ D The City Hall's way up the street.

この時間

1 《早朝・深夜の異常な時間》
⟨この時間に開いているレストランをご存知ですか⟩
- ◎ A Do you know a restaurant that's open at this time [hour]?
- ○ B Do you know a restaurant that's open at this time [hour] of the day?
- ○ C Do you know a restaurant that's open at this time of day?
- △ D Do you know a restaurant that's open at this hour of day?

2 《普通の時間》
⟨車はこの時間は混んでいます⟩
- ◎ A The traffic's heavy at this time [hour].
- ◎ B The traffic's heavy at this time [hour] of the day.
- ◎ C The traffic's heavy at this time of day.
- △ D The traffic's heavy at this hour of day.

この時期としては

⟨この時期としては珍しく涼しいです⟩
- ◎   It's unusually cool for this time of (the) year.

この辺に

1 《近い場所を意味しているとき》
⟨この辺に金物屋がありますか⟩
- ◎ A Is there a hardware store near [around] here?
- ◎ B Is there a hardware store in this neighborhood?
- ○ C Is there a hardware store nearby [close by]?

2 《広い地域を頭に置いているとき》
〈この辺にギリシャレストランはありますか〉
- ◎ A Is there a Greek restaurant around?
- ○ B Is there a Greek restaurant in the area?
- ○ C Is there a Greek restaurant anywhere?
  ❖ around は広い地域, around here は狭い地域を指している.

この前
1 《前回》
〈この前会ったところで会いましょう〉
- ◎ A Let's meet where we met (the) last time.
- ○ B Let's meet where we met last.
- ○ C Let's meet where we met the time before.

2 《前々回》
〈この前の前に会ったところで会いましょう〉
- ◎ A Let's meet where we met the time before last.
- ○ B Let's meet where we met two times ago.
- △ C Let's meet where we met the second to the last time.

このままで
1 《単数のとき》
〈サイズはこのままで結構です〉
- ◎ A The size is fine as it is.
- ◎ B The size is fine as is.

2 《複数のとき》
〈このズボンはこのままでは,はけないと思います〉
- ◎ A I'm afraid I can't wear these pants as they are.
- × B I'm afraid I can't wear these pants as are.

3 《居抜きで》
〈彼は店を居抜きで売りたいんです〉
- ◎ A He wants to sell his store as it is.
- ◎ B He wants to sell his store as is.

好みがうるさい
1 《食物》
〈彼女は食べ物の好みがうるさい〉
- ☆ A She's picky about food.
- ☆ B She's a picky eater.
- ◎ C She's a fussy eater.
- ○ D She's particular about food.
- △ E She's fussy [choosy] about food.

2 《人》
〈彼女はボーイフレンドのことになると,好みがうるさいんです〉
- ◎ A She's picky [choosy, particular] when it comes to boyfriends.
- △ B She's fussy when it comes to boyfriends.

コピーを取る
〈この本の 10 ページから 20 ページまでコピーを取って下さい〉
- ◎ A Copy pages 10 through 20 in this book.
- ○ B Make copies of pages 10 through 20 in this book.
- ○ C Xerox [Photocopy] pages 10 through 20 in this book.

五分五分だ
〈ジム:彼は当選すると思いますか〉

Jim: Do you think he'll be elected?
〈ビル：五分五分です〉
Bill:
- ☆ A It's too close to call.
- ☆ B It's too close to tell.
- ◎ C It's a tossup.
- ◎ D It's up in the air.
- ◎ E It's anybody's guess.
- ◎ F It's a close election.
- ◎ G It's a fifty-fifty chance.
- ◎ H He's got a fifty-fifty chance.
- △ I An evenly matched election.
- △ J The odds're even.
- △ K The chances're even.

ごまかす

1 《目方》
〈肉屋が目方をごまかしたんです〉
- ☆ A The butcher gypped me.
- ◎ B The butcher ripped me off.
- ◎ C I got cheated [screwed] at the meat market.
- ○ D The butcher shorted me.
- × E The butcher short-weighted me.
- × F The butcher gave me short weight.
  - ❖ E, F が辞典に出ているが使われていない．

2 《数字》
〈彼は数字をごまかしたんです〉
- ◎ A He doctored the figures.
- ○ B He fudged [tampered with] the figures.
- △ C He falsified the figures.

3 《年令》
〈彼は年令をごまかしたんです〉
- ◎ A He lied about his age.
- ○ B He told a lie about his age.
- ▽ C He fudged his age.
- × D He cheated his age.
  - ❖ D が辞典に出ているが使われていない．C を口語表現として大きく紹介している辞典があるが，使われてもまれ．

4 《ミス》
〈彼はミスをごまかそうとしているんです〉
- ☆ A He's trying to cover up his mistake.
- ◎ B He's trying to cover [correct] his mistake.
- ○ C He's trying to smooth over his mistake.
- △ D He's trying to gloss over his mistake.

ごますり

1 《下品な表現》
〈彼はごますりだ〉
- ◎ A He kisses his boss's ass.
- ◎ B He's an ass-kisser.
- ○ C He's a butt-kisser [a kiss ass].

× D He's a butt-kiss.
- ❖(1) D が辞典に出ているが使われていない．
- ❖(2) A, B, C は下品な表現であるが，親しい者同士，またはかしこまって話す必要がないときは，教育レベルに関係なくよく使われている．

2 《下品でない表現》
〈彼はごますりだ〉
- ◎ A He kisses up to his boss.
- ◎ B He brown-noses.
- ◎ C He's a brown-noser.
- ○ D He brown-noses (to) his boss.
- ○ E He plays up to his boss.
- ○ F He butters up his boss.
- ▽ G He's a brown-nose.

3 《文章で使われる表現》
〈彼はごますりだ〉
- ◎ A He's an apple-polisher.
- △ B He curries favor with his boss.
- ▽ C He toadies his boss.
- ▽ D He plays the sycophant to his boss.

4 《イギリスで使われる表現》
〈彼はごますりだ〉
- ◎ A He sucks up to [crawls to, creeps round] his boss.
- ◎ B He licks his boss's arse.
- ◎ C He's a crawler.
- ❖ B は下品な表現．

ごまんと →たくさん 6

ごみ
1 《通り》
〈ニューヨークの通りはごみがたくさんあります〉
- ☆ A There's a lot of trash on the streets in New York.
- ☆ B The streets in New York have a lot of trash.
- ◎ C There's a lot of garbage on the streets in New York.
- ◎ D The streets in New York're very trashy.
- ○ E There's a lot of litter on the streets in New York.

2 《台所》
〈台所のごみを外に出して下さい〉
- ◎ A Take out the kitchen trash [garbage].
- ○ B Take out the trash [garbage] in the kitchen.

3 《事務所》
〈彼の事務所はいつもごみがたくさんあります〉
- ◎ A His office always has a lot of trash [garbage].
- △ B His office always has a lot of crap.
- ▽ C His office always has a lot of rubbish.
- × D His office always has a lot of refuse [litter].

4 《「ごみが散らかっている」と述べるとき》
〈昨夜パーティーを開いたから事務所はごみが散らかっているんです〉
- ◎ A The office is messy [trashed] because we had a party last night.
- ◎ B The office is a mess because we had a party last night.
- ○ C The office is sleazy because we had a party last night.

　　　　△ D The office is in a mess because we had a party last night.
　　　　△ E The office is trashy because we had a party last night.
　5　《ごみ箱》
〈それをごみ箱に捨てて下さい〉
　　　　☆ A Throw it in the trash.
　　　　◎ B Throw it in the trash can.
　　　　◎ C Throw it in the waste basket.
　　　　○ D Throw it in the trash basket.
　　　　× E Throw it in the refuse basket.
混む　→混んでいる
小物
　1　《主語が単数》
〈彼は大物ではありません．小物です〉
　　　　◎ A He isn't a big shot. He's a nobody [a small fry].
　　　　△ B He isn't a big shot. He's small potatoes [a small potato].
　　　　△ C He isn't a big shot. He's nobody [nothing].
　2　《主語が複数》
〈彼らは大物ではありません．小物です〉
　　　　☆ A They aren't big shots. They're nobody.
　　　　◎ B They aren't big shots. They're nothing [peons].
　　　　○ C They aren't big shots. They're nobodies.
　　　　△ D They aren't big shots. They're small fries [potatoes].
ご用件　→用件
コレラ　→病気 10
頃
　1　《昼頃》
〈昼頃お電話します〉
　　　　◎ A I'll call you around noon.
　　　　○ B I'll call you about [just around] noon.
　　　　△ C I'll call you just about noon.
　2　《明日の今頃》
〈私は明日の今頃は大阪にいます〉
　　　　☆ A I'm going to be in Osaka around this time tomorrow.
　　　　◎ B I'm going to be in Osaka about this time tomorrow.
　　　　○ C I'm going to be in Osaka at about this time tomorrow.
　　　　△ D I'm going to be in Osaka round this time tomorrow.
転ぶ
〈転ばないように気を付けて下さい〉
　　　　◎ A Be careful not to fall [fall down, trip].
　　　　△ B Be careful not to stumble.
怖い
　1　《人が主語のとき》
〈夫：お隣のご夫婦が昨夜殺されたんだよ〉
Husband: The couple next door were killed last night.
〈妻：怖い〉
Wife:
　　　　☆ A I'm scared.
　　　　◎ B I'm frightened.
　　　　◎ C I'm terrified.

○ D I'm afraid.
　❖怖さの程度はCが一番強い．A, Bは同じ．Dは一番弱い．

2 《人が主語でないとき》
〈夫：角のご夫婦が昨夜殺されたんだよ〉
Husband: The couple on the corner were killed last night.
〈妻：怖い〉
Wife:
　☆ A That's scary.
　◎ B That's frightening.
　○ C That's terrifying.
　❖怖さの程度はCが一番強い．A, Bは同じ．ただし，Bは少し堅い響きがある．

3 《おじけづく》
〈田中さん：グリコの株を買わなかったんですか〉
Mr. Tanaka: Didn't you buy Glico stock?
〈中村さん：はい，買いませんでした．怖かったんです〉
Mr. Nakamura:
　◎ A No. I got cold feet.
　◎ B No. I chickened out.
　◎ C No. I lost my nerve.

根源

1 《原因を主語にしたときの》
〈権力欲が強いことが諸悪の根源なのである〉
　◎ A Being power-hungry's the root of all evil.
　○ B Being power-hungry's solely causing [bringing about, inviting, creating] all evil.
　△ C Being power-hungry's solely causing all evils.
　× D Being power-hungry's the root of all evils.
　× E Being power-hungry's the source [origin] of all evil.
　❖(1) D, Eが辞典に出ているが使われていない．
　❖(2) allは複数名詞を従えるので，Dを正しいと思うであろう．しかし，これは決まり文句なので単数．

2 《諸悪を主語にしたとき》
〈権力欲が強いことが諸悪の根源なのである〉
　○ A All evils come solely from being power-hungry.
　△ B All evils're caused solely by being power-hungry.
　△ C All evils're solely brought by being power-hungry.
　△ D All evils originate solely from being power-hungry.

今後

〈今後うちはXYZ会社との取引をやめます〉
　◎ A We'll stop doing business with XYZ Company from now on.
　△ B We'll stop doing business with XYZ Company from here on in.
　○ C We'll stop doing business with XYZ Company from this time on.
　▽ D We'll stop doing business with XYZ Company from hereafter [henceforth].
　❖Dは辞典に出ているが使われてもまれ．

混んでいる

1 《レストラン・スーパーなどの場合》
〈レストランは混んでいました〉

- ☆ A The restaurant was crowded.
- ◎ B The restaurant had wall to wall people.
- ○ C The restaurant was jampacked [packed, jammed].

2 《空港などの場所の場合》
〈空港は混んでいました〉
- ◎ A The airport was jampacked [packed, crowded, busy].
- ○ B The airport was congested [jammed].
- × C The airport was in a jam.
  - ❖ C は辞典に出ているが使われていない.

3 《通り・高速道路の場合》
〈通りは混んでいました〉
- ◎ A The street was jampacked [packed].
- ◎ B The street was crowded.
- ◎ C The street was busy.
- ○ D The street was congested.
- ○ E The street was jammed.
- × F The street was in a jam.
- × G The street was bustling.
  - ❖(1) F, G が辞典に出ているが使われていない.
  - ❖(2) A は人と車の両方の混雑に使われているが, 約70％は人, 約30％は車の混雑を意味している. B は100％人の混雑に, D は100％車の混雑に使われている. C は人, 車, 自転車すべてに言及している.

4 《車》

a) The traffic が主語のとき
〈ここへ来る途中, 車が混んでいました〉
- ◎ A The traffic was bumper to bumper on the way here.
- ◎ B The traffic was crowded on the way here.
- ◎ C The traffic was bad [heavy] on the way here.
- ○ D The traffic was packed [jampacked, jammed] on the way here.
- ○ E The traffic was stop and go on the way here.
- △ F The traffic was nasty [busy] on the way here.
- × G The traffic was back-up on the way here.
  - ❖ G は辞典に出ているが使われていない.

b) There was...が文頭のとき
〈ここへ来る途中, 車が混んでいました〉
- ◎ A There was a lot of [heavy, bad] traffic on the way here.
- ○ B There was a traffic jam on the way here.
- △ C There was nasty traffic on the way here.
- △ D There was a lot of traffic congestion on the way here.
- ▽ E There was nasty [bad] traffic congestion on the way here.

c) Car が主語のとき
〈高速道路は車が混んでいました〉
- ☆ A Cars were backed up on the highway.
- ◎ B Cars were bumper to bumper on the highway.
- ○ C Cars were jampacked on the highway.
- △ D Cars were jammed on the highway.
- × E Cars were stop and go on the highway.
- × F Cars were crowded on the highway.

5 《人》

〈通りは人で混んでいました〉
- ☆ A People were everywhere on the street.
- ◎ B People were crowded [jampacked] on the street.
- ○ C People were packed on the street.
- △ D People were jammed on the street.

6 《電車・バス》

〈電車は混んでいました〉
- ☆ A The train was crowded.
- ◎ B The train was packed [jampacked].
- ◎ C Passengers were packed like sardines on the train.
- ◎ D The train was full of passengers.
- ◎ E The train had wall to wall passengers.
- ○ F The train was jammed.

7 《ごった返す》

〈メイシーはクリスマスの買物客でごった返していました〉
- ◎ A Macy's was overcrowded [crammed, overflowing, filled, jampacked, packed] with Christmas shoppers.
- ○ B Macy's had wall to wall Christmas shoppers.
- ○ C Macy's was overrun [swarming] with Christmas shoppers.
- △ D Macy's was buzzing [bustling, stuffed] with Christmas shoppers.
- × E Macy's was thronged [milling, teeming, seething] with Christmas shoppers.

❖ E が辞典に出ているが使われていない.

コンピュータ学校　→各種学校 5

混乱している

1 《店・場所などが混乱しているとき》

〈店全体がしばらく混乱していました〉
- ◎ A The whole store was a madhouse for a while.
- ◎ B The whole store was chaotic for a while.
- ○ C The whole store was in chaos [confusion, disorder] for a while.
- △ D The whole store was at sixes and sevens for a while.

2 《人が混乱しているとき》

〈私は息子が交通事故で重症を負ったという電話を受けていたから、レポーターの人たちに取材されたとき混乱していたんです〉
- ◎ A I was confused when I was interviewed by reporters because I'd gotten a phone call that my son'd been seriously hurt in a car accident.
- ○ B I was in a state of confusion when I was interviewed by reporters because I'd gotten a phone call that my son'd been seriously hurt in a car accident.
- ○ C I was mixed up when I was interviewed by reporters because I'd gotten a phone call that my son'd been seriously hurt in a car accident.
- △ D I was at sixes and sevens when I was interviewed by reporters because I'd gotten a phone call that my son'd been seriously hurt in a car accident.

3 《交通機関のダイヤが大雪などで混乱しているとき》

〈飛行機のダイヤが混乱しているんです〉
- ◎ A The flights' schedules're screwed up.

- ◎ B The flights' schedules're messed up.
- ○ C The flights' schedules're fucked up.
- ▽ D The flights' schedules're chaotic.
- ▽ E The flights' schedules're a madhouse.
- ▽ F The flights' schedules're in confusion.
  - ❖(1) D は辞典に出ているがまれ．
  - ❖(2) A, C については 4 の注を参照のこと．
4 《混乱していることに腹を立てて述べるとき》
〈飛行機のダイヤが混乱していやがる〉
- ◎ A The flights' schedules're fucked up.
- ◎ B The flights' schedules're screwed up.
  - ❖ A のほうが B より腹を立てている．A, B とも性行為を表す表現なので気を使う人がいる前では使われていない．しかし，気を使う人がいないときは話者の教育レベルに関係なく広く使われている．

5 《事態が混乱しているとき》
〈事態は混乱しているんです〉
- ◎ A The situation's out of control.
- ◎ B The situation's chaotic.
- ◎ C The situation's screwed [fucked] up.
- ◎ D The situation's messed up.
- ◎ E The situation's a madhouse [a problem].
  - ❖ C については 4 の注を参照のこと．

〈ウォール街はあの 9 月 11 日以後，しばらくごった返していました〉
- ◎ A Wall Street was in chaos [turmoil] for a while after that September 11th.
- ◎ B Wall Street was chaotic for a while after that September 11th.
- ○ C Wall Street was a madhouse for a while after that September 11th.
- ○ D Wall Street was in confusion for a while after that September 11th.
- ▽ E Wall Street was in an upheaval for a while after that September 11th.

6 《情報が多すぎて頭が混乱しているとき》
〈みんながいろいろな情報をくれるので，今，頭が混乱しています〉
- ☆ A Everybody gives me different information, so my head's spinning now.
- ◎ B Everybody gives me different information, so I'm confused now.
- △ C Everybody gives me different information, so my head's swimming now.

混乱なく
〈株主総会は混乱なく終った〉
- ◎ The stockholders' meeting ended peacefully [calmly, quietly].

サービス

1 《一般の店で》
〈これはサービスしておきます〉
- ☆ A You can have this for free.
- ◎ B You can have this free of charge.
- ○ C You can have this for nothing.
- ○ D You can have this without charge.
- × E We'll give you this for nothing.

2 《高級店で》
〈これはサービスさせていただきます〉
- ☆ A You may have this for free.
- ◎ B You may have this free of charge.
- ○ C You may have this for nothing.
- ○ D You may have this without charge.

最近

1 《現在文》
〈最近・地価は高くなってきた〉
- ◎　Lately [These days] land prices're getting higher.

2 《習慣的な内容の現在文》
〈彼は最近アルコールを飲んでいません〉
- ◎　He doesn't drink these days [lately].

3 《現在進行形》
〈彼らは最近お互いに口をきいていません〉
- ◎　They aren't talking to each other these days [lately].

4 《過去形》
〈息子は最近車の事故にあったんです〉
- ◎　My son was in a car accident recently.

5 《短い期間を指している現在完了》
〈ラリーは最近太ってきたね. 彼は休暇中はいつもたくさん食べるんだ〉
- ◎ A Larry's been gaining weight recently. He always eats like a pig during the holidays.
- ○ B Larry's been gaining weight lately. He always eats like a pig during the holidays.

6 《現在の一時点，または継続状態のいずれともとれる現在完了》
〈私は最近彼に会っていません〉
- ◎　I haven't seen him recently [lately].

7 《長い継続状態を指している現在完了》
〈ラリーは最近太ってきました. 彼は結婚してから食事を食べそこなうことがあまりなかったんです〉
- ◎ A Larry's been gaining weight lately. He hasn't missed too many meals since he got married.
- ○ B Larry's been gaining weight recently. He hasn't missed too many meals since he got married.

債券

1 《国債》
〈私は国債に投資しています〉
- ◎ A I'm investing in TB.
- ◎ B I'm investing in Treasury bonds.
- ◎ C I'm investing in Treasury bills.
- ○ D I'm investing in government bonds [securities].
  - ❖ A, B は 10 年以上の長期国債. C は 1 年未満 (13 週, 26 週, 52 週) の短期国債.

2 《社債》
〈私は XYZ 社の社債に投資しようと考えています〉
- ◎ A I'm thinking of investing in XYZ's (corporate) bonds.
- ◎ B I'm thinking of investing in XYZ's securities.
- ▽ C I'm thinking of investing in XYZ's debentures.
  - ❖ C は金融界ではよく使われている.

財産

1 《一般的に言う場合》
〈彼は財産をたくさん持っています〉
- ◎ A He has a large fortune.
- ◎ B He has a lot of assets [wealth].

2 《比喩的に言う場合》
〈あなたのフランス語は将来あなたに大きな財産になるでしょう〉
- ◎ A Your French'll be a great asset to [for] you in the future.
- ◎ B Your French'll be a great advantage for [to] you in the future.
- ◎ C Your French'll be a great benefit for [to] you in the future.
- ○ D Your French'll be a big benefit for [to] you in the future.
- ○ E Your French'll be a big plus for you in the future.
- ○ F Your French'll be a great plus to you in the future.
- ○ G Your French'll be a big asset to [for] you in the future.
- △ H Your French'll be a big plus to you in the future.
- △ I Your French'll be a great plus for you in the future.

3 《「財産家」と言う場合》
〈彼は非常に財産家です〉
- ☆ A He has a lot of money.
- ◎ B He's a very wealthy man.
- ◎ C He's a man of great wealth.
- ◎ D He's very rich.
- ◎ E He has a lot of assets.
- ○ F He has a large fortune.
- ○ G He's a man with a large fortune.
- ○ H He's a man with a lot of wealth.
- △ I He's a very rich man.
- △ J He's a man of great means [substance].
- × K He's a man of means [fortune].
  - ❖ K が辞典に出ているが使われていない.

最新型

1 《車》
〈この車は最新型です〉
- ◎ A This car's the latest model [style].

- ◎ B This car's the newest model [style].
- ◎ C This car's the most recent model.
- ○ D This car's the most up-to-date model [style].
- ○ E This car's the latest edition.
- ▽ F This car's the most recent style.
- ▽ G This car's the most newly-developed model.

2 《洗濯機》

〈この洗濯機は最新型です〉
- ◎ A This washing machine's the latest [the newest, the most recent] model.
- ○ B This washing machine's the most up-to-date model.
- △ C This washing machine's the latest style [version].
- ▽ D This washing machine's the most recent style.
- ▽ E This washing machine's the most newly-developed model [style].

3 《コピー機・カメラなど》

〈このコピー機は最新型です〉
- ◎ A This copy machine's the latest [the newest, the most up-to-date, the most recent] model.
- △ B This copy machine's the newest [the latest, the most up-to-date] style.
- ▽ C This copy machine's the most recent style.

4 《ソフトウェア》

〈このソフトウェアは最新型です〉
- ☆ A This software's the latest version.
- ◎ B This software's the latest edition.
- ◎ C This software's the newest version [edition].
- × D This software's the latest revision [model, style].

5 《カーナビ》

〈このカーナビは最新型です〉
- ☆ A This GPS's the latest model.
- ◎ B This GPS's the latest version.
- ◎ C This GPS's the newest model [version].
- ○ D This GPS's the latest edition.
- ○ E This GPS's the newest edition.
- × F This GPS's the latest revision.

財政状態

1 《一般的に言う場合》

〈彼の財政状態は混乱しています〉
- ◎ A His financial affairs're [situation's] a mess.
- ○ B His financial state's a mess.
- △ C His financial condition's [picture's, circumstances're] a mess.

2 《財政状態が悪いことを言う場合》

〈この会社は財政状態が苦しいんです〉
- ◎ A This company's in trouble financially.
- ◎ B This company's financially in trouble.
- ◎ C This company's in financial trouble.
- ◎ D This company's hurting for money.
- ○ E This company's pressed for money.

最先端
1 《科学技術》

〈このコンピュータは最先端をいっています〉
- ◎ A This computer's on the cutting edge (of technology).
- ◎ B This computer's (the) state of the art.
- ◎ C This computer's (the) top of the line.
- ◎ D This computer's the most up-to-date.
- ○ E This computer's the most sophisticated.
- △ F This computer's on the leading edge (of technology).
    - ❖元来は A, B, D, E, F は技術と質の両方に言及しているが, 技術の方に焦点がある. C は質のことを言及していたが, 両方のニュアンスがある. どちらであるかは文脈で判断する.

2 《洋服の流行》

〈彼女のドレスはいつも流行の最先端をいっています〉
- ◎ A Her dress's always the latest style.
- ◎ B Her dress's always really in style [in fashion].
- ◎ C Her dress's always really stylish [fashionable].

3 《「精巧な」というニュアンスのあるとき》

〈このコンピュータは最新型です〉
- ◎ A This computer's sophisticated [advanced].
- ○ B This computer's highly developed.

最前列

〈ジムは最前列に座っていました〉
- ◎ A Jim was sitting in the front [first] row.
- ◎ B Jim was sitting in the very front.

サイト

1 《ビジネス上のサイト》

a）ページ数が多いとき

〈うちはこの製品のサイトをインターネットに載せる予定です〉
- ☆ A We're going to create a web site for this product.
- ☆ B We're going to create a site for this product on the internet.
- ◎ C We're going to set up a web site for this product.
- ◎ D We're going to set up a site for this product on the internet.
- ○ E We're going to put up [make, start, build, establish] a web site for this product.
- ○ F We're going to put up [make, start, build, establish] a site for this product on the internet.
- △ G We're going to construct [produce] a web site for this product.
- △ H We're going to construct a site for this product on the internet.
    - ❖A, C, E, G は文尾に on the internet または on the net を付け加えても使用頻度は同じ.

b）1～2 ページのとき

〈うちはこの製品のサイトをインターネットに載せる予定です〉
- ☆ A We're going to create a web page for this product.
- ◎ B We're going to set up a web page for this product.
- ○ C We're going to put up [make, start, build, establish] a web page for this product.
- △ D We're going to produce [construct] a web page for this product.
    - ❖A～D はいずれも文尾に on the internet または on the net を付け加えても

使用頻度は同じ．
2　《出会い系サイト》
〈私はインターネットに出会い系サイトを載せるつもりです〉
- ◎ A I'm going to set up [put up, create] a chat site on the internet.
- ○ B I'm going to build [make] a chat site on the internet.

3　《家庭》
〈私たちはインターネットにホームページを載せるつもりです〉
- ☆ A We're going to create a home page on the internet.
- ◎ B We're going to set up [put up] a home page on the internet.
- ○ C We're going to make [start, build, establish] a home page on the internet.

❖(1) A, B, C はいずれも文尾の on the internet はなくてもよい．
❖(2) home page は1ページの場合もページ数が多い場合も使われている．

才能

1　《…の才能がある》
〈彼は音楽の才能があるんです〉
- ☆ A He's musically gifted.
- ◎ B He's gifted musically.
- ◎ C He has a musical gift.
- ◎ D He has a gift for music.
- ◎ E He's talented musically.
- ◎ F He's musically talented.
- ◎ G He has a talent for music.
- ○ H He's gifted with musical talent.
- ○ I He has a musical flair.
- ○ J He's musically inclined.
- ○ K He has an unusual aptitude [flair] for music.
- △ L He has an unusual ability for music.
- × M He has an unusual endowment [faculty, capability] for music.

❖(1) M が辞典に出ているが使われていない．
❖(2) 才能の上では, A, B, C, D, H が一番強い．E, F, G が2番．I, J, K, L が3番．

2　《「才能のある…」と述べるとき》
〈彼は才能のあるバイオリニストです〉
- ☆ A He's a gifted violinist.
- ◎ B He's a talented [brilliant] violinist.

再発する

1　《病気の場合》
〈彼のガンは6ヵ月ほどで再発するでしょう〉
- ◎ A His cancer will return in six months or so.
- ◎ B He'll have a recurrence of cancer in six months or so.
- ○ C He'll have a relapse of cancer in six months or so.
- ○ D He'll suffer from a relapse of cancer in six months or so.
- ○ E His cancer will reappear in six months or so.
- × F He'll return of cancer in six months or so.

❖ F が辞典に出ているが使われていない．

2　《問題・トラブルの場合》
〈この種のトラブルは再発するだろう〉
- ◎ A This kind of trouble will occur [happen] again.

- ○ B This kind of trouble will take place again.
- △ C This kind of trouble will crop up [come about] again.

裁判
1 《訴訟》
a) 被害者が「裁判にかける」と述べるとき
〈彼らを裁判にかけてやる〉
- ☆ A I'll sue them.
- ◎ B I'll take them to court.
- ◎ C I'll take legal steps against them.
- ◎ D I'll bring a suit against them.
- ◎ E I'll file a lawsuit [suit] against them.
- ◎ F I'll take legal action against them.

b) 裁判中（長期間にわたって行われている意味での）
〈それは裁判中です〉
- ◎ A That's on trial now.
- ◎ B That's being tried now.
- ◎ C That's in litigation [the courts] now.
- ○ D That's being brought for trial now.
- △ E That's in a legal action [a lawsuit, trial] now.
- △ F That's being put on trial now.

c) 裁判中（開廷中の意味での）
〈それは今裁判中です〉
- ◎ A That's on [in] trial right now.
- ◎ B That's in court right now.
- ○ C That's being tried right now.

d) 原告または被告を主語にして述べるとき
〈彼は裁判に勝つでしょう〉
- ☆ A He'll win the [his] case.
- ◎ B He'll win the [his] suit.
- ◎ C He'll win the [his] lawsuit.
- △ D He'll win the (legal) action.
- △ E He'll win the litigation.
- × F He'll win the legal steps.
- × G He'll gain the case [the suit, the lawsuit].
  - ❖ F, G が辞典に出ているが使われていない.

2 《「裁判にかける」と言うとき》
a) 検察が事件を裁判にかける
〈この事件は裁判になるでしょう〉
- ◎ A They'll try this case.
- ○ B They'll bring this case to trial.
- △ C They'll put this case to trial.

b) 検察が容疑者を裁判にかける
〈彼は詐欺事件で裁判にかけられるでしょう〉
- ◎ A They'll put him on trial for fraud.
- ○ B They'll try him for fraud.
- △ C They'll bring him to trial [justice] for fraud.

c) 容疑者を主語にして述べるとき
〈彼は殺人事件で裁判にかけられるんです〉
- ◎ A He'll be tried for murder.

◎ B He'll be (put) on trial for murder.
△ C He'll come up for [face, be brought to] trial for murder.

3 《「裁判を取り下げる」と言うとき》
a) 検察を主語にして述べるとき
〈検察は起訴を取り下げるだろう〉
☆ A They'll drop the charges against the suspect.
◎ B They'll withdraw the indictment against the suspect.
◎ C They'll drop the indictment [the case] against the suspect.
○ D They'll stop prosecuting the suspect.
○ E They'll stop the prosecution of the suspect.
○ F They'll drop the charges on the suspect.
○ G They'll withdraw the indictment on the suspect.
△ H They'll drop the prosecution on the suspect.

b) 原告を主語にして述べるとき
〈彼は裁判[訴訟]を取り下げるだろう〉
◎ A He'll drop the case [the suit, the lawsuit].
○ B He'll drop the (legal) action.
○ C He'll drop the litigation.
○ D He'll withdraw the case.
○ E He'll call off the case.
△ F He'll abandon the case.
△ G He'll discontinue the case.
△ H He'll withdraw the suit [the lawsuit, the legal action].
△ I He'll abandon the suit [the lawsuit, the legal action].

裁判官 →職業 6
裁判所
1 《地方裁判所》
〈郵便局は地裁の少し先です〉
◎ A The post office is a little past the District Courthouse.
× B The post office is a little past the District Court building.

2 《州裁判所》
〈郵便局は州裁判所の少し先です〉
◎ A The post office is a little past the State Courthouse.
× B The post office is a little past the State Court building.

3 《連邦裁判所》
〈郵便局は連邦裁判所の少し先です〉
◎ A The post office is a little past the Federal Courthouse.
○ B The post office is a little past the Federal Court building.

4 《控訴裁判所》
〈郵便局は控訴裁判所の少し先です〉
◎ A The post office is a little past the Appellate Court building.
◎ B The post office is a little past the Appellate Courthouse.

5 《最高裁判所》
〈郵便局は最高裁判所の少し先です〉
◎ A The post office is a little past the Supreme Court building.
× B The post office is a little past the Supreme Courthouse.

6 《訴訟で出廷するとき》
〈私は今日の午後,裁判所へ行かなければならないんです〉
◎ A I'll have to be in court this afternoon.

△ B I'll have to be in the courthouse this afternoon.
× C I'll have to be in the court this afternoon.

財布
〈彼は誕生日にお財布をプレゼントしてくれたんです〉
◎ A He gave me a wallet for my birthday.
× B He gave me a purse for my birthday.
❖(1) ほとんどの辞典で purse＝「財布」とあるが，アメリカでは purse と言えばまず思い浮かべられるのはハンドバッグ．ただし，小銭入れの意味では change purse, coin purse としてよく使われている．
❖(2) アメリカ人は日本人がお札だけを入れるような財布は使っていない．

財務部 →…部 9

最優先
〈あなたのスケジュールが最優先です〉
◎ A Your schedule comes first.
◎ B Your schedule is No.1 priority.
◎ C Your schedule is the top priority.
◎ D Your schedule comes before anything [everything] else.
◎ E Your schedule is a top priority.
○ F Your schedule comes before anything [everything].
○ G Your schedule is the first priority.
❖ E は C より語調が弱くなる．

サイン
1 《歌手・スポーツ選手などに求める場合》
〈サインして下さい〉
◎ A Please give me your autograph.
× B Please write me your autograph.
× C Please give me your signature [sign].

2 《伝票・請求書・契約書などに求める場合》
〈ここにサインして下さい〉
◎ A We need your signature here.
◎ B Give us [Write] your signature here.
◎ C Sign here.
× D We need your sign here.
× E Give us [Write] your sign here.

…さえすれば [しなければ] いいんです
1 《「…さえすればいいんです」と言う場合》
〈彼に連絡をしてくれさえすればいいんです〉
◎ A All you have to do is get a hold of him.
○ B All you have to do is to get a hold of him.
△ C You have only to get a hold of him.
❖ C が多くの辞典に出ているが時々使われている程度．

2 《「…さえしなければいいんです」と言う場合》
〈彼と口をききさえしなければいいんです〉
◎ A Don't speak to him. That's all.
◎ B Don't speak to him. That's it.
× C All you have to do is not to speak to him.
× D All you mustn't do is to speak to him.
❖ 日本語につられて C を使いがちだが，All you have to do is...の構文では否定の語句を使えない．したがって C も D も使われていない．

探す

1 《不動産・車などを購入するため探している場合》
〈私たちは5LDKの家を探しています〉
- ☆ A We're shopping around for a 5-bedroom house.
- ☆ B We're shopping [looking] for a 5-bedroom house.
- ◎ C We're searching for a 5-bedroom house.
- ○ D We're hunting for a 5-bedroom house.
  - ❖ Aは多くの物件を見てまわり，広く，深く，比較検討しているニュアンスが他の表現より強い．

2 《仕事を探している場合》
〈私は仕事を探しています〉
- ◎ A I'm looking for a job.
- ○ B I'm hunting [searching] for a job.
- △ C I'm shopping (around) for a job.

3 《見つけるのが困難な人を探している場合》
〈私は生みの母親を探してきました〉
- ◎ A I've been searching [looking] for my biological mother.
- ◎ B I've been trying to locate [find] my biological mother.
- ◎ C I've been tracking down my biological mother.

4 《警察が容疑者・脱獄者を探している場合》
〈警察が容疑者を探している〉
- ◎ A The police're hunting for [tracking down] the suspect.
- ○ B The police're looking (out) for [searching for] the suspect.

5 《警察が行方不明者を探している場合》
〈警察が行方不明の男性を探しています〉
- ◎ A The police're searching [looking] for the missing man.
- ◎ B The police're trying to locate the missing man.
- ◎ C The police're trying to find the missing man.
- ○ D The police're hunting for [looking out for] the missing man.
  - ❖ Bは日常会話よりもテレビのニュースや新聞などでよく使われている．

6 《弁護士・通訳・大工・水道屋などを探すよう指示依頼するとき》
〈(上司が秘書に) 上手な水道屋さんを探してくれるかい〉
- ☆ A Can you get a good plumber for me?
- ☆ B Can you get me a good plumber?
- ◎ C Can you find a good plumber for me?
- ◎ D Can you find me a good plumber?
- ○ E Can you get [find] a good plumber?

7 《「しらみつぶしに探す」と言う場合》
〈警察が近所をシラミつぶしに容疑者を探している〉
- ◎ A The police're combing the neighborhood looking for the suspect.
- ◎ B The police're searching the neighborhood for the suspect.
- △ C The police're scouring the neighborhood for the suspect.
  - ❖ AはB, Cより徹底さにおいて強い響きがある．

8 《「手さぐりで探す」と言う場合》
〈彼はポケットの中を手さぐりで車の鍵を探していました〉
- ☆ A He was looking in his pockets for the car key.
- ☆ B He was feeling for the car key in his pockets.
- ◎ C He was fishing in his pockets for the car key.
- ◎ D He was looking for the car key in his pockets.

- ○ E He was fumbling for the car key in his pockets.
- ○ F He was fumbling in his pockets for the car key.

9 《「方々探す」と言う場合》

〈私は今朝からあなたを方々探してきたのよ〉
- ☆ A I've been looking all over for you since this morning.
- ◎ B I've been looking everywhere for you since this morning.
- ○ C I've been looking for you all over [everywhere] since this morning.
- △ D I've been looking in several [various] places for you since this morning.
- △ E I've been looking here and there for you since this morning.

魚屋 →店 2

さかのぼる

1 《昇給・法律や契約の効力》

〈昇給は9月までさかのぼります〉
- ◎ A The pay raise'll be retroactive from September.
- ○ B The pay raise'll be retroactive to September.

2 《家系》

〈彼の家系はメイフラワーまでさかのぼります〉
- ◎ A His family goes [dates] back to the Mayflower.
- ◎ B His family is traced (back) to the Mayflower.

酒屋 →店 7

下がる

1 《物価》

〈物価は最近下がってきました〉
- ◎ A Prices're coming down these days.
- ◎ B Prices're going down [downhill] these days.
- ◎ C Prices're dropping these days.
- ◎ D Prices're falling (down) these days.
- ○ E Prices're getting lower these days.
- △ F Prices're dropping down [decreasing, declining] these days.
- △ G Prices're becoming lower these days.
- △ H Prices're letting up these days.
- ❖ A, H は物価が下がって喜んでいるという響きが強い.

2 《税金》

〈所得税が来年下がるでしょう〉
- ◎ A The income tax'll come down next year.
- ◎ B The income tax'll go down next year.
- ◎ C The income tax'll be cut next year.
- ○ D The income tax'll be [get] lower next year.
- △ E The income tax'll become lower next year.
- △ F The income tax'll drop [decrease] next year.
- ▽ G The income tax'll fall next year.
- × H The income tax'll drop [fall] down next year.
- ❖ A は喜んでいる響きが強い.

3 《支持率》

〈彼の支持率は下がるでしょう〉
- ☆ A His approval rating's falling.
- ◎ B His approval rating's going down [dropping].
- ○ C His approval rating's declining.

△ D His approval rating's coming down [decreasing].
4 《売れ行き》
a) 普通に述べるとき
〈新築住宅の売れ行きが下がりました〉
 ☆ A New home sales've dropped [fallen].
 ◎ B New home sales've gone [come] down.
 ○ C New home sales've decreased [declined].
b) 大きく下がったことを述べるとき
〈新築住宅の売れ行きがすごく下がりました〉
 ☆ A New home sales've fallen [dropped] a lot.
 ◎ B New home sales've fallen dramatically [drastically].
 ◎ C New home sales've dropped dramatically [drastically].
 ◎ D New home sales've gone down dramatically [drastically, a lot].
 ◎ E New home sales've come down dramatically [drastically, a lot].
 ○ F New home sales've decreased dramatically [drastically].
 ○ G New home sales've declined dramatically [drastically].
 ○ H New home sales've gone downhill dramatically [drastically].

5 《気温》
〈気温が7度に下がった〉
 ◎ A The temperature's fallen [dropped] to seven degrees.
 ○ B The temperature's gone down to seven degrees.

6 《下落する》
〈地価は下落しました〉
 ◎ A Land prices have dropped [fallen].
 ◎ B Land prices have declined.
 ◎ C Land prices have gone [come] down.
 ❖Aが一番大幅な下落を意味している。2番目はB。Cは3番目.

7 《急落する》
〈不動産の値段が急落しています〉
 ◎ A Real estate prices're plummeting.
 ◎ B Real estate prices're plunging.
 ◎ C Real estate prices're spiraling downward.
 ◎ D Real estate prices're falling [declining] very fast.
 ◎ E Real estate prices're going down [decreasing, coming down] very fast.
 ○ F Real estate prices're plummeting downward.
 ○ G Real estate prices're plunging downward.
 ○ H Real estate prices're spiraling down.
 ❖急落の程度はA, Fが一番強く, B, Gが2番, C, Hは3番目, Dは4番, Eは5番目.

8 《暴落する》
a) 単に暴落した事実のみを述べるとき
〈株式市場が暴落したんです〉
 ◎ A The stock market's nosedived.
 ◎ B The stock market's taken a nosedive.
 ◎ C The stock market's plunged [plummeted, tumbled, slumped, tobogganed].
 ◎ D The stock market's fallen drastically [dramatically, tremendously].
 ◎ E The stock market's dropped drastically [dramatically, tremendous-

◎ F The stock market's crashed.
❖ F は「底を打った」という意味でも非常によく使われている．
b) 下落した数字を述べるとき
〈私の株は 100 ドルに暴落したんです〉
◎ A My stock's taken a nosedive to $100.
◎ B My stock's plunged [plummeted, tumbled, slumped, crashed] to $100.
○ C My stock's nosedived to $100.
○ D My stock's fallen drastically [dramatically] to $100.
○ E My stock's dropped drastically [dramatically] to $100.

詐欺(師)
1 《起きたことを詐欺だと言及するとき》
a) 弁護士，または法律関係者
〈これは詐欺だ〉
  ◎ A This is fraud.
  △ B This is a scam.
b) 一般の人
〈これは詐欺だ〉
  ◎ A This is a scam.
  △ B This is fraud.
2 《詐欺のため逮捕に言及するとき》
a) 弁護士，または法律関係者
〈彼は詐欺で逮捕されるだろう〉
  ◎ A He'll be arrested for fraud.
  △ B He'll be arrested for a scam.
b) 一般の人
〈彼は詐欺で逮捕されるだろう〉
  ◎ A He'll be arrested for a scam.
  ○ B He'll be arrested for fraud.
3 《訴えることに言及するとき》
a) 弁護士，または法律関係者
〈詐欺で彼を訴えることができるよ〉
  ◎ A We can sue him for committing fraud.
  △ B We can sue him for scamming you.
b) 一般の人
〈私たちは詐欺で彼を訴えるつもりです〉
  ◎ A We're going to sue him for committing fraud against us.
  ○ B We're going to sue him for scamming us.
  ❖ arrest（逮捕する），sue（訴える）というような法律上の言葉があるときは，一般の人の間でも法律用語の fraud の使用頻度は上がる．
4 《検察による告発に言及するとき》
〈彼は詐欺で告発されるだろう〉
  ◎ A He'll be charged with fraud.
  × B He'll be charged with a scam.
  × C He'll be charged with fraudulence.
  ❖ 検察（prosecutor）は証拠があって「告発する」．fraud は証拠があることを示唆する語であるのに対して，scam はそういう響きがない．
5 《詐欺師》

a) 特定の人になりすます人

〈彼はレーガン大統領の親戚だと言ったのですが,実は詐欺師であることがわかったんです〉

- ◎ A He said he was one of President Reagan's relatives, but he turned out to be an imposter [a fraud].
- ○ B He said he was one of President Reagan's relatives, but he turned out to be a fake [a phony].
- △ C He said he was one of President Reagan's relatives, but he turned out to be bogus.

b) 職業・地位を偽る人を指すとき

〈彼は外科医だと言ったのですが,本当ではなかったのです.彼は詐欺師だったのです〉

- ☆ A He said he was a surgeon but it wasn't true. He was a fraud.
- ◎ B He said he was a surgeon but it wasn't true. He was a fake [a phony].
- ○ C He said he was a surgeon but it wasn't true. He was an imposter.
- △ D He said he was a surgeon but it wasn't true. He was bogus.

c)「人をだまして」という意味を含む場合

〈彼は車の調子は最高だと言ったんだ.だから私は買ったんだ.しかし,エンジンは故障する寸前だった.彼は詐欺師だ〉

- ◎ A He said his car was in great shape, so I bought it but the engine was ready to break any second. He was a crook [a fraud].
- ○ B He said his car was in great shape, so I bought it but the engine was ready to break any second. He was a swindler.
- × C He said his car was in great shape, so I bought it but the engine was ready to break any second. He was an impostor.
- × D He said his car was in great shape, so I bought it but the engine was ready to break any second. He was bogus.

d) 信用詐欺師の場合

・男性

〈彼は詐欺師だよ〉

- ☆ A He's a con.
- ◎ B He's a con man [artist].
- ○ C He's a smooth talker.

・女性

〈彼女は詐欺師だよ〉

- ☆ A She's a con.
- ◎ B She's a con artist.
- ○ C She's a smooth talker.

6 《ぺてん師》

〈ニクソン大統領:アメリカ人はニクソン大統領がぺてん師でないことを是非覚えておいていただきたい〉

President Nixon:

- ◎ A The American people must know that their President Nixon is not a crook.
- ○ B The American people must know that their President Nixon is not a fraud.

作品

1 《映画監督・作曲家の作品の場合》

〈これは彼の最近の作品です〉
- ◎ A This is his latest production [work].
- △ B This is his latest product.

2 《画家・小説家・写真家の作品の場合》
〈これは彼の最近の作品です〉
- ◎ A This is his latest work.
- △ B This is his latest product.

避ける

1 《動作として言うとき》
〈ラッシュアワーを避けましょう〉
- ☆ A Let's avoid the rush hour traffic.
- ◎ B Let's stay [keep] away from the rush hour traffic.
- △ C Let's skirt [miss, dodge from] the rush hour traffic.
- ▽ D Let's avert from the rush hour traffic.

2 《状態として言うとき》
〈あなたは彼らを避けておいたほうがいいですよ〉
- ☆ A You'd better stay away from them.
- ◎ B You'd better keep away from them.
- ○ C You'd better steer [stay, keep] clear of them.
- ○ D You'd better keep them at arm's length.
- △ E You'd better shy away from them.
- × F You'd better give a wide berth to them.

❖ Fが辞典に出ているが使われていない.

下げる

1 《値段》

a）大幅に下げるとき
〈この車の値段を大幅に下げなければならないな〉
- ☆ A We have to slash the price on this car.
- ◎ B We have to lower [cut, bring down, reduce] the price on this car a lot.
- ○ C We have to lower [cut, bring down, reduce] the price on this car drastically.

b）普通の値下げ
〈この家の値段を下げなければならないね〉
- ☆ A We have to drop the price on this house.
- ◎ B We have to lower [bring down] the price on this house.
- ○ C We have to cut [reduce] the price on this house.
- ○ D We have to lower this house's price.
- ○ E We have to lower this house price.

c）値下げのパーセンテージを述べるとき
〈2割値下げします〉
- ☆ A We'll take 20% off the price.
- ☆ B We'll take a 20% discount off the price.
- ◎ C We'll give you a 20% discount.
- ◎ D We'll discount 20% off the price.
- ○ E We'll cut [lower, mark] 20% off the price.
- ○ F We'll bring the price down 20%.

2 《税金》
〈政府は景気をてこ入れするために税金を下げるでしょう〉

- ☆ A The government'll cut taxes to boost the economy.
- ◎ B The government'll lower taxes to boost the economy.
- ○ C The government'll bring down [reduce] taxes to boost the economy.

3 《質》

〈うちは質を下げなければならないね〉
- ◎ A We have to lower the quality.
- ○ B We have to drop the quality.
- ▽ C We have to degrade the quality.
- × D We have to make the quality worse.

4 《テレビのボリューム》

〈テレビのボリュームを下げてください〉
- ◎ A Please turn down the TV.
- ◎ B Please turn the TV down.
- △ C Please lower the TV's volume.

5 《日よけ》

〈日よけを下げて下さい〉
- ◎ A Please pull down the shades.
- ○ B Please close the shades.

支える

1 《精神的に》

〈私が交通事故で娘を失ったとき、とてもさびしかったんです。リンダはそんな私をとても支えてくれたんです〉
- ☆ A When I lost my daughter in the car accident, I felt really lonely. Linda was really supportive to [of] me.
- ◎ B When I lost my daughter in the car accident, I felt really lonely. Linda was really supporting [encouraging] me.
- ○ C When I lost my daughter in the car accident, I felt really lonely. Linda was really comforting me.
- △ D When I lost my daughter in the car accident, I felt really lonely. Linda was really propping me up.
- △ E When I lost my daughter in the car accident, I felt really lonely. Linda was really backing me (up).

2 《士気》

〈私たちは彼らの士気を支えなければならない〉
- ◎ A We have to keep up [support] their morale.
- △ B We have to hold up their morale.
- ▽ C We have to prop [prop up, back up] their morale.

3 《会社の経営》

〈私たちは彼の会社を支えなければならないね〉
- ☆ A We have to back [support] his company.
- ◎ B We have to stand behind [by] his company.
- ○ C We have to back his company up.
- ❖ B は「非常に強く支える」というニュアンスがある．

4 《屋根のような重いもの》

a) 長期

〈屋根を支えるのに少なくとも 10 本の柱が必要です〉
- ◎ A We need at least ten pillars to support the roof.
- ◎ B We need at least ten pillars to hold the roof (up).

b) 短期

〈屋根を支えるのに少なくとも 10 本の柱が必要です〉
- ◎ A We need at least ten pillars to prop up the roof.
- ◎ B We need at least ten pillars to prop the roof up.
- ◎ C We need at least ten pillars to hold the roof (up).
- △ D We need at least ten pillars to prop the roof.

差し込み

1 《電話・テレビなどコードのあるもの》

a) 入れる場合

〈電話のコードを差し込みに入れて下さい〉
- ☆ A Plug the phone in.
- ◎ B Plug in [Connect] the phone.
- ○ C Plug the phone cord in.
- ○ D Plug [Connect] the phone cord into the wall.
- △ E Plug the phone cord into the outlet [the wall socket].
- △ F Connect the phone into the wall.
- × G Insert the phone plug in the wall outlet.

b) 抜く場合

〈電話のコードを差し込みから抜いてください〉
- ☆ A Unplug the phone.
- ◎ B Disconnect the phone.
- ○ C Unplug the phone cord.
- ○ D Disconnect the phone (cord) from the wall.
- △ E Disconnect [Unplug] the phone cord from the socket.

2 《胃などの痛み》

〈私は演説をしていたとき胃に差し込みがきたんです〉
- ◎ A I had [felt] a sharp pain in the stomach while I was making the speech.
- × B I had a stitch [a gripping pain] in the stomach while I was making the speech.

❖ B が辞典に出ているが使われていない.

指図

〈私はあなたから指図を受けたくないんです〉
- ☆ A I don't want to take orders from you.
- ◎ B I don't want to take instructions from you.
- ○ C I don't want to take directions from you.
- × D I don't want to take dictates from you.

作曲家 →職業 28

ざっと

1 《本をざっと読む》

〈私はこの本をよく読まなかったんですがざっとは読みました〉
- ☆ A I didn't read this book carefully but I skimmed through it.
- ☆ B I didn't read this book carefully but I took a quick look at it.
- ◎ C I didn't read this book carefully but I had a quick look at it.
- ◎ D I didn't read this book carefully but I skimmed over it.
- ◎ E I didn't read this book carefully but I looked at it quick.
- ○ F I didn't read this book carefully but I glanced over [glanced through, scanned] it.
- ○ G I didn't read this book carefully but I looked at it quickly.

○ H I didn't read this book carefully but I gave it the once-over.
2 《ざっと話をする》
a) 上司が部下に尋ねるとき
〈会議の内容をざっと話してくれるかい〉
- ◎ A Will you give me a summary [a review] of the meeting?
- ○ B Will you give me the essence [an overview, the substance] of the meeting?
  - ❖普通，上司が部下に使う．しかし，当事者の人間関係により同僚間で使われることもある．

b) 同僚に尋ねるとき
〈会議の内容をざっと話してくれるかい〉
- ◎ Will you give [tell] me the gist of the meeting?

3 《損害額》
〈損害額はざっと10万ドルです〉
- ◎ A The damages're roughly [about] $100,000.
- ◎ B The damages're somewhere around [about] $100,000.
- ○ C The damages're approximately $100,000.

査定する
〈この家は3億円と査定されました〉
- ◎ A The value of this house was estimated [appraised, assessed] at 300 million yen.
- ◎ B This house was valued at 300 million yen.
- △ C This house was evaluated at 300 million yen.
- × D The value of this house was rated [put down] at 300 million yen.
  - ❖Dが辞典に出ているが使われていない．

さびしい
1 《相手，また話題になっている人が必要であることを意味しているとき》
〈(出張中の夫に妻が話している) 私はあなたがいなくてとてもさびしいです〉
- ☆ A I really miss you.
- ◎ B I miss you a lot.
- ○ C I miss you terribly [very much, a great deal].

2 《孤独でさびしい気持ちだけを言いたいとき》
〈(出張中の夫に妻が話している) 私はとてもさびしいんです〉
- ◎ A I feel so [really] lonely.
- ◎ B I'm so [really] lonely.
- ○ C I feel very lonely.
- ○ D I'm very lonely.
- △ E I feel so [really] lonesome.
- △ F I'm so [really, very] lonesome.
- △ G I'm very lonesome.
  - ❖相手のことをいつも考えていることと，そのため孤独でさびしいことの2つの気持ちを言いたいときは次のように言う．I really miss you. I feel so lonely.

さびつく
1 《道具・車などについて言う場合》
〈私の車はさびついてきた〉
- ◎ A My car's getting rusty.
- ◎ B My car's rusting.
- ○ C My car's rusting out.

さんせいする

2 《技術・技能について言う場合》

〈私のフランス語は最近さびついてきた〉

◎ A My French is getting rusty these days.
◎ B My French isn't what it was [used to be] these days.
○ C My French is becoming rusty these days.
△ D My French is getting bad these days.

ざらざらした

〈このソファーはざらざらしている〉

◎ A This sofa feels rough [scratchy].
× B This sofa touches rough.
  ❖ B が辞典に出ているが使われていない.

…叉路

1 《三叉路》

〈三叉路の所までずうっと歩いて下さい〉

◎ A Keep walking until you get to a fork in the road.
○ B Keep walking until the road splits.
○ C Keep walking until the road comes to a Y.
△ D Keep walking until you get to a Y.

2 《五叉路》

〈ラルフ：あなたの家はどうやって行けばよいのですか〉

Ralph: How do I get to your house?

〈ビル：この道を五叉路に出るまで，ずうっと歩いて行って下さい〉

Bill:

◎ A Keep walking until you get to the five-way intersection.
△ B Keep walking until you get to the five-street intersection.

賛成する

1 《提案に対して》

〈(ビルが数人の友人たちに提案している) ビル：角のレストランへ行こうよ〉

Bill: Let's go to the restaurant on the corner.

〈ジム：賛成〉

Jim:

◎ A I'll go along with [go for] that.
○ B I'll buy that.
○ C I('ll) second that.
△ D I go along with that.
△ E I'm for that [it].
△ F I'll agree to that.
△ G I'll buy it.
△ H I agree with that [your idea].

2 《述べられた意見に対して》

a) すでに持っている信念として述べるとき

〈A：この国では人は法律の前に平等ではないですね〉

A: People aren't treated equally in the eyes of law in this country.

〈B：賛成です〉

B:

☆ A I agree with that.
◎ B I agree with you.
○ C I agree with your opinion.
△ D I share your opinion.

　　　　❖ D は知識人の間では非常によく使われている．
　b）信念ではなく同調して述べるとき
〈賛成です〉
　　　◎　A　I'll go along with that.
　　　○　B　I'll go along with your opinion.
　　△　C　I('ll) buy that.
　　△　D　I('ll) buy your opinion.
　3　《「大賛成です」と述べるとき》
〈私はあなたの計画に大賛成です〉
　　　☆　A　I totally agree with your plan.
　　　◎　B　I strongly [completely] agree with your plan.
　　　○　C　I absolutely agree with your plan.
　　　○　D　I'm all for your plan.
　　△　E　I'm strongly [completely, absolutely] for your plan.

残念だ

〈(電話で) ジム：ひどい咳が出るのでパーティーに行かれないんだ〉
Jim: I have a bad cough, so I can't come to the party.
〈ビル：それは残念だね〉
Bill:
　　　☆　A　That's too bad.
　　　◎　B　That's a shame.
　　　◎　C　Oh, no.
　　　◎　D　I'm sorry to hear that.
　　　◎　E　That's great [terrific, fantastic].
　　　◎　F　That's a drag [bummer].
　　　◎　G　What a drag [bummer] !
　　　○　H　What a disappointment!
　　　○　I　How disappointing!
　　　○　J　That's disappointing.
　　　○　K　Oh, boy.
　　▽　L　That's a pity.
　　×　M　That's regrettable.
　　❖(1) M は多くの辞典に出ているが使われていない．L は 60 代以上の人の間ではよく使われているが，若年の人の間（40歳くらいまで）では使われていない．
　　❖(2) D は改まった響きがある．しかし，女性の間では親しくても非常によく使われているが，親しい男性の間では使われていない．
　　❖(3) E は下降調で述べる．上昇調で言えば「それはすばらしい」の意味になる．
　　❖(4) F, G は大学生・高校生・中学生の間では非常によく使われている．しかし，それ以外の年代の人の間では使われていない．
　　❖(5) H, I, J には改まった響きがあるので，親しい人たちの間ではあまり使われていない．
　　❖(6) K は女性の間ではよく使われているが，男性の間ではまれ．

散髪する

　1　《女性が言うとき》
〈私は明日散髪するんです〉
　　　◎　A　I'm going to get [have] my hair cut tomorrow.
　　　○　B　I'm going to get a haircut tomorrow.

× C I'm going to have a haircut tomorrow.
　2 《男性が言うとき》
〈私は明日散髪するんです〉
　　　◎ A I'm going to get a haircut tomorrow.
　　　○ B I'm going to get [have] my hair cut tomorrow.
　　　× C I'm going to have a haircut tomorrow.
産婦人科医　→医者 3
散歩する
　1 《1回の散歩のとき》
〈散歩しよう〉
　　　◎ A Let's take [go for] a walk.
　　　○ B Let's go out for a walk.
　　　△ C Let's go on a walk.
　2 《毎朝散歩するとき》
〈私は毎朝散歩します〉
　　　◎ A I take a walk [take walks] every morning.
　　　◎ B I go for a walk [go for walks] every morning.
　　　○ C I go on a walk [go on walks] every morning.
　3 《1日に2回以上散歩するとき》
〈彼は1日2回散歩します〉
　　　☆ A He takes two walks a day.
　　　☆ B He goes for two walks a day.
　　　◎ C He takes walks [a walk] twice a day.
　　　◎ D He goes for walks [a walk] twice a day.
　　　◎ E He goes on walks twice a day.
　　　○ F He goes on two walks a day.
　　　○ G He goes on a walk twice a day.
　4 《犬の散歩を言うとき》
〈私は毎朝犬を散歩させます〉
　　　◎ A I walk my dog every morning.
　　　◎ B I take my dog for a walk every morning.
　　　◎ C I exercise my dog every morning.
　　　❖ C は walking と running を意味する．
三流の
　1 《弁護士》
〈彼は三流弁護士だ〉
　　　◎ A He's a second-rate lawyer.
　　　◎ B He's a third-rate lawyer.
　　　△ C He's a two-bit lawyer.
　2 《大学》
〈彼は三流大学を卒業したんです〉
　　　◎ A He graduated from a second-rate college.
　　　△ B He graduated from a third-rate college.
　　　▽ C He graduated from a two-bit college.
　　　▽ D He graduated from a Podunk college.
　　　❖ D は堅い文章英語では時々使われている．

〔し〕

字

1 《読めない》
〈彼の字は読めません〉
- ☆ A I can't read his handwriting.
- ◎ B His handwriting isn't legible [readable].
- ◎ C I can't make out his handwriting.
- ◎ D His handwriting's unreadable.
- ○ E His handwriting's illegible.
- × F His handwriting is crabbed.

2 《字が上手》
a) 普通にほめるとき
〈あなたの字は上手ですね〉
- ☆ A You have beautiful [nice] handwriting.
- ◎ B You have good [neat] handwriting.
- △ C You have pretty [lovely] handwriting.
- × D You write well.
- × E You write a good [beautiful, nice] hand.

❖ D, E が辞典に出ているが使われていない。

b) 強調してほめるとき
〈あなたの字はとても上手ですね〉
- ◎ A You have really beautiful handwriting.
- ◎ B You have excellent handwriting.
- ◎ C You have terrific handwriting.
- ○ D You have fantastic handwriting.
- ○ E You have wonderful [amazing] handwriting.
- ○ F You have incredible handwriting.
- ○ G You have really lovely handwriting.
- ○ H You have really pretty handwriting.

❖ B が一番強くほめている。F が 2 番、C が 3 番、D が 4 番、E が 5 番、A、G が 6 番、H が 7 番。

3 《字が下手》
a) 普通に述べるとき
〈彼の字は下手です〉
- ☆ A He has bad handwriting.
- ◎ B He has poor handwriting.
- ○ C He writes poorly.
- △ D He writes bad [poor].
- × E He writes a bad handwriting.

b) 強調して述べるとき
〈彼の字はひどく下手です〉
- ◎ A He has horrible [terrible, awful] handwriting.
- ◎ B He has really bad handwriting.
- △ C He has really poor handwriting.

4 《大文字で書く》

a）文字が単数のとき
〈America は大文字で書き始めます〉
- ◎ A America starts with a capital letter.
- ○ B You have to capitalize America.
- ○ C You have to write America with a capital letter.

b）文字が複数のとき
〈U.S.A.は大文字で書きます〉
- ◎ A U.S.A. is written in capital letters.
- ◎ B You have to write U.S.A. with [in] capital letters.
- ○ C You have to use capital letters for U.S.A.
- ○ D You have to write U.S.A. in upper case letters.

5 《字が大きい》
〈彼は字が大きいです〉
- ◎ A He has large handwriting.
- △ B His handwriting's large.

6 《「文盲で字が読めない」の意味のとき》
〈彼は字が読めないんです〉
- ◎ A He can't read.
- ○ B He's illiterate.

痔 →病気 11

試合

1 《テニス・卓球》
a）1試合のとき
〈テニスの試合をしましょう〉
- ◎ A Let's play a game of tennis.
- △ B Let's play a tennis game.
- × C Let's play a tennis match.

b）トーナメントのとき
〈今晩テレビでテニスの試合を見よう〉
- ◎ Let's watch the tennis match [game] on TV tonight.
  - ❖ 1試合のときは game，複数の試合のときは match を使う．

2 《ボクシング・柔道》
〈今晩テレビでボクシングの試合を見よう〉
- ◎ A Let's watch the boxing match on TV tonight.
- △ B Let's watch the boxing bout on TV tonight.
- × C Let's watch the boxing game on TV tonight.
  - ❖ B はプロの間でよく使われている．

3 《ラグビー》
〈今晩テレビでラグビーの試合を見よう〉
- ◎ Let's watch the rugby game [match] on TV tonight.

4 《ゴルフ》
〈ゴルフの試合をしよう〉
- ◎ A Let's play a round of golf.
- △ B Let's play a game of golf.
- × C Let's play a match of golf.

自営業
〈私は自営業です〉
- ◎ A I'm in business for myself.
- ◎ B I run [own, have] my own business.

- ◎ C I'm running my own business.
- ◎ D I'm self-employed.
- × E I have my own company.
- × F I do business my own.
- × G I do business on my own account.
  - ❖(1) E, F, G は辞典に出ているが使われていない．
  - ❖(2) D が一番小さい規模という響きがある．E は「大きい会社」という響きがあるので「自営業」には使えない．

市会議員 →議員 2

司会をする

1 《討論会》

〈ブッシュとゴアの討論会の司会は誰がやるのですか〉

- ◎ A Who's going to be the moderator for the debate between Bush and Gore?
- ○ B Who's going to act as the moderator for the debate between Bush and Gore?
- △ C Who's going to emcee the debate between Bush and Gore?
- △ D Who's going to be the MC for the debate between Bush and Gore?

2 《アカデミー賞などの授賞式》

〈アカデミー賞の授賞式の司会は誰がやるのですか〉

- ◎ A Who's going to be the MC for the Academy's ceremony?
- ◎ B Who's going to emcee the Academy's ceremony?
- ○ C Who's going to emcee for [host] the Academy's ceremony?

3 《ラジオ・テレビのトークショー》

〈彼女はラジオのトークショーの司会をしています〉

- ◎ A She hosts the talk show on the radio.
- ◎ B She is the host for the talk show on the radio.
- ○ C She is the host of the talk show on the radio.
- × D She emcees the talk show on the radio.

4 《美人コンテスト》

〈美人コンテストの司会は誰がやるのですか〉

- ◎ A Who's going to host the beauty pageant?
- ○ B Who's going to emcee (for) the beauty pageant?
- △ C Who's going to be the MC for the beauty pageant?

5 《結婚披露宴》

〈披露宴の司会は誰がやるのですか〉

- ◎   Who's going to emcee [host] your wedding reception?
  - ❖ emcee は盛大なときにしか使えない．

字が大きい →字 5

資格がある

1 《法律上備わっている》

〈もし日本人と結婚すればこの国に永住する資格を持ちます〉

- ☆ A If you marry a Japanese, you'll be eligible to live in this country permanently.
- ◎ B If you marry a Japanese, you'll be entitled to live in this country permanently.
- ○ C If you marry a Japanese, you'll qualify [be qualified] to live in this country permanently.

2 《試験に合格して得る》

〈彼女は医院を開業する資格があります〉
- ☆ A She's qualified to practice medicine.
- ◎ B She qualifies to practice medicine.
- ○ C She's eligible [entitled] to practice medicine.

3 《現在条件を満たしている》

〈彼は今, 厚生年金の受給資格があります〉
- ◎ A He's eligible for [to receive] Social Security now.
- ◎ B He's entitled to receive Social Security now.
- ○ C He qualifies for Social Security now.
- ○ D He's qualified to receive Social Security now.
- △ E He qualifies to receive Social Security now.

4 《将来条件を満たせる》

〈彼は 10 年したら厚生年金を受給する資格があります〉
- ◎ A He'll be eligible for [to receive] Social Security in ten years.
- ◎ B He'll qualify for [to receive] Social Security in ten years.
- ◎ C He'll be entitled to (receive) Social Security in ten years.
- △ D He'll be qualified for [to receive] Social Security in ten years.

5 《努力した結果》

〈第1位優等での卒業資格には, 3.92 またはそれ以上の成績が必要なんです〉
- ◎ A You must have a 3.92 or better GPA to qualify to graduate summa cum laude.
- ◎ B You must have a 3.92 or better GPA to be eligible [entitled, qualified] to graduate summa cum laude.
- ◎ C You must have a 3.92 or better GPA to qualify for graduating summa cum laude.

6 《受けるに値する》

〈私は彼の財産の一部を相続する資格があります〉
- ◎ A I'm entitled [eligible] to inherit a part of his property.
- × B I'm qualified [I qualify] to inherit a part of his property.

しがみつく

〈みんなひっくり返ったボートにしがみついていた〉
- ☆ A Everybody was hanging [holding, clinging] onto the capsized boat.
- ◎ B Everybody was clinging to [hanging on] the capsized boat.
- ○ C Everybody was holding [clinging] on the capsized boat.

叱られる

1 《部下が上司に》

a) 普通に言うとき

〈このお客を失ったら, あなたは上司に叱られるでしょう〉
- ☆ A You'll be in big [a lot of] trouble with your boss if you lose this customer.
- ◎ B The boss'll tell you off if you lose this customer.
- ◎ C You'll get [catch] it from your boss if you lose this customer.
- ○ D The boss'll let you have it if you lose this customer.
- ○ E You'll be told off by your boss if you lose this customer.
- ○ F The boss'll give you a talking to if you lose this customer.
- △ G You'll be called on the carpet by your boss if you lose this customer.
- △ H The boss'll call you on the carpet if you lose this customer.
- ▽ I The boss'll give you a good dressing down if you lose this customer.

▽ J The boss'll scold you if you lose this customer.
× K The boss'll give you a tongue-lashing [lay you out in lavender, tell you where to get off] if you lose this customer.
❖ K が辞典に出ているが使われていない.

b)「こっぴどく（ガミガミ）叱る」というとき
〈私は重要なお客を失ったことで社長にこっぴどく叱られたんです〉
☆ A The boss chewed me out for losing our important customer.
◎ B The boss gave me hell [came down hard on me, gave it to me] for losing our important customer.
○ C The boss lit into me for losing our important customer.
△ D The boss told me off for losing our important customer.
▽ E The boss gave me a good dressing down for losing our important customer.

c) 叱責するとき
〈社長は会長に叱責されたんです〉
◎ A The CEO was reprimanded by the chairman.
○ B The CEO was called on the carpet by the chairman.
○ C The CEO was rebuked [reproached] by the chairman.
× D The CEO was scolded [reproved, rated, upbraided] by the chairman.
❖辞典に D が出ているが使われていない.

2 《子供が親に》
〈8時までに帰らないと私はお母さんに叱られるんです〉
◎ A I'll be in big [a lot of] trouble with my mother if I don't get home by 8:00.
◎ B My mother'll yell at me if I don't get home by 8:00.
○ C I'll get [catch] it from my mother if I don't get home by 8:00.
△ D My mother'll tell me off [scold me] if I don't get home by 8:00.

3 《雷を落とす》
〈社長はあなたに雷を落とすだろう〉
◎ A The boss'll give you hell.
○ B The boss'll light into you.
○ C The boss'll read you the riot act.
× D The boss'll thunder you.
❖ D が辞典に出ているが全く使われていない.

時間通り
〈飛行機は時間通り3時に離陸しました〉
◎ A The plane took off on time [on schedule] at 3:00.
◎ B The plane took off exactly at 3:00.
◎ C The plane took off at exactly 3:00.
◎ D The plane took off at 3:00 sharp.
○ E The plane took off at 3:00 on schedule.
○ F The plane took off promptly at 3:00.
○ G The plane took off at 3:00 exactly.
▽ H The plane took off punctually at 3:00.
❖ H はイギリス英語では非常によく使われている.

時間をつぶす
1 《漠然と述べるとき》
〈どこかで時間をつぶそう〉

◎　Let's (go) kill time somewhere.
2　《時間に言及するとき》
〈私たちは1時間かそこら時間をつぶさなくてはならない〉
- ◎ A We have to kill an hour or so.
- △ B We have to kill time for an hour or so.

敷地
〈敷地に入らないで下さい〉
- ☆ A Keep off the property.
- ◎ B Keep off the premises.
- ○ C Keep off the grounds.

刺激
1　《励まし》
〈社長：もし1週間の合計の売り上げ高が10万ドルに達したら，毎週特別賞与を出すよ〉
Boss: If the total weekly sales reach $100,000, I'll give you a special bonus every week.
〈支配人：それを聞いてうれしいですよ．それはここにいる全員にとっていい刺激になります〉
Manager:
- ◎ A I'm glad to hear that. That'll be good incentive for everybody here.
- ○ B I'm glad to hear that. That'll be good motivation [encouragement] for everybody here.

2　《興奮させること》
〈ジュディ：どうしてニューヨークへ引っ越したいの．物価は高いし，もっと悪いことにはとても危険なところよ〉
Judy: Why do you want to move to New York? Prices are high and what's worse, it's a very dangerous city.
〈ダン：分かってるよ．でもここには刺激がないんだよ．僕には刺激が必要なんだ〉
Dan:
- ◎ A I know, but there's no stimulation here. I need some excitement.
- ◎ B I know, but there's no excitement here. I need some stimulation.
  - ❖前の文に stimulation を使ったら次は excitement，またはその逆でもよいが，同じ単語を繰り返さないこと．

試験
1　《医師の資格試験》
〈彼はたぶん医師の資格試験に受かるでしょう〉
- ◎ A He'll probably pass the boards.
- ◎ B He'll probably pass the medical exam.
- △ C He'll probably pass the medical licensing exam.
  - ❖B は「健康診断」の意味もあるので文脈から判断する．

2　《司法試験》
〈彼はたぶん司法試験に失敗するでしょう〉
- ◎ A He'll probably fail the bar.
- ○ B He'll probably fail the bar exam.

3　《外交官試験》
〈彼はたぶん外交官試験に受かるでしょう〉
- ◎ A He'll probably pass the foreign service exam.
- ○ B He'll probably pass the foreign service test.
- △ C He'll probably pass the exam for foreign service.

4 《教員免許試験》
〈彼はたぶん教員免許試験に受かるでしょう〉
　　◎ A He'll probably pass the teachers certification exam.
　　△ B He'll probably pass the teachers certificate exam.
5 《会計士の試験》
〈彼はたぶん会計士の試験に受かるでしょう〉
　　◎　He'll probably pass the CPA exam [test].
6 《大学入試》
〈彼はたぶん中央大学に合格するでしょう〉
　　◎ A He'll probably pass the entrance exam for Chuo University.
　　○ B He'll probably pass the entrance exam to Chuo University.
　　× C He'll probably pass the entrance exam of Chuo University.
7 《期末試験》
〈私たちは来週期末試験があるんです〉
　　☆ A We're going to have finals next week.
　　◎ B We're going to have final exams next week.
　　○ C We're going to have final tests next week.
8 《中間試験》
〈私たちは来週中間試験があるんです〉
　　☆ A We're going to have mid-terms next week.
　　◎ B We're going to have mid-term exams next week.
　　○ C We're going to have mid-term tests next week.

事件

1 《主観的に述べるとき・マスコミの騒々しい報道を念頭に置いたとき》
〈ニクソン大統領はウォーターゲート事件のために辞任を余儀なくされた〉
　　◎　President Nixon was forced to resign because of the Watergate scandal.
2 《客観的に述べるとき》
〈ニクソン大統領はウォーターゲート事件のために辞任を余儀なくされた〉
　　◎　President Nixon was forced to resign because of the Watergate incident [affair].
3 《裁判を念頭に置いたとき》
〈ニクソン大統領はウォーターゲート事件のために辞任を余儀なくされた〉
　　◎　President Nixon was forced to resign because of the Watergate case.
　　❖「民事事件」「刑事事件」は裁判上の事件．したがって，前者は civil case，後者は criminal case という．

事故

1 《車の事故》
a) 口語英語
〈彼は交通事故でけがしたんです〉
　　◎ A He was hurt in a car crash [wreck].
　　◎ B He was hurt in a car accident.
　　◎ C He was hurt in a fender-bender.
　　○ D He was hurt in an auto accident.
　　❖ A は激しい事故の意味．B, D は客観的な表現で特に激しさを表していない．C は一番軽い事故．
b) 文章英語
〈交通事故の数が近年増加しました〉
　　◎　The number of traffic accidents has increased in recent years.

2 《飛行機の事故》
〈彼はヘリコプターの事故で死んだんです〉
- ◎ He was killed in a helicopter collision [accident, crash].
- ❖ crash は墜落したことを意味する.

3 《車・飛行機などの故障の事故》
〈彼の車に事故があったのかもしれない〉
- ◎ A His car might've had a problem.
- ◎ B His car might've broken down.
- ◎ C His car might've died on him.
- ○ D His car might've quit on him.
- ○ E His car might've developed trouble.

4 《漠然と述べるとき》
〈彼に何か事故があったのかもしれない〉
- ◎ Something bad might've happened to him.

自業自得

1 《強い調子で言いたいとき》
〈(ジムが首になったのは) 自業自得だ〉
- ◎ A He asked for it.
- ◎ B He had it coming (to him).
- ◎ C It [That] serves him right.
- ◎ D He deserves it.

2 《あまり強く言いたくないとき》
〈(ジムが首になったのは) 自業自得ですね〉
- ◎ A That's too bad!
- ○ B That's tough [hard]!
- △ C As one sows, so one reaps.
- △ D As a man sows, so he shall reap.
- × E That's difficult [too hard]!
- ❖ A, B を下降調で言えば「それはお気の毒ですね」と同情表現になる.

仕事

1 《ブルーカラー・臨時の仕事の場合》
〈私は仕事を探しています〉
- ◎ I'm looking for work [a job].

2 《ホワイトカラーの場合》
〈私は仕事を探しています〉
- ◎ A I'm looking for a job.
- △ B I'm looking for work.

3 《医師・弁護士・大学の教授の場合》
〈私は仕事を探しています〉
- ◎ A I'm looking for a job.
- ▽ B I'm looking for work.

4 《専門職の場合》
〈私は放送業界での仕事を探しています〉
- ◎ A I'm looking for a career in broadcasting.
- ○ B I'm looking for a job in broadcasting.
- △ C I'm looking for work in broadcasting.

5 《重役の場合》
〈私は管理職の仕事を探しています〉
- ◎ A I'm looking for a position [job] in management.

△ B I'm looking for work in management.
 6 《「一生の職業」という意味で大学生などが言う場合》
 〈私はまだ仕事を決めていません〉
　　　◎ A I haven't decided on my career yet.
　　　△ B I haven't decided on my profession yet.
 7 《保険・出版・新聞・株式市場・不動産・広告業の場合》
 〈息子は広告の仕事をしています〉
　　　◎ 　 My son's in the advertising industry [game, business].

仕事がひける →終わる 1 b)

仕事で
〈私はよく仕事でヨーロッパへ行きます〉
　　　◎ 　 I often go to Europe for [on] business.

仕事をする
〈私は 10 年間 2 つの仕事をしています〉
　　　◎ A I've been working [holding down] two jobs for ten years.
　　　○ B I've been working at [doing] two jobs for ten years.
　　　△ C I've been at two jobs for ten years.

自殺する
 1 《1 人の場合》
 a) 愛情を持っている人
 〈夫は去年自殺したんです〉
　　　◎ A My husband took his own life last year.
　　　▽ B My husband killed himself last year.
　　　▽ C My husband committed suicide last year.
　　❖家族以外の人，例えば親近感を持っている人のときも A が一番よく使われている．
 b) 親近感を持っていない人
 〈彼は自殺したんです〉
　　　☆ A He committed suicide.
　　　◎ B He killed himself.
　　　○ C He took his own life.
　　　× D He did [made] away with himself.
　　　× E He put himself to death.
　　　× F He destroyed himself.
　　❖D, E, F が辞典に出ているが使われていない．
 2 《心中する》
 a) 一家族
 ・話者が同情して述べるとき
 〈5 人家族が経済的な理由で心中したんです〉
　　　☆ A A family of five took their own lives because of their financial problems.
　　　◎ B A family of five took their lives because of their financial problems.
　　　◎ C A family of five killed themselves because of their financial problems.
　　❖同情の度合いは A が一番強く，B, C の順で下がる．
 ・客観的に述べるとき
 〈5 人家族が経済的な理由で心中したんです〉
　　　◎ 　 A family of five committed suicide because of their financial problems.

・批判的に述べるとき
〈5人家族が経済的な理由で心中したんです〉
- ◎ A A family of five committed suicide because of their financial problems.
- △ B A family of five committed murder suicide because of their financial problems.

・強く批判的に述べるとき
〈父親が妻と3人の子供を殺害して自殺したんです〉
- ◎ A A father committed murder suicide, taking the lives of his wife and three children.
- △ B A father committed suicide, taking the lives of his wife and three children.

b) 恋人

・話者が同情して述べるとき
〈2人は心中したんです〉
- ☆ A They took their own lives for love.
- ◎ B They took their lives for love.
- ◎ C They killed themselves for love.

・客観的に述べるとき
〈2人は心中したんです〉
- ◎ A They committed (a) double suicide for love.
- ◎ B They committed suicide together for love.
- × C They committed suicide together.
  - ❖多くの辞典にCが出ているが、これは単に2人、またはそれ以上の数の人が一緒に自殺したことを表し、「恋人同士が心中した」という意味にはならない。

3 《自殺を図る》

〈彼は自殺を図ったんです〉
- ◎ A He attempted [tried] to commit suicide.
- ◎ B He tried committing suicide.
- ○ C He attempted committing suicide.

4 《集団の場合》

〈彼らは集団自殺したんです〉
- ◎ A They committed a mass suicide.
- ○ B They committed a group suicide.
- × C They committed a multiple suicide.
  - ❖数の上ではAの方がBより多い。

5 《首つり》

〈彼は首つり自殺したんです〉
- ◎ A He hanged himself.
- ○ B He hanged himself to death.

6 《ピストルで》

〈彼はピストル自殺したんです〉
- ◎ A He shot and killed himself.
- ◎ B He shot himself to death.
- ○ C He committed suicide with a gun.
- △ D He committed suicide with a pistol.

7 《服毒》

〈彼は服毒自殺したんです〉

- ◎ A He killed himself by taking poison.
- ◎ B He committed suicide by taking poison.

8 《入水》

〈彼は湖で入水自殺したんです〉

- ◎ A He drowned himself in the lake.
- ◎ B He committed suicide by throwing himself in the lake.
- ◎ C He died by drowning himself in the lake.

9 《焼身》

〈彼は焼身自殺したんです〉

- ◎ A He burned himself to death.
- ◎ B He committed suicide by burning himself.

10 《船から海へ身投げする》

〈彼は海へ船から身を投げて自殺したんです〉

- ◎ A He committed suicide by throwing himself overboard.
- ○ B He committed suicide by jumping off the ship into the ocean.

11 《電車に飛び込む》

〈彼はホームに入ってきた電車の前に飛び込んで自殺したんです〉

- ◎   He killed himself by throwing himself [jumping] in front of a train as it just arrived.

12 《ビルから飛び降りる》

〈彼は 30 階建てのビルから飛び降り自殺したんです〉

- ◎ A He killed himself by jumping off [throwing himself from] a 30-story building.
- ◎ B He threw himself from [jumped off] a 30-story building and died.
  - ❖ B は and died を言わないほうがよく使われている．

13 《ガス》

〈彼はガス自殺したんです〉

- ◎ A He killed himself by breathing fumes from the gas heater.
- ◎ B He killed himself by turning on the gas heater.
- ○ C He killed himself by inhaling fumes from the gas heater.

支持者

〈彼は国会に支持者が大勢います〉

- ◎ A He has a lot of support [supporters, backers] in Congress.
- ○ B He has a lot of followers in Congress.
- ○ C He has a large following in Congress.

支持する

1 《120％支持する場合》

a） 人を支持する場合

〈彼は会合で私を支持してくれました〉

- ◎ A He went to bat for me at the meeting.
- ◎ B He stuck up for me at the meeting.

b） 強く支持したと述べる場合

〈彼は私を会合で強く支持してくれました〉

- ◎ A He really went to bat for me at the meeting.
- ◎ B He really stuck up for me at the meeting.
- ▽ C He strongly [powerfully] went to bat for me at the meeting.
- ▽ D He strongly [powerfully] stuck up for me at the meeting.

c） 提案・意見を支持する場合

〈彼は会合で私の提案を支持しました〉

◎ A He stuck up for my proposal at the meeting.
　　○ B He went to bat for my proposal at the meeting.
2 《100％支持する場合》
〈彼は会合で私の提案を支持しました〉
　　◎ A He stood behind [up for, by] my proposal at the meeting.
　　○ B He stuck up for my proposal at the meeting.
　　○ C He went to bat for my proposal at the meeting.
3 《100％ではないが強く支持する場合》
〈彼は会合で私の提案を支持しました〉
　　◎ A He backed [supported] my proposal at the meeting.
　　○ B He was in support of my proposal at the meeting.
　　○ C He backed up my proposal at the meeting.
　　○ D He backed my proposal up at the meeting.
4 《支持するニュアンスが弱いとき》
〈彼は会合で私の提案を支持してくれました〉
　　◎ A He approved of my proposal at the meeting.
　　○ B He favored my proposal at the meeting.
　　○ C He was in favor of my proposal at the meeting.
　　○ D He was supportive of my proposal at the meeting.
　　× E He was loyal of my proposal at the meeting.
　　❖ B は選択の余地が2つ、またはそれ以上あるときに使われている。C は選択の余地はなく、賛成か反対かという場面で支持するというときに使われる。
5 《支持する人が権限を持っているとき》
〈社長が会合で私の提案を支持してくれました〉
　　☆ A The President endorsed my proposal at the meeting.
　　◎ B The President stood behind [by, up for] my proposal at the meeting.
　　◎ C The President backed my proposal at the meeting.
　　○ D The President stuck up for my proposal at the meeting.
　　○ E The President went to bat for my proposal at the meeting.
　　○ F The President backed up my proposal at the meeting.
　　○ G The President backed my proposal up at the meeting.
　　❖ B～G は支持する人が権限を持っていない場合でもよく使われている。
6 《議論していない内容にさっと同意するとき》
〈私は会合を終わらせる動議を出しました。ビルは支持しました〉
　　◎ A I made a motion to end the meeting. Bill seconded it.
　　△ B I made a motion to end the meeting. Bill was in favor of it.
　　△ C I made a motion to end the meeting. Bill favored [supported] it.
　　△ D I made a motion to end the meeting. Bill backed it (up).
　　△ E I made a motion to end the meeting. Bill went along with it.

自首する
〈彼は警察に自首しました〉
　　◎ A He surrendered (voluntarily) to the police.
　　◎ B He turned himself in (to the police).
　　◎ C He gave himself up (to the police).
　　△ D He surrendered [delivered] himself to the police.
　　× E He turned [gave, denounced] himself to the police.
　　❖ E は辞典に出ているが使われていない。

市場

1 《market（市場）を使えるとき》

〈テレビ市場はダブついている〉

- ◎ A　There are too many TVs on the market.
- ○ B　There's a glut of TVs on the market.
- ○ C　The market is flooded with TVs.
- △ D　There's an overabundance of TVs on the market.
- × E　There's a glut on the TV market.
- × F　The TV market is glutted.
- × G　There's a TV glut on the market.
   - ❖ TV（テレビ），apple（リンゴ），apartment（アパート）のようなひとつひとつの機械，農産物，住宅には market は使えない．テレビは electronics market（電子市場），リンゴは produce market（野菜果物市場），アパートは housing market（住宅市場）として表現する．以下に market が使える代表例を列挙する．beverage market（飲料市場），buyer's market（買手市場），clothing market（衣料品市場），financial market（金融市場），gold market（金市場），home entertainment market（家庭娯楽市場），investment market（投資市場），job market（求人市場），labor market（労働市場），money market（金融市場），oil market（石油市場），real estate market（不動産市場），seller's market（売り手市場），silver market（銀市場），stock market（株式市場），vegetable market（野菜市場）

2 《「市場に出ている」と述べるとき》

〈この新しいテレビはすでに市場に出ています〉

- ◎ A　This new TV's already on the market.
- ◎ B　This new TV's already in stores.
- ◎ C　This new TV's already available.
- ○ D　This new TV's already selling.
- △ E　This new TV's already in the market.

3 《「市場に出す」と述べるとき》

〈(記者会見で) リポーター：いつこの型を市場に出すのですか〉

Reporter:

- ☆ A　When're you going to put this new model on the market?
- ◎ B　When're you going to market [offer] this new model?
- ◎ C　When's this model going to be into the market?
- ○ D　When's this model going to hit [come on] the market?
- ○ E　When're you going to place [offer] this new model on the market?

4 《売り手市場》

〈住宅市場は今売り手市場です〉

- ◎ A　The housing market has more buyers than sellers now.
- ◎ B　The market's good for selling houses now.
- ○ C　Housing's a seller's market now.

5 《買い手市場》

〈求人市場は今，買い手市場です〉

- ◎ A　The job market's limited now.
- ◎ B　The jobs're scarce now.
- ◎ C　The labor market has more job-seekers than jobs now.

史上最高の

〈今年日本の貿易黒字は史上最高です〉

- ◎ A This year Japan's trade surplus is at an all-time high.
- ◎ B This year Japan's trade surplus is at a record-high.
- × C This year Japan's trade surplus is a record-high.
- × D This year Japan's trade surplus is record-breaking high [all-time high].

❖ C, D が辞典に出ているが使われていない.

辞書を引く　→調べる 5

支持率

1 《当選前の選挙戦中》

〈ブッシュの支持率は今後もっと高くなるでしょう〉

- ☆ A Bush'll have better [higher] support ratings from now on.
- ◎ B Bush'll have a better [higher] support rating from now on.
- ○ C Bush'll have a better [higher] support rate from now on.
- △ D Bush'll have better [higher] support rates from now on.

2 《在職中》

〈ブッシュの支持率は今後もっと高くなるでしょう〉

- ☆ A Bush'll have better [higher] approval ratings from now on.
- ◎ B Bush'll have a better [higher] approval rating from now on.
- ○ C Bush'll have a better [higher] support ratings from now on.
- ○ D Bush'll have a better [higher] support rate from now on.
- △ E Bush'll have better [higher] support rates from now on.

静かに

1 《「動かないで」の意味のとき》

〈髪の毛を切っている間は静かに座っていて〉

- ◎　Sit still while I cut your hair.

2 《「音をたてないで」の意味のとき》

〈静かにここにいてください〉

- ◎　Stay here quietly.

3 《「乱暴ではなく」の意味のとき》

〈トミー：ねえお母さん，このオレンジで奇術するのを見てよ〉

Tommy: Hey Mom, watch me juggle these oranges.

〈母親：静かにやってね．おばあちゃんの一番お気に入りの花びんに近すぎるから〉

Mom:

- ◎　Easy does it. You're awfully close to grandma's favorite vase.

私生児

〈彼は私生児なんです〉

- ☆ A He was born to a single mother.
- ◎ B He's a child born out of wedlock.
- ◎ C He's an illegitimate child.
- ○ D He was born without the benefit of marriage.
- △ E He's a love child.

自然な

〈この英語の表現は自然ですか〉

- ◎ A Does this English expression work well?
- ◎ B Is this English expression natural?

下

《下の階》

〈下の喫茶店へ行こう〉

- ◎ A Let's go to the coffee shop downstairs.

- ◎ B Let's go downstairs to the coffee shop.
- ○ C Let's go to the coffee shop below us.
- △ D Let's go to the coffee shop under us.
- △ E Let's go to the coffee shop on the lower level.
- ▽ F Let's go to the downstairs coffee shop.

(…の)下
〈彼は人の下で働く人ではない〉
- ◎ A He isn't one to work for others [other people].
- ◎ B He isn't one to work for anybody [somebody] else.
- ◎ C He isn't one to work for anybody.
- ○ D He isn't one to work for somebody.
  - ❖ A~D はいずれも「独立心が強いので」人の下で働けるような人ではない，というニュアンスのときによく使われている．

死体
1 《死体かどうかはっきりしていないとき》
〈私は死体が川に浮かんでいるのを見ました〉
- ◎ A I saw a (dead) body floating down the river.
- × B I saw a corpse floating down the river.

2 《死体だとはっきりしているとき》
〈警察が来る前に死体を動かすな〉
- ◎ A Don't move the body before the police arrive.
- ▽ B Don't move the dead body before the police arrive.
- ▽ C Don't move the corpse before the police arrive.
  - ❖ 医師が葬儀屋に述べるときには C は時々使われている．

事態
〈事態は変わりました〉
- ◎ A Things have [The situation has] changed.
- ▽ B Matters have changed.
  - ❖ B が辞典に出ているがまれにしか使われていない．

…次第だ
1 《一般的に述べるとき》
〈すべてあなた次第です〉
- ◎ A Everything is up to you.
- ◎ B Everything is in your hands.
- ◎ C Everything depends on you.
- ○ D Everything is left in your hands.
- △ E Everything rests with you.

2 《whether 節が主語のとき》
〈私たちが出発するか否かは天気次第です〉
- ◎ A Whether we leave or not depends on the weather.
- ◎ B Whether we leave or not is up to the weather.
- ○ C Whether we leave or not rides on the weather.
- △ D Whether we leave or not rests [lies] with the weather.

3 《the decision が主語のとき》
〈決定はあなた次第です〉
- ◎ A The decision is up to you.
- ◎ B The decision is (left) in your hands.
- ◎ C The decision depends on [rides on, rests with, lies with] you.

下書きする
〈私はライオンズクラブでするスピーチの下書きをしなければならないんです〉
- ◎ A I have to make [write, work on] a (rough) draft for the speech I'm going to make at the Lions Club.
- ◎ B I have to draft the speech I'm going to make at the Lions Club.

支度する
1 《食事を作る》
a) オーブンのように「火」を使って支度するとき
〈私は今昼食の支度に忙しいんです〉
- ◎ I'm busy cooking [making, fixing] lunch now.

b) 「火」を使うか使わないか言及しないとき
〈私は今昼食の支度に忙しいんです〉
- ◎ A I'm busy fixing [making] lunch now.
- ○ B I'm busy getting lunch now.
- ▽ C I'm busy preparing lunch now.
  - ❖(1) C は日常の食事には使われていない。「パーティーの支度をする」ときならよく使われている。
  - ❖(2) cook は火を使わないで「支度する」とき（例：サンドイッチ）には使えない。
  - ❖(3) B の get には「テーブルをセットする」ことや「食器を食前に洗う」ことも含まれている。

c) 時間を明示して食事を支度させるとき
〈6時までに夕食を支度して下さい〉
- ◎ A Please have dinner ready by six.
- ○ B Please get dinner ready by six.
- △ C Please make [set] dinner ready by six.
  - ❖ A は B よりソフトな響きがあるので一番よく使われる。

2 《場所を整える》
〈2時までに手術室を支度して下さい〉
- ◎ A Please have the operating room ready by 2:00.
- ◎ B Please get the operating room ready by 2:00.
- ◎ C Please have the operating room prepared by 2:00.
- ◎ D Please get the operating room prepared by 2:00.
- ○ E Please make the operating room ready by 2:00.
- △ F Please set the operating room ready by 2:00.
  - ❖(1) 家庭内の食事の支度と違ってソフトな話し方が求められていないので、B も A と同様よく使われている。
  - ❖(2) C の have...prepared, D の get...prepared は、1 c)のような家庭内での食事の支度を言うときには使えない。

…したくてたまらない
1 《どこかへ行きたいとき》
a) 計画がすでにあるとき
〈私は本当にフランスへ行きたくてたまらないんです〉
- ◎ A I'm really dying to go to France.
- ◎ B I can hardly wait to go to France.
- ◎ C I can't wait to go to France.
- ○ D I'm really anxious [eager] to go to France.
- △ E I'm really itching to go to France.
- × F I'm really tickling [burning, impatient] to go to France.

× G I'm really keen on going to France.
  ❖(1) F, G が辞典に出ているが使われていない.
  ❖(2) E は「すぐに」という響きが一番強い.
b) 計画がないとき
〈私は本当にフランスへ行きたくてたまらないんです〉
  ◎ A I'm really dying to go to France.
  ○ B I'm really anxious [eager] to go to France.
  △ C I'm really itching to go to France.
2 《人に会いたいとき》
a) 計画がすでにあるとき
〈私はあなたにとても会いたくてたまらないんです〉
  ◎ A I can hardly wait to see you.
  ◎ B I can't wait to see you.
  ◎ C I'm really dying to see you.
  ○ D I'm really anxious [eager] to see you.
  △ E I'm really itching to see you.
b) 計画がないとき
〈私はあなたにとても会いたくてたまらないんです〉
  ◎ A I'm really dying to see you.
  ○ B I'm really anxious [eager] to see you.
  △ C I'm really itching to see you.

下っ端 →地位 8
下手に出る
〈そんなに高飛車に出ないで下手に出たほうがいいよ〉
  ◎ A I'd suggest you take a humble attitude instead of such a high-handed one.
  ○ B I'd suggest you take a low-key attitude instead of such a high-handed one.
  △ C I'd suggest you assume a humble [low-key] attitude instead of such a high-handed one.
  × D I'd suggest you take [assume] a low attitude instead of such a high-handed one.
  ❖(1) 辞典に D が出ているが使われていない.
  ❖(2) 文章英語では A, B, C いずれもよく使われている.

示談にする
〈あなたはこれを示談にしたほうがいいよ〉
  ☆ A You should settle this out of court.
  ◎ B You should work this out, out of court.
  ◎ C You should straighten [resolve, take care of] this out of court.
  ◎ D You should settle this without taking legal action.
  ◎ E You should settle this without taking it to court.
  ◎ F You should settle this without suing them.
  ○ G You should handle [solve] this out of court.
  ○ H You should find a solution on this out of court.

質屋 →店 30
視聴率
1 《テレビ》
〈この番組がすべての中で一番視聴率が高いんです〉
  ◎ A This program has the highest viewer rating [ratings] of all.

× B This program has the highest viewer rate of all.
　2　《ラジオ》
〈このラジオ番組の視聴率は高いんです〉
　　　◎ A This radio program has a high listener rating [has high listener ratings].
　　　○ B This radio program has a high rating [has high ratings].
　　　× C This radio program has a high listening rating [has high listening ratings].

歯痛　→痛い　3

失格
　1　《親として》
　a）子供に関心がなく自分のことを優先させる
〈彼は父親失格です〉
　　　◎ A He's a failure as a father.
　　　◎ B He's a lousy father.
　　　△ C He's no good as a father.
　b）子供・母親を虐待，アル中，女狂い，賭け事にのめり込む
〈彼は父親失格です〉
　　　◎　　He's a rotten [a terrible, an awful, a shitty] father.
　2　《スポーツ》
〈彼は麻薬を飲んだことがわかったので失格となったのです〉
　　　◎　　He was disqualified because it turned out he took drug.

失業
　1　《失業している》
〈彼は失業中です〉
　　　◎ A He's out of work [a job].
　　　◎ B He doesn't have work [a job].
　　　◎ C He's unemployed.
　　　◎ D He's between jobs.
　　　○ E He has no job.
　　　○ F He's got no job.
　　　○ G He's jobless.
　　　○ H He's without work [a job].
　　　❖ G は「失業中だが仕事をする気がないので失業している」の意味で普通使われている．
　2　《失業率》
　a）一般的に述べるとき
〈失業率はさらにあがるだろう〉
　　　◎ A The unemployment rate'll go up further.
　　　○ B The jobless rate'll go up further.
　　　○ C The rate of unemployment'll go up further.
　b）パーセンテージを示すとき
〈失業率は 10 ％にあがるだろう〉
　　　◎ A The unemployment rate'll go up to 10%.
　　　○ B The jobless rate'll go up to 10%.
　　　○ C The rate of unemployment'll go up to 10%.

実業家　→職業　9
実業界　→…界

実現する
1 《「実現させる」と述べるとき》
〈私は夢を実現させたいんです〉
- ☆ A I want to make my dreams come true.
- ◎ B I want to make my dreams happen.
- ◎ C I want to make my dreams a reality.
- ◎ D I want to fulfill my dreams.
- ◎ E I want to make my dream come true.
- ○ F I want to make my dream happen.
- ○ G I want to carry out my dreams.
- △ H I want to fulfill my dreams take place.
- △ I I want to realize [accomplish] my dreams.
- △ J I want to carry out my dreams a reality.
- × K I want to actualize [materialize, bring about] my dream.

❖(1) K が辞典に出ているが使われていない．
❖(2)「夢を実現させる」のときは単数の dream よりも dreams の方がよく使われている．

2 《「実現する」と述べるとき》
〈あなたの夢は実現するでしょう〉
- ☆ A Your dreams'll come true.
- ◎ B Your dreams'll happen.
- ◎ C Your dreams'll be a reality.
- △ D Your dreams'll materialize.
- △ E Your dreams'll be realities.
- △ F Your dreams'll be realized.
- × G Your dreams'll be true.

実行可能な
〈彼の提案は実行可能です〉
- ☆ A His proposal's practical.
- ◎ B His proposal's feasible [doable, workable].
- ○ C His proposal's achievable.
- ○ D His proposal works.
- × E His proposal's practicable.

❖各種の辞典で「実行可能な」は practicable で practical でない旨が力説されている．また，最近出版された辞典には，「実行可能な」は practicable であるが practical が使われることもあると書いてあるが，実際はアメリカの大学院卒のレベルの人の間でも practicable の存在さえ知られていない．

実際に…しているところ
〈あなたはテニスが上手だそうですね．実際にやっているところを見たいです〉
- ◎ A I hear you're a good tennis player. I'd like to see you in action.
- ◎ B I hear you're a good tennis player. I'd like to see you play.
- ○ C I hear you're a good tennis player. I'd like to see you playing.
- △ D I hear you're a good tennis player. I'd like to see you while (you're) playing.

実際は
〈彼は仕事を辞めたと言ったのですが，実際は解雇されたんです〉
- ◎ A He said he quit his job but in fact he was dismissed.
- ◎ B He said he quit his job but actually [really] he was dismissed.
- ○ C He said he quit his job but as a matter of fact he was dismissed.

△ D He said he quit his job but in actuality he was dismissed.
　　　× E He said he quit his job but in point of fact he was dismissed.
　　❖ E が多くの辞典に出ているが使われていない．
実施される
　〈新しい交通法は5月1日から実施されます〉
　　　◎ A The new traffic law goes [comes] into effect as of May 1st.
　　　◎ B The new traffic law becomes effective as of May 1st.
　　　◎ C The new traffic law takes effect as of May 1st.
　　　◎ D The new traffic law is in effect as of May 1st.
　　　× E The new traffic law is enforced as of May 1st.
　　　× F The new traffic law becomes operative as of May 1st.
　　　× G The new traffic law comes [goes] into force as of May 1st.
　　❖ E, F, G が辞典に出ているが使われていない．
叱責する　→叱られる 1 c)
…し続ける　→続く
知っている
　1　《うわさ・人づてに聞いて》
　〈私は六本木にいいロシアレストランがあることを知っています〉
　　　☆ A I know of a good Russian restaurant in Roppongi.
　　　◎ B I know about a good Russian restaurant in Roppongi.
　　　◎ C I know Roppongi has a good Russian restaurant.
　　　◎ D I know there's a good Russian restaurant in Roppongi.
　2　《そばを通るため》
　〈私は六本木にいいロシアレストランがあることを知っています〉
　　　◎ A I know about a good Russian restaurant in Roppongi.
　　　◎ B I know Roppongi has a good Russian restaurant.
　　　△ C I know that Roppongi has a good Russian restaurant.
　　　× D I know there's a good Russian restaurant in Roppongi.
　3　《非常によく知っている》
　a) 住んでいた人のことを述べるとき
　・普通に述べるとき
　〈彼はニューヨークのことを非常によく知っています〉
　　　☆ A He knows New York really well.
　　　◎ B He knows New York very well.
　　　◎ C He really knows New York.
　　　◎ D He knows a lot about New York.
　　　△ E He knows a really lot about New York.
　・強調して述べるとき
　〈彼はニューヨークのことはすごくよく知っています〉
　　　◎ A He knows every (little) corner of New York.
　　　◎ B He knows every inch of New York.
　　　◎ C He knows New York like the back of his hand.
　　　◎ D He knows all there's to know about New York.
　　　○ E He knows New York like the palm of his hand.
　b) 住んだことがないが書物で研究して知っているとき
　〈彼はアメリカのことを非常によく知っています〉
　　　☆ A He knows about America really well.
　　　◎ B He really knows about America.
　　　◎ C He knows a lot (of stuff) about America.

- ◎ D He knows about America very well.
- ◎ E He has a lot of information about America.
- ◎ F He knows all there's to know about America.
- ○ G He knows a lot of things about America.
- × H He knows of America really well.

4 《知りませんよ》

〈息子:僕のめがね,どこにあるか知ってる〉

Son: Do you know where my glasses are?

〈母親:知りませんよ〉

Mother:
- ☆ A I don't know.
- ◎ B I have no idea.
- ◎ C You('ve) got me.
- ○ D You('ve) got me there.
- ○ E Beats me.
- △ F Search me.
  - ❖人によっては現在 E, F を非常によく使っているが,将来この2つは使われなくなるであろう.

5 《「ぜんぜん知らない」と述べるとき》

〈息子:僕の時計,どこにあるか知らない?〉

Son: Do you know where my watch is?

〈母親:ぜんぜん知りませんよ〉

Mother:
- ☆ A I haven't the slightest [foggiest] idea.
- ☆ B I have no idea at all.
- ◎ C I have no idea whatsoever.
- ◎ D I don't have any idea whatsoever [at all].
- ○ E God only knows.

失敗

1 《試験》

〈彼はまた司法試験に落ちるでしょう〉
- ◎ A He'll fail [flunk] the bar again.
- ◎ B He won't pass the bar again.
- × C He'll fail in the bar again.
  - ❖多くの辞典に C が出ているが使われていない.

2 《ビジネス・実験・手術など》

〈彼は新しいビジネスに失敗したんです〉
- ◎ A He failed in his new business.
- ◎ B He was unsuccessful in his new business.
- ○ C He wasn't successful in his new business.

3 《パーティー》

〈パーティーは失敗だった〉
- ◎ A The party stunk.
- ◎ B The party was a flop.
- ○ C The party flopped [bombed].
- ○ D The party was a failure.
- × E The party fell through [miscarried].
- × F The party was dashed to the ground.
  - ❖ E, F が辞典に出ているが使われていない.

実力
〈うちの会社での昇進は実力次第です〉
- ☆ A Promotion in our company's based on merit.
- ◎ B Promotion in our company's based on your capability.
- ◎ C Promotion in our company's based on (your) job performance.
- ○ D Promotion in our company's based on the merit system.
- × E Promotion in our company's based on the capability system.

失礼です
1 《一般的に述べる場合》
〈あなたは私に失礼です〉
- ☆ A You're rude.
- ◎ B You're rude to me.
- ◎ C You were rude (to me).
- ○ D You're impolite.
- △ E You were impolite (to me).
- △ F You're impolite to me.

2 《強調して述べる場合》
〈失礼ね〉
- ☆ A Excuse me!
- ☆ B Excuse you!
- ◎ C Sorry!
- ◎ D I'm sorry!

❖(1) 相手が失礼であったときはいつでも使える．
❖(2) A～D いずれも文尾を上がり調子で言う．
❖(3) B，C はいずれの年代でも使われているが，特に30歳くらいの人の間で非常によく使われている．

…していただけますか
1 《非常に丁重に依頼する場合》
〈少しお金を貸していただけますでしょうか〉
- ◎ A Could I possibly ask you to lend me some money?
- ◎ B I was wondering if I could [might] ask you to lend me some money.
- ◎ C Would you mind lending me some money?
- ○ D Would you be kind enough [so kind as] to lend me some money?
- ▽ E Would you be good enough [so good as] to lend me some money?

❖(1) 一番丁重な表現としてEが多くの本で紹介されているが，ほとんど使われていない．
❖(2) 丁重さは D が1番，A，B，C はほぼ同じで2番．

2 《丁重に依頼する場合》
〈少しお金を貸していただけますか〉
- ◎   Could [Would] you lend me some money?

❖ could の方が丁重な響きがある．Will you lend me some money? という言い方も非常によく使われているが，これは丁重表現ではない．丁重どころかむしろ命令に近い響きがある．

…してもいい　→…するといいでしょう

…してもらう
〈角の写真館で写真を撮ってもらいましょう〉
- ◎   Let's have [get] our picture taken at the photo studio on the corner.

〈誰かに写真を撮ってもらおう〉
- ◎ Let's ask somebody to take our picture.

支店長 →地位 17

自動

1 《自動改札機》
〈日本のほとんどの駅には自動改札機があります〉
- ◎ A Most stations in Japan have automatic ticket taker.
- × B Most stations in Japan have automatic ticket checker.

2 《自動消火装置》
〈このビルには自動消火装置がついています〉
- ◎ A This building has a sprinkler system.
- ○ B This building has an automatic sprinkler system.

3 《自動販売機》
〈角に自動販売機があります〉
- ◎ A There's a vending machine on the corner.
- × B There's a slot machine [a dispenser] on the corner.
  - ❖辞典に B が出ているが使われていない．

4 《自動ピアノ》
〈私は自動ピアノを買おうと思っています〉
- ◎ A I'm thinking of buying a player piano.
- △ B I'm thinking of buying an automatic piano.

自動車

1 《自動車の運転の能力に言及するとき》
〈彼は自動車に乗れるんですか〉
- ◎ A Can he drive?
- ○ B Can he drive a car?
- × C Can he drive an auto [an automobile]?

2 《自動車メーカー》
〈彼女は自動車メーカーに勤めています〉
- ☆ A She works for a car company.
- ◎ B She works for a car manufacturer.
- ○ C She works for a car [an auto] maker.
- ○ D She works for an auto [an automobile] manufacturer.

3 《自動車産業》
〈彼は自動車産業の大物です〉
- ☆ A He's a big shot in the auto industry.
- ◎ B He's a big shot in the car industry.
- ○ C He's a big shot in the automobile industry.

4 《発明に言及するとき》
〈誰が自動車を発明したのですか〉
- ◎ A Who invented the automobile?
- × B Who invented the car?

5 《開発に言及するとき》
〈ヘンリー・フォードが自動車を開発したんです〉
- ☆ A Henry Ford developed an automobile.
- ◎ B Henry Ford developed the automobile.
- ○ C Henry Ford developed a car.
- ▽ D Henry Ford developed the auto.

自動車教習所 →各種学校 4

自動車組立て工場 →工場 2
自動車修理所 →店 19
…しながら
1 《over を使う場合》
a) 飲物
〈私たちは Aコーヒー B紅茶 Cワイン Dカクテル E飲物 Fビール を飲みながら話しました〉
- ◎ A We talked over coffee.
- ◎ B We talked over tea.
- ◎ C We talked over a glass of wine.
- ◎ D We talked over cocktails.
- ◎ E We talked over drinks.
- ◎ F We talked over a beer.
  - ❖(1) A over a cup of coffee, B over a cup of tea, E over a drink, F over a bottle of beer も非常によく使われている.
  - ❖(2) 決まり文句なので over が従える名詞は無制限ではなく, A～F の名詞以外はあまり使われていない.

b) 食物
〈私たちは Aアイスクリーム B朝食 C昼食 D夕食 Eデザート Fケーキ を食べながら話しました〉
- ◎ A We talked over ice cream.
- ◎ B We talked over breakfast.
- ◎ C We talked over lunch.
- ◎ D We talked over dinner.
- ◎ E We talked over dessert.
- ◎ F We talked over cake.
  - ❖ over を使える必要条件は, ① breakfast, lunch, dinner のような時間を示す語, および② ice cream, dessert, cake のようにリラックスできることを示す語. したがって, apple, banana, sandwich などには使えない.

2 《talk のような口を動かす動詞が使われているとき》
〈私たちはコーヒーを飲みながら話しました〉
- ◎ A We talked over (a cup of) coffee.
- ○ B We talked while (we were) drinking coffee.
- ○ C We talked while we drank coffee.
- × D We talked drinking coffee.
  - ❖口を動かす動詞のときは D はあまり使われていない.

3 《talk のような口を動かす動詞が使われていないとき》
〈私たちはコーヒーを飲みながらテレビを見ました〉
- ◎ A We watched TV over (a cup of) coffee.
- ◎ B We watched TV while (we were) drinking coffee.
- ◎ C We watched TV while we drank coffee.
- ◎ D We watched TV drinking coffee.

…しなければならない
1 《現在の内容》
〈私は毎朝 5 時に起きなければならないんです〉
- ◎ A I have to [I've got to] get up at 5:00 every morning.
- ▽ B I must get up at 5:00 every morning.
  - ❖堅い文章英語では B が非常によく使われている.

2 《未来の内容》

〈私は今晩彼らに会わなければならないんです〉
　　◎　A　I have to see them this evening.
　　○　B　I'll have to see them this evening.
　3　《過去の内容》
〈私は8時まで会社にいなければならなかったんです〉
　　◎　　I had to be at the office until 8:00.

…しに行く　→行く

　1　《運動を表す動詞を従えるとき》
〈彼は海へ泳ぎに行きました〉
　　◎　　He went swimming in the ocean.
〈彼は湖へスケートをしに行きました〉
　　◎　　He went skating on the lake.
〈彼はジョギングに行きました〉
　　◎　　He went jogging.
　2　《レジャーに関する動詞を従えるとき》
〈彼はニューヨークへ観光に行きました〉
　　◎　A　He went sightseeing in New York.
　　◎　B　He went to New York to sightsee.
　　×　C　He went to New York for sightseeing.
〈彼は湖へキャンプに行きました〉
　　◎　A　He went camping by the lake.
　　○　B　He went to the lake to camp.
　　×　C　He went to the lake for camping.
　3　《前述以外の動詞を従えるとき》
〈彼はアメリカへ英語を勉強しに行きました〉
　　☆　A　He went to America to study English.
　　◎　B　He went to America so that he could study English.
　　◎　C　He went to America in order to study English.
　　×　D　He went to America for studying English.
　　×　E　He went studying English in America.

死ぬ

　1　《事故で》
〈彼は交通事故で死んだんです〉
　　◎　A　He was killed in a car accident.
　　△　B　He died in a car accident.
　2　《病気・老齢で》
　a）婉曲な表現
〈彼は亡くなられたんです〉
　　◎　A　He passed away.
　　◎　B　He left us.
　　○　C　He went to a better place.
　　△　D　He went to a big golf course in the sky.
　　△　E　He passed on.
　b）一般的な表現
〈彼が死んでから5年になります〉
　　◎　A　He died five years ago.
　　◎　B　It's been five years since he died.
　　◎　C　He's been dead for five years.
　　△　D　It's five years since he died.

c) 残酷な表現
〈彼は死んだよ〉
- ◎ He kicked the bucket.

3 《病名・死因に言及するとき》
a) 長い闘病生活の場合
〈彼はガンで死んだんです〉
- ◎ A He died of cancer.
- ○ B He died from cancer.
- △ C He died because of cancer.

b) 突発的病気
〈彼は心臓発作で死んだんです〉
- ◎ A He died from a heart attack.
- ○ B He died of a heart attack.
- △ C He died because of a heart attack.

c) 出血多量などで
〈彼は出血多量で死んだんです〉
- ◎ A He died from excessive bleeding.
- ○ B He died of excessive bleeding.
- △ C He died because of excessive bleeding.

d) けが
〈彼はけがの傷口が感染して死んだんです〉
- ◎ A He died from his infected wounds.
- ○ B He died of his infected wounds.
- △ C He died because of his infected wounds.

e) 過労
〈彼は過労で死んだんです〉
- ◎ A He died from overworking.
- ◎ B He died from working too much [hard].
- ○ C He died from overwork.
- ○ D He died because of working too much [hard].
- △ E He died because of overwork.
- ▽ F He died because of overworking.

支払う

1 《店などで代金を》
a) 主語が1人称のとき
〈私が支払います〉
- ◎ A I'll pay the check [bill, tab].
- ◎ B I'll take care of the check [bill, tab].
- ◎ C I'll pick up the check [bill, tab].
- ◎ D I've got it.
- ○ E I'll foot the check [bill, tab].
  - ❖ check, bill はレストラン, バーのいずれにも使われているが, tab は主としてバーで使われている.

b) 主語が2人称のとき
〈支払ってくれますか〉
- ☆ A Will you take care of the check [bill, tab]?
- ◎ B Will you pay the check [bill, tab]?
- ◎ C Will you pick up the check [bill, tab]?
- ▽ D Will you foot the check [bill, tab]?

2 《長期間未払いのお金を》
〈いつ残金を支払ってくれますか〉
- ◎ A When will you pay the balance?
- ○ B When will you take care of the balance?
- △ C When will you clear up [settle] the balance?
- × D When will you fix [square] the balance?
  - ❖ D は辞典に出ているが使われていない．

3 《多額な支払い，または割賦の支払いなどを「全部支払う」》
〈あなたは家の支払いを全部支払ったの〉
- ☆ A Did you pay off your house?
- ◎ B Did you get your house paid off?
- ◎ C Did you finish paying off your house?
- ○ D Did you finish paying for your house?
- △ E Did you finish making all the payments on your house?
- △ F Did you finish all the payments for your house?

4 《長期間にわたって支払うとき》

a） 一般的に述べるとき
〈母：住宅ローンは全部支払ったの〉
Mother: Have you paid off the home loan?
〈息子：まだ払っていますよ〉
Son:
- ☆ A I'm still working on it.
- ◎ B I'm still paying (it).
- ◎ C I'm still going for it.

b） 支払いに苦労している気持ちで述べるとき
〈母：住宅ローンは全部支払ったの〉
Mother: Have you paid off the home loan?
〈息子：なんとか支払っています〉
Son:
- ○ A I'm scraping it together.
- ○ B I'm struggling away with it.
- ○ C I'm struggling to make the payments on [for] it.

c） 長年支払い続けている気持ちを述べるとき
〈母：住宅ローンは全部支払ったの〉
Mother: Have you paid off the home loan?
〈息子：まだ支払い続けていますよ〉
Son:
- ◎ 　I'm still plugging away at it.

5 《自腹を切る》
〈あなたは自腹を切る必要はありません〉
- ◎ A You don't have to pay out of your own pocket.
- × B You don't have to pay out of your own wallet [purse].

耳鼻咽喉科医 →医者 4

自分で

1 《「自分自身で」の意味のとき》
〈私は自分で見るまではそれを信じません〉
- ◎ A I won't believe it until I see it (for) myself.
- × B I won't believe it until I see it by myself [on my own].

2 《「他人の力を借りずに」と「自分自身で」の両方の意味のとき》

〈私は退職した後で子供たちに頼らないように，自分でこのレストランを開いたんです〉
- ☆ A I opened this restaurant for myself so that I might not depend on my children after I retired.
- ◎ B I opened this restaurant by myself so that I might not depend on my children after I retired.
- ○ C I opened this restaurant on my own so that I might not depend on my children after I retired.

司法試験 →試験 2

死亡率

〈(友人同士の会話で) ガンは死亡率が高いんだ〉
- ◎ A Cancer has a high death rate.
- △ B Cancer has a high mortality [fatality] rate.
- × C Cancer has a high mortality.
  - ❖(1) C が辞典に出ているが使われていない．
  - ❖(2) 患者が医師に尋ねるような会話，または堅い文章では，B の mortality rate は非常によく使われている．

…しましょう

1 《肯定の提案の場合》

〈地下鉄で行きましょう〉
- ◎ A Let's take the subway.
- ◎ B Why don't we take the subway?
- ○ C Why not take the subway?
- ○ D How [What] about taking the subway?
- ○ E What do you say we take the subway?
- △ F What do you say to taking the subway?

2 《否定の提案の場合》

〈彼らを夕食に招待しないことにしましょう〉
- ◎ A Let's not invite them to dinner.
- ◎ B How [What] about not inviting them to dinner?
- ◎ C What do you say about not inviting them to dinner?

…しましょうか

1 《友人・家族・または見知らぬ人が相手で，改まった話し方を必要としないとき》

a) 相手に都合がよいとき

〈駅まで車で送りましょうか〉
- ◎ A Do you want me to drive you to the station?
- ◎ B Can I drive you to the station?
- △ C Would you like me to drive you to the station?

b) 許可を求めているという誤解の恐れがあるとき

〈窓を開けましょうか〉
- ◎ A Do you want me to open the window?
- ◎ B Can I open the window for you?
- ○ C Would you like me to open the window?
  - ❖B の場合，文尾の for you がないと「窓を開けてもいいですか」と許可を求めている意味になる．

2 《丁重な話し方が求められている場合》

〈(高級レストランで) 窓をお開けいたしましょうか〉
- ◎ A Would you like me to open the window (for you)?
- ◎ B Shall I open the window (for you)?

- ◎ C Could I open the window for you?
- ◎ D May I open the window for you?
- △ E Might I open the window for you?
    - ❖(1) A, B は for you のある方が丁重に聞こえる．
    - ❖(2) C, D の文尾の for you を消すと許可の意味になり「…してもいいですか」になる．
    - ❖(3) B の Shall I...?は少し堅い響きがある．

しみ
〈あなたのドレスにしみが付いていますよ〉
- ◎ A Your dress has a stain.
- ◎ B Your dress is stained.
- ◎ C Your dress has a spot.
- ○ D Your dress is spotted.
- ○ E Your dress has a smear.
- △ F Your dress is smeared.
    - ❖(1) F が辞典に出ているがあまり使われていない．
    - ❖(2) A は洗っても取れないという響きがある．B はしみをこぼしたばかりのときに使われている．

地味な
1 《色に言及するとき》
〈あなたのネクタイの色はスーツには地味すぎます〉
- ◎ A The colors in your tie're too conservative [soft, boring] for your suit.
- ○ B The colors in your tie're too subdued [subtle] for your suit.
- × C The colors in your tie're too discreet [sober] for your suit.

2 《柄に言及するとき》
〈柄が地味だからこのネクタイが好きなんです〉
- ◎ A I like this tie because of its discreet [conservative, subtle] pattern.
- △ B I like this tie because of its subdued [sedate] pattern.

市民権
1 《居住》
〈彼女は日本人と結婚したから市民権を得たんです〉
- ◎ A She got her citizenship because she married a Japanese.
- × B She got her citizens' [civil, civic] rights because she married a Japanese.
    - ❖ B が辞典に出ているが使われていない．

2 《従来否定されていた考え方・生き方》
〈ほとんどのアメリカ人は結婚する前に同棲し，このことは完全に市民権を得ています〉
- ◎ A Most American people live together before they get married, and this is accepted.
- ◎ B Most American people live together before they get married, and society accepts this.
- ◎ C Most American people live together before they get married, and this is OK with society.
- ○ D Most American people live together before they get married, and society takes it for granted.

3 《「公民権」と表現する「市民権」》
〈彼は公民権運動により有名になったのです〉

- ◎ A He became well-known through the civil rights movement.
- × B He became well-known through the citizens' rights movement.

事務所
1 《賃貸用として見た場合》
〈このビルが完成したらいくつ事務所ができるのですか〉
- ◎ How many office spaces'll be available when this building's finished?

2 《勤務先として見た場合》
〈彼は今事務所にいます〉
- ◎ He's at [in] the office now.

3 《法律事務所》
〈彼女は法律事務所に勤めています〉
- ◎ A She works for a law firm.
- ○ B She works for a law office.
- △ C She works for a lawyer's office.
  - ❖ A は大きい事務所, B, C は小さい事務所.

4 《経理事務所》
〈彼女は経理事務所に勤めています〉
- ◎ A She works for an accounting firm.
- ○ B She works for an accounting office.
  - ❖ A は大きい事務所, B は小さい事務所.

5 《会計事務所》
〈彼女は会計事務所に勤めています〉
- ◎ A She works for a CPA.
- ○ B She works for a CPA office.
- ○ C She works for a CPA firm.
  - ❖ C は大きい事務所, B は小さい事務所. A は大きくても小さくても使える.

事務職
〈私は来週から事務職に変わるんです〉
- ◎ A I'm going to get a desk job next week.
- ○ B I'm going to work in the office next week.
- ○ C I'm going to get an office work next week.
- △ D I'm going to get a desk work next week.

事務用品
1 《品物に言及する場合》
〈どこで事務用品を買えますか〉
- ◎ A Where can I buy office supplies?
- × B Where can I buy office supply?

2 《会社に言及する場合》
〈私は事務用品の会社に勤めています〉
- ◎ A I work for an office supply company.
- ○ B I work for an office supplies company.

指名する
1 《美容師など》
〈私は美容院へ行くといつも同じ美容師を指名します〉
- ◎ A Whenever I go to my beauty shop, I always ask for the same beautician.
- ○ B Whenever I go to my beauty shop, I always request the same beautician.

2 《選挙の立候補者など》
   〈彼は共和党の候補者として指名されるでしょう〉
   - ◎ A He'll be nominated as the Republican candidate.
   - ○ B He'll be named as the Republican candidate.

示す
   1 《「模範を示す」の意味》
   〈彼らによい見本を示してください〉
   - ◎ A Set a good example for them.
   - ○ B Show a good example for them.
   - ○ C Be a role model for them.
   2 《数値の場合》
   〈失業率は7％を示している〉
   - ◎ A The unemployment rate stands [is] at 7%.
   - × B The unemployment rate reads [shows, indicates, says] at 7%.
   3 《計器の場合》
   〈寒暖計は90度を示している〉
   - ◎ A The thermometer reads [says] 90 degrees.
   - ○ B The thermometer shows [registers] 90 degrees.
   - △ C The thermometer stands [indicates] at 90 degrees.
   - × D The thermometer records [gives] 90 degrees.
      ❖ Dが辞典に出ているが使われていない．
   4 《証拠の場合》
   〈この証拠は被告が有罪であることを示している〉
   - ◎ This evidence proves [demonstrates, shows] that the accused's guilty.

締め出す
〈会社側は労働者を工場から締め出した〉
   - ☆ A The management locked the workers out of the factory.
   - ◎ B The management kept the workers out of the factory.
   - ○ C The management shut the workers out of the factory.
   - △ D The management closed the workers out of the factory.

占める
〈ユダヤ人はアメリカの全人口の約4％を占めている〉
   - ◎ A Jewish people account for [make up, comprise, constitute] about 4% of the total American population.
   - △ B Jewish people compose [amount to, form] about 4% of the total American population.
   - ▽ C Jewish people come (up) to about 4% of the total American population.
      ❖辞典にCが出ているが使われてもまれである．

閉める
   1 《店の場合》
   a) 毎日の閉店を意味するとき
   〈毎日何時に店を閉めるのですか〉
   - ☆ A What time do you close the store every day?
   - ◎ B What time do you close down the store every day?
   - ○ C What time do you shut down the store every day?
   - △ D What time do you shut the store every day?
   b) 閉まっている状態を意味するとき

〈角の店は閉まっています〉
- ◎ A　The store on the corner is closed.
- ◎ B　The store on the corner isn't open.
- × C　The store on the corner is shut.

c) 店をやめる場合
〈うちは来月店を閉めます〉
- ◎ A　We're going to close (down) the store next month.
- ○ B　We're going to shut down the store next month.
- △ C　We're going to shut the store next month.

2　《ドアの場合》

a) 一般に
〈後ろのドアを閉めて下さい〉
- ◎　　Shut [Close] the door behind you.

b) 建物・部屋・事務所から出て行くとき
〈出て行くときドアを閉めて下さい〉
- ◎ A　Close [Shut] the door when you leave.
- ◎ B　Close [Shut] the door behind you.
- ○ C　Close [Shut] the door after you.

c) 建物・部屋・事務所などへ入ったとき
〈入ったらドアを閉めて下さい〉
- ☆ A　Close [Shut] the door when you come in.
- ◎ B　Close [Shut] the door behind you.
- ○ C　Close [Shut] the door after you.

社員

1　《集合的な意味でのホワイトカラーの社員》
〈うちは社員を減らさなければならない〉
- ◎ A　We have to cut back on our personnel.
- ◎ B　We have to cut back on our (working) staff.
- ◎ C　We have to cut back on our payroll.
- ◎ D　We have to cut back on the number of our employees.
- ◎ E　We have to cut back on our workforce.
  - ❖ A の personnel は会社の大小に関係なく使われている．B の(working) staff は小規模の会社か大会社，または小さい会社の「…部」「…課」など所属する部署の社員を集合的に指すときによく使われる．C の payroll は大企業，中小企業だけでなく小さい事務所にも使える．D の number of our employees はほとんどの状況で使われる．E の workforce はホワイトカラー，ブルーカラーのいずれについても広く使うことができる．ただし，大企業，中小企業には使えるが，小さい事務所には使えないことに注意．

2　《集合的な意味での工場・スーパー・店・レストラン・建築会社などの社員》
〈うちは社員を減らさなければならない〉
- ◎ A　We have to cut back on our help [crew].
- ◎ B　We have to cut back the number of our employees.
- ◎ C　We have to cut back on our workforce.
  - ❖ A の help, crew は建築会社，スーパー，レストランの社員を指す場合によく使われている．

3　《個々のホワイトカラーの社員》
〈彼はうちの社員です〉
- ◎ A　He's a member of our staff.
- ◎ B　He's one of our staff.

◎ C　He's on our staff.
4　《個々のブルーカラーの社員》
〈彼はうちの社員です〉
　　◎　　He's one of our workers.
5　《ホワイトカラーの平社員》
〈彼は平社員です〉
　　◎ A　He's just an office worker.
　　◎ B　He just works in the office.
　　◎ C　He's just a worker.
　　○ D　He's a worker like everybody else.
　　△ E　He's just an office employee.
　　▽ F　He's an underling in the office.
　　▽ G　He's an ordinary employee.
　　　❖F, G がある口語辞典に出ているがまれ．
6　《工場・スーパーなどの平社員》
〈彼は平社員です〉
　　◎ A　He's just a worker.
　　○ B　He's a worker like everybody else.

弱肉強食
〈この世は弱肉強食なんだ〉
　　☆ A　This is a dog-eat-dog world.
　　◎ B　In this world, it's dog-eat-dog.
　　◎ C　In this world, it's the survival of the fittest.
　　× D　This world's the survival [right] of the fittest.
　　× E　This world's the law of the jungle.
　　　❖D, E が辞典に出ているが使われていない．

釈放する
1　《囚人》
〈彼は釈放されました〉
　　☆ A　He was let out of prison.
　　◎ B　He was released from prison.
2　《政治犯》
〈政府は政治犯を全員釈放すべきです〉
　　◎ A　The regime should let all the political prisoners go.
　　◎ B　The regime should let all the political prisoners out of prison.
　　◎ C　The regime should set all the political prisoners free.
　　◎ D　The regime should release all the political prisoners.

社交的
〈彼は社交的です〉
　　☆ A　He's outgoing.
　　◎ B　He's sociable.
　　○ C　He's social.

社債　→債権 2

写真
〈あなたはこの写真でとてもよく撮れています〉
　　◎ A　You look really good in this picture.
　　○ B　You look really good in this photo.
　　△ C　You look really good in this photograph.
　　　❖写真そのものの出来に言及して「よく撮れている」という場合は，This

picture turned [came] out well.（この写真はよく撮れている）という．

写真学校 →各種学校 6

写真館 →店 25

社長 →地位 11

邪魔者扱い

〈皆，私を邪魔者扱いするんです〉
- ◎ A Everybody treats me like I'm a pain in the ass [butt].
- ◎ B Everybody treats me like I'm a pain in the neck.
- ◎ C Everybody treats me like I'm a pain.
- ○ D Everybody treats me like I'm a burden [nuisance, pest].
- ○ E Everybody treats me like I'm trouble.
- ○ F Everybody treats me like I'm excess baggage.
- × G Everybody treats me like I'm a trouble.
  - ❖(1) A は少し下品な表現だが，気を使う必要のない人たちが聞き手のときは非常によく使われている．
  - ❖(2) A, B は他の表現より強い響きがある．

洒落ている

〈そのスーツは洒落ていますよ〉
- ◎ A You look sharp [great, terrific] in that suit.
- ○ B You look fantastic [incredible, stylish] in that suit.
- △ C You look smart in that suit.

じゃんじゃん

1 《商売の売れ行きを述べるとき》

〈これは今じゃんじゃん売れています〉
- ◎ A This is selling like mad [crazy] now.
- ◎ B This is a hot seller [item] now.
  - ❖ B の item は腕時計のような比較的小さいものに使われる傾向がある．

2 《電話がかかってくることを述べるとき》

〈新聞に広告を出すといつも電話がじゃんじゃんかかってきます〉
- ☆ A Every time we put an ad in the paper, the telephone rings off the hook.
- ◎ B Every time we put an ad in the paper, the telephone doesn't stop ringing.
- ◎ C Every time we put an ad in the paper, lots of phone calls come pouring in.
- ○ D Every time we put an ad in the paper, lots of phone calls pour in.
- △ E Every time we put an ad in the paper, the telephone keeps calls pour in.
- × F Every time we put an ad in the paper, the telephone goes on ringing.

…中

1 《アメリカ・中国のような横断面がある国》

〈このスーパーはアメリカ中にチェーン店があります〉
- ◎ A This supermarket has a chain of stores across the country [nation].
- ◎ B This supermarket has a chain of stores all over the country [nation].
- ◎ C This supermarket has a chain of stores throughout the country [nation].
- ◎ D This supermarket has a chain of stores from coast to coast.
- ◎ E This supermarket has a chain of stores across [throughout, all over]

America.
- ◎ F This supermarket has a chain of stores all across the country.
- △ G This supermarket has a chain of stores all through America.
- △ H This supermarket has a chain of stores (all) through the country.

2 《日本・イギリスのように細長い国》
〈このスーパーは日本中にチェーン店があります〉
- ◎ A This supermarket has a chain of stores throughout the country.
- ◎ B This supermarket has a chain of stores all over the country [nation].
- ◎ C This supermarket has a chain of stores throughout [all over] Japan.
- ◎ D This supermarket has a chain of stores all across the country.
- ◎ E This supermarket has a chain of stores everywhere in Japan.
- ○ F This supermarket has a chain of stores throughout the nation.
- ○ G This supermarket has a chain of stores across the country.
- ○ H This supermarket has a chain of stores across Japan.
- △ I This supermarket has a chain of stores (all) through the country.

3 《東京・ニューヨーク・ロンドンなどの都市中に》
〈このスーパーは東京中にチェーン店があります〉
- ◎ A This supermarket has a chain of stores throughout [all over] Tokyo.
- ◎ B This supermarket has a chain of stores throughout town [the city].
- ◎ C This supermarket has a chain of stores all over town [the city].
- ◎ D This supermarket has a chain of stores all across town [the city].
- ◎ E This supermarket has a chain of stores (all) across Tokyo.
- ◎ F This supermarket has a chain of stores across town [the city].
- ○ G This supermarket has a chain of stores everywhere in Tokyo.
- ○ H This supermarket has a chain of stores everywhere in town [the city].
- △ I This supermarket has a chain of stores all through town [the city].

4 《人間の体中》
〈毒が彼の体中にまわってしまったんです〉
- ☆ A The poison passed throughout his blood system.
- ◎ B The poison passed throughout his system.
- ○ C The poison flooded his system.
- ○ D The poison ran throughout [through] his system.
- ○ E The poison permeated his system.
- ○ F The poison permeated throughout his body [system].
- △ G The poison flooded his body.
- △ H The poison filtered throughout his body [system].
- △ I The poison permeated through his body.

5 《1日中》
〈私は1日中家にいました〉
- ☆ A I was home all day.
- ◎ B I was home the entire day.
- ◎ C I was home all day long.
- ○ D I was home the whole day.
- △ E I was home throughout the day.

❖ Cが一番強い響きがある．Bが2番，Dが3番，Eが4番，Aが一番弱い．

しゅうしょく 287

6 《冬中》
〈私は冬中フロリダにいました〉
 ☆ A I was in Florida all winter.
 ◎ B I was in Florida the entire winter.
 ○ C I was in Florida throughout the winter.
 ○ D I was in Florida the whole winter.
 △ E I was in Florida all through the winter.

7 《1年中》
〈ハワイは1年中暖かいです〉
 ☆ A Hawaii's warm year-round.
 ◎ B Hawaii's warm all-year-round.
 ○ C Hawaii's warm throughout the year.
 △ D Hawaii's warm (all) the year round.
 ❖ D だけを紹介している和英辞典があるが，時々使われる程度．

収穫物
〈私たちは昨年の収穫物をほとんど売ることができました〉
 ◎   We were able to sell most of last year's harvest [crops, crop].
 ❖ crop は収穫物が1種類，crops は2種類以上のとき．harvest は1種類でも2種類以上でも使える．

習慣
1 《個人の習慣》
〈早起きは私の習慣です〉
 ◎ A Getting up early's my habit.
 ○ B Getting up early's my custom [practice].

2 《社会の習慣》
〈アメリカの習慣はイギリスの習慣とは違います〉
 ◎ A American customs're different from those of Great Britain.
 ▽ B American practices're different from those of Great Britain.

3 《伝統的な習慣》
〈早婚はアフリカの習慣です〉
 ◎   Marrying young's the practice [custom] in Africa.

4 《商習慣》
〈これは地元の商習慣のひとつです〉
 ◎ A This is one of the local business practices.
 ▽ B This is one of the local business customs.

週休2日制 →休み 6
重視する
〈アメリカの社会は自由を重視しています〉
 ☆ A American society emphasizes freedom.
 ◎ B American society puts (an) emphasis on freedom.
 ○ C American society places (an) emphasis on freedom.
 △ D American society stresses freedom.
 ▽ E American society puts stress on freedom.
 ▽ F American society lays stress [emphasis] on freedom.
 ❖ E, F が辞典に出ているがまれ．

就職する
1 《高い地位》
〈彼は支店長としてジョージア銀行に就職したんです〉
 ☆ A He got a position at Georgia Bank as branch manager.

- ◎ B He got a job at Georgia Bank as branch manager.
- ◎ C He landed a job at Georgia Bank as branch manager.
- ○ D He landed a position at Georgia Bank as branch manager.
- ▽ E He found employment at Georgia Bank as branch manager.
- × F He got work at Georgia Bank as branch manager.
- × G He found a job at Georgia Bank as branch manager.
  - ❖(1) F, G が辞典に出ているが使われていない．
  - ❖(2) E は堅い文章英語ではよく使われている．
  - ❖(3) あこがれの会社に就職して興奮しているときは，C の land a job が一番よく使われている．
  - ❖(4) A～D は as the branch manager なら非常によく使われている．

2 《高くない地位》

〈彼はジョージア銀行に警備員として就職しました〉

- ◎ A He got [found] a job at Georgia Bank as a security guard.
- ◎ B He got work at Georgia Bank as a security guard.
- ○ C He found work at Georgia Bank as a security guard.
- × D He got a position at Georgia Bank as a security guard.
- × E He found employment at Georgia Bank as a security guard.
- × F He landed a job at Georgia Bank as a security guard.

終身雇用制

〈たいていの日本の大会社は終身雇用制を採用している〉

- ◎ A Most large Japanese corporations are adopting lifetime employment.
- ◎ B Most large Japanese corporations are adopting a lifetime employment plan [system].

住宅街 →…街 1

集中する

1 《人が何かに》

〈どういうわけか今日は仕事に集中できないんです〉

- ◎ A Somehow I can't concentrate on my work today.
- ○ B Somehow I can't get into [focus on] my work today.
- × C Somehow I can't concentrate my attention on my work today.
  - ❖ C が辞典に出ているが使われていない．

2 《交渉・会議など無生物が何かに》

〈交渉は貿易不均衡に集中した〉

- ◎ A The negotiations focused on the trade imbalance.
- ○ B The negotiations centered [concentrated] on the trade imbalance.

3 《研究・仕事などに「専心する」の意味のとき》

〈あなたは研究に集中すべきです〉

- ☆ A You should apply yourself to your studies.
- ◎ B You should devote yourself to your studies.
- ○ C You should dedicate yourself to your studies.
- ○ D You should set your mind on your studies.
- ○ E You should put your heart and soul into your studies.
- ▽ F You should bend yourself to your studies.
- × G You should assign [allot] yourself to your studies.
  - ❖ G は辞典に出ているが使われていない．F も辞典に出ているが使われてもまれ．

就任する

1 《大統領》

〈レーガンは何年に就任したのですか〉
- ◎ A When did Reagan come into [get into, take, assume] office?
- ◎ B When did Reagan inaugurated?
- ○ C When did Reagan swear into office?

2 《社長》

〈彼はいつ社長に就任するのですか〉
- ◎ A When'll he take the CEO's position?
- ◎ B When'll he come into [get into, take] office as the CEO?
- ○ C When'll he assume office as the CEO?

10人並み

〈ビル：彼女は美人なの〉
Bill: Is she beautiful?
〈トム：いや，10人並みだよ〉
Tom:
- ◎ A No, she's OK.
- ◎ B No, she's just average.
- ◎ C No, she's all right.
- ◎ D No, she isn't so bad.
- ○ E No, she's so so.
- ▽ F No, she's mediocre.
- × G No, she's on (an) average.

週末に(は)

1 《漠然と「週末に」と言う場合》

〈私は週末はおじさんの家にいます〉
- ◎ A I'm going to stay at my uncle's for the weekend.
- ○ B I'm going to stay at my uncle's over the weekend.
- △ C I'm going to stay at my uncle's on the weekend.

❖一般に「週末」と言えば金曜の夜から日曜までを指す．

2 《週末の中の「ある1日」を意味する場合》

〈私は週末に新宿でビルと偶然会いました〉
- ◎ A I bumped into Bill in Shinjuku over the weekend.
- △ B I bumped into Bill in Shinjuku on the weekend.

3 《「毎週末」を意味する場合》

〈私は週末は警備員として働いています〉
- ◎ A I work as a security guard on weekends.
- ◎ B I work as a security guard on the weekends.
- ○ C I work as a security guard on the weekend.

重役　→地位 12

修理士　→職業 20, 21

修理する

1 《(車などを)修理する》

a) 修理が終わっているか不明な場合

〈私の車を修理してみてくれましたか〉
- ◎ A Did you work on my car?
- ◎ B Did you do the work on my car?
- ○ C Did you try to fix my car?

b) 修理して動く状態になったか否かを尋ねるとき

〈私の車を修理してくれましたか〉
- ☆ A Did you fix my car?

290　しゅかんてき

- ◎ B Did you work on my car?
- ○ C Did you do the work on my car?
- ○ D Did you repair my car?
- △ E Did you make repairs on my car?
- × F Did you fix up my car?
  - ❖(1) F が辞典に出ているが使われていない．
  - ❖(2) D は「故障を修理する」の意味ではなく，車にペンキを塗り直したりして「きれいにする」という意味ではよく使われている．
  - ❖(3) D, E には少し改まった響きがある．

2　《車・時計・テレビなどの機械が作動するか否かの状態を尋ねるとき》
〈私の車は直っていますか〉
- ◎ A Did you get my car running?
- ◎ B Does my car work?
- ◎ C Is my car working?
- ◎ D Is my car fixed?
- ○ E Is my car repaired?

3　《「定期点検する」という意味のとき》
〈私は車を点検してもらっているところです〉
- ☆ A I'm having my car tuned up.
- ◎ B I'm having my car checked (out).
- ◎ C I'm having my car looked at.
- ◎ D I'm having my car serviced.
  - ❖ D は「修理する」という意味もある．どちらであるかは会話の文脈から判断する．

主観的に
〈私はあなたに主観的にならないでいただきたいのです〉
- ◎　　I'd like you not to be subjective [emotional].
  - ❖「客観的に」の項も参照のこと．

手術する
〈私は胃の手術をしなければならないんです〉
- ◎ A I need a stomach operation.
- ◎ B I've got to have a stomach operation.
- ◎ C I've got to have my stomach operated on.
- ◎ D I've got to have an operation on my stomach.

主張
〈あなたの主張は筋が通っていない〉
- ◎ A Your bottom line isn't logical.
- ◎ B Your point isn't logical.
- ◎ C Your argument isn't logical.
  - ❖ A, B は結論として述べている，つまり1点として述べている「主張」であるのに対して，C は議論のはじめから終わりまで述べている展開としての「主張」．

出演する
1　《テレビ番組》
〈彼は明日テレビに出演します〉
- ◎ A He'll be on TV tomorrow.
- ○ B He'll appear on TV tomorrow.

2　《ラジオ番組》
〈彼は明日ラジオに出演します〉

◎　A　He'll be on the radio tomorrow.
　　△　B　He'll appear on the radio tomorrow.
　3　《映画》
〈彼は多くの映画に出演しました〉
　　☆　A　He was in a lot of movies.
　　◎　B　He was in a lot of films.
　　◎　C　He appeared in a lot of movies [films].
　　○　D　He acted in a lot of movies [films].

出勤する
　1　《時間が逼迫しているとき》
〈彼が出勤したらすぐあなたにお電話させます〉
　　◎　A　As soon as he walks through [in] the door, I'll have him call you.
　　◎　B　As soon as he gets in, I'll have him call you.
　　◎　C　As soon as he arrives, I'll have him call you.
　　◎　D　As soon as he comes to work, I'll have him call you.
　　◎　E　As soon as he gets here, I'll have him call you.
　　○　F　As soon as he walks in, I'll have him call you.
　　○　G　As soon as he reports to work, I'll have him call you.
　　○　H　As soon as he comes in, I'll have him call you.
　　❖ A, B, F は「彼が帰宅したらすぐ電話させます」の意味でもよく使われている．
　2　《習慣的なこと》
〈あなたは毎日何時に出勤するのですか〉
　　◎　A　What time do you get to work every day?
　　○　B　What time do you arrive at [report to, go to] work every day?
　　×　C　What time do you walk through [in] the door every day?
　3　《ちょうど出勤してきたとき》
ａ）出勤時間にぎりぎりというニュアンスのとき
〈彼はちょうど出勤してきたところです〉
　　◎　A　He just walked through [in] the door.
　　◎　B　He just came through the door.
　　◎　C　He just walked in.
　　◎　D　He's just walked through the door.
　　○　E　He's just walked in the door.
　　○　F　He's just come through [in] the door.
ｂ）時間がぎりぎりというニュアンスがないとき
〈彼はちょうど出勤してきたところです〉
　　☆　A　He just got here.
　　☆　B　He just got to work.
　　◎　C　He's just gotten here.
　　○　D　He's just gotten to work.
　　○　E　He just reported to work.
　　△　F　He's just reported to work.
　　△　G　He just arrived at work.
　　△　H　He's just arrived at work.
　4　《出勤しているか否かを尋ねるとき》
ａ）話し手・聞き手とも会社の中にいる
〈社長は出勤していますか〉
　　◎　A　Is the boss in [here, around]?

◎ B Is the boss in the office?
◎ C Is the boss available?

b) 電話で問い合わせている

〈社長は出勤していますか〉

◎ A Is the boss in [there, around]?
◎ B Is the boss in [at] the office?
◎ C Is the boss available?

出産する

1 《予定日に出産したとき》

〈娘が昨夜男の子を出産したんです〉

◎ A My daughter had a baby boy last night.
○ B My daughter gave a birth to a baby boy last night.
○ C My daughter delivered a baby boy last night.

2 《早産したとき》

〈娘は昨夜，2週間早く男の赤ちゃんを出産したんです〉

☆ A My daughter's baby boy was born two weeks early last night.
◎ B My daughter had a two-week premature baby boy last night.
○ C My daughter gave a birth to a baby boy two weeks early last night.
○ D My daughter delivered a baby boy two weeks early last night.
○ E My daughter delivered a two-week premature baby boy last night.

出資する

〈XYZ 社はこの会社に出資しています〉

◎ A XYZ Company has a stake [an investment, capital] in this company.
◎ B XYZ Company is investing (money) in this company.
▽ C XYZ Company is laying out [sinking] money in this company.
❖(1) C が辞典に出ているがまれ．
❖(2)「共同出資する」の項も参照のこと．

出席する

1 《葬式・結婚披露宴・卒業式の場合》

〈私は葬式に出席しました〉

◎ A I went to the funeral.
○ B I attended the funeral.
× C I was present at the funeral.

2 《上記以外のフォーマルでない行事の場合》

〈私はパーティーに出席しました〉

◎ A I went to the party.
× B I was present at the party.
× C I attended the party.
❖ B, C が多くの辞典に出ているが使われていない．

出世コースに乗る

〈東大卒は出世コースに乗る〉

☆ A Tokyo University graduates are on their way to the top.
◎ B Tokyo University graduates are on their way up the ladder.
○ C Tokyo University graduates are going up the ladder.
○ D Tokyo University graduates are on their way up.
○ E Tokyo University graduates are up and coming.
× F The graduates of Tokyo University are on the promotional track.
❖ F を模範訳として紹介している口語辞典もあるが，使われていない．

出廷する
〈彼は裁判所に出廷しました〉
- ◎ A He appeared [turned up] in court.
- ◎ B He made his appearance in court.
- ○ C He showed up in court.
- ○ D He put in an appearance at court.
- × E He presented himself in court.
- × F He reported himself at court.

❖ E, F が辞典に出ているが使われていない．

出版社 →会社 8

首都圏
〈首都圏の地価はとても高い〉
- ◎ A Property prices around Tokyo're very high.
- ▽ B Property prices in and around Tokyo're very high.
- ▽ C Property prices in Tokyo and its vicinity're [its surrounding area're, its suburbs're] very high.
- ▽ D Property prices in the Greater Tokyo area're very high.
- ▽ E Property prices in the Tokyo metropolitan area're very high.
- × F Property prices in Tokyo and its surrounding're [its neighborhood're] very high.

❖ 堅い文章英語ではB〜Eはよく使われている．Aも非常によく使われている．

寿命

1 《人》

a）平均寿命を言う場合
〈日本人の平均寿命はどのくらいなのですか〉
- ◎ A How long's the average Japanese life span?
- △ B How long's the average Japanese span of life?

b）寿命の長さを言う場合
〈今タバコをやめれば，あなたの寿命は長くなりますよ〉
- ◎ If you stop smoking now, it'll increase the longevity [length] of your life.

c）短命だと述べるとき
〈彼はアルコールを飲みすぎて寿命を縮めたんです〉
- ◎ A He shortened his days [life] by drinking too much.
- ◎ B He took years off his life by drinking too much.
- ◎ C He cut his life short by drinking too much.

2 《機械》
〈この機械の寿命はどのくらいあるのですか〉
- ◎ A What's the service life [the life expectancy] of this machine?
- ◎ B How durable's this machine?
- ◎ C How long'll this machine last?

授与する
〈ハーバード大学は彼に名誉博士号を授与しました〉
- ☆ A Harvard University awarded him an honorary Ph.D.
- ◎ B Harvard University granted [gave] him an honorary Ph.D.
- ◎ C Harvard University bestowed an honorary Ph.D. on him.
- ◎ D Harvard University presented him with an honorary Ph.D.
- ○ E Harvard University gave [presented] an honorary Ph.D. to him.

- ○ F Harvard University conferred him with an honorary Ph.D.
- ○ G Harvard University conferred an honorary Ph.D. on him.
- △ H Harvard University bestowed him with an honorary Ph.D.
- △ I Harvard University bestowed on him an honorary Ph.D.

順応する

《環境などに》

〈私はどこに住んでも新しい環境に順応できます〉

- ◎ A No matter where I live, I can adapt [adjust].
- ○ B No matter where I live, I can adapt [adjust] (myself) to my new surroundings.
- △ C No matter where I live, I can acclimate.
- △ D No matter where I live, I can acclimate (myself) to my new surroundings.
- ▽ E No matter where I live, I can conform to my new surroundings.

準備する

1 《重要な行事の非直前の準備》

・クリスマスパーティーなどの2, 3週間前に, 親・友人などから電話がかかってきたとき

〈パーティーの準備でとても忙しいんです〉

- ☆ A I'm really busy getting ready for the party.
- ◎ B I'm really busy getting things ready for the party.
- ◎ C I'm really busy getting organized for the party.
- ◎ D I'm really busy organizing [preparing] for the party.
- ○ E I'm really busy doing stuff for the party.
- ○ F I'm really busy getting stuff ready for the party.
- △ G I'm really busy making arrangements [preparations] for the party.

・クリスマスパーティーなどの2, 3週間前に, 顧客・弁護士・上司などなれなれしく話せない人から電話がかかってきたとき

〈パーティーの準備で非常に忙しいんです〉

- ☆ A I'm very busy getting ready for the party.
- ◎ B I'm very busy getting organized for the party.
- ◎ C I'm very busy organizing [preparing] for the party.
- ◎ D I'm very busy making arrangements for the party.
- ○ E I'm very busy making preparations for the party.

2 《重要な行事の直前の準備》

a) クリスマスパーティーの当日, 料理のみならずいろいろなことを準備しているとき

・親・友人などから電話がかかってきたとき

〈パーティーの準備でとても忙しいの〉

- ☆ A I'm really busy getting ready for the party.
- ◎ B I'm really busy getting things ready for the party.
- ○ C I'm really busy getting stuff ready for the party.
- ○ D I'm really busy doing stuff for the party.
- ○ E I'm really busy preparing for the party.
- △ F I'm really busy making preparations for the party.
- △ G I'm really busy preparing the party.
- × H I'm really busy making arrangements for the party.

・対等に話す人でない人, 重要な取引先の顧客・上司・弁護士などなれなれしく話せない人から電話がかかってきたとき

〈パーティーの準備で非常に忙しいんです〉
- ☆ A I'm very busy preparing for the party.
- ◎ B I'm very busy getting ready for the party.
- ○ C I'm very busy making preparations [arrangements] for the party.
- △ D I'm very busy preparing the party.
- × E I'm very busy doing stuff for the party.
- × F I'm very busy getting stuff ready for the party.

b) 身支度の準備を述べるとき

〈私はパーティーの準備でとても忙しいんです〉
- ☆ A I'm very busy getting myself ready for the party.
- ◎ B I'm very busy getting ready for the party.
- ◎ C I'm very busy doing the last minute stuff [things] for the party.
- ▽ D I'm very busy preparing myself for the party.
- ▽ E I'm very busy making myself ready for the party.

c) クリスマスパーティーなどの当日の料理の準備を述べるとき
- 親友・友人などから電話がかかってきたとき

〈私はパーティーの料理を作るのにとても忙しいんです〉
- ☆ A I'm really busy fixing the food for the party.
- ◎ B I'm really busy cooking for the party.
- ◎ C I'm really busy making the food for the party.
- ◎ D I'm really busy getting (things) ready for the party.
- ○ E I'm really busy cooking [fixing] food for the party.
- ○ F I'm really busy getting stuff ready for the party.
- ○ G I'm really busy doing stuff for the party.

❖ D, F, G は料理以外のことも入っている．

- 重要な顧客・上司・牧師さんなどから電話がかかってきたとき

〈私はパーティーの料理を作るのに非常に忙しいんです〉
- ☆ A I'm very busy cooking for the party.
- ◎ B I'm very busy making the food for the party.
- ◎ C I'm very busy preparing (the food) for the party.
- ◎ D I'm very busy getting (things) ready for the party.
- ○ E I'm very busy fixing (the) food for the party.
- ▽ F I'm very busy getting stuff ready for the party.
- ▽ G I'm very busy doing stuff for the party.

3 《弁護士・会計士の試験，大学受験などの非直前の準備》

〈私は試験の準備で忙しいんです〉
- ☆ A I'm busy getting ready for the exam.
- ◎ B I'm busy preparing [studying] for the exam.
- × C I'm busy making preparations for the exam.
- × D I'm busy preparing the exam.

4 《弁護士・会計士の試験，大学受験などの直前の準備》
- 親・友人などから電話がかかってきたとき

〈私は試験の準備でとても忙しいんです〉
- ☆ A I'm really busy getting ready for the exam.
- ◎ B I'm really busy preparing for the exam.
- ○ C I'm really busy making preparations for the exam.
- ○ D I'm really busy getting things [stuff] ready for the exam.

- 丁重に話す必要がある人から電話がかかってきたとき

〈わたしは試験の準備で非常に忙しいんです〉

☆ A I'm very busy preparing for the exam.
◎ B I'm very busy getting ready for the exam.
○ C I'm very busy making preparations for the exam.

5 《「最終の準備で忙しい」と言いたいとき》
a) 友人・親と電話で話している
〈私は司法試験の最終準備に忙しいんです〉
◎ A I'm busy getting some last minute things ready for the bar exam.
◎ B I'm busy doing some last minute stuff to get ready for the bar exam.
◎ C I'm busy doing some last minute things for the bar exam.
◎ D I'm busy doing the last minute arrangements for the bar exam.
○ E I'm busy doing the last minute preparations for the bar exam.
○ F I'm busy making the final arrangements [preparations] for the bar exam.

b) 上司・教授のような丁重に話す人と電話で話している
〈私は司法試験の最終準備に忙しいんです〉
◎ A I'm busy doing the last minute arrangement [preparations, things] for the bar exam.
◎ B I'm busy making the final arrangements [preparations] for the bar exam.

6 《悪い知らせなどの心の準備》
〈悪い知らせがあるの, 準備して下さい〉
☆ A I have bad news. Please brace yourself.
◎ B I have bad news. Please prepare yourself.
◎ C I have bad news. Please brace [prepare] yourself for it.
○ D I have bad news. Please get ready for it.
△ E I have bad news. Please get ready.

7 《教師の試験作成の準備》
〈私はテストを作る準備で忙しいんです〉
☆ A I'm busy preparing the test.
◎ B I'm busy working on the test.
○ C I'm busy writing [making] the test.

8 《時間を明示して準備させるとき》
〈2時までに手術室を準備して下さい〉
◎ A Please have the operating room ready by 2:00.
◎ B Please get the operating room ready by 2:00.
◎ C Please have the operating room prepared by 2:00.
◎ D Please get the operating room prepared by 2:00.
○ E Please make the operating room ready by 2:00.
△ F Please set the operating room ready by 2:00.
❖(1) 家庭内の食事の支度と違ってソフトな話し方が求められていないので, B も A と同様よく使われている.
❖(2) C, D の表現は家庭内では使えない.

純利益

1 《会社が主語になるとき》
〈私の会社は昨年一億円の純利益をあげました〉
◎ A My company cleared a hundred million yen last year.
○ B My company made [had] a net profit of a hundred million yen last year.

2 《利益が主語になるとき》

⟨純利益は 2000 万円でした⟩
- ◎ A The bottom line was twenty million yen profit.
- ◎ B The final figure [tally] was twenty million yen profit.
- ◎ C The net profit was twenty million yen.
- ○ D The (net) balance was twenty million yen profit.
- × E The clear [pure, clean, neat] profit was twenty million yen.
  - ❖(1) E は辞典に出ているが使われていない．
  - ❖(2)「利益」の項も参照のこと．

障害
⟨彼の皮膚の色が昇進の障害となるでしょう⟩
- ◎ A His color'll keep him from getting promoted.
- ◎ B His color'll block his promotion.
- ◎ C His color'll be a stumbling block [a barrier] to promotion.
- ○ D His color'll prevent him from getting promoted.
- △ E His color'll be an obstacle [a block] to promotion.

紹介する
1 《個人に対して紹介する場合》
a) 顔を合わせて紹介する場合
・親しげに紹介するとき

⟨トム，友人のジェームズ・ブラウンを紹介するよ⟩
- ☆ A Tom, I want you to meet my friend James Brown.
- ◎ B Tom, meet my friend James Brown.
- ◎ C Tom, I'd like you to meet my friend James Brown.
- ○ D Tom, let me introduce James Brown to you.
- △ E Tom, let me introduce to you James Brown.

・かしこまって紹介するとき

⟨トム，私の友人のジェームズ・ブラウンをご紹介します⟩
- ◎ A Tom, allow me to present to you, my friend James Brown.
- ◎ B Tom, let me present to you, my friend James Brown.
- ○ C Tom, allow me to present my friend James Brown.
- ○ D Tom, let me present my friend James Brown.

b) 顔を合わせて紹介することと，名前や電話番号を教えるだけのいずれにも取れる場合

⟨すてきな男性をご紹介しますよ⟩
- ◎ A I'll fix [set] you up with a great guy.
- ◎ B I'll introduce you to a great guy.
  - ❖ A, B いずれも男女間のみならず，弁護士，会計士などのビジネス上の紹介にも非常によく使われている．

2 《大勢の人に対して紹介する場合》

⟨皆さん，ニューヨーク州知事をご紹介します⟩
- ◎ A Ladies and gentlemen, I give you the governor of New York.
- ◎ B Ladies and gentlemen, let me introduce [present] to you the governor of New York.
- ○ C Ladies and gentlemen, allow me to present to you the governor of New York.
  - ❖ C は非常に改まった響きがある．かしこまった表現を使う人の間ではよく使われている．

照会する
⟨私にいい弁護士さんを照会してくれますか⟩

しょうがくせ

◎ Will you refer me to a good lawyer?

小学生 →…学生 4

小規模で

〈彼はビジネスを小規模で始めたんです〉
- ◎ A He started his business on a small scale.
- ◎ B He started out small.
- △ C He started his business in a small way.

昇給

〈昇給していただきたいのですが〉
- ◎ A I'd like to have a raise.
- ◎ B I'd like to get a raise.
- ◎ C I'd like a raise.
- × D I'd like to have [get] my salary raised.
  - ❖(1) D は辞典に出ているが使われていない．
  - ❖(2) A は要求するニュアンスが弱いので，B，C より丁重な響きになる．

上級 →級 3

条件

1 《労働条件》

a) 給料・諸手当

〈私はここで働くことに興味はあるのですが条件が合わないんです〉
- ☆ A I'm interested in working here but I can't agree to the job terms.
- ◎ B I'm interested in working here but I can't agree to the terms of the job.
- ◎ C I'm interested in working here but I can't agree to the terms.
- × D I'm interested in working here but I can't agree to the working conditions.
- × E I'm interested in working here but I can't agree to the work conditions.
  - ❖英和辞典・和英辞典に労働条件として D が紹介されているが，全く意味が違う．D，E は「職場環境」という意味．詳細は「職場の環境」の項を参照されたい．

b) 仕事上求められる内容

・出張・残業など

〈私はここで働くことに興味があるのですが，条件に応じることができないんです〉
- ◎ A I'm interested in working here but I can't agree to the job requirements [description].
- ○ B I'm interested in working here but I can't agree to the work requirements.
- × C I'm interested in working here but I can't agree to the work description.

・経験年数・学歴・推薦状など

〈私はここで働くことに興味はあるんですが条件を満たせないんです〉
- ◎ A I'm interested in working here but I can't meet the job requirements.
- ○ B I'm interested in working here but I can't agree to the work requirements.

2 《取引の条件》

〈私は取引の条件を受け入れられません〉
- ◎ A I can't accept the terms [condition] of the deal.
- △ B I can't accept the requirements of the deal.

3 《「…という条件つきで」と言うとき》

〈私は残金を年末に支払えるという条件でなら，この工場を買います〉
- ☆ A I'll buy this factory with the condition that I can buy the balance at the end of the year.
- ◎ B I'll buy this factory on the condition that I can buy the balance at the end of the year.

証券会社 →会社 9

証拠

〈私は彼が犯人だという証拠を握っている〉
- ◎ I have evidence [proof] that he's the criminal.
  - ❖(1) 証拠の数に言及したいときは proof を使うことができない．次のように evidence で表現する：I have two pieces of evidence that he's the criminal.（私には彼が犯人だという証拠が2つあるんです）．
  - ❖(2) 辞典には proof は証明できる証拠であり，evidence は証明できない証拠であると解説されているが，実際には両者の使い分けはあいまいである．ただし，法廷，法曹会では evidence が主として使われている．

上司 →地位 2

常識

1 《知識》

〈ケンタッキーはバーボンウイスキーで有名なんです．それはアメリカ人の中では常識です〉
- ◎ A Kentucky's famous for its bourbon whiskey. That's common knowledge among the American people.
- × B Kentucky's famous for its bourbon whiskey. That's common sense among the American people.

2 《礼儀》

〈人からプレゼントをもらった後には礼状を書くべきです．それは常識です〉
- ◎ A You should write a thank-you note after you got a present from somebody. That's common sense.
- × B You should write a thank-you note after you got a present from somebody. That's common knowledge.

上昇する

《じりじりと上昇する場合》

〈新しい分譲住宅の売り上げは昨年と比較してじりじり上昇して5月に15％になりました〉
- ☆ A New condo sales edged up 15% in May over last year's.
- ◎ B New condo sales edged up to 15% in May over last year's.
- ◎ C New condo sales went up [rose] gradually to 15% in May over last year's.
- △ D New condo sales inched [crept] up to 15% in May over last year's.

少食

〈彼は小食です〉
- ◎ A He's a light eater.
- ◎ B He eats very little.
- ◎ C He eats a little bit.
- ○ D He eats like a bird.
- ○ E He eats a little.
- △ F He eats little.
- ▽ G He eats only little.

▽ H He's a small eater.
❖ D は主語が女性であれば非常によく使われている．また，男女問わずよく使われている．

昇進
〈この会社の昇進は実力主義です〉
◎ A Advancements [Promotions] in this company are based upon each employee's merit.
◎ B Advancement [Promotion] in this company is based upon each employee's merit.
△ C Advances in this company are based upon each employee's merit.

昇進する
1 《非常に低い地位からのとき》
〈彼はまもなく支配人に昇進します〉
◎ He'll work his way up [make it up] to manager soon.

2 《平社員からのとき》
〈彼はまもなく支配人に昇進します〉
◎ He'll work up [move up, make it up] to manager soon.

3 《支配人と平社員の中間のとき》
〈彼はまもなく支配人に昇進します〉
◎ A He'll be [get] promoted to manager soon.
○ B He'll advance to manager soon.

上手です
1 《語学》
a) ぺらぺらというニュアンスのとき
〈彼女は英語が上手です〉
☆ A She speaks English good.
◎ B She speaks good English.
◎ C She speaks English well.
❖(1) A は正しくないと言われているが，アメリカ人の間で一番よく使われ，「ぺらぺらです」という日本語の俗語的表現にぴったり．
❖(2) B, C は「ぺらぺら」という日本語の俗語的ニュアンスに欠けるが，非常によく使われている．

b)「流暢に」というニュアンスのとき
〈彼女は英語が上手です〉
☆ A She speaks fluent English.
☆ B She speaks English fluently.
◎ C She's proficient in the English language.
◎ D She has a good command of the English language.
▽ E She's a good [fluent] speaker of English.
❖ C, D の the English language を English としている辞典が多いが，その場合は使用頻度が下がる．

2 《演説の場合》
〈彼女は演説が上手です〉
◎ A She's a good speaker.
○ B She makes good speeches.
△ C She's a good orator.
△ D She makes speeches well.

3 《楽器の場合》
〈彼女はピアノが上手です〉

◎ A She's a good pianist.
◎ B She plays the piano well.
4 《スポーツの場合》
a）泳ぐ
〈彼女は泳ぐのが上手です〉
◎ A She's a good swimmer.
○ B She swims well [good].
b）テニス
〈彼女はテニスが上手です〉
◎ A She's a good tennis player.
◎ B She plays tennis well.
c）ゴルフ
〈彼女はゴルフが上手です〉
◎ A She's a good golfer.
○ B She plays golf well.
△ C She's a good golf player.
5 《扱い方》
a）子供
〈彼は子供の扱い方が上手なんです〉
◎ A He has a way with his children.
◎ B He knows how to treat [take care of] his children.
b）部下
〈彼は部下の扱い方が上手なんです〉
◎ A He knows how to treat [take care of] his staff.
○ B He has a way with his staff.
c）強調するとき
〈彼は部下の扱い方が非常に上手なんです〉
◎ A He really knows how to treat [take care of] his staff.
◎ B He really has a way with his staff.
◎ C He knows how to treat [take care of] his staff very well.

情勢

1 《変化していることを述べるとき》
〈中東情勢は毎日変化している〉
☆ A The situation in the Middle East's changing every day.
◎ B Things in the Middle East're changing every day.
○ C The circumstances in the Middle East're changing every day.
○ D The picture in the Middle East's changing every day.
△ E The state of affairs in the Middle East's changing every day.
△ F The scenery [ball game, landscape] in the Middle East's changing every day.
  ❖ F の landscape は，新聞・テレビなどマスコミでは非常によく使われている．

2 《詳しいことを述べるとき》
〈彼は中東の政治情勢に詳しいんです〉
◎ A He's very familiar with the political situation in the Middle East.
○ B He's very familiar with the political scene in the Middle East.
○ C He's very familiar with the political picture in the Middle East.
△ D He's very familiar with the political landscape [scenery] in the Middle East.

❖ B, D は新聞・テレビなどのマスコミでは非常によく使われている．

上層部
1 《会社》
〈上層部の許可が必要なんです〉
- ◎ A We need the green light from management [upstairs, the higher-ups].
- ○ B We need the green light from higher-up.
- △ C We need the green light from the administration.

2 《政党・組合・大学》
〈上層部の許可が必要なんです〉
- ◎ A We need the green light from upstairs [the higher-ups].
- △ B We need the green light from higher-up.

3 《中央政府》
〈上層部の許可が必要なんです〉
- ☆ A We need the green light from the administration.
- ◎ B We need the green light from upstairs.
- ○ C We need the green light from the higher-ups.
- × D We need the green light from higher-up [management].

4 《県庁・市役所》
〈上層部の許可が必要なんです〉
- ◎ A We need the green light from the administration.
- △ B We need the green light from the higher-ups.
- × C We need the green light from higher-up [upstairs, management].

私用で
〈彼は私用でいつも電話を使っています〉
- ◎ A He's always using the phone for personal reasons [calls].
- ○ B He's always using the phone for (his) personal use.
- ○ C He's always using the phone for (his) personal purposes.

衝動買い
〈彼は衝動買いをするんです〉
- ◎ A He buys things impulsively [on impulse].
- ◎ B He's an impulsive shopper.

衝突する
1 《車》
〈この先でバスがタクシーに衝突したんです〉
- ◎ A A bus smashed [crashed] into a taxi down the street.
- ○ B A bus rammed [slammed] into a taxi down the street.
  ❖ A の smash は破損がひどいという響きがある．B の slam は非常にスピードを出していたとの響きがある．

2 《警察とデモ隊》
〈警察と反政府のデモ隊が衝突したんです〉
- ◎ A The police clashed [fought] with anti-government demonstrators.
- ○ B The police got into it with anti-government demonstrators.
- ○ C The police had a fight with anti-government demonstrators.
  ❖ A は暴力，B, C は暴力か非暴力かは不明．

3 《意見》
〈私の意見と彼の意見はしばしば衝突します〉
- ◎ A My opinion often clashes with his.
- ○ B My opinion often conflicts with his.

△ C My opinion's often in opposition to his.
　4 《配偶者・上司・同僚》
〈私は昨夜夫と衝突したんです〉
　　　◎ A I had a fight [an argument] with my husband last night.
　　　◎ B I argued with my husband last night.
　　　× C I clashed with my husband last night.

場内アナウンス
〈あなたの名前が場内アナウンスされているのを聞きましたよ〉
　　　◎ A I heard your name being paged over the PA (system).
　　　◎ B I heard your name being paged over the loud speaker.
　　　△ C I heard your name being paged over the public address system.

小児科医　→医者 5
承認する
〈彼らは私たちの提案を承認してくれました〉
　　　☆ A They approved our proposal.
　　　◎ B They gave our proposal their approval.
　　　○ C They gave our proposal the go-ahead [the green light].
　　　○ D They OK'd our proposal.
　　　○ E They endorsed our proposal.
　　　△ F They gave our proposal their endorsement.
　　　△ G They gave our proposal their permission.
　　　△ H They gave our proposal a green light [a go-ahead].
　　　❖ E, F は権限を持った人(たち)が主語のときに使われる．したがって，非常に強い響きがある．

消費税　→税金 2
上品です
　1 《女性》
〈彼女は上品です〉
　　　☆ A She has style.
　　　☆ B She has class.
　　　◎ C She's classy.
　　　◎ D She's stylish.
　　　◎ E She's sophisticated.
　　　◎ F She's graceful.
　　　○ G She has grace.
　　　○ H She's elegant.
　　　○ I She's polished.
　　　○ J She's refined.
　　　○ K She's distinguished.
　　　△ L She's chic.
　　　△ M She has elegance.
　　　△ N She's a jet-setter.
　　　❖ A, D は容姿・服装・ヘアスタイル・身のこなし，B, C, N は容姿・服装・ヘアスタイル・身のこなしにも言及しているが，態度・振舞いのことに一番強く言及している．E は服装を含めた多くのものに対して趣味がよく磨かれていて，知性を強く感じさせるという意味．F, G は歩き方・食事の仕方・話し方などの身のこなし方に言及している．H, M は容姿・服装・ヘアスタイル・身のこなし方・マナー・知性など広く言及している．H, M とも教育レベルの高い人の間では非常によく使われている．I, J はマナ

ー・服装の身につけ方．Kは仕事上で成功しているというニュアンスが強い．したがって，約45歳以上の人に言及するときに使われる．Lは容姿・服装．

2 《男性》
〈彼は上品です〉
- ☆ A He has style [class].
- ◎ B He's classy [stylish, sophisticated, distinguished].
- ○ C He's polished [elegant, refined].
- △ D He has elegance.
- △ E He's a jet-setter.
- × F He has grace.
- × G He's graceful.

消防士
〈彼女は消防士です〉
- ◎ A She's a fireman.
- ◎ B She's a fire fighter.
- ▽ C She's a firewoman.
    - ❖(1) 女性でもAが非常によく使われている．
    - ❖(2) 男性のときはA，Bだけが使われている．

譲歩する
1 《互いに譲歩する場合》
a） 約50％ずつ互いに譲歩するとき
〈彼はその点で彼らに譲歩しました〉
- ◎ A He met them halfway on that point.
- △ B He split the difference with them on that point.

b） 約50％ずつ互いに（または一方が約70％）譲歩するとき
〈彼はその点で彼らに譲歩しました〉
- ◎ A He compromised with them on that point.
- ○ B He made a compromise with them on that point.

2 《一方だけが100％譲歩する場合》
〈彼はその点で彼らに譲歩しました〉
- ◎ A He conceded with them on that point.
- ○ B He made [gave] a concession to them on that point.
- × C He gave a compromise to them on that point.
- × D He made an effect to them on that point.
- × E He came round to them on that point.

❖ C, D, Eが辞典に出ているが使われていない．

上流階級 →階級 1 a), 5 a)
初級 →級 1
職業
1 《通訳》
a） ただ通訳であることを述べるとき
〈彼女は通訳です〉
- ◎ A She's an interpreter.
- ○ B She's a translator.
    - ❖ translatorを「翻訳者」としてのみ紹介している辞典がほとんどだが，「通訳」の意味でもよく使われている．

b） 何語の通訳であるかを述べるとき
〈彼女はフランス語から英語への通訳です〉

◎ A She's a French-English interpreter.
○ B She's a French-English translator.
○ C She's an interpreter from French to English.
△ D She's a translator from French to English.

c) 同時通訳
〈彼女は同時通訳です〉
◎ She's a simultaneous interpreter.

2 《観光ガイド》
〈彼は観光ガイドです〉
◎ A He's a tour guide.
△ B He's a tour conductor.

3 《旅行業者》
〈彼は旅行業者です〉
◎ A He's a travel agent.
× B He's a traveling agent.
❖ B を紹介している辞典があるが使われていない．

4 《公認会計士》
〈彼は公認会計士です〉
◎ A He's a CPA.
◎ B He's an accountant.
❖ A, B は厳密には同じではないが一般には混用されている．

5 《弁護士》
a) 客観的に述べるとき
〈彼は弁護士です〉
◎ He's a lawyer.

b) 上品な響きを出すとき
〈彼は弁護士です〉
◎ He's an attorney.

c) 否定的なニュアンスで述べるとき
〈彼は弁護士です〉
◎ A He's an ambulance chaser.
△ B He's a shyster.
❖ A は交通事故・職場・アパート・店内などでのけがの事故を扱う弁護士を揶揄して述べるときに使われている．B は「悪徳弁護士」というニュアンスで使われている．

6 《裁判官》
a) 最高裁判所
〈彼は裁判官です〉
◎ A He's a justice.
× B he's a judge.
❖最高裁判所はアメリカの各州に1つあり，連邦最高裁判所が1つ，合計51ある．

b) 最高裁以外の裁判所
〈彼は裁判官です〉
◎ A He's a judge.
× B He's a justice.

7 《刑事》
〈彼は刑事です〉
☆ A He's a police detective.

◎　B　He's a police investigator.
　　　△　C　He's a G-man.
　8　《私立探偵》
〈彼は私立探偵です〉
　　　☆　A　He's a private investigator.
　　　◎　B　He's a private detective.
　　　◎　C　He's a PI.
　　　○　D　He's a private eye.
　9　《実業家》
　a）一般的
〈彼は実業家です〉
　　　◎　A　He's a businessman.
　　　▽　B　He's a businessperson.
　　　❖一般の「サラリーマン」の意味にも使われている．
　b）製造業
〈彼は実業家です〉
　　　◎　　　He's an industrialist.
　10　《銀行家》
〈彼は銀行家なんです〉
　　　◎　　　He's a banker [a bank executive].
　　　❖banker は以前は He owns a bank. の意味でも使われていた．
　11　《銀行員》
〈彼は銀行員です〉
　　　◎　A　He's a bank employee.
　　　×　B　He's a bank clerk.
　　　❖多くの辞典に B が出ているが今は使われていない．
　12　《(銀行の) 貸付係》
〈彼女は貸付係です〉
　　　◎　A　She's a loan officer.
　　　△　B　She's a mortgage officer.
　13　《経理》
〈彼女は経理をしています〉
　　　◎　A　She's a bookkeeper.
　　　×　B　She's an accountant.
　　　❖辞典は A を「簿記係」として照会しているが，日本語では普通「経理」と言う．B は「計理士」の意味でなら非常によく使われている．
　14　《秘書》
　a）重役の秘書
〈彼女は重役の秘書です〉
　　　◎　　　She's an executive secretary.
　b）社長の秘書
〈彼女は社長の秘書です〉
　　　◎　A　She's the CEO's secretary.
　　　◎　B　She's the boss's secretary.
　　　○　C　She's the President's secretary.
　　　❖B は場面により社長以外，つまり「上司の秘書」の意味でもよく使われている．
　c）一般的に述べるとき
〈彼女は秘書です〉

- ◎ A She's an administrative secretary.
- ▽ B She's a secretary.
    - ❖ 辞典では secretary＝「秘書」と出ている．しかし，1970 年頃から secretary は「事務員」，つまり事務所で事務の仕事をしていて，特別の肩書きがない女性たちを第三者に聞こえよくするために，それ以前までよく使われていた clerk-typist に取って代わって広く使われるようになった．したがって，「社長の秘書＝the CEO's secretary」「部長の秘書＝the General Manager's secretary」「ブラウン氏の秘書＝Mr. Brown's secretary」と特定な人の「秘書」を述べるとき，または She's a good secretary.（彼女は有能な秘書です）と形容詞が先行するとき以外は，secretary は「事務員」の意味で使われることが多い．

15 《アパートの管理人》
〈彼は管理人です〉
- ◎ A He's a superintendent.
- ○ B He's a super.
- × C He's a caretaker.

16 《ボディーガード》
〈彼は社長のボディーガードです〉
- ◎ A He's the boss's body guard.
- △ B He's the boss's guard.

17 《警備員》
a）警備員だと述べるとき
〈彼は警備員です〉
- ◎ A He's a security guard.
- ○ B He's a watchman [guard].

b）警備を担当していると述べるとき
〈XYZ がうちの警備をやっています〉
- ☆ A XYZ handles [takes care of] our security.
- ◎ B Our security's (being) handled [run] by XYZ.
- ◎ C We contract our security to XYZ.
- ○ D Our security's (being) provided by XYZ.
- ○ E We contract out our security to [with] XYZ.
- ○ F We contract our security with XYZ.

18 《駐車場の係員》
a）駐車ビル
〈彼は駐車ビルの係員なんです〉
- ◎ He's a parking attendant.

b）地上の駐車場
〈彼は駐車場の係員なんです〉
- ◎ He's a parking (lot) attendant.

19 《タクシーの運転手》
〈彼女はタクシーの運転手です〉
- ☆ A She's a taxi driver.
- ◎ B She's a cab driver.
- △ C She's a cabbie.

20 《車の修理士》
〈彼は車の修理士です〉
- ☆ A He's a car mechanic.
- ◎ B He's an auto mechanic.

21 《時計の修理士》
〈彼女は時計の修理士です〉
- ◎ A She's a watch repairman.
- × B She's a watch repairwoman.

22 《電気技師》
〈彼は電気技師です〉
- ◎ A He's an electrician.
- ○ B He's an electric engineer.

23 《編集長》
a）社内で述べるとき
〈彼は編集長です〉
- ◎ A He's the chief editor.
- ○ B He's the editor-in-chief.

b）社外で述べるとき
- ◎ A He's a chief-editor.
- ○ B He's an editor-in-chief.

24 《テレビの総合司会者》
〈彼女はテレビの総合司会者です〉
- ☆ A She's a TV anchorwoman.
- ◎ B She a TV anchor [anchorman].

25 《監督》
a）スポーツ
〈彼はジャイアンツの監督です〉
- ☆ A He's the manager for the Giants.
- ◎ B He's the Giants' manager.
- △ C He's the manager to the Giants.

b）映画
〈彼は映画監督です〉
- ◎ A He's a movie director.
- ○ B He's a film director.

26 《カメラマン》
a）新聞・雑誌
〈彼は雑誌のカメラマンです〉
- ☆ A He's a photographer.
- ◎ B He's a magazine photographer.
- △ C He's a photographer for a magazine.

b）ビデオ
〈彼女はカメラマンです〉
- ◎ A She's a cameraman.
- × B She's a camerawoman.

27 《写真師》
〈彼は写真師です〉
- ☆ A He's a photographer.
- ○ B He's a studio photographer.
- △ C He's a photographer at a studio.

28 《作曲家》
a）クラシック音楽
〈彼は作曲家です〉
- ☆ A He's a composer.

◎ B He writes music.
　　○ C He writes classical music.
 b) ジャズ音楽
〈彼は作曲家です〉
　　◎ A He writes music.
　　◎ B He writes jazz music.
　　○ C He's a jazz music composer.
　　○ D He composes jazz music.
　　△ E He's a composer.
 c) ロック音楽
〈彼は作曲家です〉
　　☆ A He writes rock music.
　　◎ B He's a rock music composer.
　　○ C He writes music.
　　△ D He composes rock music.
　　× E He's a composer.
29 《栄養士》
〈彼女は栄養士です〉
　　◎ A She's a nutritionist.
　　○ B She's a specialist nutrition.
30 《薬剤師》
〈彼女は薬剤師です〉
　　◎ A She's a pharmacist.
　　○ B She's a chemist.
　　▽ C She's a druggist.
　　× D She's a pharmaceutist [dispenser].
　　❖ D が辞典に出ているが使われていない．B はイギリスでよく使われている．
31 《看護婦長》
〈彼女は看護婦長です〉
　　◎ A She's the head nurse.
　　× B She's the chief nurse.
32 《看護婦長補佐》
〈彼女は婦長補佐です〉
　　◎　　She's the acting [assistant] head nurse.
33 《(医療) 検査官》
〈彼は検査官です〉
　　☆ A He's a lab tech.
　　◎ B He's a lab technician.
　　△ C He's a medical tester.
　　× D He's a medical examiner.
34 《検死官》
〈彼は検死官です〉
　　◎ A He's a medical examiner.
　　○ B He's a coroner.
　　❖ B は州により使われていない．
35 《税関吏》
〈彼は税関吏です〉
　　◎ A He's a customs officer [inspector].
　　○ B He's a customs agent.

310 しょくぎょう

- △ C He's a customs examiner.
- × D He's a customs searcher.
- × E He's a customs house officer [inspector, agent].
- ❖辞典に D, E が出ているが使われていない．

36 《造園技師》
〈彼は造園技師です〉
- ☆ A He's a landscape architect.
- ◎ B He's a landscape designer.
- ◎ C He's a landscaper.
- △ D He's a landscape engineer.

37 《庭師 (植木屋)》
〈彼は庭師です〉
- ◎ A He's a gardener.
- × B He's a garden designer.
- × C He's a landscape gardener.
- ❖B, C が A と共に辞典に出ているが，A と同じでは使われていない．

38 《ボーイ長》
〈彼はボーイ長です〉
- ◎ A He's the maitre d'hotel.
- ◎ B He's the headwaiter.
- ◎ C He's the host.
- ❖A は高級レストランのボーイ長を言う．給仕はせずに，客をテーブルへ案内するのが仕事．B は普通のレストランのボーイ長を言い，客をテーブルに案内して給仕もする．C はコーヒーショップなどのボーイ長で，テーブルにお客を案内するが，給仕はしない．

39 《店員》
a ）コンビニ・スーパーのように店員が買物客を説得する必要のない店
〈彼はコンビニで店員として働いています〉
- ◎ A He works at a convenience store as a cashier.
- ○ B He works at a convenience store as a clerk.

b ）デパートの婦人服売り場，宝石店など店員が買物客を説得する必要のある店
・単数のとき
〈彼女は店員としてメイシーに勤めています〉
- ☆ A She works at Macy's as a salesperson.
- △ B She works at Macy's as a salesman [saleswoman].
- △ C She works at Macy's as a salesclerk.
- ❖C はデパートで買物客に説得が求められていないセール（大売り出し）のような所でしか使えない．

・複数のとき
〈リンダとメアリーは店員としてメイシーに勤めています〉
- ☆ A Linda and Mary're working at Macy's as salespeople.
- ○ B Linda and Mary're working at Macy's as salesclerks.
- △ C Linda and Mary're working at Macy's as salesmen [saleswomen, salespersons].

c ）ガソリンスタンドの店員
〈彼はガソリンスタンドの店員です〉
- ◎ A He's a gas station attendant.
- ○ B He's attendant at a gas station.
- △ C He's a filling station attendant.

40 《営業マン》
 a）一般的に述べるとき
 〈彼は繊維会社に営業マンとして勤めています〉
  ◎　He works for a textile company as a salesman [salesperson].
 b）相手に聞こえよく言おうとするとき
 〈彼は繊維会社に営業マンとして勤めています〉
  ◎ A He works for a textile company as a sales rep.
  ○ B He works for a textile company as a sales representative.

職業(訓練)学校 →各種学校 7

食事
 1 《常食の意味で》
 〈日本の食事は米，魚，野菜で構成されている〉
  ◎　The Japanese diet consists of rice, fish and vegetables.
 2 《breakfast, lunch, supper の総称として》
 〈毎食後にこの薬を飲みなさい〉
  ◎　Take this medicine after each meal.
 〈間食をしてはいけません〉
  ◎　Don't eat between meals.
 3 《食事会の意味で》
 〈私たちは彼らを感謝祭の日の食事に招く予定です〉
  ◎　We're going to have them over for dinner on Thanksgiving Day.
 4 《食餌療法の意味で》
 a）糖分抜きの食事
 〈あなたは糖分抜きの食事をしなければなりません〉
  ◎ A You have to go on [be on, stay on, stick to] a sugar-free diet.
  ◎ B You have to go on [be on, stay on, stick to] a no-sugar diet.
  ◎ C You have to put yourself on a sugar-free diet.
  ○ D You have to follow a sugar-free [no-sugar] diet.
  △ E You have to go on [be on, stick to] a sugar-less diet.
  ▽ F You have to follow a sugar-less diet.
 b）糖分の低い食事
 〈あなたは糖分の低い食事をしなければなりません〉
  ◎ A You have to be on [go on, stick to, put yourself on] a low-sugar diet.
  ○ B You have to follow a low-sugar diet.

食事する
 1 《マクドナルドなどで食事をするとき》
 〈マクドナルドで軽く食事しよう〉
  ◎ A Let's have a bite to eat at McDonald's.
  ◎ B Let's grab a bite to eat at McDonald's.
   ❖ B はマクドナルドで買って車の中，または戸外で食事する意味でもよく使われている．
 2 《マクドナルドなどで買ってマクドナルド以外の場所で食事するとき》
 〈マクドナルドで買って外で食事しよう〉
  ◎ A Let's grab a bite (to eat) from McDonald's.
  ◎ B Let's grab a bite at McDonald's.
   ❖ B はマクドナルドの中で食べる意味にも使われているが，「外で」の意味のほうがよく使われている．

食中毒 →病気 13

職場で

1 《事務系の職場》

〈私は彼と職場で知り合ったんです〉
- ☆ A I met him at work.
- ◎ B I met him at the office.
- ○ C I met him in the office.
- ○ D I met him on the job.
- △ E I met him at the job.

2 《非事務系の職場》

〈私は彼と職場で知り合ったんです〉
- ◎ A I met him at work.
- ◎ B I met him on the job.
- ○ C I met him at the job.

3 《同じ職場》

〈私は彼と職場で知り合ったんです〉
- ☆ A I met him at work.
- ◎ B I met him at [in] the office.
- ○ C I met him on [at] the job.

4 《別の職場》

〈私は彼と職場で知り合ったんです〉
- ☆ A I met him at my work.
- ◎ B I met him at [in] my office.
- ○ C I met him on [at] my job.

職場の環境

〈社員：私は職場の環境に耐えられないんです．ですから辞めます〉

Employee:
- ☆ A I can't stand the work environment, so I'm going to quit.
- ◎ B I can't stand the working environment, so I'm going to quit.
- ◎ C I can't stand the work conditions, so I'm going to quit.
- ◎ D I can't stand the working conditions, so I'm going to quit.
- ○ E I can't stand the circumstances I'm working under, so I'm going to quit.
    - ❖ Dが「労働条件」として英和辞典，和英辞典に出ているが誤訳．詳細は「条件」の項を参照．

食料品店 →店 9

初旬

〈彼らは5月の初旬に日本に来ました〉
- ☆ A They came to Japan in early May.
- ◎ B They came to Japan early in May.
- ○ C They came to Japan in [at] the beginning of May.
- △ D They came to Japan at the start of May.
- × E They came to Japan in the start of May.

女性…

〈職業について言う場合〉

〈あなたは女性の弁護士をご存知ですか〉
- ◎ A Do you know of a female lawyer?
- ○ B Do you know of a woman lawyer?
    - ❖弁護士に限らず，いつも female の方が woman よりよく使われていることに注意．female professor（女性の教授），female doctor（女医），female

police officer（女性の警官），female firefighter（女性の消防士），female executive（女性の重役），female pilot（女性パイロット）．

所属している
1 《収入を得ている場合》
〈私は ABC モデル紹介所に所属しています〉
- ◎ I work for the ABC Modeling Agency as a model.

2 《収入に関係がない場合》
〈私は小金井ゴルフクラブに所属しています〉
- ◎ I belong to the Koganei Golf Club.

ショッピングセンター
〈一番近いショッピングセンターまでどのくらい距離がありますか〉
- ◎ A How far is it to the nearest shopping center?
- ◎ B How far is it to the nearest mall?
- ○ C How far is it to the nearest shopping mall?

❖ A は1軒1軒の店が独立して密集しているものを指す．B, C は大きなビルの中に多数の店が入っている場合．

所得税 →税金 1

処罰
〈飲酒運転の処罰は何だったのですか〉
- ◎ What was the punishment [penalty] for drunk driving?

❖ punishment, penalty とも免許証の一時没収を意味している．

除名する
1 《議員・弁護士協会・ロータリークラブなど》
〈下院はリベートを受け取ったことでトラフィカントを除名した〉
- ☆ A The House threw Traficant out for taking kickbacks.
- ◎ B The House kicked Traficant out for taking kickbacks.
- ○ C The House tossed [booted] Traficant out for taking kickbacks.
- △ D The House forced Traficant out for taking kickbacks.
- △ E The House expelled Traficant out [from] for taking kickbacks.
- △ F The House dismissed Traficant out [from] for taking kickbacks.

❖(1) E, F は新聞，ニュース英語などではよく使われている．
❖(2) Traficant はオハイオ州選出の下院議員．

2 《理由を述べるとき》
〈彼は依頼人のお金を横領したことで弁護士協会から除名されたんです〉
- ☆ A He was thrown out of the bar association for embezzling his client's money.
- ◎ B He was kicked out of the bar association for embezzling his client's money.
- ○ C He was tossed [booted] out of the bar association for embezzling his client's money.
- ○ D He was blackballed from the bar association for embezzling his client's money.
- △ E He was blackballed out of the bar association for embezzling his client's money.
- △ F He was expelled [dismissed, drummed, bounced] from the bar association for embezzling his client's money.
- △ G He was expelled [dismissed, drummed, bounced] out of the bar association for embezzling his client's money.
- × H He was banished [excluded, evicted] out of the bar association for

embezzling his client's money.
- × I He was run off the bar association for embezzling his client's money.
    - ❖(1) H, I は辞典に出ていない.
    - ❖(2) A〜G は for embezzling...の代わりに because he embezzled..., because of embezzling...としてもよく使われている.

所有権
〈所有権をできるだけ早く移したほうがいいよ〉
- ◎ A You'd better transfer the title [ownership] to you ASAP.
- ▽ B You'd better transfer the right of ownership [proprietorship] to you ASAP.
- ▽ C You'd better transfer the proprietary [proprietorial] rights to you ASAP.
- × D You'd better transfer the dominium [dominion] to you ASAP.
    - ❖ D が辞典に出ているが使われていない. B, C も辞典に出ているが使われてもきわめてまれである.

書類
1 《1枚のとき》
〈書類を取りに市役所へ行きましょうか〉
- ◎ A Can I go to City Hall to get the paper?
- △ B Can I go to City Hall to get the document?
    - ❖1枚のときは A, B よりも書類の名前を明示化して述べることが多い.

2 《2枚またはそれ以上のとき》
〈書類を取りに市役所へ行きましょうか〉
- ◎ A Can I go to City Hall to get the papers?
- ○ B Can I go to City Hall to get the documents?

知らせる
〈彼に注文品が入荷したことを知らせなければならない〉
- ◎ A We have to let him know that his order came in.
- ○ B We have to inform [notify] him that his order came in.
- ○ C We have to give notice that his order came in.
    - ❖ B はよく使われているが少し堅い響きがある.

調べる
1 《警察が》
〈警察は行方不明の男性の事件を調べています〉
- ◎ A The police're investigating the case of the missing man.
- ◎ B The police're studying the case of the missing man.
- ◎ C The police're looking into [over] the case of the missing man.
- ○ D The police're going over the case of the missing man.
- ○ E The police're checking up on the case of the missing man.
- ○ F The police're inquiring into the case of the missing man.
- △ G The police're digging into the case of the missing man.
    - ❖調べている程度の点では A が一番深い響きがあり, G, B がそれに続く. C, E, F は初期の段階というニュアンスがある. D が一番弱い.

2 《国税庁が》
〈国税庁はうちの帳簿を調べています〉
- ☆ A The IRS is auditing our books.
- ◎ B The IRS is digging into our books.
- ◎ C The IRS is going over our books.
- ○ D The IRS is investigating our books.

- ○ E The IRS is taking a look at our books.
- ○ F The IRS is looking over [into] our books.
- ○ G The IRS is checking (out) our books.
  - ❖調べている深さの点ではAが1番，B，Dが2番，C，E，F，Gはほぼ同じで3番．

3 《市場を》
〈あなたはまず市場を調べたほうがいいです〉
- ☆ A You'd better research the market first.
- ◎ B You'd better check out [look at] the market first.
- ○ C You'd better look into [check] the market first.
- ○ D You'd better do research work on the market first.

4 《地図を》
〈出かける前に地図を調べてくれますか〉
- ◎ A Will you look at [check] the map before we go out?
- ◎ B Will you take a look at the map before we go out?
- ○ C Will you have a look at the map before we go out?
- ○ D Will you look [go] over the map before we go out?

5 《辞書で》
a）目的語をともなうとき
〈それを辞書で調べてください〉
- ◎ A Look it up in a dictionary.
- ◎ B Look it up in your [the] dictionary.
- ◎ C Check it out in a dictionary.
- ◎ D Check it out in your [the] dictionary.
- ○ E Consult it in a dictionary.
- ○ F Consult it in your [the] dictionary.
- × G See it in a dictionary.
- × H Refer it to a dictionary.
  - ❖(1) G, Hが辞典に出ているが使われていない．
  - ❖(2) A, C, Eは一般的に述べているのに対して，B, D, Fは相手または特定の辞書に言及している．

b）目的語をともなわないとき
〈私は新しい単語に出会うといつも辞書で調べます〉
- ◎ A Whenever I come across a new word, I refer to a dictionary.
- ○ B Whenever I come across a new word, I consult a dictionary.
- × C Whenever I come across a new word, I see a dictionary.
  - ❖Cが辞典に出ているが使われていない．

知り合う

1 《かしこまらない会話のとき（プロセスがある場合）》
〈どうやって奥さんと知り合ったのですか〉
- ◎ A How did you get to know your wife?
- ○ B How did you meet your wife?
- × C How did you get acquainted with your wife?
- × D How did you become acquainted with your wife?
- × E How did you make your wife's acquaintance?
- × F How did you contract [strike up] an acquaintance with your wife?
- × G How did you come to know your wife?
  - ❖(1) C〜Gが辞典に出ているが使われていない．
  - ❖(2)「奥さんと知り合う」ということはプロセスがある．しかし，Cのget

acquainted はプロセスを持つイディオムではない．
- ❖(3) 夫と妻の間柄は表面的なものではなく精神的にも肉体的にも知り合った仲．しかし，get acquainted は表面的に浅く知り合うというニュアンスがある．したがってかみ合わないのである．
- ❖(4) get acquainted はくだけた会話には使われていない．フォーマルな文脈で使われている．

2 《かしこまらない会話のとき（プロセスがない場合）》

〈私はパーティーで彼女と知り合ったんです〉
- ◎ A I met her at a party.
- ○ B I got to know her at a party.
- × C I came to know her at a party.
- ❖パーティーで「知り合う」というのにはプロセスがない．偶然話などをして知り合うことである．たとえ意識して，ある女性に近づいて知り合ったとしても，こういう場合プロセスは問題になっていない．くだけた会話なので get to know を使いたくなる人もいるであろう．しかし，get to know はプロセスがないとかみ合わない．

3 《かしこまった会話のとき（プロセスがない場合）》

〈面接者：あなたのことを知りたいのです．少しあなたのことを話して下さいませんか〉

Interviewer:
- ◎ A I'd like to get to know you. Why don't you tell me a little about yourself?
- ○ B I'd like to get acquainted with you. Why don't you tell me a little about yourself?

4 《かしこまった会話のとき（親しさが求められているとき）》

（新しい患者が精神科医の診察室に入る．医師はこの患者がどんな人か，直接知りたがっている）

〈患者：家族の友人に先生を紹介されました．治療していただけたらと思います〉

Patient: I was referred to you by a family friend. I hope you can work with me.

〈精神科医：私もそう願っていますが，まずお互いに知り合ったほうがいいと思います〉

Psychiatrist:
- ◎ A I hope so too, but first, maybe we should get to know each other better.
- ○ B I hope so too, but first, maybe we should get better acquainted.
- ❖かしこまった場面でも親しさが求められているときは，get to know が使われている．

5 《かしこまった会話のとき（プロセスがある場合）》

〈(裁判中の法廷で) 弁護士：ウエーバーさんはあなたの友人の１人ですね〉

Attorney: Mrs. Weber is a friend of yours, is she not?

〈証人：そうです，私たちは長年友人です〉

Witness: Yes, we've been friends for many years.

〈弁護士：ウエーバーさんとどのようにしてお知り合いになったのか，法廷で話して下さいますか〉

Attorney:
- ☆ A Would you tell the court how you came to know Mrs. Weber?
- ◎ B Would you tell the court how you became acquainted with Mrs. Weber?
- ○ C Would you tell the court how you got to know Mrs. Weber?

6 《耳にするという意味の「知る」のとき》
〈どうやってうちの会社のことを知ったのですか〉
- ☆ A How did you hear about our company?
- ◎ B How did you learn about our company?
- △ C How did you come to know about our company?
- ▽ D How did you get to know (about) our company?
- ▽ E How did you come to know our company?

7 《初めて紹介されたとき》
a）改まった口調で述べるとき
〈お知り合いになれてとてもうれしく思っています〉
- ◎ A I'm very pleased to meet you.
- ○ B I'm delighted to meet you.
- × C I'm very delighted to meet you.
  - ❖(1) be delighted には very の意味が入っている．したがって，C は使われていない．
  - ❖(2) B の方が A より改まった響きがある．

b）普通の口調で述べるとき
〈お知り合いになれてとてもうれしいです〉
- ◎ A I'm really [very] glad to meet you.
- ◎ B It's really [very] nice to meet you.
- ○ C I'm really glad to (get to) know you.
- ○ D It's really nice to (get to) know you.
  - ❖ C, D の get to know you は男性同士の間ではよく使われているが，女性から男性にはそれほど使われていない．

c）くだけた調子で述べるとき
〈お知り合いになれてうれしいです〉
- ◎ A Nice [Glad, Happy] to meet you.
- ○ B Nice to get to know you.

8 《パーティーなどの退出時に「お知り合いになれてよかった」と述べるとき》
a）普通に言う場合
〈お知り合いになれてよかったです〉
- ☆ A It was nice meeting [to meet] you.
- ◎ B Nice meeting [to meet] you.
- ○ C It was nice getting [to get] to know you.
- △ D I was glad to meet you.
- △ E I was glad to get to know you.

b）強調して言う場合
- ◎ A It was really good meeting [to meet] you.
- ◎ B It was really good to get to know you.
- ○ C Really good meeting [to meet] you.
- △ D It was really good getting to know you.

c）改まった口調で言う場合
〈お知り合いになれてよかったです〉
- △ A It was nice getting [to get] acquainted with you.
- △ B I was pleased [glad] to meet you.

自立する

1 《1人のことを述べるとき》
〈あなたは自立していい年よ〉
- ◎ A You're old enough to be independent.

- ◎ B　You're old enough to be on your own.
- △ C　You're old enough to be standing on your own two feet.
- △ D　You're old enough to be self-reliant.

2　《比較して述べるとき》

〈あなたは彼より自立しています〉
- ◎ A　You're more independent than him.
- ○ B　You're more self-reliant than him.

私立探偵　→職業 8

市立の

1　《病院の場合》

〈市立病院はどこにありますか〉
- ◎ A　Where's the City Hospital?
- × B　Where's the Municipal Hospital?

2　《学校の場合》

〈日本には市立高校はたくさんあります〉
- ◎ A　There are a lot of city high schools in Japan.
- × B　There are a lot of municipal high schools in Japan.

視力

〈ジョン：近眼なんです〉

John: I'm near-sighted.

〈アン：あなたの視力はいくつですか〉

Anne:
- ◎ A　How good is your vision?
- ○ B　How good is your eyesight?

じろじろ見る

1　《興味を持って》

〈彼女がとてもセクシーなドレスを着ていたんです．だからみんなが彼女をじろじろ見たんです〉
- ☆ A　She was wearing a really sexy dress, so everybody checked her out.
- ◎ B　She was wearing a really sexy dress, so everybody looked her over (from head to toe).
- ○ C　She was wearing a really sexy dress, so everybody looked her up and down.
- ○ D　She was wearing a really sexy dress, so everybody eyeballed her.
- △ E　She was wearing a really sexy dress, so everybody eyed her (from head to toe).

2　《驚いて》

〈彼が突然大声をあげたんです．だから皆，彼をじろじろみたんです〉
- ◎ A　He shouted all of a sudden, so everybody stared at him.
- △ B　He shouted all of a sudden, so everybody gazed at him.
- ▽ C　He shouted all of a sudden, so everybody gawked at him.

しわ

1　《顔・皮膚》

〈彼の顔はしわだらけです〉
- ☆ A　He has a lot of wrinkles on his face.
- ◎ B　His face is very wrinkled.
- ◎ C　His face has a lot of wrinkles.
- ○ D　His face has a lot of lines.
- △ E　He has a lot of lines on his face.

2 《衣服》
〈あなたの上着はしわだらけですよ〉
- ◎ A Your jacket has a lot of wrinkles.
- ◎ B Your jacket is very wrinkled.

3 《生地のしわ》
〈この生地はしわになりやすいんです〉
- ◎ A This fabric wrinkles [gets wrinkled] easily.
- △ B This fabric is easy to wrinkle [get wrinkled].

4 《生地と折り目》
〈この生地は折りじわがつきやすいです〉
- ◎ A This fabric creases easily.
- ○ B This fabric gets creased easily.
- △ C This fabric is easy to crease.

5 《折り目》
〈ズボンにアイロンをかけてくれるかい．折り目がはっきりしないんだ〉
- ◎ A Will you press my pants? The creases aren't sharp enough.
- × B Will you press my pants? The lines aren't sharp enough.

人員
〈クライスラーは人員を削減する予定です〉
- ☆ A Chrysler's going to cut its workforce.
- ◎ B Chrysler's going to cut its payroll [its personnel].
- ◎ C Chrysler's going to cut the number of its employees.
- ○ D Chrysler's going to cut its employees.

人員削減 →リストラする 1

信号
1 《信号機・信号機のある場所》
〈信号までずっと歩いて行きなさい〉
- ◎ A Keep walking until you get to a stoplight.
- ○ B Keep walking until you get to a traffic light [signal].
- ○ C Keep walking until you get to a light.
- △ D Keep walking until you get to a signal.
- × E Keep walking until you get to a traffic [stop] lamp.
   ❖ E が辞典に出ているが使われていない．

2 《信号》
〈信号が変わるまで待とう〉
- ◎ A Let's wait until the light changes.
- ○ B Let's wait until the stoplight changes.
- △ C Let's wait until the signal changes.
   ❖ ここでは文脈上，stoplight と明示しなくても，light が信号を指していることがわかるので，light の方がよく使われている．

進行する
1 《病状などが》
a）未来のことを述べているとき
〈彼のガンは進行するでしょう〉
- ◎ A His cancer'll get worse [more serious].
- ◎ B His cancer'll grow.

b）現在の状況
〈彼のガンは進行しています〉
- ◎ A His cancer's in [at] an advanced stage.

× B He's in an advanced stage of cancer.
　❖ B が辞典に出ているが使われていない．
2 《プロジェクト》
a）普通に述べるとき
〈私たちのプロジェクトは進行しています〉
　◎ A Our project's making progress.
　◎ B Our project's moving forward.
　○ C Our project's advancing [progressing].
b）強く述べるとき
〈私たちのプロジェクトは非常に進行しています〉
　◎ A Our project's making headway.
　◎ B Our project's making big progress.
　◎ C Our project's making a lot of progress.
　◎ D Our project's doing well.
　○ E Our project's making remarkable progress.
　❖強さは C が1番で，B, E が2番，D が3番，A が4番．
c）「順調に」と述べるとき
〈私たちのプロジェクトは順調に進行しています〉
　☆ A Our project's advancing without any problems.
　◎ B Our project's making progress without any problems.
　◎ C Our project's progressing smoothly without any problems.
　○ D Our project's progressing without any problems.
　○ E Our project's making progress without any trouble.
　○ F Our project's advancing smoothly.
　○ G Our project's moving forward smoothly [without any problems].
　○ H Our project's making smooth [favorable] progress.
　△ I Our project's advancing favorably.

信号無視

1 《車の場合》
〈私はタクシーが信号を無視するのを見ました〉
　☆ A I saw a cab run a red light.
　◎ B I saw a cab run through a red light.
　○ C I saw a cab blow (through) a red light.
　△ D I saw a cab drive through a red light.
2 《歩行者の場合》
〈私はジムが信号を無視するのを見ました〉
　◎ A I saw Jim walk [go] through the traffic light.
　○ B I saw Jim walk against the traffic light.

人材銀行

1 《幹部職対象》
〈私は人材銀行に勤めています〉
　◎ A I work for a headhunting firm.
　◎ B I work for a headhunter.
　○ C I work for a human resource agency [service].
　○ D I work for an executive search firm.
　× E I work for a talent bank.
　× F I work for a pool of talent persons.
　× G I work for a pool of capable and experienced persons.
　❖(1) E, F, G が辞典に出ているが使われていない．

❖(2) B, C は小規模な会社についても用いることができる．
2 《一般の人対象》
〈角に人材銀行があります〉
- ◎ A There's an employment agency on the corner.
- △ B There's an employment agent on the corner.
- × C There's a job bank on the corner.
  ❖ C が辞典に出ているが使われていない．

審査部 →…部 11

人事
〈私は人事に発言権はないんですよ〉
- ☆ A I have no say in personnel matters.
- ◎ B I have no say in personnel management.
- ○ C I have no say in personnel affairs [administration].
- ○ D I have no say in personnel.
- △ E I have no say in personnel business.

信じている
1 《「能力がある」ことを意味しているとき》
〈息子：ハーバードに入れるかどうか自信がないんです〉
Son: I'm not confident if I'll be accepted by Harvard.
〈母：お母さんはあなたが入れることを信じていますよ〉
Mother:
- ◎ A I know you can do it.
- ◎ B I have confidence in you.
- ○ C I believe [have faith] in you.
- × D I trust you.
- × E I have trust in you.

2 《「効果を信じている」と述べるとき》
〈私は流暢に話すためにフランス語の基本文型を暗記することはよいことだと信じています〉
- ◎ I believe in memorizing basic French patterns to become fluent.

3 《「存在」を意味しているとき》
〈私は神様がいると信じています〉
- ◎ I believe in God.

〈私は幽霊がいると信じています〉
- ◎ I believe in ghosts.

4 《「信仰している」ことを意味しているとき》
〈私はカトリックを信仰しています〉
- ◎ A I'm a Catholic.
- ◎ B I'm Catholic.
- × C I believe [have faith] in Catholicism.

5 《「相手が言った言葉」を意味しているとき》
〈私はあなたが言ったことを信じます〉
- ◎ A I'll take your word.
- ◎ B I believe [trust] you.
- ◎ C I believe what you said.

人事部 →…部 12
人事部長 →地位 14
心中する →自殺する

進出する
1 《場所へ》
a) 会社などの場合
〈うちの会社はニューヨークへ進出するんです〉
- ☆ A Our company's going to expand its market into [to] New York.
- ◎ B Our company's going to expand its business into [to] New York.
- ◎ C Our company's going to expand its operations into [to] New York.
- ◎ D Our company's going to branch out to [into] New York.
- ○ E Our company's going to expand its operation to [into] New York.

b) 軍事的な侵攻を意味する場合
〈ソ連は中国へ進出しようとしてきた〉
- ◎ The Soviet Union has been trying to advance into China.

2 《分野へ》
a) 会社の場合
〈あの会社は映画産業への進出を計画している〉
- ◎ A That company's planning to branch out into the movie industry.
- ○ B That company's planning to go into the movie industry.

b) 人の場合
〈あの歌手は映画界への進出を計画している〉
- ◎ That singer's planning to go into movies.

3 《上位へ》
〈あのチームはたぶん決勝へ進出するだろう〉
- ◎ That team will probably advance to [move into, go into, make, reach, get to] the finals.

親戚
〈彼はあなたの親戚ですか〉
- ◎ A Is he a relative of yours?
- ◎ B Is he one of your relatives?
- ◎ C Is he related to you?
- ◎ D Is he your relative?
- △ E Is he a relation of yours?
- △ F Is he one of your relations?
- △ G Is he your relation?
  - ❖ E, F, G は 70 代以上の人たち，また南部の黒人たちの間ではよく使われている．

信念
1 《一般的な信念》
〈これは私の信念です〉
- ◎ A This is my belief [conviction].
- × B This is my faith [creed].
  - ❖ B がどの辞典にも出ているが使われていない．

2 《宗教的信念》
〈これは私の宗教上の信念です〉
- ◎ A This is my religious belief [faith].
- ◎ B This is my faith.
- × C This is my religious conviction [creed].
  - ❖(1) C が辞典に出ているが使われていない．
  - ❖(2) faith は「信念」の意味では宗教上でしか使えない．

心配する
1 《動作として述べること》
〈私のことは心配しないで下さい〉
- ◎ A Don't worry about me.
- ◎ B Don't be worried about me.
- ○ C Don't be concerned about me.
- × D Don't be anxious about me.
  - ❖ D は辞典に出ているが使われていない．

2 《状態として述べるとき》
〈私は彼の安全が心配なんです〉
- ☆ A I'm worried about his safety.
- ◎ B I worry about his safety.
- ◎ C I'm concerned about his safety.
- ○ D I'm concerned for his safety.
- × E I'm anxious about his safety.

3 《待ち遠しいというニュアンスがあるとき》
〈私はテストの結果が非常に心配だったので夜寝られなかったんです〉
- ☆ A I was so anxious about the test results that I had a sleepless night.
- ◎ B I was so worried about the test results that I had a sleepless night.
- ◎ C I worried about the test results that I had a sleepless night.
- ○ D I was so concerned about the test results that I had a sleepless night.
- △ E I was so concerned for the test results that I had a sleepless night.

新品
1 《新品で》
〈私はこの車を新品で買ったんです〉
- ☆ A I bought this car new.
- ◎ B I bought this car brand-new.
- ○ C I bought this car from the dealer.

2 《新品の》
〈私は新品の車を買おうと思っているんです〉
- ◎ A I'm thinking of buying a new car.
- ◎ B I'm thinking of buying a brand-new car.
  - ❖ A は中古車だが「別の車」という意味でも使われている．

心不全 →病気 14

新聞配達をする
1 《1軒1軒配達している場合》
〈彼は新聞配達をしています〉
- ◎ A He has a paper route.
- ◎ B He delivers the paper.
- × C He has [does] a paper round.
  - ❖ C はイギリスでは非常によく使われている．

2 《新聞の代理店・販売店・自動販売機などに配送している場合》
〈彼はニューヨークタイムズを配達しているんです〉
- ◎ He delivers *The New York Times*.

3 《どこの新聞を配達しているのか尋ねるとき》
〈彼はどこの新聞を配達しているのですか〉
- ◎ A Which paper does he have a route with?
- ◎ B Which paper does he deliver?
- × C Which paper round does he do?

❖イギリスでは C が非常によく使われている．

進歩

1 《広い意味で述べるとき》

a）期間を示す語がないとき

〈アメリカほど科学の進歩に貢献した国はない〉

- ☆ A No other country has contributed more to the advancement of science than America.
- ☆ B No other country has contributed more to scientific advancements than America.
- ◎ C No other country has contributed more to scientific advancement than America.
- ◎ D No other country has contributed more to the advancements of science than America.
- ○ E No other country has contributed more to scientific advance(s) than America.
- ○ F No other country has contributed more to the progress of science than America.
- △ G No other country has contributed more to scientific progress than America.
- △ H No other country has contributed more to the advance(s) of science than America.

b）期間を示す語があるとき

〈20世紀の技術上の進歩は，目を見張らせるものがあった〉

- ☆ A The technological advancements in the 20th century was astounding.
- ◎ B The advancement of technology in the 20th century was astounding.
- ◎ C The technological advancement in the 20th century was astounding.
- ○ D The advancements [advances] of technology in the 20th century was astounding.
- △ E The technological advances in the 20th century was astounding.
- △ F The advance [progress] of technology in the 20th century was astounding.
- △ G Technological progress in the 20th century was astounding.

2 《特定の分野について述べるとき》

a）一般的に言う場合

〈20世紀のコンピュータ科学における進歩は，目を見張らせるものがあった〉

- ◎ A The advances [advancements] in computer science in the 20th century was amazing.
- ○ B The progress in computer science in the 20th century was amazing.
- ▽ C The advancement [advance] in computer science in the 20th century was amazing.

b）質・程度が高まることに焦点がある場合

〈医学は過去10年間著しく進歩した〉

- ◎ A Medicine has advanced remarkably over the last ten years.
- ◎ B Medicine made remarkable advances [advancements, progress] over the last ten years.
- ◎ C Medicine has seen remarkable advancements over the last ten years.
- ◎ D Medical advancement has been remarkable over the last ten years.
- ○ E Medical advancements have been remarkable over the last ten years.
- ○ F Medicine has made a remarkable advance over the last ten years.

3 《人の能力について述べるとき》
〈あなたの英語はすごく進歩しましたね〉
- ◎ A Your English has improved a lot.
- ◎ B You have made a lot of progress with English.
- ○ C You have made a lot of progress in English.
  - ❖ A は誰でも使えるが，B, C は主として先生が使う表現.

信用できる →信頼できる

信頼できる

1 《人の場合》
〈彼は信頼できる〉
- ◎ A He's dependable.
- ◎ B You can depend on him.
- ○ C You can rely on him.
- ○ D He's reliable.
- △ E You can bank on him.

2 《物事の場合》
〈彼の話は信頼できる〉
- ◎ A His story's reliable [creditable].
- ◎ B His story's believable.
  - ❖ A には証拠があるというニュアンスがあり，B には証拠はないが信じられるというニュアンスがある.

〔す〕

睡眠不足だ

1 《最近の状態》
〈私は最近睡眠不足なんです〉
- ◎ A I haven't been sleeping well lately.
- ◎ B I haven't been getting enough sleep lately.
- ◎ C I haven't been able to get enough sleep lately.
- ◎ D I've been suffering from a lack of sleep lately.
- ○ E I've been suffering from lack of sleep lately.
- ○ F I'm not getting enough sleep these days.
- △ G I've been suffering from the lack of sleep lately.
- × H I've been suffering from the want of sleep lately.
  - ❖ H が辞典に出ているが使われていない.

2 《特定の日》
〈昨夜は睡眠不足なんです〉
- ◎ A I didn't [couldn't] get enough sleep last night.
- ◎ B I didn't [couldn't] sleep well last night.
- ▽ C I didn't get sufficient sleep last night.
  - ❖ C が辞典に出ているがまれ.

数字に強い
〈彼は数字に強いんです〉
- ☆ A He's good with numbers [math].
- ◎ B He's good at math [arithmetic].
- ◎ C He's good with figures.

- ◎ D He's good at calculation [calculating].
- △ E He's good at figures.
- ❖「計算」の項も参照のこと.

スーパー →店 8

好きです

1 《不特定なもの》
〈私は骨董品の家具がすごく好きなんです〉
- ◎ A I have a thing for antique furniture.
- ◎ B I really love [like, enjoy] antique furniture.
- ◎ C I like [love] antique furniture a lot.
- ○ D I have a thing about antique furniture.
- ○ E I really go for antique furniture.

2 《特定なもの》
〈私はバドワイザーがとても好きなんです〉
- ◎ A I have a thing for Bud.
- ◎ B I really love [like, enjoy] Bud.
- ◎ C I love [like] Bud a lot.
- ○ D I have a thing about Bud.
- △ E I really go for Bud.

3 《甘いもの》
〈私は甘いものが好きなんです〉
- ☆ A I like sweets.
- ◎ B I have a sweet tooth.
- ◎ C I like sweet stuff.
- ○ D I have a weakness for sweets.
- △ E I like something sweet.

4 《異性》
〈私は彼をとても好きなんです〉
- ◎ A I'm in love with him.
- ◎ B I really love him.
- ◎ C I love him a lot.

❖ A には「夢中になっている」というニュアンスがある. したがって, 初期の段階の愛を述べるときにぴったり. しかし, 初期でなくてもその気持ちを述べたいときには, I'm still in love with you. のように still を入れて使う.

5 《両親・兄弟・動物》
〈娘:お父さん, 私はお父さんをとても好きよ〉
Daughter:
- ◎ A Dad, I love you a lot.
- × B Dad, I'm in love with you.

6 《否定文で述べるとき》
〈私はこういう音楽は好きじゃないんです〉
- ◎   I don't care for [like] this kind of music.

❖ care for は「好きです」の意味では否定文・疑問文で使われているが, 肯定文では使われていない.

すぐ

1 《場所を表す場合》
a） 目的地までもうすぐと励ますとき
〈娘:歩き疲れちゃった. タクシーに乗ったほうがいいと思うわ〉
Daughter: I'm tired of walking. We should take a cab.

〈母親：その必要はないわよ．すぐそこですよ〉
Mother:
- ☆ A　We don't need to. We're almost [just about] there.
- ◎ B　We don't need to. We're very close.
- ○ C　We don't need to. We're nearly there.
- △ D　We don't need to. We're practically there.

b）通行人に所在地を尋ねられたとき

〈通行人：郵便局はどこにありますか〉
Passerby: Where's the post office?

〈リンダ：すぐそこですよ〉
Linda:
- ◎ A　It's just down [up] the block.
- ◎ B　It's just down [up] the street.
  - ❖ B の方が A より距離がある．

2　《順序を表す場合》

〈あなたの名前はリストで，私の名前のすぐ前です〉
- ☆ A　Your name comes right [just] before mine on the list.
- ◎ B　Your name comes directly before mine on the list.
- ◎ C　Your name comes just [directly] ahead of mine on the list.
- ○ D　Your name comes immediately before [ahead of] mine on the list.
- △ E　Your name comes right ahead of mine on the list.

3　《時間を表す場合》

〈すぐ彼に連絡して下さい〉
- ☆ A　Please get a hold of him right now.
- ☆ B　Please get a hold of him right away.
- ◎ C　Please get a hold of him immediately.
- ○ D　Please get a hold of him at once.
- ▽ E　Please get a hold of him without delay.
- × F　Please get a hold of him right off.
  - ❖(1) A の right now が「すぐ」の意味で非常によく使われているが，ほとんどの辞典は紹介していない．
  - ❖(2) 多くの辞典が B の right away は F の right off とイコールだと紹介しているが，F は使われていない．

すぐできるようになる

〈ビル：僕はいまだに君と同じようにはフランス語が話せないね〉
Bill: I still can't speak French as well as you.

〈ジム：すぐに話せるようになるよ〉
Jim:
- ◎ A　You'll pick it up [catch on] soon.
- ○ B　You'll get it soon.
- ○ C　It'll come soon.

少ない資本で

〈彼は少ない資本でビジネスを始めました〉
- ◎ A　He started his business on a shoestring (budget).
- ◎ B　He started his business on a tight budget.

すぐに

1　《ほんの数分先の未来を述べる場合》

〈(レストランで) お客：あとどのくらい待たなければならないのですか〉
Customer: How much longer do I have to wait?

〈ウエイター:すぐに来ます〉
Waiter:
- ◎ A It's coming.
- ◎ B It's on the way.
- ◎ C It'll be here in a minute.
- ◎ D It'll be a minute.
- ◎ E It won't be long.
  - ❖ Aが一番すぐ来るという響きがあり，B，C，D，Eの順で遅くなるとのニュアンスがある．

2 《「直ちに」という意味を示す場合》
a) 話し手が述べるとき
〈上司:車を車庫から出してくれるかい．すぐに必要なんだ〉
Boss:
- ◎ A Will you get my car out of the garage? I need it yesterday.
- ◎ B Will you get my car out of the garage? I need it right away [right now].
- ◎ C Will you get my car out of the garage? I'm in a big hurry.
- △ D Will you get my car out of the garage? I'm in a big rush.
  - ❖ Aは上司・親のように敬意を示して話す必要のある人には使えない．

b) 聞き手が述べるとき
〈上司:手紙のワープロ打ち終わったかい〉
Boss: Are you done typing the letters on the word processor?
〈秘書:まだです．すぐにやります〉
Secretary:
- ◎ A Not yet. I'll get right on it.
- ◎ B Not yet. I'll do it right away [right now].
- ◎ C Not yet. I'll do it immediately.
- △ D Not yet. I'll do it promptly [at once, in a jiffy].

優れた

〈彼は優れた経済学者です〉
- ◎ A He's a brilliant economist.
- ◎ B He's an outstanding economist.
- ◎ C He's an excellent economist.
- × D He's a crack economist.
  - ❖(1) Dが辞典に出ているが使われていない．
  - ❖(2) 優れている度合いはAが一番強く，B，Cの順で下がる．

すごく

1 《寒さなどの程度》
〈すごく寒い〉
- ☆ A It's freezing.
- ◎ B It's freezing [damn, awfully, terribly] cold.
- ○ C It's absolutely freezing.
- × D It's bitingly [piercing] cold.
  - ❖ Dが辞典に出ているが使われていない．

2 《増減などの程度》
〈交通事故の件数がすごく増えました〉
- ◎ A The number of car accidents has increased dramatically [drastically, greatly, tremendously].
- ◎ B The number of car accidents has increased a great deal [a lot].

- ○ C The number of car accidents has increased substantially.
- ○ D The number of car accidents has increased in a big way.

少し前に →前に［で］2

少しも…でない

1 《動詞も名詞も従えるとき》

〈私は彼を少しも信用していません〉
- ☆ A I don't trust him at all.
- ◎ B I don't have any trust in him (at all).
- ◎ C I don't have the least bit of trust in him.
- ○ D I don't trust him whatsoever ［in the least］.
- ○ E I don't have any trust in him whatsoever.
- △ F I don't have any trust in him in the least.

2 《形容詞を従えるとき》

〈私は少しも寒くありません〉
- ◎ A I'm not cold at all.
- ○ B I'm not cold whatsoever ［in the least］.
- ○ C I'm not even a little ［a bit］ cold.
- ○ D I'm not the least bit cold.

3 《過去分詞を従えるとき》

〈彼は少しも酔っ払っていません〉
- ◎ A He isn't drunk at all.
- ○ B He isn't the least bit ［a bit］ drunk.
- ○ C He isn't drunk whatsoever.
- ○ D He isn't even a little drunk.
- △ E He isn't even a bit drunk.
- △ F He isn't drunk in the least.
- △ G He isn't drunk even a little ［a bit］.
- × H He isn't a little drunk.

筋

1 《筋が通っている》

a) 肯定で述べるとき

〈彼が言っていることは筋が通っている〉
- ☆ A What he's saying makes sense.
- ◎ B What he's saying's logical.
- ○ C There's a logic to ［in］ what he's saying.
- ○ D What he's saying adds up.
- △ E What he's saying holds water.
- △ F What he's saying comes across as logical.
- × G What he's saying has (a) logic.

    ❖ G が辞典に出ているが使われていない．

b) 否定で述べるとき

〈彼が言っていることは筋が通っていない〉
- ☆ A What he's saying doesn't make sense.
- ◎ B What he's saying isn't logical.
- ◎ C What he's saying's illogical.
- ○ D What he's saying doesn't add up.
- ○ E There's no logic to ［in］ what he's saying.
- △ F What he's saying has no logic.
- △ G What he's saying doesn't hold water.

△　H　What he's saying doesn't stand to reason.
　　　△　I　What he's saying doesn't come across as logical.
　　　×　J　What he's saying doesn't stand to logic.
　　　　❖ J が辞典に出ているが使われていない．
　2　《野菜》
　〈筋の多い野菜をもっと食べるといいですよ〉
　　　◎　A　You should eat more vegetables with a lot of fiber.
　　　×　B　You should eat more stringy vegetables.
　　　　❖ B が辞典に出ているが使われていない．
　3　《足首》
　〈私は足首の筋をちがえてしまったんです〉
　　　◎　A　I sprained [twisted] my ankle.
　　　○　B　My ankle was sprained.
　　　△　C　I got my ankle sprained.
　　　×　D　I had my ankle sprained.
　　　×　E　My ankle was twisted.
　4　《首筋》
　〈私は首の筋をちがえてしまったんです〉
　　　◎　A　I have a crick in my neck.
　　　○　B　I got a crick in my neck.

筋金入りの
〈彼は筋金入りの共和党員です〉
　　　◎　A　He's a staunch [an out-and-out, a steadfast] republican.
　　　◎　B　He's a republican to the core.
　　　○　C　He's a through and through republican.
　　　○　D　He's a thorough republican.
　　　▽　E　He's a dyed-in-the wool republican.
　　　　❖ E は多くの辞典に出ているが，現在ではほとんど使われていない．

すし詰め
〈電車はすし詰めでした〉
　　　◎　A　Passengers were packed like sardines on the train.
　　　◎　B　The train was jampacked [very crowded].
　　　△　C　The train had wall to wall passengers.

寿司屋　→店 5

進む
　1　《時計の場合》
　〈私の時計は1日5分進むんです〉
　　　◎　A　My watch runs [goes] five minutes fast each day.
　　　○　B　My watch gains five minutes each day.
　　　△　C　My watch advances five minutes each day.
　　　　❖「進んでいる」の項の1も参照のこと．
　2　《大学院の場合》
　〈私は大学院へ進もうと思っています〉
　　　　A　I'm thinking of going onto [to] graduate school.
　　　△　B　I'm thinking of advancing to graduate school.
　3　《大学の場合》
　〈私は大学へ進もうと思っています〉
　　　☆　A　I'm thinking of going to college.
　　　◎　B　I'm thinking of going onto college.

△ C I'm thinking of advancing to college.
 4 《高校の場合》
〈私は高校へ進もうと思っています〉
  ◎ A I'm thinking of going to high school.
  △ B I'm thinking of advancing to high school.
  × C I'm thinking of going onto high school.
 5 《病状を述べるとき》→進行する 1
 6 《クラスでの授業の進度を尋ねるとき》
〈この前はどこまで進みましたか〉
  ◎ A How far did we get [go] last time?
  ◎ B Where did we leave off last time?
  ◎ C How much did we cover last time?

進んでいる
 1 《時計が》
 a）「…分進んでいる」と述べるとき
〈私の時計は5分進んでいます〉
  ☆ A My watch's five minutes fast.
  ◎ B My watch's five minutes ahead.
  ○ C My watch's five minutes early.
 b）進んでいる分数を尋ねるとき
〈あなたの時計は何分進んでいるのですか〉
  ◎ A How fast's your watch?
  ◎ B How many minutes fast is your watch?
  ○ C How many minutes ahead is your watch?
  △ D How many minutes is your watch fast [ahead]?
  ❖「進む」の項の1も参照のこと．
 2 《技術力を比較して》
〈日本はこの分野では外国よりも進んでいる〉
  ◎ A Japan's ahead of the rest of the world in this field.
  ◎ B Japan's more advanced than the rest of the world in this field.
  ◎ C Japan's further along than the rest of the world in this field.
  ◎ D Japan's making more progress than the rest of the world in this field.
  ❖A, B, Cはすでに確立しているとの響きがあり，Dは現在も進行しているというニュアンスがある．
 3 《学科の習熟度を比較して》
〈邦雄はフランス語がクラスメートより進んでいます〉
  ◎ A Kunio's ahead of his class in French.
  ◎ B Kunio's French's more advanced than his classmates'.
  ◎ C Kunio's making more progress than his class in French.
  ❖A, Bはすでに確立しているとの響きがあり，Cは現在進行しているというニュアンスがある．
 4 《病状を述べて》→進行する 1

スタイルがいい
 1 《男女のスタイルを客観的に述べるとき》
 a）聞き手が肥満でないとき
〈あなたはスタイルがいいですね〉
  ◎ A You're in good shape.
  ○ B You have a fine [good, nice] physique.
 b）肥満または同様のことが言及されたとき

〈あなたはスタイルがいいですよ〉
- ◎ A You're athletic.
- ◎ B You're an athlete.
- ◎ C You're in good shape.
- ○ D You have a fine [good, nice] physique.
  ❖肥満が話題になっていないときにA, Bを使うと、「あなたはスポーツマンですね」の意味になる。

c) 強調して述べるとき
〈あなたはすごくスタイルがいいですよ〉
- ◎ A You look like quite an athlete.
- ◎ B You're a great athlete.
- ◎ C You're really in good shape.
- ◎ D You're really athletic.
- ◎ E You have a great [terrific] physique.

2 《女性がセクシーであるという意味のとき》
a) 普通に述べるとき
〈彼女はスタイルがいい〉
- ☆ A She's hot.
- ◎ B She has a great [terrific, sexy] body.
- ◎ C She has a good build.
- ○ D She has a fantastic body.
- ○ E She's well-built.
- △ F She's really-built.
- △ G She has an incredible body.
- △ H She has some build.

b) 強調して述べるとき
〈彼女はすごくスタイルがいい〉
- ☆ A She's really hot.
- ◎ B She's a real babe.
- ◎ C She's such a babe.
- ◎ D She's really sexy.
- ○ E She's very hot.
- △ F She's really hot stuff.
- ▽ G She's a real fox.

3 《女性の上半身のことに言及しているとき》
〈彼女はスタイルがいいね〉
- ☆ A She's got big boobs.
- ☆ B She's got big breasts.
- ◎ C She's stacked.
- ◎ D She's big-chested.
- ◎ E She's got big hooters [a big chest].
- ◎ F She's top-heavy [loaded].
- ◎ G She's got big jugs [a big rack].
  ❖B, Gは女性より男性の間でよく使われている。

4 《男性がセクシーであるという意味のとき》
〈彼はスタイルがいい〉
- ☆ A He's hot.
- ◎ B He has a some [good] build.
- ◎ C He has a great [sexy] body.

すてる 333

- ◎ D He's really-built [well-built].
- ○ E He has a terrific body.
- △ F He has a fantastic [an incredible] body.

すたれている

1 《ファッション・柄・洋服のスタイル》
〈グリーンはすたれています〉
- ☆ A Green isn't in style.
- ◎ B Green is out of fashion [style].
- ◎ C Green isn't in fashion.
- ○ D Green isn't stylish [fashionable].

2 《機械の型》
〈このタイプのファックスはもうすたれています〉
- ☆ A This type of fax machine isn't being used any more.
- ◎ B This type of fax machine is outdated any more.
- △ C This type of fax machine is dated any more.
- × D This type of fax machine is out of use any more.

❖辞典に D が出ているが使われていない．

3 《歌》
〈この歌は最近はもうすたれています〉
- ◎ This song's no longer popular these days.

スタンド

1 《電気スタンド》
a）机の上に置くタイプ
〈私はスタンドを買わなければならない〉
- ◎ I have to buy a desk lamp.

b）床に置くタイプ
〈床のスタンドを2つ買わなければならない〉
- ◎ We have to buy two floor lamps.

2 《観覧席》
a）長いす式
〈スタンドは一杯でした〉
- ◎ A The bleachers were full.
- △ B The stands were full.

b）一人ずつの座席式
〈スタンドは一杯でした〉
- ◎ A The stands were full.
- △ B The bleachers were full.

頭痛 →痛い 1
すっからかん →底をつく
ずっと前に →前に［で］2 f）
すっ飛んで行く →急ぐ 13

捨てる

1 《不要品を捨てる》
〈もしその本が必要なければ捨ててください〉
- ◎ A If you don't need that book, throw it away.
- ◎ B If you don't need that book, junk it.
- ○ C If you don't need that book, chuck it.

2 《放棄する》
a）義務を

⟨彼は妻子を捨てたんです⟩
　　◎　A　He left his wife and children.
　　◎　B　He deserted his wife and children.
　　◎　C　He abandoned his wife and children.
　　◎　D　He walked out on his wife and children.
　　◎　E　He ran out on his wife and children.
　　❖非難する気持ちは C が一番強い．B, D, E の順で下がり A が一番弱い．
b) 権利を
⟨私は遺産の権利を全部捨てます⟩
　　◎　A　I'll waive all my rights to the inheritance.
　　○　B　I'll give up all my rights to the inheritance.
3 《やむを得ず見捨てる》
⟨彼らは沈みかかっている船を捨てたんです⟩
　　◎　A　They abandoned the sinking ship.
　　○　B　They jumped off the sinking ship.
　　×　C　They jumped the sinking ship.
4 《計画などをあきらめる》
⟨私はこのプロジェクトを捨てる用意があります⟩
　　◎　A　I'm ready to quit [give up on] this project.
　　◎　B　I'm ready to let this project go.
　　○　C　I'm ready to give up this project.
5 《恋人・夫・妻と別れる》
a) 恋人を捨てる
⟨彼女はボーイフレンドを捨てたんです⟩
　　◎　A　She dumped her boyfriend.
　　○　B　She dropped her boyfriend.
　　▽　C　She jilted her boyfriend.
b) 恋人を捨てて別の男性に走る
⟨彼女は彼を捨てて別の男性に走ったんです⟩
　　◎　A　She broke up with him for another guy.
　　○　B　She split up with him for another guy.
c) 夫を捨てて別の男性に走る
⟨彼女は夫を捨てて別の男性に走ったんです⟩
　　☆　A　She walked out on her husband for another guy.
　　☆　B　She ran around on her husband with another guy.
　　◎　C　She dumped her husband for another guy.
　　○　D　She ran out on her husband for another guy.
　　△　E　She walked out on her husband with another guy.
　　△　F　She abandoned her husband for another guy.

ストライキ

1 《状態（ストをやっている）》
⟨社員は全員ストライキ中である⟩
　　◎　A　All the employees're on strike.
　　○　B　All the employees're on a walkout [a strike].
2 《動作（ストを決行する）》
a) 一般的に言うとき
⟨組合は明日ストライキをやるだろう⟩
　　☆　A　The union'll go on strike tomorrow.
　　◎　B　The union'll go on [carry out, stage] a strike tomorrow.

◎ C The union'll walk out tomorrow.
　　○ D The union'll come out on (a) strike tomorrow.
　b)「座りこみスト」と言うとき
〈組合は座り込みストをした〉
　　◎ A The union went on [carried out, staged] a sit-down strike.
　　× B The union came out on a sit-down strike.
　　❖ B は辞典に出ているが使われていない.
　c)「ゼネスト」と言うとき
〈明日, 東京中でゼネストが行われるだろう〉
　　◎ A A general strike'll go on all over Tokyo tomorrow.
　　◎ B A general strike'll be carried out [be staged] all over Tokyo tomorrow.
　　× C A general strike'll come out all over Tokyo tomorrow.
　3 《ストを中止する》
〈組合はストライキを中止するだろう〉
　　◎ A The union'll call off the strike.
　　○ B The union'll call off the walkout.

すなわち
　1 《前出の単語を詳細に述べるとき》
〈アメリカの国会は2院, すなわち上院と下院で構成されている〉
　　◎ A Congress consists of two houses, namely, the Senate and the House of Representatives.
　　△ B Congress consists of two houses, that it to say, the Senate and the House of Representatives.
　　△ C Congress consists of two houses, that is, the Senate and the House of Representatives.
　　△ D Congress consists of two houses, i.e. the Senate and the House of Representatives.
　　❖ D は文章ではよく使われている.
　2 《前出の単語を言い換えて述べるとき》
〈相撲, すなわち日本のレスリングは, 何百年も前からあるのです〉
　　◎ A Sumo, or Japanese wrestling, dates back hundreds of years.
　　○ B Sumo, in other words Japanese wrestling, dates back hundreds of years.

すねをかじる
〈彼はまだ親のすねをかじっているんです〉
　　☆ A He's still living off his parents.
　　◎ B He's still sponging [mooching] off his parents.
　　○ C He's still leeching off his parents.
　　× D He's still sponging on his parents.
　　❖(1) D が辞典に出ているが使われていない.
　　❖(2) C が一番批判しているニュアンスが強い. B は2番目. A は一番弱い.

すばらしい
〈私たちの今度の上司はすばらしい人です〉
　　☆ A Our new boss is great.
　　☆ B Our new boss is terrific [wonderful].
　　◎ C Our new boss is fantastic [amazing, incredible].
　　○ D Our new boss is super.
　　○ E Our new boss is the bomb.

- △ F Our new boss is superb [marvelous].
- △ G Our new boss is spectacular.
  - ❖(1) すばらしさの程度は C, E, G が一番強い. 2番目は B, 3番目は A, D, F.
  - ❖(2) E の the bomb は 10 代, 20 代前半の若い人の間では非常によく使われている.

スピーチをする

1 《披露宴での場合》

〈披露宴でスピーチをしていただけますか〉

- ◎ A Would you say a few words at the wedding reception?
- × B Would you give [make] a speech at the wedding reception?

2 《社会問題などについての場合》

〈彼は日米間の貿易不均衡についてスピーチをしました〉

- ☆ A He gave a speech on the trade imbalance between America and Japan.
- ◎ B He made a speech on the trade imbalance between America and Japan.
- ○ C He delivered a speech on the trade imbalance between America and Japan.
- ○ D He spoke on the trade imbalance between America and Japan.
  - ❖詳細は「演説をする」の項を参照のこと.

スピード違反　→違反 2

スピードを出す

1 《数字を明示しないとき》

〈トラックはバスと衝突したときスピードを出していました〉

- ☆ A The truck was going fast when it crashed into a bus.
- ○ B The truck was traveling [driving, moving] fast when it crashed into a bus.
- × C The truck was running fast when it crashed into a bus.
  - ❖B は新聞では非常によく使われている.

2 《数字を明示するとき》

〈トラックはバスと衝突したとき時速 100 マイルのスピードを出していました〉

- ☆ A The truck was going a hundred miles an hour when it crashed into a bus.
- ◎ B The truck was going at a hundred miles an hour when it crashed into a bus.
- ◎ C The truck was traveling (at) a hundred miles an hour when it crashed into a bus.
- ○ D The truck was driving (at) a hundred miles an hour when it crashed into a bus.
- ○ E The truck was speeding along (at) a hundred miles an hour when it crashed into a bus.
- ○ F The truck was moving (at) a hundred miles an hour when it crashed into a bus.

3 《車の速度》

〈スピードを出して〉

- ☆ A Step on it.
- ◎ B Drive [Go] faster.
- ◎ C Speed up.

- ○ D Gun it.
- ○ E Hit [Step on] the gas.
- ○ F Speed it up.
- △ G Get the lead out.
- △ H Give it some gas.
- × I Give it a [the] gun.
- × J Give her the gun.

すべり止め
〈私はすべり止めにXYZ大学に出願するつもりです〉
- ◎ A I'm going to apply to XYZ University as a safe bet.
- ◎ B I'm going to apply to XYZ University just to be safe.
- ◎ C I'm going to apply to XYZ University just in case.
- × D I'm going to apply to XYZ University as a safety school.

滑る
1 《車》
〈バスが氷の張った道路で滑ってタクシーに衝突したんです〉
- ◎ A The bus skidded on the icy road and crashed into a taxi.
- ○ B The bus slid on the icy road and crashed into a taxi.
- × C The bus slipped on the icy road and crashed into a taxi.

2 《人》
〈彼女は氷の張った道路で滑って転んだんです〉
- ◎ A She slipped on the icy road and fell down.
- △ B She lost her balance [footing] on the icy road and fell down.
- ▽ C She slid on the icy road and fell down.
- × D She skidded on the icy road and fell down.

スポーツクラブ
1 《主として男性向き》
〈この先にスポーツクラブがあります〉
- ◎ A There's a sports club down the street.
- ◎ B There's a gym down the street.
- ○ C There's an athletic club down the street.
- △ D There's an athletic gym down the street.

2 《男女の出会いのイメージがあるスポーツクラブ》
〈この先にスポーツクラブがあります〉
- ◎ There's a fitness [health] club down the street.

3 《主として女性向き》
〈この先にスポーツクラブがあります〉
- ◎ There's a health spa down the street.
  - ❖(1) a health spa は spa (エステ) の意味でもよく使われているのであいまいな語.
  - ❖(2) 精神修養の瞑想, ヨガの設備もある.
  - ❖(3) 会員になるには会費が非常に高いので, ステイタスシンボルになる.

スポーツマン
1 《スポーツ愛好家》
〈彼はスポーツマンなんです〉
- ◎ A He's athletic.
- ◎ B He enjoys sports.
- × C He's a sportsman.

2 《ヨット・魚釣り・狩猟の愛好家》

〈彼はスポーツマンです〉
- ◎ He's a sportsman.

スポーツ洋品店 →店 29

図星 →当たり

すみません

1 《謝罪するとき》

a) 謝罪する内容に言及しないとき

〈本当にすみません〉
- ☆ A I'm very sorry.
- ◎ B I feel very sorry.
- ○ C I'm terribly [really] sorry.
- ○ D I feel terribly [really] sorry.
- ○ E I really feel sorry.

  ❖謝ることで弁償することが発生してくる交通事故のようなときは、たとえ話し手は自分に落ち度があったことを認めていても A〜E を使わない点が日本語と違う。アメリカ人はこのような場面で相手の非をできるだけ多く並べ立てる。

b) 今現在相手に迷惑をかけている内容に言及して謝罪するとき

〈お邪魔してすみません〉
- ☆ A I'm sorry to bother you.
- ◎ B I'm sorry for bothering you.
- ○ C I'm sorry I'm bothering you.

c) 迷惑の内容が現在完了の継続内容のとき

〈こんなに長くお待たせしてしまってすみません〉
- ☆ A I'm sorry I've kept you waiting this long.
- ◎ B I'm sorry to have kept you waiting this long.
- ○ C I'm sorry for having kept you waiting this long.

2 《ウエイトレス・ウエイターを呼ぶとき》

a) 高級レストランでウエイトレスを呼ぶとき

・普通に呼ぶとき

〈すみませんが水をもう一杯いただけますか〉
- ☆ A Excuse me, may I have another glass of water?
- ◎ B Miss, may I have another glass of water?
- ○ C Ma'am, may I have another glass of water?
- ▽ D Hello, may I have another glass of water?
- × E Waitress, may I have another glass of water?

・特に丁重にウエイトレスを呼ぶとき

〈すみませんが水をもう一杯いただけますか〉
- ◎ A Excuse me, Miss [ma'am], may I have another glass of water?
- × B Excuse me, waitress, may I have another glass of water?

b) 高級レストランでウエイターを呼ぶとき

・普通に呼ぶとき

〈すみませんが水をもう一杯いただけますか〉
- ☆ A Excuse me, may I have another glass of water?
- ○ B Sir, may I have another glass of water?
- △ C Waiter, may I have another glass of water?
- ▽ D Hello, may I have another glass of water?

  ❖B は年上、特に話し手よりずっと年配のウエイターを呼ぶときによく使われている。

・特に丁重にウエイターを呼ぶとき
〈すみませんが水をもう一杯いただけますか〉
- ◎ Excuse me, sir, may I have another glass of water?

c) 大衆レストランでウエイトレスを呼ぶとき
〈すみません，水をもう一杯もらえますか〉
- ☆ A Excuse me, can I have another glass of water?
- ◎ B Miss, can I have another glass of water?
- ○ C Waitress, can I have another glass of water?
- ○ D Ma'am, can I have another glass of water?
- ▽ E Hello, can I have another glass of water?
  - ❖(1) B は年上の男性または女性が年下の女性に使う．
  - ❖(2) D は年下の男性または女性が年上（約 30 歳以上）の女性に使う．

d) 大衆レストランでウエイターを呼ぶとき
〈すみません，水をもう一杯もらえますか〉
- ☆ A Excuse me, can I have another glass of water?
- ◎ B Waiter, can I have another glass of water?
- ▽ C Sir [Hello], can I have another glass of water?

3 《デパートなどで店員を呼ぶとき》

a) 女性の店員に呼びかけるとき
〈すみません，お願いできますか〉
- ☆ A Excuse me, can you help me?
- ◎ B Ma'am [Miss], can you help me?
- × C Young lady, can you help me?

b) 男性の店員に呼びかけるとき
〈すみません，お願いできますか〉
- ◎ A Excuse me, can you help me?
- △ B Sir [Hello], can you help me?

すみを折る
《ページなどの》
〈本のすみを折らないでくれ〉
- ◎ Don't dog-ear the book.

すらっとしている
1 《女性の場合》
〈彼女はすらっとしている〉
- ◎ A She's skinny.
- ○ B She's trim.
- △ C She's slim [slender, thin].
  - ❖(1) A は「やせこけている」という意味でもよく使われている．どちらであるかは文脈による．
  - ❖(2) C は中年以上の人の間では非常によく使われている．

2 《男性の場合》
〈彼はすらっとしている〉
- ◎ A He's skinny [thin].
- ○ B He's slim.
- △ C He's trim.

スラム街
1 《一般的なスラム街》
〈ニューヨークにはたくさんスラム街があります〉
- ◎ A New York has a lot of slums.

- ◎ B New York has a lot of slum areas [neighborhoods].
- ◎ C New York has a lot of run-down areas [neighborhoods].
- ▽ D New York has a lot of slum [poor] quarters.

2 《特定の少数民族が住んでいるスラム街》
〈ニューヨークにはたくさんスラム街があります〉
- ◎ New York has a lot of ghettoes.

…するそうだ

1 《会話で》
〈彼が部長に昇進するそうですね〉
- ◎ A I hear [heard] he's going to be promoted to General Manager.
- ◎ B They say he's going to be promoted to General Manager.
- ○ C I understand [see] he's going to be promoted to General Manager.
- ○ D People say he's going to be promoted to General Manager.
- ○ E I'm told he's going to be promoted to General Manager.
  - ❖ A, B, D, E は人から聞いたとき, C は人から聞いた場合と掲示板・社内報などで読んだ場合の両方に使える.

2 《堅い文章英語で》
〈XYZ 銀行は HIJ 銀行と合併するそうです〉
- ◎ A I see that XYZ Bank will merge with HIJ Bank.
- ○ B I understand that XYZ Bank will merge with HIJ Bank.
- ○ C People [They] say that XYZ Bank will merge with HIJ Bank.
- ○ D It's said that XYZ Bank will merge with HIJ Bank.
- △ E XYZ Bank is said to be merging with HIJ Bank.

…するつもりだ

1 《肯定》

a) 未来
〈私は明日, 日本を発つつもりです〉
- ◎ A I'll leave Japan tomorrow.
- ◎ B I'm leaving Japan tomorrow.
- ◎ C I'm going [planning] to leave Japan tomorrow.
- ○ D I plan [intend] to leave Japan tomorrow.
- × E I mean to leave Japan tomorrow.
  - ❖(1) E が辞典に出ているが使われていない.
  - ❖(2) 話し手の意志の強さの点では A が一番強く, B が 2 番, C, D はほぼ同じで 3 番目.
  - ❖(3) D の intend は会話でも使われているが, 少し堅い響きがある.

b) 過去
・その行為を実行しなかったとき
〈私は昨夜あなたに電話するつもりだったのですが, できなかったのです〉
- ☆ A I was going to call you last night.
- ◎ B I was going to call you last night, but I couldn't.
- ◎ C I meant to call you last night(, but I couldn't).
- ○ D I was planning to call you last night(, but I couldn't).
- △ E I'd intended to call you last night(, but I couldn't).
- △ F I intended to call you last night(, but I couldn't).
- ▽ G I intended to have called you last night(, but I couldn't).
  - ❖ G は本に出ているがほとんど使われていない. E, F も多くの辞典に出ているが, 会話で時々使われる程度.

c) 過去から現在までの深刻な内容を述べるとき

〈私は夫とずうっと別れるつもりできました〉
- ◎ A I've been planning to leave my husband.
- ◎ B I've been planning on leaving my husband.
- × C I've been meaning [intending, going] to leave my husband.

d）過去から現在までの非深刻な内容を述べるとき
〈私はずうっとあなたとお話しするつもりできました〉
- ◎ A I've been meaning to talk to you.
- ○ B I've been planning to talk to you.
- ○ C I've been planning on [thinking of] talking to you.
- ▽ D I've been intending to talk to you.
- × E I've been going to talk to you.

2 《否定》
a）現在
〈私はあなたに失礼をするつもりはありません〉
- ◎ A I don't mean to be rude to you.
- △ B I don't intend to be rude to you.

b）過去
〈私はあなたを侮辱するつもりはありませんでした〉
- ◎ A I didn't mean to insult you.
- ○ B I didn't intend to insult you.

3 《第三者に「…させるつもりだ」と言うとき》
〈私は息子に会社を継がせるつもりはありませんでした〉
- ◎ A I didn't intend [mean, plan] for my son to take over my company.
- ◎ B I wasn't planning for my son to take over my company.
- × C I wasn't going for my son to take over my company.
- × D I didn't intend [mean] my son to take over my company.

❖ D が辞典に紹介されているが使われていない．

…するといいでしょう

1 《質問されていないで丁重に言いたいとき》
〈グレーのスーツにうすい黄色のシャツを着るといいでしょう〉
- ◎ A You could wear a light yellow shirt with your gray suit.
- ◎ B You might like [want] to wear a light yellow shirt with your gray suit.
- × C You should wear a light yellow shirt with your gray suit.
- × D You'd better wear a light yellow shirt with your gray suit.

2 《質問されて丁重に答えたいとき》
〈客：このグレーのスーツにはどちらのネクタイのほうが似合うと思いますか〉
Customer: Which tie do you think goes better with this gray suit?
〈店員：黄色いネクタイをなさるといいでしょう〉
Salesperson:
- ☆ A I suggest the yellow one.
- ○ B You might want [like] to wear the yellow one.
- ▽ C You should wear the yellow one.
- × D You'd better wear the yellow one.

3 《質問されて意見を述べるとき》
〈学生：私は大学院へ行こうと思っているんですが私立は全部高すぎるんです〉
Student: I'm thinking of going to graduate school but all the private schools're too expensive.
〈カウンセラー：州立の大学へ行くといいでしょう〉

Counselor:
- ☆ A I suggest you go to a state university.
- ◎ B You should [could, might] go to a state university.
- ○ C It might be better for you to go to a state university.
- ○ D It'd be better for you to go to a state university.
- ○ E I advise [recommend] you to go to a state university.
- × F You'd better go to a state university.

4 《弁護士が提案として述べるとき》

〈あなたは証拠が十分でないのでこれは示談にしたほうがいいでしょう〉

Lawyer:
- ☆ A You'd better settle this out of court because you don't have enough evidence.
- ◎ B You should [could, might] settle this out of court because you don't have enough evidence.
- ◎ C I suggest you settle this out of court because you don't have enough evidence.
- ◎ D It'd be better for you to settle this out of court because you don't have enough evidence.
- ◎ E It might be better for you to settle this out of court because you don't have enough evidence.

5 《「忠告を受け入れないと大変なことになる」というニュアンスのとき》

〈医者：タバコをやめたほうがいいですよ〉

Doctor:
- ☆ A You'd better stop smoking.
- ◎ B You should stop smoking.
- ◎ C I strongly advise [recommend] you to stop smoking.
- × D It'd be better for you to stop smoking.
- × E It might be better for you to stop smoking.
- × F I suggest [propose] you should stop smoking.
- × G You might want [like] to stop smoking.
- × H I suggest you stop smoking.
  - ❖「従わないと大変なことになる」というニュアンスなしに軽く助言するのなら，D，E は時々使われている．

6 《許可を求められたとき》

〈ビル：木曜日に休んでもいいですか〉

Bill: Can I take Thursday off?

〈支配人：いいよ．この頃は景気がよくないから君がいなくてもやれるよ〉

Manager:
- ◎ A You may as well. Business is bad these days, so we can spare you.
- ◎ B You might as well. Business is bad these days, so we can spare you.
- ◎ C It's no big deal. Business is bad these days, so we can spare you.
- ○ D It doesn't make any difference. Business is bad these days, so we can spare you.
- ○ E It doesn't matter. Business is bad these days, so we can spare you.
- ○ F It makes no difference. Business is bad these days, so we can spare you.
- ○ G There's no problem. Business is bad these days, so we can spare you.
  - ❖(1) You may as well. は辞典で正しく意味を紹介していないので，ここで整理されたい．この表現は次の3つの意味を持っている．A: It makes no

difference. (a) …してもいい, (b) …してもどうってことはない, (c) …しても同じ, (d) …しても問題はない. B: It's a good idea. (a) …してもよい, (b) …するのはいい考えだ, (c) …するのは賢明だ. C: It's a good opportunity. (a) …してもいい, (b) …するのはいい機会だ.

❖(2) You may as well...＝You'd better...と解説・紹介している本が多数あるが, 両者は全くニュアンスを異にする.

7 《「…するのはいい機会です」というニュアンスのとき》
〈妻：床に戻って寝た方がいいわよ．電車がストなの．だから今日は誰も仕事に行かないわよ〉
Wife:
◎　　You may as well go back to bed. There's a train strike. So nobody will be going to work today.

〈夫：すばらしい．今日は本当に疲れているんだ〉
Husband: Great. I'm really tired today.

8 《「…するのはいい考えです」というニュアンスのとき》
〈ロン：ボストンの兄さんを訪ねるのかい〉
Ron: Are you going to visit your big brother in Boston?
〈クリス：うん，訪ねてもいいね．ニューヨークの帰り道ボストンを通らなきゃならないんだから〉
Chris:
◎　　Yeah, I may as well. I have to go through there on my way back from New York.

座る

1 《席をすすめるとき》
a）丁重に述べる場合
〈お座り下さい〉
- ◎　A　Have a seat, please.
- ◎　B　Be seated, please.
- ◎　C　Sit down, please.
- ○　D　Take a [your] seat, please.
- ×　E　Have your seat, please.
- ×　F　Get seated, please.

❖(1) E, Fが辞典に出ているが使われていない．
❖(2) Bが一番丁重な響きがある．

b）2人以上の人をディナーに招いて着席してもらう場合
〈どうぞお座り下さい〉
- ◎　A　Please be seated.
- ◎　B　Please have a seat.
- ◎　C　Please take your seats.
- ◎　D　Please sit down.
- ▽　E　Please get seated.
- ×　F　Please have your seats.

❖Aはフォーマルな響きがあるので友人，親類がお客のときは不自然．ただし，会社の上司，取引先のお客様が相手のときにはよく使われている．

c）1人のお客様をディナーに招いた場合
〈どうぞお座り下さい〉
- ◎　A　Please be seated.
- ◎　B　Please have a seat.
- ◎　C　Please sit down.

○ D Please take a seat.
2 《席が空いているかどうか尋ねるとき》
〈この席に誰か座っていますか〉
- ◎ A Is this seat taken?
- ◎ B Is somebody sitting here?
- × C Is somebody sitting on this seat?
  ❖ C が参考書に出ているが使われていない．

〔せ〕

…製 →どこの 5, 6, 7
青果物 →野菜 8
税関
1 《一般に「税関で」と述べる場合》
〈彼女は税関に勤めています〉
- ◎ A She works at [in] customs.
- ◎ B She works for customs.
- ◎ C She works at [in] the customs department.
- ◎ D She works for the customs department.
- ◎ E She works at the customs checkpoint.
- × F She works at the customshouse.
  ❖(1) F が辞典に出ているが，現代アメリカ英語では使われていない．
  ❖(2) A, C は税関の事務職，または検問所．B, D は普通は事務職を，E は検問所を指している．

2 《名前に言及するとき》
〈私は成田税関に勤めています〉
- ◎ A I work at [for] Narita Customs.
- ◎ B I work at the customs department in Narita.
- ◎ C I work in [for] the customs department at Narita.
- ◎ D I work in [for] the customs division at Narita.

税関吏 →職業 35
税金
1 《所得税》
〈所得税は今年の秋下がるでしょう〉
- ☆ A Income tax'll go down this fall.
- ◎ B Income taxes'll go down this fall.
- ○ C The income tax'll go down this fall.
- × D The income taxes'll go down this fall.

2 《消費税》
〈消費税は近い将来上がるでしょう〉
- ☆ A Sales tax'll go up in the near future.
- ◎ B The sales tax'll go up in the near future.
- △ C Sales taxes'll go up in the near future.
- ▽ D The sales taxes'll go up in the near future.
- × E The consumption tax'll go up in the near future.
  ❖ E が辞典に出ているがこれは日本語の直訳．

3 《法人税》

〈景気が悪いので政府はまもなく法人税を下げるでしょう〉
- ◎ A The economy's bad, so the government'll reduce corporate taxes soon.
- ○ B The economy's bad, so the government'll reduce the corporate tax soon.
- △ C The economy's bad, so the government'll reduce corporate tax soon.
- × D The economy's bad, so the government'll reduce (the) corporation taxes soon.

4 《不動産税》

〈景気が悪いので政府は不動産税を下げるだろう〉
- ◎ A Since the economy's bad, the government'll lower real estate [property] taxes.
- ○ B Since the economy's bad, the government'll lower the real estate [property] tax.

5 《関税》

〈これらの時計は 20 %の関税を払わなければなりません〉
- ☆ A You have to pay 20% tax on these watches.
- ◎ B You have to pay 20% customs [duty] on these watches.
- × C You have to pay 20% customs duty [duties] on these watches.

整形外科医 →医者 7

政権

1 《アメリカの政権》

〈ブッシュ政権は国民の間で人気がある〉
- ◎ A The Bush administration's popular with the people.
- ◎ B Bush's administration's popular with the people.
- × C The Bush government's popular with the people.
- × D Bush's government's popular with the people.

2 《アメリカ以外の民主的な国》

〈小泉政権は国民に人気がある〉
- ◎ A The Koizumi government's popular with the people.
- ◎ B Koizumi's government's popular with the people.
- △ C The Koizumi administration's popular with the people.
- △ D Koizumi's administration's popular with the people.

3 《独裁政権または軍事政権》

〈フセイン政権は早晩倒されるであろう〉
- ◎ A The Saddam Hussein regime will be brought down sooner or later.
- ○ B The Saddam Hussein junta will be brought down sooner or later.

❖ B はアメリカの新聞でよく使われている．

4 《「政権につく」と言う場合》

a）民主的な政権

〈ルーズヴェルトは何年に大統領の座についたのですか〉
- ☆ A When was Roosevelt president?
- ◎ B When did Roosevelt take office?
- ○ C When was Roosevelt inaugurated?
- ○ D When did Roosevelt come into [to] office?

b）独裁政権または軍事政権

〈ヒトラーは何年に政権についたのですか〉
- ◎ A When did Hitler come to [into] power?
- × B When did Hitler come to [into] office?

税控除できる
〈この費用は税控除できます〉
- ◎ A This expense's tax-deductible.
- ◎ B We can write off this expense.
- ◎ C This expense's a tax write-off.
- ○ D This expense's deductible.

生産力がある
〈この工場はクリーブランドの工場より生産力があります〉
- ◎ A This factory is more productive than the one in Cleveland.
- ○ B This factory has more productivity than the one in Cleveland.

製紙工場 →工場 5
精神科医 →医者 8

成績

1 《会社》
〈うちの会社の業績はいいんです〉
- ☆ A Our company's doing well.
- ◎ B Our company's doing a good [a lot of] business.
- ◎ C Our company has a lot of business.
- ○ D Our company's doing good business.
- ○ E Our company('s) performance's good.

2 《社員》
a）仕事ぶりだけを述べるとき
〈彼女の成績はいいです〉
- ◎ A She does good job [work].
- ◎ B She's a good employee.

b）昇進を述べるとき
〈昇進は全く成績次第です〉
- ◎ The promotion depends solely on your performance [achievement].

3 《学生》
〈息子は成績がいいんです〉
- ◎ A My son's doing well in school.
- ◎ B My son's a good student.
- ◎ C My son gets [has] good grades.
- ◎ D My son has high grades.
- ◎ E My son has a good [high] GPA.

❖(1) A は勉強と行動面の両方，B は主として勉強面のこと．C は勉強上の成績のみに言及している．
❖(2) high のほうが good より意味が強い．
❖(3) E は高校・大学生にしか使えない．

〈誰が最高成績（最高点）を取ったのですか〉
- ◎ A Who scored (the) highest?
- ◎ B Who got the best [highest] score?

❖(1) A，B は成績（A，B，C，D，F，日本での優，良，可など）と点数のいずれについても言うことができる．これに対して，Who got the best [the highest] grade? は，点数ではなく成績のことを尋ねるときにのみ使われる．
❖(2) アメリカでは A，B，C，D の次は F（failure：不可）になる．
❖(3) テストの「点数」であるからといって，score の代りに point を使わないこと．

4 《「成績の面で」と述べるとき》
a) 大学生の場合
〈彼は成績はあまり優秀ではないけれど，付き合いではクラス一番の人気者なんだ〉
- ◎ Academically [Grade-wise], he's not a good student but he's the most popular student in his class.

b) 小学生〜高校生までの場合
〈息子は成績のほうはよくないんだけど，付き合いではクラスで一番の人気者なんですよ〉
- ◎ A Grade-wise, my son's not a good student but he's the most popular student in his class.
- ○ B Academically, my son's not a good student but he's the most popular student in his class.

贅沢に暮らす
〈彼は贅沢に暮らしている〉
- ◎ A He's living like a king.
- ◎ B He's living extravagantly.
- ◎ C He's living luxuriously [high].
- ◎ D He's living [leading] a luxurious life.
- ◎ E He's rolling in money [luxury].
- ▽ F He's rolling in wealth.
- ▽ G He's living in clover.
- ▽ H He's living like a lord [fighting cock].
- ▽ I He's living lapped in the luxury.
- ▽ J He's living in the lap of luxury.
- ▽ K He's buttering his bread on both sides.
  - ❖(1) F〜K が辞典に出ているが実際にはほとんど使われていない．
  - ❖(2) 贅沢の程度が一番高いのは A, B.

贅沢品
〈電話は以前は贅沢品と見なされていた〉
- ◎ A The telephone used to be regarded as a luxury (item).
- △ B The telephone used to be regarded as an item of luxury.
- ▽ C The telephone used to be regarded as a luxury article.
- ▽ D The telephone used to be regarded as an article of luxury.
  - ❖ C, D が辞典に出ているが，使われてもまれ．

正当化
〈あなたが言っていることは自分のミスの正当化にすぎない〉
- ◎ What you're saying's nothing but a rationalization [justification] for your mistake.

正当化する
1 《職場で》
〈自分のミスを正当化しようとするのはやめなさい〉
- ◎ A Stop trying to justify your mistake.
- ◎ B Stop trying to make excuses for your mistake.
- ○ C Stop trying to rationalize your mistake.
  - ❖ C の rationalize を「合理化する」の意味で紹介している英和辞典が多いが，この語は「正当化する」の意味でしか使われていない．「合理化する」の項も参照のこと．

2 《夫婦・友人間で》
〈自分のミスを正当化するのはやめなさい〉

- ◎ A Stop trying to make excuses for your mistake.
- ◎ B Stop trying to justify your mistake.
- ○ C Stop trying to rationalize your mistake.

正当な

1 《ビジネス上で》
〈彼の要求は正当です〉
- ☆ A His claim's legitimate.
- ◎ B His claim's justifiable [rational, valid].
- ○ C His claim's just.
- △ D His claim's legit.

2 《夫婦・友人間で》
〈彼の要求は正当です〉
- ◎ A His claim's legitimate.
- ○ B His claim's legit [valid].
- △ C His claim's just [rational].
- ▽ D His claim's justifiable.

ぜい肉

〈長生きしたければあなたはぜい肉を落とさなければならないよ〉
- ◎ A If you want to live a long life, you've got to drop your extra weight.
- ○ B If you want to live a long life, you've got to drop your extra [excess] fat.
- ○ C If you want to live a long life, you've got to drop your excess weight.
- × D If you want to live a long life, you've got to drop your excess [extra, surplus] flesh.
- × E If you want to live a long life, you've got to drop your surplus fat.

 ❖ D, E が辞典に出ているが使われていない．

政府

1 《アメリカ人がアメリカ政府をアメリカ国民に向けて話すとき》
〈政府の財政は巨額な黒字である〉
- ◎ A The Federal Government has a huge financial surplus.
- ◎ B The Government has a huge financial surplus.
- △ C Uncle Sam has a huge financial surplus.

 ❖ B は「州の政府」の意味でもよく使われている．したがって，誤解を生まない文脈でのみしか B は使えない．

2 《アメリカ人が政府を外国との関係で話すとき》
〈政府は日本の経済政策に干渉するのをやめるべきである〉
- ◎ A The American Government should stop interfering in Japan's economic policy.
- △ B Uncle Sam should stop interfering in Japan's economic policy.
- △ C Our Federal Government should stop interfering in Japan's economic policy.

 ❖ アメリカ以外の国の政府に言及するときは，The British Government（イギリス政府），The French Government（フランス政府），The Japanese Government（日本政府）のように言う．

生物

〈火星に生物はいるのですか〉
- ☆ A Is there life on Mars?
- ◎ B Are there any living things on Mars?
- △ C Are there any creatures [organisms] on Mars?

製粉工場 →工場 4
製薬会社 →会社 22
成立する
 1 《取引》
 a ）売り主・買い主が普通に述べるとき
 〈私はこの取引は成立すると思う〉
  ◎ A I think this deal will be closed [finished].
  ◎ B I think this deal will go through.
  ◎ C I think this deal will be wrapped up.
  ◎ D I think this will be a done deal.
  △ E I think this deal will be done [concluded].
   ❖ C は最終の段階を念頭において述べる響きがある．
 b ）売り主・買い主が強く望んでいる気持ちを述べるとき
 〈私はこの取引は成功すると思う〉
  ◎   I think this deal will come through.
 2 《内閣》
 〈小泉政権は成立するでしょう〉
  ☆ A The Koizumi Cabinet'll be put together.
  ◎ B The Koizumi Cabinet'll be organized.
  ○ C The Koizumi Cabinet'll be formed.
  ▽ D The Koizumi Cabinet'll come into being [existence].
 3 《条約》
 〈日米間で条約が成立した〉
  ☆ A The treaty was put in place between America and Japan.
  ◎ B The treaty was agreed on [signed] between America and Japan.
  ○ C The treaty was enacted [concluded] between America and Japan.
セールストーク
〈あなたはセールストークを磨かなければならないね〉
  ◎ A You have to improve your sales pitch.
  × B You have to improve your sales talk.
   ❖ B は辞典に出ているが使われていない．
世界で
〈東京は世界で最大の都市です〉
  ◎ A Tokyo's the world's largest city.
  ◎ B Tokyo's the largest city in the world.
世界の
〈世界経済は当分停滞するはずです〉
  ◎   The world-wide [world, global] economy should be sluggish for a while.
背が低い
 1 《単に身長が低いと述べるとき》
 〈彼は背が低いんです〉
  ◎ A He's a short man.
  ◎ B He's short.
 2 《背が低くてやせていると述べるとき》
 〈彼は背が低くてやせています〉
  ◎ A He's a small man.
  ◎ B He's small.
責任を転嫁する →負わせる 1

セックスアピール
1 《「ある」と述べる場合》
a) くだけた会話で
〈彼はセックスアピールがあります〉
- ◎ A He turns me on.
- ◎ B He's hot.
- ◎ C He's sexy to me.
- △ D He's hot stuff to me.
- × E He's hot to me.

b) かしこまって述べるとき
〈彼はセックスアピールがあります〉
- ◎ A He's physically [sexually] attractive to me.
- ◎ B I'm physically [sexually] attracted to him.
- ○ C He appeals to me physically [sexually].

❖友人同士の会話でも A, B, C が時々使われることがある.

2 《「ない」と述べる場合》
a) くだけた会話で
〈彼はセックスアピールがありません〉
- ◎ A He turns me off.
- ◎ B He doesn't turn me on.
- ○ C He isn't sexy.
- × D He isn't hot.

b) かしこまって述べるとき
〈私にとって彼はセックスアピールがありません〉
- ◎ A He isn't physically [sexually] attractive to me.
- ◎ B I'm not physically [sexually] attracted to him.
- ○ C He doesn't appeal to me physically [sexually].
- ○ D He doesn't have sexual appeal to me.

❖友人同士の会話でも A～D が時々使われることがある.

設計事務所
1 《設計士が1人のとき》
〈私は設計事務所に勤めています〉
- ◎ A I work for an architect.
- △ B I work at an architect's office.

2 《設計士が多いとき》
〈私は設計事務所に勤めています〉
- ◎ A I work for an architectural firm.
- ◎ B I work for an architect.
- △ C I work for an architectural company [office].

説得する
1 《人に…するように説得する》
〈私は彼に店を手放すように説得しました〉
- ◎ A I persuaded him to sell [into selling] the store.
- ◎ B I convinced him to sell [into selling] the store.
- ◎ C I talked him into selling the store.
- ▽ D I prevailed on him to sell [into selling] the store.
- × E I worked on [talked to] him to selling the store.

❖(1) persuade は「説得する」, convince は「納得させる」と辞典に出ているが, 同意語として使われている.

❖(2) D は堅い文章英語ではよく使われている．
2 《人に…しないように説得する》
〈私は彼に店を手放さないように説得しました〉
  ◎ A I persuaded [convinced] him not to sell the store.
  ◎ B I talked him out of selling the store.
  × C I dissuaded him from [out of] selling the store.
  ❖ C が辞典に出ているが使われていない．
3 《説得して手を引かせるとき》
〈私は彼を説得して取引から手を引かせました〉
  ◎ A I talked him out of the deal.
  ○ B I persuaded [convinced] him out of the deal.
  × C I dissuaded him out of the deal.
4 《説得している進行状態》
〈私たちは彼女たちを説得しようとしています〉
  ◎ A We're trying to persuade [convince] them.
  ◎ B We're working on them.
  × C We're trying to work on them.

説明書
〈消火器を使う前に必ず説明書を読みなさい〉
  ◎ A Be sure to read the instructions [directions] before you use the fire extinguisher.
  ◎ B Be sure to read the instruction booklet [book] before you use the fire extinguisher.
  ❖ A は貼りつけてある紙，B は小冊子を指す．

説明する
1 《一般的なこと》
〈あのお客をどうして失ったのか，説明しなければならない〉
  ◎ A You have to explain why you lost that client.
  × B You have to account for why you lost that client.
2 《金銭的なこと》
〈あなたは使ったお金を全部説明しなければならない〉
  ◎ A You have to account for every penny you spent.
  ○ B You have to provide a record for every penny you spent.
  △ C You have to explain every penny you spent.
3 《詳しく》
a) 専門分野
・予備知識がある人に対して
〈彼は金融市場について私に詳しく説明してくれました〉
  ◎ A He elaborated to me on the money markets.
  ○ B He expanded to me on the money markets.
  △ C He elaborated [expanded] on the money markets to me.
・予備知識がない人に対して
〈彼は金融市場について私に詳しく説明してくれました〉
  ☆ A He told me all about the money markets.
  ☆ B He explained all about the money markets to me.
  ◎ C He explained the money markets to me in detail.
  ○ D He explained the money markets to me at length.
  ○ E He spelled out all the details to me on the money markets.
  ❖ A〜E いずれも金融市場に対する知識がある人にも使える．

b) 非専門分野
・予備知識がある人に対して
〈あなたの計画を詳しく説明してくれますか〉
- ◎ A Will you elaborate [expand] on your plan to me?
- △ B Will you elaborate [expand] to me on your plan?

・予備知識がない人に対して
〈あなたの計画を詳しく説明してくれますか〉
- ◎ A Will you explain your plan to me in detail?
- ◎ B Will you tell [talk to] me your plan in detail?
- ○ C Will you detail your plan to me?
- ○ D Will you explain your plan to me at length?
- △ E Will you spell out your plan to me?

設立する
〈いつこの会社は設立されたのですか〉
- ◎ A When was this company started [established, founded]?
- ○ B When was this company set up [formed]?
- ○ C When did this company start [form]?
  - ❖(1) start と form は大きな会社(ただし巨大企業を除く),小さい会社の両方に使われている.
  - ❖(2) set up は小さい会社にしか使われていない.
  - ❖(3) establish と found は小さい会社にも使われているが,主として大会社に使われている.

瀬戸物屋　→店 28

責める
1 《証拠があるとき》
〈あなたは契約を破ったことで彼を責めるべきです〉
- ☆ A You should accuse him of breaking the contract.
- ◎ B You should point the finger at him for breaking the contract.
- ◎ C You should hold him responsible for breaking the contract.
- ○ D You should hold him accountable for breaking the contract.
- △ E You should stick breaking the contract on him.
  - ❖ E は教育レベルの低い人の間での方がよく使われている.

2 《証拠がないとき》
〈あなたは彼が契約を破ったことで彼を責めるべきです〉
- ◎ A You should blame him for breaking the contract.
- × B You should charge him for breaking the contract.

3 《理由を述べないとき》
〈あなたは私を責めているように聞こえます〉
- ◎ A You sound like you're accusing [blaming] me.
- △ B You sound like you're taking me to task.
- △ C You sound like you're calling me to account.

世話する
1 《店のお客》
〈あのお客は,お世話するのが大変です〉
- ◎ That customer's tough to wait on [take care of, help].

2 《病気の成人》
〈私は病気の父親の世話をしなければならないんです〉
- ◎ A I have to take care of my sick father.
- ○ B I have to look after [care for] my sick father.

△　C　I have to watch [attend to] my sick father.
　　　×　D　I have to see after my sick father.
　3　《子供》
　〈私には世話をする子供が5人いるんです〉
　　　◎　A　I have five children to take care of [watch].
　　　○　B　I have five children to look after [care for].
　　　×　C　I have five children to see after.

栓
　1　《栓をする》
　a）浴槽・台所の流し
　〈浴槽に栓をして下さい〉
　　　☆　A　Plug the bathtub.
　　　◎　B　Put the plug in the bathtub.
　　　○　C　Put the stopper in the bathtub.
　　　△　D　Stopper the bathtub.
　b）ビン
　〈ビンに栓をしてください〉
　　　☆　A　Cork the bottle.
　　　◎　B　Put the cork in the bottle.
　2　《栓をはずす》
　a）浴槽
　〈浴槽の栓をはずして下さい〉
　　　◎　　Unplug [Drain] the bathtub.
　b）ビン
　〈ビンの栓をはずして下さい〉
　　　◎　　Uncork the bottle.

繊維会社　→会社 23
繊維工場　→工場 6
善意で
　〈彼には悪気はなかったんです．彼は善意でそれを言ったんです〉
　　　◎　A　He didn't mean any harm. He said it in good faith.
　　　◎　B　He didn't mean any harm. He said it with good intentions.
　　　○　C　He didn't mean any harm. He said it with good intent.

前言を取り消す
　1　《重大な内容のとき》
　〈私は彼に前言を取り消させるつもりです〉
　　　◎　A　I'm going to make him eat his words.
　　　○　B　I'm going to make him eat his own words.
　　　×　C　I'm going to make him take his words back.
　　❖　Cが辞典に出ているが使われていない．
　2　《重大な内容でないとき》
　〈私は前言を取り消します〉
　　　◎　　I'll take back what I said.

専攻する
　1　《学士号》
　〈あなたは何を専攻しているのですか〉
　　　◎　A　What's your major?
　　　◎　B　What're you majoring in?
　2　《修士号・博士号》

〈あなたは何を専攻しているのですか〉
- ◎ A What're you studying?
- ◎ B What kind of research are you doing?
- ❖ major は学士号に限られていることに注意.

全焼する
〈お寺は全焼したんです〉
- ◎ A The temple burned down.
- ◎ B The temple burned to the ground.
- ◎ C The temple was destroyed by the fire.
- ◎ D The temple was entirely [totally, completely] destroyed by the fire.
- ◎ E The temple was burned down.
- ◎ F The temple was burned down to the ground.
- ◎ G The temple was burned to the ground.
- × H The temple was razed to the ground.
  - ❖ E, F, G は「放火で全焼した」というニュアンスが強い.

専心する →集中する 3

先生 →いい先生

全盛時代
1 《「全盛時代には」と述べるとき》
〈彼女は全盛時代には非常に人気のある歌手でした〉
- ◎ A She was a very popular singer in her day.
- ◎ B She was a very popular singer in her prime.
- ◎ C She was a very popular singer in her time.
- △ D She was a very popular singer in her prime of life.
- △ E She was a very popular singer in her era.
- △ F She was a very popular singer in her best days.
  - ❖ E が期間は一番長い. 2番目は C. A が期間的には短い.

2 《「…としての全盛時代」と述べるとき》
〈歌手としての彼女の全盛時代は終りました〉
- ◎ A Her days as a singer are over.
- △ B Her time as a singer's over.
- △ C Her best days as a singer are over.
- ▽ D Her best time as a singer's over.
  - ❖ D が辞典に出ているがまれ. B, C も辞典に出ているが時々しか使われていない.

喘息 →病気 15

選択肢
1 《選択肢の数を述べているとき》
〈私たちには選択肢は2つしかないんです〉
- ☆ A We have only two choices.
- ◎ B We have only two options.
- ○ C We have only two alternatives.

2 《選択肢の内容を述べるとき》
〈あなたには仕事を辞めるか, うちの条件を受け入れるか, いずれかの選択肢しかないんです〉
- ◎ A You have the option [choice] of quitting your job or accepting our condition.
- △ B You have the alternative of quitting your job or accepting our condition.

先着…名
〈先着50名様に粗品を差し上げております〉
- ◎ We're offering our first fifty customers a small gift.

前任者
1 《支配人》
〈今度の支配人は前任者よりも物分かりがいいわね〉
- ☆ A The new manager's more understanding than the old one.
- ◎ B The new manager's more understanding than the one before him.
- ○ C The new manager's more understanding than the one before [the ex-one].
- △ D The new manager's more understanding than the previous [the former] one.

2 《大統領・首相など地位の高い人》
〈ブッシュ大統領は前任者より支持率が高い〉
- ☆ A President Bush has higher approval ratings than the previous one.
- ◎ B President Bush has higher approval ratings than his predecessor.
- ◎ C President Bush has higher approval ratings than the one before him.
- ○ D President Bush has higher approval ratings than the one before.
- ○ E President Bush has higher approval ratings than the former one.
- △ F President Bush has higher approval ratings than the old one.
- ▽ G President Bush has higher approval ratings than the ex-one.

専門店
〈舶来品専門店へ行きましょう〉
- ◎ A Let's go to a store that sells [has, carries] only imported items.
- ◎ B Let's go to a store that only sells [has, carries] imported items.
- ◎ C Let's go to a store that specializes in imported items.
- ▽ D Let's go to a store that deals only in imported items.
- ❖ Dはいろいろな辞典に用例として出ているが,口語英語としてはあまり使われていない.

〔そ〕

総売上高
〈総売上高は増えたのですが純利益は減りました〉
- ◎ A Our gross [total, overall] sales increased but the net profits decreased.
- ○ B Our entire sales increased but the net profits decreased.

走行距離
1 《だいぶあるとき》
〈この車はまだ走行距離がだいぶあります〉
- ☆ A This car still has a lot of miles left in it.
- ◎ B This car still has a lot of miles left on it.
- ◎ C This car still has a lot of miles in [on] it.
- ◎ D This car still has a lot of miles.
- ○ E This car still has a lot of miles to go in it.
- ○ F This car still has a lot of mileage left on [in] it.
- ○ G This car still has a lot of mileage in [on] it.

2 《あまりないとき》
〈この車は走行距離はあまりありません〉
- ☆ A This car doesn't have many miles left on it.
- ◎ B This car doesn't have many mileage left on it.
- ◎ C This car's been driven a lot.
- ○ D This car doesn't have many mileage left in it.
- ○ E This car doesn't have many miles to go.
- △ F This car doesn't have many miles left in it.
- △ G This car doesn't have many miles to go in [on] it.
- △ H This car doesn't have many mileage to go on it.

総辞職する
〈経営陣は総辞職しました〉
- ◎ A The management resigned as a group [collectively].
- ○ B The management resigned en masse [as a body].

造船会社　→会社 24

想像する
1 《動詞を従えるとき》
〈私は彼の下で働くことは想像できません〉
- ◎ A I can't imagine working for him.
- ○ B I can't picture working for him.

❖A, B とも不定詞を従えることはできない.

2 《目的語＋as＋名詞を従えるとき》
〈自分自身を俳優だと想像してみてごらんなさい〉
- ◎ 　　Just imagine [picture] yourself as an actor.

増築する
1 《依頼する会社に言及するとき》
〈XYZ 会社に家を増築してもらおう〉
- ☆ A Let's have XYZ Company build the addition onto the house.
- ◎ B Let's have XYZ Company build the addition to the house.
- ◎ C Let's have XYZ Company add onto the house.
- ○ D Let's have XYZ Company build onto the house.
- ▽ E Let's have XYZ Company expand [extend, enlarge] the house.

2 《依頼する会社に言及しないとき》
〈家を増築しよう〉
- ◎ A Let's have our house added [built] onto.
- ◎ B Let's build an addition onto our house.
- ◎ C Let's add onto our house.
- ○ D Let's build onto our house.
- ○ E Let's build an addition to our house.

増長する
〈そんなことをしたら彼の横柄さを増長するだけだろう〉
- ☆ A That'll only encourage his arrogance.
- ◎ B That'll only boost [increase] his arrogance.
- ○ C That'll only egg on [build up] his arrogance.
- △ D That'll only stimulate his arrogance.

❖D が辞典に出ているがあまり使われていない.

相当する
1 《「占める」の意味のとき》
〈観光客が使うお金は, わが国の国民所得の約 5 分の 1 に相当します〉

- ◎ The money spent by tourists represents [constitutes, amounts to, comes to] about one-fifth of our national income.

2 《「等しい」の意味のとき》
〈アメリカの国務省は日本の外務省に相当する〉
- ☆ A The State Department in America's the same as the Foreign Ministry in Japan.
- ◎ B The State Department in America's like the Foreign Ministry in Japan.
- ◎ C The State Department in America corresponds to the Foreign Ministry in Japan.
- ○ D The State Department in America's equal to the Foreign Ministry in Japan.
- ○ E The State Department's the American counterpart of the Japan's Foreign Ministry.
- △ F The State Department in America's equivalent to the Foreign Ministry in Japan.

3 《相当する語》
〈何がこの英語の表現に相当する日本語ですか〉
- ☆ A How do you say this English expression in Japanese?
- ◎ B What's the Japanese equivalent for [translation of] this English expression?
- ○ C What's the Japanese equivalent of this English expression?

贈答用に包む
〈それを贈答用に包んでくれますか〉
- ◎ Will you gift-wrap it for me?

送別会
1 《転勤または退職する人が平社員のとき》
〈私たちは今週の金曜日ビルの送別会を開く予定です〉
- ◎ A We're going to have a going-away party for Bill this Friday.
- ○ B We're going to have a good-by [send-off] party for Bill this Friday.
- ▽ C We're going to have a farewell party for Bill this Friday.
  - ❖平社員たちがかなり上の上司に盛大な送別会を開くときは，C も時々使われている．

2 《退職していく社長，転任していく大使などに盛大な送別会を開くとき》
〈5月15日，退任される駐日アメリカ大使の送別会を開きます〉
- ☆ A We're going to hold a farewell party [reception] for the American Ambassador to Japan on May 15th.
- ○ B We're going to hold a farewell party [reception] in honor of the American Ambassador to Japan on May 15th.
- △ C We're going to have a going-away party [reception] for the American Ambassador to Japan on May 15th.
  - ❖ B はマスメディアに対して言うとき非常によく使われている．

総務部 →…部 14
創立
1 《記念日》
a) 会社
〈今日はうちの会社の創立記念日です〉
- ☆ A This is our company's anniversary.
- ◎ B This is the anniversary of our company.

◎ C　This is the anniversary of our company's establishment.
　　　△ D　This is the anniversary of our company's founding.
　b) 大学
〈今日は私たちの大学の創立記念日です〉
　　　◎ A　This is our college's anniversary.
　　　◎ B　This is the anniversary of our college.
　　　○ C　This is the anniversary of our college's founding [establishment].
　2　《「創立される」と述べるとき》
〈ハーバード大学は 1636 年に創立されました〉
　　　◎ A　Harvard was founded in 1636.
　　　○ B　Harvard was established in 1636.

即答
〈私たちはあなたの即答が必要なんです〉
　　　☆ A　We need your decision immediately.
　　　◎ B　We need your immediate decision.
　　　◎ C　We need your decision quickly [right away, promptly, right now].
　　　○ D　We need your prompt decision.
　　　○ E　We need your decision instantly.

底をつく
〈この不況で多くの企業は預金が底をついています〉
　　　◎ A　This recession's drained many companies of their savings.
　　　◎ B　This recession's exhausted [depleted] their savings of many companies.
　　　△ C　This recession's emptied their savings of many companies.

素質
　1　《素質を求められる職業に言及するとき》
　a) 普通に述べるとき
〈彼はプロの歌手になる素質があります〉
　　　☆ A　He has what it takes to be a professional singer.
　　　◎ B　He has the potential [the right stuff] to be a professional singer.
　　　◎ C　He has the potential [the right stuff] to have a professional singing career.
　　　○ D　He has what it takes to have a professional singing career.
　　　△ E　He has the makings to be a professional singer.
　　　△ F　He has the makings to have a professional singing career.
　　　△ G　He has the makings of a professional singer in him.
　　　△ H　He has it in him to be a professional singer.
　b) 強調して述べるとき
〈彼はプロの歌手になる素質がすごくあります〉
　　　☆ A　He really has what it takes to be a professional singer.
　　　◎ B　He really has the right stuff [the potential] to be a professional singer.
　　　○ C　He has a lot of stuff to be a professional singer.
　　　○ D　He really has what it takes to have a professional singer.
　　　○ E　He really has the right stuff [the potential] to have a professional singing career.
　　　○ F　He has a lot of stuff to have a professional singing career.
　2　《戦力になる期待を見せているとき》
〈その新入社員は素質がある〉

- ◎ A The new employee shows a lot of promise [potential].
- ◎ B The new employee looks promising.
- × C The new employee looks hopeful.
  - ❖ C が辞典に出ているが使われていない.

卒業式

1 《大学生に尋ねる》
〈卒業式はいつですか〉
- ◎ A When's your [the] graduation?
- ◎ B When's graduation?
- ◎ C When's the graduation ceremony?
- ◎ D When's your graduation ceremony [exercises]?
- ○ E When's the [your] commencement ceremony?
- △ F When's your commencement?
- △ G When's the commencement exercises?
- △ H When's commencement?
- × I When's your graduation exercise?
  - ❖(1) 多くの辞典にイギリスでは C を使い, アメリカでは F, G を使うという趣旨の解説が出ているが, これはアメリカ英語の慣用を歪曲している.
  - ❖(2) I が辞典に出ているが使われていない.

2 《私立の中高生に尋ねる》
〈卒業式はいつですか〉
- ◎ A When's your [the] graduation?
- ◎ B When's graduation?
- ◎ C When's the [your] graduation ceremony?
- △ D When's the [your] commencement ceremony?
- × E When's your commencement?
- × F When's the commencement exercises?
- × G When's commencement?
  - ❖ 公立の学校, 特に中学校には卒業式を行わない学校が多い.

3 《私立の小学生に尋ねる》
〈卒業式はいつですか〉
- ◎ A When's your [the] graduation?
- ◎ B When's graduation?
- ◎ C When's the [your] graduation ceremony?
- × D When's the [your] commencement ceremony?
- × E When's your commencement?
- × F When's the commencement exercises?
- × G When's commencement?
  - ❖ 公立の小学校は卒業式はやらない. 私立の小中学校もやらない学校が多い.

4 《掲示板・新聞など》
〈卒業式は10時に始まります〉
- ☆ A The commencement ceremony begins at 10:00.
- ◎ B The commencement exercises begins at 10:00.
- ○ C The commencement begins at 10:00.
- △ D The graduation ceremony begins at 10:00.
- ▽ E The graduation begins at 10:00.

卒業する[させる]

1 《学校の場合》
a) 大学

⟨彼はスタンフォード大学を卒業しました⟩
- ◎ A He graduated from Stanford University.
- ◎ B He got a degree from Stanford University.
- ○ C He got a degree at Stanford University.
- × D He was graduated from Stanford University.
- × E He finished [passed through, left] Stanford University.
  - ❖(1) D, E が辞典に出ているが使われていない．
  - ❖(2) B, C は普通，学士号を意味している．修士号なら普通 M.A., M.S., 博士号なら Ph.D. と言う．

b）高校・中学・小学校の場合

⟨彼は XYZ 高校を卒業しました⟩
- ◎ A He graduated from XYZ High School.
- × B He left [finished] XYZ High School.
  - ❖(1) 辞典に B が出ているが使われていない．
  - ❖(2) イギリスでは A の graduate は大学にのみ使われている．大学以外では leave, finish が使われている．

2 《比喩的に述べる場合》

a）卒業している状態

⟨彼はもうマリファナを卒業しました⟩
- ◎ A He's already outgrown smoking pot.
- ○ B He's all through with smoking pot.

b）未来の卒業

⟨私たちは息子にマリファナを卒業してもらいたいんです⟩
- ◎ A We want our son to stop [quit] smoking pot.
- ○ B We want our son to outgrow [grow out of, be all through] smoking pot.

3 《「卒業させる」と述べる場合》

⟨私は息子に大学を卒業させたいんです⟩
- ☆ A I want to put my son through college.
- ◎ B I want to pay for [finance] my son's college education.
- △ C I want to pay my son's way through college.

即効薬

⟨日本のデフレに即効薬はありません⟩
- ◎ A There's no quick fix to Japan's deflation.
- ◎ B There's no quick [easy] solution to Japan's deflation.
- ○ C There's no fast solution to Japan's deflation.
- ○ D There's no quick cure to Japan's deflation.
- △ E There's no fast [easy] fix to Japan's deflation.
- × F There's no quick medicine [drug] to Japan's deflation.

率先してやる

⟨あなたは率先してやらなければならない⟩
- ◎ You have to take the initiative [take the first step, make the first move].

率直に

1 《「率直に言って」》

⟨率直に言って彼はペテン師です⟩
- ☆ A Honestly speaking, he's a crook.
- ☆ B To be honest [frank] with you, he's a crook.
- ◎ C To be candid [up front] with you, he's a crook.

- ○ D To call a spade a spade, he's a crook.
- × E To be plain with you, he's a crook.
  - ❖ E は辞典に出ているが使われていない.
2 《「率直に話す」》
〈お互い率直に話しましょう〉
- ☆ A Let's be straight with each other.
- ◎ B Let's be open and honest with each other.
- ◎ C Let's level with each other.
- ○ D Let's be direct with each other.
- △ E Let's be straight forward with each other.

その上

1 《強調する必要がある内容のとき》
〈私は金曜日までにこの支払いをしなければならないんです. その上月末までにもう 10 の支払いがあるんです〉
- ☆ A I have to pay this bill by Friday. On top of that I have ten more bills to pay by the end of this month.
- ◎ B I have to pay this bill by Friday. Besides that I have ten more bills to pay by the end of this month.
- ◎ C I have to pay this bill by Friday. Besides I have ten more bills to pay by the end of this month.
- ◎ D I have to pay this bill by Friday. I also [Also I] have ten more bills to pay by the end of this month.
- ○ E I have to pay this bill by Friday. In addition (to that) I have ten more bills to pay by the end of this month.
- × F I have to pay this bill by Friday. What's more [Furthermore, Moreover] I have ten more bills to pay by the end of this month.
  - ❖(1) 残りの支払いが 10 でなく 2, 3 であれば A, B, C いずれも等しく非常によく使われている.
  - ❖(2) B の方が C より強調した表現となる.

2 《特に強調する必要がない内容のとき》
〈彼らは原宿の大きなお屋敷に住んでいます. その上箱根に美しい別荘を持っています〉
- ☆ A They lived in a big mansion in Harajuku and also they [they also] have a beautiful vacation home in Hakone.
- ○ B They lived in a big mansion in Harajuku and on top of [in addition to] that they have a beautiful vacation home in Hakone.
- ○ C They lived in a big mansion in Harajuku and besides that they have a beautiful vacation home in Hakone.
- ○ D They lived in a big mansion in Harajuku and besides they have a beautiful vacation home in Hakone.
- ○ E They lived in a big mansion in Harajuku and they have a beautiful vacation home in Hakone as well [on top of that].
- △ F They lived in a big mansion in Harajuku and in addition [what's more] they have a beautiful vacation home in Hakone.
- △ G They lived in a big mansion in Harajuku and furthermore [moreover] they have a beautiful vacation home in Hakone.
- △ H They lived in a big mansion in Harajuku and they have a beautiful vacation home in Hakone to boot.

3 《堅い内容のとき》

⟨リポーター：どのように空港の安全を強化するのですか⟩
Reporter: How're you going to increase security at the airports?
⟨報道官：空港中に警備員を配備させます．その上警備員に，手当たり次第に取調べる権限を持たせます⟩
Press Secretary:
- ☆ A We'll have more guards placed throughout the airports. Furthermore [Moreover] the guards'll have the authority to conduct random searches.
- ◎ B We'll have more guards placed throughout the airports. Also the guards'll [The guards'll also] have the authority to conduct random searches.
- ◎ C We'll have more guards placed throughout the airports. In addition (to that) the guards'll have the authority to conduct random searches.
- ○ D We'll have more guards placed throughout the airports. Beside that the guards'll have the authority to conduct random searches.
- ○ E We'll have more guards placed throughout the airports. Besides the guards'll have the authority to conduct random searches.
- ○ F We'll have more guards placed throughout the airports. What's more the guards'll have the authority to conduct random searches.

その気になれば

⟨教師：明日までにこれらの文章を全部暗記しなさい⟩
Teacher: Memorize all these sentences by tomorrow.
⟨学生：できないと思います⟩
Student: I don't think I can.
⟨教師：いや，できるよ．その気になれば，何でもできるよ⟩
Teacher:
- ◎ Yes, you can. If you put your mind to it, you can do anything.
  ❖主語が複数になれば minds となる．If we put our minds to it, there's nothing we can't do.（私たちがその気になれば，やれないものはない）．

その頃は

1 《かなり昔のことに言及しているとき》
⟨私の祖父母がアメリカへ来たとき，まだその頃はユダヤ人は見下され虐待されていたので，大変苦労したんです⟩
- ◎ When my grandparents came to America, they had a hard time because Jewish people were still looked down upon and mistreated in those days [back then, at that time, then].
  ❖いずれも非常によく使われているが，ニュアンスが多少異なる．in those days はその時代の広がりを心に描いた場合，back then はその時代を振り返ってなつかしい気持ちがあるとき，at that time はその時代をひとまとめに考えたとき，then は in those days と at that time の中間的ニュアンスのある一般的な語である．したがって，どれを一番よく使うかは，その人が何を心に描いているかによる．

2 《年数が明示されるとき》
⟨青木さん：1975 年に日本に来たのですね⟩
Mr. Aoki: You came to Japan in 1975, didn't you?
⟨スミスさん：そうです⟩
Mr. Smith: That's right.
⟨青木さん：その頃は日本はどうでしたか⟩

Mr. Aoki:
- ◎ What was Japan like at that time [then]?

3 《年数が明示されていないとき》

〈吉田さん:卒業後は何をしたのですか〉

Mr. Yoshida: What did you do after you graduated?

〈大川さん:その頃は仕事がほとんどなかったので,すぐ大学院へ行きました〉

Mr. Ookawa:
- ◎ A At that [the] time jobs were pretty scarce, so I decided to go to grad school right away.
- ◎ B Jobs were pretty scarce then, so I decided to go to grad school right away.

そのために…がここにいるのです

〈留学生:いろいろご面倒かけてすみません〉

Foreign Student: I'm afraid I'm being too much trouble.

〈留学生カウンセラー:少しもそんなことはありませんよ.そのために私がここにいるんですから〉

Foreign Student advisor:
- ◎ Of course you're not. That's what I'm here for.
  - ❖この表現はいつもIとhereとは限らない.That's what he's there for.(そのために彼がそこにいるんです)のように,そのときの意味により変えることができる.I suggest that you go to CPA's office. That's what he's there for.(会計事務所へ行くことを勧めます.会計士はそのためにいるのですから).

その調子 →調子 10

その日暮らしをする

〈彼らはその日暮らしをしています〉
- ☆ A They're living paycheck to paycheck.
- ○ B They're living day to day [hand to mouth].
- △ C They're living from paycheck to paycheck [day to day, hand to mouth].

その日しか空いていない

1 《ビジネスでの話》

〈依頼人:明日お会いできますか〉

Client: Can we get together tomorrow?

〈弁護士:いや駄目なんだ.あさってはどう〉

Lawyer: No, I can't. How about the day after tomorrow?

〈依頼人:今週はその日しか空いていないんです〉

Client:
- ◎ A That's all I have open [available] this week.
- ◎ B That's my only free [available] day this week.

2 《友人との話で》

〈今週はその日しか空いていないんです〉
- ◎ A That's my only free [available] day this week.
- × B That's all I have open [available] this week.

そのまま

1 《単数の無生物》

〈これはそのままで食べられます〉
- ◎ A You can eat this as it is.
- ◎ B You can eat this as is.

2 《複数の無生物》
〈これらはそのままで食べられます〉
- ☆ A You can eat these as they are.
- ◎ B You can eat these as is.
- × C You can eat these as are.

3 《単数の人間》
〈私をありのままで受け入れて下さい〉
- ◎ A Please take me as I am.
- △ B Please take me as is.

4 《複数の人間》
〈あなたは義理の両親をそのまま受け入れた方がいいですよ〉
- ◎ A You'd better accept your in-law as they are.
- ○ B You'd better accept your in-law as is.
- ▽ C You'd better accept your in-laws as are.

そばに

1 《非常に隣接しているとき》
〈彼は湖のそばに別荘を持っています〉
- ☆ A He has a vacation home on the lake.
- ◎ B His vacation home's on the lake.
- △ C He has a vacation home bordering the lake.
- △ D His vacation home's bordering the lake.

2 《近いが隣接していないとき》
〈彼は湖のそばに別荘を持っています〉
- ☆ A He has a vacation home by the lake.
- ◎ B His vacation home's by [beside] the lake.
- ◎ C He has a vacation home beside [at] the lake.
- ◎ D He has a lakeside vacation home.
- ○ E His vacation home's at the lake [lakeside].
- △ F He has a lakefront vacation home.

3 《かなり隣接しているが少し距離があるときにも使える》
〈彼は湖のそばに別荘を持っています〉
- ◎ A He has a vacation home at the lake.
- ◎ B He has a lakeside vacation home.
- ○ C His vacation home's at the lake [lakeside].
- △ D He has a lakefront vacation home.

そばを通る

1 《車のとき》
〈私は毎日市役所のそばを通ります〉
- ◎ I drive by the City Hall every day.

2 《徒歩のとき》
〈私は毎日市役所のそばを通ります〉
- ◎ I walk by the City Hall every day.

3 《車か徒歩か不明のとき》
〈私は毎日市役所のそばを通ります〉
- ◎ A I go by the City Hall every day.
- ○ B I pass (by) the City Hall every day.

染める

1 《一般的に述べるとき》
a) 自分で染める場合

〈私は髪を染めようと思っているんです〉
　　◎　I'm thinking of coloring [dyeing] my hair.
 b) 美容院・床屋で染める場合
〈私は髪の毛を染めてもらおうと思っているんです〉
　　◎　A I'm thinking of having my hair colored [dyed].
　　◎　B I'm thinking of coloring [dyeing] my hair.
 2 《染める色を述べるとき》
 a) 一般的に
〈私は髪の毛を黒く染めようと思っているんだ〉
　　◎　I'm thinking of coloring [dyeing] my hair black.
 b) 暗い色からうすい色に染めると言うとき
〈私は髪の毛を染めてもらおうと思っているんだ〉
　　◎　A I'm thinking of lightening [bleaching] my hair.
　　◎　B I'm thinking of having my hair lightened [bleached].
　　❖(1) bleach のほうが lighten よりずっとうすい色に染めることを言う．
　　❖(2) A は自分で染めるときと，美容院で染めるときの両方に使われている．
 3 《髪の毛の一部を染めるとき》
〈この辺を染めようと思っているんだ〉
　　◎　A I'm thinking of tinting this part on my hair.
　　×　B I'm thinking of rinsing this part on my hair.
　　❖B が辞典に出ているが使われていない．
 4 《染めてある状態を述べるとき》
〈私の髪は染めてあるんです〉
　　◎　My hair's dyed [colored].
 5 《毛染め剤》
〈この毛染め剤はとても安いわ〉
　　◎　A This hair color's very cheap.
　　○　B This hairdye's very cheap.

それ以後
〈うちはそれ以後 XYZ 会社と取引をやめました〉
　　☆　A We stopped doing business with XYZ Company from then on.
　　◎　B We stopped doing business with XYZ Company from that time on.
　　○　C We stopped doing business with XYZ Company from that point.
　　△　D We stopped doing business with XYZ Company from then on in.

それ自体
 1 《主語を修飾しているとき》
〈働くことはそれ自体が社会への貢献です〉
　　◎　A Working in itself's a contribution to society.
　　○　B Working per se's a contribution to society.
　　○　C Working alone's a contribution to society.
　　×　D Working as such's a contribution to society.
 2 《単数の目的語を修飾しているとき》
〈私はあなたの提案それ自体に反対していません〉
　　◎　A I'm not against your proposal in itself.
　　○　B I'm not against your proposal per se.
　　○　C I'm not against your proposal as such.
 3 《複数の目的語を修飾しているとき》
〈私はあなたの提案それ自体に反対していません〉
　　◎　A I'm not against your proposals in themselves.

- ○ B I'm not against your proposals per se.
- △ C I'm not against your proposals as such.

損益

〈損益は3千万円の黒字でした〉
- ☆ A The bottom line was ¥30,000,000 in the black.
- ◎ B The final figure [tally] was ¥30,000,000 in the black.
- ○ C The net balance was ¥30,000,000 in the black.

〔た〕

退院する
〈私は来週の月曜日に退院します〉
- ◎ I'm going to leave [get out of, be released from] the hospital next Monday.
- ❖「入院する」の項も参照のこと．

大学
1 《大学名に言及しないとき》
〈私は大学生です〉
- ◎ A I'm a college student.
- △ B I'm a university student.
  - ❖(1) 大学名に言及しないときは，正式名が Harvard University のように university を使っていても，college と言う方がずっと多い．
  - ❖(2) 大学名に言及するときは，大学院を持つ大学の場合，大学により，... University, ...College の両方が使われている．I graduated from Harvard University. (私はハーバード大学を卒業しました)/I graduated from The College of William and Mary. (私はウイリアム・メアリー大学を卒業しました)
  - ❖(3) 大学院を持たない大学の場合，I graduated from Mount Union College. (私はマウントユニオン大学を卒業しました) のようになる．
  - ❖(4) 総合大学には university，単科大学には college を使うという解説は事実を歪曲している．

2 《「大学で」と述べるとき》
〈ところで彼女は大学で教えているのですか〉
- ☆ A By the way does she teach at a college?
- ◎ B By the way does she teach at a university?
- ○ C By the way does she teach in a college [university]?
- × D By the way does she teach at college [university]?

3 《「大学へ」と述べるとき》
〈リンダ：息子さんは夏は何をしているのですか〉
Linda: What does your son do in the summertime?
〈メアリー：大学へ行っています〉
Mary:
- ◎ A He goes to college.
- ○ B He goes to a college.
- △ C He goes to the [a] university.
- × D He goes to university.

4 《「大学卒」を言うとき》
〈彼は大卒です〉
- ◎ A He has a degree.
- ○ B He's a college graduate.

退学する
1 《学生の意思で「退学する」と述べるとき》
〈彼は退学したんです〉
- ◎ A He dropped out of school.

- ○ B He quit [left] school.
- × C He withdrew from school.
    - ❖辞典にCが出ているが使われていない．

2 《学生側が「学校が退学させた」と述べるとき》

〈学校は彼を退学させたんです〉
- ◎ A The school kicked [threw] him out.
- ○ B The school expelled him.
- ○ C The school tossed him out.
- ○ D The school made him leave [quit].
- △ E The school forced him out.

3 《学校側が「退学させた」と述べるとき》

〈学校は彼を退学させたんです〉
- ☆ A The school kicked [threw] him out.
- ◎ B The school expelled him.
- ○ C The school dismissed him.
- ○ D The school tossed him out.
- ○ E The school made him leave [quit].
- △ F The school forced him out.

4 《退学させた理由を述べるとき》

〈学校は彼をマリファナを吸ったことで退学させるでしょう〉
- ◎ A The school'll kick [threw] him out for smoking pot.
- ○ B The school'll expel him for smoking pot.
- ○ C The school'll toss him out for smoking pot.
- ○ D The school'll make him leave [quit] for smoking pot.
- ○ E He'll have to leave school for smoking pot.
- △ F He'll have to quit school for smoking pot.
- △ G The school'll force him out for smoking pot.
- × H The school'll make him drop out for smoking pot.
    - ❖A～Gまで，because he smoked pot, because of smoking potもよく使われている．しかし，on account of, due to, owing toは堅い表現なので，会話ではあまり使われていない．

大学生 →…学生 1

大金

〈この家を建てるのに大金がかかりました〉
- ◎ A It cost me a (small) fortune to build this house.
- ◎ B It cost me an arm and a leg to build this house.
- ◎ C It cost me a great deal of money to build this house.

退屈な

〈この仕事は退屈です〉
- ☆ A This job's boring.
- ○ B This job's tedious [dull, monotonous].
- ▽ C This job's wearing [tiresome, irksome].
    - ❖Cが辞典に出ているが使われてもまれ．

対決

〈会社側はスト中の社員と対決を強行した〉
- ◎ A The company forced a confrontation with the strikers.
- △ B The company forced a showdown [a face-off] with the strikers.
    - ❖対決の度合いはAのほうが一番強い．

対決する
〈あなたは証拠をつきつけて彼と対決すべきです〉
- ◎ A You should confront him with the evidence.
- ○ B You should face him with the evidence.

大賛成　→賛成する　3

大事にする

1　《異性間での愛情》
〈私と結婚してくれたらあなたを大事にしますよ〉
- ☆ A If you marry me, I'll take good care of you.
- ◎ B If you marry me, I'll be really good to you.
- ○ C If you marry me, I'll pamper you.
- ○ D If you marry me, I'll treat you well.
- ○ E If you marry me, I'll treat you like a queen.
- △ F If you marry me, I'll treat you like a princess.

　❖ A〜D は男女を問わず使われている．女性が男性に述べるときは E は...like a king., F は...like a prince.を使う．しかし，使用頻度はいずれも△．

2　《目などを酷使しないようにと述べるとき》
〈コンピュータの仕事をやめて目を大事にしたほうがいいですよ〉
- ◎ A You'd better stop working on the computer and give your eyes a break.
- ◎ B You'd better stop working on the computer and not use your eyes too much.
- ○ C You'd better stop working on the computer and not overuse your eyes too much.

3　《身体の健康》
〈お身体を大事にして下さい〉
- ◎ A Take care of yourself, please.
- ○ B Take good care of yourself, please.
- × C Be careful of yourself, please.

退社する
〈彼女は何時に退社しましたか〉
- ◎ A What time did she leave work?
- ◎ B What time did she leave the office?
- △ C What time did she leave her work?

　❖ B は事務職にしか使えないが，A, C はデパート，工場，事務所など職種を問わず広く使われている．

大衆向き

1　《デパート》
〈J.C.ペニーは大衆向きです〉
- ☆ A J. C. Penney's for the average shopper [person].
- ◎ B J. C. Penney's for the general public.
- ◎ C J. C. Penney's for the man on the street.
- ◎ D J. C. Penney's for working people.
- ◎ E J. C. Penney's for the working class.
- ◎ F J. C. Penney's for the working guy.
- ◎ G J. C. Penney's for the average guy [man].
- ◎ H J. C. Penney's for the blue-collar worker.
- ◎ I J. C. Penney's for blue-collar workers.
- ○ J J. C. Penney's for the people at large.

- △ K J. C. Penney's for the ordinary people.
- × L J. C. Penney's for the masses.
- × M J. C. Penney's for everybody.
  - ❖(1) L が辞典に出ているが使われていない．L はアメリカ人には「共産主義の人たち」を連想させる．
  - ❖(2) M は金持ちの人たちも入ってしまうので使われていない．
  - ❖(3) C, F, G は女性も含めて述べている．これもアメリカが男性社会であることを裏書きしている好例．
  - ❖(4) 事務所で働いている OL も D, E, H に含まれる．

2 《新聞・雑誌》

〈この新聞は大衆向きです〉
- ☆ A This paper's for the average reader [person].
- ◎ B This paper's for the general public.
- ◎ C This paper's for the man on the street.
- ◎ D This paper's for the working class.
- ◎ E This paper's for working people.
- ◎ F This paper's for the working guy.
- ◎ G This paper's for the people on the street.
- ◎ H This paper's for blue-collar workers.
- ◎ I This paper's for the blue-collar worker.
- △ J This paper's for ordinary people.
- △ K This paper's for the people at large.
- △ L This paper's for the masses.

体重を減らす

1 《一般的に述べるとき》

〈私は体重を減らそうとしているんです〉
- ◎ A I'm trying to lose weight.
- ◎ B I'm trying to slim down.
- ◎ C I'm trying to take some of the weight off.
- △ D I'm trying to take off weight.
- ▽ E I'm trying to reduce [decrease] my weight.
- × F I'm trying to be on a diet.
  - ❖(1) F が辞典に出ているが使われていない．
  - ❖(2) C は「最近太った」というニュアンスがある．
  - ❖(3) A, D の weight の前に所有格を使うことはできないが，E は所有格＋weight で使われる．
  - ❖(4) F の I'm on a diet. は「規定食を食べています」という意味．つまり，脂肪，糖分，塩分の少ない料理を食べるということで，「体重を減らす」という意味は全くない．

2 《下腹部のぜい肉を頭に浮べて述べるとき》

a) 男性

〈私は体重を減らそうとしています〉
- ○ A I'm trying to get rid of my love handles.
- ○ B I'm trying to get rid of my beer [pot] belly.
- ○ C I'm trying to get rid of my belly.
- ○ D I'm trying to get rid of my spare tire.
- ○ E I'm trying to get rid of my love handle.
- △ F I'm trying to get rid of my roll.
- ▽ G I'm trying to get rid of my paunch.

❖ G が辞典に出ているが使われてもまれ．

b）女性

〈私は体重を減らそうとしています〉

- ○ A I'm trying to get rid of my love handles.
- △ B I'm trying to get rid of my belly.
- △ C I'm trying to get rid of my roll.
- △ D I'm trying to get rid of my beer [pot] belly.

退職する

〈私たちは退職する社長の送別会を開く予定です〉

- ☆ A We're going to give a farewell party for the outgoing CEO.
- ◎ B We're going to give a farewell party for the leaving CEO.
- ○ C We're going to give a farewell party for the departing CEO.
- △ D We're going to give a farewell party for the outbound CEO.
- × E We're going to give a farewell party for the taking-off CEO.

❖(1) E が辞典に出ているが使われていない．
❖(2) C には少し堅い響きがある．

態度

1 《職業上ふさわしいとされる振る舞いについて言う場合》

〈彼の態度は警察官にふさわしくなかった〉

- ◎ A His conduct was unbecoming for a policeman.
- ○ B His behavior was unbecoming for a policeman.

2 《職業上求められる言動・行状・品行について言う場合》

〈彼は道義に反する態度のために，弁護士協会から除名された〉

- ◎ A He was expelled from the bar association because of his unethical conduct.
- △ B He was expelled from the bar association because of his unethical behavior.

3 《一般的に言う場合》

〈彼の態度はすごくよくなった〉

- ◎ His conduct's [behavior's] improved a lot.

4 《否定的に言う場合》

〈私は彼の態度にうんざりしています〉

- ◎ A I'm disgusted at his behavior.
- △ B I'm disgusted at his conduct.

大反対 →反対する 4

だいぶ違う

1 《「望ましい状態になる」という意味のとき》

〈ジェーン：風邪が治らないのよ〉
Jane: I can't get rid of my cold.

〈リンダ：うがいをするのね．だいぶ違うわよ〉
Linda:
- ◎ A Gargle. It'll help you a lot.
- ◎ B Gargle. It'll make a big difference.

2 《「話が変わってくる」という意味のとき》

〈花子：大学を卒業したら，どんな仕事をしたいの〉
Hanako: What kind of work do you want to do after you graduate from college?

〈ポール：日本で就職するか，アメリカで就職するかによってだいぶ違ってくるよ〉
Paul:

◎ It'll make a big difference depending on whether I get a job in Japan or in the States.

逮捕する

1 《会話の場合》

〈私たちは警察ができるだけ早く犯人を逮捕することを願っています〉

☆ A We hope the police'll get [catch, arrest] the suspect as soon as possible.

○ B We hope the police'll nab [bust, nail] the suspect as soon as possible.

△ C We hope the police'll apprehend the suspect as soon as possible.

2 《新聞・ニュースの場合》

〈私たちは警察ができるだけ早く犯人を逮捕することを願っています〉

◎ A We hope the police'll arrest the suspect as soon as possible.

△ B We hope the police'll apprehend the suspect as soon as possible.

大量生産する

〈自動車はヘンリー・フォードによって初めて大量生産されました〉

◎ A The automobile was first mass-produced by Henry Ford.

○ B The automobile was first assembled in mass production by Henry Ford.

代理を務める

1 《不在者の代行でそのポストの仕事をするとき》

〈部長の不在中,誰が代理を務めるのですか〉

☆ A Who's going to act [fill in] as the General Manager while he's gone?

☆ B Who's going to stand in [fill in, substitute, sub] for the General Manager while he's gone?

◎ C Who's going to take the General Manager's place [take the place of the General Manager] while he's gone?

◎ D Who's going to cover for the General Manager while he's gone?

○ E Who's going to replace the General Manager while he's gone?

○ F Who's going to act on the General Manager's behalf while he's gone?

2 《弁護士が述べるとき》

〈私はXYZ会社の弁護士として代理を務めています〉

☆ A I represent XYZ Company.

◎ B I work for XYZ Company as a lawyer.

○ C I represent XYZ Company as a lawyer.

楕円形

1 《数学で図形を言うとき》

〈彼は黒板に楕円形を書きました〉

◎ A He drew an oval (shape) on the blackboard.

◎ B He drew an oblong shape on the blackboard.

× C He drew an oblong on the blackboard.

❖ Cが辞典に出ているが使われていない.

2 《家具などの形を言うとき》

〈私は楕円形のテーブルを買いたいんです〉

◎ I want to buy an oblong [oval] table.

倒れる

1 《人が》

a) 体力的にきつくて
〈彼は毎日働きすぎてついに倒れてしまったんです〉
- ◎ A He worked too hard every day and finally fell down.
- ○ B He worked too hard every day and finally collapsed.
- × C He worked too hard every day and finally gave way [succumbed].
- ❖ C が辞典に出ているが使われていない．

b) 精神的にきつくて
〈彼は毎日研究でとても長い時間働いて，とうとう倒れてしまったんです〉
- ☆ A He worked very long hours every day on his research and finally had a breakdown.
- ◎ B He worked very long hours every day on his research and finally broke down.
- △ C He worked very long hours every day on his research and finally cracked up.
- ❖ C が辞典に出ているが時々使われている程度．

2 《ビルが》
〈銀行の裏のビルが地震のために倒れたんです〉
- ☆ A The building behind the bank collapsed because of [was destroyed by] the earthquake.
- ◎ B The building behind the bank fell down because of the earthquake.
- ○ C The building behind the bank toppled over because of the earthquake.
- △ D The building behind the bank came down [toppled] because of the earthquake.

3 《政権が》
a) 能動態
〈フセイン政権はまもなく倒れるだろう〉
- ◎ A The Saddam Hussein regime'll collapse soon.
- ○ B The Saddam Hussein regime'll fall (apart) soon.
- △ C The Saddam Hussein regime'll crumble [come apart] soon.
- × D The Saddam Hussein regime'll fall down soon.
- ❖ D が辞典に出ているが使われていない．

b) 受動態
〈フセイン政権はまもなく倒されるでしょう〉
- ☆ A The Saddam Hussein regime'll be beaten soon.
- ◎ B The Saddam Hussein regime'll be toppled [overthrown] soon.
- × C The Saddam Hussein regime'll be pulled down soon.
- ❖ C が辞典に出ているが使われていない．

高い

1 《金額の場合》
a) 品物の価値を客観的に述べるとき
〈この車は高かった〉
- ◎ A This car was expensive.
- ◎ B This car cost a lot of money.

b) 値段を客観的に述べるとき
〈値段が高かった〉
- ◎ The price was high [expensive].

c) 品物の価値が支払った金額の価値がないと主観的に文句を述べるとき
〈この車は高かった〉

374　たかくなる

- ☆ A This car wasn't a good deal.
- ◎ B This car wasn't a good buy.
- ◎ C This car was a bad deal.
- ○ D This car was a bad buy.
- ○ E This car was a terrible [an awful] deal.
- ○ F This car was a terrible buy.
- ○ G This car wasn't a good bargain.
- △ H This car was a bad purchase.

d)「ぼられる」と言うとき

〈私はこの車を修理してもらうのにぼられました〉

- ◎ A I was ripped off when I had this car fixed.
- ◎ B I was taken advantage of when I had this car fixed.
- ○ C I was overcharged when I had this car fixed.
  - ❖「ぼられる」というニュアンスはAが一番強い．以下B，Cの順で弱くなる．

e)「法外な代金」と言うとき

〈私は車を修理してもらったとき法外な代金を支払ったんです〉

- ☆ A They ripped me off when I had my car fixed.
- ◎ B I was ripped off when I had my car fixed.
- ◎ C I paid a huge [tremendous] amount of money when I had my car fixed.
- ○ D I paid through the nose when I had my car fixed.
- ○ E I paid a (small) fortune when I had my car fixed.
- ○ F I paid a bundle when I had my car fixed.

2 《長さ・大きさの場合》

a) 建物のとき

〈これがこの町で一番高いビルです〉

- ◎ A This is the tallest building in this city.
- ○ B This is the highest building in this city.

b) 山のとき

〈世界で一番高い山はどこですか〉

- ◎ A What's the highest mountain in the world?
- ○ B What's the tallest mountain in the world?

c) 身長のとき

〈彼の身長は6フィートです〉

- ◎ A He's six feet tall.
- × B He's six feet high.
  - ❖ Bは，木に登っているなどしていて「地上から6フィートの高さの所にいる」の意味でならよく使われている．

高くなる

1 《通貨のレートを述べるとき》

〈円はまもなく高くなるでしょう〉

- ☆ A The yen'll go [come] down soon.
- ◎ B The yen'll get stronger soon.
- ○ C The yen'll fall soon.
- ○ D The yen'll drop soon.
- ○ E The yen'll get [become, be] expensive soon.
- △ F The yen'll devaluate soon.
- ▽ G The yen'll depreciate soon.

❖ 円が今より高くなるということは，対ドル交換レートは￥130から￥120，￥110と数字が下がる．このことは日本人にとっては値上がりすることを意味する．しかし，一般のアメリカ人は次の2つの理由で「値下がりする」という言い方をする．
①円の交換レートが￥120，￥110になることは数字が下がるからである．
②アメリカのドルは1971年8月15日に金と交換するというIMFの国際条約を一方的に破り，以後破約したままにしてあるにもかかわらずドルを世界基軸通貨，つまり中心通貨と考えているからである．

2 《主語に値段を示す抽象名詞があるとき》
〈石油の値段はまもなく高くなるでしょう〉
◎ A Oil prices'll be higher soon.
◎ B Oil prices'll go up [rise] soon.
◎ C Oil prices'll be up soon.
○ D Oil prices'll be more expensive soon.
○ E Oil prices'll become [get] higher soon.
○ F Oil prices'll come up soon.
  ❖(1) rent（家賃），fare（運賃），tuition（授業料），tax（税金），toll（通行料），fee（謝礼）のような値段を示す語が主語のときはいつも上記の使用頻度になる．
  ❖(2) Dは値段を示す語のときは使えないと辞典に出ているが，実際にはよく使われている．

高値で取引を終える
〈アメリカのドルは円に対して高値で取引を終えた〉
◎ A The U.S. dollar closed [ended, finished] (the day) strong against the yen.
△ B The U.S. dollar wound up (the day) strong against the yen.

だから言ったでしょ
〈邦雄：フィアットを修理するのに20万かかったんだよ〉
Kunio: It cost me ￥200,000 to have my Fiat fixed.
〈花子：だから言ったでしょ〉
Hanako:
◎ A What did I tell you?
◎ B I told you so.
○ C I told you that'd happen.
▽ D What did I say to you?

たかる
1 《たかる物を明示しないとき》
〈彼にたかるのはやめろ〉
☆ A Stop bumming off him.
◎ B Stop bumming from him.
○ C Stop mooching off [from] him.
2 《たかる物を明示するとき》
〈彼にタバコをたかるのはやめろ〉
◎ A Stop bumming cigarettes from [off] him.
○ B Stop mooching cigarettes from [off] him.

たくさん
1 《不可算名詞を修飾する場合》
a）肯定文
〈彼女はたくさんお金を稼いでいます〉

たくさん

☆ A She makes a lot of money.
◎ B She makes a good [great] deal of money.
○ C She makes a bunch of money.
× D She makes much money.

b) 疑問文
〈彼女はたくさんお金を稼いでいるのですか〉
◎ A Does she make a lot of money?
○ B Does she make much money?
○ C Does she make a good deal [a great deal, a bunch] of money?

c) 否定文
〈彼女はたくさんお金を稼いでいません〉
☆ A She doesn't make a lot of money.
◎ B She doesn't make much [a bunch of] money.
○ C She doesn't make a good [great] deal of money.
❖堅い文章英語では肯定, 疑問, 否定いずれの場合も a bunch of は使われていない.

2 《可算名詞を修飾する場合》
a) 肯定文
〈ニューヨークにはたくさん日本レストランがあります〉
☆ A There are a lot of Japanese restaurants in New York.
◎ B There are many [a bunch of] Japanese restaurants in New York.
○ C There are a large number of Japanese restaurants in New York.
▽ D There are numbers of Japanese restaurants in New York.

b) くだけた肯定文
〈彼女にはたくさんボーイフレンドがいます〉
◎ A She has a lot [bunch] of boyfriends.
○ B She has many boyfriends.
❖(1) 可算名詞の修飾に関しては, 上の2つの肯定文での区別が疑問文, 否定文にもあてはまる.
❖(2) 堅い文章英語では many, a large number of がよく使われている.

3 《to 不定詞を使って「…するものがたくさんある」と述べる場合》
〈私は今度の週末にやることがたくさんあるんです〉
☆ A I have a lot to do this weekend.
○ B I have a lot of things [stuff] to do this weekend.
○ C I have lots [a great deal] to do this weekend.

4 《「山ほど」と言うとき》
a) 可算名詞
〈私は結婚のプレゼントを山ほどもらいました〉
☆ A I got lots of wedding presents.
◎ B I got tons of wedding presents.
○ C I got loads of wedding presents.

b) 不可算名詞
〈私はやる仕事が山ほどあるんです〉
☆ A I have lots of work to do.
◎ B I have tons of work to do.
○ C I have loads of work to do.
○ D I have a (whole) slew of work to do.

5 《「うなるほど」「くさるほど」と言うとき》
〈彼はうなるほどお金を持っています〉

◎ A He's loaded.
◎ B He has tons [loads] of money.
○ C He's rolling in dough [money].
○ D He has money to burn.
△ E He's rolling in bucks.

6 《「ごまんと」と言うとき》
〈バーバラくらいのモデルはごまんといるよ〉
☆ A Models like Barbara are a dime a dozen.
◎ B There are tons of models like Barbara.
○ C There are loads of models like Barbara.
△ D There are a whole slew of models like Barbara.

タクシー運転手 →職業 19
タクシーをとめる
〈タクシーをとめて下さい〉
◎ A Flag down a taxi, please.
◎ B Flag a taxi down, please.
◎ C Hail [Grab, Get, Catch, Stop] a taxi, please.
○ D Flag a taxi, please.

打診する
1 《whether もしくは if を従えて A か B かを尋ねるとき》
〈トムに興味があるかどうか打診してくれますか〉
◎ A Will you find out if [whether] Tom's interested or not?
◎ B Will you see if [whether] Tom's interested or not?
◎ C Will you feel out if [whether] Tom's interested or not?
◎ D Will you check and see if [whether] Tom's interested or not?
◎ E Will you check [look] into whether Tom's interested or not?
○ F Will you check [ask] to see if Tom's interested or not?
△ G Will you check [look] into if Tom's interested or not?
△ H Will you feel Tom out whether [if] he's interested or not?
△ I Will you look to see if Tom's interested or not?

2 《ある社会的な問題について意見を尋ねるとき》
〈この公害について彼の意見を打診してくれますか〉
☆ A Will you find out [ask] his opinion on this pollution?
◎ B Will you check (into) his opinion on this pollution?
○ C Will you check and see [look into] his opinion on this pollution?
△ D Will you sound [feel] out his opinion on this pollution?

出す
1 《洋服の一部分をひろげて大きくする》
〈私はスーツの肩を出してもらっているんです〉
◎ A I'm having my suit altered at the shoulders.
○ B I'm having my suit let out at the shoulders.
❖ A の alter は B の let out (出して大きくする) 以外の意味 (「詰める」など) もあるので, あいまいになる.

2 《卒業生を世の中に出す》
〈中央大学は多数の弁護士を出しています〉
◎ A Chuo University's been graduating a lot of lawyers.
○ B Chuo University's been producing a lot of lawyers.
▽ C Chuo University's been sending a lot of lawyers.
❖ C が辞典に出ているがまれ.

3 《看板を出す》
〈私は店を開いたとき看板を出すつもりはありません〉
- ◎ A I'm not going to put up a sign when I open the store.
- ○ B I'm not going to hang out a sign when I open the store.
- △ C I'm not going to set up [set out, erect] a sign when I open the store.

4 《旗を出す》
〈私たちは祭日には旗を出します〉
- ◎ A We put up our flag on legal holidays.
- ○ B We fly our flag on legal holidays.
- △ C We display our flag on legal holidays.
- × D We hoist our flag on legal holidays.
  ❖ D が辞典に出ているが使われていない．

5 《舌を出す》
a) 怒ったとき
〈彼は怒るといつも舌を出す〉
- ◎ A He sticks out his tongue whenever he gets mad.
- × B He puts out his tongue whenever he gets mad.
  ❖ アメリカの子供たちは親に言われたことに対して怒ると舌を出すことが多い．

b) 医師が患者に対して言うとき
〈舌を出してください〉
- ◎ A Please stick out your tongue.
- × B Please put out your tongue.

6 《投資する》
〈うちはこのプロジェクトに 10 万ドルを出せます〉
- ◎ A We can invest $100,000 in this project.
- △ B We can make an investment of $100,000 in this project.
- × C We can advance the capital of $100,000 in this project.
  ❖ C が辞典に出ているが使われていない．

7 《一人一人がお金を出し合う》
〈入院しているビルに何か買うのに 5 ドル出すのはどうですか〉
- ☆ A How about chipping in five bucks to buy something for Bill in the hospital?
- ◎ B How about pitching [putting] in five bucks to buy something for Bill in the hospital?
- ○ C How about kicking [tossing] in five bucks to buy something for Bill in the hospital?

訪ねる

1 《初めて訪ねるので道順を知らないとき》
〈東京に来たらどうぞ訪ねてください〉
- ☆ Please look us up when you come to Tokyo.

2 《道順を知っているとき》
〈近所に来たら訪ねて下さい〉
- ◎ A Please come around [stop by] when you're in the neighborhood.
- ◎ B Please visit (us) when you're in the neighborhood.
- ▽ C Please call on us when you're in the neighborhood.

3 《親しい間柄のとき》
〈私たちはおじさんを訪ねるためにニューヨークへ行くところなんです〉
- ◎ A We're going to New York to visit [see] my uncle.

▽ B We're going to New York to call on my uncle.
❖ B は辞典に出ているがまれ．

4 《かしこまった間柄のとき》
〈新任のアメリカ大使が首相を訪ねました〉
◎ A The newly-appointed American Ambassador called on the Prime Minister.
◎ B The newly-appointed American Ambassador paid a visit to the Prime Minister.
○ C The newly-appointed American Ambassador visited the Prime Minister.

戦う
1 《戦争で》
a)「…と戦う」と言うとき
〈フランスはドイツと何度も戦った〉
◎ A France fought against Germany many times.
◎ B France fought with Germany many times.
◎ C France fought Germany many times.
❖ B は前後関係によりフランスとドイツが同盟国で共に戦った，という意味にもなる．

b)「…と同盟して戦う」と言う
〈アメリカはイギリスと共にドイツと戦った〉
◎ A America fought (together) with Great Britain against Germany.
◎ B America fought along with Great Britain against Germany.
◎ C America fought against Germany with Great Britain.
◎ D America fought against Germany together [along] with Great Britain.
❖ D はドイツとイギリスが同盟国で，その両国とアメリカが戦った，という意味にも使われている．C についても D ほどではないが，同様の響きがある．

2 《比喩的に述べるとき》
〈私は過去何年も高血圧と戦ってきたんです〉
◎ A I've been fighting high blood pressure for the past several years.
△ B I've been fighting against high blood pressure for the past several years.

たたく
1 《ドアなどを》
a) コツコツ（トントン）たたくとき
〈彼はドアをコツコツ（トントン）たたいた〉
◎ A He knocked on the door.
○ B He rapped on the door.

b) ドンドンたたくとき
・ドア
〈彼はドアをドンドンたたいた〉
◎ A He beat [pounded, banged] on the door.
× B He slogged on the door.
❖(1) B が辞典に出ているが使われていない．
❖(2) たたく強さは beat が一番強い．pound, bang の順で下がる．

・窓
〈彼は窓をドンドンたたいた〉

- ◎ A He banged on the window.
- △ B He pounded on the window.

c) 軽くたたくとき

〈彼はドアを軽くたたいた〉
- ◎ A He tapped on the door.
- ○ B He knocked softly on the door.

2 《人を》

a) 顔を手のひらでぴしゃりとたたくとき

〈彼は私の顔をぴしゃりとたたいた〉
- ◎ A He slapped my face.
- ◎ B He slapped me on [in] the face.
- ○ C He smacked me in [on] the face.
- ○ D He smacked my face.
- ❖「殴る」の項も参照のこと.

b) 赤ちゃんのお尻をたたくとき

〈彼女は赤ちゃんのお尻をたたいた〉
- ◎ She swatted [spanked, hit] the baby (on the butt).
- ❖たたく強さは swat が一番弱く, spank, hit の順で強くなる.

立ち直る

1 《会社の財政》

〈うちの会社は去年まさに倒産しそうだったのですが立ち直ったんです〉
- ◎ A Our company was about to bankrupt last year but it got back on its feet.
- ◎ B Our company was about to bankrupt last year but it bounced back [recovered].
- ○ C Our company was about to bankrupt last year but it rebounded [survived].
- △ D Our company was about to bankrupt last year but it got itself together.

2 《個人の精神》

〈彼の会社は倒産したんです. しかし, 彼はまもなく立ち直るでしょう〉
- ◎ A His company went bankrupt, but he'll be (back) on his feet soon.
- ◎ B His company went bankrupt, but he'll recover soon.
- ◎ C His company went bankrupt, but he'll land on his feet soon.
- ○ D His company went bankrupt, but he'll bounce back soon.

立ち寄る

1 《相手の事務所などへ立ち寄るとき》

a) 肯定文の場合

〈金曜日に立ち寄りますよ〉
- ☆ A I'll stop by on Friday.
- ◎ B I'll come by [swing by, drop by, stop in, come over] on Friday.
- ◎ C I'll be by [be in] on Friday.
- ○ D I'll drop in [come in] on Friday.
- × E I'll swing in on Friday.

b) 疑問文の場合

〈金曜日に立ち寄っていいですか〉
- ☆ A Can I stop by on Friday?
- ◎ B Can I drop by [come by, come over, swing by] on Friday?
- ○ C Can I stop in [drop in] on Friday?

× D Can I be by [be in] on Friday?
c) 相手の事務所に言及して尋ねるとき
〈今週の金曜日あなたの事務所に立ち寄っていいですか〉
　　　◎ A Can I stop by (at) your office this Friday?
　　　◎ B Can I drop by (at) your office this Friday?
　　　◎ C Can I swing by your office this Friday?
　　　○ D Can I stop in (at) your office this Friday?
　　　○ E Can I stop at your office this Friday?
　　　△ F Can I drop in (at) your office this Friday?
　　　× G Can I swing by [drop] at your office this Friday?
　　　❖(1) 上例の A〜F まで疑問文であるが肯定文でも使い方は同じ．
　　　❖(2) D, F のように in が付くと A, B, C より時間が長いニュアンスがある．
　　　　しかし，どのくらいを長いと考えるかは主観の問題である．以上のことは
　　　　(a)の stop in, be in, drop in, come in, (b)の stop in, drop in にも
　　　　当てはまる．
d) 相手に言及して尋ねるとき
〈今週の金曜日立ち寄っていいですか〉
　　　◎ A Can I stop in [drop in] on you?
　　　○ B Can I swing by you?
　　　△ C Can I stop by [drop by] on you?
　　　× D Can I swing by on you?
2 《相手の自宅へ立ち寄るとき》
a) 肯定文の場合
〈金曜日に立ち寄りますよ〉
　　　☆ A I'll stop by on Friday.
　　　◎ B I'll come by [come over, swing by, drop by, be by] on Friday.
　　　△ C I'll drop in on Friday.
　　　▽ D I'll stop in [come in] on Friday.
　　　× E I'll swing in [be in] on Friday.
b) 疑問文の場合
〈今日の午後立ち寄っていいですか〉
　　　☆ A Can I come over [stop by] this afternoon?
　　　◎ B Can I drop by [swing by, come by] this afternoon?
　　　○ C Can I stop in [drop in] this afternoon?
3 《聞き手と一緒に行って立ち寄るとき》
〈帰宅する途中で図書館へ立ち寄ろう〉
　　　☆ A Let's go by the library on the way home.
　　　◎ B Let's stop by [stop at, stop by at] the library on the way home.
　　　◎ C Let's stop in (at) library on the way home.
　　　○ D Let's drop by [drop by at, swing by, drop in] the library on the way home.
　　　△ E Let's drop in at the library on the way home.

脱税
1 《脱税》
〈彼は脱税で逮捕されたんです〉
　　　☆ A He was arrested for cheating on his taxes.
　　　◎ B He was arrested for tax evasion.
　　　△ C He was arrested for tax dodging.
　　　△ D He was arrested for fudging his taxes.

だっせんする

2 《脱税者》
〈彼は脱税者で有名になったんです〉
- ○ A He became well-known for being a tax cheat [evader].
- × B He became well-known for being a tax cheater [dodger, shirker].

3 《脱税する》
〈彼は脱税したんです〉
- ◎ A He cheated on his taxes.
- △ B He evaded his taxes.
- × C He dodged his taxes.

脱線する

1 《電車の場合》
〈8時10分の電車が脱線しました〉
- ◎ A The 8:10 train was derailed.
- ◎ B The 8:10 train jumped the tracks.
- ○ C The 8:10 train derailed.
- ○ D The 8:10 train went [ran] off the tracks.

2 《話が脱線する場合》
〈話が脱線しないようにしよう〉
- ☆ A Let's stick to the subject.
- ◎ B Let's stick to what we're talking about.
- ◎ C Let's not get off the subject.
- ◎ D Let's not get sidetracked.
- ◎ E Let's stay on track [the subject].
- ◎ F Let's get back to the subject.
- ◎ G Let's not get away from the subject.
- ○ H Let's not move away from the subject.
- ○ I Let's not move away from what we're talking about.
- △ J Let's not veer off [deviate from] the subject.

3 《行動で「道を踏み外す」場合》
〈彼は悪友と脱線してしまったんです〉
- ◎ A He got [fell] in with the wrong crowd.
- ○ B He got involved with [in] the wrong crowd.
- △ C He deviated [went astray] from the right path with his bad friends.
- × D He got on the loose [went wild, went out of compass] from the right path with his bad friends.

脱走する

1 《兵隊が》

a) 1人の場合
〈彼は陸軍から脱走した〉
- ◎ A He went AWOL from the army.
- ○ B He was a deserter from the army.
- △ C He fled from [deserted (from)] the army.

❖ A の AWOL は absent without leave の略.

b) 複数の場合
〈今日10人が陸軍から脱走した〉
- ◎ A Ten people went AWOL from the army today.
- ○ B There were ten cases of desertion from the army today.
- △ C Ten people fled from [deserted (from)] the army today.

2 《囚人が》

〈10人が今日刑務所から脱走したんです〉
- ☆ A Ten people escaped from prison today.
- ◎ B Ten people busted out of prison.
- △ C Ten people broke [fled] from prison.

脱党 →離党

建てる

1 《建物が主語のとき》

〈たくさんの分譲マンションが東西線沿線に建てられています〉
- ☆ A A lot of condos're going up along the Tozai Line.
- ◎ B A lot of condos're popping up along the Tozai Line.
- ○ C A lot of condos're being build [constructed] along the Tozai Line.
- ○ D A lot of condos're springing up along the Tozai Line.
  - ❖(1) B にはどんどん建てられているというニュアンスが1番強い．2番目は D．
  - ❖(2) A, C はどんどん建てられているというニュアンスはない．

2 《建築依頼人が主語のとき》

a）建築中の場合

〈私は今家を建てているんです〉
- ◎ A I'm building a house now.
- ○ B I'm having a house built now.
  - ❖進行形のときは，大工さんや建築会社に依頼していても，A の方が B よりもよく使われている．

b）建築が済んでいる場合

〈私は去年家を建てたんです〉
- ◎ A I built my house last year.
- ◎ B I had my house built last year.

3 《建築会社が主語のとき》

〈XYZ建築会社は東西線沿線にたくさん分譲マンションを建てています〉
- ◎ A XYZ Construction Company's building a lot of condos along the Tozai Line.
- △ B XYZ Construction Company's constructing a lot of condos along the Tozai Line.

たとえば

1 《一般的に》

〈私は大都会，たとえばニューヨークとかシカゴに住みたいんです〉
- ☆ A I want to live in a big city, like New York or Chicago.
- ◎ B I want to live in a big city, for example, New York or Chicago.
- ◎ C I want to live in a big city, such as New York or Chicago.
- ○ D I want to live in a big city, for instance, New York or Chicago.
- ○ E I want to live in a big city, say, New York or Chicago.
  - ❖ D は少し堅い響きがある．

2 《疑問詞を従える場合》

〈メアリー：私はこってりした料理が好きなんです〉

Mary: I like rich food.

〈リンダ：たとえばどんな料理？〉

Linda:
- ◎ A Like what?
- ○ B For example what?
  - ❖ A の like は尋ねる内容により，Like who?（たとえば誰ですか），Like

where? (たとえばどこですか), Like when? (たとえばいつですか) のような形でも使われる.

他人
〈私は影で他人の批判をしないようにしています〉
- ◎ I'm trying not to criticize others [other people] behind their backs.

楽しい
1 《ロックコンサート》
〈コンサートは楽しかったでしょう〉
- ◎ A The concert must've been great [terrific, incredible, fun, awesome].
- ◎ B The concert must've been a ball [a blast].
- ○ C The concert must've been fantastic.
- △ D The concert must've been amazing.
- × E The concert must've been enjoyable.
  - ❖楽しかった度合いは incredible が一番強い.

2 《クラシックコンサート》
〈コンサートは楽しかったでしょう〉
- ◎ A The concert must've been great [terrific, incredible, enjoyable].
- ○ B The concert must've been amazing [fantastic].
- △ C The concert must've been awesome.
- × D The concert must've been fun.

3 《人と一緒にいること》
〈私は彼と一緒にいることが楽しいです〉
- ◎ A I enjoy his company.
- ◎ B I enjoy being with him.
- ◎ C It's great being with him.
- ○ D It's terrific being with him.
- ○ E I enjoy his companionship.

4 《人と行動をしていること》
〈私は彼と働いてとても楽しんでいます〉
- ◎ A I really enjoy working with him.
- ◎ B It's terrific [really great] working with him.
- ○ C It's terrific [really great] to work with him.

楽しむ
1 《クラシックコンサートのような知的な所へ行ったとき》
a) 普通に述べるとき
〈楽しかったです〉
- ◎ A We had a good time.
- ◎ B We had a great time.
- ○ C It was enjoyable.
- ○ D We enjoyed ourselves.
- × E We had fun.
- × F It was fun.
  - ❖(1) E, F は知的なことには使われていない.
  - ❖(2) C, D は改まった響きがある.
  - ❖(3) B の方が A より少し強い.

b) 強調して述べるとき
〈非常に楽しかったです〉
- ◎ A It was really great [terrific, wonderful].
- ◎ B We had a really great [terrific, wonderful] time.

- C It was really enjoyable.
- D We really enjoyed ourselves.
- E We really had a good time.
- F It was really incredible.
- G We had a really incredible time.
  ❖(1) incredible が一番強く, wonderful, terrific, great の順で弱くなる.
  ❖(2) C, D, E は改まった響きがある.
2 《スポーツ・ピクニック・ロックコンサート》
a） 普通に述べるとき
〈楽しかったです〉
- A We had a good [great] time.
- B It was fun.
- C We enjoyed ourselves.
- D It was enjoyable.
b） 強調して述べるとき
〈とても楽しかったです〉
- A We had a really great time.
- B We had a lot of fun.
- C It was a lot of fun.
- D It was terrific.
- E We had a blast.
- F We had a ball.
  ❖ E, F は約 40 歳以下の人の間で非常によく使われている.
3 《ハネムーンのような一生に一度という経験》
〈私たちはとても楽しかったです〉
- A We had the time of our lives.
- B We had a really terrific [great] time.

だぶだぶした
1 《ズボンが》
〈このズボンは私にはだぶだぶです〉
- These pants're baggy [loose] on me.
2 《上着が》
〈この上着は私にはだぶだぶです〉
- A This jacket's too big for me.
- B This jacket's too large [loose] for me.

たぶん
1 《肯定文》
〈彼はたぶん当選するでしょう〉
- A He'll probably be elected.
- B Maybe he'll be elected.
- C Chances're he'll be elected.
- D He'll most likely be elected.
- E Most likely he'll be elected.
- F Odds're he'll be elected.
- G It's very [most] likely he'll be elected.
- H Supposedly he'll be elected.
- I Presumably he'll be elected.
- J Perhaps he'll be elected.
- K The odds're [The chances're] he'll be elected.

- △ L In all likelihood he'll be elected.
- △ M As likely as not he'll be elected.
- ▽ N In all probability he'll be elected.
- × O As like as not he'll be elected.
  - ❖(1) O が辞典に出ているが使われていない．M は教育レベルの高い人の間でよく使われている．
  - ❖(2) 可能性のパーセンテージは，L, N が一番強いニュアンスがあり約 95 % 以上，A, I が 2 番で約 90 % 以上，C, D, E, F, G, H, K, M が 3 番で約 65 % 以上，B は 4 番で約 35〜50 %，J は 5 番で約 30 %．
  - ❖(3) H には他の人が言ったこと，何かで読んだことに基づいて述べている響きがある．
  - ❖(4) I は証明できる，またはそれに似たものがあるという響きがある．
  - ❖(5) A は文中，B, J は文中・文尾でも使われるが，文頭で使われることが多い．C, F, H, L, M は文頭で使われる．

2 《質問に対して否定で答える場合》

〈ジム：リンダは来ないと思う〉

Jim: I don't think Linda'll come.

〈ジェーン：たぶんね〉

Jane:
- ☆ A Probably not.
- ◎ B Most likely not.
- ○ C Maybe not.
- ○ D Odds're [Chances're] she won't.
- △ E It's most [very] likely not.
- △ F The odds're [The chances're] she won't.
- △ G Presumably not.
- △ H Very likely not.
- × I Perhaps not.
  - ❖ E, G はくだけた会話のときは使用頻度は下がる．

3 《今までの経験から明白なとき，または証明できるとき》

〈A：フセインは国連の安保理事会の決議に従うと思いますか〉

A: Do you think Saddam Hussein'll follow the United Nations' Security Council's resolutions?

〈B：他の決議を無視してきたのでたぶん従わないでしょう〉

B:
- ☆ A He probably won't because he's been ignoring the other resolutions.
- ◎ B Presumably [Most likely] he won't because he's been ignoring the other resolutions.
- ◎ C Chances're he won't because he's been ignoring the other resolutions.
- ○ D Odds're he won't because he's been ignoring the other resolutions.
- ○ E Very likely [Supposedly] he won't because he's been ignoring the other resolutions.
- △ F The chances're [The odds're] he won't because he's been ignoring the other resolutions.
- △ G In all likelihood he won't because he's been ignoring the other resolutions.
- × H Maybe [Perhaps] he won't because he's been ignoring the other resolutions.

食べる
1 《「生活する」という意味のとき》
〈私たちは夫の給料だけでは食べていけません〉
 ◎ A We can't live just on my husband's salary.
 △ B We can't make a living just on my husband's salary.
2 《食習慣を述べるとき》
〈ヨーロッパ人はアジア人よりも肉をたくさん食べます〉
 ◎ A Europeans eat more meat than Asians.
 ▽ B Europeans have more meat than Asians.
3 《具体的に食事することを述べるとき》
〈ウエイトレス：今日は何をお召し上がりになりますか〉
Waitress:
 ◎ A What will you be having today?
 △ B What will you be eating today?
4 《進行形のとき》
〈彼女は今昼食を食べています〉
 ◎ A She's eating lunch now.
 ○ B She's having lunch now.
5 《ガツガツ食べるとき》
〈ガツガツ食べるな〉
 ☆ A Don't eat like a pig.
 ◎ B Don't eat like an animal.
 ○ C Don't shovel your food in.
6 《経験を尋ねるとき》
〈あなたはギリシャ料理を食べたことがありますか〉
 ☆ A Have you ever tried Greek food?
 ◎ B Have you ever tasted [had, eaten] Greek food?
 ○ C Have you ever sampled Greek food?

卵
《比喩的に》
〈彼は歌手の卵です〉
 ◎ A He's a budding singer.
 × B He's a singer in the making [embryo].
 × C He's an incipient [embryonic] singer.
 ❖(1) B, C が辞典に出ているが使われていない．
 ❖(2) A が使えるのは芸術分野に限られる．したがって，それ以外のときは He's a new lawyer.（彼は弁護士の卵です）のように言う．

だます
1 《「だます」行為を述べるとき》
〈彼は私をだまそうとしているのだと思います〉
 ☆ A I think he's trying to cheat me.
 ◎ B I think he's trying to pull a fast one.
 ○ C I think he's trying to pull the wool of my eyes.
 ○ D I think he's trying to pull a wool over my eyes.
 ○ E I think he's trying to deceive me.
2 《だまして何かを巻きあげるとき》
〈彼は私をだましてお金を巻きあげようとしたんです〉
 ☆ A He tried to cheat me out of my money.
 ◎ B He tried to rip me off.

- ◎ C He tried to trick me out of my money.
- ◎ D He tried to screw [fuck] me out of my money.
- ○ E He tried to bilk [milk, bamboozle] me out of my money.
- ○ F He tried to gyp me out of my money.
- △ G He tried to wheedle [dupe, hustle, swindle] me out of my money.
- × H He tried to cajole [fool, do, outsmart] me out of my money.
  - ❖(1) D は女性の間では使用頻度は少し下がる．
  - ❖(2) F は特に少額のニュアンスがある．
  - ❖(3) G が辞典に出ているが使われていない．

3 《「何に」だますかを明示して述べるとき》

〈彼は私をだましてポンコツ車を買わせたんです〉
- ◎ A He talked me into buying his piece of junk.
- ◎ B He fucked [screwed] me into buying his piece of junk.
- ◎ C He tricked me into buying his piece of junk.
- ○ D He conned [fooled] me into buying his piece of junk.
- △ E He deceived [hustled, duped] me into buying his piece of junk.
- × F He outsmarted [wheedled] me into buying his piece of junk.
  - ❖ B は性表現なので男性の間では非常によく使われているが，女性の間では使用頻度は下がる．

たまらない →…したくてたまらない

駄目だ

〈月曜日は私は駄目なんです〉
- ◎ A Monday's out for me.
- ◎ B Monday's out of the question for me.
- ◎ C Monday's impossible for me.
- △ D Monday's not available for me.
  - ❖「都合」の項も参照のこと．

頼る

1 《肯定的な意味での「頼る」》

〈私には頼る人が誰もいないんです〉
- ☆ A I don't have anybody I can depend on.
- ☆ B I don't have anybody I can count on.
- ◎ C I don't have anybody I can rely on.
- ◎ D I don't have anybody I can fall back on.
- △ E I don't have anybody I can bank on.

2 《否定的な意味での「頼りにならない」》

〈彼は頼りになりません〉
- ◎ A You can't depend [count, rely] on him.
- ◎ B He isn't reliable [dependable].
- △ C You can't bank on him.

ダンスを踊る

〈タンゴを踊れますか〉
- ◎ A Can you tango?
- ◎ B Can you do the tango?
- ○ C Can you dance the tango?
- × D Can you dance tango?
  - ❖ waltz, mambo などでも同様．

男性

1 《一般的に述べるとき》

⟨彼は魅力的な男性です⟩
- ◎ He's an attractive man.

2 《くだけた調子で述べるとき》
⟨彼は魅力的な男性です⟩
- ◎ A He's an attractive guy.
- △ B He's an attractive fellow [feller].

3 《Who が先行しているとき》
⟨リンダと話している男性はどなたですか⟩
- ◎ A Who's the gentleman talking to Linda?
- ◎ B Who's the guy talking to Linda?
- ◎ C Who's the man talking to Linda?
- ◎ D Who's that talking to Linda?
  - ❖ A は丁重に述べるときの言い方. B はややくだけた言い方.

断熱してある
⟨この家は断熱してあります⟩
- ◎ A This house's insulated.
- ◎ B This house has insulation.

担保
1 《担保に入れる》
⟨何か担保に入れなければ, 融資してくれる銀行はありませんよ⟩
- ◎ A Unless you put something up as collateral, no bank'll finance you.
- ◎ B Unless you give [list, use] something as collateral, no bank'll finance you.
- ◎ C Unless you mortgage something, no bank'll finance you.
- × D Unless you put [give, lay, place] something in pledge, no bank'll finance you.
- × E Unless you give something as a security, no bank'll finance you.

2 《抵当》
a) 抵当がついているか否かを尋ねるとき
⟨このビルには抵当がついているのですか⟩
- ◎ A Does this building have a mortgage on it?
- ◎ B Is this building mortgaged?
- ○ C Does this building have a mortgage?
- × D Does this building have a security on it?
  - ❖ D が辞典に出ているが使われていない.

b) 抵当をつけている銀行を尋ねるとき
⟨どこの銀行があなたの家に抵当をつけているのですか⟩
- ◎ A Which bank holds the mortgage on your house?
- ◎ B Which bank did you finance your house through?
- ○ C Which bank has the mortgage on your house?
- × D Which bank holds your house as a security?
  - ❖ D が辞典に出ているが使われていない.

c) 2番抵当に言及するとき
・入れるとき
⟨家を2番抵当に入れたいのですが⟩
- ◎ A I'd like to take out [get] a second mortgage on my house.
- △ B I'd like to remortgage on my house.
  - ❖ B の remortgage は 2 番抵当以外にも, 3 番抵当, 4 番抵当など多重の抵当を表すことができる.

・つけるとき
〈XYZ銀行が私の家に2番抵当をつけています〉
- ◎ A XYZ Bank has a second mortgage on my house.
- ○ B XYZ Bank holds a second mortgage on my house.

暖房

1 《機械に言及する場合》
〈あなたの事務所には暖房がついていますか〉
- ◎ A Does your office have heat?
- △ B Does your office have a heater?
- ▽ C Does your office have heating?

2 《稼動に言及する場合》
〈暖房を消しておいて下さい〉
- ☆ A Please keep the heat off.
- ◎ B Please keep the heater off.
- ○ C Please keep the heating off.

短命である

1 《人》
〈息子は短命でした〉
- ◎ A My son had a short life.
- ◎ B My son died young.
- ◎ C My son didn't live long.
- ◎ D My son didn't have a long life.
- ○ E My son didn't live a long life.

2 《動物》
〈犬は短命です〉
- ◎ A Dogs have a short life span [expectancy].
- ◎ B Dogs have short lives.
- ○ C Dogs don't live long.
- ○ D Dogs don't live [have] a long life.

3 《人気・栄光・任期・成功など》
〈彼の人気は短命でした〉
- ☆ A His popularity didn't last long.
- ◎ B His popularity didn't last for a long time.
- ○ C His popularity was short-lived.
- ▽ D His popularity had a short life.

〔ち〕

治安

〈政府は治安を維持しなければならない〉
- ◎ A The Government must keep the peace.
- ○ B The Government must keep order.

地位

1 《上の人》
〈彼は上の人から長いお説教をされたんです〉
- ☆ A He got a long lecture from management.
- ◎ B He got a long lecture from the supervisors.

- ○ C He got a long lecture from upstairs [the higher-ups, the head honchoes, the top-dogs].
2 《上司》
a) 一般的に述べるとき
〈彼は私の上司です〉
- ◎ A He's my boss [supervisor].
- ◎ B I work for him.
- ○ C I report to him.
- ○ D I work under him.
- × E He's my superior.
- × F He's my service superior.
  - ❖ Eは軍隊，警察などの組織では非常によく使われている．

b) くだけた口調で述べるとき
〈上司は外出しているの〉
- ◎ A Is the head honcho out?
- ○ B Is the top dog out?
- △ C Is the big cheese out?
  - ❖(1) A, B, C いずれも会長，社長，専務，部長，課長，支店長，支配人，つまり上司なら誰でも使える．
  - ❖(2) He's my head honcho., He's my top dog., He's my big cheese.のように，A, B, C は my のみならず，our, her, his, their, つまり所有格と共に使うことはできない．

c) 直属の上司
〈彼は私の直属の上司です〉
- ☆ A I work directly under him.
- ☆ B I report directly to him.
- ◎ C He's my immediate [direct] supervisor.
- ○ D He's my immediate [direct] boss.
- ○ E I work right under him.
- △ F I work immediately under [directly for] him.

3 《最高管理職》
〈彼は最高管理職なんです〉
- ◎ A He's in senior [top] management.
- × B He's in the highest management.

4 《中間管理職》
〈彼は中間管理職なんです〉
- ◎ A He's in middle management.
- ○ B He's a middle manager.
- × C He's a middle management member.
- × D He's a member of middle management.

5 《管理職の下っ端》
〈彼は管理職の下っ端なんです〉
- ☆ A He's the low man on the totem pole in management.
- ◎ B He's a low-ranking manager.
- ○ C He's low man on the totem pole in management.
- △ D He's a low man on the totem pole in management.

6 《同僚》
a) 管理職のとき
〈彼は私の同僚です〉

- ☆ A He's my colleague.
- ◎ B He's my associate.
- △ C He's my coworker.
  - ❖(1) associate は非常にあいまいな語で，出資している場合もある．A, C には出資しているニュアンスは全くない．
  - ❖(2) 管理職にも上，中，下がある．C は下の方の管理職（課長，係長クラス）ならよく使われている．

b) 非管理職のとき

〈彼は私の同僚です〉
- ☆ A We work together.
- ◎ B He's my coworker.
- △ C He's my colleague.

c) 非管理職で似た仕事に従事しているが依存してはいない

〈彼は私の同僚です〉
- ◎ He's my fellow worker.
  - ❖互いに依存していないので coworker のように親密感はない．ホワイトカラー，ブルーカラーの両方で使われている．

d) 同じ会社で働いている

〈彼は私の同僚です〉
- ◎ A We work for the same company.
- ○ B He's my fellow employee.
  - ❖同じ会社で働いてさえいれば地位に関係なく使える．

7 《部下》

a) 1人の部下に言及するとき

〈彼は私の部下です〉
- ◎ A He works for me.
- ◎ B He's my assistant.
- ◎ C He's on my staff.
- ○ D He reports to me.
- △ E He works under me.
- △ F He's my subordinate.
- × G He's my inferior [follower].
  - ❖(1) G が辞典に出ているが使われていない．
  - ❖(2) A は直属の部下の場合でも直属の部下でない場合でも使われている．D, E, F は主として直属の部下に，B, C は直属の部下の場合のみに使われている．

b) 複数の部下に言及するとき

〈部長は部下に人気がないんです〉
- ◎ A The General Manager isn't popular with his employees [staff].
- ○ B The General Manager isn't popular with his people.
- △ C The General Manager isn't popular with his subordinates.
  - ❖A の employee は「従業員」「社員」の意味なので，主語が会社の所有者，つまりオーナーのときしか使えないと考えがちである．しかし，現代アメリカ英語では，主語が「社主」の場合だけでなく「上司」の場合でも広く使われている．

8 《下っ端》

a) 1人しかいないとき

〈彼女は職場で一番下っ端なんです〉
- ◎ A She's (the) low man on the totem pole at work.

◎ B She's just the peon at work.
△ C She's at the bottom of the food chain at work.
× D She's low woman on the totem pole at work.
❖(1) 女性の場合でも low woman ではなく low man という．
❖(2) A, B, C いずれも職種を問わず，ホワイトカラー，ブルーカラーの両方に使われている．

b) 2人以上いるとき
〈彼女は会社で一番下っ端なんです〉
◎ A She's a low man on the totem pole at work.
◎ B She's just a peon at work.

9 《会長》
a) 男性
〈彼は会長です〉
☆ A He's the Chairman of the board.
◎ B He's the Chairman (of the board of directors).
❖アメリカの chairman (会長) は，日本と違って社長 (CEO or President) の上司で権限を持っている．

b) 女性
〈彼女はこの会社の会長です〉
☆ A She's the chairman of this company.
○ B She's the chairwoman [chairperson] of this company.

10 《副会長》
〈彼は副会長です〉
◎ A He's the Vice-Chairman.
× B He's the Acting-Chairman.
❖ B が辞典に出ているが使われていない．「副会長」が病気かどこかへ出張している間の「臨時副会長」の意味ならよく使われている．

11 《社長》
〈彼は社長です〉
◎ A He's the CEO.
◎ B He's the President.
○ C He's the Chief Executive Officer.
❖(1) 会社により A, B 両方いる場合，または A, B が同一職の場合もある．
❖(2) 日本と違うのは，会長に選ばれ現場の最高責任者であることである．

12 《重役》
a) 一般の会社
〈彼は会社の重役です〉
☆ A He's a corporate executive.
◎ B He's a company executive.
○ C He's a corporate director.
△ D He's a company director.

b) 銀行
〈彼は銀行の重役です〉
◎ A He's a bank executive.
◎ B He's a banker.
△ C He's a bank director.

13 《営業部長》
〈彼は営業部長です〉
◎ A He's the Director [Manager] of Sales.

- ◎ B He's the Sales Director [Manager].
- × C He's the executive of Sales.
  - ❖ director は manager よりも高い地位であることがはっきりしているという響きがある．

14 《人事部長》

〈彼は人事部長です〉
- ◎   He's the Manager [Director] of Personnel.

15 《平社員》

a) ホワイトカラー

・客観的に述べるとき

〈彼は平社員です〉
- ◎ A He's just [only] an (office) employee.
- ◎ B He just works in the office.
- ◎ C He isn't in management.
- ○ D He's just an office worker.
- △ E He's an ordinary employee.
- △ F He's just a worker.
- △ G He's a worker like everybody else.

・軽蔑的に述べるとき

〈彼はただの平社員です〉
- ◎   He's just a peon.

b) ブルーカラー
- ◎ A He's just a worker [an employee].
- ◎ B He's a worker like everybody else.
- △ C He's only a worker [an employee].
- △ D He's an ordinary employee.

16 《銀行の頭取》

a) 銀行名に言及しない

〈彼は銀行の頭取です〉
- ◎ A He's a bank president.
- △ B He's a banker.

b) 銀行名に言及するとき

〈彼はカリフォルニア銀行の頭取です〉
- ☆ A He's the president of California Bank.
- × B He's the president at [for, to] California Bank.

17 《支店長》

a) どこの支店ではなく広く一般的に述べるとき

〈彼は支店長です〉
- ◎ A He's a branch manager.
- × B He's a branch head.

b) 支店内，または支店外でも特定の支店を頭に入れて述べるとき

〈彼は支店長です〉
- ◎   He's the branch manager.

c) 支店名と共に述べるとき

〈彼は中野支店長です〉
- ◎ A He's the manager at [of] the Nakano branch.
- ○ B He's the head of the Nakano branch.
- △ C He's the head at the Nakano branch.
- × D He's the chief at [of] the Nakano branch.

18 《副支店長》
〈彼は中野支店の副支店長です〉
　　◎　He's the assistant manager of [at] the Nakano branch.
19 《教頭》
〈彼は教頭です〉
　　◎　He's the assistant principal [vice-principal].
20 《教授》
a) 学園の外で一般的に述べるとき
〈彼は教授です〉
　　☆　A　He's a professor.
　　◎　B　He's a college professor.
　　○　C　He's a university professor.
b) 学園の中で述べるとき
〈彼は教授です〉
　　◎　A　He's a professor.
　　◎　B　He's on the faculty.
　　◎　C　He's a member of the faculty.
　　○　D　He's a faculty member.
　　❖ faculty には学校の事務職員，また学生も入ると書いてある辞典があるが，これはアメリカ英語の慣用事実を歪曲している．
c) 学園の外で大学名を明示して述べるとき
〈彼女はコーネル大学の教授です〉
　　☆　A　She's a professor at Cornell.
　　☆　B　She's on the faculty at Cornell.
　　◎　C　She's a member of the faculty at Cornell.
　　◎　D　She's on the faculty of Cornell.
　　○　E　She's a faculty member of Cornell.
　　○　F　She's a member of the faculty of Cornell.
d) 大学と学部を明示して述べるとき
〈彼女はプリンストン大学の経済学部の教授です〉
　　◎　A　She's a professor of economics at Princeton.
　　×　B　She's a professor of economics of Princeton.
　　❖ B が辞典に出ているが使われていない．
e) 呼びかけるとき
〈(ブラウン) 教授，おはようございます〉
　　☆　A　Good morning, Dr. Brown.
　　◎　B　Good morning, Professor Brown.
　　○　C　Good morning, Professor.
　　△　D　Good morning, Doctor.
f) 教授の種類を明示する必要があるとき
・正教授
〈彼は正教授です〉
　　◎　He's a full professor.
・準教授
〈彼は準教授です〉
　　◎　He's an associate professor.
・助教授
〈彼は助教授です〉
　　◎　He's an assistant professor.

・非常勤教授
〈彼女は非常勤教授です〉
- ◎ She's a part-time [an adjunct] professor.

・客員教授
〈彼は客員教授です〉
- ◎ He's a visiting professor.

・名誉教授
〈彼は名誉教授です〉
- ◎ A He's a professor emeritus.
- × B He's an emeritus professor.
  - ❖ B が辞典に出ているが使われていない.

21 《学部長》
〈彼女は史学部の学部長です〉
- ☆ A She's the dean of the History Department.
- ◎ B She's the head of the History Department.
- ○ C She's the chairman of the History Department.
- △ D She's the chairperson [chairwoman] of the History Department.

22 《講師》
a) 各種学校・大学の場合
〈彼は英語学校の講師です〉
- ◎ A He's an instructor at an English school.
- × B He's a lecturer at an English school.
  - ❖ イギリスの大学では B が使われている.

b) 講演講師の場合
・大学
〈皆さん本日の講師であるジェームズ・ブラウンさんをご紹介いたします〉
- ◎ A Ladies and gentlemen, let me introduce today's guest lecturer, Mr. James Brown.
- ○ B Ladies and gentlemen, let me introduce today's visiting lecturer, Mr. James Brown.

・会社
〈皆さん本日の講師であるジェームズ・ブラウンさんをご紹介いたします〉
- ◎ A Ladies and gentlemen, let me introduce today's guest speaker, Mr. James Brown.
- ○ B Ladies and gentlemen, let me introduce today's speaker, Mr. James Brown.
- △ C Ladies and gentlemen, let me introduce today's visiting speaker, Mr. James Brown.

地価
〈東京の地価は非常に高い〉
- ◎ A The price of land [property] in Tokyo is very high.
- ○ B Land [Property] prices in Tokyo are very high.
  - ❖ property には土地だけでなく建物も含まれている. しかしながら, land＝property の意味でもよく使われている.

近い
1 《場所》
a) 場所を従えないとき
〈郵便局は近くにありますか〉
- ◎ A Is the post office around [near] here?

◎ B Is the post office in this neighborhood?
○ C Is the post office close by [nearby]?

b) 場所を従えるとき
〈郵便局は市役所の近くです〉
◎ A The post office is near City Hall.
○ B The post office is close to [close by, nearby] City Hall.
○ C The post office is not far from City Hall.

c) 比較級で場所を従えるとき
〈彼は私より駅の近くに住んでいます〉
◎ A He lives closer to the station than me.
○ B He lives nearer to the station than me.

d) 最上級で場所を従えるとき
〈彼は私たちみんなの中で駅の一番近くに住んでいます〉
◎ A He lives the closest to the station out of all of us.
○ B He lives the nearest to the station out of all of us.

e)「目と鼻の先」と言うとき
〈市役所ですか．目と鼻の先ですよ〉
◎ A The City Office? It's just ahead.
◎ B The City Office? It's right there.
◎ C The City Office? It's right [just] down there.
◎ D The City Office? It's right [just] down the block.
△ E The City Office? It's right ahead.
△ F The City Office? It's just there.
▽ G The City Office? It's a stone's throw from here.
❖(1) G が口語辞典に出ているが，会話のみならず文章でもまれ．
❖(2) 距離の点から見ると A, E が一番近く，B, F が 2 番．C が 3 番，D が 4 番．

2 《年齢》
〈彼は 50 歳に近いんです〉
◎ A He's pushing [going on] 50.
◎ B He's almost 50.
◎ C He's nearly [close to] 50.
◎ D He's near 50.
❖ A, B が 50 歳に一番近いとのニュアンスがある．

3 《時間》
〈ジェーン：今何時ですか〉
Jane: What time is it now?
〈ビル：3 時に近いです〉
Bill:
◎ A It's almost [close to, nearly] 3:00.
◎ B It's going on 3:00.
◎ C It's pushing 3:00.
❖ A, C が 3 時に一番近いとのニュアンスがある．

誓う

1 《支持すると誓うとき》
〈私たちはあなたを支持することを誓います〉
◎ A We vow to stand by you.
◎ B We give our word to you.
○ C We make a vow to you.

2 《約束を守ると誓うとき》
〈ジム：約束を守れますか〉
Jim: Can you keep your promise?
〈ビル：はい誓います〉
Bill:
   ◎ A Yes, I swear.
   × B Yes, I pledge [vow].
  3 《真実を話すと誓うとき》
〈(法廷で) 私は真実を話すことを誓います〉
   ◎ A I swear to tell the truth.
   × B I vow [pledge] to tell the truth.
  4 《忠誠を誓うとき》
〈兵士：私は合衆国に忠誠であることを誓います〉
Soldier:
   ◎ A I pledge to be loyal to the United States.
   × B I vow to be loyal to the United States.

違って

〈日本はアメリカと違って集団社会である〉
   ◎ A Japan's a group-oriented society unlike America.
   ○ B Japan's a group-oriented society as opposed to America.
   ○ C Japan's a group-oriented society in contrast to America.
   ❖「違って」を強調する点では B が一番強く，C, A の順で弱くなる．

力になってくれる

 1 《精神面》
〈私がこのレストランを開いたとき，おじさんが力になってくれたんです〉
   ◎ A When I opened this restaurant, my uncle supported me.
   ◎ B When I opened this restaurant, my uncle was supportive (of me).
   ◎ C When I opened this restaurant, my uncle was behind me.
   ○ D When I opened this restaurant, my uncle backed me up.
   ○ E When I opened this restaurant, my uncle was my backer.
   ○ F When I opened this restaurant, my uncle stood behind [by] me.
   ❖ A, B, E は精神面と経済面の両方の意味がある．C, D, F は経済面のニュアンスもあるが精神面の響きが強い．

 2 《経済面》
〈私がこのレストランを開いたとき，おじさんが力になってくれたんです〉
   ◎ A When I opened this restaurant, my uncle financed me.
   ◎ B When I opened this restaurant, my uncle supported me [backed me up, stood behind me] financially.
   ◎ C When I opened this restaurant, my uncle was behind [supportive of] me financially.
   ○ D When I opened this restaurant, my uncle stood by me financially.
   ○ E When I opened this restaurant, my uncle was in support of me financially.

力を合わせる

〈私たちは問題を解決するために，力を合わせなければならない〉
   ◎ A We have to work together [join hands] to solve the problem.
   ○ B We have to join forces [cooperate] to solve the problem.

知識階級 →階級 5 d)

着服する
1 《少額のお金》
〈彼は会社のお金を着服したことで逮捕されたんです〉
- ☆ A He was arrested for pocketing the company's money.
- ◎ B He was arrested for helping himself to the company's money.
- ◎ C He was arrested for skimming money from [out of] the company.
- ○ D He was arrested for siphoning money from [out of] the company's account.
- ○ E He was arrested for siphoning the company's money.
  - ❖ A, B は少額だが何度もやった，C は何度もやった，D, E は改まった響きがあり，また回数は不明．

2 《高額のお金》
〈彼は公金を着服したことで逮捕されたんです〉
- ◎ A He was arrested for embezzling public funds.
- ○ B He was arrested for misappropriating public funds.
- ○ C He was arrested for diverting public funds into his own pocket.
- △ D He was arrested for appropriating public funds for him.
  - ❖ B, C, D はテレビ，ラジオ，新聞などのマスメディアの英語では非常によく使われている．

ちゃちな
〈これはちゃちなアパートだ〉
- ◎ A This is a lousy [a terrible, an awful] apartment building.
- △ B This is a crummy apartment building.
- × C This is a cheesy apartment building.
  - ❖ C が辞典に大きく紹介されているが使われていない．

チャンス
1 《自分の努力で変えられないチャンス》
a) 見送る
〈私はこのチャンスを見逃したくないね〉
- ◎ A I don't want to pass this chance.
- △ B I don't want to pass this opportunity.

b) 失敗して「もう一度チャンスを下さい」と頼むとき
〈私にもう一度チャンスを下さい〉
- ◎ A Give me one more chance.
- ▽ B Give me one more opportunity.

c) 次のチャンス
〈次のチャンスを待とう〉
- ◎ A Let's wait for another chance.
- ▽ B Let's wait for another opportunity.

d) 使ってみるチャンス
〈私にはフランス語を使うチャンスがないんです〉
- ◎ A I have no chance to use my French.
- △ B I have no opportunity to use my French.

2 《実現させることが可能なチャンス》
a) 利用できるチャンス
〈彼はこのチャンスを利用するかもしれません〉
- ◎ A He might take advantage of this opportunity.
- △ B He might take advantage of this chance.

b) 絶好のチャンス

〈これは私にとって絶好のチャンスですよ〉
- ◎ A This is a golden opportunity for me.
- × B This is a golden chance for me.

c) すばらしいチャンス

〈これは私たちにとってすばらしいチャンスになるかもしれません〉
- ◎ A This might be a terrific opportunity for us.
- △ B This might be a terrific chance for us.

3 《慣用的にchance, opportunityが使われるとき》

a) 改革するチャンス

〈この不景気は日本を改革するいいチャンスになるかもしれない〉
- ◎ A This bad economy may be a good chance [opportunity, time] to reform Japan.
- ○ B This bad economy may be a good occasion to reform Japan.
- × C This bad economy may be a good crack to reform Japan.
  - ❖ C は辞典に出ているが使われていない.

b) 「チャンスがあれば」と言うとき

〈チャンスがあれば私はホワイトハウスに入ってみたいと思っています〉
- ◎ If I have a chance [an opportunity], I want to go in the White House.

注意を引く

1 《会話で》

〈彼の方針は我々の注意を引きました〉
- ◎ His policy got [caught] our attention.

2 《改まった調子で述べるとき》

〈彼の方針は我々の注意を引きました〉
- ◎ A His policy attracted [drew] our attention.
- ○ B His policy arrested [engaged] our attention.

中学生 →…学生 3
中間管理職 →地位 4
中間試験 →試験 8
中級 →級 2
中古

1 《車の場合》

〈私は中古車を買おうと思っているんです〉
- ◎ I'm thinking of buying a used [secondhand, previously-owned] car.
  - ❖広告では previously-owned がよく使われている.

2 《「中古で」と述べる場合》

〈私はこの車を中古で買った〉
- ◎ I bought this car used [secondhand].

注射

〈先生, 注射を打ってくれますか〉
- ◎ A Doctor, will you give me a shot?
- △ B Doctor, will you give me an injection?
- ▽ C Doctor, will you give me a booster [booster shot, needle]?
- × D Doctor, will you give me a dose [an overdose]?
  - ❖(1) D は辞典に出ているが使われていない.
  - ❖(2) B は堅い文章英語ではよく使われている.

駐車場

1 《有料駐車場》

〈XYZ 銀行の後ろに駐車場があります〉

- ◎ A There's a parking lot behind XYZ Bank.
- ◎ B There's parking behind XYZ Bank.
  - ❖ B の parking は不可算名詞扱いのため不定冠詞は不要である．free parking（無料駐車場），big parking（大きい駐車場）のように形容詞が付いても不定冠詞は不要．

2 《お客・社員のための無料駐車場》

〈XYZ 銀行の後ろに駐車場があります〉

- ◎ A There's a parking lot behind XYZ Bank.
- ◎ B There's parking behind XYZ Bank.
- △ C There's a parking area behind XYZ Bank.
  - ❖ C は A，B と違って「駐車場」として特に作ったものではない．したがって，草が生えている単なる空き地を言うこともある．

3 《パーキングビル》

〈角を曲がったところにパーキングビルがあります〉

- ◎ A There's a parking garage around the corner.
- ◎ B There's a multi-story car park around the corner.
- × C There's a parking building [stall, structure] around the corner.
  - ❖(1) C は辞典に出ているが使われていない．
  - ❖(2) A はアメリカ英語，B はイギリス英語．

4 《地下駐車場》

〈あのビルの後ろに地下駐車場があります〉

- ◎ A There's an underground parking garage [parking lot] behind that building.
- ◎ B There's underground parking behind that building.

5 《1 台ずつの仕切りのある駐車場》

〈(駐車場で係員に尋ねて) 駐車する所はありますか〉

- ◎ A Are there any parking spots [spaces] available?
- ◎ B Are there any spots [spaces] available?
- ○ C Is there any parking available?
- △ D Are there any (parking) places available?

中旬

〈彼女らは 7 月中旬に日本に来ます〉

◎ They'll come to Japan in the middle of July [in mid-July].

中心

1 《中心街》

a ）中心街の [に]

〈私は東京の中心街 [都心] で事務所を持ちたいんです〉

- ☆ A I want to have an office in downtown Tokyo.
- ◎ B I want to have an office in the downtown area of Tokyo.
- ◎ C I want to have an office in the heart of Tokyo.
- ○ D I want to have an office in the center of Tokyo.
- △ E I want to have an office in Tokyo, downtown.
- △ F I want to have an office in downtown in Tokyo.
  - ❖(1) C，D は厳密には地理上の中心地である．しかし，アメリカ人はビジネス上の中心街の意味でよく使っている．
  - ❖(2) 辞典には downtown を名詞としても紹介しているが使われていない．

b) 中心街へ
〈中心街へ行こう〉
- ◎ A Let's go downtown.
- ○ B Let's go to the downtown area.
- × C Let's go to the downtown.

2 《中心に回る》
〈(事実を客観的に述べて) 世界経済はアメリカを中心に回っている〉
- ◎ A The global economy revolves around America.
- ○ B The global economy centers around America.
- △ C The global economy moves around America.
- ▽ D The global economy orbits [goes] around America.
- × E The global economy works around America.

3 《「支配している」という意味の「中心の」》
〈アメリカは男性中心の社会です〉
- ◎ A America's a male dominated society.
- ◎ B In America it's a men's world.
- ○ C America's a society for men.
- △ D America's a male centered [chauvinistic] society.
- △ E America's a men's society.
- × F America's a men's centered [dominated] society.
- × G America's a male ruled society.

中毒

1 《ニコチン中毒》
〈彼はニコチン中毒です〉
- ◎ A He's addicted to nicotine.
- ◎ B He's a nicotine addict.
- ◎ C He's hooked on nicotine.

2 《麻薬中毒》
〈彼は麻薬中毒です〉
- ◎ A He's addicted to drugs.
- ○ B He's a drug addict.
- ○ C He's hooked on drugs.

3 《アルコール中毒》
a) 否定的に述べるとき
〈彼女はアル中なんです〉
- ◎ A She's an alcoholic.
- ○ B She's alcoholic.

b) 婉曲に述べるとき
〈彼女はアル中なんです〉
- ◎ A She has a drinking problem.
- ▽ B She has an alcoholic problem.

4 《仕事中毒》
a) 否定的に述べるとき
〈彼は仕事中毒なんです〉
- ◎ A He's married to his work.
- ◎ B He's working too much [hard].
- ◎ C He's a workaholic.
- △ D He's addicted to (his) work.

b) 冗談として述べるとき

〈彼は仕事中毒なんです〉
- ◎ A He's married to his work.
- ◎ B He's a workaholic.

注目されている
〈彼のスキャンダルは全米で注目されている〉
- ◎ A All American eyes're wrapped up in his scandal.
- ◎ B All American eyes're on his scandal.
- ◎ C All American eyes're focusing on his scandal.
- ○ D All American eyes're focused on his scandal.
- △ E His scandal's the object of all American people's attention.

❖教育レベルの高い人の間では E は非常によく使われている．

注文
1 《注文する》

〈紙を注文してくれますか〉
- ☆ A Will you order paper?
- ◎ B Will you place an order for paper?
- ○ C Will you put in an order for paper?
- △ D Will you give an order for paper?

2 《注文する会社を明示するとき》

〈紙を XYZ 会社に注文してくれますか〉
- ☆ A Will you order paper from XYZ Company?
- ◎ B Will you place an order for paper with XYZ Company?
- ○ C Will you put in an order for paper with XYZ Company?
- ○ D Will you place an order with XYZ Company for paper?
- △ E Will you put in an order with XYZ Company for paper?

3 《「注文してある」状態を述べるとき》

〈それは XYZ 会社に注文してあります〉
- ☆ A That's on order from XYZ Company.
- ◎ B That's on order with XYZ Company.
- ◎ C We've ordered that from XYZ Company.

4 《注文が殺到している》

a) 製品を明示しないで述べるとき

〈注文がじゃんじゃん入ってきています〉
- ◎ A Orders're pouring in.
- ◎ B We're flooded with orders.
- △ C Orders're flying [rushing] in.
- △ D We're snowed with orders.
- × E We have a pressure of orders.
- × F We're submerged with [snowed by] orders.

❖辞典に E, F が出ているが使われていない．

b) 製品を明示して述べるとき

〈この製品の注文がじゃんじゃん入ってきています〉
- ◎ A Orders're pouring [flooding] in for this product.
- ◎ B Orders for this product're pouring [flooding] in.
- ○ C Orders're flying [rushing] in for this product.

5 《注文がものすごく入っている状態》

〈この製品はものすごく注文があるんです〉
- ☆ A We have tons of orders for this product.
- ◎ B We have pile of orders for this product.

○ C　We have a flood [a rush] of orders for this product.
中流階級　→階級 1
長期的視野で
〈我々はこのプロジェクトを長期的視野でやるつもりです〉
　　　◎ A　We're going to carry out this project with a long-range point of view.
　　　○ B　We're going to carry out this project with a long-term focus.
　　　○ C　We're going to carry out this project with a long-range viewpoint.
　　　△ D　We're going to carry out this project with a long-term point of view.
調子
　1　《頭の働き》
　〈私は夜，頭の調子がとてもいいんです〉
　　　☆ A　I do my best thinking at night.
　　　◎ B　I can think most [very] clearly at night.
　　　○ C　I'm very clear-headed at night.
　　　○ D　My brain works very well at night.
　　　× E　My head works very well at night.
　2　《おなかの働き》
　〈おなかの調子がよくないんです〉
　　　☆ A　I have an upset stomach.
　　　◎ B　I'm having some problems with my stomach.
　　　◎ C　There's something wrong with my stomach.
　　　○ D　I'm having some problem with my stomach.
　　　○ E　My stomach's upset.
　　　△ F　I have some problems [problem] with my stomach.
　　　△ G　I'm having some trouble with my stomach.
　3　《試合・競技での》
　〈私は試合で調子がよくなかったんです〉
　　　◎ A　I wasn't at my best for the game.
　　　◎ B　I wasn't in good shape [condition] for the game.
　　　◎ C　I was in bad shape for the game.
　　　○ D　I was in bad condition for the game.
　　　△ E　I wasn't in good form for the game.
　4　《健康上の》
　〈私は今日調子がよくないんです〉
　　　◎ A　I feel bad today.
　　　◎ B　I don't feel good today.
　　　△ C　I'm in bad shape [condition] today.
　5　《機械》
　〈コピー機の調子がよくないんです〉
　　　◎ A　The copy machine's acting up.
　　　◎ B　There's something wrong with the copy machine.
　　　◎ C　There's a problem with the copy machine.
　　　◎ D　The copy machine isn't working well.
　　　△ E　The copy machine doesn't work well.
　　　△ F　There's trouble with the copy machine.
　6　《相手・まわりの人に合わせる》
　〈彼らの冗談に調子を合わせるのは私には難しい〉
　　　◎ A　It's tough for me to play along (with their joke).

◎ B It's tough for me to go along with their joke.
7 《現在の状態・程度が続けば》
〈この調子でいけばうちの会社は早晩倒産するでしょう〉
- ◎ A At this rate our company'll go bankrupt sooner or later.
- ◎ B The way things're going, our company'll go bankrupt sooner or later.
- ◎ C If things continue at this rate, our company'll go bankrupt sooner or later.
- ○ D If things continue the way they're now, our company'll go bankrupt sooner or later.

8 《生活様式・仕事のやり方》
〈ここニューヨークでは万事がこの調子なんだ〉
- ☆ A This is the way things're done here in New York.
- ◎ B This is the way things go here in New York.
- ◎ C This is how things're done here in New York.
- ◎ D This is how things go here in New York.

9 《文章の書き方》
〈大衆向きに調子を下げて書いた方がいいよ〉
- ◎ A You'd better dumb it down for the public.
- ◎ B You'd better simplify it for the public.
- ○ C You'd better write it down for the public.
- × D You'd better lower the tone for the public.
  ❖辞典に D が出ているが使われていない．

10 《「その調子」と励まして》
〈教習所の指導員：さあ車線を守って，あまり左へ行かないように．その調子，いいよ〉
Driving Teacher:
- ◎ A Now stay on the road. Don't go far to the left. That's it [right]. Good.
- ◎ B Now stay on the road. Don't go far to the left. There you go. Good.
- ◎ C Now stay on the road. Don't go far to the left. You got it. Good.
- ◎ D Now stay on the road. Don't go far to the left. You're getting it. Good.
- ○ E Now stay on the road. Don't go far to the left. That's the way. Good.

挑戦する
1 《試みるという意味の場合》
〈私は5回司法試験に落ちたんです．合格するまで挑戦します〉
- ◎ A I've failed the bar exam five times. I'll keep on [continue, go on] trying until I pass it.
- × B I've failed the bar exam five times. I'll keep on challenging until I pass it.

2 《個人・国などと競う意味の場合》
〈私は世界テニス選手権をかけて彼に挑戦する〉
 ◎ I'll challenge him for the world tennis title.
〈私は今年の最高売上賞でジョーに挑戦したい〉
 ◎ I want to challenge Joe for the company's top prize in sales this year.
〈アメリカはドイツに製鉄生産において挑戦している〉
 ◎ Americans are challenging Germans in steel-making.
〈今，アメリカの工業会社は工業技術において日本の会社に挑戦するために，設備改

良に投資を迫られている〉
- ◎ Now American industrial companies are forced to invest in renovating their facilities in order to challenge Japanese companies in industrial technology.

腸チフス →病気 16

調停する

1 《調停委員またはそれに準ずる人が調停したとき》

〈彼は労使の調停をしました〉
- ◎ A He acted as the go-between for management and labor.
- ○ B He mediated [arbitrated] between management and labor.
- △ C He intervened [stepped in] between management and labor.

2 《調停をするのが職業でない人が調停したとき》

〈彼は労使の調停をしました〉
- ◎ A He acted as the go-between for management and labor.
- ○ B He stepped in [intervened] between management and labor.
- △ C He bargained between management and labor.

❖クリントンが大統領の在任中, 大リーグのストライキを調停したのが好例.

ちょうど

1 《時刻》

〈ビル: 今何時〉

Bill: What time is it now?

〈ジェーン: ちょうど5時です〉

Jane:
- ☆ A It's exactly 5:00.
- ◎ B It's 5:00 on the dot [nose].
- ○ C It's 5:00 exactly.
- △ D It's precisely 5:00.
- △ E It's 5:00 precisely.
- × F It's just 5:00.

❖Fが多くの辞典に出ているが使われていない.

2 《スケジュール》

〈飛行機はちょうど3時に離陸しました〉
- ☆ A The plane took off at 3:00 sharp.
- ☆ B The plane took off on time at 3:00.
- ○ C The plane took off at 3:00 on the nose [dot].
- ○ D The plane took off exactly [promptly] at 3:00.
- ○ E The plane took off at exactly 3:00.
- ○ F The plane took off at 3:00 exactly.
- △ G The plane took off at promptly [precisely] 3:00.
- △ H The plane took off at 3:00 promptly [precisely].
- △ I The plane took off precisely at 3:00.

3 《金額・数字》

〈ちょうど200ドルです〉
- ◎ A $200 even.
- ◎ B An even $200.
- ○ C Exactly $200
- △ D $200 exactly.
- △ E $200 on the nose.
- △ F Precisely $200.

▽　G　$200 on the dot.
　　　×　H　Just $200.
　4　《数字と関係ないとき》
〈それはちょうど私が言おうとしていたことです〉
　　　☆　A　That's just what I was going to say.
　　　◎　B　That's exactly what I was going to say.
　　　△　C　That's precisely what I was going to say.
　　　❖「ちょうど…するところだった」の項も参照のこと．

ちょうど…するところだった

〈(それは) 私がちょうど言おうとしていたことです〉
　　　◎　A　You took the words right out of my mouth.
　　　◎　B　That was just what I was going to say.
　　　◎　C　I was just going to say that.
　　　◎　D　I was about to say that.
　　❖(1) Aが一番強い響きがある．以下B, C, Dの順で弱くなる．
　　❖(2)「ちょうど」の項の 4 も参照のこと．

ちょうど…のとき

　1　《短い時間帯》
〈ちょうど私が家を出ようとしていたとき，彼から電話があったんです〉
　　　◎　　Just as [when] I was leaving home, I got a phone call from him.
　　❖英文法書や辞典では just as しか出ていないが，just when もよく使われている．
　2　《広い時間帯》
〈ちょうど私がイギリスを旅行していたときにその事件が起きたのです〉
　　　◎　　That incident occurred while I was traveling in England.

帳簿をつける

〈誰が帳簿をつけているのですか〉
　　　◎　A　Who's keeping the books?
　　　△　B　Who's keeping the accounts?

調理師学校　→各種学校 9

貯金する

　1　《未来の内容》
〈あなたはまさかの日に備えてお金を貯金したほうがいいですよ〉
　　　◎　A　You should save money for a rainy day.
　　　◎　B　You should put money away [put away money] for a rainy day.
　　　○　C　You should put money aside [put aside money] for a rainy day.
　　　△　D　You should save money up [save up money] for a rainy day.
　　　△　E　You should deposit for a rainy day.
　　　△　F　You should stash money away [stash away money] for a rainy day.
　　　△　G　You should sock away money [sock money away] for a rainy day.
　　❖Dには長期間という響きがある．
　2　《過去から現在まで》
〈私たちは新しい家のために毎月1千ドル貯金をしてきています〉
　　　◎　A　We've been saving (up) $1,000 every month for our new home.
　　　◎　B　We've been putting aside $1,000 every month for our new home.
　　　◎　C　We've been putting $1,000 aside every month for our new home.
　　　△　D　We've been putting $1,000 away every month for our new home.
　　　△　E　We've been putting [stashing, socking] away $1,000 every month for our new home.

3 《習慣的内容》
〈私は毎月銀行へ 500 ドル貯金しています〉
- ◎ A I put [deposit] $500 in the bank every month.
- ○ B I put $500 aside in the bank every month.
- ○ C I put aside $500 in the bank every month.
- △ D I put [stash, sock] $500 away in the bank every month.
- △ E I put [stash, sock] away $500 in the bank every month.

4 《隠して貯金しているというニュアンスのとき》
〈アラファトは外国の多くの銀行に巨額のお金を貯金していると多くの新聞は報じている〉
- ☆ A Many papers say Arafat's hiding (away) tremendous amount of money in many banks overseas.
- ◎ B Many papers say Arafat's stashing (away) tremendous amount of money in many banks overseas.
- ○ C Many papers say Arafat's socking away tremendous amount of money in many banks overseas.
- △ D Many papers say Arafat's socking [hoarding] tremendous amount of money in many banks overseas.

直接

1 《会って話すこと》
〈今晩会ったときあなたは彼に直接尋ねるべきです〉
- ◎ A You should ask him face to face [yourself, in person] when you see him tonight.
- ○ B You should ask him personally [directly, straight out] when you see him tonight.
- △ C You should ask him up front when you see him tonight.

2 《会わないで電話で話すとき》
〈あなたは今晩彼に電話したとき直接尋ねるべきです〉
- ☆ A You should ask him yourself when you call him tonight.
- ◎ B You should ask him personally [directly] when you call him tonight.
- ○ C You should ask him straight out when you call him tonight.
- × D You should ask him in person [up front] when you call him tonight.

直面している

1 《国・会社などの場合》
〈日本は 50 年振りの不況に直面しています〉
- ◎ A Japan's facing its worst recession in 50 years.
- ◎ B Japan's faced with its worst recession in 50 years.
- ◎ C Japan's confronted with [by] its worst recession in 50 years.
- ◎ D Japan's confronting its worst recession in 50 years.
- ◎ E Japan's up against its worst recession in 50 years.
    - ❖ C, D, が一番困難という響きがある．2 番目は E．一番弱いのは A, B．

2 《個人の場合》
〈彼は倒産に直面しているんです〉
- ☆ A He's facing bankruptcy.
- ◎ B He's come face to face with bankruptcy.
- ○ C He's faced with bankruptcy.
- △ D He's up against bankruptcy.

        △ E He's confronted with bankruptcy.
        ▽ F He's confronting bankruptcy.
        ▽ G He's in (the) face of bankruptcy.
        ▽ H He's confronted by bankruptcy.
         ❖ F, G, H が辞典に出ているがまれにしか使われていない.

直行する
〈この便はシカゴへ直行します〉
        ◎ A The flight'll take you straight [directly, nonstop] to Chicago.
        ◎ B The flight'll take you to Chicago nonstop.
        ○ C The flight'll get you straight [directly, nonstop] to Chicago.
        ○ D The flight'll get you to Chicago nonstop.

ちょっと
〈あなたとちょっとお話ししたいのですか〉
        ◎ A I'd like to talk to you for a sec [a second, a moment, a minute].
        ○ B I'd like to talk to you for a few seconds [a little bit, a little while, a short time, a short while].
         ❖時間的に sec が一番短いという響きがある. 一番長いのは a little while, 次が a short while.

散らかす
1 《散らかす (動作)》
〈部屋を散らかさないで〉
        ◎ A Don't mess the room up with a lot of papers.
        ◎ B Don't mess up the room with a lot of papers.
        ◎ C Don't make a mess in the room with a lot of papers.
        ○ D Don't letter the room up with a lot of papers.
        × E Don't clutter up the room with a lot of papers.
         ❖ E が辞典に出ているがこの意味では使われていない.「一杯にする」という意味なら使われている. 詳細は「一杯にする」の項を参照されたい.
2 《散らかっている (状態)》
a) 単に「散らかっている」と言うとき
〈彼の事務所はいつも散らかっている〉
        ◎ A His office is always messy.
        ◎ B His office is always a mess.
        ○ C His office is always a dump [a wreck, a disaster].
        △ D His office is always in disaster.
b) 散らかっていて汚いとき
〈彼の事務所はいつも散らかっている〉
        ☆ A His office is always a pigsty.
        ◎ B His office is always a pig pen.
        △ C His office is always a garbage pile [heap].
         ❖ C は A, B ほど汚れていない.

チラシ
1 《1枚のチラシ》
〈新聞に入っているお宅の会社のチラシを見ました〉
        ◎   I saw your flier inserted in the paper.
2 《折ってあるチラシ》
〈新聞に入っているお宅の会社のチラシを見ました〉
        ◎   I saw your leaflet that was inserted in the paper.

賃貸している

1 《アメリカの場合》
a) 家主が
〈私は事務所を 600 ドルで貸している〉
- ◎ A I'm leasing [renting] (out) the office for $600.
- ◎ B I lease [rent] (out) the office for $600.

b) テナントが
〈私は事務所を 600 ドルで借りている〉
- ☆ A I'm renting the office for $600.
- ◎ B I'm leasing the office for $600.
- ○ C I lease [rent] the office for $600.
- △ D I'm renting out the office for $600.
- × E I'm leasing out the office for $600.
- × F I lease [rent] out the office for $600.

2 《イギリスの場合》
a) 家主が
〈私は 600 ドルで事務所を貸している〉
- ◎ A I let [rent out] the office for $600.
- ◎ B I'm renting out the office for $600.
- ○ C I'm letting (out) the office for $600.
- ○ D I let out the office for $600.
- △ E I lease out the office for $600.
- △ F I'm renting the office for $600.
- ▽ G I rent the office for $600.

b) テナントが
〈私は 600 ドルで事務所を借りている〉
- ☆ A I'm renting the office for $600.
- ◎ B I rent [lease] the office for $600.
- ◎ C I'm leasing the office for $600.
- △ D I let the office for $600.
- × E I'm letting (out) the office for $600.
- × F I lease out the office for $600.
- × G I let [rent] out the office for $600.
- × H I'm renting out the office for $600.

❖ lease, rent, let は基本的には同じで，それぞれ置き換えられる．lease は特に 2 年以上の長期契約に使われ，かしこまった響きがある．rent は契約期間の長さには関係なく使われ，rent はくだけた響きがある．let はイギリス英語のくだけた表現．

陳列する

1 《動作として述べるとき》
〈これらのドレスをウィンドウに陳列しなさい〉
- ◎ A Display these dresses in the window.
- ◎ B Put these dresses on display in the window.
- × C Put these dresses on show in the window.
- × D Exhibit these dresses in the window.
- × E Put these dresses on exhibition in the window.
- × F Lay these dresses out in the window.

❖ C~F は辞典で紹介されているが使われていない．

2 《状態として述べるとき》

〈私はこの店の商品の陳列の仕方が好きではない〉
- ◎ A I don't like the way the merchandise is (being) displayed in this store.
- ◎ B I don't like the way the merchandise is on display in this store.
- × C I don't like the way the merchandise is exhibited in this store.

❖辞典に C が出ているが使われていない．

〔つ〕

ツアー
《演奏旅行などの意味で》
〈彼らはヨーロッパツアーの最中です〉
- ◎ A They're touring Europe.
- ○ B They're touring around Europe.
- ○ C They're on a tour of Europe.

❖「旅行」の項も参照のこと．

付いている

1 《冷房・コピー機などの機械》
〈クーラーは付いていますか〉
- ☆ A Is the air-conditioner on?
- ◎ B Is the air-conditioner running?
- ◎ C Is the air-conditioner turned on?
- ○ D Is the air-conditioner working?
- △ E Is the air-conditioner switched on?

2 《売るとき》
〈このスーツにはこれらのネクタイが3本付いています〉
- ◎ A This suit comes with these three ties.
- ◎ B These three ties come with this suit.

3 《アパートの家具》
〈(不動産屋で) 客：あのアパートは全室冷蔵庫が付いているのですか〉
Customer:
- ☆ A Do all the apartments in that building have fridges?
- ◎ B Are all the apartments in that building equipped with fridges?
- ○ C Do all the apartments in that building furnished with fridges?

4 《ホテルの設備》
〈(ホテルのフロントで) 客：どの部屋にもテレビは付いているのですか〉
Customer:
- ☆ A Do all the rooms come with TVs?
- ◎ B Do all the rooms have TVs?
- ◎ C Are all the rooms equipped with TVs?

5 《同時通訳などの設備》
〈産経会館には同時通訳の設備が付いているのですか〉
- ◎ A Does the Sankei Kaikan have simultaneous interpretation facilities?
- ○ B Is the Sankei Kaikan equipped with simultaneous interpretation facilities?

6 《ジムの設備》
〈あのジムは設備がたくさん付いています〉

412 ついている

- ◎ A That gym has a lot of equipment.
- ◎ B That gym's well-equipped.
- △ C That gym has a lot of facilities.
- × D That gym's equipped with a lot of facilities.

ついている
〈私は今日，ついていた〉
- ◎ A Today I had a run of good luck.
- ◎ B Today I was in luck.
- ◎ C Today luck was with me.

…通
1　《コンピュータを自由自在に駆使できると述べるとき》
a） 主語が3人称のとき
〈彼はコンピュータ通です〉
- ◎ A He's a computer genius.
- ◎ B He's a computer expert.
- ◎ C He's a computer wiz.
- ◎ D He's a computer pro.
- ○ E He's a computer guru.
- △ F He's computer savvy.
    - ❖(1) F の savvy は形容詞なので不定冠詞の a は不要．
    - ❖(2) C は年配者の間では非常によく使われている．
    - ❖(3) 強さの点では A が一番強く，B, C が2番，D, E, F はほぼ同じで3番．

b） 主語が1人称のとき
〈私はコンピュータ通です〉
- ◎ A I'm a computer expert.
- ○ B I'm a computer wiz [guru].
- △ C I'm computer savvy.
- × D I'm a computer genius.

c） 会社・営業部・人事部のような場所を限定して述べるとき
〈私は会社でコンピュータ通です〉
- ☆ A I'm the computer expert at the office.
- ◎ B I'm the computer guru at the office.
- ○ C I'm the computer wiz at the office.
- △ D I'm the computer pro at the office.
- × E I'm the computer genius [savvy] at the office.

2　《車・コンピュータなどの機械の構造のことを念頭において述べるとき》
〈彼は車の通です〉
- ☆ A He really knows a lot about cars.
- ◎ B He really knows his stuff [shit] about cars.
- ◎ C He really knows his stuff [shit] when it comes to cars.

3　《深い学識が要求される分野》
〈彼は中国通です〉
- ☆ A He's an authority [expert] on China.
- ◎ B He's quite knowledgeable about China.
- ◎ C He's really familiar with China.
- ○ D He knows all there's to know about China.
    - ❖ A のほうが B, C, D より強いニュアンスがある．

ツーカーです

1 《上司が秘書や部下のことを言うとき》
〈私たちは過去10年間一緒に働いてきたんです．だからツーカーなんです〉

- ☆ A We've been working together for the last ten years, so we communicate very well.
- ◎ B We've been working together for the last ten years, so she can read my mind.
- ○ C We've been working together for the last ten years, so we can communicate very well.
- ○ D We've been working together for the last ten years, so we're communicating very well.
- ○ E We've been working together for the last ten years, so we're on the same wave length.
- ○ F We've been working together for the last ten years, so we're in sync with each other.
- △ G We've been working together for the last ten years, so we're in tune with each other.
- △ H We've been working together for the last ten years, so we're just like that.

❖ H は V サインの人差し指の上に中指をクロスさせて that を強く発音する．

2 《秘書や部下が上司のことを言うとき》
〈私たちは過去10年間一緒に働いているんです．だからツーカーなんです〉

- ☆ A We've been working together for the past ten years, so we communicate very well.
- ◎ B We've been working together for the past ten years, so I can read his mind.
- ◎ C We've been working together for the past ten years, so we're on the same wave length.
- ◎ D We've been working together for the past ten years, so we can communicate very well.
- ◎ E We've been working together for the past ten years, so I can tell what he's thinking.
- ○ F We've been working together for the past ten years, so we're in sync with each other.
- ○ G We've been working together for the past ten years, so he and I can communicate very well.
- ○ H We've been working together for the past ten years, so we're just like that.

3 《女性同士》
〈私たちは大学時代から知っているんです．だからツーカーなんです〉

- ☆ A We've known each other since in college, so we communicate very well.
- ◎ B We've known each other since in college, so she can read my mind.
- ◎ C We've known each other since in college, so we can read each other's mind.
- ◎ D We've known each other since in college, so she and I can read each other's mind.
- ◎ E We've known each other since in college, so we're on the same wave length.

- ○ F We've known each other since in college, so we're in tune [sync] with each other.
- ○ G We've known each other since in college, so we're just like that.

4 《男性同士の友人》

〈私たちは20年友人なんです。だからツーカーなんです〉

- ☆ A We've been friends for twenty years, so we communicate very well.
- ◎ B We've been friends for twenty years, so he can read my mind.
- ○ C We've been friends for twenty years, so we can communicate very well.
- ○ D We've been friends for twenty years, so we can read each other's mind.

5 《恋人・夫婦》

〈ジェーン：私たちは長い間付き合っているんです。だからツーカーなんです〉

Jane:

- ☆ A We've been seeing each other for a long time, so we communicate very well.
- ◎ B We've been seeing each other for a long time, so she can read my mind.
- ◎ C We've been seeing each other for a long time, so we can read each other's mind.
- ◎ D We've been seeing each other for a long time, so she and I can read each other's mind.
- ◎ E We've been seeing each other for a long time, so we're on the same wave length.
- ○ F We've been seeing each other for a long time, so we're just like that.
- ○ G We've been seeing each other for a long time, so we're communicating very well.
- △ H We've been seeing each other for a long time, so we're in sync each other.

通過する

1 《税関》

〈これは税関を通過しないでしょう〉

- ◎ A This won't go through customs.
- ○ B This won't pass through customs.

2 《試験》

〈私はなんとか筆記試験は通過したのですが口頭試験に落ちてしまったんです〉

- ◎ I managed to pass [get through, squeak through, scrape through] the written test but I failed the oral one.

3 《電車》

〈この電車は代々木は通過します〉

- ◎ A This train'll pass Yoyogi.
- ◎ B This train won't stop at Yoyogi.

4 《車》

〈私は大きなトラックがあなたの事務所のそばを通過するのを見ました〉

- ◎ A I saw a big truck passing by your office.
- ◎ B I saw a big truck driving by [past] your office.
- ◎ C I saw a big truck going by [past] your office.
- ○ D I saw a big truck passing your office.

5 《法案が議会を》

⟨この法案は議会を通過するでしょう⟩
- ◎ A The bill will go [pass] through the House.
- ◎ B The bill will be passed by the House.
- ○ C The bill will get through the House.
- ○ D The bill will be ratified by the House.
- △ E The bill will clear through the House.
- △ F The bill will be carried by the House.
- × G The bill will ride the House.
  - ❖(1) G が辞典に出ているが使われていない．
  - ❖(2) C には「難しさがある」という響きがある．

通信社 →会社 26

通報する

1 《客観的に述べるとき》

⟨誰かが警察へ行って私たちのことを通報したんです⟩
- ◎ A Somebody went to the police and told [informed] them about us.
- ◎ B Somebody went to the police and reported us.

2 《主観的に「密告する」というニュアンスで述べるとき》

⟨誰かが警察へ行って私たちのことを通報したんです⟩
- ◎ A Somebody went to the police and ratted us out [ratted on us].
- ○ B Somebody went to the police and squealed [snitched, put the fingers] on us.
  - ❖ B の snitch は 20 代前半以下の人の間では非常によく使われている．

通訳 →職業 1

通路

1 《スーパー》

⟨通路を開けておいて下さい⟩
- ◎ A Keep the aisle clear.
- △ B Keep the lane clear.
- × C Keep the walkway clear.

2 《アパート・ビル》

⟨通路を開けておいて下さい⟩
- ☆ A Keep the hall clear.
- ◎ B Keep the hallway clear.
- △ C Keep the corridor clear.
- ▽ D Keep the passageway clear.

3 《劇場》

⟨通路を開けておいて下さい⟩
- ◎ A Keep the aisle clear.
- ○ B Keep the walkway [path] clear.
- △ C Keep the pathway clear.

4 《工場・倉庫》

⟨通路を開けておいて下さい⟩
- ◎ A Keep the walkway clear.
- ○ B Keep the pathway [path] clear.
  - ❖ A には，いろいろなものが置いてあるので歩くのに唯一安全な道路という響きがある．

5 《飛行機》

⟨通路を開けておいて下さい⟩
- ◎ A Keep the aisle clear.

416 つかいやすい

　　　△ B Keep the walkway clear.
　6 《ビルとビル，家と家の間》
　〈通路を開けておいて下さい〉
　　　◎ A Keep the aisle clear.
　　　× B Keep the walkway [pathway] clear.
　7 《公園》
　〈XYZ公園にはたくさん通路があります〉
　　　☆ A XYZ Park has a lot of paths.
　　　◎ B XYZ Park has a lot of pathways.
　　　○ C XYZ Park has a lot of walkways.
　　　△ D XYZ Park has a lot of trails.
　　❖ D は狭い通路.

使いやすい
〈このワープロは使いやすい〉
　　　◎ A This word processor's easy to use.
　　　○ B This word processor's user-friendly.

使う
1 《一般的に述べるとき》
〈このペンを使って下さい〉
　　　◎　Use this pen, please.
2 《機械を使えるかを尋ねるとき》
〈あなたはこの機械を使えますか〉
　　　☆ A Can you run this machine?
　　　◎ B Can you use [operate] this machine?
3 《時間を使うことを述べるとき》
〈私は時間を有効に使いたいんです〉
　　　◎ A I want to use my time well.
　　　○ B I want to use my time good.
　　　○ C I want to make good use of my time.
　　　△ D I want to use my time efficiently.
4 《人を使っていることを述べるとき》
〈彼は大勢人を使っています〉
　　　◎ A He has a lot of people working for him.
　　　◎ B He has a lot of employees.
　　　◎ C He has a large staff.
　　　◎ D A lot of people work for him.
　　　○ E He has a lot of people on his payroll.
　　　○ F He's employing a lot of people.
　　　○ G He employs a lot of people.
5 《人を使うのが上手であることを述べるとき》
〈彼は社員を使うのが上手です〉
　　　◎　He's good at managing [directing, handling] his employees.
6 《共同で使う》
〈私は他のテナントたちとお手洗いを共同で使うことにうんざりしています〉
　　　◎ A I'm sick and tired of sharing the bathroom with the other tenants.
　　　△ B I'm sick and tired of using the bathroom with the other tenants.
7 《「1人で使っている」というとき》
a) 批判的なニュアンスがある場合
〈彼は1人でこの大きな事務所を使っています〉

◎ A He's keeping this big office (all) to himself.
○ B He keeps this big office (all) to himself.
× C He's using this big office all to himself.

b）批判的なニュアンスのない場合
〈彼は1人でこの大きな事務所を使っています〉
◎ A He has this big office (all) to himself.
× B He's using this big office all to himself.

捕まる
1 《軽犯罪で「パクられる」というニュアンスのとき》
〈彼は酔っ払い運転で捕まったんです〉
◎ A He got picked up [busted] for drunk driving.
○ B He got nabbed for drunk driving.

2 《軽犯罪で「捕まる」というニュアンスのとき》
〈彼は酔っ払い運転で捕まったんです〉
◎ A He was caught for drunk driving.
○ B He was arrested for drunk driving.

3 《大きな犯罪で「捕まる」というニュアンスのとき》
〈彼は殺人容疑で逮捕されたんです〉
☆ A He was arrested for murder.
◎ B He was caught for murder.
△ C He was apprehended [got busted] for murder.
▽ D He got picked up [got nabbed, was captured] for murder.

付き合いで →付き合っている 6

突き当たり
1 《ビルの中》
〈彼の事務所は突き当たりです〉
◎ A His office is at the (other) end of the hall.
○ B His office is at the far end of the hall [hallway].
○ C His office is at the (other) end of the hallway.
△ D His office is at the (other) end of the corridor.
△ E His office is at the far end of the corridor.
× F His office is at the top [bottom] of the hall.

2 《道路》
〈彼の事務所は突き当たりです〉
◎ A His office is at the (other) end of the road.
○ B His office is at the far end of the road.

3 《路地》
〈彼の事務所は突き当たりです〉
◎ A His office is at the (other) end of the alley.
○ B His office is at the far end of the alley.

4 《スーパー・コンビニなどの中》
〈それは突き当たりにあります〉
◎ A That's at the (other) end of the aisle.
○ B That's at the far end of the aisle.

付き合っている
1 《成人》
〈ビルはジェーンと付き合っています〉
◎ A Bill's going out with Jane.
◎ B Bill and Jane're going out (together).

- ◎ C Bill's seeing Jane on the side.
- ◎ D Bill and Jane're seeing each other.
- ○ E Bill's dating Jane.
- ○ F Bill and Jane're dating.
- ○ G Bill and Jane go out together.
- △ H Bill goes out with Jane.
- △ I Bill and Jane go out [date].
- △ J Bill dates Jane.
- △ K Bill's in a relationship with Jane.
- △ L Bill and Jane're in a relationship.
- △ M Bill has a relationship with Jane.
- △ N Bill and Jane have a relationship.
- × O Bill keeps company with Jane.

❖(1) O が多くの辞典に出ているが使われていない．
❖(2) K〜N は少し改まった場面では非常によく使われている．
❖(3) A〜N はいずれも片方，または 2 人共が別の人と結婚している，つまり不倫で「付き合っている」の意味でも使われている．C, D は「独身」「不倫」のパーセンテージは 50 %で，一番この点があいまいな表現．2 番目にこのニュアンスが強いのは K〜N で，約 70 %は独身，約 30 %が不倫との響きがある．A, B, E〜J は独身である意味で使われるが，約 10 %は不倫上で「付き合っている」の意味でも使われている．

2 《10代〜20歳くらい》

〈ビルはジェーンと付き合っているんだよ〉

- ◎ A Bill's going out with Jane.
- ◎ B Bill and Jane're going out (together).
- ○ C Bill's seeing [dating] Jane.
- ○ D Bill and Jane're dating.
- ○ E Bill goes out with Jane.
- △ F Bill and Jane're seeing each other.
- △ G Bill and Jane go out (together).
- △ H Bill dates Jane.
- ▽ I Bill and Jane date.
- ▽ J Bill's in a relationship with Jane.
- ▽ K Bill and Jane're in a relationship.
- ▽ L Bill has a relationship with Jane.
- ▽ M Bill and Jane have a relationship.
- × N Bill keeps company with Jane.

3 《年齢差が非常にあるとき》

a) 女性が主語のとき

〈彼女は若い男性と付き合っている〉

- ◎ A She's robbing the cradle.
- ◎ B She has a boy toy.
- ◎ C She's seeing a young guy.

❖辞典に A は結婚しているときにも使われると書いてあるが，約 95 %は 2 人は結婚していないという響きがある．B は She が非常に金持ちというニュアンスがある．A, B は She が独身のときだが，C は別の男性と結婚しているときも独身のときも使われている．

b) 男性が主語のとき

〈彼は若い女性と付き合っているんです〉

- ◎ A He's robbing the cradle.
- ◎ B He's seeing a young woman.
- ○ C He's her sugar daddy.
  - ❖(1) A は He が普通結婚していないとき，B は He が別の女性と結婚しているときもある．
  - ❖(2) C は He が別の女性と結婚しているか否かはっきりしない．
  - ❖(3) C は She が He からお金やプレゼントをたくさんもらっているという響きが強い．

4 《社交上の交際》

a) 中流の上，または上流階級

〈私たちは彼らと付き合っています〉
- ◎ A We socialize with them.
- ◎ B We spend time with them.
- △ C We hang out [around] with them.
  - ❖ A は豪華なパーティーや，有名なホールでのクラシック音楽のコンサートへ行くこと，有名なカントリークラブでゴルフをすることなど．C はスポーツ観戦，ボウリング，テニス，また，ディスコへ行くこと．B はあいまいな表現で，多くのことが意味される．

b) 中流，下層階級，若い人

〈私たちは彼らと付き合っています〉
- ◎ A We hang out with them.
- ◎ B We spend time with them.
- ○ C We hang around with them.
- △ D We socialize with them.
  - ❖ D は下層階級では使われていない．

5 《ビジネス》

〈うちは XYZ 社と付き合っています〉
- ◎ A We do business with XYZ Company.
- ◎ B We deal with XYZ Company.
- ◎ C We're dealing with XYZ Company.
- ◎ D We associate with XYZ Company.
  - ❖ A, B, C はビジネス上での取引があるときに使われている．しかし，D は表面的な付き合いで具体的には言えないあいまいな語．

6 《「付き合いで」というとき》

〈私はしばしば付き合いで飲みに行きます〉
- ◎ A I often go drinking to socialize.
- ◎ B I often go drinking for the companionship [the company].
- ◎ C I often go drinking just for the companionship [the company].
  - ❖ C はあまり自発的ではなく「ただ社交上必要なので付き合う」というニュアンスが強い．

突きとめる

1 《故障・病気・死因》

a) 車の修理工

〈エンジンの故障の原因が突きとめられないんです〉
- ◎ A I can't find [locate, pinpoint, figure out] the problem with the engine.
- ○ B I can't detect [determine] the problem with the engine.

b) 一般の人

〈エンジンの故障の原因が突きとめられないんです〉

◎ A I can't find [figure out, find out] the problem with the engine.
○ B I can't pinpoint [determine] the problem with the engine.
△ C I can't locate [detect] the problem with the engine.

2 《事務所・家の場所》

〈私は彼の事務所を突きとめることができなかったんです〉

◎ A I couldn't find his office.
○ B I couldn't locate his office.
× C I couldn't find out his office.

着く

1 《一般的に言う場合》

a) 場所を述べるとき

〈駅へ着いたら電話して下さい〉

◎ A When you get to the station, please call me.
▽ B When you arrive at the station, please call me.
× C When you reach the station, please call me.

❖文章英語ではBを使い，A，Cは使われていない．

b) 場所を明示しないとき

〈あなたは何時に着いたのですか〉

◎ A What time did you get in [arrive]?
× B What time did you reach [get to]?

2 《飛行機・長距離バスなどで遠方から着くことを強調する場合》

〈(電話で)(飛行機は)何時に着くのですか〉

☆ A What time're you getting in [arriving]?
◎ B What time'll your plane be here?
◎ C What time'll your plane get in?
○ D What time're you landing?
○ E What time'll your plane arrive?
△ F What time'll your plane land?

❖get in を使うのは，30分または1時間に1本のスケジュールで走っている交通機関を利用した場合．したがって，どんなに遠くから来たときでも，頻繁に走っている電車を乗り継いで着いたときには get in は使えない．

3 《困難を乗り越えて着くことを強調する場合》

〈ついに彼らは山の頂上にたどり着きました〉

◎ A Finally they reached [made it to] the top of the mountain.
△ B Finally they got to the top of the mountain.
▽ C Finally they arrived at the top of the mountain.

作り笑い

1 《表情の場合》

〈彼は私に作り笑いをしました〉

◎ A He gave me a forced smile.
◎ B He forced a smile at me.

2 《声を出した場合》

〈彼は作り笑いをしました〉

◎ A He forced a laugh.
○ B He made [gave] a forced laugh.

つくる

1 《会社》

〈私たちは新しい会社を作るんです〉

☆ A We're going to start (up) a new company.

つくる 421

◎ B We're going to set up a new company.
○ C We're going to organize [establish] a new company.

2 《組合》
〈組合を作ろう〉
☆ A Let's start a union.
◎ B Let's organize a union.
○ C Let's put together a union.
△ D Let's form [establish, make] a union.
× E Let's make up [create] a union.
❖ E が辞典に出ているが使われていない．

3 《半導体》
〈うちの会社は半導体を作っています〉
☆ A Our company makes semiconductors.
◎ B Our company manufactures semiconductors.
○ C Our company produces semiconductors.
❖ B, C は大量生産を意味している．

4 《生地》
〈うちの会社は生地を作っているのです〉
◎ A Our company's making fabrics.
○ B Our company's manufacturing fabrics.
▽ C Our company's producing fabrics.

5 《作物》
〈私たちはトウモロコシを作っています〉
◎ A We grow corn.
△ B We raise [cultivate] corn.

6 《ワイン》
〈うちの会社はワインを作っています〉
◎ A Our company's making wine.
○ B Our company's producing wine.
× C Our company's manufacturing [brewing, distilling] wine.

7 《ウイスキー》
〈うちの会社はウイスキーを作っているんです〉
◎ A Our company's making whiskey.
○ B Our company's distilling whiskey.
× C Our company's brewing whiskey.

8 《ビール》
〈うちの会社はビールを作っています〉
☆ A Our company brews beer.
◎ B Our company makes beer.
○ C Our company produces beer.
× D Our company manufactures beer.

9 《庭》
〈私は庭を造るつもりです〉
☆ A I'm going to plant a garden.
◎ B I'm going to grow [make] a garden.

10 《犬小屋》
〈私は明日犬小屋を作るつもりです〉
☆ A I'm going to build a doghouse tomorrow.
◎ B I'm going to make a doghouse tomorrow.

- △ C I'm going to construct a doghouse tomorrow.
- × D I'm going to fit up a doghouse tomorrow.

11 《橋》

a) エンジニア

〈私たちは川に橋を作る予定です〉
- ☆ A We're going to build a bridge on the river.
- ◎ B We're going to construct a bridge on the river.
- △ C We're going to make a bridge on the river.

b) 一般の人

〈私たちは川に橋を作る予定です〉
- ☆ A We're going to build a bridge on the river.
- ◎ B We're going to make a bridge on the river.
- △ C We're going to construct a bridge on the river.

12 《新語》

〈この小説家は多くの新語を作りました〉
- ◎ A This novelist made up many new words [phrases].
- ◎ B This novelist came up with many new words [phrases].
- ◎ C This novelist coined many new phrases.
- × D This novelist coined many new words.

つけがまわってくる

1 《普通の語調で言うとき》

〈一生懸命働かないと，後でつけがまわってくるよ〉
- ◎ A If you don't work hard, you'll pay for it later [in the end].
- ◎ B If you don't work hard, you'll pay the price later.
- ◎ C If you don't work hard, it'll bite you in the ass.
- ○ D If you don't work hard, you'll pay the price in the end.
- ○ E If you don't work hard, it'll bite you in the butt.
  ❖ C, E は下品な表現であるが，教養のある人の間でも広く使われている．

2 《強い調子で言うとき》

〈一生懸命働かなければ，後で必ずつけがまわってくるよ〉
- ◎ A If you don't work hard, you'll have to pay for it later [in the end].
- ◎ B If you don't work hard, you'll have to pay the price later.

告げ口する

1 《子供の場合》

〈ジムが僕のことをお母さんに告げ口したんだ〉
- ◎ A Jim went to Mom and told [tattled] on me.
- ○ B Jim went to Mom and squealed [ratted] on me.
- △ C Jim told [tattled] on me to Mom.

2 《成人の場合》

〈ジムが私のことを上司に告げ口したんです〉
- ◎ A Jim went to my boss and reported [told on] me.
- ○ B Jim went to my boss and ratted [squealed] on me.
- △ C Jim reported [told on] me to my boss.

つけ込む

〈私は彼の無知につけ込みたくないんです〉
- ◎ A I don't want to take advantage of his ignorance.
- ○ B I don't want to play on [exploit] his ignorance.
- △ C I don't want to capitalize on his ignorance.
- △ D I don't want to cash in on his ignorance.

- × E I don't want to presume on [impose on, practice on, trespass upon] his ignorance.
- × F I don't want to avail myself of his ignorance.
- × G I don't want to make advantage of his ignorance.
  - ❖(1) D は金銭的ニュアンスがはっきりしているときにのみ使われている．
  - ❖(2) E, F, G が辞典に出ているが使われていない．

つけひげ →ひげ 2

つける

1 《電気機器のスイッチなどを》

〈テレビをつけて下さい〉
- ◎ A Turn on the TV.
- ○ B Switch on the TV.
- △ C Flip on the TV.

2 《香水・口紅などを》

〈このコロンをつけなさい〉
- ◎ A Wear this cologne.
- ○ B Put on [Use] this cologne.

都合

1 《都合がいい》

a) 一般的に言う場合

〈月曜日は私には都合がいいです〉
- ◎ A Monday's good for me.
- ◎ B Monday's all right with [for] me.
- ◎ C Monday's OK with [for] me.
- ◎ D Monday works for me.

b) 強調して言う場合

〈月曜日は私には非常に都合がいいです〉
- ◎ A Monday's very [really] good for me.
- ◎ B Monday works well [works good] for me.
- ○ C Monday's very convenient for me.
- △ D Monday's quite all right for [with] me.
- ▽ E Monday's quite OK for [with] me.
  - ❖ B の work good はアメリカ人の間で誤りとして言われているがよく使われている．

c) 改まった口調で言う場合

〈月曜日は私には都合がいいです〉
- ☆ A Monday's suitable for me.
- ◎ B Monday's convenient for me.
- ○ C Monday suits me just fine.
- ○ D Monday's convenient with me.

2 《都合が悪い》

a) 一般的に言う場合

〈月曜日は私は都合がよくないんです〉
- ◎ A Monday isn't good for me.
- ◎ B Monday is bad for me.
- ○ C Monday isn't convenient for me.
- ○ D Monday doesn't work for me.
- △ E Monday isn't OK [all right] for me.
- △ F Monday doesn't suit [fit] my schedule.

△ G Monday doesn't suit me.
　　　× H Monday doesn't fit me.
　　　❖ H が辞典に出ているが使われていない.
　b) 強調して言う場合
　〈月曜日は私には一番都合がよくないんです〉
　　　◎ A Monday's the worst (day) for me.
　　　△ B Monday's the most inconvenient for me.
　　　△ C Monday's the least suitable for me.
　　　△ D Monday works the worst [the least] for me.
　3 《都合を尋ねる》
　a) 普通に尋ねる場合
　〈いつが一番都合がよいですか〉
　　　☆ A When'd be the best for you?
　　　◎ B When'd work the best for you?
　　　○ C When'd be the most convenient for you?
　　　▽ D When'd suit you the best?
　b) 丁寧な口調で尋ねる場合
　〈いつが一番ご都合がよろしゅうございますか〉
　　　◎ A What time'd be the most convenient for you?
　　　◎ B What time'd be [work] the best for you?
　　　○ C What time'd suit you the best?
　　　○ D What time'd be the most suitable for you?

続く
《状態の継続》
a) 一般に述べる場合
〈この寒さは 1 週間続くでしょう〉
　　　☆ A This cold weather'll last [continue] for a week.
　　　◎ B This cold weather'll stay on [go on] for a week.
　　　○ C This cold weather'll keep going for a week.
　　　△ D This cold weather'll keep [carry on, hold] for a week.
b) 非人称の It を主語にとるある種の動詞を従える場合
〈明日まで雨が降り続くでしょう〉
　　　☆ A It'll continue to rain [raining] until tomorrow.
　　　◎ B It'll keep (on) raining until tomorrow.
　　　○ C It'll go on raining until tomorrow.
　　　❖同様の文型をとる動詞は, snow (雪), sleet (みぞれ), sprinkle (霧雨) など.

続けて
〈10 日間続けて雨が降っています〉
　　　☆ A It's been raining for ten days straight.
　　　◎ B It's been raining for ten days in a row.
　　　◎ C It's been raining nonstop [continuously] for ten days.
　　　○ D It's been raining for ten days continuously [consecutively].
　　　△ E It's been raining for ten days running [on end].
　　　▽ F It's been raining for ten days successively [in succession].

集い　→集まり
勤めている
　1 《平社員》
　〈彼はデトロイト銀行に勤めています〉

☆ A　He works at Detroit Bank.
　　　◎ B　He's working at Detroit Bank.
　　　○ C　He's employed at Detroit Bank.
　　　△ D　He's employed by Detroit Bank.
　2　《平社員・管理職のどちらにも使える》
〈彼はデトロイト銀行に勤めています〉
　　　☆ A　He works for Detroit Bank.
　　　◎ B　He's working for Detroit Bank.
　　　◎ C　He's with Detroit Bank.
　　　○ D　He works with Detroit Bank.
　　　○ E　He's working with Detroit Bank.

つなぐ
　1　《手を》
〈両側の人たちと手をつないで下さい〉
　　　◎　　Join hands with the people on both sides of you.
　2　《犬を》
　a）単に「つなぐ」と述べるとき
〈犬をつないで下さい〉
　　　◎　　Tie up the dog, please.
　b）つなぐ対象を述べるとき
〈犬をあの木につなぎなさい〉
　　　◎ A　Tie your dog to that tree.
　　　▽ B　Tie up [Fasten] your dog to that tree.
　　　❖ Bは辞典に出ているが使われてもまれ.
　3　《車を》
〈あなたの車を私の車につなぎなさい〉
　　　◎ A　Hitch your car to the back of mine.
　　　○ B　Hook your car up to mine.
　　　△ C　Hook your car onto mine.
　　　× D　Tie [Connect] your car to mine.
　　　× E　Join [Couple] your car with mine.
　　　❖ D, Eが辞典に出ているが使われていない.
　4　《電話を》
〈内線15番につないで下さい〉
　　　◎ A　Please get [give] me extension 15.
　　　◎ B　Please put me through to extension 15.
　　　◎ C　Please transfer me to extension 15.
　　　◎ D　Please connect me to extension 15.
　　　○ E　Please transfer me through to extension 15.
　　　○ F　May I have extension 15, please?
　　　❖(1) Fは非常に丁重な響きになる.
　　　❖(2) 間違った内線につながれたときはC, Eが一番よく使われている.

つまずく
　1　《足を踏み外すこと》
　a）ただ単につまずく
〈彼は岩につまずいた〉
　　　◎　　He tripped on [over] a rock.
　b）つまずいてよろける
〈彼は石につまずいた〉

つま(らせ)

- ◎ A He stumbled on a stone.
- ○ B He stumbled over a stone.
- ▽ C He faltered over a stone.
  - ❖ C が辞典に出ているが使われてもまれ.

2 《比喩的に述べるとき》

〈彼は仕事ではずっと成功しているのですが，結婚でつまずいてしまったんです〉

- ◎ A He's been really successful in business but he messed up (in) his marriage.
- ◎ B He's been really successful in business but he messed his marriage up.
- ◎ C He's been really successful in business but he wrecked his marriage.
- ◎ D He's been really successful in business but he screwed up his marriage.
- ◎ E He's been really successful in business but he screwed his marriage up.
- ◎ F He's been really successful in business but he made a mess of his marriage.
- ○ G He's been really successful in business but he made a wrong [bad] choice in his marriage.
- ○ H He's been really successful in business but he made a mistake in his marriage.
- △ I He's been really successful in business but he made a false step in his marriage.
- × J He's been really successful in business but he took a wrong step in his marriage.
- × K He's been really successful in business but he met with a setback in his marriage.
  - ❖(1) 辞典に J, K が出ているが使われていない.
  - ❖(2) D, E が一番強い響きがある. 2番目は A, B, F. 3番目は C, G, H, I.
  - ❖(3) G は女性の方に非があったニュアンスがある.

詰ま(らせ)る

1 《コピー機》

〈コピー機を詰まらせないで下さい〉

- ☆ A Don't jam the copy machine.
- ◎ B Don't jam up the copy machine.
- ○ C Don't jam the copy machine up.
- △ D Don't clog (up) the copy machine.
- × E Don't plug [block, stop] (up) the copy machine.
  - ❖ E が辞典に出ているが使われていない.

2 《トイレ・流し・その他パイプ状のもの》

〈トイレを詰まらせないで下さい〉

- ☆ A Don't clog up the toilet, please.
- ◎ B Don't clog [stop] the toilet up, please.
- ◎ C Don't plug [stop] up the toilet, please.
- ◎ D Don't clog the toilet, please.
- ○ E Don't back up [jam] the toilet, please.

3 《鼻が風邪などで》

〈私はよく鼻が詰まるんです〉

- ◎ A My nose gets stuffed up quite often.
- ○ B My nose plugs up quite often.
- △ C My nose stuffs [gets plugged] up quite often.

4 《詰まっている》

a）コピー機

〈コピー機が詰まっているんです〉
- ☆ A The copy machine's jammed.
- ◎ B The copy machine's jammed up.
- △ C The copy machine's clogged (up).
- × D The copy machine's plugged [stopped, blocked, stuffed] (up).

b）流し・トイレ・その他パイプのもの

〈流しが詰まっているんです〉
- ☆ A The sink's clogged.
- ◎ B The sink's clogged [backed, stopped, plugged] up.
- ○ C The sink's plugged.
- ○ D The sink's blocked up.
- △ E The sink's blocked.
- × F The sink's stopped.
- × G The sink's bunged [stuffed] (up).

c）食物がのどに

〈早く食べすぎたの。そうしたらのどに詰まっちゃったの〉
- ◎ A I ate too fast and something got stuck in my throat.
- ◎ B I ate too fast and I was choking.

d）鼻

〈鼻が詰まっているんです〉
- ◎ A My nose is stuffed [plugged] up.
- ○ B My nose is plugged.
- ○ C I have a stuffy nose.
- △ D My nose is stuffed.
- △ E I have a stuffed nose.

5 《感激して胸が詰まる》

〈私は感動的な映画を見るといつも胸が詰まるんです〉
- ☆ A Whenever I see a touching movie, I get choked up.
- ◎ B Whenever I see a touching movie, I get a lump in my throat.
- ○ C Whenever I see a touching movie, I choke up.
- ○ D Whenever I see a touching movie, I have a lump in my throat.
- △ E Whenever I see a touching movie, I feel a lump in my throat.
- × F Whenever I see a touching movie, my throat gets choked up.

詰めこむ

1 《詰めこむ中身について言及しない場合》

〈彼女はスーツケースに詰めこんでいました〉
- ☆ A She was cramming her suitcase full.
- ◎ B She was stuffing [jamming] her suitcase full.
- ◎ C She was stuffing her suitcase.
- △ D She was cramming [squeezing, jamming] her suitcase.

2 《詰めこむ中身について言及する場合》

〈これらを全部スーツケースに詰めこむことができるかどうかわかりません〉
- ☆ A I don't know if I can cram all this stuff into the suitcase.
- ◎ B I don't know if I can stuff all this stuff into the suitcase.

つめる

- ◎ C I don't know if I can squeeze all this stuff into the suitcase.
- ○ D I don't know if I can jam all this stuff into the suitcase.
  - ❖(1) 詰めこみ方が一番強いのは A. 以下，D, C, B の順で弱くなる．
  - ❖(2)「詰める」の項も参照のこと．

詰める

1 《洋服の丈などを》
〈袖を詰めてくれますか〉
- ☆ A Will you hem my sleeves?
- ◎ B Will you shorten my sleeves?
- ○ C Will you take up my sleeves?
- ○ D Will you take my sleeves up?

2 《座席を》
〈(電車・バスなどで) 詰めてくれますか〉
- ◎ A Will you scoot over for me?
- ○ B Will you move [slide] over for me?
- ○ C Will you make room [space] for me?
- △ D Will you scooch over for me?
  - ❖ D は 40 歳以上の女性にはよく使われている．特に子供に話しかけるときは非常によく使われている．

3 《かばんなどに》
〈彼女はスーツケースに (荷物を) 詰めていました〉
- ◎ A She was packing her suitcase.
- ○ B She was packing up her suitcase.
- ○ C She was filling (up) her suitcase.
  - ❖「詰めこむ」の項も参照のこと．

強い

1 《暖房器具などの設定について言う場合》

a) 一般的に述べるとき
〈暖房を強くしておいて下さい〉
- ◎ A Keep the heat on high.
- ◎ B Keep the heat turned on [up] high.
- ○ C Keep the heat running on high.
- △ D Keep the heat up.
- △ E Keep the heat at its maximum.
  - ❖ A〜D は温度を「(その暖房器具の設定温度の中で) 最強にしておく」と，一般的に「(温度を) 高くしておく」の両方の意味で使われている．E は教育レベルの高い人の間では非常によく使われている．

b) 「最強」の意味のとき
〈暖房を最強にしておいて下さい〉
- ◎ A Keep the heat turned all the way up.
- ◎ B Keep the heat turned up all the way.
- ◎ C Keep the heat all the way up.
- ◎ D Keep the heat up all the way.
- ◎ E Keep the heat (turned) on high.
- ○ F Keep the heat turned on all the way.
- ○ G Keep the heat on full blast.
- ○ H Keep the heat turned up [running on] high.
- △ I Keep the heat at its maximum.
- △ J Keep the heat switched all the way up.

- △ K Keep the heat switched up all the way.
- × L Keep the heat switched on all the way.
- × M Keep the heat switched on high.
  - ❖(1) A〜K は冷房, テレビ, 水道, ガスなど操作できるものに広く使われている.
  - ❖(2) E, H は「今より強く」の意味でも多少使われているが, 普通は「最強にしておく」の意味で使われている.
 2 《酒などについて言う場合》
 〈彼は強い酒が好きなんです〉
  - ☆ A He likes the hard stuff.
  - ◎ B He likes the strong stuff.
  - ◎ C He likes hard [strong] liquor.
  - ◎ D He likes liquor.
  - ○ E He likes hard [strong] alcohol.
  - ▽ F He likes spirits.
  - ❖ F は辞典に出ているがあまり使われていない.

強くなる
 1 《要望としての意見》
 〈政府は規制を撤廃すべきだという意見がますます強まるだろう〉
  - ◎ A The opinion that the Government should deregulate its restrictions'll become more and more popular.
  - ○ B The opinion that the Government should deregulate its restrictions'll become more and more common.
  - ○ C The opinion that the Government should deregulate its restrictions'll become more widespread.
  - △ D The opinion that the Government should deregulate its restrictions'll become stronger and stronger.
 2 《権限・勢力・発言力》
 〈彼の人事への発言力がますます強くなるだろう〉
  - ☆ A He'll have more and more power in personnel.
  - ◎ B His power in personnel will be stronger and stronger.
  - ◎ C He'll have more and more pull [influence] in personnel.
  - ◎ D He'll have a bigger and bigger say [voice] in personnel.
 3 《風》
 〈今日の午後もっと風が強くなるだろう〉
  - ☆ A It'll be windier this afternoon.
  - ◎ B The wind'll get stronger this afternoon.
  - ○ C The wind'll be stronger this afternoon.
  - ▽ D It'll blow harder this afternoon.
 4 《「確証を得る」意味で》
 〈彼が今言ったことで私の彼に対しての疑いが強くなりました〉
  - ◎ A What he just said's confirmed my suspicion in him.
  - ○ B What he just said's increased [validated] my suspicion in him.
  - △ C What he just said's strengthened [secured, settled, assured] my suspicion in him.
  - × D What he just said's guaranteed my suspicion in him.

連れて行く
 1 《話し手が行くと決めているとき》
 〈父親:今年の夏みんなをニューヨークへ連れて行くよ〉

430　つれていく

Father:
- ◎ A I'm going to take you to New York this summer.
- ◎ B I'm going to bring you to New York this summer.
- ○ C I'm going to let you come with me to New York this summer.
- ○ D I'm going to let you come to New York with me this summer.
    - ❖ どの辞典も B を紹介していないが非常によく使われている．これは一時的な俗語表現としてではなく，以前から定着している慣用である．

2　《話し手が行くと決めていないとき》

〈父親：今年の夏ニューヨークへみんなを連れて行くかもしれないよ〉

Father:
- ◎ A I might take you to New York this summer.
- △ B I might bring you to New York this summer.

3　《話し手と聞き手が一緒に行くとき》

a）聞き手がどこかへ行くのを決めているとき

〈お父さん，私たちをニューヨークへ連れて行ってくれますか〉

- ☆ A Dad, will you take us with you to New York?
- ◎ B Dad, will you let us go with you to New York?
- ◎ C Dad, can we go to New York with you?
- ◎ D Dad, can we go with you to New York?

b）聞き手がどこかへ行くのをまだ決めていないとき

〈お父さん，今年の夏ニューヨークへ連れて行ってくれますか〉

- ◎ A Dad, can [will] you take us to New York this summer?
- ◎ B Dad, can we go to New York this summer?

4　《話し手と聞き手が一緒になるとき》

〈ジムを明日連れて行っていいですか〉

- ◎ A Can I bring [take] Jim tomorrow?
- ◎ B Can I bring [take] Jim along tomorrow?
- ◎ C Can I bring Jim with me tomorrow?.
- ◎ D Can I come with Jim tomorrow?
    - ❖ bring＝「連れて来る」と覚えている人が多いであろう．しかし，話し手と聞き手が一緒になるときは take と同じ「連れて行く」の意味としてよく使われている．

5　《「車で目的地まで乗せて行く」の意味のとき》

〈明日動物園へ連れて行くよ〉

- ☆ A I'll take you to the zoo tomorrow.
- ◎ B I'll drive you to the zoo tomorrow.
- ◎ C I'll give you a ride to the zoo tomorrow.
- ○ D I'll give you a lift to the zoo tomorrow.
- △ E I'll take you to the zoo by car tomorrow.
    - ❖ A, E は動物園へ行って一緒に楽しむの意味で普通使われているが，B, C, D は動物園まで車で連れて行って，自分はどこかへ別のところへ行くというニュアンスで普通使われる．

6　《「すぐ連れて行く」の意味のとき》

〈私たちは彼を車ですぐ病院へ連れて行かなければならない〉

- ◎ A We have to get [rush] him to the hospital.
- ◎ B We have to take him to the hospital immediately.
- △ C We have to race him to the hospital.
- ▽ D We have to dash him to the hospital.
    - ❖ get, rush, race, dash に immediately の意味が入っているが，B の take

にはimmediatelyの意味が入っていないので言及する必要がある。なお，getに「すぐ連れて行く」の意味を紹介している英和辞典，和英辞典はないが，よく使われている．
7 《連れて来てもらう》
〈彼にここへ連れて来てもらったんです〉
　　☆ A He gave me a ride here.
　　☆ B He drove me here.
　　◎ C I got a ride [lift] here from him.
　　◎ D He gave me a lift here.
　　◎ E He brought me here by car.

〔て〕

提案
1 《一般に》
a) かしこまらない内容
〈ジェーンの提案は私たちが動物園へ行くことなんです〉
　　◎ A Jane's suggestion [idea] is that we go to the zoo.
　　◎ B Jane's suggesting that we go to the zoo.
　　△ C Jane's proposal is that we go to the zoo.
　　△ D Jane's proposing that we go to the zoo.
b) かしこまった内容
〈新しい企画に対する彼の提案は却下されたんです〉
　　☆ A His proposal for the new project was rejected.
　　◎ B His suggestion for the new project was rejected.
　　△ C His proposition for the new project was rejected.
2 《議案・法律》
〈提案13は通過すると思いますか〉
　　◎ A Do you think Proposition 13 will pass?
　　× B Do you think Proposal [Suggestion] 13 will pass?

提案する
1 《かしこまった場面》
〈弁護士は私が訴えた会社と妥協するように提案しました〉
　　◎ A My lawyer suggested [proposed] (to me) that I compromise with the company I sued.
　　◎ B My lawyer suggested [proposed] compromising with the company I sued.
　　◎ C My lawyer suggested to me to compromise with the company I sued.
　　△ D My lawyer proposed to me to compromise with the company I sued.
　　△ E My lawyer suggested [proposed] my compromising with the company I sued.
　　❖ suggest には親しみを込めた響きがある．propose にはかしこまった響きとよく考えたというニュアンスがある．
2 《かしこまらない場面》
〈ジェーンは私たちがハワイで夏休みを過ごすことを提案しています〉
　　◎ A Jane's suggesting that we spend the summer vacation in Hawaii.
　　◎ B Jane's suggestion is that we spend the summer vacation in Hawaii.

- △ C Jane's proposing that we spend the summer vacation in Hawaii.
- △ D Jane's proposal is that we spend the summer vacation in Hawaii.

定員

1 《定員以上に受け入れているとき》

〈最近定員より 15 ％以上の学生を入学させている大学が多い〉

- ☆ A Lately many colleges accept 15% more applications than they can enroll.
- ◎ B Lately many colleges accept 15% more applications than they can admit.
- ◎ C Lately many colleges accept 15% more applications than they should have.
- ◎ D Lately many colleges accept 15% more applications than they're supposed to.
- ○ E Lately many colleges accept 15% more applications than they can take (in).
- ○ F Lately many colleges accept 15% more applications than they're allowed to.
- △ G Lately many colleges accept 15% more applications than they have room for.
- △ H Lately many colleges accept 15% more applications than their maximum capacity.
- × I Lately many colleges accept 15% more applications than the prescribed [set, fixed] number.

❖ I が辞典に出ているが使われていない．

2 《大学の学部の定員》

〈経済学部の定員は何人ですか〉

- ◎ A What's the total number of students in the economics department?
- ◎ B How many students're you going to have [enroll, admit, accept] in the economics department?
- ◎ C How many students're you going to accept into the economics department?
- ○ D How many students can you join the economics department?
- ○ E How many students're you going to admit into the economics department?
- △ F What's the maximum number of students in the economics department?
- △ G How many students can you allow in the economics department?

3 《団体観光旅行の定員》

〈このツアーの定員は何人ですか〉

- ☆ A How many people're going on this tour?
- ◎ B What's the maximum [total] number of people on this tour?
- ◎ C How many people're you going to take on this tour?
- ◎ D How many people can join this tour?
- ◎ E How many people can you take on this tour?
- ◎ F How many people're you going to accept for [on] this tour?

4 《飛行機の定員》

〈この飛行機の定員は何人ですか〉

- ☆ A What's the total number of passengers on this plane?
- ◎ B How many passengers can you take on this plane?

- ◎ C What's the seating capacity on this plane?
- ◎ D How many seats does this plane have?
- ○ E What's the maximum number of passengers on this plane?
- ○ F How many passengers can you have on this plane?
- ○ G What's the maximum seating capacity on this plane?
- ○ H What's the total seating capacity on this plane?
- △ I How many passengers can you fly on this plane?

低下する

1 《学生の学力》

〈最近日本の大学生の学力が著しく低下しました〉

- ◎ A Lately Japanese college students' scholastic ability's declined dramatically [drastically, a lot].
- ◎ B Lately Japanese college students' scholastic ability's gone down dramatically [drastically].
- ○ C Lately Japanese college students' scholastic ability's fallen dramatically [drastically].
- ○ D Lately Japanese college students' scholastic ability's dropped dramatically [drastically].
- ○ E Lately Japanese college students' scholastic ability's gone [come] down a lot.
- △ F Lately Japanese college students' scholastic ability's come down dramatically [drastically].
- △ G Lately Japanese college students' scholastic ability's fallen a lot.

❖下がる程度は drop が一番強く，fall が2番，残りはほぼ同じで3番．

2 《生産性》

〈日本の生産性は今後低下するだろう〉

- ☆ A Japan's productivity'll slow down from now on.
- ◎ B Japan's productivity'll decrease from now on.
- ○ C Japan's productivity'll decline [go down, fall, drop] from now on.
- △ D Japan's productivity'll come down [get worse] from now on.

3 《道徳》

〈日本の10代の少女の道徳が低下している〉

- ☆ A The morals of Japanese teenage girls're changing for the worse.
- ◎ B The morals of Japanese teenage girls're getting worse.
- ○ C The morals of Japanese teenage girls're declining [going down, falling].
- △ D The morals of Japanese teenage girls're dropping [coming down].

定義する

〈あなたが使う用語をもっとはっきり定義してくれますか〉

- ◎ A Will you spell out [explain] your terms more clearly?
- ○ B Will you define your terms more clearly?
- × C Will you expound [throw light on] your terms more clearly?

❖C が辞典に出ているが使われていない．

定期預金 →預金 1

提出する

1 《レポートを》

〈私は月曜日までに歴史のレポートを提出しなければならないんです〉

- ◎ A I've got to turn in [hand in, send in] my history paper by Monday.
- × B I've got to give in my history paper by Monday.

- ❖(1) B が辞典に出ているが使われていない．
- ❖(2) hand in は手で渡すとき，send in は郵便で送るときに使い分けられている．turn in は「手渡し」「郵便」のいずれにも使われている．

2 《証拠を》

〈私は彼が犯人であるという証拠を提出しなければならない〉

- ◎ A I've got to provide [produce, present] the evidence that he's the criminal.
- ○ B I've got to hand over the evidence that he's the criminal.
- △ C I've got to bring forward [submit] the evidence that he's the criminal.
  - ❖(1) A, C は郵便，または手渡しの両方に使えるが，B は手渡しにしか使えない．
  - ❖(2) produce には相手が証拠を隠しているというニュアンスがある．

3 《陳情書を》

〈私たちは当局に陳情書を提出するつもりです〉

- ◎ A We're going to present [submit, turn in] the petition to the authorities.
- ◎ B We're going to file the petition with the authorities.
- ○ C We're going to register the petition with the authorities.

提訴する

〈アメリカはフランスを WTO に提訴するだろう〉

- ◎ A America'll file an action against France with the WTO.
- ◎ B America'll appeal [take, present] the case against France to the WTO.
- ○ C America'll take action against France with the WTO.

停滞している

〈日本の経済は過去10年間停滞している〉

- ◎ A Japan's economy has been stagnant [sluggish] for the past ten years.
- ○ B Japan's economy has been at a standstill for the past ten years.
- ▽ C Japan's economy has been idle for the past ten years.
- ▽ D Japan's economy has been inactive for the past ten years.
- × E Japan's economy has been dull for the past ten years.
  - ❖(1) E が辞典に出ているが使われていない．
  - ❖(2) 停滞の深刻度は stagnant が一番強い．以下 sluggish, at a standstill の順になる．

定着率

1 《「定着率が高い」と言うとき》

〈この会社は社員の定着率が高い〉

- ◎ A This company has a low employee turnover rate.
- ○ B This company has loyal employees.
- △ C This company's employees stay for a long time.

2 《「定着率が悪い」と言うとき》

〈この会社は社員の定着率が悪い〉

- ◎ A This company has a high employee turnover rate.
- ○ B This company has a high turnover rate of its employees.

停電

1 《工事により》

〈建築工事のために2時間停電になります〉

◎ A We're going to have a two-hour power outage because of the construction work.
　　　○ B We're going to have a two-hour blackout because of the construction work.
　　　▽ C We're going to have a two-hour power cut because of the construction work.
　　　× D We're going to have a two-hour power failure because of the construction work.
　2　《災害などにより》
〈今日の午後，嵐のために2時間停電になりました〉
　　　◎ A This afternoon we had a two-hour blackout [power outage] because of the storm.
　　　○ B This afternoon we had a two-hour power failure because of the storm.
　　　△ C This afternoon we had a two-hour power blackout because of the storm.
　　　× D This afternoon we had a two-hour power stoppage [power breakdown, failure] because of the storm.
　　　❖ D が辞典に出ているが使われていない．
　3　《状態を述べる場合》
〈停電だ〉
　　　◎ A The power's out.
　　　○ B The electricity's off.
　　　○ C The power's (gone) off.
　　　△ D The juice's off.
　　　× E The current's off.
　　　❖(1) E は辞典に出ているが使われていない．
　　　❖(2) 電気が消えたときに「停電だ！」と叫ぶときには Blackout! という．

手紙を書く

〈彼は昨日私に手紙を書いてきました〉
　　　◎ A He wrote me yesterday.
　　　○ B He wrote (a letter) to me yesterday.
　　　○ C He wrote me a letter yesterday.

敵意

〈彼は彼らに対して敵意を持っている〉
　　　◎ A He has hostility [animosity] towards them.
　　　○ B He has hatred towards them.
　　　▽ C He has antagonism towards them.
　　　× D He has enmity [spite, maliciousness, ill feeling] towards them.
　　　❖ D が辞典に出ているが使われていない．

適材適所

〈スミス氏が総支配人に昇格した．適材適所だ〉
　　　◎ A Mr. Smith has been promoted to General Manager. He's the right man for the job.
　　　▽ B Mr. Smith has been promoted to General Manager. He's the right man in the right place.
　　　× C Mr. Smith has been promoted to General Manager. He's the right man for the right place.
　　　❖辞典に C が出ているが使われていない．B も多くの辞典に出ているがまれ

に使われる程度.

手頃な
〈私たちは手頃な家を探しています〉
- ☆ A We're looking for an affordable house.
- ◎ B We're looking for a reasonably-priced house.
- ○ C We're looking for an affordably-priced house.

…でしょう (現在の推量)
1 《現在のことを話題にしていることを明示する副詞句があるとき》
〈車はもう混んでいるでしょう〉
- ☆ A The traffic must be heavy by now.
- ☆ B I'm sure the traffic's heavy by now.
- ◎ C The traffic's got to be heavy by now.
- ◎ D The traffic has to be heavy by now.
- ◎ E The traffic'll be heavy by now.
- ◎ F The traffic'd be heavy by now.
- ◎ G I'm positive the traffic's heavy by now.
- ○ H I bet [I betcha, I'll bet] the traffic's heavy by now.
- △ I I'm certain the traffic's heavy by now.
    - ❖断定度はGが一番強く，Dが2番，Cが3番，A，Bが4番，Hが5番，Eが6番．Fが一番弱い．

2 《関係詞が文中にあるとき》
〈あの人が私たちに会おうとしている人なんでしょう〉
- ☆ A That must be the person we're going to meet.
- ☆ B I'm sure that's the person we're going to meet.
- ◎ C That's got to be the person we're going to meet.
- ◎ D That has to be the person we're going to meet.
- ◎ E That'll be the person we're going to meet.
- ◎ F That'd be the person we're going to meet.
- ◎ G I'm positive that's the person we're going to meet.
- ○ H I bet [I betcha, I'll bet] that's the person we're going to meet.
- △ I I'm certain that's the person we're going to meet.
    - ❖上記の文のpersonとweの間に関係詞のwhomが省略されている．

3 《副詞・副詞句・関係詞がないとき》
〈お疲れでしょう〉
- ☆ A You must be tired.
- ☆ B I'm sure you're tired.
- ◎ C You have to be tired.
- ◎ D You've got to be tired.
- ◎ E I bet you're tired.
- ○ F I'll bet you're tired.
- ○ G I betcha you're tired.
- × H You'll be tired.
- × I You'd be tired.
    - ❖副詞句 (by now)，関係詞が文中にないときはwill, wouldは推量で使えないことが多い．

鉄鋼工場 →工場 3

手伝う
1 《名詞を従えるとき》
〈彼は私の研究を手伝ってくれました〉

- ☆ A He helped me with my research.
- ◎ B He helped with my research.
- ○ C He helped me in my research.
  - ❖手伝う仕事が知的なときは with でなく in を使うと説明している辞書があるが，実際は名詞の内容に関係なく A が一番よく使われている．

2 《動詞を従えるとき》

〈彼は私がビジネスを始めるのを手伝ってくれました〉
- ◎ A He helped me to start my business.
- ◎ B He helped me start my business.
- ◎ C He helped start my business.

鉄道会社　→会社 27
撤廃する　→規制を撤廃する
出て行く

1 《一般的に言うとき》

〈彼は少し前に事務所を出ていきました〉
- ◎ 　He went out of [walked out of, left] the office a few minutes ago.

2 《ちょっと出て行く》

〈彼はちょっと事務所を出て行きました〉
- ◎ A He stepped out of his office.
- ◎ B He stepped away from his desk.
- ◎ C He walked out of his office for a minute.
- ◎ D He just walked away from his desk.
- ◎ E He just walked away from his desk for a moment [a second, a sec].
- ◎ F He went out of his office for a minute [a moment].
- ○ G He went out of his office for a second [a sec].
- ○ H He left his office for a minute [a moment].
- △ I He left his office for a second [a sec].

3 《怒って出て行く》

〈彼は怒って出て行きました〉
- ☆ A He stormed out of his office.
- ◎ B He bolted [stomped, flew] out of his office in a rage.
- ◎ C He bolted out of his office in a huff.
- ○ D He stomped [flew] out of his office in a huff.
- ○ E He ran out of his office in a rage [a huff].
- △ F He bolted out of his office in anger.
  - ❖F の in anger は上記の他の動詞にも使えるが，時々使われる程度．

4 《命令的に述べるとき》

〈出て行け〉
- ◎ A Get out.
- ◎ B Get away.
- ◎ C Get lost.
- ◎ D Beat it.

出ている

1 《水道》

〈水道が出ている〉
- ◎ A The water's running.
- ○ B The water's on.

2 《よだれ》

〈あなたはよだれが出ていますよ〉

◎ A Your mouth's watering.
× B Your mouth's running.
❖ B が辞典に出ているが使われていない.

3 《鼻》
〈鼻が出ていますよ〉
◎ A Your nose is running.
◎ B You've got a runny nose.

4 《外出している》
〈彼は出ています〉
◎ He's out.

5 《新聞に載っている》
〈彼のスキャンダルが新聞に出ています〉
◎ His scandal is in the papers.

6 《テレビ・ラジオ》
〈彼女は毎日テレビに出ています〉
◎ A She's on TV every day.
○ B She appears on TV every day.

出て来る

1 《建物から》
〈私は彼女が XYZ 銀行から出て来るのを見ました〉
◎ A I saw her leaving [coming out of] XYZ Bank.
△ B I saw her coming out (from) XYZ Bank.

2 《入口・裏口から》
〈私は彼が裏口から出て来るのを見ました〉
◎ A I saw him coming out through [of] the backdoor.
◎ B I saw him coming out the backdoor.
○ C I saw him leaving out the backdoor.
▽ D I saw him leaving the backdoor.
▽ E I saw him coming out from [by, at] the backdoor.

3 《駅の東口・西口・南口・北口から》
〈私は彼が東口から出て来るのを見ました〉
☆ A I saw him leaving [coming out] the east exit.
◎ B I saw him coming out of [through] the east exit.
○ C I saw him coming out from the east exit.
△ D I saw him out by [at] the east exit.

手取り

〈私は手取りで月に3千ドル稼がなければならないんです〉
◎ A I have to clear [net] $3,000 a month.
◎ B I have to earn [make] $3,000 after taxes a month.
◎ C My take-home-pay has to be $3,000 a month.
○ D My net-income has to be $3,000 a month.
❖ A は低い給料には使われていない. C は非常に高額の給料には使われていない.

手に汗を握って

〈私たちは手に汗を握って試合中ずっと見ていました〉
◎ A We were on the edge of our seats during the whole game.
○ B We were on the pins and needles during the whole game.
▽ C We were in breathless suspense during the whole game.
❖ C は辞典に出ているがまれ. ただし, 文章では非常によく使われている.

手に入る
〈ニューヨークタイムズは日本で手に入ります〉
- ◎ A You can buy [get] *The New York Times* in Japan.
- ◎ B *The New York Times* is available in Japan.
- ◎ C You can have access to *The New York Times* in Japan.
- ○ D You can get access to *The New York Times* in Japan.
- × E You can access to *The New York Times* in Japan.

手本となる
〈私はあなたに他の人たちのお手本になっていただきたいのですが〉
- ◎ A I'd like you to set a good example for the others.
- ○ B I'd like you to be a good example for the others.
- △ C I'd like you to show a good example for the others.

出前
1 《会話で》
〈角のレストランは出前をしていますよ〉
- ☆ A The restaurant on the corner has catering service available.
- ◎ B The restaurant on the corner offers catering service(s).
- ○ C The restaurant on the corner has catering services available.
- ○ D The restaurant on the corner offers catering.
- △ E The restaurant on the corner supplies catering service(s).
- ▽ F The restaurant on the corner supplies catering.

2 《広告・看板》
〈出前いたします〉
- ☆ A Catering available.
- ◎ B Catering service(s) available.
- ○ C Catering service(s) offered.
- △ D Catering offered.
- △ E Catering service(s) supplied.
- ▽ F Catering supplied.

出まわる
〈偽100ドル札が国中に出まわっている〉
- ◎ A Counterfeit one hundred-dollar bills're (being) circulated all over the country.
- ◎ B Counterfeit one hundred-dollar bills're going around all over the country.
- ○ C Counterfeit one hundred-dollar bills're (being) passed around all over the country.

デリカショップ →店 10

出る
1 《雑誌が出版される》
〈5月号は火曜日に出ます〉
- ◎ The May issue'll come out [be out, be published] Tuesday.

2 《電話に応答する》
〈電話が鳴っています．出て下さい〉
- ◎ A The phone's ringing. Get [Answer] it, please.
- ◎ B The phone's ringing. Pick it up, please.
- ◎ C The phone's ringing. Grab it, please.
  - ❖(1) C は A, B より何度も鳴っているときに使われるので「急いで出なさい」というニュアンスがある．

❖(2)「出て行く」「出ている」「出て来る」の項も参照のこと．

テレビ

1 《一般に機械を指すとき》

〈私はテレビを買わなければならないんです〉

◎ A I have to buy a TV.
▽ B I have to buy a television [a TV set].
❖ B は以前はよく使われていたが，今はたまに使われる程度．

2 《特定の機械を指すとき》

〈それはテレビの上にあります〉

◎ A It's on the TV.
△ B It's on the television.

3 《映像・番組を述べるとき》

〈彼は明日テレビに出演します〉

◎ A He'll appear on TV tomorrow.
× B He'll appear on the TV tomorrow.

手を打つ

1 《売主が》

〈私は彼の値段で手を打つつもりです〉

◎ A I'm going to accept [agree to] the price he offered.
○ B I'm going to go with the price he offered.

2 《買主が》

〈私は彼の値段で手を打つつもりです〉

◎ A I'm going to meet the price he asked.
○ B I'm going to agree to [go with] the price he asked.

手を引く

〈彼はたぶん取引から手を引くだろう〉

☆ A He'll probably back out of the deal.
◎ B He'll probably pull out of the deal.
○ C He'll probably back down from the deal.
△ D He'll probably withdraw from the deal.

点

1 《正誤の対象として述べるとき》

〈あなたはその点で間違っています〉

◎ A You're wrong on that point.
◎ B You're wrong in that respect.
○ C You're wrong in that regard.
▽ D You're wrong on that score.

2 《同意・不同意の対象として述べるとき》

〈私はその点であなたに同意します〉

◎ A I agree with you on that point.
○ B I agree with you in that respect [regard, situation].

3 《多くの点から性格・行動を述べるとき》

〈彼は私に多くの点で親切でした〉

◎ A He was nice to me in many ways.
○ B He was nice to me in many respects.
▽ C He was nice to me in many regards.
× D He was nice to me on many points [scores].

4 《単に多くの点を意味するとき》

〈多くの点で私はシカゴよりもニューヨークのほうが好きです〉

◎ A In many ways I like New York more than Chicago.
○ B In many respects I like New York more than Chicago.
△ C In many regards I like New York more than Chicago.
▽ D On many points [scores] I like New York more than Chicago.

5 《特定の点を述べるとき》
〈彼は非常に忍耐強いんです．その点では彼はよい教師です〉
◎ A He's really patient. In that respect he's a good teacher.
○ B He's really patient. In that regard he's a good teacher.
× C He's really patient. On that point he's a good teacher.

6 《「他の点では」と述べるとき》
〈ニューヨークは物価の高い都市ですが，他の点では魅力的です〉
◎ A New York's an expensive city, but it's fascinating in other respects.
◎ B New York's an expensive city, but it's fascinating otherwise.
○ C New York's an expensive city, but it's fascinating in other areas [ways, regards].

7 《(…の) 点では》
〈XYZ会社は売り上げの点では日本で一番大きいんです〉
◎ A XYZ Company's the largest in Japan sales-wise.
○ B XYZ Company's the largest in Japan in terms of (its) sales.
△ C XYZ Company's the largest in Japan from the standpoint of its sales.
▽ D XYZ Company's the largest in Japan from the viewpoint of its sales.
❖ Cも「(…の) 点では」の英訳として辞典で紹介しているが，時々使われる程度．

店員 →職業 39
天気 →いい天気
電気会社 →会社 28
天気図
〈この天気図を見て下さい〉
◎ A Look at this weather map.
○ B Look at this weather chart.
△ C Look at this meteorological chart.
× D Look at this weather graph.
❖ Dは辞典に出ているが使われていない．Cも辞典に出ているが時々使われている程度．

電気屋 →店 15
転勤になる

1 《一般的に述べるとき》
〈彼はシカゴ支店に転勤になるでしょう〉
☆ A He'll be moved to the Chicago branch.
◎ B He'll be transferred [sent] to the Chicago branch.
○ C He'll be assigned [relocated] to the Chicago branch.
△ D He'll be shifted to the Chicago branch.
❖ Cはかしこまった響きがあるが，ビジネスの世界ではA, Bと同じように非常によく使われている．

2 《栄転》
〈彼はシカゴ支店に栄転になったんです〉
☆ A He was moved to the Chicago branch with a promotion.
◎ B He was transferred [sent] to the Chicago branch with a promotion.

- ◎ C He was reassigned to the Chicago branch and was promoted.
- ◎ D He was promoted to the Chicago branch.
- ○ E He was assigned [relocated] to the Chicago branch with a promotion.
- ○ F He was moved [transferred, sent] to the Chicago branch and was promoted.

3 《降格転勤》

〈彼は大阪支店へ降格転勤になったんです〉
- ◎ A He was moved [transferred, sent, reassigned] to the Osaka branch with a demotion.
- ◎ B He was demoted to the Chicago branch.
- ○ C He was relocated [assigned] to the Osaka branch with a demotion.

4 《転属になる》

〈彼は人事部に転属になったんです〉
- ☆ A He was moved to Personnel.
- ◎ B He was transferred [reassigned] to Personnel.
- ○ C He was assigned [relocated, shifted, sent] to Personnel.

伝言

1 《人に頼むとき》

a) 緊急なとき

〈秘書に伝言をしておいて下さい〉
- ◎ A Please leave word with my secretary.
- ○ B Please leave a message with my secretary.

b) 緊急でないとき
- ◎ A Please leave a message with my secretary.
- △ B Please leave word with my secretary.

2 《「伝言がある」というとき》

〈ビルからあなたへの伝言があります〉
- ◎ A I have a message for you from Bill [from Bill for you].
- △ B I have word for you from Bill [from Bill for you].

転職する

〈いつあなたは転職したのですか〉
- ◎ A When did you change jobs?
- ○ B When did you change your job?

電子レンジ

〈私は電子レンジを買わなければならないんです〉
- ☆ A I have to buy a microwave.
- ◎ B I have to buy a microwave oven.
- × C I have to buy an electronic oven.

❖ C が辞書に出ているが使われていない．

伝染する

1 《接触伝染病》

〈エイズは伝染病です〉
- ◎ AIDS is a contagious [an infectious] disease.

2 《空気伝染病》

〈結核は伝染します〉
- ◎ Tuberculosis is infectious [contagious].

❖ 辞典では接触伝染病の場合は contagious，空気伝染病の場合は infectious を使うのが正しいとしているが，実際には区別なく使われている．

電柱
1 《電気の電柱》
〈電柱が倒れたんです〉
- ◎ A The light pole fell over.
- ○ B The utility pole fell over.
- × C The electricity [electric-light, electric] pole fell over.
- ❖ C が辞典に出ているが使われていない．

2 《電話の電柱》
〈電柱が倒れたんです〉
- ◎ A The telephone pole fell over.
- × B The telegraph pole fell over.

点滴を受ける →病気 17
てんてこ舞い →忙しい 6
転覆する
1 《大きい船》
〈船は嵐のために転覆したんです〉
- ◎ A The ship turned over because of the storm.
- ○ B The ship overturned because of the storm.
- △ C The ship capsized because of the storm.
- × D The ship keeled [heeled] over because of the storm.
- ❖(1) D が辞典に出ているが使われていない．
- ❖(2) C はテレビ，新聞では非常によく使われている．

2 《小さい船》
〈彼らのボートは湖で転覆したんです〉
- ◎ A Their boat turned over [overturned] on the lake.
- ○ B Their boat tipped over on the lake.
- △ C Their boat capsized over on the lake.

電力会社 →会社 30
電話
1 《電話線を意味しているとき》
〈電話を開けておいて下さい〉
- ◎ A Keep the line open for me.
- △ B Keep the phone [telephone] open for me.

〈彼の電話はまだ話し中ですか〉
- ☆ A Is his line still busy?
- ◎ B Is his phone still busy?
- △ C Is his telephone still busy?

2 《「電話で」というとき》
〈別の電話でジムと話しているんだよ〉
- ◎ A I'm talking to Jim on another line.
- △ B I'm talking to Jim on another phone [telephone].

3 《電話口を意味しているとき》
〈彼を電話に出してくれますか〉
- ◎ A Will you put him on the phone [telephone]?
- △ B Will you put him on the line?

4 《(…のことで) 電話する》
〈新聞に出ている貴社の広告のことでお電話しています〉
- ☆ A I'm calling about your ad in the paper.
- ◎ B I'm calling in response to your ad in the paper.

○ C I'm answering your ad in the paper.
△ D I'm replying your ad in the paper.

5 《切らないでおく》
a) 電話で丁重に話すことが求められているとき
〈切らないでおいていただけますか〉
◎ A Will you hold on (a minute [a second])?
△ B Would you hold the line?

b) 電話で特に丁重に話すことが求められていないとき
〈切らないでおいてくれますか〉
◎　 Will you hang on?

6 《公衆電話》
〈あの公衆電話は故障しています〉
◎ A That pay phone's out of order.
△ B That public phone's out of order.

7 《携帯電話》
〈あなたは携帯電話をお持ちですか〉
☆ A Do you have a cell phone?
○ B Do you have a mobile [cellular] phone?

8 《(ホテルなどの) 館内電話》
〈この階に館内電話がありますか〉
◎　 Is there a house phone on this floor?

〔と〕

…という題の
〈彼は「日本の将来」という題の本を書きました〉
◎ A He wrote a book called Japan's Future.
○ B He wrote a book titled [named] Japan's Future.
△ C He wrote a book by [with] the name of Japan's Future.

…と言えば
〈音楽と言えば, あなたが一番好きな歌手は誰ですか〉
◎ A Speaking of music, who's your favorite singer?
× B Speaking about [Talking of, Talking about] music, who's your favorite singer?
❖辞典に B が出ているが使われていない.

同意する
1 《意見が同じであることを述べるとき》
a) 肯定文
〈私はあなたの提案に同意します〉
◎ A I agree with your proposal.
○ B I think it's a good proposal.
△ C I'm with your proposal.

b) 疑問文
〈(就職の面接で) 面接者:仕事の給与の条件は同意できるのですか〉
Interviewer:
☆ A Can you agree to the terms of the job?
◎ B Can you accept the terms of the job?

2 《契約書，またはそれに準ずるような文中で》
〈たとえあなたがこの規約の条件が気に入らなくても
- ◎ A Even if you don't like the terms of this agreement,
- ○ B Even if you don't agree with the terms of this agreement,

このサービスを受けるには履行しなければなりません〉
- ☆ A you have to agree to them to use this service.
- ◎ B you have to accept them to use this service.
- ○ C you have to abide by [follow, honor] them to use this service.

3 《「120％同意する」と述べるとき》
〈私はあなたに120％同意します〉
- ◎ A I agree with you 110%.
- ◎ B I totally [completely] agree with you.
- ○ C I agree with you totally [completely, entirely].
- ○ D I entirely agree with you.
- △ E I thoroughly [wholeheartedly] agree with you.
- △ F I 110% agree with you.
- △ G I agree with you thoroughly [wholeheartedly].
    - ❖ A を日本語の「120％」に引かれて a hundred and twenty percent としてはならない．「完全（以上）に」のニュアンスは英語では110％として表される．

4 《決裁権を持っている人が要請・依頼・計画・提案などを許可するという意味の「同意する」のとき》
〈社長は私たちの提案に同意してくれるでしょう〉
- ☆ A The boss'll agree to our proposal.
- ◎ B The boss'll approve [accept] our proposal.
- ◎ C The boss'll give us the go-ahead [the approval] on our proposal.
- ○ D The boss'll give the green light to our proposal.
- ○ E The boss'll go along with [go for] our proposal.
- △ F The boss'll consent to our proposal.
    - ❖ F は少し堅い響きがある．

5 《動詞を従えるとき》
〈私たちはこの候補者を支持することに同意します〉
- ◎ A We agree to support this candidate.
- ◎ B We agree supporting this candidate.
    - ❖ A は直接支持運動をするとき，B は間接的に支持運動をするときに使い分けられている．

6 《「…の点で合意する」と述べるとき》
〈彼はその点について彼らに同意しました〉
- ◎ A He reached an agreement [a compromise] with them on that point.
- ◎ B He came to terms with them on that point.
- △ C He arrived at an agreement with them on that point.

どういたしまして

1 《深く謝罪する I'm sorry. と言われたとき》
〈どういたしまして〉
- ☆ A That's [It's] all right.
- ☆ B That's [It's] OK.
- ◎ C Don't worry about it.
- ◎ D Don't mention it.
- ○ E It was [It's] nothing.

- △ F Don't be worried about it.
- △ G That was [That's] nothing.

2 《軽く詫びる Excuse me. と言われたとき》
〈どういたしまして〉
- ◎ A That's all right [OK].
- ◎ B No problem.
- ○ C Don't worry about it.

3 《スーパー・コンビニなどで客が礼を述べたとき》
〈どういたしまして〉
- ◎ A You're welcome.
- ◎ B Don't mention it.
- ◎ C Sure thing.
- ◎ D You bet.
- ○ E Sure.
- ○ F You betcha.
- △ G My pleasure.
- △ H It's my pleasure.

4 《スーパー・コンビニより高級な店でお客がお礼を述べたとき》
〈どういたしまして〉
- ◎ A It's my pleasure.
- ◎ B My pleasure.
- ◎ C You're welcome.
- ○ D Certainly.

5 《友人・家族同士など丁重な話し方を求められないとき》
〈どういたしまして〉
- ◎ A You're welcome.
- ○ B Don't mention it.
- ○ C Sure (thing).
- △ D You bet [betcha].

どう思いますか →思う 8

動機
〈何が動機でこの研究に興味を持ったのですか〉
- ◎ A What motivated [prompted, encouraged] you to become interested in this research?
- ◎ B What made you become interested in this research?

騰貴する
〈土地が騰貴している〉
- ◎ A Land's skyrocketing in value.
- ◎ B Land's soaring in value.
- ◎ C Land's going up in value.
- ◎ D Land's rising [increasing] in value.
- ○ E Land's shooting up in value.
- ○ F Land's appreciating in value.
  ❖騰貴している程度はAが一番高く，Bが2番目，Eが3番目，Dは4番目，C，Fが5番目．

同居する
1 《現在同居しているとき》
〈私たちは義理の両親と同居しています〉
- ◎ A We live with my in-laws.

- ◎ B My in-laws live with us.
- ○ C We live together with my in-laws.

2 《「これから同居する」という意味のとき》
〈私の義理の両親は私たちの家に同居したいと言っているんです〉
- ☆ A My in-laws want to move in with us.
- ◎ B My in-laws want to move into [in] our house.
- ◎ C My in-laws want to move into our place.
- ○ D My in-laws want to move in our place.

当座預金 →預金 3
倒産する →破産する
どうして
1 《肯定文が先行している場合》
〈ビル：私は来週ニューヨークへ行くんです〉
Bill: I'm going to go to New York next week.
〈トム：どうして〉
Tom:
- ◎ A What for?
- ◎ B Why?
- ◎ C How come?

2 《否定文が先行している場合》
〈ビル：私はトムが好きではないんです〉
Bill: I don't like Tom.
〈ボブ：どうして〉
Bob:
- ◎ A Why (not)?
- ◎ B How come?
- × C How come not?

3 《文は肯定文だが否定的な内容の場合》
〈ビル：私はトムが嫌いだよ〉
Bill: I hate Tom.
〈ボブ：どうして〉
Bob:
- ◎ A Why?
- ◎ B How come?
- × C Why not?
- × D How come not?

どうしようもない
1 《ひどい交通渋滞》
〈都心で車を運転することはどうしようもないね〉
- ◎ A Driving in downtown Tokyo's a nightmare.
- ◎ B Driving in downtown Tokyo's a torture.
- ◎ C Driving in downtown Tokyo's next to [almost] impossible.
- ○ D Driving in downtown Tokyo's an ordeal.
- ○ E Driving in downtown Tokyo's torture.
- ○ F Driving in downtown Tokyo's all but [nearly] impossible.
- △ G Driving in downtown Tokyo's hardly [barely] possible.
  - ❖ B は a torture, E は無冠詞.

2 《他の選択肢がないとき》
〈デトロイトの工場を売る以外他にどうしようもないね〉

☆ A We have no other choice but to sell the factory in Detroit.
◎ B We have no other solution [alternative, option] but to sell the factory in Detroit.
△ C We have no other way but to sell the factory in Detroit.

3 《会社の倒産》
〈この会社の倒産はどうしようもないね〉
◎ A We can't help this company out of (its) trouble.
◎ B We can't prevent this company from going bankrupt.
○ C We can't save this company from its bankruptcy.

4 《患者が絶望的なとき》
〈医師:お母様はどうしようもありませんね〉
Doctor:
◎ A There's nothing more we can do for your mother.
◎ B We've done everything possible [we could] for your mother.
× C Your mother's helpless.
× D Your mother doesn't have a hope of survival.

同性愛

1 《客観的に述べるとき》
a) 女性
〈彼女は同性愛者なんです〉
◎ A She's a homosexual [a lesbian].
◎ B She's homosexual [gay].

b) 男性
〈彼は同性愛者なんです〉
◎ A He's gay.
○ B He's a homosexual.
○ C He's homosexual.

2 《否定的に述べるとき》
a) 女性
〈彼女はレズなんです〉
◎ A She's a dyke.
△ B She's very butch.
△ C She's a lesbo.

b) 男性
〈彼はオカマなんです〉
◎ A He's a fag [a faggot, a queer, a homo].
◎ B He's queer.
○ C He's a flamer.
○ D He's a Queer.
○ E He's a gay-bob.
❖ C は女装をしているオカマに使われている。D は若い男性を好む中年の男性を言うときに使われている。

3 《「同性愛結婚」と述べるとき》
〈同性愛結婚はほとんどの国で認められていません〉
◎ A Same sex marriage isn't allowed in almost all countries.
× B Same gender marriage isn't allowed in almost all countries.
× C Homosexual [Gay] marriage isn't allowed in almost all countries.

同棲する

1 《批判的に述べる場合》

〈2人は同棲しているんです〉
- ◎ A They're shacking up (together).
- ○ B They're living in sin.

2 《中立的に述べる場合》
〈2人は同棲しています〉
- ◎ A They're living together.
- ▽ B They're cohabiting.
- ▽ C They're cohabitating.
  - ❖(1) 堅い文章では B, C はよく使われている．
  - ❖(2) C は多くの辞典に出ていないが使われている．

当選する

1 《当選した事実だけを述べるとき》
〈彼は知事に当選しました〉
- ◎ A He was elected (as) Governor.
- ○ B He was elected to the Governorship.
- △ C He was elected to Governor.
- × D He was returned to [as] Governor.
- × E He was returned Governor.
  - ❖ D, E が「当選する」の意味で辞典に出ているが使われていない．ただし，「再選される」の意味では使われている．

2 《僅差での当選》
〈彼は僅差で当選しました〉
- ◎ A He was elected by a narrow [small] margin.
- × B He was elected by a narrow [small] majority.
  - ❖ 辞典に B が出ているが使われていない．

3 《僅差で知事（市長，その他公職の地位）に当選する》
〈彼は僅差で知事に当選しました〉
- ☆ A He was elected Governor by a small margin.
- ◎ B He was elected as Governor by a small margin.
- ○ C He got into office as Governor by a small margin.
- ○ D He got in as Governor by a small margin.
- ○ E He got into [in] the Governor's mansion by a small margin.
- △ F He got the position [job] as Governor by a small margin.
- △ G He was put into office as Governor by a small margin.
- △ H He was elected to Governor [the Governorship] by a small margin.
- ▽ I He got a lease on the Governor's mansion by a small margin.
  - ❖ I は英字新聞の社説，または政治コラムなどではよく使われている．

4 《大差での当選》
〈彼は大差で当選しました〉
- ☆ A He was elected by a landslide.
- ☆ B He was elected by an overwhelming victory.
- ◎ C He was elected by a landslide victory.
- ○ D He was elected in a landslide [an overwhelming] victory.
- ○ E He was elected by a large majority [margin].
- △ F He was elected by a big majority [margin].
- × G He was elected in a large majority [margin].
  - ❖ G が辞典に出ているが使われていない．

5 《最高得票で》
〈彼は最高得票で当選しました〉

- ◎ A He got more votes than any other candidate elected.
- ◎ B He got the most votes in the election.
- ◎ C He got into office with the most [the largest number of] votes.
- ◎ D He carried the election with the most [the largest number of] votes.
- ○ E He was elected with the largest number of votes.
- △ F He tallied the most votes in the election.
- × G He was elected with the highest poll.
- × H He was elected polling the largest number of votes.
- × I He was elected at the head [top] of the poll.
  - ❖辞典に G, H, I が出ているが使われていない.

6 《再選させる》

〈私たちは彼を知事に再選しなければならない〉

- ☆ A We have to reelect him as Governor.
- ◎ B We have to reelect him Governor.
- ○ C We have to put him back in the Governor's mansion.
- ○ D We have to get him into office Governor again.
- △ E We have to return him to the Governor's mansion.
- △ F We have to reelect him to the Governorship.

7 《再選される》

〈彼は上院議員に再選されるでしょう〉

- ☆ A He'll be elected to the Senate again.
- ◎ B He'll be reelected as senator.
- ○ C He'll be reelected senator.
- ○ D He'll get into office as senator again.
- ○ E He'll be returned to the Senate.
- △ F He'll be put back in office as senator.
- △ G He'll be elected to senator again.

同窓会

1 《パーティーを開く集い》

a） 同窓生と話すとき

〈同窓会をやろうよ〉

- ◎ A Let's have a reunion.
- △ B Let's have a class reunion.
- × C Let's have an alumni meeting.
  - ❖C が A, B の意味で辞典に出ているが使われていない.

b） 同窓生以外の人と話すとき

〈(上司に伺いをたてている) 同窓会に行きたいので火曜日の午後休ませてもらえますか〉

- ◎ A May I take Tuesday afternoon off because I want to go to the class reunion?
- × B May I take Tuesday afternoon off because I want to go to the reunion?

c） 同窓会の種々の活動の会合

〈(ジェーンとリンダが話している) 近いうちに同窓会の会合を開こうよ〉

- ◎ A Let's have an alumni meeting one of these days.
- × B Let's have an alumna meeting one of these days.
  - ❖(1) 辞典には A が男性, B が女性と出ているが, 実際は女性でも B を使っていない.
  - ❖(2) アメリカの alumni association (同窓会) は日本とはだいぶ違い, 母校

のための資金集め運動，校友雑誌の出版などのような活動をしている．
  2 《組織》
〈彼は同窓会の一員です〉
    ◎ A He's a member of the alumni association.
    × B He's a member of the graduates' [old boys'] association.
    ❖ B が辞典に出ているが使われていない．
  3 《同窓生》
〈彼は私の同窓生なんです〉
    ☆ A We went to the same school together.
    ◎ B He went to the same school as me.
    ◎ C He's one of my old [former] classmates.
    △ D He's one of my ex-classmates.

統率力

  1 《「統率力がある」と言うとき》
〈彼には統率力があります〉
    ☆ A He has leadership skills.
    ☆ B He shows leadership skills.
    ◎ C He shows leadership qualities [abilities].
    ◎ D He has leadership qualities.
    ◎ E He demonstrates leadership skills [qualities, abilities].
    ○ F He has good leadership.
    ○ G He shows (good) leadership.
    ○ H He demonstrates leadership.
    ○ I He has leadership abilities.
    △ J He has leadership.
    × K He has (the) capacity as a leader.
  2 《「統率力を見せる」と言うとき》
〈統率力を見せてくれた後，あなたを昇進させますよ〉
    ◎ A After you show your leadership skills [qualities, abilities], we'll promote you.
    ◎ B After you demonstrate your leadership skills [qualities, abilities], we'll promote you.
    ◎ C After you prove your leadership skills [qualities, abilities], we'll promote you.
    × D After you have leadership skills [qualities, abilities], we'll promote you.

どうぞどうぞ

  1 《丁重に話す必要があるとき》
〈ブラウン氏：お電話をお借りしてもいいですか〉
Mr. Brown: Can I use the telephone?
〈スミス氏：どうぞどうぞ〉
Mr. Smith:
    ◎ A Certainly.
    ◎ B By all means.
    ◎ C Yes, please.
    ◎ D Of course, please.
  2 《友人などに話すとき》
〈トム：電話を借りてもいいですか〉
Tom: Can I use the telephone?

⟨ビル:どうぞ⟩
Bill:
- ◎ A Sure.
- ◎ B Sure thing.
- ◎ C Be my guest, please.
- ◎ D Yes, go ahead, please.
- ◎ E Go ahead, please.
- ◎ F By all means.
- ◎ G Yes, please.
- ◎ H Of course, please.
- ◎ I Why not?

どうってことない
⟨母:どうして運転を習いたくないの⟩
Mother: Why don't you want to learn how to drive?
⟨娘:分からないわ,お母さん.車が怖いんだと思うわ⟩
Daughter: I don't know, Mom. I guess I'm afraid of cars.
⟨母:何をばかなことを言っているの.やってみなさいよ.どうってことないわよ⟩
Mother:
- ◎ A Oh come on, give it a try. It won't hurt you.
- ◎ B Oh come on, give it a try. It won't [can't] kill you.

どうでしたか
1 《訪れた国・会った人などの印象を主観的に尋ねるとき》
⟨パリはどうでしたか⟩
- ◎ A How did you like Paris?
- ◎ B What did you think of Paris?
- ◎ C Did you have a good time in Paris?
- △ D How did you find Paris?

2 《訪れた国・会った人などの印象を客観的に尋ねるとき》
⟨パリはどうでしたか⟩
- ◎ A What was Paris like?
- ◎ B How was Paris?

道徳
1 《全体の道徳》
⟨日本の主婦の道徳は最近低下している⟩
- ☆ A The morals of Japanese housewives're declining these days.
- ◎ B The morality of Japanese housewives is declining these days.
- ◎ C The morals among Japanese housewives're declining these days.
- ○ D The morality among Japanese housewives is declining these days.

2 《個人に対して言うとき》
⟨彼には道徳がない⟩
- ◎ A He doesn't have morals.
- ◎ B He has no morals.
- ◎ C He's immoral.
- ◎ D He doesn't have high moral standards [principles].

3 《職業上の道徳を言うとき》
⟨彼には道徳がない⟩
- ◎ A He doesn't have ethics.
- ◎ B He has no ethics.
- ◎ C He isn't ethical.

- ◎ D He's unethical.
- △ E He doesn't have morals.
- △ F He has no morals.

頭取 →地位 16

どうにか…する

〈私は夫とは決してずっと幸せではなかったのですが，子供たちのためにどうにか過去 30 年間やってきたのです〉
- ◎ A I've never been happy with my husband, but for my children's sake I've managed to [I've been able to] get along with him for the past 30 years.
- ○ B I've never been happy with my husband, but for my children's sake I've succeeded at [I've been successful at] getting along with him for the past 30 years.

盗品

〈これは盗品だ〉
- ◎ A This is a stolen item.
- △ B This is a hot item.
- △ C This is hot stuff.
- △ D This is a hot [stolen] product.

当分

〈私は当分忙しくなるでしょう〉
- ◎ A I'm going to be busy for a while.
- △ B I'm going to be busy for the time being.
- × C I'm going to be busy for the present.
  - ❖(1) C が多くの辞典に出ているが使われていない．
  - ❖(2) 堅い文章英語では A, B とも非常によく使われている．

どう見ても

〈彼女はどう見ても 40 歳以上でしょう〉
- ◎ A She must be at least forty.
- ○ B She must be forty at least.
- × C She must be forty if a day.
- × D She must be forty to all appearances.
- × E She must be over at least forty.
  - ❖(1) C, D は以前は使われていたが今は死語で使われていない．
  - ❖(2) E の over at least が辞典に出ているが，重複になるので使われていない．

動揺

〈彼女が社長に選ばれたことが会社中に動揺を引き起こした〉
- ◎ A Her selection as the CEO caused a commotion [turmoil] throughout the company.
- △ B Her selection as the CEO caused a disturbance throughout the company.
- × C Her selection as the CEO caused a tumult throughout the company.
  - ❖ C はどの辞典にも出ているが使われていない．

盗用する

〈この一節は私の本から盗用したものです〉
- ◎ A This passage was lifted [plagiarized] from my book.
- ○ B This passage was stolen from my book.

どうりで

〈(ニューヨークで) 京子:日本語がとても上手ですね〉
Kyoko: You speak Japanese really well.
〈バーバラ:私は日本で生まれて日本の学校へ行ったんです〉
Barbara: I was born in Japan and went to school there.
〈京子:どうりで〉
Kyoko:
- ◎ A No wonder.
- ○ B That explains it [everything].
- ○ C It's no wonder.
- △ D It's no surprise.
- △ E No surprise.

登竜門

〈東大は日本では出世のための登竜門です〉
- ◎ A A Todai diploma assures [guarantees] you a successful career in Japan.
- ◎ B A Todai diploma is your key to a successful career in Japan.

同僚 →地位 6

遠い

〈フランス大使館はここから遠いですよ〉
- ◎ A The French Embassy's far from here.
- ◎ B The French Embassy's a long ways from here.
- ○ C The French Embassy's a long way from here.
- ○ D The French Embassy's far away from here.
- △ E The French Embassy's a long distance from here.
- △ F The French Embassy's a great distance from here.

❖多くの辞典にA, Eは疑問文・否定文, B, Cは肯定文で使われるという解説が出ているが,現代アメリカ英語の慣用を歪曲している.

遠ざける

〈彼のわがままが多くの人を遠ざけているんです〉
- ☆ A His selfishness turns off a lot of people.
- ◎ B His selfishness alienates a lot of people.
- ○ C His selfishness separates him from a lot of people.
- △ D His selfishness cuts off [estranges] a lot of people.
- ▽ E His selfishness turns away a lot of people.

❖Eが辞典に出ているがまれにしか使われていない.

遠まわしに言う

1 《「やめて下さい」とやめるを強調するとき》
〈遠まわしに言うのはやめて下さい〉
- ◎ A Stop beating around the bush.
- ○ B Stop talking in a roundabout way.
- △ C Stop hedging.
- × D Stop being mealy-mouthed.
- × E Stop saying in a roundabout way.
- × F Stop making an indirect reference.

❖D, E, Fが辞典に出ているが使われていない.

2 《言いたいことをずばり言って下さいというニュアンスで述べるとき》
a) 普通に述べるとき
〈遠まわしに言うのはやめて下さい〉

☆　A　Get to the point.
　　　◎　B　Cut to the chase.
　　　○　C　Get [Come] to the bottom line.
　　　△　D　Cut to the point.
　b) いらいらした気持ちで述べるとき
〈遠まわしに言うのはやめて下さい〉
　　　☆　A　Just get to the point.
　　　◎　B　Just cut to the chase.
　　　○　C　Just get to the bottom line.

遠回りする
〈危険な所を通って行きたくないんだ．だから遠回りしよう〉
　　　◎　A　I don't want to drive through the tough neighborhood, so let's take a detour.
　　　◎　B　I don't want to drive through the tough neighborhood, so let's go the long way around.
　　　△　C　I don't want to drive through the tough neighborhood, so let's make a detour.
　　　△　D　I don't want to drive through the tough neighborhood, so let's detour.
　　　△　E　I don't want to drive through the tough neighborhood, so let's go a long way around.

通る
 1　《交通機関が通る》
 a) 路線を主語にしたとき
〈東西線は代々木を通っていますか〉
　　　◎　　Does the Tozai Line run [go] through Yoyogi?
 b) 人を主語にしたとき
〈東西線は代々木を通っていますか〉
　　　◎　A　Can you take [catch, get on, use] the Tozai Line at Yoyogi?
　　　◎　B　Can you take [catch, get on] the Tozai Line in Yoyogi?
　　　○　C　Can you use [take, ride] the Tozai Line from Yoyogi?
 2　《歩いて通る》
〈私は彼が少し前私の事務所のそばを歩いて通るのを見ました〉
　　　◎　A　I saw him walking [going, passing] by my office a while ago.
　　　◎　B　I saw him going [walking] past my office a while ago.
　　　○　C　I saw him passing my office a while ago.
 3　《車で通る》
〈私は彼が少し前私の事務所のそばを車で通るのを見ました〉
　　　◎　A　I saw him driving by my office a while ago.
　　　◎　B　I saw him going past my office in his car a while ago.
　　　○　C　I saw him passing by my office in his car a while ago.
 4　《声》
〈彼の声はよく通ります〉
　　　◎　A　His voice carries well.
　　　◎　B　He projects his voice well.
　　　○　C　He has a booming voice.
　　　△　D　He has a far-reaching [penetrating] voice.
 5　《法案》
〈この法案は上院を通るでしょう〉

- ◎ A This bill will be approved [passed] by the Senate.
- ◎ B This bill will pass through the Senate.
- ○ C This bill will be ratified by the Senate.

6 《年令》

〈母はとても若く見えるので30歳で通るんです〉

- ◎ A My mother looks so young she can pass for 30.
- ◎ B My mother looks so young people often guess [believe] she's 30.

時がたつのは速い

〈時がたつのは速いですね〉

- ◎ A Time flies, doesn't it?
- ◎ B Time goes by fast, doesn't it?
- ○ C Time passes [goes by] so quickly, doesn't it?

時々

〈私は時々彼に会います〉

- ☆ A I see him sometimes.
- ◎ B Sometimes I see him.
- ◎ C I sometimes see him.
- ◎ D I see him (every) now and then.
- ◎ E I see him once in a while.
- ○ F I see him occasionally.
- ○ G I see him every now and again.
- ○ H I see him from time to time.
- ○ I At times I see him.
- △ J I see him now and again.
- △ K I see him at times.

どきどきする

1 《異性・重要人物などに会ったとき》

〈初めて彼女に紹介されたとき,私はどきどきしました〉

- ◎ A The first time I was introduced to her, my heart was racing.
- ◎ B The first time I was introduced to her, my heart was beating fast.
- ◎ C The first time I was introduced to her, my stomach was in knots.
- ◎ D The first time I was introduced to her, I couldn't breathe.
- ◎ E The first time I was introduced to her, I had butterflies in my stomach.
- ◎ F The first time I was introduced to her, she took my breath away.
- ○ G The first time I was introduced to her, my heart went pit-a-pat.
- ○ H The first time I was introduced to her, my jaw dropped.
- △ I The first time I was introduced to her, I lost my breath.

❖「どきどきしていた」度合いはHが一番強い.

2 《健康上のとき》

〈心臓がどきどきしているんです〉

- ◎ A My heart's pounding.
- ◎ B My heart's beating fast.
- ○ C My heart's racing.
- △ D My heart's pounding fast.

❖どきどきしている速さの点ではCが1番,Bが2番,Dが3番,Aが4番.

解く

1 《誤解》

a) ビジネス上の改まった間柄で

〈私はあなたが彼と私の間の誤解を解いてくれることを願っています〉
- ☆ A I hope you can clear up the misunderstanding between him and me.
- ☆ B I hope you can resolve the misunderstanding between him and me.
- ◎ C I hope you can work out the misunderstanding between him and me.
- ◎ D I hope you can straighten out the misunderstanding between him and me.
- ○ E I hope you can take care of the misunderstanding between him and me.
- ○ F I hope you can iron out [fix] the misunderstanding between him and me.
- △ G I hope you can solve [settle] the misunderstanding between him and me.

❖ Bが一番誤解を解くのが難しいという響きがある．D, Fが2番，A, C, Gが3番，Eが4番．

b）友人同士

〈私はあなたが彼と私の誤解を解いてくれることを希望しています〉
- ☆ A I hope you can clear up the misunderstanding between him and me.
- ◎ B I hope you can take care of [work out, straighten out] the misunderstanding between him and me.
- ○ C I hope you can iron out [solve] the misunderstanding between him and me.
- △ D I hope you can fix [resolve, settle] the misunderstanding between him and me.

2 《数学の問題》

〈あなたはこの数学の問題を解けますか〉
- ◎ A Can you work out this math problem?
- ◎ B Can you work this math problem out?
- ◎ C Can you find the answer to [for] this math problem?
- ○ D Can you solve this math problem?

得意である

1 《科目》

〈私はフランス語が得意です〉
- ☆ A I'm good at French.
- ◎ B I have a knack for French.
- ◎ C French's my strong suit.
- ○ D French's my forte.
- ○ E French's my cup of tea.

2 《スポーツ》

〈彼女はスポーツが得意なんです〉
- ◎ A She's athletic.
- ◎ B She's good at sports.
- ◎ C She's an athlete.

❖ A, Cは「スポーツが得意です」の他に「スポーツが好きなんです」，「スタイルがいい」の3つの意味がある．どれであるかは会話の前後からわかる．「スタイルがいい」の詳細はその項を参照されたい．

独学

1 《学校へ全く行かなかったとき》

〈彼は独学したんです〉
- ☆ A He didn't go to school.

- ◎ B He didn't have a formal education.
- ○ C He didn't get a formal education.
- ○ D He didn't have [get] an education.
- ○ E He's self-taught [self-educated].
- △ F He didn't get [receive] schooling.

2 《ある科目を独学したとき》

〈彼は独学でフランス語を勉強したんです〉
- ☆ A He studied French on his own.
- ◎ B He studied French by himself.
- ◎ C He taught himself French.
- ○ D He studied French alone.

独身

1 《女性》

〈彼女は独身です〉
- ◎ A She's single.
- ◎ B She isn't married.
- ○ C She's a single (woman).
- △ D She's unmarried.
- ▽ E She's an unmarried woman [person].
- × F She's a bachelor-girl [a bachelorette].
- × G She's a spinster.

❖(1) F, G は辞典に出ているが使われていない．
❖(2) G がある辞典に口語英語として紹介されているが全く使われていない．しかし，堅い文章英語では，約50歳以上の女性にまれに使われる．

2 《男性》

〈彼は独身です〉
- ☆ A He's single.
- ◎ B He isn't married.
- ◎ C He's a bachelor.
- ○ D He's a single guy.

❖ C は離婚して再び独身になった男性には使わない傾向がある．

時計とにらめっこで

〈私は時計とにらめっこでやっています〉
- ◎ A I'm working against the clock.
- ◎ B I'm working under the gun.
- ○ C I'm working against time.
- × D I'm working against the gun.
- × E I'm working under the clock.

どこかに

1 《漠然と尋ねるとき》

〈どこかにロシアレストランがありますか〉
- ◎ A Is there a Russian restaurant around?
- △ B Is there a Russian restaurant anywhere [somewhere]?

2 《限定して尋ねるとき》

〈東京のどこかにロシアレストランがありますか〉
- ◎ A Is there a Russian restaurant anywhere in Tokyo?
- ○ B Is there a Russian restaurant around Tokyo?

どこでもいいから

〈どこでもいいですから，あなたにお目にかかりたいんです〉

◎ A I want to see you no matter where (it is).
○ B I want to see you anywhere.

どことどこが →どこの 8

どこにいらっしゃいますか
〈(落ち合うとき) どこにいらっしゃいますか〉
◎ A Where will I find you?
◎ B Where will you be?
○ C Where will I see you?

どこの
1 《会社を尋ねる場合》
a) 相手の住んでいる場所を知らずに勤務先の会社名を尋ねるとき
〈どこの会社にお勤めですか〉
◎ A Who do you work for?
× B What [Which] company do you work for?
× C Where do you work?

b) 相手の住んでいる場所を知っていて勤務先を尋ねるとき
〈どこの会社にお勤めですか〉
◎ A Where do you work?
○ B Who do you work for?

c) 相手の職種を知っているとき
〈ブラウン氏：ところで, どういう方面のお仕事についているのですか〉
Mr. Brown: By the way what line of business are you in?
〈スミス氏：銀行に勤めています〉
Mr. Smith: I work for a bank.
〈ブラウン氏：どこの銀行にお勤めですか〉
Mr. Brown:
◎ A Which [What] bank do you work for?
◎ B Who do you work for?
◎ C Where do you work?

2 《学校を尋ねる場合》
a) 一般的に
〈この辺ではどこの学校でフランス語の講座を開いていますか〉
◎ A Who's offering French courses around here?
◎ B What [Which] school's offering French courses around here?

b) 卒業した学校を尋ねる場合
・高卒者に尋ねる場合
〈どこの学校を卒業したのですか〉
◎ A Where did you go to high school?
◎ B What [Which] high school did you go to?
◎ C What [Which] high school did you graduate from?

・大卒者に尋ねる場合
〈どこの学校を卒業したのですか〉
◎ A What college did you go to?
◎ B Where did you graduate (from)?
○ C Where did you go to school [collage]?
○ D What college [school] did you graduate from?
○ E Which college [school] did you graduate from?

c) 通っている学校を尋ねる場合
・各種学校名を尋ねる場合

⟨どこの英語学校へ行っているのですか⟩
 ◎ Which [What] English school do you go to?
・小・中・高校生に尋ねる場合
⟨どこの学校へ行っているのですか⟩
 ◎ Where do you go to school?
・大学生に尋ねる場合
⟨どこの大学に行っているのですか⟩
 ◎ A Where do you go to school [college]?
 △ B What college [school] do you go to?
 △ C Which college [school] do you go to?
  ❖ what と which は厳密には違いがある．which はいくつかの学校が話題になっていて，その中のどこの学校かと尋ねる場合，what は不特定多数のどこの学校かと尋ねる場合に使うのが正しいが，実際の会話ではこの違いはあまり守られていない．

3 《国を尋ねる場合》
⟨どこの国が世界で一番犯罪率が低いのですか⟩
 ◎ A Who has the lowest crime rate in the world?
 ◎ B What [Which] country has the lowest crime rate in the world?

4 《店を尋ねる場合》
⟨この辺ではどこの店でドイツ食品を売っているのですか⟩
 ◎ A Who sells German food around here?
 ◎ B Which [What] store sells German food around here?

5 《機械のメーカー》
⟨あなたの車はどこ製ですか⟩
 ☆ A What kind of car are you driving?
 ◎ B What sort of car are you driving?
 ◎ C Who makes [made] your car?
 ◎ D What [Which] company makes your car?
 ◎ E What make's your car?
 ○ F What make of car are you driving?
 ○ G Which kind of car are you driving?
 △ H Which sort of car are you driving?
 △ I Which make's your car?
 △ J Which make of car are you driving?
 △ K Which [What] company manufactures your car?
  ❖ A, B, G, H は次の3つの意味があり，どれも非常によく使われている．どの意味であるかは話の前後で普通わかる．①会社名　②何年型　③(種類で) どんな車．②および③の詳細はその項を参照されたい．

6 《化粧品のメーカー》
⟨その口紅はどこ製ですか⟩
 ☆ A Who makes that lipstick?
 ☆ B What kind of lipstick's that?
 ◎ C What brand of lipstick's that?
 ◎ D Who puts that lipstick out?
 ◎ E What [Which] company makes that lipstick?
 ○ F Who made that lipstick?
 ○ G What [Which] company puts that lipstick out?
 △ H What company manufactures [produces] that lipstick?

7 《生地のメーカー》

⟨その生地はどこ製ですか⟩
  ☆ A Who makes that fabric?
  ◎ B What [Which] company makes that fabric?
  ○ C What [Which] company puts that fabric out?
  △ D What [Which] company manufactures that fabric?
8 《スポーツの対戦チームを尋ねるとき》
⟨ジム：今晩野球の試合があるんだ⟩
Jim: There's going to be a baseball game tonight.
⟨トム：どことどこがやるの⟩
Tom:
  ◎ A Who's playing?
  ○ B Who's playing who?

床屋 →店 36

所

1 《ビジネス》
⟨新宿はこの種のビジネスには理想的な所です⟩
  ◎ A Shinjuku's an ideal location [area, place] for this kind of business.
  ▽ B Shinjuku's an ideal district for this kind of business.
  × C Shinjuku's an ideal neighborhood for this kind of business.

2 《犯罪上の危険》
⟨ハーレムは危険な所ですか⟩
  ☆ A Is Harlem a bad neighborhood?
  ◎ B Is Harlem a dangerous neighborhood [area, place]?
  ◎ C Is Harlem a bad area [place]?
  ○ D Is Harlem a tough neighborhood [area, place]?
  ○ E Is Harlem a rough neighborhood [area, place]?

土砂降り

⟨雨が土砂降りです⟩
  ☆ A It's really pouring [coming down].
  ☆ B It's raining really hard.
  ☆ C It's really raining hard.
  ◎ D It's raining very hard.
  ◎ E The rain's really coming down.
  ◎ F The rain's really falling hard.
  ◎ G The rain's falling really hard.
  ○ H It's really raining fast [heavy].
  ○ I It's raining really fast [heavy].
  ○ J It's raining cats and dogs.
  ○ K It's really raining in buckets.
  ○ L It's coming down in buckets.
  △ M The rain's falling very hard [in buckets].
  △ N It's really raining heavily.
  △ O It's raining really heavily.
  △ P The rain's really falling heavy [heavily].
  △ Q The rain's falling really heavy [heavily].
  × R It's raining in sheets [in torrents].

どたん場

⟨彼はどたん場で気が変わったんです⟩
  ◎ A He changed his mind at the last minute.

× B He changed his mind at the last moment.
　　❖ B が辞典に出ているが使われていない．

土地
1 《ある目的のために》
〈私は家を建てるために土地を買おうと思っています〉
　　☆ A I'm going to buy a piece of land to build my house.
　　◎ B I'm going to buy a lot [some land] to build my house.

2 《開発されている町・市の中の土地》
a） 土地をひとつと述べるとき
〈私は原宿に土地をひとつ持っています〉
　　◎ A I have a piece of land in Harajuku.
　　◎ B I have a lot in Harajuku.
　　❖ A は建物があるかないか不明．B は建物がない．

b） 土地を2つと述べるとき
〈私は原宿に土地を2つ持っています〉
　　◎ A I have two pieces of land in Harajuku.
　　◎ B I have two lots in Harajuku.
　　❖ A は 2 つが離れていることが多い．B は 2 つが隣接していることが多い．

3 《森の中の土地》
〈私はあの森に土地をひとつ持っています〉
　　◎ A I have some land in that forest.
　　○ B I have a piece of land in that forest.
　　× C I have a lot in that forest.

4 《農業用の土地として述べるとき》
〈この土地は非常に不毛です〉
　　◎ A This soil's really poor.
　　○ B This land's really poor.
　　× C This lot's really poor.

5 《空地》
〈私の家の裏に空地があります〉
　　◎ A There's a vacant lot behind my house.
　　◎ B There's vacant land behind my house.
　　❖ A の lot は可算名詞，B の land は不可算名詞であることに注意．

途中
1 《目的地への途中》
a） 行き先を明示したとき
〈私は駅へ行く途中で彼を見ました〉
　　◎ 　I saw him on the [my] way to the station.

b） 行き先を明示しないとき
〈彼は途中で事故にあったのかもしれない〉
　　◎ A He might've been in a car accident on the [his] way.
　　◎ B He might've been in a car accident along the way.
　　× C He might've been in a car accident along his way.

2 《途中で引き返す》
〈私は携帯電話で父が倒れたことを知ったので途中で引き返さなければならなかったのです〉
　　◎ A I had to turn back halfway because I learned on my cell phone that my father collapsed.
　　○ B I had to turn back midway because I learned on my cell phone that

my father collapsed.

3 《身体の器官》

〈お餅が彼ののどの途中にひっかかってしまったんです〉

◎ A The rice cake got stuck in his throat.
▽ B The rice cake caught midway in his throat.
× C The rice cake got stuck midway in his throat.
× D The rice cake caught [got stuck] on its way in his throat.

4 《「…の最中」の意味》

〈私たちは今会議の途中なんです〉

◎ A We're in the middle of the meeting.
○ B We're halfway through the meeting.
△ C We're midway through the meeting.
▽ D We're in the course of the meeting.

5 《終了までいる [やる] べきであることが念頭にあるとき》

a) パーティー

〈私は披露宴の途中で退席しなければならなかったんです〉

☆ A I had to leave the wedding reception before it was over.
◎ B I had to leave in the middle of the wedding reception.
◎ C I had to leave midway through the wedding reception.

b) 車の修理中

〈私は今彼の車を修理しているんです．途中で放り出せないよ〉

◎ A I'm fixing his car. I can't stop it halfway.
○ B I'm fixing his car. I can't stop it in the middle way.
○ C I'm fixing his car. I can't stop it midway through.
○ D I'm fixing his car. I can't stop it before I finish it.

どちらにしても

〈どちらにしても電話します〉

◎ A Either way, I'll call you.
◎ B I'll call you no matter what.
○ C In any case, I'll call you.
○ D I'll call you regardless.
△ E At any rate, I'll call you.

❖ B, D, E は本来3つ以上の場面がある場合に使われるが，2つの場合でもよく使われている．

特権

1 《外交官》

〈特権を乱用している外交官が多い〉

◎ A Many diplomats abuse their privileges.
△ B Many diplomats abuse their special rights.
× C Many diplomats abuse their prerogatives.

❖ C が辞典に出ているが使われていない．

2 《外交官以外》

〈泣くことは女性の特権だね〉

☆ A Crying's a women's prerogative.
◎ B Crying's a women's right.
△ C Crying's a women's weapon [privilege].

取っておく

〈客：このドレスを明日まで取っておいてくれますか〉

Customer:

とってくる

◎ A Can you hold this dress until tomorrow?
◎ B Can you put this dress on hold until tomorrow?
○ C Can you hold onto [set aside, put aside] this dress until tomorrow?
○ D Can you keep a hold of this dress until tomorrow?
▽ E Can you keep this dress until tomorrow?
❖ E が辞典に出ているが使われてもまれ．

取って来る

〈市役所から書類を取って来ましょうか〉

◎ A Can I get the papers at [from] City Hall?
◎ B Can I go get the papers at [from] City Hall?
◎ C Can I pick up the papers at [from] City Hall?
○ D Can I go and get the papers at [from] City Hall?

とどまる

《数値が》

〈失業率は5％近辺にとどまっている〉

◎ A The unemployment rate stays [is staying] around five percent.
◎ B The unemployment rate is around five percent.
△ C The unemployment rate hovers [fluctuates] around five percent.
❖ C はテレビ，新聞などでは非常によく使われている．

怒鳴り込む → 怒鳴る 3

怒鳴る

1 《人に》

a ）過去形

〈上司はジムに怒鳴っていました〉

☆ A The boss was yelling at Jim.
◎ B The boss was shouting at Jim.
◎ C The boss was chewing Jim out loudly.
○ D The boss was screaming at Jim.
△ E The boss was barking at Jim.
△ F The boss was blasting (at) Jim.
❖ D が一番強い響きがある．F が2番，A, B, C が3番，E が4番．

b ）未来形

・少し改まって話す必要がある人と話している

〈4時までに会社へ戻らないと上司に怒鳴られるんです〉

◎ A If I don't get back to the office by 4:00, my boss'll yell at [kill] me.
◎ B If I don't get back to the office by 4:00, my boss'll chew me out.
○ C If I don't get back to the office by 4:00, my boss'll scream at me.
▽ D If I don't get back to the office by 4:00, my boss'll shout at [blast, bark at] me.
✗ E If I don't get back to the office by 4:00, my boss'll blast at me.
❖ shout at は未来形ではまれにしか使われていない．

・親しい友人と話している

〈7時までに帰らないと妻に怒鳴られるんです〉

◎ A If I don't get home by 7:00, my wife'll yell at [kill] me.
◎ B If I don't get home by 7:00, my wife'll chew [bitch] me out.
○ C If I don't get home by 7:00, my wife'll scream at me.
▽ D If I don't get home by 7:00, my wife'll shout [bark] at me.
▽ E If I don't get home by 7:00, my wife'll blast (at) me.
❖ B の bitch は親しい間でなければ使われていない．

2 《怒鳴る理由も言及するとき》
〈上司はジムが遅刻して出勤したことで怒鳴った〉
- ☆ A The boss yelled at Jim for coming in late.
- ◎ B The boss shouted at Jim for coming in late.
- ○ C The boss blasted [screamed at] Jim for coming in late.
- △ D The boss barked at Jim for coming in late.
  - ❖ C が一番強い響きがある．A, B が2番，D が一番弱い．

3 《怒鳴って入ってくることに言及するとき》
〈彼は私の事務所に怒鳴りこんできた〉
- ◎ A He stormed [busted] into my office.
- ◎ B He barged [burst] into my office angrily.
- ○ C He flew [rushed] into my office angrily.
- ○ D He fumed into my office.
- △ E He stomped into my office.

飛ぶように売れている

1 《動詞で述べるとき》
a) いかなる商品でも使える
〈この本は飛ぶように売れています〉
- ◎ A This book's selling like mad [crazy].
- △ B This book's selling like hot cakes.
  - ❖ B は 1970 年代まではよく使われていた．

b) 棚に陳列してある商品
〈この本は飛ぶように売れています〉
- ◎ A This book's selling like mad [crazy].
- ○ B This book's flying off the shelves.
- △ C This book's selling like hot cakes.

2 《名詞で述べるとき》
a) 時計
〈これは最近飛ぶように売れているんです〉
- ☆ A This is a best seller these days.
- ◎ B This is a hot seller these days.
- ◎ C This is a hot product these days.
- ○ D This is a hot item these days.
- △ E This is hot stuff these days.
  - ❖(1) E は不定冠詞の a が不要．
  - ❖(2) C, D, E は these days を消すと「これは盗品だ」の意味にもなる．

b) コンピュータ
〈これは最近飛ぶように売れているんです〉
- ◎ A This is a hot seller [product, item] these days.
- ◎ B This is a best seller these days.
- × C This is hot stuff these days.

c) ハンドバッグのようなブランド物
〈これは最近飛ぶように売れているんです〉
- ◎ A This is a hot item [product] these days.
- ◎ B This is a best seller these days.
- ○ C This is a hot seller these days.
- ▽ D This is hot stuff these days.

d) 香水
〈この香水は最近飛ぶように売れているんです〉

- ◎ A This is best-selling perfume these days.
- ◎ B This perfume's a hot product these days.
- ○ C This perfume's a hot [best] seller these days.
- ▽ D This perfume's hot stuff these days.

とぼける
〈彼はあなたがそのことを尋ねても多分とぼけるでしょう〉
- ☆ A He'll probably play dumb even if you ask him about it.
- ◎ B He'll probably pretend not to know even if you ask him about it.
- ○ C He'll probably pretend ignorance even if you ask him about it.
- × D He'll probably play possum [act possum, act blank] even if you ask him about it.
- × E He'll probably sham [play, feign] innocence even if you ask him about it.

❖ D, E が辞典に出ているが使われていない.

ドライヤー
1 《髪を乾かすドライヤー》
〈ドライヤーを借りてもいいですか〉
- ◎ A Can I use your blow [hair] dryer?
- × B Can I use your dryer?

❖ drier も広く使われている.

2 《衣類の乾燥機》
〈この乾燥機は故障しています〉
- ◎ A This dryer's broken.
- △ B This clothes dryer's broken.
- × C This hot-air dryer's broken.

❖ C が辞典に出ているが使われていない.

取り組む
1 《難しい問題のとき》
〈私たちはこの問題に取り組まなければならないんです〉
- ☆ A We have to get a grip on this problem.
- ◎ B We have to tackle this problem.
- ○ C We have to come to grips with this problem.
- ○ D We have to wrestle with this problem.
- △ E We have to battle [grapple] with this problem.

❖ A, C が一番難しいという響きがある. B, D が2番, E が3番.

2 《1 より難しさの下がる問題のとき》
〈私たちはこの問題に取り組まなければならない〉
- ◎ A We have to work on [deal with, take care of] this problem.
- ○ B We have to face (up to) this problem.
- ○ C We have to address to this problem.
- × D We have to address ourselves to this problem.

❖ B がこの中では一番難しいという響きがある.

取り壊す
〈あなたのビルを取り壊すのにいくらかかりましたか〉
- ◎ A How much did it cost to tear down [demolish, knock down] your building?
- ◎ B How much did it cost to have your building torn down [demolished]?
- △ C How much did it cost to have your building knocked down?

とりしきる
〈彼はすべてを自分でとりしきりたいんです〉
- ◎ A He's wants to run everything himself.
- ◎ B He wants to run the show himself.
- ○ C He wants to control everything himself.

取締役
1　《一般的に言うとき》
〈彼は取締役です〉
- ◎ A He's an executive.
- × B He's a director.
  - ❖ B はよく使われているが,非常にあいまいな語で,部長,課長,支配人なのか不明.したがって B のように述べたとき,「取締役」の意味にはならない.

2　《「会社の取締役」と言うとき》
〈彼は会社の取締役です〉
- ◎ A He's a corporate executive.
- ○ B He's a company executive.

3　《会社名を明示して言うとき》
〈彼は XYZ 会社の取締役です〉
- ◎ A He's an executive with [at] XYZ Company.
- ◎ B He's an XYZ Company executive.
- ○ C He's an executive of XYZ Company.
- △ D He's an executive for XYZ Company.

4　《政策を決定する「取締役理事会の一人」の意味の「取締役」と言うとき》
〈彼は取締役です〉
- ☆ A He's on the board of directors.
- ◎ B He's a member of the board of directors.
- ○ C He's a board of directors member.
- × D He's on the board of executives.
  - ❖(1) executive は「政策を決定する取締役理事会の一人」の意味には使えない.
  - ❖(2) アメリカの会社は the board of directors(取締役理事会)が会社運営の最高責任者 chairman(会長)を選び,chairman が現場の最高責任者である the President(社長)を選ぶ.President は会社により CEO(Chief Executive Officer)とも呼ばれる.会社により Chairman が President または CEO を兼任することもある.したがって,普通日本の会社で名誉職である chairman は,アメリカでは会社の最高責任者である.

取り付ける
1　《車に》
〈車にクーラーを取り付けてもらおう〉
- ◎　Let's have an air conditioner put [installed] in the car.

2　《壁に》
〈北の壁にクーラーを取り付けてもらおう〉
- ◎ A Let's have an air conditioner put in [installed] on the north wall.
- ○ B Let's have an air conditioner put on the north wall.

取りに来る
〈(クリーニング店で)客:いつこれを取りに来ていいですか〉
Customer:
- ☆ A When can I pick this up?

☆ B When can I come get this?
◎ C When can I come and get this?
○ D When can I come [drop, stop] by and pick this up?
○ E When can I stop [drop] by and get this?

取引
1 《特定の取引》
〈うちは XYZ 会社と取引ができると思います〉
☆ A I think we can make a deal with XYZ Company.
◎ B I think we can do business with XYZ Company.
○ C I think we can strike a deal with XYZ Company.
△ D I think we can swing a deal with XYZ Company.

2 《継続的な取引》
a) 一般の会社
〈うちは XYZ 会社と取引があります〉
◎ A We're doing business [dealing] with XYZ Company.
◎ B We do business [deal] with XYZ Company.

b) 銀行
・会社と銀行
〈うちは XYZ 銀行と取引があります〉
☆ A We do [We're doing] business with XYZ Bank.
◎ B We deal [We're dealing] with XYZ Bank.
◎ C We have an account with XYZ Bank.
◎ D We're banking with XYZ Bank.
○ E We bank with XYZ Bank.
❖ A, B は融資・預金以外，つまり銀行の本来の業務とは関係がない建築・警備員・人材派遣などで取引がある場合にも使われている．

・個人と銀行
〈私は XYZ 銀行と取引があります〉
☆ A I have an account with XYZ Bank.
◎ B I'm banking with XYZ Bank.
○ C I bank with XYZ Bank.
○ D I deal [I'm dealing] with XYZ Bank.
△ E I do [I'm doing] business with XYZ Bank.

取引をまとめる
1 《取引の条件・契約書の交換・金銭の授受を意味するとき》
〈いつまでに取引をまとめられますか〉
◎ A By when can we close the deal?
○ B By when can we get the deal closed?

2 《契約書の署名・交換，金銭の授受だけを意味するとき》
〈いつまでに取引をまとめられますか〉
◎ A By when can we finish [complete] the transaction?
○ B By when can we get through [be through, be done] with the transaction?

努力する
1 《夢・望むものを達成するため》
〈私は経営修士号を得るために努力しています〉
☆ A I'm working hard on my MBA.
◎ B I'm working hard for my MBA.
◎ C I'm working [trying] hard to get my MBA.

- ○ D I'm working hard at my MBA.
- △ E I'm putting forth an effort towards my MBA.
- △ F I'm making a big effort to get my MBA.
- × G I'm making an effort [a lot of effort] to get my MBA.
- × H I'm striving hard at [for] my MBA.
- × I I'm aiming hard at [for, on] my MBA.
- × J I'm putting forth an effort at [on] my MBA.

2 《獲得を目指しているとき》

〈私は優等を取ろうと努力しています〉

- ◎ A I'm aiming [striving, trying] to get honors.
- ○ B I'm working to get honors.

3 《望んでいないが義務上》

〈私は義理の両親とうまくやっていくために努力しています〉

- ☆ A I'm trying hard to get along with my in-laws.
- ◎ B I'm working hard to get along with my in-laws.
- ○ C I'm making an effort to get along with my in-laws.
- ○ D I'm doing my best to get along with my in-laws.
- △ E I'm putting forth an effort to get along with my in-laws.
- × F I'm striving to get along with my in-laws.

4 《とまどい・動揺を隠す》

〈彼はとまどいを隠そうと努力した〉

- ☆ A He tried hard to hide his embarrassment.
- ◎ B He worked to hide his embarrassment.
- ○ C He struggled [worked hard] to hide his embarrassment.
- △ D He strove to hide his embarrassment.
- △ E He made an effort to hide his embarrassment.

取る

1 《新聞》

〈私はジャパンタイムズを取っています〉

- ◎ A I get *the Japan Times*.
- ○ B I take *the Japan Times*.
- △ C I subscribe to *the Japan Times*.
- × D I take in *the Japan Times*.
  - ❖(1) D は辞典にイギリス英語と書いてあるが現在は使われていない．A を紹介している辞典はほとんどないが，一番よく使われている．
  - ❖(2) C はイギリスでは雑誌によく使われている．

2 《賞》

〈誰が1等を取りましたか〉

- ◎ A Who won [got] first prize?
- ○ B Who took first prize?

3 《食事》

〈昼食を取りましたか〉

- ◎ A Did you have [eat] lunch?
- × B Did you take lunch?

4 《家賃》

〈角の人からいくら家賃を取っているの〉

- ◎ How much are you charging [getting from] the tenant on the corner?

5 《給料》

〈給料をひと月いくら取っているのかい〉
　　◎　　How much do you make [get] a month?
6　《免許証》
〈いつ車の免許証を取ったの〉
　　◎　A　When did you get your driver's license?
　　×　B　When did you take your driver's license?
7　《成績》
〈テストで何点取ったの〉
　　◎　A　What did you get on the test?
　　×　B　What did you take on the test?
8　《博士号》
〈どこで博士号を取ったのですか〉
　　◎　A　Where did you get [receive] your Ph.D?
　　△　B　Where did you obtain your Ph.D?
　　×　C　Where did you take your Ph.D?
9　《時間》
a）感謝するとき
〈お時間を取っていただいてありがとうございます〉
　　◎　A　Thank you for your time.
　　○　B　Thank you for letting me take up your time.
　　○　C　Thank you for sharing [giving me] your time.
　　×　D　Thank you for taking a lot of your time.
b）文句を言うとき
〈あなたは私の時間をすごく取っています〉
　　◎　A　You're taking (up) [wasting] a lot of my time.
　　◎　B　You're taking too much of my time.
10　《手渡す意味で》
〈その本を私に取って下さい〉
　　◎　A　Hand [Pass, Give] me that book.
　　◎　B　Let me have that book.
　　❖　give は場面により「その本を私に下さい」の意味でもよく使われている．

取るに足りない
1　《人》
〈彼は自分が重要な人物だと思っているのですが，実際は取るに足りない人なんです〉
　　☆　A　He thinks he's important but in fact he's a nobody.
　　◎　B　He thinks he's important but in fact he's nothing [worthless].
　　○　C　He thinks he's important but in fact he's a man of little importance.
　　△　D　He thinks he's important but in fact he's a man of no importance.
　　▽　E　He thinks he's important but in fact he's a nothing.
　　▽　F　He thinks he's important but in fact he's a man of small [no] account.
　　×　G　He thinks he's important but in fact he's a snippet.
　　×　H　He thinks he's important but in fact he has nothing in him.
　　×　I　He thinks he's important but in fact he doesn't have anything in him.
　　×　J　He thinks he's important but in fact he's nonentity.
　　❖　G～J が辞典に出ているが使われていない．

2　《事》
〈そんな取るに足りない事で口論するのはよそう〉

どんな 471

　　◎ A Let's not argue over such small stuff.
　　○ B Let's not argue over such small things [problems].
　　○ C Let's not argue over such trivial things.
　△ D Let's not argue over such small matters.
　△ E Let's not argue over such trivial matters [problems].
　× F Let's not argue over such trifling problems [matters].
　× G Let's not argue over such trifles.
　❖ F, G が辞典に出ているが使われていない．

ドル箱
〈この商品はうちの会社のドル箱です〉
　　◎ A This product's a real gold mine for our company.
　　◎ B This product's a money-maker for our company.
　　◎ C This product's making our company rich.
　× D This product's a cashbox [a money box] for our company.
　❖ D が多くの辞典に出ているが使われていない．

取れかかっている
〈あなたのベストのボタンが取れかかっている〉
　　◎ A A button on your vest's loose.
　　◎ B A button on your vest's coming [falling] off.
　　◎ C A button on your vest's about to fall [come] off.
　△ D A button on your vest's just going to fall [come] off.

泥
1 《一般的に言うとき》
〈車は泥だらけだった〉
　　◎　The car was covered with mud [dirt].
　❖ mud は湿った泥，dirt は乾いた泥をいう．

2 《「はねかける」と言うとき》
〈トラックに泥をはねかけられたんです〉
　　◎ A A truck splashed mud on me.
　　○ B A truck splashed me with mud.
　× C A truck splashed mud over [about] me.
　❖ C が辞典に出ているが使われていない．

3 《比喩的な意味で「ドロをはく」と言うとき》
〈容疑者は数日したらドロをはくだろう〉
　　◎　The suspect'll come clear [spill his guts, confess] in a few days.

どんな
1 《職業を尋ねるとき》
〈どんなお仕事をしているのですか〉
　☆ A What do you do for a living?
　　◎ B What do you do?
　　◎ C What kind of work do you do?
　　◎ D What line of business're you in?
　　○ E What business're you in?
　　○ F What's your occupation?
　△ G What kind of job're you doing?
　❖ G を紹介している辞典があるが，あまり使われていない．

2 《好きな食べ物を尋ねるとき》
〈どんな食べ物が一番好きですか〉
　☆ A What's your favorite food?

- ☆ B What kind of food's your favorite?
- ☆ C What kind of food do you like best?
- ◎ D What food do you like best?
- ◎ E What type [sort] of food do you like best?
- ○ F Which type [kind] of food do you like best?

3 《好きなタイプの異性を尋ねるとき》
〈どんなタイプの男性がお好きですか〉
- ☆ A What type of guy do you like?
- ◎ B What kind of guy do you like?
- ○ C What sort of guy do you like?

4 《好きな音楽を尋ねるとき》
〈どんな音楽がお好きですか〉
- ◎ A What kind [type] of music do you like?
- ◎ B What music do you like?
- ○ C What sort of music do you like?

5 《車の種類を尋ねるとき》
〈どんな車に乗っているのですか〉
- ◎ A What type [kind] of car are you driving?
- ○ B What sort of car are you driving?
- ○ C Which kind of car are you driving?
- × D Which sort of car are you driving?

問屋 →卸売り

〔な〕

内科医 →医者 10

(…が)ないことに気付く
〈いつ身分証がないのに気が付いたのですか〉
- ☆ A When did you notice you didn't have your ID card?
- ◎ B When did you realize you didn't have your ID card?
- △ C When did you find you didn't have your ID card?
- △ D When did you miss your ID card?

内容

1　《就職する仕事の内容》
〈仕事の内容を教えていただけますか〉
- ☆ A Could you tell me what the job is exactly?
- ☆ B Could you tell me exactly what the job is?
- ◎ C Could you tell me what the job involves [entails]?
- ○ D Could you tell me the nature of the job?
- △ E Could you tell me what exactly is the job?
- ❖ C は教育レベルの高い人ほどよく使われている.

2　《本・映画などの内容》
〈私が読む前にこの本の内容を言わないで下さい〉
- ☆ A Please don't tell me what happens in the story before I read this book.
- ◎ B Please don't tell me how the story ends before I read this book.
- ○ C Please don't tell me the plot [details] before I read this book.
- △ D Please don't tell me the contents before I read this book.

ないよりまし
〈ないよりましだ〉
- ◎ A Anything's better than nothing.
- ○ B It's better than nothing.
- ○ C Something's better than nothing.
- × D Half a loaf is better than none.
- ❖ D が口語辞典に出ているが使われていない.

直す

1　《(くつ下などを) 修繕する》
〈お母さん, くつ下を直してくれますか〉
- ◎ A Mom, will you fix my socks?
- ○ B Mom, will you mend my socks?
- ▽ C Mom, will you repair my socks?

2　《癖を直す》
〈私はこの悪い癖を直したいんです〉
- ◎ A I want to get rid of [break, kick] this bad habit.
- ◎ B I want to break myself of this bad habit.
- ○ C I want to beat [lick] this bad habit.
- △ D I want to get over [cure] this bad habit.
- △ E I want to cure myself of this bad habit.
- × F I want to cure [get] me of this bad habit.

❖(1) F が辞典に出ているが使われていない．
❖(2) 「修理する」の項も参照のこと

治る
1 《重病・重傷の場合》
〈彼は心臓発作から回復したばかりです〉
◎ A He's just recovered from a heart attack.
○ B He's just gotten over a heart attack.
△ C He's just recuperated [overcome] from a heart attack.
× D He's just gotten rid of a heart attack.

2 《軽い病気・けがの場合》
〈風邪は治りましたか〉
☆ A Are you over your cold yet?
◎ B Is your cold better yet?
◎ C Is your cold gone yet?
◎ D Did you get rid of your cold?
◎ E Have you gotten your cold yet?
◎ F Has your cold gone away yet?
△ G Have you gotten rid of your cold?
× H Have you thrown off [recovered from, gotten well of] your cold?

(…の)中
1 《「(建物の) 中へ」》
〈彼らはバーの中に入って行った〉
☆ A They went inside [into] the bar.
◎ B They went in the bar.
△ C They went inside of the bar.

2 《「(建物の) 中に」》
〈ビルの中には誰もいません〉
☆ A There's no one inside the building.
◎ B There's no one in the building.
○ C There's no one inside of the building.

3 《建物に言及せず「中に」と述べる場合》
〈彼は中にいます〉
◎   He's inside.

長生きする
1 《一般的に言う場合》
〈両親が一緒に長生きしてくれることを願っています〉
◎ A I hope my parents'll live [enjoy] a long life together.
◎ B I hope my parents'll live [enjoy] long lives together.

2 《「…より長生きする」と言う場合》
〈彼は私より長生きするでしょう〉
◎ A He'll live longer than me.
○ B He'll outlive me.
○ C He'll be around longer than me.
△ D He'll survive [hang on] longer than me.

長いものには巻かれろ
1 《市役所・町役場が相手のとき》
〈長いものには巻かれろ〉
◎ A You can't fight City Hall.
◎ B You can't fight the Government.

△ C You can't fight the City Hall.
 × D You can't fight city fathers.
   ❖ D が辞典に出ているが使われていない.
 2 《県庁が相手のとき》
 〈長いものには巻かれろ〉
 ◎ A You can't fight the government.
 ◎ B You can't fight the county government.
 × C You can't fight the prefectural government.
   ❖ アメリカでは prefecture は全く使われていないので意味をなさない. 日本の県に相当するのは A, B. A の the government は中央政府とは限らない.
 3 《日本の中央政府が相手のとき》
 〈長いものには巻かれろ〉
 ◎ A You can't fight the government.
 ◎ B You can't fight the Japanese government.
 △ C You can't fight the central government.
   ❖ B は外国人が使うときよく使われる.
 4 《アメリカ政府のとき》
 〈長いものには巻かれろ〉
 ◎ A You can't fight the Federal government.
 ○ B You can't fight Uncle Sam.

長くもたない →長持ちする 4
仲直りする
 1 《男女間の場合》
 〈メアリーとトムはまもなく仲直りするでしょう〉
 ◎ A Mary and Tom'll get back [make up] soon.
 ◎ B Mary and Tom'll work things out soon.
 ○ C Mary and Tom'll patch things up soon.
 △ D Mary and Tom'll reconcile soon.
 △ E Mary and Tom'll settle their differences soon.
 △ F Mary and Tom'll bury the hatchet soon.
 2 《同性同士の場合》
 〈トムとジムはまもなく仲直りするでしょう〉
 ◎ A Tom and Jim'll settle their differences soon.
 ◎ B Tom and Jim'll work things out soon.
 ○ C Tom and Jim'll patch things up soon.
 ○ D Tom and Jim'll make up [reconcile] soon.
 ○ E Tom and Jim'll bury the hatchet soon.
 △ F Tom and Jim'll get reconciled soon.
 × G Tom and Jim'll get back together soon.
   ❖ D の make up は女性同士の場合には非常によく使われている.

眺めがいい
 1 《一般的に述べる場合》
 〈眺めが素敵でした〉
 ◎ A The view was enjoyable.
 △ B The view was pleasing [pleasant].
 × C The view was entertaining [swell].
   ❖ C が辞典に出ているが使われていない.
 2 《「…の眺めがいい」と述べる場合》

〈ホテルは湖の眺めがいいんです〉
- ◎ A The hotel has a nice view of the lake.
- ◎ B The hotel looks out over the lake.
- ◎ C The hotel overlooks the lake.
- × D The hotel commands a nice view of the lake.
  - ❖(1) D が辞典に出ているが使われていない.
  - ❖(2) A は湖からの距離にかかわらず，また高台にあるか否かにかかわらず使われている. B は A, C と比べてより湖に隣接しており，湖より高い場所であっても同じ高さであっても使われている. C は A, B と異なり，高台にあるという響きがある.

長持ちする

1 《生地》
〈この生地は長持ちします〉
- ☆ A This fabric lasts a long time.
- ◎ B This fabric lasts long [for a long time].
- ◎ C This fabric is durable.
- ○ D This fabric is long-lasting.
- ○ E This fabric wears well.
- ○ F This fabric stands up.
- × G This fabric stands a good deal of wear.
- × H This fabric keeps long.
  - ❖ G, H が辞典に出ているが使われていない.

2 《機械》
〈この機械はあの機械よりも長持ちするでしょう〉
- ☆ A This machine'll last longer than that one.
- ◎ B This machine'll last for a longer time than that one.
- ◎ C This machine'll be more durable than that one.
- ○ D This machine'll have a longer life than that one.
- ○ E This machine'll be longer lasting than that one.
- ○ F This machine'll give longer service than that one.

3 《ヘアカラー》
〈このヘアカラーはあれより長持ちします〉
- ☆ A This hair color lasts longer than that one.
- ◎ B This hair color lasts a longer time than that one.
- ◎ C This hair color stays in [holds up, holds up well, wears well] for a longer time than that one.
- ○ D This hair color is longer lasting than that one.
- △ E This hair color keeps for a longer time than that one.

4 《(人の命が) 長く持たない》
〈彼はあまり長く持たないでしょう〉
- ☆ A He won't live much longer.
- ◎ B He won't last much longer.
- ○ C He won't survive much longer.

仲を取り持つ
〈私がジェーンとビルの仲を取り持ったんですよ〉
- ◎ A I got Jane and Bill together.
- ◎ B I fixed Jane and Bill up.
- ○ C I matched Jane and Bill up.
- ○ D I played the matchmaker for Jane and Bill.

◯ E I was the matchmaker for Jane and Bill.
　　　△ F I played cupid for Jane and Bill.
　　　△ G I hooked Jane and Bill up.
泣きくずれる
　〈彼女は突然泣きくずれた〉
　　　◎ A She suddenly broke down (crying).
　　　◎ B She suddenly burst into tears.
　　　△ C She suddenly broke into tears.
殴る　→たたく　2
　1　《顔・腹部などを殴るとき》
　〈彼は私の顔を殴ったんです〉
　　　☆ A He punched me in the face.
　　　◎ B He hit me in the face.
　　　◯ C He struck me in the face.
　　　△ D He punched [hit] my face.
　　　▽ E He struck my face.
　　　❖ strike という動詞を用いると堅い響きがある．
　2　《「…で殴る」と言うとき》
　a）本などで
　〈彼は私の頭を本で殴ったんです〉
　　　◎ A He hit me on the head with a book.
　　　◎ B He hit my head with a book.
　　　◎ C He knocked me upside the head with a book.
　　　◯ D He struck me on the head with a book.
　　　◯ E He struck my head with a book.
　　　◯ F He hit me in the head with a book.
　　　△ G He struck me in the head with a book.
　　　▽ H He punched me in [on] the head with a book.
　　　▽ I He punched my head with a book.
　　　❖ H, I は辞典に出ているがまれ．
　b）げんこつで
　〈彼は私の頭をげんこつで殴ったんです〉
　　　◎ A He knocked me upside the head with his fist.
　　　◎ B He hit [struck] me on the head with his fist.
　　　◎ C He hit [struck] my head with his fist.
　　　△ D He hit me in the head with his fist.
　　　△ E He struck me in the head with his fist.
　　　❖ D, E が辞典に出ているが時々使われている程度．
納得させる
　1　《一般的に述べる場合》
　〈私はやっと彼を納得させました〉
　　　◎ A I finally convinced [persuaded] him.
　　　◎ B I finally got through to him.
　2　《内容に言及する場合》
　a）「…であることを納得させる」
　〈私は彼女が無罪であることを，陪審員に納得させることができませんでした〉
　　　◎ A I couldn't convince [persuade] the jury that she was innocent.
　　　◯ B I couldn't get through to the jury that she was innocent.
　b）「…することを納得させる」

〈私はやっと彼に妥協するよう納得させました〉
- ☆ A I finally convinced [persuaded] him to compromise.
- ◎ B I finally talked [persuaded] him into a compromise.
- ◎ C I finally talked [persuaded] him into compromising.
- ○ D I finally convinced him into a compromise.
- ○ E I finally convinced him into compromising.
- ▽ F I finally got through to him to compromise.

何かやっている

〈母：一晩中どこへ行っていたの〉
Mother: Where have you been all night?
〈息子：マイクの家にいたんだよ〉
Son: I was at Mike's.
〈母：それは変ね．マイクはあなたを探してここへ来たのよ．あなた何かやっているのね〉
Mother:
- ◎ A That's funny. Mike came here, looking for you. You're up to no good, aren't you?
- ◎ B That's funny. Mike came here, looking for you. You're up to something, aren't you?

❖ B の方が怒っているニュアンスは強い．

何から何まで

〈リンダ：デイヴと私は仲良くやって行くのが難しいのよ〉
Linda: Dave and I are having trouble getting along.
〈リズ：何のことでけんかするの〉
Liz: What do you argue about?
〈リンダ：何から何までよ〉
Linda:
- ◎ A You name it.
- ○ B Anything and everything.
- ○ C Everything.
- ○ D Anything.

❖ You name it は次のように例を列挙したあとに使うことも多い．

〈ジョン：今晩の料理は何〉
John: What's cooking tonight?
〈シンディ：何でもいいわよ．スパゲッティ，ハンバーグ，鶏の唐揚，カレーライス，ビーフシチュー，ポークカツ…何でも言ってちょうだい〉
Cindy: Whatever you want; spaghetti, hamburgers, fried chicken, curried rice, beef stew, pork cutlet—you name it.

何を

1 《出し物・番組などを尋ねる》

a） 起こっていることについて尋ねるとき
〈あそこで何をやっているんですか〉
- ◎ A What's going on [happening] over there?
- △ B What's cooking over there?

b） テレビの番組を尋ねるとき
〈5チャンネルでは何をやっているの〉
- ◎ A What's on Channel 5?
- △ B What's being aired [broadcast, televised] on Channel 5?

c） 映画館のスケジュールを尋ねるとき

〈銀行の裏の映画館では何をやっているの〉
- ◎ A What's playing [showing] at the movie theater behind the bank?
- ○ B What's on at the movie theater behind the bank?

d) 劇場のスケジュールを尋ねるとき

〈あの劇場では何をやっているの〉
- ◎ A What're they performing at that theater?
- ◎ B What's being performed at that theater?

2 《相手の言いたいことを尋ねる》

〈何を言おうとしているのですか〉
- ◎ A What's the bottom line?
- ◎ B What's the [your] point?
- ◎ C What're you driving [getting] at?
- ◎ D What're you trying to say?
  - ❖話し手がまわりくどい話し方をするため何を言いたいのかわからない場合に, 聞き手が使う表現.

生意気な口をきく

〈両親にそんな生意気な口をきくべきではないよ〉
- ◎ A You shouldn't be so smart with your parents.
- ◎ B You shouldn't be such a smart-aleck with your parents.
- ○ C You shouldn't have [use] such a smart mouth with your parents.
- △ D You shouldn't be so sassy [smart-alecky] with your parents.
- × E You shouldn't be so fresh with your parents.
  - ❖Eが辞典に出ているが使われていない.

悩む

1 《すでに起こったことに対して》

〈何を悩んでいるのですか〉
- ◎ A What's bugging [bothering, eating] you?
- ○ B What's on your mind?
- ○ C What's irritating you?
- △ D What's annoying you?
  - ❖Bは悩みの程度としては最も弱い響きがある.

2 《今起こっていることに対して》

〈彼の言っていることがあなたを悩ませているのですか〉
- ◎ A Is what he's saying bugging [bothering, eating] you?
- ○ B Is what he's saying getting on your nerves?
- ○ C Is what he's saying getting to [irritating] you?
- ○ D Is what he's saying getting under your skin?
- △ E Is what he's saying annoying you?

並ぶ

〈お客様に並んでくださるように言いましたか〉
- ◎ A Did you ask the customers to line up?
- ◎ B Did you ask the customers to get in [make, form] a line?
- ◎ C Did you ask the customers to stand in a line?
  - ❖Cには「(今現在列をはずれているので) きちんと列に入って並ぶ」という意味もある.

なる

1 《名詞を従えるとき》

a) 目標・夢を述べるとき

〈私は弁護士になりたいんです〉

- ◎ A I want to be a lawyer.
- ○ B I want to become a lawyer.
- × C I want to get [make] a lawyer.

b）素質を言及するとき

〈彼はいいヴァイオリニストになるでしょう〉

- ◎ A He'll make a good violinist.
- ◎ B He'll be a good violinist.
- △ C He'll become a good violinist.
    - ❖(1) 名詞を従える場合は get は使えない．
    - ❖(2) make が「なる」の意味で使われるときは，本人に素質が備わっていることを意味する．

2 《形容詞を従えるとき》

a）天気・体調・景気に言及するとき

〈明日は暑くなるでしょう〉

- ☆ A It'll be hot tomorrow.
- ◎ B It'll get hot tomorrow.
- ○ C It'll become hot tomorrow.

b）自立した・有名な・重要なを言及するとき

〈あなたはもっと自立しなければならないね〉

- ◎ A You have to be [become] more independent.
- × B You have to get more independent.
    - ❖形容詞を従えるときは使用頻度に違いはあるが，be, become, get いずれも使われることが多い．しかし，famous（有名な），independent（自立した），important（重要な）などのときは get は使えないことに注意．

3 《特に「(悪い状態に) なる」の意味のとき》

〈ミルクを冷蔵庫に入れなさい．さもないと悪くなるでしょう〉

- ◎ A Put the milk in the fridge, or it'll turn [get] sour.
- △ B Put the milk in the fridge, or it'll become [go, be] sour.
    - ❖turn および go が「なる」の意味で使われるのはよくない状態に「なる」場合である．

鳴る

1 《おなかが空腹で》

〈おなかが鳴っている〉

- ☆ A My stomach's growling.
- ◎ B My stomach's grumbling.
- ○ C My stomach's talking [rumbling].
- × D My stomach's chiming.
- × E My belly's chiming [rumbling, growling].
    - ❖D, E が辞典に出ているが使われていない．

2 《耳》

〈私の左の耳が鳴るんです〉

- ☆ A I hear a ringing in my left ear.
- ◎ B I have a ringing in my left ear.
- ○ C My left ear's ringing.

3 《各種のベル》

〈ドアのベルが鳴っている〉

- ◎ A The doorbell's ringing.
- × B There's a ring at the door.

4 《「そら，ベルが鳴っている」と述べるとき》

a) 鳴らしている人が視界にないとき
〈そら，ドアのベルが鳴っている〉
  ◎ There goes the doorbell.
    ❖上記の表現は doorbell に限らず駅，映画館，空港どこでも「そら」という気持ちで述べるときは使える．
b) 鳴らしている人が視界にあるまたはあったとき
〈そら，ドアのベルが鳴っている〉
  ◎ Here comes the doorbell.

5 《サイレン》
〈救急車のサイレンが鳴っている〉
  ☆ A The ambulance siren's blaring.
  ◎ B The ambulance siren's piercing [loud].
  ○ C The ambulance siren's screaming.
  × D The ambulance siren's blowing [whistling] hard.
    ❖辞典に D が出ているが使われていない．

6 《教会の鐘》
〈教会の鐘が鳴っている〉
  ◎ A The church bell's ringing [chiming].
  ○ B The church bell's tolling.
  △ C The church bell's sounding [singing].

7 《雷》
〈雷が鳴っている〉
  ☆ A It's thundering.
  ○ B The thunder's rolling [rumbling].
  ○ C It's rumbling.
    ❖C は天気のことを言及していることがはっきりしているときにしか使えない．

8 《クツ》
〈私のクツが鳴るんです〉
  ☆ A My shoes squeak.
  ○ B My shoes're squeaky.
  × C My shoes creak.
    ❖C が辞典に出ているが使われていない．

馴れ合い

1 《相手が個人の場合》
〈学生とあまり馴れ合いになることはよくありません〉
  ◎ A Being too friendly with your students isn't good.
  ○ B Being too close with your students isn't good.
  △ C Having a cozy relationship with your students isn't good.

2 《相手が組織の場合》
〈政府が軍事産業と馴れ合いになるべきではない〉
  ☆ A The government shouldn't be in such a cozy relationship with the military industry.
  ◎ B The government shouldn't be in such a close relationship with the military industry.
  ○ C The government shouldn't be in such a comfortable relationship with the military industry.
  △ D The government shouldn't be in such a comfy [snug] relationship with the military industry.

なれなれしい
  1 《一般的に述べる場合》
  〈彼は私になれなれしいんです〉
      ◎ A He's too friendly with [to] me.
      ○ B He's overly-friendly with [to] me.
  2 《特に性的ななれなれしさを表す場合》
  a) その場限りのとき
  〈私になれなれしくするのをやめてください〉
      ☆ A Stop hitting on me.
      ◎ B Stop getting fresh with me.
      ◎ C Stop making a pass [passes] at me.
      △ D Stop making an advance at [towards] me.
      △ E Stop making advances at [towards] me.
      × F Stop giving [making] attentions to me.
      ❖(1) F が辞典に出ているが使われていない.
      ❖(2) なれなれしさの程度は A が一番強い. B が 2 番, C が 3 番, D 4 番.
  b) 繰り返し起こるとき
  〈彼は毎日私になれなれしいんです〉
      ◎ A He hits on [gets fresh with] me every day.
      ◎ B He makes passes [a pass] at me every day.
      △ C He makes advances at [towards] me every day.
      △ D He makes an advance at me every day.
      × E He makes an advance towards me every day.

慣れる →順応する

何…
  1 《何時》
  a) 時刻
  〈何時ですか〉
      ☆ A Can you tell me the time?
      ◎ B What time is it?
      ◎ C What time do you have?
      ◎ D Do you have the time?
      ○ E What's the time?
  b) 「何時に」
  〈明日何時に電話したらいいですか〉
      ◎   When [What time] can I call you tomorrow?
  c) 「何時まで」
  〈このお店は何時まで開いているのですか〉
      ◎ A How late is this [your] store open?
      ◎ B How late are you open?
      ○ C When do you close?
      ○ D When [At what time] does this store close?
      △ E Until what time are you open?
      △ F Until what time is this store open?
      ❖「何時まで」は常に How late...? の方が Until what time...? よりもよく使われている. How late can you stay here? (何時までここにいられますか)/How late can I call you tonight? (今晩何時までお電話してもいいですか)
  2 《何度》

a) 体温
〈患者：熱があるんです〉
Patient: I have a fever.
〈医師：何度ありますか〉
Doctor:
- ◎ What's your temperature?

b) 気温
〈気温は何度ですか〉
- ◎ A How hot is it?
- ◎ B What's the temperature?
- ◎ C How cold is it?
  - ❖ A は暑いとき，C は寒いとき，B はいつでも使える．

3 《何年生》

a) 大学生に尋ねるとき
〈あなたは何年生ですか〉
- ◎ A What year are you?
- ○ B What year are you in(, in college)?
- ○ C How far along're you?
- ○ D How far along're you in college?
- △ E How far along're you at college?
- △ F What year're you in, at college?

b) 中高生に尋ねるとき
〈あなたは何年生ですか〉
- ◎ A What grade're you?
- ◎ B What year are you?
- ○ C What year are you in, in high school?
- ○ D How far along're you in high school?
- △ E What grade're you in?
- △ F What year are you in(, at high school)?
- △ G What year are you in high school?

c) 小学生に尋ねるとき
- ◎ A What grade're you?
- ○ B What grade're you in(, in elementary school)?
- ○ C How far along're you in elementary?
- ○ D How far along're you in school?
- ○ E How far along're you in elementary school?
- ○ F What grade're you in, at elementary school?
- △ G How far along're you at elementary school?

4 《何年に》
〈何年に博士号を取ったのですか〉
- ◎ A When [What year] did you get a Ph.D?
- △ B In what year did you get a Ph.D?
- △ C What year did you get a Ph.D in?
  - ❖ 学校英文法では B を強調している．

5 《何番目》

a) 駅
〈新宿はここから何番目の駅ですか〉
- ◎ A How many stations are there between here and Shinjuku?
- ◎ B How many stations are there before Shinjuku?

△ C How many stations come before Shinjuku?
b）兄弟
〈あなたは兄弟の中で何番目なの〉
　　　◎ A Which (number) child are you in your family?
　　　◎ B Where do you come in your family?
　　　△ C Where are you in your family?
　　　△ D Where do you fall in your family?
c）成績
・学校
〈君はクラスで何番目なの〉
　　　◎ A What's your class rank?
　　　◎ B What's your rank in class?
　　　◎ C What do you do in your class?
　　　○ D What's your class standing?
・会社
〈預金高でXYZ銀行は何番目ですか〉
　　　◎ A What's XYZ's rank among the other banks in terms of amount of savings?
　　　◎ B Where does XYZ rank among the other banks in terms of amount of savings?
　　　◎ C In terms of amount of savings how high does XYZ rank among the other banks?
　　　❖ Aのrankの代わりにposition, Bのrankの代わりにstandを使うこともできるが, rankの方がもっとよく使われている.
d）チームの順位
〈ジャイアンツは何番［何位］ですか〉
　　　◎ A Where do the Giants stand in the pennant race?
　　　◎ B What's the Giants' position in the pennant race?
　　　△ C Where do the Giants rank in the pennant race?
e）打順
〈清原選手は何番を打っているのですか〉
　　　◎ A Where does Kiyohara bat?
　　　◎ B When does Kiyohara bat?
　　　◎ C Where is Kiyohara up?
　　　× D In what order does Kiyohara hit?
f）GNP
〈日本はGNPの点で何番目なのですか〉
　　　◎ A Where does Japan rank (in the world) in terms of GNP?
　　　○ B In what position does Japan rank in terms of GNP?
　　　○ C What's Japan's (world) position in terms of GNP?
g）大統領（首相, 社長など）
〈レーガンは何代目の大統領ですか〉
　　　◎ A How many presidents have there been before Reagan?
　　　◎ B How many presidents were there before Reagan?
　　　○ C Which president of the United States is Reagan?
　　　△ D What number president is Reagan?
　　　× E Where does Reagan rank among the American Presidents?
何…から何…まで
1　《何階から何階までアパートになるのですか》

◎ What [Which] floors is this building going to be apartments?

2 《何曜日から何曜日まで》
〈何曜日から何曜日まで大売出しなのですか〉
◎ What [Which] days're the sales?

3 《何年から何年まで》
〈何年から何年まであなたはフランスにいたのですか〉
◎ What [Which] years were you in France?

4 《何番から何番まで》
〈何番から何番までの電話番号をあなたの会社で専用で使っているのですか〉
◎ What [Which] telephone numbers does your company have all to itself?

5 《何ページ》
〈何ページから何ページまでが落丁しているんですか〉
☆ A Which pages're missing?
◎ B What pages're missing?
× C From what page to what page's missing?
❖日本語につられて C を使わないこと．

(聞き返して) 何ですって

1 《丁重に尋ねるとき》
〈何とおっしゃいましたか〉
◎ A I beg your pardon?
◎ B Beg your pardon?
◎ C Pardon me?
◎ D I'm sorry?
◎ E Excuse me?
◎ F Would you repeat that [it] please?
❖A が一番丁重な響きがある．その他はほぼ同じ．

2 《普通に尋ねるとき》
〈何て言いましたか〉
◎ A Pardon?
◎ B Sorry?
◎ C Can you say that again?
◎ D Can you come again?
◎ E Come again?
◎ F What did you say?
◎ G What's that?
◎ H What?

3 《乱暴に尋ねるとき》
〈何だって〉
◎ A What's that?
◎ B What?
❖A, B とも強い語調で発言する．

〔に〕

似合う
1 《物が主語の場合》

a）強調しないで述べるとき

〈そのドレスはあなたに似合います〉

- ☆ A That dress looks good on you.
- ◎ B That dress fits [suits] you.
- ○ C That dress does something for you.
- ○ D That dress becomes you.
- △ E That dress is becoming on you.
- ▽ F That dress is becoming to you.
- × G That dress fits [sits] well on you.
  - ❖ G が辞典に出ているが使われていない．

b）強い形容詞または名詞を使って強調するとき

〈そのドレスはあなたにすごく似合いますよ〉

- ☆ A That dress looks great on you.
- ◎ B That dress looks terrific [wonderful] on you.
- ◎ C That dress looks fantastic [incredible, amazing] on you.
- ○ D That dress looks super on you.
- △ E That dress looks the bomb on you.
- △ F That dress looks superb on you.
- △ G That dress looks marvelous on you.
  - ❖(1) ほめている強さはCが一番強く，B，E，Gが2番，A，D，Fが3番．
  - ❖(2) Eは若年層，特に20歳前後の人たちの間では非常によく使われている．

c）形容詞を強調して述べるとき

〈そのドレスはあなたにすごく似合いますよ〉

- ☆ A That dress looks really great on you.
- ◎ B That dress looks really terrific [fantastic, incredible, wonderful, amazing] on you.
- ○ C That dress looks really super on you.
- △ D That dress looks really superb on you.

d）動詞を強調して述べるとき

〈そのドレスはあなたにものすごく似合いますよ〉

- ☆ A That dress really looks great on you.
- ◎ B That dress really looks terrific [incredible, wonderful, fantastic, amazing] on you.
- ○ C That dress really looks super on you.
- ○ D That dress really suits [fits] you.
- ○ E That dress really does something for you.
- ○ F That dress really becomes you.
- △ G That dress really looks the bomb on you.
- △ H That dress really looks superb on you.
- △ I That dress is really [very] becoming on you.
- ▽ J That dress is really [very] becoming to you.

2 《人が主語のとき》

a）in を使って言うとき

〈あなたはそのドレスものすごく似合いますよ〉

- ◎ A You look really great [terrific, fantastic, incredible, wonderful, amazing] in that dress.
- ○ B You look really good [nice] in that dress.
- △ C You really look the bomb in that dress.
- △ D You look really super [superb] in that dress.

b) with を使って言うとき
〈あなたはそのドレスものすごく似合いますよ〉
- ☆ A You look really great with that dress on.
- ◎ B You look really terrific [fantastic, incredible, wonderful, amazing] with that dress on.
- ○ C You look really good [nice] with that dress on.
- △ D You really look the bomb with that dress on.
- △ E You look really super [superb] with that dress on.

2位につける
〈アメリカは GNP において1位で，日本は2位につけている〉
- ◎ A America ranks first in GNP, followed by Japan.
- ◎ B America ranks first in GNP, with Japan coming in second.
- ○ C America ranks first in GNP, and Japan's second.
- ○ D America ranks first in GNP, and Japan's in the second place.
- ○ E America ranks first in GNP, with Japan following close behind.

臭いをかぐ
〈この魚の臭いをかいでごらん〉
- ◎ A Smell this fish.
- ◎ B Take a smell of this fish.
- ○ C Have a smell of this fish.
- × D Take a smell at this fish.
- ❖ Dが辞典に出ているが使われていない．

苦手だ
1 《科目》
〈私は数学が苦手なんです〉
- ◎ A Math's my weak point.
- ◎ B I'm terrible at [awful at, bad at, weak in] math.
- ○ C I'm lousy at math.
- ○ D Math's my weak subject.
- ▽ E Math's my Achilles heel.
- ❖ E は教育レベルの高い人の間では非常によく使われている．

2 《人》
〈あのお客は苦手なんです〉
- ◎ A That customer's hard [tough] to deal with.
- ○ B That customer's difficult to deal with.

3 《食べ物》
〈私は肉ならどんなものでも食べますが魚は苦手なんです〉
- ◎ A I like all kinds of meat but I don't like fish.
- ○ B I like all kinds of meat but fish isn't for me.

肉離れ →病気 18
肉屋 →店 1

逃げる
1 《人が走って》
〈彼は警察官を見たとき，逃げたんです〉
- ☆ A When he saw a policeman, he took off.
- ◎ B When he saw a policeman, he ran away [off].
- △ C When he saw a policeman, he fled.
- △ D When he saw a policeman, he made tracks.
- △ E When he saw a policeman, he beat it.

❖ C は堅い文章英語，または警察の間では非常によく使われている．

2 《車で》

〈彼は警察官を見たとき，逃げたんです〉

　☆　A　When he saw a policeman, he took off.
　◎　B　When he saw a policeman, he sped away.
　△　C　When he saw a policeman, he fled.
　△　D　When he saw a policeman, he made tracks.
　△　E　When he saw a policeman, he beat it.
　×　F　When he saw a policeman, he ran away [off].

にこにこする

〈彼はにこにこしていた〉

　◎　A　He was all smiles.
　◎　B　He was smiling ear to ear.
　○　C　He was smiling from ear to ear.

にせもの

1 《絵》

〈この絵はにせものだ〉

　☆　A　This picture's a fake.
　◎　B　This picture's fake.
　◎　C　This picture's a rip-off.
　○　D　This picture's a fraud [a phony].
　○　E　This picture's counterfeit [phony, imitation].
　△　F　This picture's bogus.

2 《ダイヤモンド》

〈これはにせのダイヤモンドだ〉

　☆　A　This is a fake diamond.
　◎　B　This is a faked diamond.
　○　C　This is a phony [a bogus, an imitation, a counterfeit, a mock] diamond.
　×　D　This is a false [a sham, a spurious] diamond.

3 《署名》

〈この署名はにせものだ〉

　☆　A　This signature's a forgery.
　◎　B　This signature's forged.
　○　C　This signature's a fraud.
　○　D　This signature's phony [bogus].
　△　E　This signature's a fake.
　△　F　This signature's fake [falsified].
　▽　G　This signature's falsification.
　×　H　This signature's sham.
　×　I　This signature's a rip-off.

4 《医者》

〈彼はにせ医者です〉

　☆　A　He's practicing medicine without a license.
　◎　B　He isn't a licensed doctor.
　○　C　He's an unlicensed doctor.
　○　D　He's a quack.

5 《偽札》

a）金額を明示しない場合

〈偽札が国中に出まわっている〉
- ☆ A Counterfeit bills're circulated all over the country.
- ◎ B Fake bills're circulated all over the country.
- △ C Phony [Bogus] bills're circulated all over the country.

b) 金額を明示するとき

〈これは偽 100 ドル札だ〉
- ☆ A This is a counterfeit (one) hundred-dollar bill.
- ◎ B This is a fake (one) hundred-dollar bill.
- ◎ C This is a phony (one) hundred-dollar bill.
- ○ D This is a bogus (one) hundred-dollar bill.

似ている

1 《人と人が》

a) 容姿

〈彼は父親にとてもよく似ています〉
- ☆ A He looks a lot [just] like his father.
- ☆ B He really looks like his father.
- ☆ C He looks like his father a lot.
- ◎ D He really takes after his father.
- ◎ E He takes after his father a lot.
- ○ F He looks a great deal like his father.
- ○ G He looks like his father a great deal.
- ○ H He really resembles his father.
- ○ I He resembles his father a lot.
- ○ J He has a strong [striking] resemblance to his father.
- ○ K He bears a strong resemblance to his father.

b) 性格

〈彼は父親にとてもよく似ています〉
- ◎ A He really takes after his father.
- ◎ B He takes after his father a lot.
- ◎ C He's a lot [just] like his father.
- ○ D He's a great deal [very much] like his father.
- ○ E He favors his father a lot.
- ○ F He really favors his father.

❖(1) A, B は容姿が似ていることを言うのにも使うことができる．
❖(2) E, F は「彼はお父さんの方がとても好きなんです」の意味でもよく使われている．

c) 瓜ふたつ

〈彼は父親に瓜ふたつです〉
- ◎ A He's a carbon copy of his father.
- ◎ B He's a chip off the old block.
- ◎ C He's the spitting [the exact] image of his father.
- △ D He's the perfect likeness [image] of his father.
- △ E He's the very picture of his father.
- △ F He's his father's double.
- × G He's a chip of the old block.

❖ G が辞典に出ているが使われていない．

2 《無生物が》

〈彼の意見はあなたの意見に似ています〉
- ◎ A His opinions're similar to yours.

- ◎ B His opinions match yours.
- ◎ C You and he have the similar opinions.
- ◎ D His opinions're really [very] like yours.
- ○ E Your opinions resemble his.

3 《長い歴史の流れのある内容を述べるとき》

〈英国の政治制度は両国が君主制である点で日本と似ている〉

- ☆ A British political system's similar to Japan's in that both have a monarchy system.
- ◎ B British political system matches Japan's in that both have a monarchy system.
- ◎ C British political system's very [really] like Japan's in that both have a monarchy system.
- ○ D British political system resembles Japan's in that both have a monarchy system.
- △ E British political system's very parallel to Japan's in that both have a monarchy system.

二度としません

1 《上司に対して言うとき》

〈社長：これで今週3回目の遅刻だ．もう1回遅刻したら首にするぞ〉

Boss: This is the third time you've been late this week. If you come in late once more I'll fire you.

〈従業員：わかりました．二度と致しません〉

Employee: Yes, sir.

- ◎ A It won't happen again.
- ▽ B I won't do it again.
  ❖ 親しい友人，親子のような関係のときはA, Bとも非常によく使われている．

2 《親，友人に対して言うとき》

〈二度としません〉

- ◎ A It won't happen again.
- ◎ B I won't do it again.

二の足を踏む

〈私は彼らの提案に，二の足を踏んでいます〉

◎ I'm having second thoughts [hesitating] about their proposal.

入院する

1 《話し手が「入院する」》

〈私は胃の手術で入院しなければならないんです〉

- ☆ A I have to check into [go to] the hospital for stomach surgery.
- ◎ B I have to be checked [admitted] into the hospital for stomach surgery.
- ○ C I have to go into the hospital for stomach surgery.
- ○ D I have to be hospitalized for stomach surgery.
- ○ E I have to admit [check] myself into the hospital for stomach surgery.
- ○ F I have to stay [be] at the hospital for stomach surgery.
- △ G I have to get [have] myself checked into the hospital for stomach surgery.
- △ H I have to get [have] myself admitted into the hospital for stomach surgery.

2 《「入院させる」というとき》

〈私は息子を胃の手術で入院させなければならないんです〉
- ◎ A I have to take [check, admit] my son into the hospital for the stomach surgery.
- ◎ B I have to put my son into [in] the hospital for stomach surgery.
- ◎ C I have to get [have] my son checked into the hospital for stomach surgery.
- ◎ D I have to have my son hospitalized for stomach surgery.
- ○ E I have to get [have] my son admitted into the hospital for stomach surgery.
- ○ F I have to hospitalize my son for stomach surgery.

入居する
1 《名詞を従えるとき》

〈いつ新しい家に入居なさるのですか〉
- ◎ A When're you going to move into the new house?
- ○ B When're you going to start living in the new house?

2 《名詞を従えないとき》

〈いつ入居なさるのですか〉
- ◎ A When're you going to move in?
- ○ B When're you going to start living?

入国管理事務所
〈入国管理事務所は彼にビザの延長を許可しませんでした〉
- ◎ A The Immigration Office refused to grant him an extension on his visa.
- ○ B Immigration refused to grant him an extension on his visa.

(コンピュータに)入力する
〈データを全部コンピュータに入力しなさい〉
- ☆ A Enter all the data into the computer.
- ◎ B Enter all the data in the computer.
- ◎ C Put all the data into [in] the computer.
- ◎ D Feed all the data into [in] the computer.
- ○ E Input all the data into [in] the computer.
- ○ F Input all the data.

にらんでいる
1 《一般的に述べるとき》

〈彼は私をにらんでいました〉
- ◎ A He was glaring at me.
- △ B He was staring angrily at me.
- △ C He was staring at me angrily.

2 《比喩的に述べるとき》

〈彼は社長に，にらまれているんです〉
- ◎ A He's on the boss's shit list.
- ○ B He's on the boss's black list.
  - ❖ shit は下品な表現なので男性の間の方がよく使われている．

庭
1 《前庭》

〈彼らの家には大きな前庭があります〉
- ☆ A Their house has a big front yard.
- ◎ B Their house has a big yard [lawn].

- × C Their house has a big garden.
- 2 《裏庭》

〈彼らの家には小さい裏庭があります〉
- ◎ A Their house has a small yard.
- ○ B Their house has a small backyard.
- × C Their house has a small garden.
  - ❖(1) アメリカの garden は菜園か花壇を意味し，普通裏庭の片隅にある．前者は vegetable garden とも言う．後者は flower garden, flower bed と言い，共によく使われている．
  - ❖(2) 日本人は「庭＝garden」と思っている人が多いようだ．日本人が普通思い浮べる庭は yard と言うのが適切．
  - ❖(3) 中庭は courtyard と言う．

庭師　→職業 37

人気のある

1 《商品が》

〈これは今非常に人気のある商品です〉
- ◎ A This is a hot product now.
- ○ B This is a hot item now.
- △ C This is a hot stuff now.

2 《場所が》

〈新宿は商業地として人気があります〉
- ◎ 　Shinjuku's a sought-after [popular] business district.

人間

〈人間は死を免れない（死すべき運命にある）〉
- ☆ A Man's mortal.
- ☆ B Men're mortal.
- ◎ C Mankind's mortal.
- ◎ D Human beings're mortal.
- ◎ E Humans're mortal.
- ◎ F Our species is mortal.
- △ G People're mortal.
- △ H Humankind's mortal.
- △ I The human race's mortal.
- △ J The humanity's mortal.
- △ K Our species are mortal.

忍耐

1 《肯定的な内容のとき》

〈忍耐は成功につながる〉
- ☆ A Perseverance brings success.
- ◎ B Perseverance leads to success.
- ○ C You can get success from perseverance.
- △ D Patience leads to success.

2 《否定的な内容》

〈私は彼に対して忍耐が尽きました〉
- ◎ A I'm running out of [I'm losing] patience with him.
- ◎ B My patience with him's running out.
- ○ C My patience with him's wearing thin.
- × D My patience with him's getting thin.

〔ぬ〕

抜け穴
《比喩的に》
〈この法律にはいくつか抜け穴がある〉
☆　This law has some loopholes.

〔ね〕

値上がりする
1　《為替の対ドルレートの場合》
〈円のレートは今年の秋までに上がるでしょう〉
◎　A　The yen rate'll go down [drop] by this fall.
◎　B　The yen rate'll fall by this fall.
○　C　The yen rate'll come down by this fall.
○　D　The yen rate'll spiral [decrease] by this fall.
○　E　The yen rate'll depreciate by this fall.
△　F　The yen rate'll decline by this fall.
△　G　The yen rate'll be higher [stronger] by this fall.
❖(1) B, C は円を通貨としない人たちが，自分たちにとって得であるという気持ちで述べるときに使われている．
❖(2) E, F は改まった響きがある．また，アメリカ人でも為替に無関心な人は E を知らない人も多い．
❖(3)「円が値上がりする」ということは¥125 から数字が少なくなることである．このことは日本人にとっては「値上がりする」ことになる．しかし，為替相場に従事している人以外のアメリカ人は次の理由で「値下がりする」と言う．
① 円とドルの交換レートが現在の 120 円台から 100 円近くなることは数字が下がるからである．
② アメリカはアメリカのドルを世界の基軸通貨と考えているからである．

2　《勢いを強調する場合》
〈地価は急速に値上がりしています〉
◎　A　Land prices're skyrocketing.
◎　B　Land prices're going up quickly [very fast].
○　C　Land prices're going up dramatically [tremendously].
○　D　Land prices're shooting up.
○　E　Land prices're jumping [soaring].
○　F　Land prices're going up rapidly.
○　G　Land prices're increasing very fast.
○　H　Land prices're increasing dramatically [tremendously].
○　I　Land prices're rising fast [quickly, dramatically, rapidly].
△　J　Land prices're surging.
▽　K　Land prices're spiraling.
❖(1) 多くの辞典に K が出ているがまれ．

❖(2) 強調の度合いは A が一番強く，C，D，H が 2 番，残りはほぼ同じ．

ネイティブのように
〈彼女はフランス語をネイティブのように話します〉
- ◎ A She speaks French like a native.
- ○ B She speaks French as if she were French.
- ○ C She speaks French like a native speaker.
- ○ D She speaks French like a Frenchman.
- △ E She speaks French like it's her native language.

❖D の主語は She であるが Frenchwoman とはしない．

値切る
〈最初，彼は 50 ドルと言っていたが 35 ドルまで値切ってやった〉
- ◎ A At first he asked for $50 but I got [talked] him down to $35.
- ○ B At first he asked for $50 but I brought him down to $35.
- × C At first he asked for $50 but I beat him down to $35.

❖C がある辞典に出ているが使われていない．

値下がりする
〈円のレートは今年の秋までに約 180 円に値下がりするでしょう〉
- ◎ A The yen rate'll rise [go up, come up, increase, climb] to about 180 by this fall.
- ◎ B The yen rate'll be higher [stronger, more expensive] to about 180 by this fall.
- × C The yen rate'll revaluate [upvaluate] to about 180 by this fall.

❖「値上がりする」の項も参照のこと．

熱 →病気 19

熱心な
1 《仕事》
〈彼は仕事に熱心です〉
- ◎ A He's dedicated to his work.
- ◎ B He's enthusiastic about his work.
- △ C He's zealous about his work.

❖A は献身的な，B は仕事に興味を持っているさまを表し，C は熱心すぎるというニュアンスがある．

2 《宗教》
a) 肯定的な意味

〈彼は熱心な信者です〉
- ◎ He's a devout [a dedicated, an enthusiastic] believer.

❖熱心さの度合いでは，enthusiastic がもっとも弱い．

b) 否定的な意味

〈彼は熱心な信者です〉
- ◎ He's a zealous [pious] believer.

❖どちらも独善的というニュアンスがあり，特に zealous は他派の人を改宗させようとするという響きがある．

熱中する
〈彼らは新興宗教に熱中しているんです〉
- ☆ A They're all excited about the new cult.
- ◎ B They're all wrapped up in the new cult.
- ○ C They're all gung-ho about the new cult.

値引きする
1 《金額・パーセンテージを示さないとき》

- 車・家具・不動産のような大きな買物のとき
〈少し値引きしてくれますか〉
- ☆ A Will you give me a better deal?
- ◎ B Will you come down (on the price) a little?
- ◎ C Will you give me a little discount?
- ◎ D Will you go down (on the price) a little?
- ○ E Will you reduce the price a little?
- △ F Will you mark it down a little?
    - ❖ A〜E は車の販売店, 家具屋などではよく使われているが, F は時々使われる程度, しかし, 小売店などでは F も非常によく使われている.

2 《値引きのパーセンテージに言及するとき》
- 車・家具・不動産のような大きな買物のとき
〈1割値引きしてくれますか〉
- ◎ A Can you give me a 10% discount?
- ◎ B Can you take 10% off (the price)?
- ◎ C Can you come down 10% (on the price)?
- ○ D Can you go down 10% (on the price)?
- ○ E Can you lower [reduce] the price 10%?
- ○ F Can you lower 10% on the price?
- △ G Can you mark it down 10%?

3 《金額を示すとき》
- 車・家具・不動産のような大きな買物のとき
〈値段を 500 ドルに値引きしてくれますか〉
- ◎ A Can you cut [lower, come down on] the price to $500?
- ◎ B Can you bring [make] the price down to $500?
- ○ C Can you reduce [go down] the price to $500?
- △ D Can you mark the price down to $500?

4 《社員同士で話すとき》
- 2人の支配人が話している
〈売り上げが下がってきたからすべての商品を 10 %かそこら値引きしなければならない〉
- ☆ A We have to lower the price 10% or so on all the merchandise because sales're low.
- ◎ B We have to mark down all the merchandise 10% or so because sales're low.
- ○ C We have to reduce the price 10% or so on all the merchandise because sales're low.

根も葉もない
〈ちょっと待って下さい. あなたが言っていることは根も葉もないことです〉
- ◎ A Wait a minute. What you're saying makes no sense.
- ○ B Wait a minute. What you're saying isn't based on fact [reality].
- △ C Wait a minute. What you're saying has no basis in reality.
- △ D Wait a minute. What you're saying's absolutely [utterly] groundless.
    - ❖辞典では D を紹介しているが使用頻度は高くない.

寝る
1 《床につくことに言及するとき》
〈私は普通 9 時頃寝ます〉
- ☆ A I usually go to bed around 9:00.

- ◎ B I usually get to sleep [fall asleep] around 9:00.
- ○ C I usually turn in around 9:00.
- ○ D I usually hit the hay [the sack] around 9:00.
- △ E I usually retire around 9:00.

2 《眠りにつくことに言及するとき》

〈私は普通，床につくとすぐ寝てしまいます〉

- ◎ A I usually go to sleep [fall asleep] the moment I go to bed.
- △ B I usually drop off the moment I go to bed.

3 《眠りに入ることが難しかったとき》

〈昨夜，上の階の人が遅くまでどんちゃん騒ぎをしていたんです．それで私は寝られなかったんです〉

- ☆ A My upstairs neighbors had a wild party last night, so I couldn't get to sleep.
- ◎ B My upstairs neighbors had a wild party last night, so I couldn't go to sleep.
- ○ C My upstairs neighbors had a wild party last night, so I couldn't fall asleep.

4 《眠ることに言及するとき》

〈あなたは毎日どのくらい眠るのですか〉

- ◎ How long do you sleep every day?

5 《寝ている状態に言及すること》

〈私は6時頃には寝ていました〉

- ◎ A I was asleep around 6:00.
- ◎ B I was sleeping around 6:00.

6 《ぐっすり眠っている》

〈彼はぐっすり眠っています〉

- ◎ A He's sleeping like a baby [like a log].
- ◎ B He's fast [sound] asleep.
- ◎ C He's sleeping soundly.
- ○ D He's sleeping deeply.

❖主語が成人の場合でも，Aの sleep like a baby はよく使われている．

7 《一睡もできない》

〈私は結果がとても心配で一睡もできなかったんです〉

- ◎ A I was so anxious about the results that I had a sleepless night.
- ◎ B I was so anxious about the results that I couldn't sleep at all.
- ◎ C I was so anxious about the results that I didn't sleep a wink.

❖日本語と同じく英語の場合も，多少眠っていたとしてもこのように言う．

年収

1 《極めて少ないとき》

〈彼の年収は約80万円です〉

- ◎ His yearly income's about ¥800,000.

2 《多いとき》

〈彼の年収は約3000万円です〉

- ◎ His yearly [annual] income's about ¥30,000,000.

3 《普通のとき》

〈彼の年収は約600万円です〉

- ◎ A His yearly income's about ¥6,000,000.
- △ B His annual income's about ¥6,000,000

燃費

1 《燃費が悪い》
〈この車は燃費が悪いんです〉
- ◎ A This car gets bad [low] gas mileage.
- ○ B This car has bad [low] gas mileage.
- △ C This car delivers bad [low] gas mileage.

2 《燃費がいい》
〈この車は燃費がいいんです〉
- ◎ A This car gets good [high] gas mileage.
- ○ B This is a gas-efficient [fuel-efficient, fuel-saving] car.
- △ C This car delivers good [high] gas mileage.
- △ D This car has good gas mileage.

3 《ガソリンを食う》
a) 話し手が怒っているとき
〈この車はガソリンをがぶ飲みするんだよ〉
- ◎ A This is a gas guzzler.
- ◎ B This car guzzles a lot of gas.
- △ C This car eats a lot of gas.
- △ D This car is a gas hog.
- △ E This car swallows up [drinks] a lot of gas.
  - ❖ D, E は人により使用頻度はかなり上下する.

b) 客観的に述べるとき
〈この車はガソリンをすごく使うんですよ〉
- ◎ A This car uses [consumes] a lot of gas.
- ○ B This car takes a lot of gas.
- △ C This car puts away a lot of gas.

〔の〕

…の

1 《大学の》
a) 学生
〈彼はハーバードの学生です〉
- ◎ A He's a student at Harvard.
- × B He's a student of [for, to] Harvard.

b) 教授
〈彼はハーバードの教授です〉
- ◎ A He's a professor at Harvard.
- × B He's a professor of [for, to] Harvard.

c) 学長
〈彼はハーバードの学長です〉
- ☆ A He's the president of Harvard.
- ◎ B He's president of Harvard.
- ○ C He's president at Harvard.
- △ D He's president at Harvard.

2 《会社の》
a) 社員

〈彼はシカゴ銀行の社員です〉
- ☆ A He's an employee of Chicago Bank.
- ◎ B He's an employee at Chicago Bank.
- ○ C He's an employee for Chicago Bank.
- × D He's an employee in Chicago Bank.
  - ❖ D が辞典に出ているが使われていない．

b) 社長・頭取

〈彼はシカゴ銀行の頭取です〉
- ☆ A He's the president of Chicago Bank.
- ◎ B He's the president for Chicago Bank.
- ○ C He's the president at Chicago Bank.
- × D He's the president in Chicago Bank.
  - ❖頭取でなく「…会社の社長」のときも，前置詞の使い方は同じ．

c) 支店長

〈彼はシカゴ支店の支店長です〉
- ☆ A He's the manager of the Chicago branch.
- ◎ B He's the manager for the Chicago branch.
- ○ C He's the manager at the Chicago branch.
- × D He's the manager in the Chicago branch.

3 《前置詞の使い分け》

a) on を使う例

〈彼は日米関係の権威です〉
- ◎　He's an authority on Japanese-American relations.

〈私はウィル・ハーバーグの書いたアメリカの宗教の本を何冊か読んだことがある〉
- ◎　I've read some books on religion in America written by Will Herberg.

〈昨日 4 チャンネルで真珠湾のニュースを放映した〉
- ◎　Yesterday they showed a newsreel on Pearl Harbor on Channel 4.

b) from を使う例

〈政府は東京湾の埋立てをしている〉
- ◎　The government's reclaiming land from Tokyo Bay.

〈通りを歩いていたとき，10 年振りで大学時代の友人にばったり会った〉
- ◎　I ran into a friend from college that I hadn't seen in ten years while I was walking on the street.

〈これらはアイダホのジャガイモです〉
- ◎　These're potatoes from Idaho.

c) for を使う例

〈私は風邪の薬を買わなければならないのです〉
- ◎　I have to buy medicine for a cold.

〈私は東大の入学試験を受けた〉
- ◎　I took the entrance examination for Tokyo University.

〈彼は日航のパイロットです〉
- ◎　He's a pilot for JAL.

d) to を使う例

〈私, コンサートの切符が 2 枚あるんです〉
- ◎　I've got two tickets to the concert.

〈日本のアメリカ大使は誰ですか〉
- ◎　Who's the Japanese ambassador to the United States?

e) about を使う例

〈昨日4チャンネルで私は統一教会のニュース映画を見た〉
- ◎ Yesterday I saw a newsreel on Channel 4 about the Unification Church.

〈ここにMXミサイルの記事が出ている〉
- ◎ Here's an article about the MX missile.

〈ベティのおもしろいうわさを聞いたよ〉
- ◎ I heard some interesting gossip about Betty.

脳外科医　→医者 11

能率

1　《能率》

〈この会社は能率がすべてなんです〉
- ☆ A Efficiency's [Productivity's] everything in this company.
- ◎ B Being efficient's [productive's] everything in this company.
- ○ C Getting things done's everything in this company.
- × D Effectiveness's [Effectivity's, Productiveness's] everything in this company.

❖ D が辞典に出ているが使われていない．

2　《能率的》

〈私たちのシステムのほうがあなた方よりも能率的です〉
- ◎ A Our system is more efficient [effective, productive] than yours.
- ◎ B Our system works better than yours.
- ◎ C Our system produces more than yours.

3　《能率的に》

〈私は能率的に時間を使いたいんです〉
- ◎ I want to use my time efficiently [effectively, productively].

能力開発部　→…部 15

脳裏を占めている

〈彼は部長に昇進したいという思いがどんなに自分の脳裏を占めているかに，気がついていないようだ〉
- ◎ A He doesn't seem to realize how much wanting to be promoted to General Manager occupies his mind.
- △ B He doesn't seem to realize how much wanting to be promoted to General Manager fills his mind.

ノーブランドの

〈この店はノーブランドの食品しか置いていません〉
- ◎ This store only sells generic brand of food.

残りなさい

〈放課後残りなさい〉
- ◎ A Stay (behind) after school.
- ▽ B Remain after school.

❖ B の remain はフォーマルな語．

喉から手が出るほど欲しい

〈私はあの家が喉から手が出るほど欲しいんです〉
- ◎ A I want that house so badly it hurts.
- ◎ B I want that house so badly I can taste it.
- ◎ C I'd kill [die] for that house.
- ◎ D I'm dying [anxious] to buy that house.
- ○ E I'm eager [itching] to buy that house.

のぼる
1 《建築物》
〈東京タワーに上ったことがありますか〉
   ◎ A Have you ever been (up) to the top of Tokyo Tower?
   ◎ B Have you ever gone to the top of Tokyo Tower?
   × C Have you ever climbed the top of Tokyo Tower?
2 《山》
〈富士山に登ったことがありますか〉
   ◎ A Have you ever climbed Mt. Fuji?
   ◎ B Have you ever climbed up (to) Mt. Fuji?
   ◎ C Have you ever climbed to the top of Mt. Fuji?
   ◎ D Have you ever been to the top of Mt. Fuji?
   ○ E Have you ever gone to Mt. Fuji?
   ○ F Have you ever gone up to the top of Mt. Fuji?
3 《崖》
a) 一般の人
〈あの崖を登ろう〉
   ◎ A Let's climb (up) that cliff.
   △ B Let's scale that cliff.
b) 登山家のベテラン
〈あの崖を登ろう〉
   ◎   Let's climb (up) [scale] that cliff.
4 《川》
〈この川は船で何マイル上れますか〉
   ◎ A How many miles up this river can we go by ship?
   ○ B How many miles up is this river navigable?
5 《木》
〈私は木を登るのが得意なんです〉
   ◎ A I'm good at climbing trees.
   ○ B I'm good at climbing up trees.
6 《太陽など》
〈太陽が昇ってきた〉
   ◎ A The sun's coming up.
   ○ B The sun's rising.
7 《損害額》
〈損害額は2千万円以上にのぼるだろう〉
   ◎ A The loss'll amount to [exceed] more than ¥20,000,000.
   ○ B The loss'll total [add up to, come to, run to] more than ¥20,000,000.

飲む
1 《アルコール》
〈私はアルコールは飲みません〉
   ☆ A I don't drink.
   ◎ B I don't drink liquor [alcohol].
   ○ C I don't touch the stuff.
2 《薬》
a) 一般に
〈この薬を飲みなさい〉
   ◎ A Take this medicine.

△ B　Swallow this medicine.
b) 液体
〈この薬を飲みなさい〉
　　◎ A　Take this medicine.
　　○ B　Drink this medicine.
3 《スープ》
〈私は普通夕食にスープを飲むます〉
　　◎ A　I usually have [eat] some soup for dinner.
　　× B　I usually drink some soup for dinner.

乗り換える
〈中野で東西線に乗り換えられます〉
　　◎ A　You can change [transfer] to the Tozai Line at Nakano.
　　◎ B　You can change trains to the Tozai Line at Nakano.
　　◎ C　You can change trains at Nakano to the Tozai Line.
　　△ D　You can change trains at Nakano for the Tozai Line.

乗り切る
〈会社は不況を乗り切るだろう〉
　　☆ A　The company'll survive the recession.
　　◎ B　The company'll make it [get, live] through the recession.
　　○ C　The company'll outlast the recession.
　　△ D　The company'll outlive the recession.

乗り越す
〈今日私は読書に非常に夢中になっていたので乗り越してしまったんです〉
　　◎ A　Today I was so absorbed in my reading I went past [went beyond, rode past] my stop.
　　▽ B　Today I was so absorbed in my reading I went beyond [past] my destination.
　　× C　Today I was so absorbed in my reading I was carried beyond my stop.
　　× D　Today I was so absorbed in my reading I overshot my stop.
　　❖ C，D が辞典に出ているが使われていない．

乗る
1 《命令・提案》
〈あのバスに乗りなさい〉
　　◎ A　Take [Catch, Get on] that bus.
　　○ B　Ride on [Ride] that bus.
　　△ C　Board [Use] that bus.
2 《乗る駅名を明示するとき》
〈中野で東西線に乗りなさい〉
　　◎ A　Take the Tozai Line from Nakano.
　　○ B　Use [Catch, Get on] the Tozai Line from Nakano.
3 《目的地を明示するとき》
〈私たちは中野まで東西線に乗って行きました〉
　　◎ A　We took the Tozai Line to Nakano.
　　○ B　We rode the Tozai Line to Nakano.
　　△ C　We rode on [use] the Tozai Line to Nakano.
4 《乗っている状態に言及するとき》
〈彼女は私と同じ電車に乗っていました〉
　　◎ A　She was taking the same train as I was.

◎ B She was on the same train as I was.
○ C She was riding (on) the same train as I was.

5 《行先を尋ねるとき》
〈どこまで地下鉄に乗って行ったのですか〉
☆ A Where did you take [ride] the subway to?
◎ B Where did you take the subway?
○ C Where did you ride the subway?

6 《乗った駅名を尋ねるとき》
〈あなたはどこで地下鉄に乗ったのですか〉
◎ A Where did you catch [get on] the subway?
△ B Where did you catch [get on] the subway at?

7 《「乗ったことがある」という経験を述べるとき》
a) 地下鉄
〈私は東京で地下鉄に乗ったことがありません〉
◎ A I've never taken [been on, used] the subway in Tokyo.
○ B I've never ridden the subway in Tokyo.
△ C I've never ridden on the subway in Tokyo.
❖使用頻度は肯定文, 疑問文, 否定文でも同じ.

b) タクシー
〈あなたはロンドンでタクシーに乗ったことがありますか〉
◎ A Have you ever taken [been in, used] a taxi in London?
○ B Have you ever taken a ride in a taxi in London?

c) 飛行機
・一般的に言うとき
〈あなたは飛行機に乗ったことがありますか〉
☆ A Have you ever flown?
◎ B Have you ever been [traveled] on a plane?
◎ C Have you ever taken a flight?
○ D Have you ever ridden on a plane?
△ E Have you ever ridden a plane?
× F Have you ever used a plane?

・航空会社を明示したいとき
〈あなたはノースウエストに乗ったことがありますか〉
◎ A Have you ever flown on [flown with] Northwest?
◎ B Have you ever taken [gone on] a Northwest flight?
◎ C Have you ever used Northwest?
◎ D Have you ever been [traveled] on Northwest?
○ E Have you ever ridden on Northwest?
△ F Have you ever ridden [traveled with] Northwest?

・等級を明示したいとき
〈私はファーストクラスの飛行機に乗ったことはありません〉
☆ A I've never flown first class.
◎ B I've never traveled [flown in, sat in] first class.
○ C I've never sat in first class on a plane.
○ D I've never traveled in a first class seat.
△ E I've never traveled in the first class section.
△ F I've never taken a first class seat on a plane.

8 《相乗りする》
〈私たちは毎日駅まで車に相乗りして行きます〉

- ◎ A We car-pool to the station every day.
- ○ B We go to the station in a car-pool every day.

9 《乗り込む》

〈みんな彼の小さい車に乗り込みました〉

- ◎ A Everybody crammed into his small car.
- ○ B Everybody packed into his small car.
- ○ C Everybody jammed into [in] his small car.
- ○ D Everybody squeezed into [in] his small car.

載る

1 《編集者・リポーター・記者が述べるとき》

〈スキャンダルはワシントンポストが第1面に載せたほど衝撃でした〉

- ◎ A The scandal was shocking enough to land [print, run, put] on the front page of *The Washington Post*.
- ○ B The scandal was shocking enough to carry on the front page of *The Washington Post*.
    - ❖ A, Bとも読者が述べるときも多少使われている．

2 《読者が述べるとき》

〈スキャンダルはワシントンポストが第1面に載せたほど衝撃でした〉

- ☆ A The scandal was shocking enough to be printed on the front page of *The Washington Post*.
- ◎ B The scandal was shocking enough to be put on the front page of *The Washington Post*.
- ○ C The scandal was shocking enough to be run [carried] on the front page of *The Washington Post*.
    - ❖ A, B, Cは編集者・リポーター・記者が述べるときも多少使われている．

ノルマ

《売り上げ》

〈今月は売り上げのノルマを達成できないと思う〉

- ◎ A I'm afraid I can't reach the sales quota this month.
- △ B I'm afraid I can't reach the sales requirement this month.
    - ❖ Bが辞典に出ているがあまり使われていない．

のんきな

1 《物事を深刻に取らない》

〈彼はのんきです〉

- ◎ He's easy-going [happy-go-lucky, laid-back].

2 《運まかせ・行き当たりばったり》

〈彼はのんきです〉

- ◎ He's happy-go-lucky.

飲ん兵衛

〈彼は飲ん兵衛だ〉

- ◎ A He's a heavy drinker.
- ○ B He's a boozer.
- △ C He's a drunkard.
- ▽ D He's a tipper.
- × E He's a sot [a drunk sot, a souse].
    - ❖ Eが辞典に出ているが使われていない．

〔は〕

場当り的に

〈この会社は場当り的にほとんどの仕事をやっているようだ〉

- ☆ A This company seems to carry out most of its work in a disorganized way.
- ◎ B This company seems to carry out most of its work in a haphazard way.
- ○ C This company seems to carry out most of its work in a disorganized [random, haphazard] manner.
- ○ D This company seems to carry out most of its work in a haphazard [random, disorganized] fashion.
- △ E This company seems to carry out most of its work on a random basis.
- × F This company seems to carry out most of its work on a piecemeal basis.
  - ❖ F は辞典に出ているが使われていない.

肺炎 →病気 20

廃業している

〈角のレストランは廃業している〉

- ◎ A The restaurant on the corner's out of business.
- ◎ B The restaurant on the corner's closed [shut] down.
- ◎ C The restaurant on the corner's gone.

バイキングレストラン →店 4

買収する

1 《ワイロ》

〈たぶん我々はあの政治家を買収できるだろう〉

- ☆ A Maybe we can bribe that politician.
- ◎ B Maybe we can pay [buy] that politician off.
- ○ C Maybe we can slip that politician some cash.
- △ D Maybe we can corrupt that politician.
- ▽ E Maybe we can grease that politician's palm [hand].
  - ❖ E は以前はよく使われていた.

2 《企業の買収》

〈XYZ 会社は STU 会社を買収しようとしているんです〉

- ◎ A XYZ Company's trying to take over [buy out] STU Company.
- ○ B XYZ Company's trying to get ownership of STU Company.
- ○ C XYZ Company's trying to purchase [acquire] STU Company.
- △ D XYZ Company's trying to buy off STU Company.
  - ❖ A は 100％または 51％以上の株の取得, B, C, D は 100％の株取得を意味する.

輩出する →出す 2

売春婦

1 《客観的に述べるとき》

〈彼女は売春婦です〉

- ◎ She's a prostitute.

2 《軽蔑的に述べるとき》
〈彼女は売春婦です〉
- ☆ A She's a hooker.
- ◎ B She's a whore.
- ○ C She's a streetwalker.
- △ D She's a lady of the evening.
- ❖軽蔑の気持ちはBが一番強い．

3 《売春夫》
a) 客観的に述べるとき
〈彼は売春夫です〉
- ◎ He's a male prostitute.

b) 軽蔑の気持ちで述べるとき
〈彼は売春夫です〉
- ○ A He's a gigolo.
- △ B He's a whore [streetwalker].

梅毒 →病気 21
肺病 →病気 22
配布される

1 《製品の場合》
〈この新製品は月曜日までに日本中に配布されます〉
- ◎ A This new product'll be distributed [delivered] all over Japan by Monday.
- ◎ B This new product'll be in stores all over Japan by Monday.
- ▽ C This new product'll be circulated all over Japan by Monday.
- ❖(1) Cが辞典に出ているがほとんど使われていない．
- ❖(2) Cの be circulated は主として新聞，通貨について使われている．

2 《本の場合》
〈この新しい本は月曜日までに日本中に配布されます〉
- ◎ A This new book'll be distributed all over Japan by Monday.
- ○ B This new book'll be circulated all over Japan by Monday.

3 《新聞・雑誌の場合》
〈この新聞はアメリカ中に配布されています〉
- ◎ A This paper's distributed all over America.
- ○ B This paper's circulated all over America.

俳優養成所 →各種学校 11
入る

1 《建物・部屋などに入る》
a) 建物の名前に言及する場合
〈このレストランに入ろうよ〉
- ☆ A Let's go into this restaurant.
- ◎ B Let's go in this restaurant.
- ○ C Let's walk into this restaurant.
- ○ D Let's walk [step] in this restaurant.
- ▽ E Let's enter this restaurant.

b) 建物の名前に言及しない場合
〈彼女たちがこのコーヒーショップで待っています．入りましょう〉
- ◎ They're waiting in this coffee shop. Let's go [walk, step] in.

c) 場所に言及して「入って来る」の意味で述べるとき
〈(秘書に向かって) 彼らに私の事務所に入るように言って下さい〉

☆ A Please tell them to come into my office.
◎ B Please tell them to come on in my office.
○ C Please tell them to come in my office.

d）場所に言及しないで「入って来る」の意味で述べるとき
〈(訪問者に) どうぞお入りください〉

◎　　　Please come (on) in.

2 《入学する》
a）大学に（合格して）入る
・日本の大学の場合
〈私は東大に入れないと思います〉

☆ A I don't think I can pass the entrance exam for Todai.
☆ B I don't think I can make it into Todai.
◎ C I don't think I could get into Todai.
◎ D I don't think Todai'll take me.
◎ E I don't think they'll take [accept] me into Todai.
○ F I don't think I'll be accepted by [to] Todai.
○ G I don't think I'll get into Todai.
○ H I don't think Todai'll accept me.
△ I I don't think I'll be accepted into Todai.

・アメリカの大学の場合
〈私はハーバードに入れないと思います〉

☆ A I don't think I can make it into Harvard.
◎ B I don't think Harvard'll take [accept] me.
◎ C I don't think I could get into Harvard.
◎ D I don't think they'll take [accept] me into Harvard.
○ E I don't think I can get into Harvard.
○ F I don't think I'll be accepted by [to] Harvard.
○ G I don't think I'll get accepted into Harvard.
△ H I don't think I'll be accepted into Harvard.

❖アメリカの大学は日本のような入試はない．SAT，高校時代の成績，教師の推薦状で受け入れるか否かを決める．したがって，日本の大学の場合に使う pass the entrance exam という表現は使えない．

b）講座などに入る
〈私は YMCA の水泳のクラスに入ろうと思っています〉

☆ A I'm going to sign up for the swimming class at the YMCA.
◎ B I'm going to register for the swimming class at the YMCA.
○ C I'm going to enroll in the swimming class at the YMCA.
△ D I'm going to be enrolled in the swimming class at the YMCA.

3 《入会する》
〈私は YMCA に入ろうと思っています〉

◎ A I'm going to register [enroll, sign up] at the YMCA.
○ B I'm going to be enrolled at the YMCA.

4 《入社する意味のとき》
a）平社員
〈あなたはこの会社にいつ入社したのですか〉

◎ A When did you start working for this company?
◎ B When did you get a job at this company?
◎ C How long've you been working for this company?
▽ D When did you join this company?

▽ E When did you find employment at this company?
× F When did you enter this company?
❖辞典にはD, E, Fしか出ていないが，よく使われるのはA, B, C.
b) 役員・管理職
〈いつ彼はこの会社に入ったのですか〉
◎ A When did he join this company?
◎ B When did he start working for this company?
◎ C How long's he been working for this company?
× D How long did he get a job at this company?
× E How long did he enter this company?
5 《品物が店に入る》
〈私の注文したものが入ったら，すぐ電話してくれますか〉
◎ A As soon as my order comes [gets] in, will you call me?
○ B As soon as my order arrives, will you call me?
6 《電車がホームに入る》
〈私たちの乗る電車が入ってきた〉
☆ A Here comes our train.
◎ B Our train's almost here.
◎ C Our train's pulling [coming] in.
○ D Our train's nearly here.
○ E Our train's getting in [arriving, approaching].
❖Cのpull inが一番近い距離にあるという響きがある．Aが2番目，以下approach, arrive, come in, get in, Bの順．
7 《交渉などに入る》
〈労使はまもなく話し合いに入るでしょう〉
☆ A The management and the union'll start talks soon.
☆ B The management and the union'll start to talk [start talking] soon.
◎ C The management and the union'll begin [go into] talks soon.
◎ D The management and the union'll begin to talk [begin talking] soon.
○ E The management and the union'll enter into talks soon.

パイロット養成所 →各種学校 12

博士号
〈彼はハーバードから博士号を取ったんです〉
◎ A He got his [a] Ph.D. from Harvard.
◎ B He got his [a] doctorate from Harvard.
△ C He got his [a] doctor's degree from Harvard.

はかる
1 《「殺害を」図る》
〈彼らは首相の殺害を図っています〉
☆ A They're plotting the murder of the prime minister.
◎ B They're planning on the murder of the prime minister.
○ C They're planning to murder the prime minister.
2 《「体重を」計る》
〈私は毎日体重を計っています〉
◎ A I weigh myself every day.
◎ B I check my weight every day.
○ C I get on the scale every day.
3 《「目方を」計る》

⟨(店で) この目方を計ってくれますか⟩
- ◎ A Will you see [check] how much this weighs?
- ○ B Will you weigh this (for me)?

4 《「人の価値を」測る》

⟨人の価値はお金では測れません⟩
- ☆ A A person's worth can't be measured in terms of money.
- ◎ B A person's worth can't be judged in terms of money.
- ○ C A person's worth can't be gauged [calculated] in terms of money.

5 《「計画を」諮る》

⟨私たちはこの計画を会議に諮る予定です⟩
- ◎ A We're going to submit [turn in] this plan to a conference for deliberation.
- ○ B We're going to present [hand in] this plan to a conference for deliberation.

吐き気がする

1 《病気のとき》

⟨私は吐き気がするんです⟩
- ☆ A I feel sick.
- ☆ B I feel sick to my stomach.
- ☆ C I feel like throwing up.
- ◎ D I feel nauseated [nauseous].
- ○ E I feel like I'm going to barf.
- ○ F I feel like my stomach's turning.
- ○ G I feel queasy.
- × H I feel sickish.
- × I I feel sick at the stomach.
    - ❖(1) H, I が辞典に出ているが使われていない.
    - ❖(2) A は必ずしも「吐き気がする」を意味するわけではなく, 一般的に病気で「気分が悪い」の意味でも非常によく使われている.
    - ❖(3) E は 30 代以下の男性の間では非常によく使われている. 女性の間では時々使われている.

2 《比喩的に述べるとき》

⟨私は彼の横柄な態度に吐き気がするんです⟩
- ◎ A His arrogant behavior makes me sick (to my stomach).
- ◎ B His arrogant behavior is disgusting.
- × C His arrogant behavior turns my stomach.
- × D His arrogant behavior is causing [provoking] nausea.
    - ❖ C, D が辞典に出ているが使われていない.

破棄する

1 《契約》

a) 法律違反になるとき

⟨彼は契約を破棄するでしょう⟩
- ◎ A He'll break the contract.
- △ B He'll breach the contract.

b) 法律違反にならないとき

⟨彼は契約を破棄するでしょう⟩
- ◎ A He'll break the contract.
- ○ B He'll cancel the contract.

2 《婚約》

〈彼女は彼との婚約を破棄しました〉
- ☆ A She broke their engagement.
- ◎ B She broke the engagement to him.
- ○ C She broke the engagement with him.
- ○ D She broke her engagement to him.
- △ E She broke her engagement with him.

3 《裁判》

〈最高裁は原判決を破棄した〉
- ☆ A The Supreme Court reversed the original decision.
- ◎ B The Supreme Court reversed the original judgment.
- ○ C The Supreme Court overturned the original judgment [decision].
- × D The Supreme Court quashed the original decision [judgment].
    - ❖ D が数冊の辞典に出ているが使われていない．

4 《条約》

〈日米安保条約は日本人に現実を直視することを妨げているからできるだけ早く破棄されるべきだ〉
- ◎ A The Japan-U.S. Security Treaty should be abolished [ended, torn up] as soon as possible because it prevents Japanese people from facing reality.
- ○ B The Japan-U.S. Security Treaty should be put [brought] to an end as soon as possible because it prevents Japanese people from facing reality.
- ○ C The Japan-U.S. Security Treaty should be terminated [removed, scrapped] as soon as possible because it prevents Japanese people from facing reality.
- △ D The Japan-U.S. Security Treaty should be revoked [repealed, retracted, rescinded] as soon as possible because it prevents Japanese people from facing reality.

ハクがつく

〈佐藤氏はノーベル賞受賞によって，彼の経歴にハクをつけた〉
- ◎ A Sato's Nobel Prize gave him added prestige.
- ◎ B Sato's Nobel Prize added to [increased] his prestige.
- ○ C Sato's Nobel Prize boosted his prestige.
- ○ D Sato's Nobel Prize gave him added credit.
- △ E Sato's Nobel Prize enhanced his prestige.
- × F Sato's Nobel Prize boosted [enhanced, increased] him added credit.
- × G Sato's Nobel Prize added luster to his career.
    - ❖ F, G が辞典に出ているが使われていない．

白人

〈彼は白人です〉
- ☆ A He's white.
- ◎ B He's a white guy [man].
- △ C He's Caucasian.
- △ D He's a Caucasian.
- ▽ E He's a white.
    - ❖白人の女性を言う場合，B は She's a white woman. とする必要があるが，それ以外は主語を She にすればよい．

爆発する
1 《爆弾の場合》
〈2つの爆弾がXYZビルの正面で爆発したんです〉
- ◎ A Two bombs exploded [went off, blew up] in front of the XYZ Building.
- △ B Two bombs blasted [detonated] in front of the XYZ Building.
- ▽ C Two bombs burst up in front of the XYZ Building.
  - ❖ Cが辞典に出ているが使われてもまれ．

2 《火山の場合》
〈昨夜，浅間山が爆発したんです〉
- ◎ A Mt. Asama erupted last night.
- △ B Mt. Asama went off [blew up] last night.
- ▽ C Mt. Asama burst into eruption last night.
  - ❖ Cが辞典に出ているが使われてもまれ．

舶来品
〈昨日は舶来品専門店へ3軒行ったけど，買いたかったものを見つけることができなかった〉
- ◎ A Yesterday we went to three stores that sold only imported items [products, goods], but we couldn't find what we wanted.
- ○ B Yesterday we went to three stores that sold only imported merchandise [articles], but we couldn't find what we wanted.

パクられる →捕まる 1

薄利多売
〈マクドナルドは薄利多売です〉
- ◎ A McDonald's relies on high volume (sales) to make a profit.
- ◎ B McDonald's relies on volume to make a profit.
- ○ C McDonald's tries to make a profit through selling in high volume.
- × D McDonald's relies on narrow-margin high-turn-over.
  - ❖ Dが辞典に出ているが使われていない．

激しく降る →雪がすごく降る

励ます
〈初めて私がパリへ行ったとき，彼は私を励ましてくれました〉
- ◎ A The first time I went to Paris, he was supportive of me.
- ◎ B The first time I went to Paris, he was encouraging to me.

派遣
1 《会社》
〈彼女は派遣会社に勤めています〉
- ◎ A She works for a temp agency.
- ○ B She works for a temporary employment agency.
- × C She works for a temp agent.
- × D She works for a temporary agency.

2 《社員》
〈彼は派遣社員です〉
- ◎ A He's a temp.
- ◎ B He's an employee from a temp agency.
- ◎ C He's from a temp agency.
- ○ D He's from a temporary employment agency.
- △ E He's on a temp staff.

3 《「派遣する」と言うとき》

a）派遣している会社数のみを述べるとき
〈うちは約 300 の会社にスタッフを派遣しています〉
- ☆ A　We work with about 300 companies.
- ◎ B　We provide about 300 companies with staff.
- ◎ C　We staff about 300 companies.
- ○ D　We provide staff for about 300 companies.
- ○ E　We send [dispatch] staff to about 300 companies.

b）派遣している人材の内容と会社数を述べるとき
〈うちは通訳を約 300 の会社に派遣しています〉
- ☆ A　We provide about 300 companies with interpreters.
- ◎ B　We staff interpreters for about 300 companies.
- ◎ C　We send interpreters to about 300 companies.
- ○ D　We dispatch interpreters for about 300 companies.
- △ E　We provide interpreters for [to] about 300 companies.

破産する

1　《自己破産している事実のみを述べるとき》
〈彼は破産しているんです〉
- ☆ A　He's bankrupt.
- ◎ B　He's broke.
- ○ C　He's in bankruptcy.
- × D　He's belly-up [busted, bust].
- × E　He's in a bankruptcy.
  - ❖(1) D, E が辞典に出ているが今は使われていない．
  - ❖(2) B は「お金が全くない」という意味でもよく使われる．

2　《自己破産の申請手続きをしていることを述べるとき》
〈彼は自己破産をしているんです〉
- ◎ A　He's in Chapter 13 [Chapter 11].
- ◎ B　He's going through Chapter 13 [Chapter 11].
- ◎ C　He's filing for Chapter 13 [Chapter 11].
- ◎ D　He's going through (a) bankruptcy.
- ◎ E　He's in bankruptcy.
- △ F　He's filing for personal bankruptcy.
- × G　He's filing for individual bankruptcy.
  - ❖(1) 正しくは個人の破産は Chapter 13, 法人の破産は Chapter 11. しかし，弁護士以外はこれらを混用している．
  - ❖(2) B, C, D, F は，「申請中」，今後「申請する」，すでに「申請してしまっている」の 3 つの状況で使われている．

3　《法人の破産を客観的に述べるとき》
〈XYZ 会社は先週破産したんです〉
- ◎ A　XYZ Company went into bankruptcy last week.
- ◎ B　XYZ Company went bankrupt [went broke] last week.
- ○ C　XYZ Company failed last week.
- ○ D　XYZ Company folded last week.
- ○ E　XYZ Company became insolvent last week.
- △ F　XYZ Company liquidated [folded up] last week.
- △ G　XYZ Company went belly-up last week.
- ▽ H　XYZ Company went bust last week.

4　《法人が破産申請していることを述べるとき》
〈XYZ 会社は破産しているんです〉

- ◎ A XYZ Company's in Chapter 11 [Chapter 13, bankruptcy].
- ◎ B XYZ Company's filing for Chapter 11 [Chapter 13, bankruptcy].
- ○ C XYZ Company's insolvent.

始まる

1 《かしこまった式の場合》

〈葬式は何時に始まるのですか〉

- ◎ A What time does the funeral begin?
- ○ B What time does the funeral start?
- × C What time does the funeral get under way [get started]?

2 《かしこまらないパーティー・スポーツの試合などの場合》

〈彼らが来たらすぐパーティーは始まります〉

- ☆ A The party'll start [begin] as soon as they come.
- ◎ B The party'll get under way as soon as they come.
- ○ C The party'll get started as soon as they come.

3 《痛みなどの場合》

〈毎年冬になると,背中が痛み始めるんです〉

- ◎ A Every winter my back starts to hurt.
- ◎ B Every winter my backache sets in.
- ○ C Every winter my back starts to ache.
- ○ D Every winter my back decides to hurt [ache].
- ○ E Every winter my backache starts.
- △ F Every winter my backache begins.

初めから終わりまで

〈あなたはこの本を最初から最後まで読むべきです〉

- ☆ A You should read this book cover to cover.
- ◎ B You should read this book from cover to cover.
- ◎ C You should read this book from beginning to end.
- ◎ D You should read this book from start to finish.
- ○ E You should read this book from the beginning to the end.
- ○ F You should read this book from the start to the finish.
- △ G You should read this book from the first to the last page.
- △ H You should read this book beginning to end.
- △ I You should read this book start to finish.
- × J You should read this book the first to the last page.

初めて

〈私が初めて彼を見たとき,横柄だと思いました〉

- ☆ A The first time I saw him, I thought he was arrogant.
- ◎ B When I first saw him, I thought he was arrogant.
- ◎ C When I saw him for the first time, I thought he was arrogant.

初めに

1 《「最初に」の意味のとき》

〈初めにトムに電話したんです.それからビルに電話したんです〉

- ◎ A First I called Tom and then Bill.
- ○ B I called Tom first and then Bill.

❖文頭,文尾で使われている first は「まず」の意味.

2 《「何はさておき」の意味のとき》

〈もしフランス語を上手に話せるようになりたいなら,初めに基本文型を暗記しなければなりません〉

- ◎ A If you want to learn to speak French well, first of all, you have to

memorize basic patterns.
- ◎ B If you want to learn to speak French well, to start [begin] with, you have to memorize basic patterns.
- ◎ C If you want to learn to speak French well, for a starter [a start], you have to memorize basic patterns.
- ○ D If you want to learn to speak French well, above all, you have to memorize basic patterns.
- ○ E If you want to learn to speak French well, above [before] everything, you have to memorize basic patterns.
- ○ F If you want to learn to speak French well, as a starter, you have to memorize basic patterns.
- ○ G If you want to learn to speak French well, in the first place, you have to memorize basic patterns.

初めは
〈初めは彼らが嫌いだったんです〉
- ☆ A At first I didn't like them.
- ◎ B Initially I didn't like them.
- ○ C In [At] the beginning I didn't like them.
- △ D At the start I didn't like them.

初めまして →知り合う 7

始める

1 《時間に言及されないとき》
〈仕事を始めよう〉
- ◎ A Let's start working.
- ◎ B Let's get to work.
- ◎ C Let's get down to business [work].
- ○ D Let's start work.
- ○ E Let's start to work.
- △ F Let's begin working [to work].
- × G Let's set to work.
  - ❖(1) G が辞典に出ているが使われていない.
  - ❖(2) F の begin は start と違ってフォーマルな響きがあるので, 会話ではあまりよく使われていない.

2 《時間に言及されるとき》
〈何時に仕事を始めるのですか〉
- ◎ A What time do you start working [to work]?
- ○ B What time do you start [get to] work?
- △ C What time do you begin working [to work]?
- △ D What time do you get down to business [work]?
  - ❖ B の get to work は「職場に着く」「出勤する」という意味でもよく使われている. したがって, What time...?のような語があるときは使用頻度は高くない.

恥ずかしい

1 《失敗を見られるなどして「ばつが悪い」》
〈私は今日会合に遅れたんです. 部屋に入ったときみんなが私を見たんです. 本当に恥ずかしかったです〉
- ◎ I was late for the meeting today. When I got in the room, everybody looked at me. I was really embarrassed.

2 《法律に違反して》

〈私は彼の財布を盗んだんです．とても恥ずかしく思っています〉
- ◎ A I stole his wallet. I feel so ashamed.
- ◎ B I stole his wallet. I'm so ashamed of myself.

3 《モラルに反したことをして》
〈私は先週浮気をしてしまったんです．本当に恥ずかしく思っています〉
- ◎ A I cheated on my husband last week. I feel really ashamed.
- ◎ B I cheated on my husband last week. I'm really ashamed of myself.

4 《自分に能力がないことに対して怒りの気持ちで述べるとき》
〈私は弁護士の試験にまた落ちてしまったんです．恥ずかしく思っています〉
- ◎ I've failed the bar again. I'm ashamed of myself.

5 《他人に知られたくない気持ちで述べるとき》
〈私は弁護士の試験にまた落ちてしまったんです．恥ずかしく思っています〉
- ◎ I've failed the bar again. I'm embarrassed.

6 《おどおどしたり，はにかみ・内気の「恥ずかしがり」》
〈彼は恥ずかしくて，ジェーンを映画に誘えないんです〉
- ☆ A He's too shy to ask Jane to go to the movies.
- ◎ B He's too embarrassed to ask Jane to go to the movies.
- △ C He's too bashful [timid] to ask Jane to go to the movies.
  - ❖語法辞典にはこのような場合は bashful を使うとあるが，実際には shy, embarrassed, timid も使われている．

〈彼は恥ずかしがり屋で，大勢の人の前でスピーチすることはできないんです〉
- ☆ A He's too shy to make a speech before a large audience.
- ◎ B He's too timid to make a speech before a large audience.
- △ C He's too bashful to make a speech before a large audience.

肌が白い

1 《白人》
〈彼女は肌が白いです〉
- ◎ A She's fair-skinned [light-skinned].
- ◎ B She has white [fair, light] skin.
- ◎ C She has a fair [light] complexion.
- ▽ D She has a white complexion.
- ▽ E She's fair complected [complexioned].
- ▽ F She's white-skinned.
  - ❖D, E, F が辞典に出ているがまれ．

2 《非白人》
〈彼女は肌が白いんです〉
- ◎ A She has light skin.
- ◎ B She's light-skinned.
- ◎ C She has a light [fair] complexion.
- △ D She's light-complected.

働き者

〈彼は働き者です〉
- ☆ A He works hard.
- ☆ B He's a hard [good] worker.
- ○ C He's a diligent [an industrious] worker.
- ○ D He works diligently.
- △ E He works industriously.

バタンと閉まる [閉める]

1 《物が主語の場合》

〈ドアがバタンと閉まった〉
- ◎ A The door slammed.
- ◎ B The door slammed shut.
- ◎ C The door slammed closed.

2 《人が主語の場合》
〈彼は窓をバタンと閉めた〉
- ◎ A He slammed the window shut.
- △ B He slammed the window (closed).

場違いな思いをする
〈パーティーの客がほとんど皆，名士だったんです．それで私は場違いな思いをしました〉
- ◎ A Almost all the guests at the party were celebrities, so I felt like out of place.
- ○ B Almost all the guests at the party were celebrities, so I felt like a fish out of water.
- ○ C Almost all the guests at the party were celebrities, so I felt like I didn't belong.

発揮する
〈教師1：佐藤さんが中央大学の試験に落ちたのは信じられないなあ〉
Teacher 1: I can't believe that Sato failed the examination for Chuo.

〈教師2：気分が悪かったので実力を発揮できなかったと言ってたよ〉
Teacher 2:
- ◎ A He said he couldn't show [display, demonstrate] his real ability because he wasn't feeling well.
- ◎ B He said he couldn't do himself justice because he wasn't feeling well.

はっきりした
1 《名詞を修飾するとき》
〈2つの間には，はっきりした違いがある〉
- ☆ A There's a clear difference between the two.
- ○ B There's a definite difference between the two.
- △ C There's a distinct difference between the two.
- ▽ D There's a precise [decisive] difference between the two.
- ▽ E There's a marked difference between the two.
- ▽ F There's a decided difference between the two.
  - ❖(1) D, E, F は辞典に出ているが会話ではまれにしか使われていない．
  - ❖(2) 文章英語ではFはよく使われている．B, C, Eは非常によく使われている．

2 《文・節を修飾するとき》
〈彼がお金を盗んだことははっきりしている〉
- ☆ A He definitely stole the money.
- ◎ B It's obvious [evident, clear] that he stole the money.
- ◎ C It's apparent that he stole the money.
- ○ D It's certain that he stole the money.
- ○ E It's definite that he stole the money.
- △ F It's plain that he stole the money.
  - ❖ A, Eが一番強いニュアンスがある．Dが2番，Bが3番．Cはこの中でははっきりしている度合いが一番弱い．なお，Bの evident は証拠があってはっきりしているときに使われる．Fは「単純明快である」というニュアンス．

はっきりした答
〈いつはっきりした答をもらえますか〉
- ◎ A When can I have your final answer?
- ◎ B When can you let me know for sure?
- ○ C When can I have your definite answer?

罰金
1 《罰金を払う》
〈彼らは審判に暴力を振るったために1千ドルの罰金を払わされた〉
- ◎ A They were forced to pay $1,000 fine [a fine of $1,000] for their violence against the umpire.
- ◎ B They were fined $1,000 for their violence against the umpire.
- × C They were forced to pay $1,000 penalty [a penalty of $1,000] for their violence against the umpire.
  - ❖ C を紹介している辞典があるが使われていない．

2 《罰金を課す》
〈スピード違反で私は500ドルの罰金を課せられた〉
- ☆ A They fined me $500 for speeding.
- ◎ B They charged me $500 for speeding.
- ◎ C They made me pay $500 for speeding.
- △ D They penalized me $500 for speeding.

3 《契約不履行のための違約金》
〈もし契約を破ると10万ドルの違約金を払わなければならなくなります〉
- ☆ A If you break the contract, you'll be fined $100,000.
- ◎ B If you break the contract, you'll have to pay $100,000 fine [a fine of $100,000].
- ◎ C If you break the contract, you'll incur a penalty of $100,000.
- ○ D If you break the contract, you'll have to pay $100,000 penalty [a penalty of $100,000].
- ○ E If you break the contract, you'll incur a fine of $100,000.

白血病　→病気 23

発言権
〈私にはそれに関しての発言権はないんです〉
- ◎ I have no say [voice] in it.

発射する　→打ち上げる

罰する
1 《罰する当局が主語のとき》
〈学校当局は，タバコを吸ったために彼らを罰した〉
- ◎ A The school authorities punished them for smoking.
- ○ B The school authorities disciplined them for smoking.
- △ C The school authorities penalized them for smoking.
- △ D The school authorities subjected them to punishment [a penalty] for smoking.
- × E The school authorities meted out punishment to them for smoking.
- × F The school authorities visited them with punishment for smoking.
- × G The school authorities visited punishment [a penalty] upon them for smoking.
- × H The school authorities amerced a penalty upon them for smoking.
  - ❖(1) E～H が辞典に出ているが使われていない．
  - ❖(2) E は堅い文章では時々使われている．

2 《罰せられる》
〈5人の学生がタバコを吸って罰せられた〉
- ☆ A Five students were punished for smoking.
- ◎ B Five students were disciplined for smoking.
- ○ C Five students were penalized for smoking.
- △ D Five students were subjected to punishment [a penalty] for smoking.

3 《厳しく罰せられる人が主語のとき》
〈彼はマリファナを吸って厳しく罰せられたんです〉
- ◎ A He was punished severely for smoking pot.
- ○ B He was punished heavily for smoking pot.
- × C He had [got, took] his gruel for smoking pot.
- ❖ Cが辞典に出ているが使われていない.

4 《罰せられない》
〈私はスピード違反で捕まったんですが罰せられなかったんです〉
- ◎ A I was caught for speeding but I got off scot-free.
- ◎ B I was caught for speeding but I got away with it.
- ◎ C I was caught for speeding but I got off with a warning.
- ◎ D I was caught for speeding but he let me off.
- × E I was caught for speeding but I went unpunished [scot-free].
- × F I was caught for speeding but I got away with punishment.
- ❖ E, Fが辞典に出ているが使われていない.

発展する
〈彼の会社は将来発展するだろう〉
- ◎ His company'll expand [grow, get bigger, become larger] in the future.

八方美人 →美人 5

派手な
1 《(服などが) けばけばしく派手なとき》
〈これは派手すぎます〉
- ◎ A This is too tacky [showy].
- ◎ B This is too gaudy [flashy].
- ❖ Aは「(服が) 若向けである, 若作りの派手」という意味でも非常によく使われている.

2 《色・柄が派手なとき》
〈これは私には派手すぎる〉
- ◎ This is too loud [flashy] for me.
- ❖ loudは特に「柄が大きく派手」という意味でよく使われている.

鼻風邪 →風邪 1 d)
話し合いができる →話し合う 1
話し合う
1 《交渉・取引をする意味のとき》
(サッチャー元英国首相がレーガン元アメリカ大統領と話している)
〈マーガレット・サッチャー：ゴルバチョフ氏と会いました．私たちは彼と話し合えると私は思います〉
Margaret Thatcher:
- ◎ A I met Mr. Gorbachev. I think we can do business [work, negotiate, talk] with him.
- ◎ B I met Mr. Gorbachev. I think we can discuss our concerns with him.

○ C I met Mr. Gorbachev. I think we can talk about our concerns with him.
○ D I met Mr. Gorbachev. I think we can talk things over with him.
○ E I met Mr. Gorbachev. I think we can work things out with him.

2 《交渉・取引の意味でないとき》
a) 相手が言ったことに気分を害しているとき
〈部長：どうやったら売上高を上げられると思うかね〉
Manager: How do you think we can boost sales?
〈部長代理：それは先週話し合ったばかりじゃないですか〉
Assistant Manager:
◎ A We just went over that last week.
◎ B Didn't we just go over that last week?
○ C We went over that last week.
○ D Didn't we go over that last week?
❖ C, D は that と last week，またはいずれかを強くアクセントをつけて言う．

b) 相手が言ったことに気分を害していないとき
〈部長：どうやったら売上高を上げられると思うかね〉
Manager: How do you think we can boost sales?
〈部長代理：それは先週話し合ったのではないですか〉
Assistant Manager:
◎ A We went over that last week.
◎ B Didn't we go over that last week?

話したがらない
〈ビル：ジムはジェーンと結局付き合うことになったの〉
Bill: Did Jim end up going out with Jane?
〈トム：彼はそのことを話したがらないんだよ〉
Tom:
◎ A He's taking the Fifth on that.
◎ B He doesn't want to talk about that.
△ C He's taking the Fifth Amendment on that.

話にならない →問題外

話の最中
〈今，話をしているところなので，後で立ち寄ってくれますか〉
◎ We're in the middle of a conversation, so will you drop in later?

花屋 →店 3

母
1 《養母》
〈彼女は私の養母です〉
◎ A She's my adoptive mother.
△ B She's my adopted mother.

2 《生みの母》
〈彼女は私の生みの母です〉
◎ She's my natural [biological, birth] mother.

3 《育ての母》
〈彼女は私の育ての母です〉
◎ She's my foster mother.

4 《義理の母》
〈彼女は私の義理の母です〉

◎　She's my mother-in-law.
　5　《継母》
〈彼女は私の継母です〉
　　　◎　She's my stepmother.
　6　《代理母》
〈私たちは代理母を探しているんです〉
　　　◎　We're looking for a surrogate mother.
　7　《義理の両親》
〈私は義理の両親とうまくいっていないんです〉
　　　◎　A　I don't get along with my in-laws.
　　　▽　B　I don't get along with my parents-in-law.
　　　❖(1) Bは誤りではないがほとんど使われていない．
　　　❖(2) Aを英和辞典で調べると「親戚」の意味が出ているが，その意味で使われることはない．

速い・早い
　1　《仕事が速い》
〈彼は仕事が速い〉
　　　☆　A　He gets a lot done.
　　　◎　B　He's very productive.
　　　◎　C　He does a lot.
　　　◎　D　He's a fast worker.
　　　○　E　He's quick [fast] at work.
　　　△　F　He accomplishes [achieves] a lot of work.
　2　《頭の回転が速い》
〈彼は頭の回転が速いんです〉
　　　☆　A　He thinks fast.
　　　◎　B　He thinks quick.
　　　◎　C　He has a quick mind.
　　　○　D　He thinks quickly.
　　　○　E　He's a fast thinker.
　　　○　F　His brain works very fast.
　　　△　G　He has a fast mind.
　3　《計算が速い》
〈彼は計算が速いんです〉
　　　☆　A　He's good with numbers.
　　　◎　B　He's quick with numbers.
　　　◎　C　He's good with math.
　　　○　D　He's quick at figures [calculation].
　　　○　E　He's good at calculation.
　　　△　F　He's quick at calculating.
　4　《早口》
〈彼は早口です〉
　　　☆　A　He talks fast.
　　　◎　B　He speaks fast.
　　　◎　C　He talks [speaks] quick.
　　　○　D　He talks [speaks] quickly.
　　　△　E　He's a fast talker [speaker].
　5　《歩くのが速い》
〈彼は歩くのが速いんです〉

☆ A He walks fast.
◎ B He's a fast walker.
◎ C He walks quick.
○ D He walks quickly.
△ E He's a quick walker.

6 《食べるのが速い》
〈彼は食べるのが速いんです〉
☆ A He eats fast.
◎ B He eats quick.
◎ C He's a fast eater.
○ D He's a quick eater.
○ E He eats quickly.

7 《異性に対して》
〈彼は女性に手が早い〉
◎ A He can get a date anytime.
◎ B He's a ladies' man.

はやる

1 《ファッション》
a) 普通に現在の状態を述べるとき
〈ブルーが今年ははやっています〉
☆ A Blue's "in" this year.
◎ B Blue's popular [hot, fashionable] this year.
◎ C Blue's in fashion this year.
○ D Blue's in style this year.
△ E Blue's in vogue this year.

b) 強調して現在の状態を述べるとき
〈ブルーが今年はすごくはやっているんです〉
☆ A Blue's really "in" this year.
◎ B Blue's really hot this year.
◎ C Blue's really [very] popular this year.
○ D Blue's really [very] fashionable this year.
○ E Blue's really in style this year.
△ F Blue's really in vogue this year.

c) 未来
〈今年はブルーがはやるでしょう〉
☆ A Blue'll be "in" this year.
◎ B Blue'll be popular [in fashion] this year.
○ C Blue'll become popular this year.
○ D Blue'll be in style this year.
△ E Blue'll be stylish [be in vogue, come into vogue] this year.

d) 未来に「はやらなくなる」と述べるとき
〈今年ブルーははやらないでしょう〉
☆ A Blue won't be "in" this year.
◎ B Blue won't be hot [popular, fashionable, in fashion] this year.
◎ C Blue'll go [be] out of fashion this year.
◎ D Blue'll go [be] out of style this year.

2 《伝染病》
〈インフルエンザがはやっている〉
◎ A The flu's going around.

- △ B The flu's prevalent.
- × C The flu's raging.
- × D The flu's going strong.
- ❖ C, D が辞典に出ているが使われていない.

3 《商売などが繁盛する》

a) 店

〈彼のレストランははやっています〉
- ◎ A His restaurant's doing well.
- ◎ B His restaurant has a lot of business.
- ◎ C His restaurant's doing a good [a lot of] business.
- ◎ D His restaurant's successful [busy].
- ○ E His restaurant's doing good business.
- △ F His restaurant's flourishing [thriving].

b) 弁護士

〈私の弁護士ははやっています〉
- ☆ A My lawyer has a lot of clients.
- ◎ B My lawyer has a large clientele [practice].
- △ C My lawyer has a big practice.

c) 公認会計士

〈私の会計士ははやっています〉
- ◎ A My CPA has a lot of clients.
- ◎ B My CPA has a large clientele.
- △ C My CPA has a large practice.
- ❖ C は弁護士にはよく使われているが，公認会計士には時々しか使われていない.

d) 医師

〈私の医者ははやっています〉
- ☆ A My doctor has a lot of patients.
- ◎ B My doctor has a large practice.
- ○ C My doctor has a large clientele.

払い戻す

1 《店がお客に「払い戻す」と述べるとき》

〈持って来てくだされば払い戻します〉
- ◎ A We'll give you a refund if you bring it back.
- ◎ B You'll get the money back if you return it.
- ◎ C You'll get a refund if you return it.
- ○ D We'll return your money to you if you bring it back.
- × E We'll pay you the money back if you return it.

2 《「払い戻してもらう」と述べるとき》

〈私はテレビの代金を払い戻してもらいました〉
- ☆ A I got a refund for the TV.
- ◎ B I got the money back for the TV.
- ○ C I got my money back for the TV.
- △ D I was reimbursed [refunded] for the TV.

3 《「全額を払い戻してもらう」と述べるとき》

〈私はテレビのお金を全額払い戻してもらいました〉
- ☆ A I got a full refund for the TV.
- ◎ B I got all the money back for the TV.
- ○ C I got all my money back for the TV.

△ D I got refund in full for the TV.
△ E I was reimbursed [refunded] in full for the TV.

腹が出る →太っている 4

張り切っています

1 《今，または短期の仕事に》
〈彼はとても張り切っています〉
◎ A He's really raring to go.
◎ B He's really fired-up.
◎ C He's raring to go.
△ D He's really [highly] driven.
△ E He's really gung-ho.
❖ A が一番強く，B, C, E が2番，D が3番．

2 《長期のプロジェクト・仕事に》
〈彼はとても張り切っています〉
☆ A He's really motivated.
◎ B He's highly motivated.
○ C He's really driven.
△ D He's really gung-ho.
△ E He's highly driven.

3 《不定冠詞を従えるとき》
a) be＋動詞の過去分詞＋不定詞
〈彼はあなたの下で働くことにとても張り切っています〉
◎ A He's really motivated to work for you.
○ B He's really gung-ho [driven, encouraged] to work for you.

b) 動詞＋人＋不定詞
〈彼は部下を張り切らせるのがうまいんです〉
◎ A He's good at motivating [encouraging] his people to work hard.
△ B He's good at driving his people to work hard.

腫れる

1 《症状の動き》
〈私の左足が腫れ出してきたんです〉
◎ A My left foot's started to swell (up).
△ B My left foot's started to puff up.
△ C My left foot's started to blow up like a balloon.
▽ D My left foot's started to enlarge.

2 《症状の状態》
〈私の左足が腫れているんです〉
◎ A I have a swollen left foot.
◎ B My left foot's swollen.
○ C My left foot's blown up like a balloon.
○ D My left foot's puffed up.
△ E My left foot's puffed out.
▽ F I have a puffed-up left foot.

…版

1 《辞典》
〈私はこの辞典の改訂版を持っています〉
◎ I have the latest revision [edition, version] of this dictionary.

2 《機械》
〈私たちは2.6リットルエンジンの小型版を生産する予定です〉

◎ We're going to produce a downsized model [version, type] of the 2.6-liter engine.

繁華街 →…街 6

(車が)パンクする
〈私の車はニューヨークへ行く途中でパンクしたんです〉
   ◎ A My car had [got] a flat tire on the way to New York.
   ◎ B My car had [got] a flat on the way to New York.
   ◎ C My car had [got] a blowout on the way to New York.

判決を下す
 1 《有罪の場合》
 a）有罪であったことのみに言及するとき
〈彼には有罪の判決が下された〉
   ☆ A He was convicted.
   ◎ B He was found guilty.
   ○ C He was declared guilty.
   △ D He was pronounced guilty.
 b）有罪の内容を述べるとき
〈彼には死刑の判決が下された〉
   ◎ A He was sentenced to [given] the death penalty.
   ◎ B He was sentenced to death.
   △ C He was condemned to die.
   △ D He was condemned to death.
   × E He was condemned to the death penalty.
   ❖ E が辞典に出ているが使われていない.
 2 《無罪の場合》
〈彼は昨日, 殺人容疑の裁判で無罪と判決された〉
   ◎ A He was acquitted [cleared] of the murder charges yesterday.
   ◎ B He was found innocent [not guilty] of the murder charges yesterday.
   ○ C He was exonerated from the murder charges yesterday.
   × D He was in the clear of the murder charges yesterday.
   ❖ D が辞典に出ているが使われていない.

反対する
 1 《友人・家族のような間での話のとき》
〈友人のほとんどは私の提案に反対するでしょう〉
   ☆ A Most of my friends'll be against my proposal.
   ◎ B Most of my friends'll object to my proposal.
   ○ C Most of my friends'll oppose [be opposed to] my proposal.
   ❖ B が語調は一番強い.
 2 《改まった話の内容のとき》
〈取締役理事会は私たちの提案に反対するでしょう〉
   ☆ A The board of directors'll object to our proposal.
   ◎ B The board of directors'll oppose [be opposed to] our proposal.
   ○ C The board of directors'll be against our proposal.
   ❖ A を否定にするときは have no objection to が普通使われている.
 3 《強く反対すると述べるとき》
〈取締役理事会は私たちの計画に強く反対するでしょう〉
   ◎ A The board of directors'll strongly [totally] object to our proposal.
   ◎ B The board of directors'll be strongly [totally] opposed to our

proposal.
- ◎ C The board of directors'll strongly [totally] oppose our proposal.
- ○ D The board of directors'll absolutely object to [oppose] our proposal.
- ○ E The board of directors'll be absolutely opposed to our proposal.

4 《大反対していると述べるとき》
〈彼女は私たちの計画に大反対している〉
- ◎ A She's dead set against our proposal.
- ◎ B She's dead against our proposal.
- ◎ C She's set against our proposal.
- ◎ D She's absolutely [totally] against our proposal.
- ◎ E She's very much against our proposal.
- ◎ F She's really [strongly] against our proposal.
- △ G She's wholly against our proposal.
- × H She's wholly-set against our proposal.
  - ❖(1) H が辞典に出ているが使われていない.
  - ❖(2) A が一番強い響きがあり，C, D が 2 番，B が 3 番，E, F, G がほぼ同じで 4 番目.

5 《単に不賛成の意を示す場合》
〈私の両親は私たちの結婚に反対しています〉
- ◎ A Our marriage's frowned upon by my parents.
- ◎ B My parents frown upon [disapprove] our marriage.
- ◎ C My parents don't agree with our marriage.
- ○ D My parents don't think much of our marriage.
- × E My parents look askance at our marriage.
  - ❖ E が辞典に出ているが使われていない.

6 《抗議する場合》
a）反対することを公にするとき
〈彼女は開発計画に反対した〉
- ◎ A She took a stand against the development project.
- ○ B She raised an objection against the development project.
- ○ C She argued against the development project.
  - ❖ C は特に反対であることを演説で表明したり，実際に抗議を行なったりすることを意味する.

b）反対を公にすることは特に述べないとき
〈彼女は開発計画に反対した〉
- ◎ A She was against the development project.
- ◎ B She opposed the development project.
- ◎ C She was opposed to the development project.
- ◎ D She made an objection to the development project.
- ◎ E She objected to the development project.
- ○ F She raised an objection to the development project.
- △ G She said her objection to the development project.
  - ❖ 反対の強さは A が一番，B, C, D, F がほぼ同じで 2 番，G が 3 番，E が一番弱い.

7 《反対論を述べるとき》
〈彼女は開発計画に反対論を述べました〉
- ◎ A She made a [her] case against the development project.
- ○ B She presented her point [reasoning, reason] against the develop-

ment project.
- ○ C She had a convincing argument against the development project.

ハンドバッグ
〈彼は昇進祝いに私にブルーのハンドバッグをプレゼントしてくれたんです〉
- ◎ A He gave me a blue purse for my promotion.
- ▽ B He gave me a blue handbag for my promotion.
    - ❖ B はアメリカでは今はほとんど使われていない．ただし，イギリスでは B しか使われていない．

ハンドルを切りそこねる
〈老人はハンドルを切りそこねて，レンガのビルの横腹にまともにぶつかった〉
- ◎ A The old man lost control of his car and slammed into the side of the brick building.
- ◎ B The old man turned in the wrong direction and slammed into the side of the brick building.
- ◎ C The old man turned the wrong way and slammed into the side of the brick building.
- △ D The old man steered the wrong way and slammed into the side of the brick building.
- ▽ E The old man steered in the wrong direction and slammed into the side of the brick building.
    - ❖ E が辞典に出ているが使われてもまれ．

犯人
1 《容疑者の場合》
〈警察は容疑者を探している〉
- ◎ A The police're searching for the suspect.
- × B The police're searching for the criminal.

2 《罪が確定している場合》
〈犯人は10年の刑を宣告された〉
- ◎ A The criminal was sentenced to 10 years in prison.
- × B The suspect was sentenced to 10 years in prison.

3 《人質を取っているとき》
〈犯人はまだ人質を解放していません〉
- ◎ A The man [guy] hasn't released the hostage yet.
- ○ B The kidnapper hasn't released the hostage yet.
- × C The criminal hasn't released the hostage yet.

反応がいい
1 《スピーチの場合》
〈彼のスピーチの反応はよかったですか〉
- ◎ Did his speech get a good response [reaction]?

2 《広告の場合》
〈広告の反応はよかったですか〉
- ◎ A Did the ad get a good response?
- ◎ B Did the ad work well?
- △ C Did the ad get a good reaction?

販売促進部 →…部 18
販売代理店 →店 22
パン屋 →店 6

〔ひ〕

B面
〈私はB面の歌の方が好きです〉
- ☆ A I like the songs on the other side better.
- ◎ B I like the songs on the flip side better.
- ○ C I like the songs on the opposite side better.

(…と)比較して

1 《増加・上昇の場合》
〈1984年は1983年と比較して交通事故の件数が増えました〉
- ◎ A In 1984 the number of car accidents increased over [from] 1983.
- ◎ B In 1984 the number of car accidents increased compared to [with] 1983.
- ◎ C In 1984 the number of car accidents increased over [from] that of 1983.
- ○ D In 1984 the number of car accidents increased compared to [with] that of 1983.
- ○ E In 1984 the number of car accidents increased over [from] what it was in 1983.
- ○ F In 1984 the number of car accidents increased compared to [with] what it was in 1983.
- △ G In 1984 the number of car accidents increased over [from] those of 1983.
- △ H In 1984 the number of car accidents increased compared to [with] those of 1983.
- △ I In 1984 the number of car accidents increased over [from] what they were in 1983.
- △ J In 1984 the number of car accidents increased compared to [with] what they were in 1983.
  - ❖(1) Aのoverとfromには「比較して」の意味があり，堅い文章英語でも会話でも非常によく使われている．
  - ❖(2) the number of は3人称単数で呼応する場合と，意味内容が複数であるため3人称複数で呼応する場合とがある．

2 《減少・低下の問題》
〈1984年は1983年と比較して，交通事故の件数が減りました〉
- ◎ A In 1984 the number of car accidents decreased from 1983.
- ◎ B In 1984 the number of car accidents decreased compared to [with] 1983.
- ○ C In 1984 the number of car accidents decreased from that of 1983.
- ○ D In 1984 the number of car accidents decreased compared to [with] that of 1983.
- ○ E In 1984 the number of car accidents decreased from what it was in 1983.
- ○ F In 1984 the number of car accidents decreased compared to [with] what it was in 1983.
- △ G In 1984 the number of car accidents decreased from those of 1983.

△ H In 1984 the number of car accidents decreased compared to [with] those of 1983.
△ I In 1984 the number of car accidents decreased from what they were in 1983.
△ J In 1984 the number of car accidents decreased compared to [with] what they were in 1983.

❖「増加・上昇」のときは「比較して」の意味で over がよく使われているが,「減少・低下」のときは使われていない.

美化する
〈たいていのアメリカ人は暗殺された大統領を美化する強い傾向がある.特にケネディー大統領を〉
◎ Most Americans have a strong tendency to glorify [idealize] the assassinated presidents, especially John F. Kennedy.

ピカピカに
1 《ピカピカに磨く》
〈靴をピカピカに磨いてくれますか〉
◎ A Will you give my shoes a shine?
◎ B Will you put a good shine on my shoes?
▽ C Will you put a high shine on my shoes?
▽ D Will you polish my shoes well?

❖辞典に C, D が出ているがあまり使われていない.

2 《「ピカピカに磨いた」の意味の「ピカピカ」》
〈彼女はピカピカの靴を履いていました〉
◎ A She was wearing very shiny shoes.
◎ B She was wearing nicely-shined shoes.
○ C She was wearing well-polished shoes.
▽ D She was wearing highly-polished [highly-shined] shoes.

❖ D が辞典に出ているがあまり使われていない.

3 《「ピカピカ輝いている」の意味の「ピカピカ」》
〈彼女はピカピカしているネックレスをつけていました〉
☆ A She was wearing a sparkling necklace.
◎ B She was wearing a shiny necklace.
△ C She was wearing a glittering [twinkling] necklace.

ひがむ
〈父は兄にプレゼントをよくあげるんだけど,私はもらったことがないのよ.私がひがむのは当然でしょう〉
◎ My father often gives my brother presents but I've never gotten anything. Is it normal for me to be sensitive?

引き合う
〈この取引は私には引き合わない〉
◎ A This deal won't do anything for me.
◎ B This deal won't profit me.
◎ C This deal won't make me any money.
○ D This deal won't make me a profit.
○ E This deal won't turn a profit for me.
△ F This deal won't produce a profit for me.
△ G This deal won't pay off for me.

引き起こす
〈北大西洋条約機構がバルカンの惨事を引き起こしている〉

- ◎ A NATO's inviting [provoking, asking, causing] disaster in the Balkans.
- ◎ B NATO's courting disaster in the Balkans.
- ○ C NATO's prompting [inducing, generating] disaster in the Balkans.
- △ D NATO's bringing about disaster in the Balkans.
    - ❖ B の court は会話よりもテレビやラジオなどのニュース，新聞などでよく使われている．

引き金となる
1 《「口火となる」の意味のとき》
〈それが暴動の引き金となったのです〉
- ◎ A That started [triggered, sparked] a riot.
- △ B That touched off a riot.
- △ C That ignited a riot.
- × D That triggered off [touched] a riot.
    - ❖ C は堅い文章英語では非常によく使われている．

2 《「原因となる」の意味のとき》
〈それが暴動の引き金となったのです〉
- ◎ A That caused [incited, provoked] the riot.
- ○ B That led [led up to, brought about] the riot.
- △ C That brought on [induced] the riot.
- × D That gave [set fire to, occasioned] the riot.
    - ❖ D が辞典に出ているが使われていない．

引きずっている
1 《恋人などを忘れられなくて》
〈彼は初恋の人を失って，まだ引きずっているんです〉
- ◎ A He lost his first love. He still can't get over it.
- ◎ B He lost his first love. He's still stuck on her.
- ◎ C He lost his first love. He still can't forget her.
- ○ D He lost his first love. He still can't get by [overcome] it.
- ○ E He lost his first love. He still can't get back on his feet.

2 《過去の苦い経験》
〈彼は株で大損したんです．彼はまだそれを引きずっているんです〉
- ☆ A He lost a lot of money in the stock market. He still can't get over it.
- ☆ B He lost a lot of money in the stock market. He still can't get back on his feet.
- ◎ C He lost a lot of money in the stock market. He still can't get passed it.
- ○ D He lost a lot of money in the stock market. He still can't overcome it.
- △ E He lost a lot of money in the stock market. He still can't get by it.

3 《癖で足を引きずって歩くとき》
〈彼は足を引きずって歩いていました〉
- ◎ A He was dragging his feet.
- ◎ B He was scuffling his shoes.
- × C He was scuffling his feet.
    - ❖ C が辞典に出ているが使われていない．

4 《抵抗して足を引きずって》
〈彼は足を引きずっていた〉
- ◎ He was dragging his heels.

引き出す →下ろす
低くする
1 《声》
〈声を低くして下さい. 誰かが聞いているかもしれません〉
- ◎ A Lower your voice. Someone may be listening.
- ○ B Keep your voice down. Someone may be listening.
- × C Drop your voice. Someone may be listening.
    - ❖ C が辞典に出ているが使われていない.
2 《テレビ・ラジオ・CD プレイヤーの場合》
〈テレビの音を低くしておいて下さい〉
- ◎ A Keep the TV turned down (low).
- ◎ B Keep the TV volume set on low.
- ◎ C Keep the TV volume turned down low.
- ○ D Keep the TV down.

ひげ
1 《本物のひげ》
〈彼はひげをはやしている〉
- ◎ A He has a mustache.
- × B He wears [is wearing] a mustache.
- × C He has on a mustache.
    - ❖ B, C は辞典に出ているが使われていない.
2 《つけひげ》
〈彼はつけひげをつけている〉
- ◎ A He's wearing a fake mustache.
- ◎ B He has on [wears] a fake mustache.

引ける
〈ダウ平均株価は 2,246.73 で引けました〉
- ☆ A The Dow-Jones closed at 2,246.73.
- ◎ B The Dow-Jones ended [closed] the day at 2,246.73.
- ○ C The Dow-Jones finished the day at 2,246.73.
- ○ D The Dow-Jones finished [ended] at 2,246.73.
- △ E The Dow-Jones wrapped [wound up] the day at 2,246.73.
- △ F The Dow-Jones wrapped up at 2,246.73.
- × G The Dow-Jones wound at 2,246.73.

非公開の
〈会議は非公開でした〉
- ☆ A It was a closed-door meetings.
- ◎ B The meeting was behind closed-door.
- ◎ C The meeting wasn't open to the public.
- ○ D The meeting was a closed-door session.
- △ E The meeting was closed-door.

日毎に
〈日毎に寒くなってきた〉
- ◎ A It's getting colder every day.
- ○ B It's getting colder day by day [each day].
- △ C It's getting colder daily.

久し振り
1 《一般に言うとき》
a) 再会

⟨昨日久し振りに昔の友人に会いました⟩
- ◎ A Yesterday I saw an old friend for the first time in ages.
- ◎ B Yesterday I saw an old friend for the first time in a long time.
- △ C Yesterday I saw an old friend for the first time in a long while.
- × D Yesterday I saw an old friend after a long separation [interval].
- ❖(1) D が多くの辞典に出ているが使われていない.
- ❖(2) 会わなかった時間としてはAが一番長く, 以下B, Cの順.

b) 手紙を受け取ったとき

⟨久し振りにトムから手紙をもらった⟩
- ◎ A I heard from Tom for the first time in ages.
- ○ B I heard from Tom for the first time in [after] a long time.
- △ C I heard from Tom for the first time in a long while.
- × D I heard from Tom after a long silence.

c) 天気

⟨昨日は久し振りにいい天気だった⟩
- ◎ A Yesterday we had nice weather for the first time in ages.
- ◎ B Yesterday we had nice weather for the first time in a long time.
- ◎ C Yesterday we had nice weather for the first time in many days.
- ◎ D Yesterday we had nice weather for the first time in several days.
- △ E Yesterday we had nice weather for the first time in a long while.
- ❖天気の悪かった期間としてはAが一番長く, B, C, E, Dの順で短くなる.

d) 帰宅

⟨息子が久し振りに帰ってきた⟩
- ◎ A My son came home for the first time in ages [in a long time].
- △ B My son came home for the first time in a long while.
- × C My son came home after a long absence [interval].
- ❖Cが多くの辞典に出ているが使われていない.

e) 飲酒

⟨久し振りにウイスキーを飲んでいるんですよ⟩
- ◎ A This is the first whisky I've had in ages [in a long time].
- ◎ B This is my first whisky in ages [in a long time].
- △ C This is the first whisky I've had in a long while.
- △ D This is my first whisky in a long while.
- × E I'm drinking whisky after a long abstinence.
- ❖Eが辞典に出ているが使われていない.

2 《話しかけるとき》

a) 昔の部下・学生・友人に会って

⟨久し振りだね⟩
- ◎ A Long time no see.
- ◎ B Where've you been hiding [keeping] yourself?

b) 昔の上司・恩師などに会って

⟨お久し振りです⟩
- ◎ A It's been a long time!
- ◎ B It's been (quite) a while!
- ◎ C It's been ages!
- ◎ D I haven't seen you in ages [in a long time].
- ◎ E Haven't seen you in ages.

c) 女性が男性の友人に, または女性の友人に会って

⟨お久し振りね⟩

◎ A I almost [nearly] forgot what you looked like.
◎ B It's been forever.
◎ C Long time no see.
◎ D Where've you been hiding [keeping] yourself?

秘書 →職業 14

非常階段
〈このビルには非常階段はあるのですか〉
◎ A Does this building have a fire escape?
◎ B Does this building have an emergency exit?
○ C Does this building have an emergency stairway?
× D Does this building have an emergency stair [staircase]?

非常に
1 《副詞的に用いて》
a) 特筆すべきニュアンスを含まない場合
・一般的な形容詞とともに
〈彼らは非常に貧しいんです〉
◎ They're very [really] poor.
〈今日は非常に暑いです〉
◎ It's very [really] hot today.
・厳粛な意味を持つ形容詞とともに
〈彼は非常に敬虔なクリスチャンです〉
◎ A He's a very devout Christian.
○ B He's a really devout Christian.
〈彼女は非常に献身的な教師です〉
◎ A She's a very dedicated teacher.
○ B She's a really dedicated teacher.
b)「高度に」「高く」というニュアンスを含む場合
〈このコンピュータは非常に精巧です〉
◎ A This computer is highly [very] sophisticated.
○ B This computer is really sophisticated.
〈彼は非常に教育レベルが高い〉
◎ A He's highly [very] educated.
△ B He's really educated.
〈彼らの制度は非常に進んでいる〉
◎ Their system's highly [very, really] advanced.
〈彼は非常に尊敬されています〉
◎ A He's highly [very] respected.
○ B He's really respected.
〈彼は非常に賞賛されています〉
◎ A He's highly [very] admired.
○ B He's really admired.
〈彼は経済学者として非常に著名です〉
☆ A He's very prominent as an economist.
◎ B He's highly prominent as an economist.
○ C He's really prominent as an economist.
〈株式市場は今非常に危険だ〉
◎ A The stock market is very [really] risky now.
○ B The stock market is highly risky now.
〈あなたの戦略は非常に危険です〉

- ◎ A Your strategy is very [really] dangerous.
- ○ B Your strategy is highly dangerous.

〈これは非常に個人的な問題です〉
- ◎ This is a highly [very, really] personal matter.

〈これは非常にデリケートな問題です〉
- ◎ This is a highly [very, really] sensitive issue.

2 《形容詞的に用いて》

a) 通常の会話で

〈それは私に非常に影響を与えた〉
- ◎ A That has a great influence on me.
- ○ B That has a lot of influence on me.

〈あなたには非常に忍耐が必要です〉
- ◎ A You need a lot of patience.
- ○ B You need great patience.

b) くだけた会話で

〈旅行は非常に楽しい〉
- ◎ A Traveling is a lot of fun.
- ○ B Traveling is great fun.

c) 改まった会話で

〈お目にかかれて非常に光栄です〉
- ◎ A It's great honor to meet you.
- × B It's a lot of honor to meet you.

〈彼の死は私にとって非常にショックなことでした〉
- ◎ A His death was a great shock to me.
- × B His death was a lot of shock to me.

d) of＋great＋抽象名詞の形が可能な場合

〈この絵は非常に価値がある〉
- ◎ A This picture is very valuable.
- ○ B This picture is of great value.
- × C This picture is of a lot of value.

❖多くの辞典・英文法書でBを大きく紹介しているが，話し言葉では使用頻度は高くない．

美人

1 《普通に述べるとき》

〈彼女は美人です〉
- ◎ A She's a knockout.
- ◎ B She's beautiful [gorgeous, good-looking, lovely, pretty].

2 《「すごい美人」と述べるとき》

〈彼女はすごい美人です〉
- ☆ A She's very beautiful.
- ◎ B She's really beautiful.
- ◎ C She's a real knockout [stunner].
- ◎ D She's a real beauty.
- ◎ E She's really [very] gorgeous.
- ○ F She's a great [stunning] beauty.

❖多くの辞典に a beauty（美人）と出ているが，D, F のように a＋形容詞＋beauty で使う．

3 《「セクシー」であるという意味の「すごい美人」》

〈彼女はすごい美人です〉

        ◎ A She's really hot.
        △ B She's a real babe.
        ▽ C She's a doll.
  4 《いい男》
  a）身体全体の容姿
  ・普通に述べるとき
  〈彼はいい男です〉
        ◎ A He's good-looking.
        △ B He's a hunk [a babe].
  ・強調して述べるとき
  〈彼はすごくいい男です〉
        ◎ A He's gorgeous.
        ◎ B He's really good-looking.
  b）顔
  ・普通に述べるとき
  〈彼はいい男です〉
        ◎   He's handsome.
  ・強調して述べるとき
  〈彼はすごくいい男です〉
        ◎ A He's really handsome.
        ○ B He's very handsome.
  ・ずっと年上の女性が述べるとき
  〈彼はいい男です〉
        ◎   He's cute.
        ❖ 60歳以上の女性なら40歳くらいの男性にも使われている．
  c）セクシーだというニュアンスのとき
  〈彼はいい男です〉
        ☆ A He's hot.
        ◎ B He's sexy.
        ○ C He's a stud [a babe].
        △ D He's foxy.
        △ E He's a fox.
  5 《八方美人》
  〈彼は八方美人です〉
        ☆ A He's two-faced.
        ◎ B He talks out of both sides of his mouth.
        ◎ C He says whatever other people want to hear.
        △ D He's everybody's friend.
        × E He's double-faced [double-tongued].
        ❖(1) E が辞典に出ているが使われていない．
        ❖(2) D も辞典に出ているが時々使われる程度．この表現は「みんなに好かれている」という肯定的な意味でなら非常によく使われている．

ひっかかる
  1 《衣服が針に》
  〈私のコートが釘にひっかかってしまったんです〉
        ◎ A My coat (got) caught on a nail.
        ◎ B I got [had] my coat caught on a nail.
  2 《ペン》
  〈このペンはひっかかる〉

☆ A This pen doesn't work (well).
○ B This pen's a lousy pen.
○ C This pen's a piece of shit [crap, junk].
△ D This pen scratches.

3 《詐欺》

〈彼は詐欺にひっかかたんです〉
◎ A He was cheated [tricked] by a con artist.
○ C He was taken in a con artist.
○ D He was [got] sucked in a con artist.
○ F He fell for a con artist's tricks.

日付を入れる

〈小切手に日付を入れて下さい〉
◎ Date the check, please.

引越し屋

〈彼は引越し屋に勤めている〉
◎ A He works for a moving company.
◎ B He works for the movers [a mover].
❖ A は大きい会社と小さい会社の両方に使われている．引越しだけでなく，それ以外の運送もしている．B は引越しを業務としている小さい会社．

ひったくる

〈背の高い男が私からハンドバッグをひったくったんです〉
☆ A A tall guy grabbed my purse from me.
◎ B A tall guy ripped my purse out of my hands.
◎ C A tall guy took my purse from me.
◎ D A tall guy snatched my purse.
○ E A tall guy snatched my purse from me.
△ F A tall guy snatched my purse off [away from] me.
❖ひったくった強さの度合いは B が1番，A が2番，C, D は3番．

ぴったり

1 《隙間がないありさま》

〈窓をぴったり閉めて下さい〉
◎ A Shut the window all the way.
◎ B Shut the window completely.
× C Shut the window closely [tightly].
❖ C が辞典に出ているが使われていない．

〈誰かが私たちをぴったり尾行しています〉
◎ A Someone's following us closely.
× B Someone's following us on our heels.

2 《食い違いのないこと》

a) 計算

〈あなたの計算はぴったりです〉
◎ Your calculation's exactly [perfectly] correct.

b) 勘定

〈客：いくらですか〉
Customer: How much is it?
〈店員：ぴったり百ドルです〉
Cashier:
◎ A $ 100 even.
◎ B Even $100.

- ◎ C Exactly $100.
- ◎ D Just $100.

c）話の内容
〈あなたの話と彼の話はぴったりです〉
- ◎ A Your story is exactly the same as his.
- ○ B Your story is identical to his.
- ○ C Your story matches his.
- × D Your story is identical with his.
  - ❖ D が辞典に出ているが使われていない．

d）寸法
〈そのドレスはあなたにぴったりです〉
- ☆ A That dress fits you perfectly.
- ◎ B That dress fits you perfect.
- ◎ C That dress fits you like a glove.
- ◎ D That dress is a perfect fit.
- ○ E That dress fits you to a T.
- × F That dress fits you like a skin.
- × G That dress is a perfect fit to you.
  - ❖(1) F, G が辞典に出ているが使われていない．
  - ❖(2) 3 も参照のこと

3 《よく似合うという意味で》
〈そのドレスはあなたにぴったりです〉
- ☆ A That dress suits [fits] you perfectly.
- ◎ B That dress fits you perfect.
- ○ C That dress suits you perfect.
  - ❖ 2 d) も参照のこと．

匹敵する
1 《技術》
〈彼らの技術はうちのに匹敵します〉
- ☆ A Their technology's as good as ours.
- ◎ B Their technology's comparable with ours.
- ◎ C Their technology's equal to ours.
- ○ D Their technology matches [compares] ours.
- ○ E Their technology can compete with ours.
- ○ F Their technology's comparable to ours.
- △ G Their technology's a match for ours.
- △ H Their technology rivals ours.

2 《語学・テニス・ゴルフなど》
〈フランス語で彼に匹敵する人はいません〉
- ☆ A No one can speak French better than him.
- ◎ B No one's better than him in French.
- ◎ C No one can beat him in French.
- ○ D No one compares [can compare] with him in French.
- ○ E No one can match him in French.
- △ F He has no match in French.
- △ G No one's a match for him in French.
- △ H He's without a match in French.
- × I He's peerless [without a peer] in French.
- × J No one can compare favorably with him in French.

3 《貨幣の価値》
〈当時の 100 ドルは今の 10 ドルに匹敵する〉
- ☆ A $100 in those days is worth $10 now.
- ◎ B $100 in those days is equal to $10 now.
- ○ C $100 in those days equals $10 now.
- ○ D $100 in those days is equivalent to $10 now.

ヒットする

1 《歌》
〈この歌はすごくヒットするでしょう〉
- ☆ A This song'll be on [in] the top ten.
- ☆ B This song'll be a big hit.
- ◎ C This song'll be a No. 1 hit.
- ◎ D This song'll top the charts.
- ◎ E This song'll be No. 1 on the charts.
- ○ F This song'll be a great success.
  - ❖ C, E が一番強い響きがある．

2 《映画》
〈この映画はすごくヒットするでしょう〉
- ◎ A This movie'll be a blockbuster.
- ◎ B This movie'll be a huge [big] hit.
- ○ C This movie'll be a great success.
- △ D This movie'll be in [on] the top ten.
- △ E This movie'll be No. 1 on the charts.
- △ F This movie'll top the charts.
  - ❖ E が一番強い響きがある．

3 《本》
〈この本はすごくヒットするでしょう〉
- ◎ A This book'll be on the best seller list.
- ◎ B This book'll be No. 1 on the best seller list.
- ◎ C This book'll be at the top of the best seller list.
- ◎ D This book'll be on the top ten list.
- △ E This book'll be a No. 1 seller.
- △ F This book'll be a great success.
- △ G This book'll catch on.
  - ❖ B, C, E が一番強い響きがある．

4 《車》
〈この車はすごくヒットするでしょう〉
- ◎ A This car'll be a hot seller [a big hit].
- ◎ B This car'll be on the top ten list.
- ◎ C This car'll be on the best seller list.
- ○ D This car'll be a No. 1 seller.
- ○ E This car'll catch on.
  - ❖ D が一番強い響きがある．

必要である

1 《プロジェクトなどの事柄が主語のとき》
〈私たちのプロジェクトには彼の財政援助が必要なんです〉
- ◎ A Our project needs [requires] his financial help.
- ○ B Our project calls for his financial help.
- △ C Our project demands his financial help.

2 《人が主語のとき》
〈あなたがそこへ行く必要はありません〉
- ☆ A You don't have [need] to go there.
- ◎ B There's no need for you to go there.
- ○ C It's unnecessary for you to go there.
- ▽ D There's no necessity for you to go there.
  - ❖ C を You're unnecessary to go there.のように，人を主語にして言い換えることはできない．

3 《「いい弁護士・医者などになるには」が主語のとき》
〈いい弁護士になるためには，約10年の経験が必要である〉
- ☆ A Being a good lawyer requires about ten years' experience.
- ◎ B Being a good lawyer calls for about ten years' experience.
- ○ C Being a good lawyer demands about ten years' experience.
- × D Being a good lawyer needs about ten years' experience.

4 《経験年数が主語のとき》
〈約10年の経験が，いい弁護士になるためには必要である〉
- ☆ A About ten years' experience is necessary [required] to be a good lawyer.
- ◎ B About ten years' experience is needed to be a good lawyer.
- ◎ C About ten years' experience is necessary for being a good lawyer.
- ○ D About ten years' experience is required [needed] for being a good lawyer.

5 《規則上不可欠な内容のとき》
〈卒業するのに36単位が必要なんです〉
- ◎ 36 credits're mandatory [required, needed, necessary] for your graduation.
  - ❖ 必要性の度合いはmandatoryが一番強いというニュアンスがある．requiredが2番目，neededとnecessaryが3番目．

ビデオ屋 →店 26

人

1 《関係詞または不定詞を従えるとき》
a) 断定して述べるとき
〈彼は約束を破る人ではない〉
- ☆ A He isn't one to break his promise.
- ◎ B He isn't somebody [a man, one] who breaks his promise.
- ◎ C He isn't a man to break his promise.
- ○ D He isn't a person [a guy] who breaks his promise.
- △ E He isn't somebody [a person] to break his promise.

b) 断定せず婉曲に述べるとき
〈彼は約束を破る人ではない〉
- ◎ A He isn't one who would [could, will] break his promise.
- × B He isn't one who can break his promise.

2 《Who (誰が) を文頭で使うとき》
a) 女性
〈ジムとテニスをしている人は誰ですか〉
- ☆ A Who's that playing tennis with Jim?
- ◎ B Who's the woman playing tennis with Jim?
- ○ C Who's the person [the one] playing tennis with Jim?
- △ D Who's the girl playing tennis with Jim?

× E Who's somebody playing tennis with Jim?
  ❖ D は以前,若く見えるというニュアンスを持って,年令に関係なく使われていたが,今は 20 歳くらいまでに普通使われている.

b) 男性
〈ビルとテニスをしている人は誰ですか〉
  ☆ A Who's that playing tennis with Bill?
  ◎ B Who's the guy playing tennis with Bill?
  ○ C Who's the man [the person] playing tennis with Bill?
  △ D Who's the one playing tennis with Bill?
  × E Who's somebody playing tennis with Bill?

3 《「来客」の意味のとき》
〈今,人が来ているんです〉
  ◎ A I have company now.
  ○ B I have a guest [visitor] now.
    ❖ A は 1 人または 2 人以上でも使える.

4 《泥棒に対する警告》
〈人を見たら泥棒と思え〉
  ☆ A Don't trust strangers.
  ◎ B Beware of strangers.

5 《人の価値》
〈人の価値は財産にあるのではなく人柄にある〉
  ☆ A A man's worth doesn't lie in what he has but in what he is.
  ◎ B You shouldn't judge people by what they have but by what they do.

6 《「他人」の意味のとき》
〈私は人が言うことは気にしません〉
  ◎   I don't care what others [other people] say.

人影がない
〈通りには人影がなかった〉
  ◎ A The street was empty.
  ○ B The street was dead [deserted].
  △ C The street was vacant.
  ▽ D The street was desolate.

人質になる
1 《人質に取られたとき (動作)》
〈人質になったときどんなに恐ろしかったか,言葉では表現できません〉
  ◎ A I can't tell you how scared I was when I was taken hostage.
  ◎ B I can't tell you how scared I was when I was taken as a hostage.

2 《人質に取られていたとき (状態)》
〈私は人質に取られていたときどんなに怖かったか,言葉では表現できません〉
  ◎ A I can't tell you how scared I was when I was held hostage.
  ○ B I can't tell you how scared I was when I was held [kept] as a hostage.
  ○ C I can't tell you how scared I was when I was kept hostage.

3 《人質の数に言及するとき》
〈彼らは 20 人の人質を取っているんです〉
  ◎ A They're holding 20 hostages.
  ◎ B They have 20 hostages.
  △ C They keep 20 hostages.

ひとりで 539

人使いが荒い
〈彼は人使いが荒い〉
- ☆ A He's a slave driver.
- ◎ B He works his employees [staff, people] hard.
- ◎ C He works his employees [staff, people] to death.
- ○ D He runs his employees [staff, people] rugged.
  - ❖ staff はホワイトカラー，それ以外は職種を問わず広く使える．

ひと儲けする →利益 5

独り相撲を取る
〈私は独り相撲を取っているような気がします〉
- ◎ A I feel like I'm trying to do the impossible.
- ◎ B I feel like I'm beating my head against the wall.
- ◎ C I feel like I'm beating against a brick wall.
- ○ D I feel like I'm pounding my head against a brick wall.
- △ E I feel like I'm hitting my head against a brick wall.

一人っ子
1 《兄弟・姉妹がいないとき》
〈私は一人っ子なんです〉
- ◎ I'm an [the] only child.

2 《姉か妹がいるとき》
〈僕は一人息子です〉
- ◎ A I'm the only son.
- △ B I'm an only son.

ひとりで
1 《「自力で」の意味》
〈私は彼はひとりで事態に対処できると思う〉
- ◎ A I think he can cope with the situation on his own.
- ◎ B I think he can cope with the situation by himself.
- ◎ C I think he can cope with the situation himself.
- ○ D I think he can cope with the situation alone.
  - ❖ A, B はともに「聞き手の力なしで」が原義．しかし，A の方が自力の意味が強い．D は「聞き手のみならず誰の力も必要がない」というニュアンス．C は漠然とした表現．

2 《「他の人はいない」の意味》
〈彼はひとりで住んでいます〉
- ◎ A He lives alone.
- ◎ B He lives by himself.

3 《「自分で」の意味》
〈あなたはひとりで決めるべきです〉
- ◎ A You should decide for yourself.
- △ B You should decide yourself.
- × C You should decide alone [by yourself].

4 《(レストランで) お一人様ですか》
〈ボーイ長：お一人様ですか〉
Headwaiter:
- ☆ A Are you one?
- ◎ B Table for one?
- ◎ C Are you by yourself?
- ◎ D Will someone be joining you (later)?

△ E Do you have a companion?
△ F Are you alone?

ひとりでに
〈ドアはひとりでに開いたんです〉
◎ A The door opened by itself.
× B The door opened of itself [by its own accord].
❖ B が辞典に出ているが使われていない．

独り舞台
〈彼の独り舞台だった〉
◎ A He stole the show.
○ B He stole the whole show.

皮膚科医 →医者 12
ひまを出す →首になる 4
肥満 →太っている 5

秘密
1 《「秘密を守る」と言うとき》
〈これは秘密にしておいて下さい〉
◎ A Keep this a secret.
◎ B Keep this quiet.
○ C Keep this secret [confidential].
○ D Keep this under your hat.
○ E Keep this to yourself.
× F Keep this private [dark].
× G Keep this under your bonnet [derby, Stetson].
× H Keep this under wraps.
❖ F, G, H が辞典に出ているが使われていない．

2 《「秘密を漏らす」と言うとき》
〈彼が秘密を漏らしたのかもしれません〉
◎ A He may've let the cat out of the bag.
◎ B He may've spilled the beans.
◎ C He may've let the secret out.
◎ D He may've given the secret away.
◎ E He may've leaked the secret.
○ F He may've betrayed the secret.
❖ A は一番深刻でないという響きがある．B がそれに続き，C, D, E はほぼ同じ．F は一番深刻というニュアンスがある．

3 《秘密の》
〈あなたに秘密の情報があります〉
◎ A I have secret information for you.
△ B I have classified information for you.
× C I have underhand [sub-rosa, undercover, inside] information for you.
❖ C が辞典に出ているが使われていない．

〈私たちは秘密の会合を開きました〉
◎ A We had a secret meeting.
▽ B We had a clandestine meeting.
❖ B は辞典に出ているがまれ．

日焼けする
1 《普通に日焼けしている場合》

〈彼は日焼けしています〉
- ◎ A He's tan.
- ◎ B He has a tan [a suntan].
- ○ C He's suntanned [tanned].
- × D He's sunburned.
- × E He's sunburnt [sunbrowned].
  - ❖(1) E は辞典に出ているが使われていない．
  - ❖(2) D は「普通に日焼けしている」という意味では使われない．3 を参照のこと．

2 《非常に日焼けしている場合》
〈彼はすごく日焼けしています〉
- ◎ A He's real [very] tan.
- ◎ B He has a dark tan.
- ○ C He has a deep tan.

3 《炎症を起こしている場合》
〈彼は日焼けして皮膚が赤くなっている〉
- ◎ He's deeply [seriously, badly] sunburned.

美容院 →店 35

評価する

1 《過大評価する》
〈私のことを過大評価しないで下さい〉
- ◎ A Don't overestimate [overrate] me.
- △ B Don't make [think] too much of me.
- △ C Don't overvalue me.

2 《過小評価する》
〈彼を過小評価してはだめですよ〉
- ◎ A Don't underestimate [underrate] him.
- ○ B Don't minimize [undervalue, belittle] him.

病気

1 《一般的に言う場合》
〈彼は病気なんです〉
- ◎ A He's sick.
- ◎ B He's ill.
- ◎ C He's feeling ill.
- ○ D He's feeling sick.
- ○ E He feels ill [sick].
  - ❖ ill の方が sick より重い響きがある．

2 《重い病気の場合》
〈彼は重い病気なんです〉
- ◎ A He's seriously ill.
- ◎ B He's very sick.
- △ C He's very ill.
- △ D He's seriously sick.

3 《「欠勤するという電話が入る」という場合》
〈部長：ジムを呼んでくれ〉
Manager: Get Jim.
〈秘書：病気で休むという電話があったところです〉
Secretary:
- ◎　　He just called in sick.

4 《アルツハイマー病》
〈彼はアルツハイマー病なんです〉
- ☆ A He has Alzheimer's.
- ◎ B He has Alzheimer's disease.
- ○ C He's suffering from Alzheimer's disease.
- × D He has AD.
- × E He's suffering from AD.
  ❖辞典に D, E が出ているが使われていない.

5 《胃潰瘍》
〈彼は胃潰瘍なんです〉
- ◎ A He has an ulcer.
- ○ B He has a stomach ulcer.
- △ C He has a gastric ulcer.

6 《おたふく風邪》
〈彼はおたふく風邪なんです〉
- ◎ A He has the mumps.
- ○ B He's suffering from the mumps.
- × C He has (infectious) parotitis.

7 《かっけ》
〈彼はかっけなんです〉
- ☆ A He has beriberi.
- ◎ B He's suffering from beriberi.
- △ C He's suffering beriberi.

8 《肝硬変》
〈彼は肝硬変なんです〉
- ☆ A He has cirrhosis of the liver.
- ◎ B He's suffering from cirrhosis of the liver.
- △ C He's suffering of cirrhosis of the liver.
- × D He's suffering liver cirrhosis.
  ❖ D が辞典に出ているが使われていない.

9 《下痢》
〈私は昨日から下痢をしているんです〉
- ◎ A I've had diarrhea since yesterday.
- × B I've had loose bowels since yesterday.
  ❖ B が辞典に出ているが使われていない.

10 《コレラ》
〈彼はコレラなんです〉
- ◎ A He has cholera.
- ○ B He's suffering from cholera.

11 《痔》
〈彼は痔なんです〉
- ◎ A He has hemorrhoids.
- ○ B He's suffering from hemorrhoids.
- × C He has piles.
- × D He has speed bump.
  ❖辞典に C, D が出ているが使われていない.

12 《しょう紅熱》
〈彼はしょう紅熱です〉
- ◎ A He has scarlet fever.

○ B He's suffering from scarlet fever.
13 《食中毒》
〈彼は食中毒です〉
- ☆ A He has food poisoning.
- ◎ B He's suffering from food poisoning.
- ○ C He's suffering food poisoning.

14 《心不全》
〈彼は心不全を起こしているんです〉
- ☆ A He's having a stroke.
- ◎ B He's suffering from a stroke.
- ○ C He's having [suffering from] heart failure.
- × D He's having a heart stroke.

15 《喘息》
〈彼は喘息です〉
- ◎ A He has asthma.
- ○ B He's suffering from asthma.

16 《腸チフス》
〈彼は腸チフスなんです〉
- ◎ A He has typhoid fever.
- ○ B He's suffering from typhoid fever.

17 《点滴を受ける》
a) 受けている状態を述べるとき
〈彼は点滴を受けています〉
- ◎ A He's on an IV.
- △ B He's getting an intravenous drip.

b) 医者に依頼するとき
〈点滴を受けたいのですが〉
- ◎ A Will you give me an IV?
- ◎ B Can I get an IV?
- × C Can I get a DIV?
  ❖日本の病院内では DIV と言っているが，英語では使われていない．

18 《肉離れ》
〈彼は肉離れを起こしているんです〉
- ◎ A He has a pulled muscle.
- △ B He's suffering from a pulled muscle.

19 《熱》
a) 熱が高い
〈彼女は熱が高いんです〉
- ☆ A She has a high fever.
- ◎ B She's running a high fever.
- ◎ C She has a high temperature.
- ○ D She's running a high temperature.

b) 熱が出る
〈あなたは今晩高い熱が出るでしょう〉
- ◎ A You'll get [run, develop, have] a high fever tonight.
- ◎ B You'll be running [getting, developing] a high fever tonight.
- ○ C You'll develop [have, run, get] a high temperature tonight.
- ○ D You'll be running [getting, developing] a high temperature tonight.

❖ temperature より fever の方がよく使われている．

20 《肺炎》
〈彼は肺炎なんです〉
- ☆ A He has pneumonia.
- ◎ B He's suffering from pneumonia.
- ○ C He has inflammation of the lung.

21 《梅毒》
〈彼は梅毒なんです〉
- ◎ A He has syphilis.
- ○ B He's suffering from syphilis.
- × C He's syphilitic.
  ❖ C が辞典に出ているが使われていない．

22 《肺病》
〈彼は肺病なんです〉
- ☆ A He has TB.
- ◎ B He's suffering from TB.
- ○ C He has tuberculosis.
- ○ D He's suffering from tuberculosis.
- × E He has consumption.
  ❖辞典に E が出ているが今は使われていない．

23 《白血病》
〈彼は白血病なんです〉
- ◎ A He has leukemia.
- ○ B He's suffering from leukemia.

24 《不眠症》
〈彼は不眠症なんです〉
- ☆ A He has insomnia.
- ◎ B He's suffering from insomnia.
- ◎ C He can't get to sleep.
- ◎ D He's having trouble [a hard time] sleeping.
- ◎ E He can't sleep.
- ○ F He can't fall asleep.

25 《流感》
〈彼は流感にかかっているんです〉
- ☆ A He has the flu.
- ○ B He's suffering from the flu.

26 《淋病》
〈彼は淋病なんです〉
- ◎ A He has gonorrhea.
- ○ B He's suffering from gonorrhea.

美容外科医 →医者 13

氷山の一角
〈これは氷山の一角だ〉
- ☆ A This is just the tip of the iceberg.
- ◎ B This is only the tip of the iceberg.
- × C This is just the visible peak on an iceberg.
- × D This is nothing but the small part of the iceberg.
  ❖ C, D が辞典に出ているが使われていない．

美容整形手術
1 《目・鼻などの形を整える手術》
a）鼻
〈私は鼻の美容整形手術をしたんです〉
- ◎ A I had [got] a nose job.
- ○ B I had [got] my nose done.

b）あご
〈私はあごの美容整形手術をしたんです〉
- ◎ A I had [got] a chin job.
- ○ B I had [got] my chin done.

c）胸
〈私は胸の美容整形手術をしたんです〉
- ◎ A I had [got] a boob job.
- ◎ B I had [got] a breast job.
- ○ C I had [got] my breasts done.
- ○ D I had [got] my boobs done.

d）目
〈私は目の美容整形手術をしたんです〉
- ◎ A I had [got] my eyes done.
- ○ B I had [got] an eye job.

2 《しわとりの手術》
〈私は顔のしわ取りの美容整形手術をしたんです〉
- ◎ A I had [got] a face-lift.
- ○ B I had [got] my face done.

平等（の）
1 《平等》
〈私は人権の平等をよいものと思っています〉
- ◎ A I believe in the equality of human rights.
- × B I believe in the equalitarianism [egalitarianism] of human rights.
  - ❖ B が辞典に出ているが会話では使われていない．ただし，高い教育レベル対象の文章英語では使われている．

2 《平等の》
a）平等社会
〈アメリカは平等社会です〉
- ◎ A America's an equal society.
- ▽ B America's an equalitarian [egalitarian] society.
  - ❖ B は硬い文章英語では非常によく使われている．

b）平等の立場で
〈私たちはお互いに平等の立場で話すことができなければならない〉
- ◎ A We have to be able to talk to each other on an equal basis.
- ○ B We have to be able to talk to each other on an equal footing.
- ▽ C We have to be able to talk to each other on an equal standing.
- × D We have to be able to talk to each other on one footing.
  - ❖ D が辞典に出ている使われていない．

表明する
〈組合は会社の新しい方針に不満を表明した〉
- ◎ A The union voiced [expressed, stated] dissatisfaction with the company's new policy.
- ○ B The union made known its dissatisfaction with the company's new

policy.
- × C The union manifested [set forth, exhibited] dissatisfaction with the company's new policy.
- ❖ C が辞典に出ているが使われていない．

評論家
〈彼は野球評論家です〉
- ◎ A He's a baseball commentator.
- × B He's a baseball analyst [critic].
  - ❖(1) B が辞典に出ているが使われていない．
  - ❖(2) commentator, analyst, critic の 3 語は次の要領で使い分けられている．

① commentator：主としてテレビ，ラジオなどに出てきて意見を述べる人．日本語では「解説者」にあたることも多い．
例：foreign news commentator（海外ニュース評論家），football commentator（フットボール評論家），baseball commentator（野球評論家），tennis commentator（テニス評論家），boxing commentator（ボクシング評論家），soccer commentator（サッカー評論家），sports commentator（スポーツ評論家），commentator on consumer affairs（消費者問題評論家），political commentator（政治評論家）

② analyst：統計などをもとにした分析・評論を行う人．
例：economic analyst（経済評論家），military analyst（軍事評論家），legal analyst（法律評論家），historical analyst（歴史評論家），criminal analyst（犯罪評論家），education analyst（教育評論家），analyst of juvenile psychology（青少年心理学評論家），aviation analyst（航空評論家）

③ critic：主として芸術についての批評をする人．
例：photography critic（写真評論家），food critic（料理評論家），social critic（社会評論家），music critic（音楽評論家），literary critic（文芸評論家），drama critic（演劇評論家），ballet critic（バレエ評論家），movie critic（映画評論家）

肥沃な
〈これは肥沃な土壌です〉
- ☆ A This soil is fertile.
- ◎ B This soil is rich.
- ◎ C This soil has a high productivity.
- ○ D This soil is productive.

開き直る
1 《挑戦的な態度をとる》
〈彼は私に対して開き直った〉
- ◎ A He turned on me.
- △ B He suddenly got defiant towards me.
- △ C He suddenly took the offensive with me.

2 《「リラックスする」というニュアンスのあるとき》
〈ジャイアンツはペナントレースに勝つ見込みがないと悟ったとき，開き直って実力を発揮しはじめた．その結果 7 連勝した〉
- ◎ When the Giants realized they had no chance of winning the pennant, they relaxed and started displaying their true ability. As a result, they won seven games in a row.

開く
1 《パーティーなどの集まりについて言う場合》

a）ごく普通の集まりのとき
・パーティーを開くことのみに言及するとき
〈金曜日の夜，ささやかなパーティーを開くのですが，いらっしゃいますか〉
- ◎　　We're going to have [throw] a little party on Friday evening. Would you like to come?
・誰のためにパーティーを開くかに言及するとき
〈私たちはビルの昇進祝いのパーティーを開く予定です〉
- ◎　A　We're going to give [throw] Bill a promotion party.
- ◎　B　We're going to give [throw] a promotion party for Bill.
- ◎　C　We're going to have a promotion party for Bill.
- ×　D　We're going to have Bill a promotion party.
  - ❖(1) D が辞典に出ているが使われていない．
  - ❖(2) have は C の型でのみ使う．

b）披露宴・葬儀など改まった集まりのとき
〈どこで披露宴を開くのですか〉
- ◎　A　Where are you going to hold [have] your wedding reception?
- ×　B　Where are you going to throw [give] your wedding reception?

c）準備に話の焦点がある場合
〈孤児たちにクリスマスパーティーを開きましょう〉
- ◎　A　Let's organize [plan] a Christmas party for the orphans.
- ◎　B　Let's prepare [make preparations] for the Christmas party for the orphans.
- ◎　C　Let's give a Christmas party for the orphans.
  - ❖(1) C は話し手が費用を負担することを示す．
  - ❖(2) A は不定冠詞の a，B は定冠詞の the を使う．

2 《演奏会などの興行について言う場合》
a）出演者自身が言うとき
〈私たちは来年コンサートを20回開きます〉
- ☆　A　We're going to perform twenty concerts next year.
- ◎　B　We're going to give [perform in] twenty concerts next year.
- △　C　We're going to put on [hold] twenty concerts next year.

b）出演者以外（事務職員など）が言うとき
〈私たちは来年コンサートを20回開きます〉
- ◎　A　We're going to put on [hold, have] twenty concerts next year.
- △　B　We're going to give twenty concerts next year.

平社員　→地位 15

ひりひりする
〈寒くて顔がひりひりするんです〉
- ◎　A　My face hurts from the cold.
- ○　B　My face is hurting [stinging] from the cold.
- ○　C　My face stings from the cold.
- ×　D　My face smarts from the cold.
  - ❖ D が辞典に出ているが使われていない．

昼間
〈私は普通，昼間は外出しています〉
- ☆　A　I'm usually out during the day.
- ◎　B　I'm usually out in the daytime.
- ○　C　I'm usually out during the daytime.
- △　D　I'm usually out in the day.

▽ E I'm usually out by day.

昼休み →休み 1 d)

卑劣な

〈彼は卑劣な男だ〉

◎ A He's a mean guy.
○ B He's a nasty guy.
△ C He's a despicable guy.
▽ D He's a cowardly [contemptible] guy.
  ❖(1) D は辞典に出ているが会話ではまれ．
  ❖(2) 堅い文章英語では C, D もよく使われている．
  ❖(3) 卑劣さの度合いは C が一番強い．B が2番，A が3番，D は4番．

広い

1 《面積の広さ》

〈セントラル公園は広いです〉

☆ A Central Park's big.
☆ B Central Park covers a lot of ground.
◎ C Central Park covers a big [large] area.
○ D Central Park's large.
○ E Central Park covers a tremendous amount of ground.
○ F Central Park has a lot of acreage.
△ G Central Park covers a lot of acreage.
× H Central Park has a large area.

2 《広々とした感じ》

〈彼の事務所はあなたの事務所ほど広くはありません〉

◎ A His office isn't as roomy as yours.
◎ B His office doesn't have as much room as yours.
◎ C His office isn't as spacious as yours.
○ D His office doesn't have as much space as yours.
  ❖ C, D の方が A, B より広々としている響きがある．

披露宴

〈(結婚)披露宴は何時に始まりますか〉

◎ A What time does the reception start?
○ B What time does the wedding reception start?

広げる

1 《視野》

〈私は視野を広げるために世界一周旅行をしようと計画しています〉

☆ A I'm planning to travel around the world to expand my horizons.
◎ B I'm planning to travel around the world to broaden [widen] my horizons.
○ C I'm planning to travel around the world to expand [broaden] my horizon.
○ D I'm planning to travel around the world to expand [broaden] my way of thinking.
○ E I'm planning to travel around the world to expand [broaden] my outlook.
△ F I'm planning to travel around the world to expand [widen, broaden] my prospects.

2 《住宅》

〈壁を取り払って居間を広げましょう〉

    ☆ A Let's add onto the living room by removing the wall.
    ◎ B Let's enlarge [expand] the living room by removing the wall.
    ◎ C Let's increase the living room's size by removing the wall.
    ○ D Let's add onto [expand, enlarge] the living room space by removing the wall.
3 《店》
〈うちは事務所を小さくして店を広げるつもりなんです〉
    ☆ A We're going to have the store space increased by making the office smaller.
    ◎ B We're going to increase the store space by making the office smaller.
    ◎ C We're going to have the store space enlarged by making the office smaller.
    ◎ D We're going to have [get] more store space by making the office smaller.
    ○ E We're going to have the store space expanded by making the office smaller.
    ○ F We're going to enlarge [expand] the store space by making the office smaller.
    △ G We're going to have the store enlarged [expanded] by making the office smaller.
4 《事業》
〈このデパートはパリに事業を広げる計画です〉
    ◎ A This department store's planning to expand its business [market, operations] into [to] Paris.
    ◎ B This department store's planning to branch out into Paris.
    ◎ C This department store's planning to open a store in Paris.
    ○ D This department store's planning to expand its operation into [to] Paris.

びん詰工場 →工場 7

〔ふ〕

…部
1 《営業部》
〈彼女は営業部で働いています〉
    ◎ A She works in Sales.
    ○ B She works in the Sales Department.
    △ C She works in the Sales Division.
      ❖(1) A を紹介している辞典がないが一番よく使われている.
      ❖(2) C は非常に大きな会社以外では使われていない.
2 《開発部》
〈彼女は開発部で働いています〉
    ◎ A She works in R and D.
    ○ B She works in the R and D Department.
    ○ C She works in Research and Development.
    ○ D She works in the Research and Development Department.
3 《監査部》

⟨彼女は監査部で働いています⟩
- ◎ A She works in Auditing.
- ○ B She works in the Auditing Department.

4 《企画部》
⟨彼女は企画部で働いています⟩
- ◎ A She works in Planning.
- ○ B She works in the Planning Department.
- △ C She works in the Planning Division.

5 《技術部》
⟨彼女は技術部で働いています⟩
- ☆ A She works in Tech Support.
- ○ B She works in the Tech (Support) Department.
- ○ C She works in the Technical Support Department.
- ▽ D She works in the Technical Development Department.
- × E She works in Engineering Department.
  - ❖辞典にEが出ているが「工学部」の意味．したがって，技術部の意味では使われていない．

6 《経理部》
⟨彼女は経理部で働いています⟩
- ◎ A She works in Accounting.
- ○ B She works in the Accounting Department.
- × C She works in the General Accounting Department.

7 《購買部》
⟨彼女は購買部で働いています⟩
- ◎ A She works in Purchasing.
- ○ B She works in the Purchasing Department.
- × C She works in Buying [the Buying Department].

8 《広報部》
⟨彼女は広報部で働いています⟩
- ◎ A She works in Public Relations.
- ◎ B She works in PR.
- ○ C She works in the Public Relations Department.
- △ D She works in the Public Relations Division.
- × E She works at the Public Relations Division.
  - ❖(1) Eを出している辞典があるが，使われていない．
  - ❖(2) Dだけを紹介している辞典が多いが，非常に大きな会社以外では使われていない．

9 《財務部》
⟨彼女は財務部で働いています⟩
- ◎ A She works in Finance.
- ○ B She works in the Finance Department.

10 《市場調査部》
⟨彼女は市場調査部で働いています⟩
- ◎ A She works in Marketing.
- ◎ B She works in the Marketing Department.
  - ❖ある辞典で「営業部」にBを紹介しているが，「市場調査部」の意味でしか使われていない．

11 《審査部》
⟨彼女は審査部で働いています⟩

- ◎ A She works in Credit.
- ○ B She works in the Credit Department.
- △ C She works in Crediting.

12 《人事部》
〈彼女は人事部で働いています〉
- ☆ A She works in Human Resources.
- ◎ B She works in Personnel.
- ○ C She works in HR.
- ○ D She works in the Human Resources Department.
- ○ E She works in the Personnel Department.
- ❖ A, C, D は大きな会社で使われる傾向がある.

13 《生産部》
〈彼女は生産部で働いています〉
- ◎ A She works in Production.
- ○ B She works in the Production Department.
- × C She works in Producing.

14 《総務［庶務］部》
〈彼女は総務［庶務］で働いています〉
- ◎ A She works in General Affairs.
- ○ B She works in the General Affairs Department.

15 《能力開発部》
〈彼女は能力開発部で働いています〉
- ◎ A She works in Personnel Development.
- ○ B She works in Personnel Development Department.

16 《派遣部》
〈彼女は派遣部に勤めています〉
- ◎ A She works in Dispatching.
- ○ B She works in the Dispatching Department.

17 《発送部》
〈彼女は発送部で働いています〉
- ◎ A She works in Shipping.
- ○ B She works in the Shipping [Dispatching] Department.
- ○ C She works in Dispatching.

18 《販売促進部》
〈彼女は販売促進部で働いています〉
- ◎ A She works in Sales Promotion.
- ○ B She works in the Sales Promotion Department.

19 《文書部》
〈彼女は文書部で働いています〉
- ◎ A She works in Legal.
- ○ B She works in the Legal Department.

20 《輸入部》
〈彼女は輸入部で働いています〉
- ◎ A She works in Importing.
- ○ B She works in Import.
- ○ C She works in the Import Department.

不安

1 《社会・経済上の出来事が不安な気持ちを引き起こしているとき》
〈XYZ銀行の倒産は私たちを不安にさせています〉

☆ A XYZ Bank's going bankrupt's worrying us.
◎ B XYZ Bank's going bankrupt's making us insecure [uneasy].
◎ C XYZ Bank's going bankrupt's causing a lot of anxiety among us.
○ D XYZ Bank's going bankrupt's causing a lot of concern [uneasiness] among us.
○ E XYZ Bank's going bankrupt's making us worried [anxious, concerned].

2 《私的な理由で不安な気持ちをいだいているとき》
〈ご主人がハンサムなので彼女は不安なんです〉
◎ A Her husband's good-looking, so she's (feeling) insecure.
◎ B Her husband's good-looking, so she feels insecure.
△ C Her husband's good-looking, so she's apprehensive.
× D Her husband's good-looking, so she's ill at ease.
× E Her husband's good-looking, so she's skittish.

3 《態度・言動に不安を感じているとき》
〈私は息子の態度に不安を感じたんです〉
◎ A I felt like there was a problem with my son's attitude.
◎ B I felt like there was something wrong with my son's attitude.
○ C I felt like there was trouble with my son's attitude.
○ D I felt like there was something up with my son's attitude.
○ E I sensed some concerns [worries] about my son's attitude.
△ F I sensed some anxiety [apprehension, misgiving] about my son's attitude.

不案内だ

1 《住宅地の場合》
〈私はこの辺は不案内なんです〉
◎ A I don't know this neighborhood [area].
◎ B I'm not from around here.
◎ C I'm new to this neighborhood [area].
◎ D I'm a stranger around here.
△ E I'm quite new around here.
△ F I'm quite new in this neighborhood [area].

2 《ビジネス街の場合》
〈私はこの辺は不案内なんです〉
◎ A I'm a stranger around here.
◎ B I'm new to this area.
◎ C I'm not from around here.
◎ D I don't know this area.
△ E I'm quite new around here.
△ F I'm quite new in this area.

部下 →地位 7

不可欠な

1 《どうしても必要なこと》
〈運動は健康に不可欠です〉
☆ A Exercise's absolutely necessary for [to] your good health.
◎ B Exercise's essential for [to] your good health.
△ C Exercise's indispensable for [to] your good health.
△ D Exercise's mandatory for your good health.
▽ E Exercise's mandatory to your good health.

▽ F Exercise's requisite for [to] your good health.
　　❖運動は健康に必要，運動しなければ病気になる．したがって，「どうしても必要」というニュアンスが必要．
　2 《必要だが他の方法もあるとき》
　〈彼女の助言は私たちのプロジェクトに不可欠でした〉
　　◎ A Her advice was indispensable for [to] our project.
　　○ B Her advice was absolutely necessary for [to] our project.
　　△ C Her advice was essential for [to] our project.
　　❖助言は彼女のものでなく，他の人の助言でもいいことも多い．
　3 《規則・法律上の内容のとき》
　〈36 単位が卒業に不可欠です〉
　　☆ A 36 credits're mandatory for graduation.
　　◎ B 36 credits're absolutely necessary for [to] graduation.
　　○ C 36 credits're essential for [to] graduation.
　　△ D 36 credits're requisite for [to] graduation.

不器量な
〈彼女は不器量です〉
　　◎ 　She's homely [plain, plain-looking].
　　❖不器量さは homely が 1 番，plain, plain-looking が 2 番．

副会長　→地位 10
副作用
〈この薬には副作用がありますか〉
　　◎ A Does this medicine have any side effects?
　　△ B Is this medicine free of [from] side effects?
　　▽ C Does this medicine have any aftereffects [secondary effects]?
　　× D Does this medicine have any ill effects?
　　❖D が辞典に出ているが使われていない．

復習する
　1 《理解の確認のためのおさらいを言う場合》
　〈月曜日の授業の前に 8 課を復習しなさい〉
　　◎ A Review Lesson 8 before Monday's class.
　　○ B Go over Lesson 8 before Monday's class.
　2 《もう一度詳しくやり直すことを言う場合》
　〈8 課を復習しなさい〉
　　◎ A Redo Lesson 8.
　　◎ B Do Lesson 8 again [over].
　　❖A, B いずれも，ミスをしたので練習問題などをやり，詳しく復習するという場合に使われている．

腹痛　→痛い 6
ふさぎ込んでいる
〈彼はふさぎ込んでいる〉
　　◎ 　He's moping [gloomy].

不時着する
〈飛行機はハイジャックされたため不時着した〉
　　◎ A The plane made a forced landing because it was hijacked.
　　△ B The plane made an emergency landing because it was hijacked.

無精ひげ
〈社長は無精ひげをはやしていた〉
　　◎ A The boss had a three-day old beard.

- ◎ B The boss was sporting a three-day old beard.
- ○ C The boss had a three-day beard.
- △ D The boss had three days' growth of beard.
- △ E The boss was wearing a three-day beard.
- △ F The boss was wearing three days' growth of beard.
    - ❖「無精ひげをはやす」を wear a three-day beard であると紹介している辞典もある．これは誤りではないが，使用頻度は高くない．「ひげをはやす」にあたる動詞は現代口語では wear よりも have が一般的であることと，three-day old beard のように old を入れた形の方が多いためである．

侮辱する
〈私はあなたを侮辱するつもりはありませんでした〉
- ◎ A I didn't mean to insult you.
- ◎ B I didn't mean to put you down.

婦人科医　→医者 14

ブス
〈彼女はブスだ〉
- ◎ A She's ugly.
- ◎ B She's a butt-ugly.
- ◎ C She looks like she was beaten with an ugly stick.
- ◎ D She's a real dog.
    - ❖(1) B, C は特に若年層に広く使われている．なお，A〜D いずれも男性に対しても等しくよく使われている．
    - ❖(2)「不器量な」の項も参照のこと．

豚小屋
1　《一般的に述べる場合》
〈私は豚小屋を作っているんです〉
- ◎ A I'm building a pigpen.
- ▽ B I'm building a pigsty.

2　《比喩的に述べる場合》
〈彼の事務所は豚小屋です〉
- ◎ A His office is a pigpen [pigsty, dump].
- △ B His office is a garbage heap [pile].
- × C His office is a hogpen [hogsty].
    - ❖ C が辞典に出ているが使われていない．

(道の)二股　→…叉路

2人きりで
〈トムと奥さんは彼の両親と一緒に住む前に，2人きりで暮らしていたのよ〉
- ◎ A Tom and his wife lived (all) by themselves before they moved in with his parents.
- ○ B Tom and his wife lived alone before they moved in with his parents.

負担する
〈私は1人で費用を全部負担することはできません〉
- ◎ A I can't pay [handle] all the expenses by myself.
- ○ B I can't foot [shoulder, bear, assume] all the expenses by myself.
- × C I can't stand [take] all the expenses by myself.
    - ❖ C が辞典に出ているが使われていない．

不通になる
〈東西線は事故のため不通になっています〉
- ◎ A The Tozai Line isn't running because of the accident.

△　B　The Tozai Line has stopped because of the accident.
普通の人
　1　《会話》
　〈普通の人はこの単語を知りません〉
　　◎　A　The average person [guy] doesn't know this word.
　　◎　B　The man on the street doesn't know this word.
　　○　C　The people on the street don't know this word.
　　○　D　Average people don't know this word.
　　○　E　The general public doesn't know this word.
　　○　F　Ordinary people don't know this word.
　　△　G　The people at large don't know this word.
　　▽　H　John Doe [John Q. Public] doesn't know this word.
　　❖Aのguy，Bのmanには女性も入っている．これもアメリカが男性社会で あることを裏書きしている一例．
　2　《新聞》
　〈普通の人はこの単語を知りません〉
　　◎　A　The average person doesn't know this word.
　　◎　B　The people on the street don't know this word.
　　◎　C　Average people don't know this word.
　　○　D　The general public doesn't know this word.
　　○　E　The people at large don't know this word.
　　○　F　John Doe [John Q. Public] doesn't know this word.
普通預金　→預金 2
物価
　1　《一般的に述べるとき》
　〈最近は物価が高い〉
　　◎　A　These days prices're high [expensive].
　　◎　B　These days living costs're high [expensive].
　　○　C　These days the cost of living's high [expensive].
　　×　D　These days prices of commodities're high.
　　❖Dが辞典に出ているが使われていない．
　2　《地域を明示して述べるとき》
　〈東京の物価は高い〉
　　☆　A　Tokyo's very expensive.
　　☆　B　Tokyo prices're very high [expensive].
　　◎　C　Prices in Tokyo're very high [expensive].
　　○　D　Living costs in Tokyo're very high [expensive].
　　○　E　The cost of living in Tokyo's very high [expensive].
　　△　F　Commodity prices in Tokyo're very high [expensive].
　　×　G　Tokyo living costs're very high.
　　×　H　Prices of commodities in Tokyo're very high [expensive].
二日酔い　→酔っ払っている 5
復旧する
　〈東西線はまもなく復旧するでしょう〉
　　☆　A　The Tozai Line'll start [begin] running again soon.
　　◎　B　The Tozai Line'll resume (its) service soon.
　　○　C　The Tozai Line'll resume (its) normal [regular] service soon.
　　○　D　The Tozai Line'll resume its services soon.
　　○　E　The Tozai Line'll resume its normal [regular] services soon.

- ▽ F The Tozai Line'll reopen (its) service soon.
- ▽ G The Tozai Line'll reopen its services soon.
- ▽ H The Tozai Line'll be open to traffic again soon.
- ▽ I The Tozai Line'll return to normal [normalcy] soon.
- ▽ J The Tozai Line'll resume its normal conditions soon.
- ▽ K The Tozai Line'll get back to normal [normalcy] soon.
- ▽ L The Tozai Line'll be restored [brought back] to normalcy soon.
  - ❖ F〜L が辞典に出ているがほとんど使われていない．

ぶつける

1 《車》

a）故意

・非常に強くぶつけたとき

〈彼は車を私の車に激しくぶつけたんです〉

- ◎ He rammed [smashed, slammed, crashed] his car into mine.
  - ❖故意にぶつけたとの響きは ram が 100 %，smash は約 90 %，slam は約 70 %，crash は約 50 % という程度の違いがある．

・強くぶつけたとき

〈彼は車を私の車に強くぶつけたんです〉

- ◎ He ran [drove] his car into mine.
  - ❖故意にぶつけたとの響きは run, drive とも 100 %．

・普通にぶつけたとき

〈彼は車を私の車にぶつけたんです〉

- ◎ A He hit my car.
- ◎ B He bumped his car into mine.

b）非故意

・非常に強くぶつかった

〈彼の車が私の車に激しくぶつかったんです〉

- ◎ A His car smashed [crashed, slammed, rammed] into mine.
- ◎ B He crashed his car into mine.
- △ C He slammed [smashed] his car into mine.
  - ❖ C は故意に「ぶつける」意味では非常によく使われているが，非故意の「ぶつかる」の意味では時々しか使われていないことに注意されたい．

・激しくぶつかったとき

〈彼の車が私の車に激しくぶつかったんです〉

- ◎ A His car crashed [ran] into mine.
- ○ B He ran [drove] his car into mine.
- △ C His car drove into mine.

・普通にぶつかったとき

〈彼の車が私の車にぶつかったんです〉

- ◎ A His car bumped into [hit, collided with] mine.
- ◎ B He bumped [hit] my car.
- ◎ C He bumped his car into mine.
- × D He hit his car into mine.
  - ❖ B は故意・非故意の両方に使われ，そのパーセンテージは両方とも約 50 %．

2 《足をイス・頭を壁などに》

a）普通にぶつけたとき

〈彼は足をイスにぶつけたんです〉

- ◎ A He bumped his leg on [against] the chair.

◎ B He hit his leg on [against] the chair.
○ C He bumped his leg into the chair.
△ D He hit his leg into the chair.
b) 非常に強くぶつけたとき
〈彼は足をイスに非常に強くぶつけたんです〉
◎ A He really whacked his leg on the chair.
◎ B He really slammed his leg on the chair.
◎ C He really smashed his leg on [into, against] the chair.
◎ D He really crashed his leg on the chair.
◎ E He really bumped his leg on [against] the chair.
◎ F He really hit his leg on [against] the chair.
◎ G He really smacked his leg on the chair.
○ H He really smacked his leg against the chair.
○ I He really knocked his leg on [against, into] the chair.
△ J He really slammed his leg against [into] the chair.
△ K He really bumped his leg into the chair.
▽ L He really smacked his leg into the chair.
❖ 強さの度合いは smash, slam が一番強い. crash が 2 番, whack が 3 番, hit が 4 番, smack が 5 番, knock が 6 番, bump が一番弱い.

不動産税 →税金 4
不動産屋 →店 39
太っている
1 《主観的に述べるとき》
a) 男性
〈彼は太っている〉
◎ A He's heavy [big, flabby].
◎ B He's large.
◎ C He's stout.
○ D He's portly.
× E He's plump.
❖ B は背が高く, 腕・胸などの筋肉が隆々としていて, 横幅も広いという響きがある. C, D は背が低くずんぐりしているというニュアンス.

b) 女性
〈彼女は太っている〉
◎ A She's heavy [big, large, flabby].
△ B She's plump [beerbellied].
× C She's stout [corpulent, corn-fed, portly].
2 《客観的に述べるとき》
〈彼は太っています〉
◎ He's overweight [obese].
3 《でぶと述べるとき》
〈彼女はでぶです〉
☆ A She's fat.
◎ B She's as big as a house.
◎ C She's chubby [chunky].
○ D She's pudgy.
○ E She's a fatso [a cow].
○ F She's as big as a whale.
△ G She's a tab of lard.

- △ H She's as big as a cow.
- ▽ I She's tubby.
- ❖太っている程度はA, Bが一番強い．D〜Iはほぼ同じで2番．Cは3番．

4 《ビール腹》
a）男性の場合
〈私はおなかが出てき始めた〉
- ☆ A I'm starting to get a spare tire.
- ☆ B I'm starting to get love handles.
- ☆ C I'm starting to get a beer belly.
- ◎ D I'm starting to get a (pot) belly.
- ○ E I'm starting to get a roll.
- △ F I'm starting to get a paunch.

b）女性の場合
〈私はおなかが出てきたんです〉
- ◎ A I'm starting to get my belly.
- △ B I'm starting to get my roll.

5 《肥満》
〈肥満はアメリカの社会では大きな問題です〉
- ☆ A Obesity's a big health problem in American society.
- ◎ B Being obese's [overweight's] a big health problem in American society.
- ○ C Obesity's a big problem in American society.
- × D Obesity's a big social problem in America.
  - ❖アメリカでは問題を社会問題と言わずに健康問題，経済問題などとひとつひとつの問題として表現する．一方，日本では全体，つまり社会全体の問題と考える．したがって，英語と日本語との表現に差が出てくるのはどうしようもない．

6 《太り気味》
〈彼女は太り気味です〉
- ☆ A She's a little heavy.
- ◎ B She's kind of heavy.
- ◎ C She's on the heavy side.
- ◎ D She's a little large [big].
- ○ E She's kind of big [large].
- ○ F She's somewhat heavy [large].
- △ G She's sort of heavy [large, big].
- △ H She's on the large [big] side.
- △ I She's somewhat big.
- △ J She's heavish.
- × K She's biggish [largish].

腐敗している

1 《社会》
〈私たちの社会は腐敗している〉
- ◎ A Our society's corrupt.
- ○ B Our society's corrupted.
- △ C Our society's rotten [dirty].
- ▽ D Our society's filthy.

2 《人の心》
〈この国の政治家はほとんど腐敗している〉

◎ A Most Politicians in this country're corrupt.
　　△ B Most Politicians in this country're corrupted [dirty].
　　▽ C Most Politicians in this country're rotten [filthy].
　3　《「非常に腐敗している」と述べるとき》
　　〈私たちの社会は非常に腐敗している〉
　　◎ A Our society's rotten to the core.
　　◎ B Our society's really corrupt.
　　○ C Our society's very corrupt.
　　○ D Our society's really corrupted.
　　△ E Our society's very corrupted.

不法侵入
〈彼は建物に不法侵入した科で逮捕されたんです〉
　　☆ A He was arrested for breaking and entering the building.
　　◎ B He was arrested for trespassing in the building.
　　○ C He was arrested on charges of forced entry into the building.
　　▽ D He was arrested on charges of forcible entry into the building.
　　× E He was arrested on charges of intrusion of the building.
　　× F He was arrested on breach of close of the building.
　　❖ E, F が辞典に出ているが使われていない．D も辞典に出ているがまれに使われる程度．

不眠症　→病気 24

増やす
　1　《語彙》
　　〈私は語彙を増やさなければならないんです〉
　　◎ A I have to improve [expand, increase, enlarge] my vocabulary.
　　○ B I have to make my vocabulary bigger.
　　○ C I have to build up [strengthen] my vocabulary.
　2　《人員》
　　◎ A We have to increase the staff.
　　○ B We have to beef up [expand, boost, build up] the staff.
　3　《資本》
　　〈うちは資本を増やさなければならないんです〉
　　◎ A We have to increase the capital.
　　○ B We have to build up [boost] the capital.
　　× C We have to expand [beef up] the capital.
　4　《予算》
　　〈私たちは研究開発の予算を増やすように，会社にお願いしているんです〉
　　◎ A We're asking the management to boost [increase, raise, beef up, add to] the R and D budget.
　　○ B We're asking the management to hike the R and D budget.
　　× C We're asking the management to multiply the R and D budget.
　　❖ C が辞典に出ているが使われていない．

プライド
　1　《違法的および道徳的な内容》
　　〈私はプライドがあるから不法なことは何もできません〉
　　◎ A I can't do anything illegal because of my morals [ethics, integrity].
　　○ B I can't do anything illegal because of my conscience.
　　× C I can't do anything illegal because of my pride.
　　❖ break the law（法律を破る），steal（盗む），break the contract（契約を

破る), tell a lie（うそをつく）は英米人にとっては道徳（morals），倫理（ethics），良心（conscience），誠実（sincerity）の問題で，pride（誇り）とは無関係．しかし，日本人は文化上体面を大きな問題にするので「プライド」と言う．

2 《道徳上かつプライド的な内容》

〈私はプライドのために妻が不倫したことを許せなかったんです〉

◎ A I couldn't forgive my wife's cheating on me because of my pride [morals].
× B I couldn't forgive my wife's cheating on me because of my ethics.
❖ B の ethics は職業上の道徳に関係がないときは使われていない．

ふらふらする

1 《多忙のとき》

〈私はとても忙しいんです．頭がふらふらするんです〉

◎ A I'm so busy. My head's spinning.
○ B I'm so busy. My head's swimming.
△ C I'm so busy. My head spins [swims].
× D I'm so busy. My head's reeling.
❖ D が辞典に出ているが使われていない．

2 《身体の不調のとき》

〈熱があるんです．頭がふらふらするんです〉

◎ A I have a fever. My head's spinning.
◎ B I have a fever. I feel dizzy.
○ C I have a fever. My head's swimming.

3 《重い物を持ったとき》

〈足がふらふらだよ〉

◎ My legs're giving way [giving out].

4 《疲れたとき》

〈ふらふらだよ〉

◎ I'm groggy [exhausted, tired out].

5 《決心がつかないとき》

〈彼は心がふらふらしてるんです〉

◎ A He hasn't made up his mind.
◎ B He hasn't made his decision yet.
○ C He's wavering on his decision.
× D He's swaying [faltering] in his mind.
❖ D が辞典に出ているが使われていない．

ぶらぶらする

1 《「さぼる」という意味のとき》

〈上司：ぶらぶらするな．仕事に戻れよ〉

Supervisor:

◎ A Don't fool [mess] around. Go back to work.
◎ B Don't goof off. Go back to work.
◎ C Don't screw around. Go back to work.
○ D Don't play [goof] around. Go back to work.
❖語調は C が一番強い．A が 2 番，D が 3 番，B が 4 番．

2 《「時間をつぶす」という意味のとき》

〈今忙しくて話せないんだ．だからしばらくぶらぶらしててくれますか〉

◎ I'm too busy to talk to you now, so will you stick [hang] around for a while?

振られる
  1 《一定の期間交際した後で振られる場合》
〈彼はガールフレンドに振られたんです〉
- ◎ A His girlfriend dumped him.
- ○ B His girlfriend dropped him.
- ○ C He was dumped by his girlfriend.
- ▽ D His girlfriend jilted him.
  - ❖(1) D が辞典に紹介されているが，今は老人の間でしか使われていない．
  - ❖(2) dump にはおどけた響きがあるとしている辞典もあるが，そういった事実はない．

  2 《初めてデートなどに誘って振られる場合》
〈ジム：元気がないね．どうしたんだい〉
Jim: You're in low spirits. What happened?
〈ビル：リンダを誘ったら振られたんだ〉
Bill:
- ◎ A I asked Linda out. She turned me down.
- ◎ B I asked Linda out. She blew me off.
- ○ C I asked Linda out. She gave me the cold shoulder.

❖ A は主として 35 歳以上，B は若年層の間で使われている．

ふりをする
〈彼は寝ているふりをした〉
- ◎ A He pretended to be sleeping.
- ◎ B He pretended that he was sleeping.
- ○ C He made believe that he was sleeping.
- ○ D He acted like he was sleeping.
- ○ E He faked sleeping.

フル回転する
〈工場はフル回転しています〉
- ☆ A The factory's in full swing.
- ☆ B The factory's operating at full capacity.
- ◎ C The factory's going in full swing.
- ○ D The factory's in full operation.
- ○ E The factory's going (at) full steam.
- △ F The factory's hitting on all cylinders [eight].

ブレーキをかける
  1 《一般的に述べる場合》
〈どうしてブレーキをかけなかったのですか〉
- ☆ A Why didn't you step on the brakes?
- ◎ B Why didn't you put on [push] the brakes?
- ○ C Why didn't you use the brakes?
- ▽ D Why didn't you apply the brakes?
  - ❖ D は辞典に出ているがまれ．

  2 《急ブレーキをかける場合》
〈急ブレーキをかけるな〉
- ◎ A Don't jam on [hit] the brakes.
- ◎ B Don't slam your foot on the brakes.
- ◎ C Don't brake hard.

ブレーン
〈A 氏はブッシュ大統領のブレーンです〉

- ◎ A Mr. A is an advisor to President Bush.
- ◎ B Mr. A is one of President Bush's closest advisors.
- △ C Mr. A is a member of President Bush's Brain Trust.
- ❖ C が辞典に出ているがあまり使われていない．

プレゼント

1 《一対一のような場面》
〈これ私のプレゼントです〉
- ☆ A This is for you.
- ◎ B Here's a little something [gift, present] for you.
- ◎ C Here's something for you.
- ○ D This is a present [gift] for you.
- × E This is my present for you.
- ❖ gift と present は全く同じで，ニュアンス上の違いはない．

2 《祝福される人に多数の人がプレゼントを渡しているとき》
〈これ私のプレゼントです〉
- ◎ A This is my present for you.
- ◎ B Here's my present for you.
- ○ C This is for you.
- ○ D Here's something for you.
- ○ E Here's a little present [gift, something] for you.
- ○ F This is a present [gift] for you.
- ❖ 多数の人がプレゼントを渡しているとき，自分のと他の人との区別がつかなくなる心配から，A, B が C～F より多く使われる．

プレゼントする
〈彼は私の昇進祝いにこの時計をプレゼントしてくれたんです〉
- ◎ A He gave me this watch for my promotion.
- × B He presented me with this watch for my promotion.
- ❖(1) B が辞典に出ているが使われていない．
- ❖(2) 動詞の present は「贈呈する」という意味ではよく使われているが，日常的な「贈物をする」という意味では使われない．

プレッシャーをかける
〈プレッシャーをかけないで下さい〉
- ◎ A Don't pressure me.
- ○ B Don't put pressure on me.
- △ C Don't put the squeeze on me.

プレハブ →家 11

風呂に入る

1 《1回のとき》
〈私は毎日お風呂に入ります〉
- ◎ A I take a (hot) bath every day.
- ○ B I have a (hot) bath every day.
- △ C I use a (hot) bath every day.
- ❖ C は辞典に出ているが時々使われる程度．

2 《2回以上のとき》
〈私は毎日3回お風呂に入ります〉
- ◎ A I take three (hot) baths every day.
- ◎ B I take a (hot) bath three times every day.
- ○ C I have three (hot) baths every day.
- ○ D I have a (hot) bath three times every day.

3 《お風呂に入れる》
〈彼女は赤ちゃんをお風呂に入れています〉
- ◎ A She's giving her baby a bath.
- △ B She's bathing [washing] her baby.

プロポーズする
〈なぜかモリスには彼女にプロポーズする勇気がどうしても出なかった〉
- ◎ A Somehow, Morris could never summon up the courage to propose to her.
- ◎ B Somehow, Morris could never summon up the courage to ask her to marry him.
- ▽ C Somehow, Morris could never summon up the courage to seek her hand in marriage.
- ▽ D Somehow, Morris could never summon up the courage to pay court [his addresses] to her.
- ▽ E Somehow, Morris could never summon up the courage to court [woo] her.
- ▽ F Somehow, Morris could never summon up the courage to ask [sue] for her hand.
    - ❖ C〜F が多くの辞典・英文法書に出ているが、いずれも古い表現で、今ではほとんど使われていない。

不渡り手形を出す
1 《会社》
〈XYZ 会社は昨日不渡り手形を 10 枚出したんです〉
- ◎ A XYZ Company wrote [issued] ten bad checks yesterday.
- ○ B XYZ Company bounced ten checks yesterday.
- × C XYZ Company wrote ten rubbers [dishonored checks] yesterday.
- × D XYZ Company failed ten checks yesterday.
- × E XYZ Company passed ten drafts yesterday.
    - ❖ C, D, E が辞典に出ているが使われていない。

2 《個人》
〈彼は昨日不渡り手形を 10 枚出したんです〉
- ◎ A He wrote ten bad checks yesterday.
- ○ B He bounced ten bad checks yesterday.
- × C He issued ten bad checks yesterday.

分別がある
〈彼は分別があります〉
- ◎ A He has common [good] sense.
- ○ B He's a sensible man.
- △ C He has a lot of sense.
- △ D He's a man of sense.
- × E He's prudent [discreet].
    - ❖ D は堅い文章英語では非常によく使われている。

文房具店　→店 32

分類する
〈アルファベット順にそれらを分類しよう〉
- ◎ A Let's categorize [group, divide] them in alphabetical order.
- ○ B Let's classify [break, class] them in alphabetical order.
- △ C Let's sort [distribute] them in alphabetical order.

[へ]

…へ…しに行く

1 《スーパー・デパートなどへ買い物に行くとき》
〈彼女は西友へ買い物に行きました〉
- ◎ A She went shopping at Seiyu.
- ○ B She went shopping in Seiyu.
- × C She went shopping to Seiyu.

2 《湖へ泳ぎに行くとき》
〈湖へ泳ぎに行こう〉
- ◎ A Let's go swimming in the lake.
- ○ B Let's go swimming at the lake.
    - ❖ 湖から離れた所にいるときは at の方がよく使われている。そばにいれば in の方がよく使われている。

3 《湖へ釣りに行くとき》
〈湖へ釣りに行こう〉
- ◎ A Let's go fishing at the lake.
- ○ B Let's go fishing by the lake.
- ○ C Let's go fishing in the lake.
    - ❖ A, B は湖のそばにいないとき、C は主として湖のそばにいるときに使われている。

4 《湖へキャンプに行くとき》
〈湖へキャンプに行こう〉
- ◎ A Let's go camping at [by] the lake.
- ○ B Let's go camping beside the lake.

5 《湖へスケートに行くとき》
〈湖へスケートに行こう〉
- ◎ Let's go skating on [at] the lake.
    - ❖ on the lake は湖のそばにいるときに、at the lake は湖のそばにいないときに主として使われている。

閉鎖する

1 《工場など》
〈うちはデトロイトの工場を閉鎖する予定です〉
- ◎ A We're going to close [close down, shut down] the factory in Detroit.
- ○ B We're going to close up the factory in Detroit.
- △ C We're going to shut the factory in Detroit.
    - ❖(1) A, B, C のいずれも、一時的閉鎖、永久的閉鎖の両方について用いられる。
    - ❖(2) 辞典に永久的閉鎖には close down、一時的閉鎖には shut down を用いるとあるが、慣用的にはこのような区別はなされていない。

2 《学級閉鎖》
〈流感のため当分学校は閉鎖されます〉
- ◎ A School will be closed [closed down, shut down] for a while because of the flu.
- × B School will be shut for a while because of the flu.

平日は
〈私は平日はあなたにお会いできません〉
- ◎ A I can't see you during the week.
- ○ B I can't see you on weekdays.
  - ❖ A は特定の週,または不特定の週の両方に使われている.B は特定の週には使われていない.

平和を愛する
〈日本人は平和を愛する国民です〉
- ◎ A The Japanese're a peaceful people.
- ◎ B The Japanese're a peace-loving people.
- × C The Japanese're a peaceable people.
  - ❖(1) C は辞典に出ているが使われていない.
  - ❖(2) 多くの辞典で C は「平和を愛する」,A は「平和な」としているが,A を使うのが一般的.C はアメリカでは使われず,イギリスでも使われてもまれ.

別居する
1 《どちらが望んだかを明示しない場合》
〈トムとメアリーは別居したんです〉
- ◎ A Tom and Mary separated.
- ◎ B Tom and Mary got [were] separated.
- ◎ C Tom and Mary got a separation.
- ○ D Tom was separated from Mary.
  - ❖ D は Mary が望んだというニュアンスは約 40 %,Tom が望んだというニュアンスは約 60 %.

2 《一方が望んだことを明示する場合》
〈リンダは夫と別居したんです〉
- ◎ A Linda separated from her husband.
- ◎ B Linda was separated from her husband.
- ○ C Linda got separated from her husband.
- ○ D Linda got a separation from her husband.
  - ❖ B は夫が望んだというニュアンスもありうるが,リンダが望んだというニュアンスの方が 6 対 4 程度の割合で強い.

別荘
1 《分譲マンション・一軒家のどちらにも使える》
〈彼らはサンフランシスコに別荘を持っています〉
- ◎ They have a vacation [second] home in San Francisco.

2 《一軒家》
〈彼らはサンフランシスコに別荘を持っています〉
- ◎ They have a vacation [second] house in San Francisco.

3 《山荘》
〈彼らは別荘を持っています〉
- ◎ A They have a cottage.
- ○ B They have a country cottage [house].

4 《夏だけの別荘》
〈彼らは別荘を持っています〉
- ☆ A They have a summer home.
- ◎ B They have a summer house.
- ○ C They have a summer place.

5 《豪邸》

〈彼らはフロリダに別荘を持っています〉
- ◯ They have a villa in Florida.
  ❖ villa はほとんどの辞典で紹介しているが，アメリカ人は知らない人が多い．教育レベルの高い人または上流階級の人たちの間ではよく使われている．

別に
〈リンダ：おなかが空いているの〉
Linda: Are you hungry?
〈ジム：別に〉
Jim:
- ◎ A Not really.
- ◯ B Not quite.
- ◯ C Not exactly.

ぺてん師 →詐欺師 6

へとへと
〈私はへとへとです〉
- ☆ A I'm exhausted.
- ☆ B I'm really tired.
- ◎ C I'm worn [tired] out.
- ◎ D I'm dead tired.
- ◯ E I'm very tired.
- ◯ F I'm run down.
- ◯ G I'm wiped out.
- ◯ H I'm pooped.
- △ I I'm bushed.
- △ J I'm dog [quite] tired.
- △ K I'm used up.
- × L I'm all in.
- × M I'm done [knocked] up.
- × N I'm tired to death.
  ❖(1) L, M, N が辞典に出ているが使われていない．
  ❖(2) A が一番へとへとの度合いが強いという響きがある．

減らす
1 《体重》
〈私は体重を減らさなければならないんです〉
- ☆ A I have to lose (some) weight.
- ◎ B I have to take off [drop] a few pounds.
- ◯ C I have to take off some weight.
- ◯ D I have to get rid of a few pounds.
- △ E I have to get rid of [drop] some weight.
- △ F I have to shed a few pounds.
- × G I have to reduce [decrease] some weight.
- × H I have to drop weight.

2 《アルコール・タバコ・食べ物・嗜好品など》
〈私はアルコールを減らさなければならないな〉
- ☆ A I have to cut back [down] on the alcohol.
- ◎ B I have to take it easy [go easy] on the alcohol.
- ◯ C I have to reduce the alcohol.
- △ D I have to slow down [decrease] the alcohol.

3 《社員》
〈うちは社員を減らさなければならないんです〉
- ☆ A We have to downsize.
- ◎ B We have to cut the personnel.
- ○ C We have to cut back [down] on personnel.
- ○ D We have to cut [downsize] personnel.
- △ E We have to reduce [decrease] (the) personnel.

❖詳細は「リストラする」を参照のこと．

ぺらぺら →上手です 1 a)

偏見を持つ

〈彼は彼らに対して偏見を持っている〉
- ◎ A He is prejudiced [biased] against them.
- ◎ B He has a prejudice against them.
- ○ C He has a bias against them.
- △ D He has a warped attitude towards them.
- △ E He is prejudiced towards them.

❖ D, E が辞典に出ているが時々使われる程度．

弁護士 →職業 5
編集長 →職業 23
編成する

1 《予算を》
〈私たちは予算を編成しなければならない〉
- ◎ A We have to write (up) our budget.
- ○ B We have to put together [make up] our budget.
- △ C We have to make our budget.

2 《番組を》
〈私の仕事はテレビ番組を編成することです〉
- ◎ A My job is to produce TV programs.
- ○ B My job is to put TV programs together.

3 《人材を》
〈学生をテストの結果によって編成すべきだと思う〉
- ◎ A I think we should place students based on the results of their tests.
- ○ B I think we should assign students based on the results of their tests.

変装する

1 《状態を述べるとき》
〈彼は修道士に変装していた〉
- ◎ A He was disguising himself as a monk.
- ◎ B He was wearing a monk outfit.
- ◎ C He was dressed up [disguised] as a monk.
- ○ D He wore a disguise as a monk.
- ○ E He had a disguise on as a monk.

2 《動作を述べるとき》
〈彼は修道士に変装した〉
- ◎ A He dressed up [disguised himself] as a monk.
- × B He camouflaged [costumed] as a monk.
- × C He put into a costume as a monk.

❖ B, C が辞典に出ているが使われていない．

ベンツ

〈私はベンツを買おうと思っています〉

◎ A I'm thinking of buying a Mercedes.
△ B I'm thinking of buying a Mercedes-Benz.
× C I'm thinking of buying a Benz.

変動する

〈ドルと円の為替相場は当分変動し続けるでしょう〉

☆ A The exchange rate between the dollar and the yen'll fluctuate for a while.
◎ B The exchange rate between the dollar and the yen'll vary for a while.
○ C The exchange rate between the dollar and the yen'll move up and down for a while.
○ D The exchange rate between the dollar and the yen'll yo-yo for a while.
△ E The exchange rate between the dollar and the yen'll waver for a while.

便利な

1 《近くて便利》

〈彼の家は駅の近くの便利なところにある〉

◎ A His house is really close to the station.
◎ B His house is right around the corner from the station.
◎ C His house is right next to the station.
△ D His house is conveniently located near the station.

❖(1)「便利な」というとまず convenient という語を思い浮かべる人が多いだろう．しかし，この語は改まった話以外ではあまり使われない．

❖(2)「近くて便利な」という言い方は英語ではあまりせず，A, B, C のように「とても近い」ということによって便利だというニュアンスも同時に表すのが普通．

2 《辞書などが「役に立つ」という意味のとき》

〈これは便利な辞書です〉

◎ A This is a useful dictionary.
◎ B This dictionary's useful.
○ C This dictionary comes in handy.
△ D This is a handy dictionary.

〔ほ〕

防音の

〈この家は防音してあります〉

◎ A This house is soundproof.
△ B This house is soundproofed.

法外な →高い 1 e)
忙殺される →忙しい 4
法人税 →税金 3

法人組織になっている

〈林さん：あなたの会社は法人組織になっているのですか〉
Mr. Hayashi:
　　◎　Is your company incorporated?
〈阿部さん：はい，そうです．節税のために5年前に法人組織にしました〉

Mr. Abe:
◎ Yes, it is. I incorporated it five years ago to save on taxes.

宝石

1 《イヤリング・ネックレス・腕輪・時計などの宝石品》
〈彼女はたくさん宝石類を持っています〉
- ◎ A She has a lot of jewelry.
- × B She has a lot of jewels [gems].
  - ❖ B が辞典に出ているが使われていない．

2 《ダイヤモンドなどの非加工品としての宝石》
〈彼女はたくさん宝石類を持っています〉
- ◎ A She has a lot of jewels.
- × B She has a lot of jewelry.

3 《イヤリング・ネックレス・腕輪・時計などの宝石店》
〈彼女は宝石店に勤めています〉
- ◎ A She works for a jewelry store.
- × B She works for a jewels store.
  - ❖「店」の項も参照のこと．

呆然とする

1 《ショック》
〈私は父が突然死亡して呆然としていました〉
- ◎ I was shocked [stunned] by my father's sudden death.

2 《ショックだけでなく対処の困難さを述べるとき》
〈私は父が突然死亡して悲しみで呆然としていました〉
- ◎ A I was overcome with grief because of my father's sudden death.
- ○ B I was overwhelmed with grief because of my father's sudden death.
  - ❖ overwhelm は父の死後，精神的にショックを受けただけでなく，その後に起きた事態に対しての精神的・肉体的な困難さを意味している．

放送する

1 《テレビの場合》
〈NBC がこのボクシングの試合をテレビで放送します〉
- ◎ NBC'll televise [show, telecast, air, broadcast] this boxing match.
  - ❖ air, broadcast はともに，「テレビで放送する」場合にも「ラジオで放送する」場合にも使われる．どちらの意味になるかは文脈によって判断する．

2 《ラジオの場合》
〈野球の試合は NPR によってラジオで放送されます〉
- ◎ The baseball game'll be aired [broadcast] on NPR.

方法

1 《選択肢がないと言いたいとき》
〈うちにはデトロイトの工場を売る以外，他に方法がないね〉
- ☆ A We have no other choice but to sell the factory in Detroit.
- ◎ B We have no other option [solution] but to sell the factory in Detroit.
- ○ C We have no other alternative but to sell the factory in Detroit.
- △ D We have no other way but to sell the factory in Detroit.
- ▽ E We have no other selection but to sell the factory in Detroit.
  - ❖辞典，参考書の例文に「(…以外の)方法」に way を出しているが，あまり使われていない．

2 《「(…するのに一番いい)方法」と言いたいとき》
〈フランス語を話せるようにする方法は何ですか〉

- ☆ A What's the best way to learn to speak French?
- ◎ B What's the best method to learn to speak French?
- △ C What's the best manner to learn to speak French?

暴落する →下がる 8

法律で認められている

1 《行為を述べるとき》

〈この通りに駐車することは法律で認められていない〉

- ☆ A Parking on this street's against the law.
- ◎ B Parking on this street isn't legal.
- ◎ C Parking on this street isn't allowed.
- ◎ D Parking on this street's illegal.
- ○ E Parking on this street's prohibited.
- ○ F Parking on this street isn't legalized.
- △ G Parking on this street isn't permitted.
- ▽ H Parking on this street's never lawful.
- × I Parking on this street isn't legitimate.
    - ❖ I がある辞典に出ているが全く使われていない．H が数冊の辞典に lawful の模範文例として出ているがまれ．lawful は下記の 3「合法的」というニュアンスのとき以外は多くの辞典に例文が出ているがまれにしか使われていない．

2 《「正統な」というニュアンスのとき》

〈チャールズ王子は正統な王位継承者なのですが，たぶん彼はなれないでしょう〉

- ◎ A Prince Charles is the legitimate heir to the throne but he probably can't be.
- △ B Prince Charles is the legal heir to the throne but he probably can't be.
- ▽ C Prince Charles is the lawful heir to the throne but he probably can't be.

3 《「合法的に」というニュアンスのとき》

〈あなたはそれを合法的に解決しなければなりません〉

- ◎ A You have to solve it legally.
- ◎ B You have to solve it the right way.
- ◎ C You have to solve it by legitimate means.
- ○ D You have to solve it by lawful means.
- ○ E You have to solve it legitimately [lawfully].
    - ❖ B は法的手続き以外のことにも使える．

暴力団

1 《成人の暴力団》

a) 漠然と述べるとき

〈彼は暴力団なんです〉

- ☆ A He's in the mob.
- ◎ B He's in the Mafia.
- ◎ C He's in the (crime) family.
- ◎ D He's a member of the mob [the Mafia].
- ◎ E He's a part of the mob [the Mafia].
- ○ F He's a part of the crime family.
- △ G He's a mob member [a mobster].
- △ H He's a part of the family.
- × I He's a gangster [a gangsta].

❖(1) 暴力団はアメリカではひとつの組織が広い地域を支配している．したがって，A は He's in a mob.ではなく He's in the mob.と定冠詞の the を使う．B〜F までも同じ理由で a ではなく the を使う．
❖(2) I が辞典に出ているが今は使われていない．
b）所属暴力団名に言及するとき
〈彼はカポネ暴力団の一員です〉
- ☆ A He's in the Capone Mob [Mafia].
- ◎ B He's a member of the Capone Mob [Mafia].
- ◎ C He's a member of the Capone (Crime) Family.
- ◎ D He's in the Capone (Crime) Family.
- ◎ E He's a part of the Capone Mob [Mafia].
- ◎ F He's a part of the Capone (Crime) Family.
- ◎ G He belongs to the Capone Mob [Mafia].
- ○ H He belongs to the Capone (Crime) Family.
- ○ I He's a Capone Mob [Mafia] member.
- ○ J He's a Capone (Crime) Family member.

2 《10代の若者の暴力団》
〈彼は暴力団員です〉
- ◎ A He's in a gang.
- ◎ B He's a gang member.
- ◎ C He's a member of a gang.
- ◎ D He belongs to a gang.
- ○ E He's a part of a gang.
- × F He's a gangster [a gangsta].
  ❖F が辞典に出ているが今はもう使われていない．

暴力をふるう
〈彼は怒るといつも暴力をふるうんです〉
- ☆ A Whenever he gets angry, he gets violent.
- ◎ B Whenever he gets angry, he becomes violent.
- ○ C Whenever he gets angry, he resorts to violent.
- △ D Whenever he gets angry, he uses violence.

ボーイ長　→職業 38

ホームページを開く
〈あなたはいつインターネットにホームページを開くのですか〉
- ☆ A When're you going to create a home page on the internet?
- ◎ B When're you going to set up [put up] a home page on the internet?
- ○ C When're you going to make [start, build, establish] a home page on the internet?
  ❖詳細は「サイト」の項を参照のこと．

ボーリング場
〈ボーリング場へ行こう〉
- ◎ A Let's go to the bowling alley.
- × B Let's go to the bowling center [ground].
  ❖B が辞典に出ているが使われていない．

墓穴を掘る
〈あなたは墓穴を掘っているよ〉
- ◎ A You're going to get yourself in trouble.
- ◎ B You're asking for trouble.
- ○ C You're digging your own grave.

- ○ D You're inviting trouble.
- △ E You're getting yourself in trouble.

保険をかける

1 《ただ保険に加入することのみを言う場合》

〈私はこのビルに火災保険をかけようと思っているんです〉

- ◎ A I'm thinking of buying [taking out, getting] (some) fire insurance on this building.
- ◎ B I'm thinking of buying [taking out, getting] a fire insurance policy on this building.

2 《保険の金額を明示する場合》

〈このビルには2億円の火災保険をかけています〉

- ☆ A This building has a ¥200,000,000 fire insurance policy.
- ◎ B This building is insured against fire for ¥200,000,000.
- ◎ C This building has fire insurance in the amount of ¥200,000,000.
- △ D This building carries [keeps] a ¥200,000,000 fire insurance policy.

3 《保険の金額と保険会社を明示する場合》

〈私は三井でこのビルに1億円の火災保険をかけました〉

- ◎ A I bought a hundred million yen fire insurance policy on [for] this building with Mitsui Fire Insurance Company.
- ◎ B I bought a hundred million yen worth of fire insurance for this building with Mitsui Fire Insurance Company.

誇りを持っている

1 《自分自身に対して》

〈私は自分自身に誇りを持っています〉

- ◎ A I'm proud of myself.
- ◎ B I take [have] pride in myself.
- ◎ C I'm proud the way I am.
- ◎ D I'm proud who I am.
- ○ E I'm proud to be myself.
- × F I'm proud I'm myself.

2 《現在の幸運・現在の状態に感謝して述べるとき》

〈私はフランス人であることに誇りを持っています〉

- ☆ A I'm proud to be French.
- ◎ B I'm proud of being French.
- ◎ C I'm proud I'm French.
- ○ D I take pride in being French.
- △ E I have pride in being French.

3 《今やっていることに対して》

〈あなたはやっていることに対して誇りを持つべきです〉

- ☆ A You should have pride in what you're doing.
- ◎ B You should take pride in what you're doing.
- ◎ C You should be proud of what you're doing.
- ○ D You should show pride in what you're doing.

4 《達成したこと・内容に対して》

〈あなたはやったことに誇りを持つべきです〉

- ☆ A You should be proud of what you did.
- ◎ B You should take [show] pride in what you did.
- ○ C You should have pride in what you did.

5 《達成した地位に対して》

〈私は弁護士であることに誇りを持っています〉
- ☆ A I'm proud of being a lawyer.
- ◎ B I'm proud to be a lawyer.
- ○ C I'm proud of I'm a lawyer.
- ○ D I take pride in being a lawyer.
- △ E I have pride in being a lawyer.

保証されている

1 《製品が》

〈この時計は 10 年間保証されています〉
- ◎ A This watch has [carries] a ten-year warranty.
- ◎ B This watch has [carries] a ten-year guarantee.
- ◎ C This watch is guaranteed [warranted] for ten years.

2 《人の将来などが》

〈彼はハーバードの卒業生なんです．だから彼の将来は保証されています〉
- ◎ He's a Harvard graduate, so his future's secured [guaranteed, assured].

保証人 →連帯保証人

補助金

1 《一般に》

〈私たち農夫は政府の補助金が必要なんです〉
- ◎ A We farmers need government subsidies [aid, assistance].
- ◎ B We farmers need subsidies [financial help] from the government.
- ◎ C We farmers need to be subsidized by the government.

2 《研究目的と明示する場合》

〈私は政府から研究のための補助金をもらいました〉
- ◎ A I got a government grant for my research.
- ◎ B I got a grant for my research from the government.
- × C I got a grant-in-aid from the government.
  - ❖ C が辞典に出ているが使われていない．

ボタン

1 《はずれている》

a) ボタンが主語のとき

〈あなたの 2 番目のボタンがはずれていますよ〉
- ◎ A Your second button's open.
- ○ B Your second button's undone.
- △ C Your second button's unfastened.
- × D Your second button's unbuttoned.

b) ボタンが主語でないとき

〈シャツのボタンがはずれていますよ〉
- ◎ A Your shirt's unbuttoned [undone].
- △ B Your shirt's unfastened.
- × C Your shirt's buttoned off.
- × D Your shirt's off the buttons.
  - ❖ C, D が辞典に出ているが使われていない．

2 《とれそうです》

〈上着のボタンがとれそうです〉
- ☆ A The button on your jacket's coming off.
- ◎ B The button on your jacket's falling off.
- ◎ C The button on your jacket's about to come off.

○ D The button on your jacket's about to fall [drop] off.
  3 《とれている》
〈上着のボタンが2つとれていますよ〉
　　　◎ A Your jacket's missing two buttons.
　　　◎ B Your jacket has two buttons missing.
　　　○ C Two buttons're missing on your jacket.
  4 《ボタンをかける》
  a) 上着
〈上着のボタンをかけて下さい〉
　　　◎ 　Button (up) your jacket, please.
  b) シャツ
〈シャツのボタンをかけて下さい〉
　　　◎ A Button your shirt, please.
　　　△ B Button up your shirt, please.
  5 《ボタンをはずす》
〈医師：シャツのボタンをはずして下さい〉
Doctor:
　　　◎ A Unbutton [Undo] your shirt, please.
　　　× B Button off your shirt, please.
　　　× C Unfasten your buttons on the shirt, please.
　　　❖ B, C が辞典に出ているが使われていない．
  6 《カフスボタン》
〈私は彼の誕生日にカフスボタンをあげました〉
　　　◎ A I gave him cuff links on his birthday.
　　　× B I gave him cuff buttons on his birthday.
　　　❖辞書には B が出ているが使われていない．

ボディーガード　→職業 16

歩道橋
〈あの歩道橋を使おう〉
　　　◎ A Let's use that overpass.
　　　○ B Let's use that bridge.
　　　○ C Let's use that pedestrian bridge [overpass].
　　　❖ B は文脈によっては「川の橋」を意味する．

ほとんどできている
  1 《相手を励ますとき》
〈ベティ：このクロスワード・パズルは終わらせられないわ〉
Betty: This crossword puzzle is impossible to finish.
〈ナンシー：いや，そんなことはないわよ．ほら，すでにできたのを見てごらんなさいよ．ほとんどできているじゃないの〉
Nancy: No, it's not. Look how much you've done already!
　　　◎ A You're almost there [finished, done].
　　　◎ B You're nearly finished [done].
  2 《やっていることが終わったか否かを尋ねられて答えるとき》
〈息子：夕食はできた〉
Son: Is dinner ready?
〈母親：ほとんどできているわよ〉
Mother:
　　　☆ A Just about.
　　　◎ B Almost.

- ◎ C I'm almost done.
- ○ D I'm almost finished.
- △ E I'm almost there.

ほとんど…ない

1 《名詞を従えるとき》
〈私には友達はほとんどいません〉
- ☆ A I don't have many friends.
- ◎ B I have hardly [hardly have] any friends.
- ◎ C I have almost no friends.
- ○ D I have barely any friends.
- △ E I barely have any friends.
  - ❖ A は B〜E と意味が違うと思う人もいるであろう．しかし，実際は同じ意味で使われている．

2 《代名詞を従えるとき》
a）文中で
〈私はこの近所ではほとんど誰も知らない〉
- ◎ A I hardly [barely] know anyone in this neighborhood.
- ◎ B I know almost no one in this neighborhood.
- ○ C I know hardly anyone in this neighborhood.
- △ D I know barely anyone in this neighborhood.

b）文頭で
〈昨日はほとんど誰もここへ来なかった〉
- ◎ A Hardly anyone came here yesterday.
- ◎ B Almost no one came here yesterday.
- ◎ C Few people came here yesterday.
- △ D Barely anyone came here yesterday.

3 《形容詞を従えるとき》
〈それはほとんど不可能です〉
- ☆ A It's almost impossible.
- ◎ B It's nearly [next to] impossible.
- ○ C It's hardly [barely] possible.
- △ D It's practically [just about, all but] impossible.
- × E It's scarcely [substantially] possible.
- × F It's as good as impossible.
  - ❖ 辞典に E, F が出ているが使われていない．

4 《動詞を従えるとき》
〈彼はほとんど英語を話しません〉
- ◎ A He speaks very little English.
- ◎ B He speaks hardly any English.
- ○ C He hardly [barely] speaks (any) English.
- ○ D He speaks little English.
- △ E He speaks barely any English.

ほとんどの①

1 《可算名詞を従えるとき》
〈日本にいるほとんどの外国人はアジア人です〉
- ☆ A Just about all the foreigners in Japan're Asians.
- ☆ B Almost all the foreigners in Japan're Asians.
- ☆ C Most of the foreigners in Japan're Asians.
- ☆ D The [A] majority of foreigners in Japan're Asians.

- ◎ E Nearly [Practically] all the foreigners in Japan're Asians.
- ◎ F Most foreigners in Japan're Asians.
- ○ G Virtually all the foreigners in Japan're Asians.
- ○ H Just about every foreigner in Japan's Asians.
- ○ I Almost [Nearly] every foreigner in Japan's Asians.
- ○ J Practically every foreigner in Japan's Asians.
- ○ K Virtually every foreigner in Japan's Asians.
- ○ L The bulk of foreigners in Japan're Asians.
  - ❖(1) D, L の形では特定の人々に言及しているが、the を使わない方がずっとよく使われている。
  - ❖(2) B, H は厳密には約98％以上、A, E, F, G, I, J は約90％以上、C, K は約80％以上、D, L は約65％以上を意味している。しかし、実際の会話ではほとんど区別なく使われている。

2 《不可算名詞を従えるとき》

〈私は人生のほとんどをフランスで過しました〉

- ◎ A I spent almost [practically] all my life in France.
- ◎ B I spent the [a] majority of my life in France.
- ◎ C I spent most of my life in France.
- ○ D I spent virtually [nearly] all my life in France.
- ○ E I spent just about all my life in France.
- ○ F I spent the greater [the better] part of my life in France.
- △ G I spent the bulk of my life in France.

ほとんどの②

1 《非特定な人・物を述べるとき》

〈ほとんどの子供たちは無邪気です〉

- ◎ A Most children're innocent.
- × B Most of the children're innocent.

2 《特定な人物を述べるとき》

a) 〈うちの事務所の社員のほとんどは英語の他にフランス語とドイツ語を話します〉

- ☆ A Most of the employees in our office speak French and German in addition to English.
- ◎ B Most employees in our office speak French and German in addition to English.

b) 〈この辺の店のほとんどは元旦は閉まっています〉

- ☆ A Most stores around here're closed on New Year's Day.
- ◎ B Most of the stores around here're closed on New Year's Day.
  - ❖多くの辞典、参考書に most of＝ほとんどの…、most＋複数名詞＝たいていの…という訳語がつけられて、さも両者は違うかのように紹介されているが、これは両者の本来の意味を歪曲している。most of と most＋複数名詞は同じで次の要領で使い分けられている。前述1の「ほとんどの子供」の例で説明したように、非特定、つまり広く一般的な人や物について言及するときは、most＋複数名詞を使う。一方、特定な人や物に言及するときに most＋複数名詞を使うときは、2 a) の B、または b) の A のように、常にその後に most＋複数名詞を説明する語または文が不可欠である。

3 《特定な国民について述べるとき》

〈ほとんどのアメリカ人はヨーロッパ人と違って理想主義者です〉

- ☆ A Most American people're idealists unlike Europeans.
- ◎ B Most of the American people're idealists unlike Europeans.

◎ C Most Americans're idealists unlike Europeans.
× D Most of the Americans're idealists unlike Europeans.
❖上記のDが使われない理由については，以下の例を比較してほしい．

〈アメリカ人は理想主義者です〉
◎ A The American people're idealists.
◎ B American people're idealists.
◎ C Americans're idealists.
▽ D The Americans're idealists.

上のA, B, Cは同じ意味で，アメリカ人全体を特定化した強い響きがある．Dはtheがあるにもかかわらず，その逆で特定した響きが全くない．B, CはDと違ってAに近い特定化した響きがある．most ofは常に特定化した名詞しか従えない．したがって，Dはまれにしか使われない．Dは日本人に理解しにくい一点であろう．それはthe+Americans, つまりthe+名詞の形は特定化したときのみ使われると一般に解説されているからである．しかし，一国民を述べるときは，アメリカ人に限らず，Dの形は特定化した国民ではなく，特定した響きが全くなく，広く一般的な意味での「国民」に言及するときに使われている．したがって，問題文DのMost of the Americans're idealists.はまれにしか使われていないのである．

ほのめかす

1 《節を従えるとき》

〈彼女は彼らが嘘をついていることをほのめかした〉
☆ A She implied that they were lying.
☆ B She suggested that they were lying.
◎ C She hinted [dropped a hint] that they were lying.
○ D She insinuated that they were lying.
△ E She alluded to the fact that they were lying.
▽ F She alluded that they were lying.
❖(1) Bは一番強い響きがある．
❖(2) Eは堅い文章では非常によく使われている．

2 《単語を従えるとき》

〈彼女は彼の横柄さをほのめかした〉
◎ A She hinted at his arrogance.
○ B She dropped [gave] a hint about his arrogance.
△ C She alluded to [insinuated] his arrogance.
× D She suggested to [implied] his arrogance.
× E She dropped [gave] a hint at his arrogance.
× F She gave an inkling of his arrogance.
❖D, E, Fが辞典に出ているが使われていない．

ほめる

1 《普通の会話で》

〈彼はあなたのことをほめていました〉
◎ A He said great things about you.
◎ B He said terrific [terrific, fantastic, wonderful] things about you.
◎ C He said incredible things about you.
◎ D He said good things about you.
○ E He said great things about you.
○ F He said terrific [fantastic, wonderful] stuff about you.
○ G He said incredible stuff about you.
○ H He said good stuff about you.

❖ほめる強さは C, G が一番強く, B, F が2番, A, E が3番, D, H が4番.

2 《改まった調子で述べるとき》

〈彼はあなたのことをほめていました〉

- ◎ A He spoke well of you.
- ◎ B He spoke [talked] highly of you.
- ◎ C He praised you.
- △ D He sang you praises.
- × E He sang his praises about you.

❖ほめる強さは B が一番強く, A, C, D が2番.

ぼられる →高い 1 d)

保留になる

1 《期限を明示しないとき》

〈彼の提案は保留になっています〉

- ◎ A His proposal's on hold.
- ○ B His proposal's on the back burner.
- △ C His proposal's in limbo.

2 《期限を明示するとき》

〈彼の提案は月曜日まで保留になっています〉

- ◎ A His proposal is on hold until Monday.
- ○ B His proposal is on the back burner until Monday.
- ○ C His proposal is being held over until Monday.
- △ D His proposal is in limbo until Monday.

ポルノ

1 《女優》

〈彼女はポルノ女優なんです〉

- ☆ A She's a porn star.
- ◎ B She's a porno star.
- ◎ C She's an adult movie star.
- ◎ D She's a porn gueen.
- ○ E She's an adult movie actress.
- △ F She's a porn actress [a porno gueen, a porno actress].

2 《男優》

〈彼はポルノ男優なんです〉

- ☆ A He's a porn star.
- ◎ B He's an adult movie actor [star].
- ○ C He's a porno star [actor].
- △ D He's a porn actor.
- ▽ E He's a porno figure.

ボロ儲け →利益 6

ほろ酔い →酔っ払っている 4

本気だ

〈私はあなたと別れます. 本気です〉

- ☆ A I'll leave you. I mean it.
- ◎ B I'll leave you. I'm serious.
- △ C I'll leave you. I mean business.

❖ B が一番強い響きがあり, C が2番, A は一番弱い.

ポンコツ

1 《普通または少し怒っているとき》

〈この車はポンコツだ〉
- ◎ A This car's a pile of crap.
- ◎ B This car's a pile [piece, hunk] of junk.
- ◎ C This car's a lemon [junker].

2 《怒っているとき》
〈この車はポンコツだ〉
- ◎ A This car's a piece of shit.
- ◎ B This car's a pile of shit.
- ❖ A, B は気を使う必要がない場面では非常によく使われているが, 下品な表現なので改まって話す場面では使わないほうがよい.

本題からはずれない
〈本題からはずれないようにしましょう〉
- ◎ A Let's stick to the subject.
- ◎ B Let's not get off the subject.
- ◎ C Let's not get off track.
- ○ D Let's not stray [move away] from the subject.
- △ E Let's not deviate [wander] from the subject.
- × F Let's not go [fly, run] off the subject.
- ❖ C の track の前には the がない.

本当ですね
1 《親しい者同士のとき》
〈リンダ:今日はすごく暑いわね〉
Linda: It's really hot today.
〈ビル:本当だね〉
Bill:
- ◎ A You said it.
- ◎ B You're telling me.
- ◎ C You can say that again.
- ◎ D I'll say.
- ◎ E Yes, it is.

2 《丁重に話すとき》
〈(高級レストランなどで) 客:今日は実に暑いね〉
Customer: It's really hot today.
〈ウエイター:本当ですね〉
Waiter:
- ◎ A Yes, it (certainly) is.
- ◎ B I'll say.

本当の姿
1 《ある国の本当の姿》
a) 本当の姿を紹介する
〈私はアメリカのあるがままの本当の姿を紹介したいんです〉
- ☆ A I want to introduce an accurate picture of the United States as it is.
- ◎ B I want to introduce a true [real] picture of the United States as it is.
- ○ C I want to introduce a truthful picture of the United States as it is.

b) 本当の姿を知っている
〈あなたはアメリカの本当の姿を知っていませんね〉
- ☆ A You don't have an accurate picture of the United States.
- ◎ B You don't have a true [real] picture of the United States.

- ◎ C You don't know what the United States is really like.
- × D You don't know an accurate [a true, a real] picture of the United States.

2 《人柄》

〈あなたは彼の本当の姿を知らないんですね〉
- ◎ A You don't know his real personality.
- ○ B You don't know his true personality.
- × C You don't know his accurate personality.
- × D You don't know his real [true] picture.
- × E You don't have his real [true, accurate] personality.

本当は

〈彼は仕事を辞めたと言ったのですが,本当は首になったんです〉
- ◎ A He said he quit his job but to tell the truth he was fired.
- ◎ B He said he quit his job but truthfully he was fired.
- ◎ C He said he quit his job but in truth he was fired.
- ◎ D He said he quit his job but to be honest (with you) he was fired.

ぽんと(肩を)たたく

1 《慰め・はげましなどを表して》

〈彼は私の肩をぽんとたたいた〉
- ◎ A He patted me on the shoulder.
- ◎ B He patted my shoulder.
- ▽ C He patted me in the shoulder.
  - ❖ C が辞典に出ているが使われてもまれ

2 《注意を引くために》

〈彼は私の肩をぽんとたたいた〉
- ◎ A He tapped me on the shoulder.
- ◎ B He tapped my shoulder.
- × C He tapped me in the shoulder.

本命

1 《役職の候補》

〈彼が次期社長の本命です〉
- ◎ A He's the most likely candidate [guy] to be the next CEO.
- ◎ B He's the most likely to be the next CEO.
- ○ C He's the favorite for [to be] the next CEO.
- ○ D He's favored to be the next CEO.

2 《大統領選の候補》

a) 予備選挙で

〈ブッシュが本命です〉
- ◎ A Bush's the favorite.
- ◎ B Bush's the favored [favorite, most likely] candidate.
- △ C Bush's the prospective winner.

b) 本選挙で

〈ブッシュが本命です〉
- ◎ A Bush's the favorite.
- ○ B Bush's the favored [favorite, most likely, prospective] candidate.

3 《知事・市長選の候補》

〈誰が本命なのですか〉
- ◎ A Who's the favorite?
- ◎ B Who's the favorite [favored] candidate?

- ◎ C Who's the most likely to win [to be elected]?
- ○ D Who's the most favored [likely] candidate?
- ○ E Who's the most likely to become the mayor [the governor]?
- ○ F Who's the most likely to get the mayor's [the governor's] job?
- ○ G Who's the prospective winner?

本物の

1 《料理》
〈私は本物のフランス料理が食べたいんです〉
- ☆ A I want to eat real French food.
- ◎ B I want to eat authentic French food.
- △ C I want to eat genuine French food.

2 《ネックレス》
〈私は本物の真珠のネックレスが買いたいんです〉
- ☆ A I want to buy a real pearl necklace.
- ◎ B I want to buy a genuine pearl necklace.
- △ C I want to buy an authentic pearl necklace.

3 《絵》
〈これは本物のピカソの絵です〉
- ◎ A This is a real [genuine] Picasso's picture.
- ○ B This is an authentic Picasso's picture.

ぼんやりした

〈彼に対する私の記憶はぼんやりしています〉
- ◎ A My memory of him's hazy [cloudy, vague, fuzzy].
- △ B My memory of him's foggy [blurred, blurry].

〔ま〕

舞い上がっている
1 《昇進・合格・成功》
a) 一般的に述べるとき
〈彼は昇進したから舞い上がっているんです〉
- ☆ A He's excited because he got promoted.
- ◎ B He's thrilled because he got promoted.
- ○ C He's in seventh heaven because he got promoted.
- △ D He's beaming because he got promoted.
- △ E He feels giddy [He's giddy] because he got promoted.
- × F He's beside himself because he got promoted.
- × G He's overjoyed because he got promoted.
  - ❖(1) G は主語が女性のときによく使われている．
  - ❖(2) F が辞典に肯定的な内容で紹介されているが使われていない．否定的な内容ならよく使われている．

b) 強く述べるとき
〈彼は昇進したからすごく舞い上がっているんです〉
- ☆ A He's really excited because he got promoted.
- ◎ B He's really thrilled because he got promoted.
- ◎ C He's ecstatic because he got promoted.
- ◎ D He's walking on air because he got promoted.
- ◎ E He's on cloud nine because he got promoted.
- ○ F He's walking on [in] the clouds because he got promoted.
- ○ G His head's in the clouds because he got promoted.

2 《異性関係で》
a) 一般的に述べるとき
〈彼女はデートに誘われたから舞い上がっているんです〉
- ☆ A She's excited because she was asked out for a date.
- ◎ B She's thrilled because she was asked out for a date.
- ○ C She's in seventh heaven because she was asked out for a date.
- ○ D She's beaming [overjoyed] because she was asked out for a date.
- △ E She feels giddy [She's giddy] because she was asked out for a date.

b) 強く述べるとき
〈彼女はデートに誘われたからすごく舞い上がっているんです〉
- ☆ A She's really excited because she was asked out for a date.
- ◎ B She's really thrilled because she was asked out for a date.
- ◎ C She's ecstatic because she was asked out for a date.
- ◎ D She's walking on air because she was asked out for a date.
- ○ E She's walking on [in] the clouds because she was asked out for a date.
- ○ F Her mind's in the clouds because she was asked out for a date.
- △ G She's on cloud nine because she was asked out for a date.

真裏
〈ミシガン銀行の真裏にフレンチレストランがあります〉
- ◎ A There's a French restaurant right [just, directly] behind Michigan

Bank.
- ○ B There's a French restaurant immediately behind Michigan Bank.
- ○ C There's a French restaurant right in back of Michigan Bank.
- ▽ D There's a French restaurant just [directly, immediately] in back of Michigan Bank.
  - ❖(1) D が辞典に出ているが使われてもまれ.
  - ❖(2) A〜D いずれも土地が隣接していても,していなくても使われている.

前貸しする
〈給料を前貸ししていただけますか〉
- ◎ A Could you give me some of my pay early?
- ◎ B Could I have an advance on my pay?
- ◎ C Could you advance me some of my pay?
- ◎ D Could you give me an advance on my pay?
- ◎ E Could you give me some of my pay ahead of time?
- △ F Could you pay me some of my salary in advance?

前に [で]
1 《場所のとき》
a) 通りをはさんで
〈うちの事務所はミシガン銀行の前にあります〉
- ☆ A Our office is across from Michigan Bank.
- ◎ B Our office is across the street from Michigan Bank.
- ◎ C Our office is on the other side of the street from Michigan Bank.
- ○ D Our office is on the opposite side of the street from Michigan Bank.
- ○ E Our office faces Michigan Bank.
- ○ F Our office is facing Michigan Bank.
- ○ G Our office is opposite Michigan Bank.
- △ H Our office is opposite from [to] Michigan Bank.
  - ❖(1) E, F, G は真ん前というニュアンスがある. A〜D は「真ん前」であっても,または「少しずれて」いても使われている. A〜D を「真ん前」の意味であることをはっきりさせるには, right, straight, directly, immediately をつける.
  - ❖(2) 「…の前」=in front of と結びつけて誤用している人が多い. この種のミスは日本の英字紙などでも多く見受けられる. 使い分けのこつとしては, street (通り), hall (廊下), aisle (通路), table (食卓) をはさんでいるときの「…の前には」には, in front of を使えないということをしっかりインプットされたい. →b), c), d).

b) 廊下をはさんで
〈彼の事務所は私の事務所の前にあります〉
- ☆ A His office is across from mine.
- ◎ B His office is across the hall from mine.
- ◎ C His office is on the other side of the hall from mine.
- ○ D His office is on the opposite side of the hall from mine.
- ○ E His office faces mine.
- △ F His office is opposite side of the hall from mine.

c) (電車の中などで) 通路をはさんで
〈私の前に座っていた男性はニューヨークタイムズを読んでいました〉
- ☆ A A guy sitting across from me was reading *The New York Times*.
- ◎ B A guy sitting across the aisle from me was reading *The New York Times*.

- ◎ C A guy sitting on the other side of the aisle from me was reading *The New York Times*.
- ○ D A guy sitting on the opposite side of the aisle from me was reading *The New York Times*.
- ○ E A guy sitting facing me was reading *The New York Times*.
- △ F A guy sitting opposite me was reading *The New York Times*.

d）テーブルをはさんで

〈彼は食卓で私の前に座っていました〉

- ☆ A He was sitting across from me.
- ◎ B He was sitting across the table from me.
- ◎ C He was sitting on the other side of the table from me.
- ○ D He was sitting on the opposite side of the table from me.
- ○ E He was sitting facing me.
- △ F He was sitting opposite me.

e）通りをはさんでいないとき

〈XYZ銀行の前に白い車が止まっています〉

- ◎　There's a white car in front of XYZ Bank.

f）名簿などの順序のとき

〈あなたの名前は私の名前の前に載っています〉

- ◎ A Your name's listed before mine.
- ○ B Your name's listed in front of mine.

g）重要人物を従えるとき

〈私たちは女王様と王様の前で5曲歌いました〉

- ☆ A We sang five songs before the Queen and the King.
- ◎ B We sang five songs in front of the Queen and the King.

h）大勢の人の前で

〈彼は大勢の聴衆の前でスピーチをしました〉

- ◎　He made a speech before [in front of] a large audience.

i）「…の前の方に」と言うとき

〈私の席は教室の前の方です〉

- ◎　My seat's in [at] the front of the classroom.
  - ❖(1) in the front of は前から1, 2, 3, 4, 5列, at the front of は前から1, 2列目をいう.
  - ❖(2) in front of は建物などの外の「正面に」, in the front of は建物の内部の「…の前の方に」である.
  - ❖(3) in front of は「…の正面に」の意味. Let's meet in front of Mitsukoshi. (三越の正面で会いましょう).「真ん前に[で]」の項も参照のこと.

2 《時間上のとき》

a）「(…より) 前に」と述べるとき

〈彼女は彼より前にここへ来ました〉

- ◎　She got here before [earlier than, ahead of] him.

b）数分前のとき

〈私は少し前に彼を見ました〉

- ◎ A I saw him a few minutes ago.
- ◎ B I saw him a minute [a moment] ago.
  - ❖時間的にはAのほうが長い. Bは同じで「ちょっと前」というニュアンス.

c）1日のうちの「少し前に」

〈私は少し前に彼が外出するのを見ました〉

- ◎ A I saw him going out a little while [bit] ago.

- ○ B I saw him going out a short time ago.
- ○ C I saw him going out a while ago.
- △ D I saw him going out a short while ago.

d) 数週間前から数ヵ月前のとき

〈2人は少し前に離婚したんです〉
- ◎ A They got divorced a little while ago.
- ○ B They got divorced a short time ago.
- △ C They got divorced a (short) while ago.

e) 節を従えるとき

〈彼らはあなたが私に電話してくる少し前に外出しました〉
- ◎ A They went out a little before you called me.
- ◎ B They went out just before you called me.
- ○ C They went out shortly before you called me.

f) ずっと前に

・離婚のような非日常的な話のとき

〈2人はずっと前に離婚しました〉
- ☆ A They got divorced a long time ago.
- ◎ B They got divorced a while ago.
- ○ C They got divorced ages ago.
- △ D They got divorced long ago.
    - ❖(1) 年数の上では C が一番長いという響きがある．A が2番，D が3番，B が4番．
    - ❖(2) 年数は人により大きく異なるが，C は少なくとも 10 年以上前．

・日常くり返される話のとき

〈ずっと前に行った角のレストランへ行こう〉
- ☆ A Let's go to the restaurant on the corner we went to a while ago.
- ☆ B Let's go to the restaurant on the corner we went to a long time ago.
- ◎ C Let's go to the restaurant on the corner we went to ages ago.
- △ D Let's go to the restaurant on the corner we went to long ago.
    - ❖期間の点では D が一番長く少なくとも 1 年以上前，C は2番目で約 10 ヵ月くらい前，B が3番目で 6〜8 ヵ月くらい前，A が4番目で 3〜5 ヵ月くらい前．

前の

1 《上司》

〈彼は前の上司です〉
- ☆ A He's my old boss.
- ◎ B He's my former boss.
- △ C He's my ex-boss.

2 《秘書》

〈彼女は私の前の秘書なんです〉
- ☆ A She's my former secretary.
- ◎ B She's my old secretary.
- △ C She's my ex-secretary.

3 《妻》

〈彼女は前の妻です〉
- ◎ A She's my ex-wife.
- ○ B She's my former wife.
- × C She's my old wife.

4 《ボーイフレンド》

〈彼は前のボーイフレンドです〉
- ☆ A He's my ex-boyfriend.
- ◎ B He's my old boyfriend.
- ○ C He's my former boyfriend.

5 《ルームメイト》
〈彼女は前のルームメイトなんです〉
- ◎ A She's my old roommate.
- ○ B She's my former roommate [ex-roommate].

6 《知事・市長・首相・大統領》
〈彼は前の知事です〉
- ◎ A He's a former governor.
- ○ B He's an ex-governor.
- △ C He's an old governor.

前もって

1 《時間に言及しないとき》
〈日本に来るときは前もって私に連絡して下さい〉
- ◎ A When you're coming to Japan, get in touch with me ahead of time.
- ○ B When you're coming to Japan, get in touch with me in advance.
- △ C When you're coming to Japan, get in touch with me beforehand.

2 《時間に言及するとき》
〈日本に来るときは前もって一週間前に連絡して下さい〉
- ☆ A When you're coming to Japan, get in touch with me one week ahead of time.
- ◎ B When you're coming to Japan, get in touch with me one week in advance [beforehand].
- △ C When you're coming to Japan, get in touch with me one week prior [early].

3 《前金》
〈合計金額の3分の1を前もって支払っていただけますか〉
- ◎ A Could you pay us one-third of the total up front?
- ○ B Could you pay us one-third of the total ahead of time [in advance, beforehand]?
- × C Could you pay us one-third of the total prior [earlier, early]?

まぎらわしい

〈ブラウン氏：契約書のこのパラグラフがよく分からないんです〉
Mr. Brown: I don't quite understand this paragraph of the contract.
〈弁護士：少しまぎらわしいですね．ご説明しましょう〉
Lawyer:
- ◎ It's somewhat misleading [unclear, confusing]. I'll try to explain it to you.

まさか

〈マイク：車はまた修理に出してあるんだ〉
Mike: My car's in the shop again.
〈ランディ：まさかまた事故を起こしたって言うんじゃないだろうね〉
Randy:
- ◎ Don't tell me you had another accident.

マザコン

〈彼はマザコンです〉
- ◎ A His mother's running [controlling] his life.

- ◎ B His mother runs his life.
- ◎ C He's controlled by his mother.
- ◎ D He's a mama's boy.
- ○ E He's tied to his mother's apron strings.
- × F He's a mom's [mother's] boy.
   ❖ E は 30 歳以下の人の間では，時々しか使われていない．

勝る
1 《統率力》
〈統率力において彼に勝る人はいません〉
- ◎ A Nobody can top [beat] him in leadership skills.
- ○ B Nobody can outdo him in leadership skills.
- ○ C Nobody can surpass him in leadership skills.
- △ D Nobody can outshine him in leadership skills.
- △ E Nobody can exceed his leadership skills.
   ❖ 教養の高い人の間では C，D，E は非常によく使われている．

2 《売上げ》
〈XYZ 会社は今年売上げの点で HHH 会社を勝るだろう〉
- ☆ A XYZ Company'll top [beat] HHH Company sales-wise this year.
- ◎ B XYZ Company'll get ahead of HHH Company sales-wise this year.
- ○ C XYZ Company'll exceed [surpass, outperform] HHH Company sales-wise this year.
- △ D XYZ Company'll outdo [outshine] HHH Company sales-wise this year.
- × E XYZ Company'll outstrip [outmatch, excel] HHH Company sales-wise this year.
   ❖ E が辞典に出ているが使われていない．

(…割)増し
1 《5割増し》
〈アメリカでは残業は5割増しです〉
- ◎ A They get time and a half for overtime in America.
- △ B They get time and a half for overtime work in America.
- × C They get time and a 50% for overtime in America.

2 《3割増し》
〈私たちは残業は3割増しです〉
- ◎ A We get 30% more for overtime.
- △ B We get 30% more for overtime work.

真正面で →真ん前で[に]
麻酔専門医 →医者 15
マスコミに騒がれている
〈彼はマスコミに騒がれている〉
- ◎ A He's getting a lot of media attention.
- ◎ B He's getting a lot of attention from the media.

貧しい家庭の出である
〈ジムは今非常に金持ちですが貧しい家庭の出なんです〉
- ◎ A Jim's very rich now, but he came from nothing.
- ◎ B Jim's very rich now, but he came from a family with no money.
- ◎ C Jim's very rich now, but he came from the bad [wrong] side of town.
- ○ D Jim's very rich now, but he came from no money.

- ○ E　Jim's very rich now, but he came from the inner city [the projects].
- ○ F　Jim's very rich now, but he came from the other [wrong] side of the tracks.

❖ E は都市の出身，A，B，C，D，F は都市・町・村のいずれにも使える．

まだ

1 《時間》

a）思ったより早い時間と思ったとき

〈まだ4時だ〉

◎　It's only [just] 4:00.

❖(1) only と just の間に違いはない．
❖(2) just は辞典に「ちょうど4時です」と出ているが，その意味では使われていない．

b）時間がたつのが遅いと思ったとき

〈まだ4時なんだ〉

◎　It's still 4:00.

2 《いまなお》

〈彼はまだ怒っています〉

◎　He's still angry.

〈私はまだそのことを覚えています〉

◎　I still remember it.

〈リンダ：頭痛はどう〉

Linda: How's your headache?

〈ジェーン：まだとれないのよ〉

Jane:

◎　It's still there.

3 《さらにもっと》

a）達成

〈スティーブ：君の車はまだ支払いが終わっていないのかい〉

Steve: Haven't you paid off your car yet?

〈ジョン：うん，まだだよ．まだかなりあるよ〉

John:

◎　No, not yet. I still have a long way to go.

b）距離

〈スティーブ：ずいぶん運転しているよ．もうそろそろかい〉

Steve: We've been driving a long time. Aren't we almost there?

〈ジョン：いや，まだかなりあるよ〉

John:

◎　No, we still have a long way to go.

4 《いまだに》

〈彼はまだ私に電話してこないんです〉

◎ A　He still hasn't called me yet.
◎ B　He still hasn't called me.
◎ C　He hasn't called me yet.
△ D　He has yet to call me.

❖(1) A はいらいらした気持ちが一番強い．B，C，D の順で弱くなる．
❖(2) D は堅い響きがある．
❖(3) C の yet を強く言えば A と同じ強いニュアンスは出る．

又貸しする　→貸す 7

間違いなく
〈間違いなくこれは当たるでしょう〉
- ☆ A This'll definitely catch on.
- ☆ B Definitely this'll catch on.
- ◎ C There's no doubt [question] this'll catch on.
- ◎ D This is certain to catch on.
- ◎ E I'm sure [positive, certain] this'll catch on.
- ○ F This is sure [bound] to catch on.
- ○ G It's certain this'll catch on.
- ○ H It's a sure bet [thing] this'll catch on.

間違える
〈私はトムをジムと間違えてしまったんです〉
- ◎ A I mistook Tom for Jim.
- ▽ B I took Tom for Jim.
    - ❖ B が辞典に出ているが使われてもまれ．

間違ったことを教える
〈あなたは，日本の教育制度について間違ったことを私に教えましたよ〉
- ◎ A You gave me the wrong information about the Japanese educational system.
- ◎ B You misinformed me about the Japanese educational system.
    - ❖ B は少し堅い表現．

待つ

1 《面接で》

〈面接者：明日3時に最終面接に来られますか〉

Interviewer: Can you come for the final interview at 3:00 tomorrow?

〈応募者：もちろん来られます〉

Applicant: I certainly can.

〈面接者：お待ちしています〉

Interviewer:
- ◎ A I'll expect you then.
- ◎ B I'll be expecting you then.
- ◎ C I'll see you then.
    - ❖ A はかしこまった口調で，大企業の面接などでよく使われている．B はややあたたかみのある口調，C はくだけた口調でアルバイトの面接などでよく使われている．

2 《友人との約束で》

〈リンダ：角のコーヒーショップで2時に会いましょうよ〉

Linda: Let's meet at 2:00 at the coffee shop on the corner.

〈ジェーン：いいわね．待ってるわ〉

Jane:
- ☆ A Good idea. I'll see you then.
- ◎ B Good idea. I'll see you there.
- ○ C Good idea. I'll be waiting for you.
    - ❖ C は会うことに興奮していて，時間より前に行って待っているというニュアンスがある．

3 《相手が遅れるとき》

〈リンダ：私は少し遅れるかもしれないわ〉

Linda: I might be a little late.

〈ビル：心配しないで．待っているよ〉

Bill:
- ◎ A Don't worry. I'll wait for you.
- ○ B Don't worry. I'll be waiting for you.
  - ❖ B には「待ち遠しい」というニュアンスがある.

4 《楽しみにしていると言うとき》
〈ジェーン:飛行機は 11 時 15 分に着きます〉
Jane: My plane'll get in at 11:15.
〈お会いできるのを楽しみに待っています〉
Bill:
- ◎ A I'm looking forward to seeing you then.
- ◎ B I look forward to seeing you then.
  - ❖ A の方が楽しみにしている気持ちが強い.

5 《相手に少し待ってもらうとき》
〈ちょっと待ってくれますか.彼はすぐ来ます〉
- ◎ A Will you wait (just) a second [a sec, a minute, a moment]? He'll be right with you.
- ◎ B Will you hang on a second [a sec, a minute]? He'll be right with you.
- ○ C Will you hang on a moment? He'll be right with you.
- ○ D Will you hold on a minute [a moment]? He'll be right with you.
- △ E Will you hold on a second [a sec]? He'll be right with you.

6 《起こそうとした行動を止めるとき》
〈ちょっと待った.雨が降り出した.ピクニックを中止しなければならないよ〉
- ◎ A Wait [Just] a minute. It's started to rain. We've got to cancel the picnic.
- ◎ B Wait [Just] a sec. It's started to rain. We've got to cancel the picnic.
- ◎ C Wait [Just] a second. It's started to rain. We've got to cancel the picnic.
- ◎ D Hang [Hold] on a minute. It's started to rain. We've got to cancel the picnic.
- ◎ E Hang [Hold] on a sec. It's started to rain. We've got to cancel the picnic.
- ◎ F Hang [Hold] on a second. It's started to rain. We've got to cancel the picnic.
- ◎ G Hold on [it]. It's started to rain. We've got to cancel the picnic.
- ○ H Wait [Just] a moment. It's started to rain. We've got to cancel the picnic.
- ○ I Hang [Hold] on a moment. It's started to rain. We've got to cancel the picnic.

7 《相手の言っていることに反論するとき》
〈ちょっと待って下さい.あなたが言っていることは全く筋が通りません〉
- ◎ A Wait [Just] a minute. What you're saying makes no sense at all.
- ◎ B Wait [Just] a second. What you're saying makes no sense at all.
- ◎ C Wait [Just] a sec. What you're saying makes no sense at all.
- ◎ D Wait a second here. What you're saying makes no sense at all.
- ◎ E Hold on [it]. What you're saying makes no sense at all.
- ◎ F Hang on. What you're saying makes no sense at all.
- ○ G Wait [Just] a moment. What you're saying makes no sense at all.
- △ H Just a second here. What you're saying makes no sense at all.

8 《もう少し待つようにすすめるとき》
a) 学校・役所などの団体
〈息子：3週間前にハーバードに願書を送ったんだけど，まだどこからも返事がないよ〉
Son: I sent my applications to Harvard three weeks ago, but I still haven't heard from them.
〈父：途中なのかもしれないよ．もう1週間待ってごらん〉
Father:
 ◎ A It might be on the way. Give it [them] another week.
 ◎ B It might be on the way. Wait another week.
b) 個人
〈ビル：リンダはここに2時までに来ることになっているんだけど，まだ来ていないんだよ〉
Bill: Linda's supposed to be here by 2 o'clock, but she still isn't.
〈ジェーン：もう10分かそこら待ったら〉
Jane:
 ◎ A Give her another ten minutes or so.
 ○ B Wait for her another ten minutes or so.
 △ C Give it another ten minutes or so.

まっすぐ行く

1 《道順を教えるとき》
〈最初の交差点までまっすぐ行きなさい〉
 ◎ A Go [Walk] straight to the first intersection.
 ○ B Go straight until the first intersection.
 × C Follow this street to the first intersection.
 × D Follow your nose on to the first intersection.
 ❖ C, D を紹介している辞典があるが，D は全く使われていない．C は使われているが「この道をずっと行きなさい」という意味．つまり，A, B のように「まっすぐ行く」という意味はなく，道は曲がりくねっているニュアンスもある．

2 《直行するという意味のとき》
〈仕事がひけたらすぐ，あなたの事務所にまっすぐ行きます〉
 ☆ A As soon as I get off work, I'll go straight [directly] to your office.
 ☆ B As soon as I get off work, I'll head straight for your office.
 ◎ C As soon as I get off work, I'll be headed to [for] your office.
 ◎ D As soon as I get off work, I'll make a beeline to your office.
 ○ E As soon as I get off work, I'll make a beeline for your office.

…まで

1 《場所》
a) 地名の名詞を従えるとき
〈渋谷まで地下鉄で行き，それから JR に乗り換えましょう〉
 ◎ A Let's take the subway to Shibuya and then change to JR.
 ○ B Let's take the subway as far as Shibuya and then change to JR.
 ▽ C Let's take the subway until Shibuya and then change to JR.
b) 節を従えるとき
〈交差点までずうっと歩いて下さい．それから左へ曲って下さい〉
 ◎ A Keep walking until [till] you get to the intersection and then turn left.
 △ B Keep walking as far as the intersection and then turn left.

2 《時間》

〈電話するまで家にいて下さい〉

   ◎ A Stay at home till I call you, please.
   ○ B Stay at home until I call you, please.

窓

1 《外側に開く窓》

〈私たちは開き窓の家を探しています〉

   ◎ A We're looking for a house with casement windows.
   × B We're looking for a house with casements.
   ❖ B が辞典に出ているが使われていない.

2 《出窓》

〈私たちは出窓の家を探しています〉

   ◎ We're looking for a house with bow windows.

3 《張り出し窓》

〈私たちは張り出し窓の家を探しています〉

   ◎ We're looking for a house with bay windows.
   ❖ bay window とは地上一階から建物の上まで窓になっている.

4 《上げ下げ窓》

〈私たちは上げ下げ窓の家を探しています〉

   ◎ We're looking for a house with sash windows.

5 《社会の窓》

〈社会の窓が開いていますよ〉

   ◎ Your fly's open [unzipped].

まとまる

1 《レポート》

〈教授:あなたのレポートは非常によくまとまっている〉

Professor:

   ◎ A Your paper's really well organized [put together].
   ○ B Your paper has a lot of organization.

2 《国会》

a)「まとまっている」と述べるとき

〈国会はこの問題になるとまとまっている〉

   ◎ A Congress is unanimous when it comes to this issue.
   ◎ B Congress is unified when it comes to this issue.
   ◎ C Congress is in total agreement when it comes to this issue.
   ○ D Congress is united when it comes to this issue.
   ❖ A は 100 %一致しているニュアンスがあり, B は約 80 %, C は約 90 %, D は 100 %. しかし, A の方が D よりコンセンサスの響きが強い.

b)「まとまっていない」と述べるとき

〈国会はこの問題では意見がまとまっていません〉

   ☆ A Congress is divided when it comes to this issue.
   ◎ B Congress isn't unanimous when it comes to this issue.
   ◎ C Congress isn't unified [united] when it comes to this issue.
   ○ D Congress isn't in total [complete] agreement when it comes to this issue.
   ○ E Congress is split when it comes to this issue.
   ❖ A, E は約 50 %, C は約 60 %, B, D は 100 %まとまっていない.

3 《取引》

〈たぶんこの取引はまとまらないでしょう〉

- ◎ A This deal will probably fall through [apart].
- ◎ B This deal probably won't be closed.
- ◎ C This deal probably won't come [go] through.
- ◎ D We probably won't be able to wrap up [close] this deal.

4 《話し手の意見・考え》
〈私はまだそれについて考えがまとまっていません〉
- ◎ A I still haven't come to a conclusion about it.
- ◎ B I still haven't made an opinion about it.
- ◎ C I still haven't made a decision on it.
- ○ D I still haven't made my decision on it.
- △ E I still haven't come to my conclusion [decision] on it.

学ぶ態度
〈ほとんどのアメリカ人は外国から学ぶ態度がありません〉
- ☆ A Most Americans aren't open-minded to ideas from the rest of the world.
- ◎ B Most Americans aren't open [receptive] to ideas from the rest of the world.
- ◎ C Most Americans aren't willing to accept ideas from the rest of the world.
- △ D Most Americans aren't accepting of ideas from the rest of the world.

マニア

1 《コンピュータ》
〈彼はコンピュータマニアなんです〉
- ☆ A He's a computer geek.
- ◎ B He's a computer nerd [nut].
- ◎ C He's crazy [nuts] about computers.
- ○ D He's addicted to computers.
- ○ E He's nuts for computers.
- ○ F He's a computer addict.
- △ G He's a computer freak [junkie].
- △ H He's computer crazy.
- △ I He's crazy for [over] computers.
- △ J He's wild [mad] about computers.
- × K He's mad [wild] for computers.

2 《競馬・映画・ダンスなど》
〈彼は競馬マニアなんです〉
- ☆ A He's crazy about horse racing.
- ◎ B He's nuts [mad] about horse racing.
- ◎ C He's a horse racing fanatic [maniac].
- ○ D He's fanatic about horse racing.
- △ E He's a horse racing nut [freak].
- △ F He's nuts for [over] horse racing.
- △ G He's mad for horse racing.
- △ H He's addicted to horse racing.
- △ I He's an aficionado of horse racing.

3 《写真》
〈彼は写真マニアなんです〉
- ◎ A He's crazy [nuts] about photography.
- ◎ B He's a photography fanatic [maniac].

- ◎ C He's mad about photography.
- ○ D He's a photography buff.
- ○ E He's fanatic about photography.
- △ F He's a photography nut [freak].
- △ G He's nuts for [over] photography.
- △ H He's mad for photography.
- △ I He's a shutterbug.
- △ J He's addicted to photography.
- △ K He's an aficionado of photography.

❖ K は教育レベルの高い人の間では非常によく使われている．

間に合う

1 《コンサート・約束のような動かないものに》
〈コンサートに間に合ったの〉
- ☆ A Did you make it to the concert?
- ◎ B Did you make the concert?
- ◎ C Were you on [in] time for the concert?
- ◎ D Did you get to the concert on [in] time?
- ◎ E Did you get to the hall in time for the concert?
- △ F Did you make it for the concert?

2 《電車のように動くもの》
〈あなたは8時の電車に間に合いましたか〉
- ☆ A Did you catch the 8:00 train?
- ◎ B Did you get on the 8:00 train?
- ◎ C Did you make (it to) the 8:00 train?
- ◎ D Did you get to the 8:00 train on [in] time?
- ◎ E Did you get to the station on [in] time for the 8:00 train?
- ○ F Did you make it on the 8:00 train?
- ○ G Did you get to the station for the 8:00 train on [in] time?
- △ H Did you arrive at the station for the 8:00 train on [in] time?
- △ I Did you arrive in [on] time for the 8:00 train?

招く

1 《家に招くとき》
〈彼らを夕食に招こう〉
- ◎ A Let's invite them over for [to] dinner.
- ◎ B Let's have them over for dinner.
- ◎ C Let's ask them over for [to] dinner.

2 《レストランなどへ招くとき》
〈彼らを夕食に招こう〉
- ◎ A Let's invite them out to [for] dinner.
- ◎ B Let's meet them for dinner.
- ◎ C Let's ask them out for [to] dinner.
- △ D Let's have them out to dinner.

3 《家・レストランの両方に使える》
〈彼らを夕食に招こう〉
- ◎ A Let's invite them for [to] dinner.
- ◎ B Let's ask them for [to] dinner.
- ◎ C Let's have them to [for] dinner.

4 《講演講師として》
a) 決定しているとき

〈私たちは 5 月 21 日に中国の専門家を講師としてお招きします〉
- ◎ A We've scheduled [We're scheduled] to have an expert on China as a guest speaker on May 21st.
- ◎ B We've booked [We're booked] to have an expert on China as a guest speaker on May 21st.
- ◎ C We've scheduled [We're scheduled] to invite an expert on China as a guest speaker on May 21st.
- ◎ D We've booked [We're booked] to invite an expert on China as a guest speaker on May 21st.
- ◎ E We're going [planning] to invite an expert on China as a guest speaker on May 21st.
- ◎ F We're planning on inviting an expert on China as a guest speaker on May 21st.

b）決定しているときと予定のときのいずれにも使える

〈5 月 21 日に中国の専門家を講師にお招きします（お招きする予定です）〉
- ◎ We're going to have [invite] an expert on China as a guest speaker on May 21st.

5 《「お返しに招く」と述べるとき》

〈いつか近いうちに彼らをお返しに夕食に招きましょう〉
- ☆ A Let's return their invitation for dinner one of these days.
- ◎ B Let's return their favor for dinner one of these days.
- ○ C Let's invite [ask] them for dinner in return one of these days.

6 《「大きな問題を招く」と言うとき》

〈あなたがそれをするなら大きな問題を招きますよ〉
- ◎ A If you do that, you'll be asking for big trouble.
- ◎ B If you do that, you'll be in big trouble.

まねる

《人の動作などを模倣する場合》

〈彼のまねをしてはだめですよ〉
- ◎ Don't copy [mimic, parrot, ape] him.

魔法ビン

〈私は魔法ビンを買わなければならないんです〉
- ◎ A I have to buy a thermos.
- △ B I have to buy a thermos jug.
- × C I have to buy a thermos bottle [flask].
- × D I have to buy a vacuum bottle [flask].

❖ C, D が辞典に出ているが使われていない．

(…の) 真向いに

〈うちの事務所はアトランタ銀行の真向いにあります〉
- ☆ A Our office is right [just] across (the street) from Atlanta Bank.
- ◎ B Our office is directly [immediately] across (the street) from Atlanta Bank.
- ◎ C Our office is right [just, directly, immediately] on the other side of the street from Atlanta Bank.
- ◎ D Our office is right [just, directly, immediately] on the opposite side of the street from Atlanta Bank.
- ◎ E Our office faces Atlanta Bank.
- ○ F Our office is right [just, directly, immediately] opposite Atlanta Bank.

マリファナ
1 《経験を尋ねるとき》
〈あなたはマリファナを吸ったことがありますか〉
- ◎ A Have you ever tried weed?
- ○ B Have you ever tried pot [grass, marijuana]?

2 《吸っている行為》
〈私は彼らがマリファナを吸っているのを見ました〉
- ◎ A I saw them smoking weed.
- ○ B I saw them smoking pot [grass, marijuana].

3 《麻薬でラリる》
〈彼は昨夜, 麻薬でラリっていた〉
- ☆ A He was high last night.
- ◎ B He was high on crack [drugs] last night.
- ◎ C He was loaded [stoned, fucked up] last night.
- ○ D He was high on pot [weed] last night.
- △ E He was doped up last night.
- △ F He was high on dope [grass] last night.

丸…
〈私は丸5年間アメリカにいました〉
- ◎ A I was in America for five full years.
- ◎ B I was in America for a full [good] five years.
- ○ C I was in America for five solid [whole] years.
- ○ D I was in America for a whole five years.
- × E I was in America for full five years.
  - ❖ E が辞典に出ているが使われていない.

まわり
1 《「場所のまわり」と言うとき》
〈私は毎日家のまわりをジョギングします〉
- ◎ A I jog around the neighborhood every day.
- ○ B I jog the neighborhood every day.
- × C I jog around the house every day.
  - ❖ around には「…じゅうを」という意味があるので,「家のまわりを」を C のように around the house とすると, 家の外側というより内部を, すなわち「家じゅうを」という意味になり, 家の中をジョギングすることになるので不自然. ただし, 次の場合は「…の外側をぐるりと」という意味になる: I jog around the lake every day. (私は毎日湖のまわりをジョギングします)

2 《「まわりの人」と言うとき》
〈まわりの人に聞いて下さい〉
- ◎ A Ask around.
- △ B Ask the [other] people around you.

回り道する
1 《一般的に言うとき》
〈道路はこの先で工事中だから私たちは回り道しなければならない〉
- ☆ A We have to take a detour because the road down the street's under construction.
- ◎ B We have to go the long way around because the road down the street's under construction.
- ◎ C We have to take the long way (around) because the road down the

street's under construction.
- ◯ D　We have to make a detour because the road down the street's under construction.
- △ E　We have to detour because the road down the street's under construction.
- △ F　We have to go a long way around because the road down the street's under construction.

2　《比喩的な意味のとき》

〈回り道かもしれませんが最終的には引き合うでしょう〉

- ◎ A　It may take longer [a long time] but it'll pay you in a long time.
- ◎ B　You may need more time but it'll pay you in a long time.
- ◎ C　You may have to spend more time but it'll pay you in a long time.
- ◯ D　It may be a detour but it'll pay you in a long time.
- ◯ E　You may have to take a detour but it'll pay you in a long time.

回る　→中心 2

満室です

《ホテル》

a） フロントのスタッフが宿泊希望者に述べるとき

〈お部屋は満室でございます〉

- ☆ A　All the rooms're taken.
- ◎ B　All the rooms're full [booked (up)].
- ◎ C　There are no rooms available.
- ◎ D　We have no vacancies [vacancy].
- ◎ E　We have no reservations available.
- ◎ F　We're booked up.
- ◎ G　The rooms're full.
- ◯ H　We're full.
- △ I　We have no vacancies available.

b） フロントのスタッフが宿泊希望者に強く述べるとき

〈お部屋は満室でございます〉

- ☆ A　We're completely booked.
- ◎ B　We're completely full [booked up].
- ◎ C　All the rooms're completely full [booked (up)].
- ◎ D　The rooms're completely full [booked (up)].
- △ E　All the rooms're fully booked up.

マンション

1　《一戸を所有しているとき》

〈彼らは湖が見えるマンションに住んでいるんです〉

- ☆ A　They live in a condo with a lakeview.
- ◎ B　They live in a condo complex with a lakeview.
- △ C　They live in a condo building with a lakeview.
- △ D　They live in a condominium with a lakeview.

2　《貸借しているとき》

〈彼らはマンションに住んでいるんです〉

- ◎ A　They live in an apartment (building).
- ▽ B　They live in an apartment house.

3　《ワンルームマンション》

〈彼女はワンルームマンションに住んでいる〉

- ☆ A　She lives in a studio apartment.

- ◎ B She lives in a studio.
- ○ C She lives in an efficiency apartment.
- △ D She lives in an efficiency.

満席です

1 《飛行機》

a）一般的に述べるとき

〈(旅行代理店で) 満席でございます〉

- ☆ A There are no seats available.
- ◎ B The flight's full.
- ◎ C All the seats're full.
- ○ D The flight's booked (up).
- ○ E There's no seat available.
- × F We have no vacancy.
- × G We have no seats available.

b）強調して述べるとき

〈(旅行代理店で) 満席でございます〉

- ☆ A The flight's completely booked up.
- ◎ B We're completely full [booked (up)].
- ◎ C All the seats're completely full.
- △ D All the seats're fully booked up.
- △ E All the seats're occupied.

c）飛行機の到着先を明示して述べるとき

〈(旅行代理店で) サンフランシスコ行きの便は満席でございます〉

- ☆ A There are no seats available on the San Francisco flight.
- ◎ B The flight to San Francisco's full.
- ◎ C The San Francisco flight's full.
- ○ D There's no seat available on the San Francisco flight.

2 《レストラン》

a）一般的に述べるとき

〈支配人：ただいま満席でございます〉

Manager:

- ◎ A We're full right now.
- ◎ B We're booked (up) right now.
- ◎ C The tables're full.
- ○ D The tables're booked (up).

b）強調して述べるとき

〈支配人：ただいま満席でございます〉

Manager:

- ☆ A We're completely full.
- ◎ B All the tables're completely booked.
- ◎ C We're completely booked.
- ○ D The tables're completely booked.
- ○ E We're completely booked up.
- △ F The tables're completely booked up.
- △ G All the tables're completely booked up.

満足させる

〈上司を満足させることは難しいんです〉

- ☆ A It's tough to please my boss.
- ◎ B My boss's tough to please.

- ○ C It's tough to make my boss happy.
- ○ D It's tough to satisfy my boss.
- △ E My boss's tough to satisfy.
- △ F It's tough to make my boss satisfied.

満点を取る

〈誰がテストで満点を取ったのですか〉
- ◎ A Who aced the test?
- ◎ B Who got a hundred [the perfect score] on the test?
- × C Who got full marks?
  - ❖ C が辞典に出ているが,アメリカでは使われていない.ただし,イギリスではよく使われている.

真ん中で [に]

1 《テニスコート》

〈校庭の真ん中にテニスコートがあります〉
- ◎ A There's a tennis court in the middle of the school yard.
- ○ B There's a tennis court in the center of the school yard.

2 《髪の毛》

〈彼の髪の毛は真ん中で分けられています〉
- ◎ A His hair's parted in the middle.
- ○ B His hair's parted in the center.

3 《都市》

〈うちの事務所はシカゴの真ん中にあります〉
- ☆ A Our office is in downtown Chicago.
- ◎ B Our office is in the center [middle] of Chicago.
- ○ C Our office is in the downtown area [district] of Chicago.
- △ D Our office is in the central Chicago.
  - ❖厳密には A, C はビジネス上, B, D は地理上の「真ん中に」であるが,アメリカ人は混用している.

万引きする

〈彼は高価なネクタイを万引きしたところを見つかったんです〉
- ◎ A He was caught lifting [shoplifting, stealing] an expensive tie.
- × B He was caught boosting an expensive tie.
  - ❖ B が辞典に出ているが使われていない.

真ん前に [で]

1 《建物の正面の場合》

〈メイシーの真ん前で会いましょう〉
- ☆ A Let's meet in front of Macy's.
- ◎ B Let's meet right in front of Macy's.
- ○ C Let's meet directly in front of Macy's.
- △ D Let's meet immediately [just] in front of Macy's.
- △ E Let's meet just before Macy's.

2 《通りをはさんでいる場合》

a) 強調して述べるとき

〈彼の店はシカゴ銀行の真ん前にあります〉
- ◎ A His store directly faces Chicago Bank.
- ◎ B His store's right [directly, just, exactly] across (the street) from Chicago Bank.
- ◎ C His store's directly opposite Chicago Bank.
- ○ D His store's directly facing Chicago Bank.

△ E His store's right [just] on the other side of the street from Chicago Bank.
▽ F His store's immediately facing Chicago Bank.
❖強調の度合いは A, D, F が一番強い.

b) 普通に述べるとき

〈彼の店はシカゴ銀行の真ん前にあります〉

◎ A His store faces [His store's facing] Chicago Bank.
◎ B His store's across (the street) from Chicago Bank.
◎ C His store's opposite Chicago Bank.
◎ D His store's on the other side of the street from Chicago Bank.
❖「真ん前」にあるという強調の度合いは A が一番強く，2 番目は C．B, D は「真ん前」ばかりでなく少し斜めでも使われている．

〔み〕

見えますか

〈男性：すみませんが，郵便局はどこにありますか〉
Man: Excuse me, where's the Post Office?
〈女性：緑色の屋根のビルが見えますか．それですよ〉
Woman:
◎ Can [Do] you see a building with the green roof? That's it.
❖Can you... は建物などに遮られて見にくいとき，Do you... は見るのに困難がないとき．

見栄を張る

1 《2 人称のことを述べるとき》

〈見栄を張るな〉
☆ A Don't try to make yourself look better than you are.
◎ B Don't try to make yourself look good.
◎ C Don't try to put up a front.
△ D Don't try to put on airs.
× E Don't try to keep up appearances.
× F Don't be vainglorious [pretentious].

2 《3 人称のことを述べるとき》

〈彼は見栄を張るためにキャデラックを買ったんです〉
☆ A He bought a Cadillac to make himself look better than he is.
◎ B He bought a Cadillac to make himself look good.
◎ C He bought a Cadillac to keep up appearances.
△ D He bought a Cadillac to put up a front.
× E He bought a Cadillac to cut a dash [a wide swath].
❖E が辞典に出ているが使われていない．

見送る

1 《人を》

a) 1 人または小人数で

〈私は彼を成田で見送るつもりです〉
◎ A I'm going to see him off at Narita.
× B I'm going to give him a send-off at Narita.
× C I'm going to send him off at Narita.

b) 大勢で
〈親戚全員が成田で私を見送ってくれました〉
- ◎ A All my relatives saw me off at Narita.
- ○ B All my relatives gave me a send off at Narita.

c) 盛大に
〈親戚全員が成田で私を盛大に見送ってくれたんです〉
- ◎ A All my relatives gave me a big send-off at Narita.
- ○ B All my relatives gave me a large send-off at Narita.
- △ C All my relatives gave me a good send-off at Narita.

2 《機会を》
〈これがいいチャンスなのは分かっているんだけど，見送らなければならないんです〉
- ◎ A I know this is a good chance but I have to pass it up [pass on it, pass it].
- ○ B I know this is a good chance but I have to let it go.
- △ C I know this is a good chance but I have to forgo it.
  - ❖ C には堅い響きがある．

見落とす
〈彼は私のミスを見落としたんです〉
- ◎ A He missed my mistake.
- ◎ B He didn't see [catch, find] my mistake.
- ○ C He skipped [overlooked] my mistake.
- △ D He passed over [by] my mistake.

未解決の →解決する 3

磨く
1 《物を》
a) 靴
〈靴を磨いてくれますか〉
- ◎ A Will you polish [shine] my shoes?
- △ B Will you give my shoes a brush [a polish]?
- △ C Will you put a shine on my shoes?
  - ❖ B, C が辞典に出ているが，多少使われている程度．

b) 銀器
〈銀のお皿を磨いてくれますか〉
- ◎ A Will you polish the silver tray?
- ○ B Will you shine the silver tray?
- △ C Will you give the silver tray a polish?
- ▽ D Will you burnish [brighten, scour] the silver tray?
- ▽ E Will you put a shine on the silver tray?
  - ❖ D, E が辞典に出ているがあまり使われていない．

2 《才能などを》
a) 語学力
〈私はフランス語力を磨かなければならないんです〉
- ◎ A I have to improve [work on, brush up on] my French.
- △ B I have to brush up my French.
- ▽ C I have to develop my French.
  - ❖ C が辞典に出ているがあまり使われていない．

b) ユーモアのセンス
〈あなたはユーモアのセンスを磨かなければなりません〉
- ☆ A You've got to work on your sense of humor.

- ◎ B You've got to improve your sense of humor.
- ◎ C You've got to get a sense of humor.
- ○ D You've got to develop your sense [a sense] of humor.
- ○ E You've got to work on a sense of humor.
- × F You've got to brush up on [get] your sense of humor.
  - ❖辞典に F が出ているが使われていない.

c) セールストーク

〈あなたはセールストークを磨かなければならないね〉

- ☆ A You've got to work on your sales pitch.
- ◎ B You've got to improve [develop] your sales pitch.
- ○ C You've got to brush up on [work at, get, polish up] your sales pitch.
- × D You've got to polish your sales pitch.
- × E You've got to get a sales pitch.

見かけ

1 《見かけで判断する》

〈人を見かけで判断すべきではない〉

- ◎ A You shouldn't go by looks [appearance(s)] only.
- ◎ B You shouldn't judge by looks [appearance(s)] only.
- ◎ C You shouldn't make a judgment by looks [appearance(s)] only.
- ◎ D You shouldn't size people up by looks [appearance(s)] only.
- ○ E You shouldn't pass judgment by looks [appearance(s)] only.
- × F You shouldn't judge from appearance(s) only.
- × G You shouldn't pass a judgment by appearances only.
  - ❖(1) F, G が辞典に出ているが使われていない.
  - ❖(2) A～E すべて, only の代わりに alone を使っても可.

2 《Looks, Appearances が主語のとき》

〈見かけは当てにならない〉

- ◎ A Looks [Appearances] can be deceiving.
- ◎ B Looks [Appearances] can deceive.
- ◎ C Looks're [Appearances're] deceiving.
- ○ D Looks're [Appearances're] misleading.
- △ E Looks're [Appearances're] deceptive.
- × F Appearances're deceitful.
  - ❖(1) 多くの辞典に F が出ているが使われていない.
  - ❖(2) A, B は can を用いているので, 断定度は他の表現より弱い.

右に出る

〈フランス語となると, 彼の右に出る人はいません〉

- ☆ A No one can beat [top] him when it comes to French.
- ◎ B No one can outshine [outdo, outperform] him when it comes to French.
- ○ C No one can surpass [exceed, overshadow] him when it comes to French.
- × D No one can outstrip [outmatch, excel, get ahead of] him when it comes to French.
  - ❖ D が辞典に出ているが使われていない.

右に曲がる

〈角を右に曲がりなさい〉

- ◎ A Make [Take, Hang] a right at the corner.

◎ B Turn right at the corner.
   △ C Turn to the right at the corner.

見込み
〈我々が試合に勝つ見込みは七三だ〉
   ◎ A The odds're 7 to 3 that we'll win the game.
   ▽ B The chances're 7 to 3 that we'll win the game.
   ❖どの辞典にも B が出ているがあまり使われていない．

未婚の母
〈彼女は未婚の母なんです〉
   ◎ A She's a single mother.
   ○ B She's an unwed mother.

未熟な
1 《職業上》
〈彼は弁護士としては未熟です〉
   ☆ A He isn't very experienced as a lawyer.
   ◎ B He doesn't have much [a lot of, enough] experience as a lawyer.
   ○ C He's very inexperienced as a lawyer.
   × D He's a greenhorn [greenhand, fresh hand] as a lawyer.
   × E He's immature as a lawyer.
   × F He isn't mature as a lawyer.
   ❖D, E, F が辞典に出ているが使われていない．

2 《人格》
〈彼はまだ未熟ですが紳士です〉
   ◎ A He still isn't perfect but he's a gentleman.
   ○ B He still doesn't do everything right but he's a gentleman.
   △ C He still doesn't do everything perfect but he's a gentleman.
   × D He's still immature but he's a gentleman.
   × E He still isn't mature but he's a gentleman.
   ❖辞典に D, E が出ているが使われていない．D, E は辞典に「未熟な」と出ているが，これは誤りで，「子供っぽい」という訳語が適切だからである．

3 《未熟児》
〈彼女は昨夜1ヵ月早く未熟児を産みました〉
   ☆ A Last night her baby was born one month early.
   ◎ B Last night she had her baby one month early.
   ◎ C Last night her baby came out one month early.
   ◎ D Last night her baby came out one month premature.
   ◎ E Last night her baby was born one month premature.
   ○ F Last night she had her baby one month premature.
   ○ G Last night she gave birth to a one-month premature.
   ○ H Last night she delivered a baby one month early.
   △ I Last night she had a one-month premie.
   × J Last night she had a one-month premature [immature] baby.
   × K Last night she delivered a baby one month early.
   ❖(1) C, D は残酷な響きがあるが非常によく使われている．
   ❖(2) A, B, C, H には「早産した」だけで未熟児の意味ではないと思うかもしれないが，1ヵ月早いとなるとアメリカでは未熟児と考える．

水着
1 《女性用の場合》
〈私は水着を買わなければならないんです〉

◎ A I have to buy a swimsuit [bathing suit].
△ B I have to buy a swimming suit.
× C I have to buy a swimming [bathing] costume.
❖ C は辞典に出ているが使われていない．

2 《男性用の場合》
〈私は水着を買わなければならないんです〉
◎ A I have to buy a swimsuit.
○ B I have to buy a swim trunks.
○ C I have to buy a bathing suit.
▽ D I have to buy a pair of (swimming) trunks.
▽ E I have to buy a swimming suit.
❖ D, E が辞典に出ているがまれ．

水増しする
1 《請求書》
a) 水増しの事実を否定的に述べるとき
〈広告代理店が水増し請求してきたんです〉
◎ A The ad agency padded the bill.
○ B The ad agency inflated the bill.

b) 水増しの事実を客観的事実として述べるとき
〈広告代理店が水増し請求してきたんです〉
◎　 The ad agency increased the bill.

c) 水増しのパーセンテージ・金額を述べるとき
〈広告代理店が2割水増し請求してきたんです〉
◎ A The ad agency padded [increased] the bill (by) 20%.
○ B The ad agency inflated the bill (by) 20%.

2 《大学の入学生の定員》
〈定員の2割またはそれ以上水増し入学させる大学が多い〉
◎　 Many colleges accept 20 or more students than they should have.

水をさす
1 《人間関係》
〈彼女は私たちの関係に水をさそうとしている〉
☆ A She's trying to come between us.
◎ B She's trying to break us up.
○ C She's trying to put a barrier between us.
○ D She's trying to spoil our relationship.
○ E She's trying to alienate us from each other.
△ F She's trying to sour our relationship.
△ G She's trying to alienate me from you.
△ H She's trying to throw cold water [a wet blanket] on our relationship.
△ I She's trying to throw a wrench into our relationship.
× J She's trying to estrange us.
× K She's trying to dash cold water [throw a chill] on our relationship.
❖(1) 辞典に J, K が出ているが使われていない．
❖(2) H は約45歳以上の人には時々使われている．60歳以上なら普通に使われているが，若い人たちの間では使われていない．

2 《博士号・弁護士の資格などを取ろうとしている努力を伴う計画・夢など》
〈私が博士号を取ろうとしていることに水をささないで下さい〉
◎ A Don't discourage me from getting my Ph.D.

- △ B Don't get [make] me discouraged from getting my Ph.D.
- △ C Don't get [bring] me down from getting my Ph.D.
  - ❖ B, C は人によってはまれにしか使われていない．したがって，相手が使ったときの知識としてインプットしておくべきだが，自分から使うことは勧めない．

3 《やかん・なべなどに水を入れる》
〈やかんに水をさして下さい〉
- ☆ A Please put some water in the kettle.
- ◎ B Please put some water into the kettle.
- ○ C Please pour some water in [into] the kettle.

店

1 《肉屋》

a) スーパーの中で店員に尋ねるとき
〈肉屋さんはどこですか〉
- ☆ A Where's the meat department?
- ○ B Where's the meat section [counter]?
- ○ C Where do you have [keep] the meat?
- △ D Where's the meat?
  - ❖アメリカでスーパーがある市や町では独立した肉屋はない．スーパーの中にある．

b) 小さい町で
〈角に肉屋があります〉
- ◎ A There's a butcher [meat market] on the corner.
- ○ B There's a butcher's on the corner.
- △ C There's a butcher shop on the corner.

2 《魚屋》

a) スーパーの中で店員に尋ねるとき
〈魚屋はどこですか〉
- ☆ A Where's the fish department?
- ◎ B Where's the fish section?
- ◎ C Where's the sea food department [section]?
- ○ D Where do you have [keep] the fish?
- ○ E Where's the sea food?
- △ F Where's the fish?
  - ❖アメリカでスーパーがある市や町では独立した魚屋はない．スーパーの中にある．

b) 小さい町で
〈角に魚屋があります〉
- ☆ A There's a fish market on the corner.
- ◎ B There's a fish shop [store] on the corner.
- × C There's a fish dealer [monger] on the corner.
  - ❖ C が辞典に出ているが使われていない．

3 《花屋》
〈角に花屋があります〉
- ◎ A There's a florist on the corner.
- ○ B There's a flower shop on the corner.
- △ C There's a flower store on the corner.
- × D There's a florist's on the corner.
  - ❖ D が辞典に出ているが使われていない．

4 《バイキングレストラン》
〈あのビルにはバイキングレストランがあります〉
- ☆ A That building has an all-you-can-eat restaurant.
- ◎ B That building has a buffet-style restaurant.
- ◎ C That building has a buffet.
- ○ D That building has a buffet restaurant.
- △ E That building has a smorgasbord.
- ▽ F That building has a smorgasbord restaurant.
- ❖ A は B〜F より大衆的な響きがある．

5 《寿司屋》
〈角に寿司屋があります〉
- ◎ A There's a sushi bar on the corner.
- × B There's a sushi shop [store] the corner.

6 《パン屋》
〈角にパン屋があります〉
- ◎ A There's a bakery on the corner.
- ○ B There's a baker's on the corner.
- △ C There's a baker on the corner.

7 《酒屋》
〈角に酒屋があります〉
- ◎ A There's a liquor store on the corner.
- △ B There's a liquor shop on the corner.
- △ C There's a package store on the corner.

8 《スーパー》
〈この先にスーパーがあります〉
- ☆ A There's a grocery store down the street.
- ◎ B There's a big grocery store down the street.
- ○ C There's a large grocery store down the street.
- △ D There's a supermarket down the street.

9 《食料品店》
〈この先に食料品店があります〉
- ☆ A There's a grocery store down the block.
- ◎ B There's a corner grocery store down the block.
- ○ C There's a neighborhood [small] grocery store down the block.

10 《デリカショップ》
〈角にデリカショップがあります〉
- ◎ A There's a deli on the corner.
- △ B There's a delicatessen on the corner.
- △ C There's a sandwich shop on the corner.
- × D There's a delica shop on the corner.
- × E There's a side dish store on the corner.
- ❖(1) D が日本のお惣菜店の看板で広く使われているが英語ではない．
- ❖(2) E が辞典に出ているが使われていない．
- ❖(3) A, B は英米ではお惣菜そのものだけを売っているのではなく，お客の好みに応じてお惣菜をサンドイッチにして売る店．

11 《お菓子屋》
〈角にお菓子屋があります〉
- ◎ A There's a candy store on the corner.
- ○ B There's a candy shop on the corner.

× C There's a confectionery store on the corner.
  ❖ C が辞典に出ているが今は使われていない.

12 《クリーニング屋》
〈このドレスをクリーニング屋へ持って行ってください〉
  ◎ A Take this dress to the cleaners, please.
  △ B Take this dress to the laundry, please.
  × C Take this dress to the cleaner's, please.
  × D Take this dress to the laundry [cleaning] shop, please.
    ❖(1) C は辞典に出ているが使われていない.
    ❖(2) 以前は水洗いのクリーニング屋は B の laundry, ドライのクリーニング屋は C の cleaner's であったが, 今はどちらにも A の cleaners が使われている.
    ❖(3) cleaners は単複同型で, 複数でも cleanerses とはしない. There are some cleaners near my office. (私の事務所の近くにクリーニング屋が何軒かあります).

13 《コインランドリー》
〈彼は5つコインランドリーを持っているんです〉
  ◎ A He owns five laundromats.
  ○ B He owns five coin laundries.
  △ C He owns five self-service laundries.

14 《生地屋》
〈角に生地屋があります〉
  ◎ A There's a fabric store on the corner.
  × B There's a material store on the corner.
  × C There's a dry-goods store [shop] on the corner.

15 《電気屋》
〈この近くに電気屋がありますか〉
  ◎ A Is there an appliance store near here?
  △ B Is there an appliance dealer near here?
  × C Is there an electric [electrical] store near here?
    ❖(1) C が辞典に出ているが使われていない.
    ❖(2) アメリカでは以前と違って, 電気屋は日本のようにない. 今は電気製品は金物店やウォルマートのような店で売られている.

16 《家具屋》
〈角に家具屋があります〉
  ◎ A There's a furniture store on the corner.
  ○ B There's a home furnishing store on the corner.

17 《リサイクルショップ》
〈角にリサイクルショップがあります〉
  ◎ A There's a thrift store [shop] on the corner.
  × B There's a recycle [recycling] store on the corner.
    ❖ A は慈善のための中古衣料品店. したがって, 日本のリサイクルショップと全く等しくはない.

18 《車の販売店》
a) 新車
〈角に車の販売店があります〉
  ◎   There's a car dealer [dealership] on the corner.
    ❖ car dealer は多くのメーカーの車を扱っている. car dealership は一社のメーカーの車しか販売していない. しかし, アメリカ人でこの違いを知って

いる人は少なく，混用されている．
 b) 中古車
〈この先に中古車の販売店があります〉
   ◎ A There's a used car dealer [lot] down the street.
   △ B There's a secondhand car dealer [lot] down the street.
19 《車の修理所》
 a) 自動車修理所を指していることがはっきりしている場合
〈彼はこの先の自動車修理所で修理工として働いています〉
   ◎ He works for the shop [garage] down the street as a mechanic.
 b) ガレージと誤解される恐れがある場合
〈ベティ：あら，高級車を持っているのね〉
Betty: Gee, that's an expensive car you have!
〈キャシー：ありがとう．でも，実を言うとお父さんのなのよ．私のは今，自動車修理所に出してあるのよ〉
Cathy:
   ◎ A Oh thank you, but to tell you the truth it's my father's. Mine's in the shop now.
   ▽ B Oh thank you, but to tell you the truth it's my father's. Mine's in the garage now.
   ❖ 上の対話でBのgarageを使うと自宅のガレージに誤解される恐れがある．
 c) shopかgarageかはっきりしない場合
〈ジェーン：どこで会いましょうか〉
Jane: Where should we meet?
〈ボブ：スミス自動車修理所で会おう〉
Bob:
   ◎ A Let's meet at Smith's Auto.
   ◎ B Let's meet at Smith's Garage.
   ◎ C Let's meet at Smith's Shop.
   ◎ D Let's meet at Smith's.
   ❖ この地域をよく知らない人にはA，Bが普通使われ，C，Dは知っている者同士で使われている．
20 《レンタカー屋》
〈角にレンタカー屋があります〉
   ◎ A There's a rental car agency on the corner.
   △ B There's a rental car agent on the corner.
21 《ガソリンスタンド》
〈この先にガソリンスタンドがあります〉
   ◎ A There's a gas station down the street.
   △ B There's a filling station down the street.
22 《販売代理店》
 a) 車の代理店の場合
〈私はフォードの代理店に勤めています〉
   ◎ A I work for a Ford Dealership.
   ○ B I work for a Ford Dealer.
 b) 車以外の代理店
〈私はソニーの代理店に勤めています〉
   ◎ A I work for a Sony Dealer.
   ○ B I work for a Sony Dealership.
23 《旅行代理店》

〈角に旅行代理店があります〉
- ◎ A There's a travel agency on the corner.
- ◎ B There's a travel agent on the corner.
- △ C There's a travel company on the corner.
  - ❖ B は小さい町では時々しか使われていない．

24 《インターネットカフェ》

〈角にインターネットカフェがあります〉
- ◎ There's a cybercafe [an internet cafe] on the corner.

25 《写真館》

〈角に写真館があります〉
- ◎ A There's a photo studio on the corner.
- ◎ B There's a photographer studio on the corner.
- ○ C There's a photographer on the corner.

26 《ビデオ屋》

a) 売っている店

〈角にビデオ屋があります〉
- ◎ A There's a video store on the corner.
- ○ B There's a video shop on the corner.

b) 貸す店

〈角にビデオ屋があります〉
- ◎ A There's a video store on the corner.
- ○ B There's a video shop on the corner.
- △ C There's a video rental store [shop] on the corner.

27 《金物屋》

〈角に金物屋があります〉
- ◎ A There's a hardware store on the corner.
- △ B There's a hardware shop on the corner.

28 《瀬戸物屋》

〈角に瀬戸物屋があります〉
- ◎ A There's a china store on the corner.
- ○ B There's a china shop on the corner.
- × C There's a chinaware store [shop] on the corner.
  - ❖ C が辞典に特記なく出ているが使われていない．ただし，chinaware store はアメリカの東南部ではよく使われている．

29 《スポーツ用品店》

〈角にスポーツ用品店があります〉
- ☆ A There's a sporting goods store on the corner.
- ◎ B There's a sporting goods shop on the corner.
- × C There's a sport goods store [shop] on the corner.

30 《質屋》

〈角に質屋があります〉
- ◎ A There's a pawn shop on the corner.
- × B There's a pawn store on the corner.

31 《事務用品店》

〈角に事務用品店があります〉
- ◎ A There's an office supply store on the corner.
- △ B There's an office supply shop on the corner.

32 《文房具店》

〈角に文房具店があります〉

- ◎ A There's a stationery store [shop] on the corner.
- × B There's a stationer('s) on the corner.

33 《宝石店》
〈角に宝石店があります〉
- ◎ A There's a jewelry store on the corner.
- ○ B There's a jewelry shop on the corner.
- △ C There's a jeweler on the corner.

34 《エステ》
〈角にエステがあります〉
- ◎ A There's a (health) spa on the corner.
- × B There's an esthetic salon [an esthetician] on the corner.

35 《美容院》
〈角に美容院があります〉
- ☆ A There's a beauty shop on the corner.
- ◎ B There's a beauty salon on the corner.
- ○ C There's a beauty parlor on the corner.
- △ D There's a beautician on the corner.
  - ❖ B は高級な美容院に使われている．C は米国南部では非常によく使われている．

36 《床屋》
〈角に床屋があります〉
- ☆ A There's a barber on the corner.
- ◎ B There's a barber shop on the corner.
- ○ C There's a barber's shop on the corner.

37 《薬局》
〈角に薬局があります〉
- ◎ There's a drug store [a pharmacy] on the corner.
  - ❖ 厳密には処方せんを扱う店が pharmacy で扱わない店が drug store. しかし，実際には混用されている．

38 《かぎ屋》
〈角にかぎ屋があります〉
- ☆ A There's a locksmith on the corner.
- ◎ B There's a key store on the corner.
- ○ C There's a key shop on the corner.

39 《不動産屋》
〈角に不動産屋があります〉
- ☆ A There's a real estate agency on the corner.
- ◎ B There's a real estate agent on the corner.
- ○ C There's a realty agency [a realtor] on the corner.
  - ❖ realtor は他の語と比べて上品な響きがあるため，不動産業者は realtor と呼ばれることを好む．

40 《画廊》
a) オリジナルの絵を置いている店
〈角に画廊があります〉
- ◎ There's an art gallery [a gallery] on the corner.

b) 複製の絵を置いている店
〈角に画廊があります〉
- ◎ A There's a printshop on the corner.
- ○ B There's a poster store on the corner.

△ C There's a poster shop on the corner.
　　　× D There's a picture shop on the corner.
　　　❖ D が辞典に出ているが使われていない．
　41 《運送屋》
〈角に運送屋があります〉
　　　◎ A There's a moving company on the corner.
　　　○ B There's a mover on the corner.
　　　× C There's a carrier [a forwarding agent] on the corner.
　　　❖ C が辞典に出ているが使われていない．

見せびらかす
　1 《非常に否定的な意味で》
〈彼女は新しい車を見せびらかしていました〉
　　　◎ A She was flaunting her new car.
　　　△ B She was parading her new car.
　　　× C She was sporting her new car.
　　　❖(1) C が辞典に出ているが使われていない．
　　　❖(2) A は B より否定的ニュアンスがずっと強い．
　2 《客観的に述べるとき》
〈彼女は新しい車を見せびらかしていました〉
　　　◎　 She was showing off her new car.

見せる
　1 《物を》
〈(生地店で) 見本を見せてくれますか〉
　　　◎ A Will you show me [let me see] some samples?
　　　◎ B Can I look at [see] some samples?
　　　◎ C Can I take a look at some samples?
　　　○ D Can I have a look at some samples?
　2 《「証明する」という意味で》
〈有能であることを見せてくれたら昇給しますよ〉
　　　◎ A After you prove that you're capable, I'll give you a raise.
　　　○ B After you demonstrate [show] that you're capable, I'll give you a raise.

満たす
　1 《就職の条件》
〈(人事部の人が話している) 彼はすべての条件を満たしていないんです〉
　　　◎ A He doesn't meet all our requirements.
　　　○ B He doesn't fit [meet] the bill.
　　　△ C He doesn't meet the bills.
　　　× D He doesn't fulfill the bill(s).
　2 《需要》
〈市場の需要を満たさなければならない〉
　　　☆ A We have to meet the market demand.
　　　◎ B We have to fill [satisfy] the market demand.
　　　△ C We have to fit the market demand.
　　　× D We have to answer the market demand.
　3 《ニーズ》
〈私たちは市場のニーズを満たさなければならない〉
　　　☆ A We have to meet the market needs.
　　　◎ B We have to meet the needs of the market.

- ○ C We have to satisfy [fulfill, fill] the market needs.
- △ D We have to meet [answer] the market's needs.

4 《空腹》

〈トースト2枚では私の空腹は満たせません〉

- ◎ A Two pieces of toast won't fill me up.
- ○ B Two pieces of toast won't make me up.
- △ C Two pieces of toast won't satisfy my hunger.
- × D Two pieces of toast won't meet [fill, fulfill] my hunger.
  - ❖ D が辞典に出ているが使われていない．

5 《食欲》

〈これでは私の食欲は満たされません〉

- ◎ A This doesn't satisfy my appetite.
- ○ B This doesn't fill [fulfill] my appetite.
- ▽ C This doesn't appease my appetite.
- × D This doesn't meet my appetite.

6 《精神》

a）精神的と述べるとき

〈リンダ：私は彼に精神上で満たされていないんです〉

Linda:
- ◎ A I'm not happy [satisfied] with our mental life.
- ◎ B He doesn't make me happy mentally.
- ◎ C He doesn't satisfy me mentally.

b）何かと欠けているものがあると述べるとき

〈私は夫との生活に何か満たされていないんです〉

- ◎　Somehow I feel like there's something missing between us.

7 《性生活》

〈リンダ：私は彼との性生活に満たされていなんです〉

Linda:
- ◎ A I'm not happy [satisfied] with our sex life.
- ◎ B He doesn't satisfy me (sexually).
- ◎ C He doesn't make me happy sexually [in bed].
- △ D He doesn't meet my sexual desires.
- △ E He doesn't fulfill my sexual requirements.

道

1 《道を尋ねるとき》

a）尋ねている人が道順をだいたい知っているとき

〈横浜へ行く一番いい道順は何ですか〉

- ☆ A What's the best way to get to Yokohama?
- ◎ B What's the best road to get to Yokohama?
- △ C What's the best route to get to Yokohama?
  - ❖(1) A, C は道順を知らなくても使えるが，B はだいたいの道順を知っているときに使う．
  - ❖(2) route は出発点から目的地，つまり端から端までの道順を聞いている響きがある．

b）尋ねている人が道順を知らないとき

〈横浜へ行く一番いい道順は何ですか〉

- ◎ A What's the best way to get to Yokohama?
- △ B What's the best route to get to Yokohama?
- × C What's the best road to get to Yokohama?

c）近い場所まで行く詳細な道順を尋ねるとき
〈市役所へ行く道順を教えていただけますか〉
- ☆ A Can you give me directions to City Hall?
- ◎ B Can you tell me how to get to City Hall?
- ◎ C Can you tell me how I can get to City Hall?
- ○ D Can you direct me to City Hall?
- ○ E Can you tell me directions [the way] to City Hall?

2 《「道に迷う」ときの「道」》
〈(電話で) 道に迷ったんです．だから遅れます〉
- ◎ A I got lost, so I'll be late.
- ○ B I was lost, so I'll be late.
- △ C I lost my way, so I'll be late.
- × D I missed my way, so I'll be late.
- × E I lost myself, so I'll be late.
- × F I went out of the right way, so I'll be late.
  - ❖ D, E, F が辞典に出ているが使われていない．

3 《地下道》
〈地下道を使おう〉
- ◎ A Let's use the underpass.
- ◎ B Let's use the underground passage.
- ○ C Let's use the underground pass.

4 《高速道路》
〈高速道路を使おう〉
- ◎ A Let's take the turnpike.
- ◎ B Let's take the thruway.
- ◎ C Let's take the parkway.
- ◎ D Let's take the expressway.
- ◎ E Let's take the freeway.
- ◎ F Let's take the highway.
- ◎ G Let's take the motorway.
  - ❖ A, B, C は主としてアメリカの東部で使われている有料道路．D, F は中西部，東部で使われている．F は本来「公道」を指しているが，西海岸を除いた多くの州で「高速道路」の意味で使われている．西海岸で使われているのは E．D, E は通行料を取らない「高速道路」を言う．G はイギリス英語．

5 《森の中の道》
a）大きな森
〈あの森にはたくさん道がある〉
- ◎ A That forest has a lot of trails.
- ○ B That forest has a lot of paths.
- △ C That forest has a lot of pathways [walkways].
- × D That forest has a lot of walks.

b）普通の森
〈あの森にはたくさん道がある〉
- ◎ A Those woods have a lot of trails.
- ○ B Those woods have a lot of paths.
- △ C Those woods have a lot of pathways [walkways].
- × D Those woods have a lot of walks.
  - ❖ woods は forest より小さい森．普通ひとつの森でも woods と複数形で使

6 《「方法」の意味での道》
〈彼の助言にしたがうより他に道がない〉
- ◎ A We have no other choice but to take his advice.
- ○ B We have no other alternative but to take his advice.
- △ C We have no other way but to take his advice.

7 《成功への道》
〈これが成功への道です〉
- ☆ A This is the route to success.
- ◎ B This is the way [road] to success.
- ▽ C This is the gateway to success.
- × D This is the street to success.

密出国[入国]する[させる]

1 《密出国する》
〈彼は日本を密出国したようだ〉
- ◎ A It looks like he sneaked [snuck] out of Japan.
- ○ B It looks like he smuggled out of Japan.

2 《密入国する》
〈多くの外国人がアメリカへ密入国しようとしている〉
- ◎ A Many foreigners're trying to sneak into America.
- ○ B Many foreigners're trying to go to America as stowaways.

3 《密入国させる》
〈彼は大勢を日本へ密入国させたために逮捕されたんです〉
- ☆ A He was arrested for helping a lot of people get into Japan illegally.
- ◎ B He was arrested for helping a lot of people come into Japan illegally.
- ◎ C He was arrested for bringing a lot of people into Japan illegally.
- ◎ D He was arrested for illegally bringing a lot of people into Japan.
- ○ E He was arrested for sneaking [smuggling] a lot of people into Japan.
- ○ F He was arrested for bringing a lot of people enter Japan illegally.

密造する

1 《アルコール》
〈彼はウイスキーを密造したために逮捕されました〉
- ◎ A He was arrested for bootlegging whiskey.
- ◎ B He was arrested for brewing (whiskey) illegally.
- ◎ C He was arrested for making whiskey [moonshine] illegally.
- × D He was arrested for manufacturing [distilling] whiskey illegally.
- × E He was arrested for making whiskey illicitly [secretly].
- × F He was arrested for moonshine.
  - ❖ D, E, F が和英辞典に出ているが使われていない.
  - ❖ D の manufacture は工業製品を「製造する」意味にしか使われない. F の moonshine はどの英和辞典でも動詞で「(酒を)密造する」の意味を紹介しているが, 現在は使われていない.

2 《武器》
〈彼らは武器を密造したことで逮捕されたんです〉
- ◎ A They were arrested for making weapons illegally.
- ○ B They were arrested for manufacturing weapons illegally.
- △ C They were arrested for producing weapons illegally.

          △ D They were arrested for making [manufacturing] arms illegally.
          × E They were arrested for producing arms illegally.

見積り
1 《一般的に述べるとき》
〈明日までに見積りしてもらえますか〉
  ☆ A Can you give me an estimate by tomorrow?
  ◎ B Can you give me your estimate by tomorrow?
  ○ C Can you give me the estimate by tomorrow?

2 《概算の見積り》
〈明日までに概算の見積りをもらえますか〉
  ☆ A Can you give me a ballpark estimate by tomorrow?
  ◎ B Can you give me a rough estimate by tomorrow?
  ○ C Can you give me your [the] ballpark estimate by tomorrow?
  ○ D Can you give me your [the] rough estimate by tomorrow?
  △ E Can you give me an approximate estimate by tomorrow?
  ▽ F Can you give me your [the] approximate estimate by tomorrow?

3 《明細の見積り》
〈工事の費用の明細の見積りをもらえますか〉
  ◎ A Can you give me an itemized [a detailed] construction cost estimate?
  ◎ B Can you give me a detailed estimate on the cost of the construction?
  ○ C Can you give me an itemized estimate on the cost of the construction?
  ○ D Can you give me an estimate specifying the cost of the construction?
  △ E Can you give me a complete construction cost estimate?
  △ F Can you give me a complete estimate on the cost of the construction?

密輸入する
〈彼は麻薬を日本へ密輸入して逮捕されたんです〉
  ☆ A He was arrested for smuggling drugs into Japan.
  ◎ B He was arrested for bringing drugs into Japan (illegally).
  ○ C He was arrested for importing drugs into Japan illegally.
  ○ D He was arrested for running drugs through illegal channels into Japan.
  ○ E He was arrested for trafficking drugs into Japan.
  ❖ D, E は新聞では非常によく使われている．

見ている
1 《見なす》
a）情勢を
〈私は事態をこのように見ています〉
  ☆ A This is how I look at [see] the situation.
  ◎ B This is my take on the situation.
  ○ C This is how I view [understand] the situation.

b）人を
〈私たちは彼を保守的であると見ています〉
  ◎ A We see [regard, think of, view] him as (being) conservative.
  △ B We look at [on] him as (being) conservative.

2 《成り行きを見守る》
〈私は株式市場の回復を見ているんです〉
  ◎ A I've been following the recovery of the stock market.

- ◎ B I've been keeping an [my] eye on the recovery of the stock market.
- ◎ C I've been paying attention to the recovery of the stock market.
- ○ D I've been watching the recovery of the stock market.
- ○ E I've been keeping my eyes on the recovery of the stock market.

3 《監視する》

a) 子供の車などの危険に対して

〈子供たちを見ていてくれますか〉

- ◎ A Will you watch my kids?
- ◎ B Will you keep an eye on my kids?
- ○ C Will you keep your eyes on my kids?
- △ D Will you keep your eye on my kids?
- △ E Will you watch over my kids?

b) 成人のしてはいけないことに対して

〈主人がリンダとデートしないように見ていてくれますか〉

- ☆ A Will you keep an eye on my husband so he won't go out with Linda?
- ◎ B Will you keep your eye on my husband so he won't go out with Linda?
- ○ C Will you keep your eyes on my husband so he won't go out with Linda?
- △ D Will you watch my husband so he won't go out with Linda?

見てまわる

1 《デパートなどを》

a) 何かを探して，または時間つぶしに

〈あのデパートを見てまわろう〉

- ☆ A Let's check out that department store.
- ◎ B Let's look around (in) that department store.
- ◎ C Let's take a look around (in) that department store.
- ◎ D Let's browse around in that department store.
- ○ E Let's browse (around) that department store.
- ○ F Let's have a look around (in) that department store.

b) 時間つぶしに

〈あのデパートを見てまわろう〉

- ◎ A Let's walk around (in) that department store.
- ○ B Let's wander around (in) that department store.

c) 目的に関する含みのない場合

〈三越の中を見てまわろう〉

- ◎ A Let's browse [look] around Mitsukoshi.
- ◎ B Let's have [take] a look around Mitsukoshi.

2 《工場・学校などを》

a) 案内者とともに

〈キャンパスを見てまわりましょう〉

- ◎ A Let's tour the campus.
- ◎ B Let's take a tour of the campus.
- △ C Let's have a tour of the campus.

❖ A, B, C の表現はいずれも建物の中と外の両方について使える．

b) 案内者なしで

・建物の外

〈キャンパスを見てまわりましょう〉

- ☆ A Let's check out the campus.
- ◎ B Let's look around the campus.
- ◎ C Let's take [have] a look around the campus.
- ◎ D Let's have a look around on the campus.
- ○ E Let's take a look around on the campus.
- ○ F Let's look around on the campus.
・建物の中
〈キャンパスを見てまわりましょう〉
- ◎ A Let's check out [look around (on)] the campus.
- ◎ B Let's take a look around the campus.
- ○ C Let's have a look around the campus.

見て見ぬふりをする
〈年取った男性が電車の中で少年のグループに殴られていたのですが，みんな見て見ぬふりをしていました〉
- ☆ A An old man was being beaten by bunch of boys on the train, but everybody looked the other way.
- ◎ B An old man was being beaten by bunch of boys on the train, but everybody closed their eyes to it.
- ○ C An old man was being beaten by bunch of boys on the train, but everybody shut their eyes to it.

認められている
〈彼は世界で有数の指揮者の1人として認められている〉
- ☆ A He's regarded as one of the best conductors in the world.
- ☆ B He's considered (to be) one of the best conductors in the world.
- ◎ C He's recognized as one of the best conductors in the world.
- ○ D He's viewed [thought of] as one of the best conductors in the world.
- △ E He's accepted as one of the best conductors in the world.

認める
1 《名詞を従えるとき》
a) 誤り
〈彼は誤りを認めました〉
- ◎ A He admitted his mistake.
- ○ B He admitted to [owned up to] his mistake.
- ○ C He acknowledged his mistake.
- × D He allowed his mistake.
  - ❖(1) D は辞典に出ているが使われていない．
  - ❖(2) C は「しぶしぶ認める」というニュアンスがあるのに対して，A，B は指摘され「気づいて」認めるというニュアンスがある．

b) 敗北
〈ゴアは敗北をもっと早く認めるべきだった〉
- ◎ A Gore should've accepted [conceded] his defeat much sooner.
- △ B Gore should've admitted [acknowledged] his defeat much sooner.
- × C Gore should've owned up to his defeat much sooner.
  - ❖ concede には「進んで」というニュアンスがある．

c) 要求
〈会社側は組合の要求を認めた〉
- ◎ The management granted [agreed to, went along with] the union's demands.

❖「すんなりと認めた」というニュアンスが一番強いのは grant. 2番目は agree to, 3番目は go along with.

2 《動名詞を従えるとき》

〈彼は契約を破ったことを認めた〉

◎ A He admitted (to) breaking his contract.
○ B He acknowledged [owned up to] breaking his contract.
× C He allowed breaking his contract.
❖ C は辞典に出ているが使われていない.

3 《that 節を従えるとき》

〈彼は契約を破ったことを認めた〉

☆ A He admitted that he had broken the contract.
◎ B He acknowledged that he had broken the contract.
◎ C He owned up to the fact that he had broken the contract.
× D He owned [allowed] that he had broken the contract.
❖ D は辞典に出ているが使われていない.

4 《補語を従えるとき》

〈彼はうわさが本当であることを認めました〉

◎ A He admitted the rumor to be true.
○ B He acknowledged the rumor to be [being] true.
△ C He acknowledged the rumor as true.
△ D He owned up the rumor to be [being, as] true.
▽ E He admitted the rumor being [as] true.
❖ that 節を用いて He admitted that the rumor was true.（彼はうわさが本当であるということを認めました）とする方が一番よく使われている.

5 《なるほど(, しかし…)》

〈ビル：日本は住むには最悪の国だよ〉

Bill: Japan's the worst country to live in.

〈トム：どうして〉

Tom: How come?

〈ビル：物価が世界一高いからさ〉

Bill: Prices're the highest in the world.

〈トム：なるほど, それはそうだが犯罪率は低いよ〉

Tom:

◎ A Granted, but it has a low crime rate.
◎ B I agree, but it has a low crime rate.
○ C I'll buy it, but it has a low crime rate.
○ D I accept that, but it has a low crime rate.
△ E I admit [acknowledge] that, but it has a low crime rate.

南(の)

〈彼は南フランスで休暇を過しています〉

◎ A He's vacationing in southern France.
◎ B He's vacationing in the south of France.
○ C He's vacationing in the southern part of France.
× D He's vacationing in South France.
❖ 国・大陸について言う場合には, South Korea（韓国）, South America（南米）のようにする.「北」「東」「西」も使い方は同じ.

見晴らしがいい

1 《人以外の無生物が主語のとき》

a）主観的に述べる場合

〈シカゴホテルは湖の見晴らしがすばらしいんです〉
◎ A The Chicago Hotel has a really nice view of the lake.
◎ B The Chicago Hotel has a great view of the lake.
◎ C The Chicago Hotel has a terrific view of the lake.
◎ D The Chicago Hotel has a wonderful view of the lake.
◎ E The Chicago Hotel has an incredible view of the lake.
○ F The Chicago Hotel has a fantastic view of the lake.
❖(1) F は年配の女性（約45歳以上）に主として使われている．
❖(2) E が一番見晴らしがよいという響きがある．D, F が2番，C が3番，A, B が4番．しかし，A は really を使わないとぐーんと弱くなる．

b ）客観的に述べる場合
〈シカゴホテルは湖の見晴らしがすばらしいんです〉
◎ A The Chicago Hotel overlooks the lake.
◎ B The Chicago Hotel looks out over [onto] the lake.
○ C The Chicago Hotel looks out on the lake.
× D The Chicago Hotel commands a nice view of the lake.
❖ D が多くの辞典に出ているが使われていない．

2 《人が主語のとき》
〈シカゴホテルは湖の見晴らしがすばらしいんです〉
☆ A You can get a really nice view of the lake from the Chicago Hotel.
◎ B You can get a great [a terrific, an incredible] view of the lake from the Chicago Hotel.
○ C You can get a wonderful [fantastic] view of the lake from the Chicago Hotel.
△ D You have a nice outlook of the lake from the Chicago Hotel.
× E You have a nice prospect of the lake from the Chicago Hotel.

見舞う
〈私は父の見舞いに病院へ行ってきたところです〉
◎ A I've just been to the hospital to visit [see] my father.
◎ B I've just been to the hospital to check on my father.
○ C I've just been to the hospital to look in my father.
× D I've just been to the hospital to ask [inquire] after my father.
❖(1) D が辞典に出ているが使われていない．
❖(2) D は医師，看護婦［士］に尋ねることを意味し，病人と話をするというニュアンスはない．C は病人と顔を合せるが時間が短いという響きがある．B は医師，看護婦［士］に病状を尋ねること，また病人と話をして見舞うの両方の意味で使われている．A は病人に会って見舞うことを意味している．

見る・診る
1 《視線を向けるという感じのとき》
〈（彼が話し手・聞き手の方へ来るとき）彼を見て〉
◎ A Look at him.
○ B Take a look at him.
△ C Have a look at him.
❖ C が時間上一番短いとの響きがある．B が2番，A が一番長い．

2 《形容詞を従えたとき》
〈新しいドレスを着ている彼女を見て〉
☆ A Look at her in her new dress.
◎ B Take a look at her in her new dress.
△ C Have a look at her in her new dress.

3 《「じっと見る」というニュアンスのとき》
〈踊り方を見せますから見ていて下さい〉
- ☆ A I'm going to demonstrate how to dance. Watch me.
- ◎ B I'm going to demonstrate how to dance. Look at me.
- ○ C I'm going to demonstrate how to dance. Take a look at me.
- △ D I'm going to demonstrate how to dance. Have a look at me.

4 《ちらりと見る》
〈私は彼を角の所でちらりと見ました〉
- ◎ A I caught [got] a glimpse of him on the corner.
- △ B I had a glimpse of him on the corner.
- × C I glimpsed him on the corner.
  - ❖ C が辞典に出ているが使われていない．

5 《夢を見る》
a) 普通に述べるとき
〈私は毎晩夢を見ます〉
- ◎ A I dream every night.
- △ B I have a dream every night.
- ▽ C I dream a dream every night.

b)「夢で…を見る」と述べるとき
〈昨夜夢であなたを見ました〉
- ☆ A You were in my dream last night.
- ◎ B I dreamed about you last night.
- ○ C I had a dream about you last night.
- ○ D I saw you in my dream last night.

6 《「鑑賞する」の意味のとき》
〈絵を見に美術館へ行こう〉
- ◎ Let's go to the art museum to see [look at] pictures.

7 《テレビで映画を見るとき》
〈私は昨夜テレビでいい映画を見ました〉
- ◎ I saw [watched] a good movie on TV last night.

8 《テレビで試合を見るとき》
〈テレビでジャイアンツとタイガースの野球の試合を見よう〉
- ◎ A Let's watch the baseball game between the Giants and the Tigers on TV.
- △ B Let's see the baseball game between the Giants and the Tigers on TV.

9 《野球場で試合を見るとき》
〈私たちは野球の試合を見にヤンキースタジアムへ行きました〉
- ☆ A We went to the Yankee Stadium to watch a baseball game.
- ◎ B We went to the Yankee Stadium to see a baseball game.

10 《医者に診てもらう場合》
a) 主語が患者の場合
〈お医者さんに診てもらいなさい〉
- ☆ A You should see your doctor.
- ◎ B You should have your doctor look at you.
- ◎ C You should have your doctor take a look at you.
- ○ D You should have your doctor have a look at you.
- ○ E You should have your doctor check you.
- △ F You should have your doctor examine you [check you out].

▽　G　You should consult your doctor.
　×　H　You should consult your doctor check on you.
　　❖辞典に H が出ているが使われていない.
 b）主語が医者の場合
〈息子は熱が高いんです. 診ていただけますか〉
　☆　A　My son has a high fever. Will you take [have] a look at him?
　☆　B　My son has a high fever. Will you look at him?
　◯　C　My son has a high fever. Will you examine [check] him?
　△　D　My son has a high fever. Will you look over him?
　×　E　My son has a high fever. Will you see him?
　　❖E の see は, a）の患者が主語の場合の A のときか, 医者に電話をして「診ていただけますか」とか, 病院の廊下で担当の医者とすれ違ったときなどに「診ていただけますか」と言うとき, つまりまだ約束を取りつけていないときならよく使われている.
 c）診てもらう患部を明示する場合
〈お医者さんにおなかを診てもらいなさい〉
　◎　A　Have [Get] your stomach examined [checked, looked at] by your doctor.
　◎　B　Have your doctor examine [check, look at] your stomach.
11　《機械の故障などを診てもらう場合》
 a）一般的に述べる場合
〈私のテレビを診てくれますか〉
　◎　A　Will you have [take] a look at my TV?
　◎　B　Will you look at [check] my TV?
　△　C　Will you look over my TV?
　▽　D　Will you examine my TV?
　×　E　Will you see my TV?
 b）故障があるか否かを述べる場合
〈私のテレビが故障しているかどうか診てくれますか〉
　☆　A　Will you check [look over] if anything's wrong with my TV?
　◎　B　Will you see if anything's wrong with my TV?
　◯　C　Will you take [have] a look if anything's wrong with my TV?
　△　D　Will you examine if anything's wrong with my TV?

未練がある
1　《愛していた女性・男性に》
 a）別れたくない気持ちを述べるとき
〈私は彼女と別れることに決めたんですがまだ未練があるんです〉
　◎　A　I decided to break up with her but I still can't let her go.
　◎　B　I decided to break up with her but I still can't forget her.
　◎　C　I decided to break up with her but I still can't get her out of my mind.
　◎　D　I decided to break up with her but I still can't stop thinking about her.
　△　E　I decided to break up with her but I still can't quit thinking about her.
　△　F　I decided to break up with her but I'm still caught up with [hooked on, stuck on, attached to] her.
　×　G　I decided to break up with her but I'm still not ready to give up our bond.

- × H I decided to break up with her but I still have a lingering feeling for her.
- × I I decided to break up with her but I still have a lingering attachment for [to] her.
- × J I decided to break up with her but I still think regretfully of her.
- × K I decided to break up with her but I still feel some regret for her.
- × L I decided to break up with her but I still have a lingering affection for [to] her.
  - ❖(1) A は B〜F より強く「別れたくない」という響きがある.
  - ❖(2) G〜L が辞典に出ているが使われていない.

b) 楽しかったときのことを思い出して非常に感傷的な気持ちを述べるとき
〈私は彼女と別れることに決めたんですがまだ未練があるんです〉
- ◎ I decided to break up with her but I still can't forget her.

2 《買おうと思った家・車・ドレスなどに》
〈私はあの家を買わないことに決めたんですがまだ未練があるんです〉
- ◎ A I decided not to buy that house but I still can't stop thinking about it.
- ◎ B I decided not to buy that house but I still can't get it out of my mind.
- ○ C I decided not to buy that house but I still can't quit thinking about it.
- ○ D I decided not to buy that house but I still can't forget (about) it.
- △ E I decided not to buy that house but I still can't let it go.

見分ける

1 《「区別する」という意味で》

a) A と B とを見分ける
〈あなたは容姿だけでギリシア人とイタリア人を見分けられますか〉
- ◎ A Can you tell Greeks from Italians just by their looks?
- ◎ B Can you tell Greeks and Italians apart just by their looks?
- ○ C Can you distinguish Greeks from Italians just by their looks?
- △ D Can you distinguish [make a distinction] between Greeks and Italians just by their looks?
- × E Can you separate [discriminate, mark off] Greeks from Italians just by their looks?
- × F Do you know Greeks from Italians just by their looks?
  - ❖ E, F が辞典に出ているが使われていない.

b) 目的語が一つのとき
〈私はあの双子を見分けられません〉
- ◎ A I can't tell those twins apart.
- ◎ B I can't distinguish between those twins.
- ▽ C I can't distinguish those twins.
  - ❖ C が辞典に出ているがまれ.

2 《「多くの物の中から見つける」という意味で》
〈(遺失物保管所で) この中でご自分の傘が見分けられますか〉
- ☆ A Do you see your umbrella here?
- ◎ B Can you see [identify] your umbrella here?
- ◎ C Do you recognize your umbrella here?
- ○ D Can you recognize your umbrella here?
- × E Do you identify your umbrella here?
  - ❖「聴き分ける」の項も参照のこと

〔む〕

向かう
1 《話し手の方へ来るとき》
〈彼らはこちらへ向かっています〉
   ◎ A They're on the way here.
   ◎ B They're coming here.
   ○ C They're headed here.
   △ D They're heading here.
2 《病人が快方に》
〈患者は日毎に快方に向かっています〉
   ◎ A The patient's improving [getting better] every day.
   ◎ B The patient's on the road to recovery every day.
   ○ C The patient's taking a turn for the recovery every day.
   × D The patient's taking a better [favorable] turn for the recovery every day.
   ❖辞典に D が出ているが使われていない.
3 《問題が解決するとき》
〈この問題は解決の方向に向かっている〉
   ◎ A We've nearly [almost] got this problem licked.
   ◎ B We've nearly [almost] got this problem solved.
   × C This problem seems to be on the way to a solution.
   ❖ C は口語辞典に出ているが, 日本語につられた不自然な英語.

迎えに行く
1 《第三者を迎えに行くとき》
〈彼を飛行場まで迎えに行っていただけますか〉
   ☆ A Could you pick him up [go get him] at the airport?
   ◎ B Could you go and get him up at the airport?
   ◎ C Could you pick him up [go get him] from the airport?
   ○ D Could you go and get him from the airport?
   ○ E Could you get him at the airport?
   △ F Could you get him from the airport?
   △ G Could you go for him at the airport?
   × H Could you call for [collect] him at the airport?
   ❖ H が辞典に出ているが使われていない.
2 《相手を迎えに行くとき》
〈何時に飛行場まで迎えに行きましょうか〉
   ☆ A What time do you want me to pick you up at the airport?
   ◎ B What time do you want me to come (and) get you at the airport?
   ◎ C What time do you want me to pick you up [come get you] from the airport?
   ○ D What time do you want me to come and get you from the airport?
   ○ E What time do you want me to get you at the airport?
   △ F What time do you want me to get you from the airport?
   △ G What time do you want me to come for you at the airport?
   × H What time do you want me to call for [collect] you at the airport?

❖ H は辞典に出ているが使われていない.

昔の仲間
1 《女性が言う場合》
〈私は最近昔の仲間の誰にも全然会っていません〉
- ◎ A I never see any of our old friends these days.
- ○ B I never see any of the old crowd these days.
- △ C I never see any of our old buddies these days.
- △ D I never see any of the old gang these days.

2 《男性が言う場合》
〈私は最近昔の仲間の誰にも全然会っていません〉
- ◎ A I never see any of our old friends these days.
- ◎ B I never see any of the old crowd [gang] these days.
- ○ C I never see any of our old buddies these days.

昔流の教育を受けた
1 《否定的に使われている場合》
〈フランセズ：間違いないのよ．私のデートの相手と兄さんたちのデートの相手のことになると，父は2つの基準を持っているのよ〉
Frances: There's no doubt about it; my father sets a double standard when it comes to who I can date and who my brothers can date.
〈スーザン：だけどそれは無理ないわよ．なんだかんだと言っても昔流の教育を受けているんだから〉
Susan:
- ◎ Well, what do you expect? After all, he's from the old school.

2 《肯定的に使われている場合》
〈コリンズ氏：今度の事務員はすごく礼儀が正しいね．うちの他の女性よりもしとやかだね〉
Mr. Collins: That secretary they just hired has perfect manners. She acts more like a lady than the other women on the staff.
〈ハリス氏：昔流の教育を受けていることを忘れちゃだめだよ．他の女性はずうっと若いんだよ〉
Mr. Harris:
- ◎ She's from the old school, remember. The other women are much younger than she is.

…向きである
1 《店を述べるとき》
〈J.C.ペニーは大衆向きです〉
- ☆ A J. C. Penney's for the average shopper.
- ◎ B J. C. Penney's targeted [geared] to the average shopper.
- ◎ C J. C. Penney's geared for the average shopper.
- ◎ D J. C. Penney's targeted at the average shopper.
- ○ E J. C. Penney's meant [intended] for the average shopper.
- △ F J. C. Penney's tailored to [geared at, suited for] the average shopper.

2 《製品を述べるとき》
〈これは輸出向きです〉
- ☆ A This is for export.
- ◎ B This is intended [made, meant] for export.
- ○ C This is targeted [geared] for export.
- ○ D This is aimed at export.

3 《素質の観点から述べるとき》
〈彼は営業マン向きではない〉
- ◎ A He doesn't have the right stuff [potential, makings] to be a salesperson.
- ◎ B He doesn't have what it takes to be a salesperson.
- ○ C He isn't cut out [meant] for a salesperson.
- × D He isn't of a salesperson turn.
  - ❖ D が辞典に出ているが使われていない.

4 《適性の観点から述べるとき》
〈彼はこの種の仕事に向いています〉
- ☆ A He's made [cut out] for this kind of work.
- ◎ B He's fit [suited] for this kind of work.
- ○ C He's suitable for this kind of work.
  - ❖ C は少し改まった響きがある.

報いる
〈私は親切に報いたいのですが〉
- ☆ A I'd like to pay back your favor.
- ◎ B I'd like to return the favor.
- ○ C I'd like to repay [reciprocate] the favor.
- △ D I'd like to respond to the favor.
- × E I'd like to reciprocate for the favor.

矛盾している
1 《矛盾していることだけを述べるとき》
〈あなたが言っていることは矛盾している〉
- ◎ What you're saying is contradictory [contradicting].

2 《言動に矛盾があることを述べるとき》
a) 人が主語のとき
〈あなたの言動には矛盾があります〉
- ◎ A You aren't practicing what you're preaching.
- ◎ B You aren't what you preach.
- ◎ C You aren't doing what you say.
- ○ D You aren't doing what you're saying.

b) what you're saying が主語のとき
〈あなたが言っていることは矛盾している〉
- ◎ A What you're saying isn't consistent with your behavior.
- ○ B What you're saying's contradictory to [inconsistent with] your behavior.
- ○ C What you're saying's contradicting your behavior.
- ○ D What you're saying's in conflict with your behavior.
- △ E What you're saying's incompatible with your behavior.
- △ F What you're saying's in contradiction to your behavior.

3 《「矛盾だらけである」ことを述べるとき》
〈あなたが言っていることは矛盾だらけだ〉
- ◎ A What you're saying's full of inconsistencies.
- ○ B What you're saying's full of contradictions.

難しい
1 《一般に》
〈ルース：テストはどうだった〉
Ruth: How was the test?

〈ラルフ:すごく難しかったよ〉
Ralph:
  ☆ A It was really tough.
  ◎ B It was really hard.
  ○ C It was really difficult.

2 《深刻な内容の場合》
〈ブラウン夫人:息子が交通事故で5年前に死んだのです〉
Mrs. Brown: My son was killed in a car accident five years ago.
〈スミス夫人:まあ,それはお気の毒ですね〉
Mrs. Smith: I'm sorry to hear that.
〈ブラウン夫人:息子がいなくてとても寂しいことがよくあるんです.彼のことを考えないようにするのですが,時々難しいんです〉
Mrs. Brown: I often miss him terribly.
  ◎ A I try not to think about him, but it's difficult sometimes.
  ○ B I try not to think about him, but it's hard sometimes.
  ▽ C I try not to think about him, but it's tough sometimes.

3 《「難しい点」と述べるとき》
a) 初心者
〈これはわたしにとって難しい点のひとつです〉
  ☆ A This is one of the major problems for me.
  ◎ B This is one of the tough [hard] problems for me.
  ○ C This is one of the main problems for me.
  △ D This is one of the difficult [tough, hard, sticking] points for me.

b) 非初心者・専門家
〈これは私にとって難しい点のひとつです〉
  ☆ A This is one of the major problems for me.
  ◎ B This is one of the tough [hard, main] problems for me.
  ○ C This is one of the difficult [tough, hard] points for me.
  △ D This is one of the sticking points for me.

4 《「…するのは難しい」と述べるとき》
〈彼の事務所を見つけるのはとても難しかったんです〉
  ◎ A I had a lot of trouble finding his office.
  ◎ B I had a really hard time finding his office.
  ◎ C It was really hard finding [to find] his office.
  ◎ D It was really tough finding [to find] his office.
  ○ E It was very difficult finding [to find] his office.
  ○ F Finding his office was really difficult.
  △ G I had a lot of difficulty finding his office.

5 《面接などで急所をつかれたときに》
〈面接官:どのぐらい日本に滞在するのですか〉
Interviewer: How long are you going to stay in Japan?
〈アメリカ人の応募者:難しい問題です.私にはよくわかりません〉
American applicant:
  ◎   That's a good question. I really don't know.
  ❖ここでは good が使われるが,これは無限制ではなく,It was a good question.(難しい質問でした)/It was a good test.(難しいテストでした)のような語と結びついて用いられている.読むときは good を強く発音する.

6 《難しい注文》

〈それは難しい注文だ〉
- ◎ A That's a tall order.
- ◎ B That's a lot to ask.
- △ C That's a tough [difficult] order.

無駄

1　《無駄足を踏む》
〈私の事務所へ来るときは，必ず電話して下さい．もし，して下さらないと，無駄足を踏むかも知れませんよ〉
- ◎ A When you come to my office, be sure to call me. If not, you may end up on a wild goose chase.
- ○ B When you come to my office, be sure to call me. If not, your trip may be for nothing.
- △ C When you come to my office, be sure to call me. If not, your trip may be for naught.
- ▽ D When you come to my office, be sure to call me. If not, your trip may be futile.

2　《無駄にさせる》
〈あなたは私にたくさんのお金を無駄にさせていますよ〉
- ☆ A You're wasting a lot of my money.
- ◎ B You're making me waste a lot of my money.
- ○ C You're forcing me to waste a lot of my money.

3　《「…するのに時間［お金］を無駄にする」と述べるとき》
〈私は彼を２週間説得しようとしましたが無駄でした〉
- ◎ A I wasted two weeks trying to persuade him.
- ◎ B I tried to persuade him for two weeks but it was useless.
- ◎ C I tried to persuade him for two weeks but I couldn't.

4　《「…しても無駄だ」と述べるとき》
〈彼を説得しようとしても無駄です〉
- ☆ A There's no point trying to persuade him.
- ◎ B There's [It's] no use trying to persuade him.
- ◎ C It's of no use to try to persuade him.
- ◎ D It's useless [pointless] to try to persuade him.
- △ E It's no good trying to persuade him.
- × F There's no good trying to persuade him.

5　《無駄になる》
〈もしあなたがそれをやればあなたの時間は無駄になりますよ〉
- ◎ A If you do that, you'll be wasting your time.
- ○ B If you do that, your time'll be wasted.
- △ C If you do that, your time'll go to waste.

6　《「努力が無駄になる」と述べるとき》
〈あなたの努力はすべて無駄になるでしょう〉
- ☆ A All your efforts'll be wasted.
- ◎ B All your efforts'll go [lead] nowhere.
- ○ C All your efforts'll go down the drain.

夢中です

1　《10代の女性が一方的に夢中になっている場合》
〈ジェーンは先生に夢中なんです〉
- ☆ A Jane has a crush on her teacher.
- ☆ B Jane's infatuated with her teacher.

- ☆ C Jane's crazy about her teacher.
- ◎ D Jane's madly in love with her teacher.
- ○ E Jane's nuts about her teacher.
- △ F Jane's mad for [about] her teacher.
- △ G Jane's wild about her teacher.
- × H Jane's dead gone on her teacher.
  - ❖(1) A は 10 代の男の子が主語の場合には多少使われている.
  - ❖(2) A, B は「一方的な恋」, C〜G は一方的, また両者が夢中になっている場合にも使われている.

2 《成人が一方的に夢中になっているとき》
〈リンダはビルに夢中なんです〉
- ☆ A Linda's infatuated with Bill.
- ☆ B Linda's crazy about Bill.
- ☆ C Linda's totally [head over heels] in love with Bill.
- ◎ D Linda's madly in love with Bill.
- ◎ E Linda's nuts about Bill.
- ○ F Linda's hooked on Bill.
- △ G Linda's mad for [about] Bill.
- △ H Linda's wild about Bill.
- △ I Linda has a crush on Bill.
- △ J Linda's pretty stuck on Bill.
- × K Linda's over (head and) ears in love with Bill.
- × L Linda's falling headlong in love with Bill.
- × M Linda has her head turned by Bill.
  - ❖(1) 辞典に K, L, M が出ているが使われていない.
  - ❖(2) A 以外は両面的な場合にも使われている.

3 《年令に関係なく両者が夢中になっている場合》
〈彼らはお互いに夢中なんです〉
- ☆ A They're crazy about each other.
- ☆ B They're head over heels in love with each other.
- ◎ C They're totally in love with each other.
- ◎ D They're nuts about each other.
- ○ E They're madly in love with each other.
- ○ F They're wild about [hooked on] each other.
- △ G They're mad for [about] each other.

4 《無生物に夢中になっている場合》
〈彼はゴルフに夢中なんです〉
- ◎ A He's crazy about golf.
- ○ B He's wild [nuts] about golf.
- △ C He's mad about [hooked on] golf.

胸が詰まる →詰ま(らせ)る 5
無理だ

1 《聞き手の第三者に対する行動を述べるとき》
〈貸付け主任:担保なしで1億円借りたいんですって. それは無理ですよ〉
Loan Officer:
- ◎ A You want to borrow a hundred million yen without any collateral? That's [You're] asking too much.
- ○ B You want to borrow a hundred million yen without any collateral? That's [You're] expecting too much.

2 《聞き手の話し手に対する期待・要求を無理だと述べる場合》
〈あなたが言っていることは無理だよ〉
- ◎ A You're [That's] asking too much from me.
- ◎ B You're [That's] expecting too much from me.
- ◎ C What do you expect from me?
- ○ D You're [That's] asking too much of me.
- ○ E You're [That's] expecting too much of me.
- ○ F What do you expect of me?
  ❖ C, F は全体を強いトーンで述べる必要がある.

〔め〕

目 →目が大きい, 目が覚める, 目が飛び出るほどのお金を払う, 目がない, 目と鼻の先, 目をつけている, 目を離さない

明記する
〈一番いい大理石が玄関に使われるように, 契約で明記した方がいいですよ〉
- ☆ A You'd better stipulate [specify] in the contract that the best marble be used in the entrance hall.
- ◎ B You'd better write down [put down, express, spell (it) out, designate] in the contract that the best marble be used in the entrance hall.
- △ C You'd better make a point [provide, qualify, set terms] in the contract that the best marble be used in the entrance hall.
- × D You'd better render [fix] in the contract that the best marble be used in the entrance hall.
  ❖ D が辞典に出ているが使われていない.

明細 →見積り 3

名士
〈パーティーのお客のほとんどは名士でした〉
- ◎ A Most of the guests at the party were celebrities.
- ◎ B Most of the guests at the party were famous people.
- ○ C Most of the guests at the party were famous figures.
- ○ D Most of the guests at the party were big names.
- × E Most of the guests at the party were socialites [personages, social lions].
  ❖ E が辞典に出ているが使われていない.

名目上の
〈うちの社長は名目上なんです〉
- ◎ A Our president's in name only.
- ◎ B Our president's just a figurehead.
- △ C Our president's just in name.
- ▽ D Our president's just a titular head.

名誉毀損
〈彼のことをそんなふうに言っちゃ駄目だよ. 名誉毀損で訴えられるよ〉
- ◎ A Don't say that about him, or he'll sue you for libel.
- ◎ B Don't say that about him, or he'll sue you for slander.
- △ C Don't say that about him, or he'll sue you for defamation of

character.
- △ D Don't say that about him, or he'll sue you for character damage.
- ▽ E Don't say that about him, or he'll sue you for character assassination.
  - ❖(1) E が辞典に出ているが，現在，口語英語ではめったに使われていない．
  - ❖(2) A は文書，B は口頭での名誉毀損と区別されていると辞書に出ているが，実際は全く区別なく使われている．

目が大きい
〈彼の目は大きい〉
- ◎ A He has big eyes.
- △ B His eyes're big.
  - ❖身体の一部に言及するときは，目に限らず have で表現する．

目が覚める
〈私は毎朝5時頃目が覚めるんです〉
- ◎ A I wake up around 5:00 every morning.
- ○ B I wake around 5:00 every morning.
- × C I awake (up) around 5:00 every morning.
  - ❖C が辞典に出ているが使われていない．

目方をごまかす →ごまかす 1

(…に)目がない
〈私はアンティーク家具に目がないんです〉
- ◎ A I have a thing for antique furniture.
- ◎ B I have a weakness for antique furniture.
- ○ C I have a passion for antique furniture.
- ○ D I'm in love with antique furniture.
- △ E I really go for antique furniture.
- △ F I have a fancy for antique furniture.
  - ❖(1) B がニュアンスとしては一番強い．
  - ❖(2) E は以前は非常によく使われていた．

めちゃめちゃになる
〈約束を守りなさい．さもないとあなたの評判はめちゃめちゃになりますよ〉
- ◎ A Keep your promise, or it'll destroy [ruin] your reputation.
- ○ B Keep your promise, or it'll trash [spoil, mess up, screw up, wreck] your reputation.
- △ C Keep your promise, or it'll mar your reputation.
- × D Keep your promise, or it'll make a mess [a muddle, a hash, a mush, a mull] of your reputation.
  - ❖(1) D が辞典に出ているが使われていない．
  - ❖(2) めちゃめちゃにする度合いは A が一番強い響きがある．B が2番目に強い．

めったに…ない
〈私はめったに車で会社に行きません〉
- ☆ A I almost never drive to work.
- ◎ B I hardly ever drive to work.
- ○ C I rarely drive to work.
- △ D I seldom drive to work.

めどがつく
〈6ヶ月もかかったが，ついにプロジェクトのめどがついた〉
- ◎ A It took no less than six months but finally we can see the [a] light

at the end of the tunnel on the project.
- ◎ B It took no less than six months but finally we can see the [an] end on the project.
- ◎ C It took no less than six months but finally we can see the [an] end to the project.
- ◎ D It took no less than six months but finally we can get close [near] to the end on the project.
- ○ E It took no less than six months but finally we're moving on toward the end on the project.
- △ F It took no less than six months but finally we're approaching the end on the project.

目と鼻の先 →近い 1 e)

めまいがする

1 《病気》

a) 普通のめまいのとき

〈私はめまいがするんです〉

- ◎ A I'm [I feel] dizzy.
- ◎ B I'm [I feel] light-headed.
- ◎ C My head's spinning.
- × D My head's swimming.
- × E I feel giddy.

❖(1) D, E が辞典に出ているが使われていない．

❖(2) B の I'm light-headed. と C はどの辞典にも出ていないがよく使われている．

b) 強いめまいのとき

〈私はすごくめまいがするんです〉

- ◎ A I'm (feeling) really dizzy.
- ◎ B I feel really [really feel] dizzy.
- ◎ C My head's really spinning.
- ◎ D The ceiling's [The rooms's] really spinning.
- ○ E I really feel like the ceiling's spinning.
- △ F My bed's spinning.

2 《多忙のとき》

〈私は忙しくてめまいがしています〉

- ◎ A I'm overwhelmed because I'm too busy.
- ◎ B I feel like I'm spinning my wheels because I'm too busy.
- ○ C My head's spinning [swimming] because I'm too busy.
- △ D I feel like I'm spinning around because I'm too busy.
- △ E My head spins [swims] because I'm too busy.
- × F My head's reeling because I'm too busy.

メモ

1 《手書きの場合》

〈外出するときはメモを書いて下さい〉

- ◎ A When you go out, be sure to leave a note.
- ○ B When you go out, be sure to write a note.
- × C When you go out, be sure to leave [write] a memo.

2 《ワープロの場合》

〈全員机を離れるときは鍵をかけるように注意したメモをもらいました〉

- ◎ A Everybody got a memo reminding people to lock their desks when

　　　　　　they leave.
　　　× B　Everybody got a note reminding people to lock their desks when they leave.

目をつけている
1 《異性に興味を持っているとき》
a) 普通に述べるとき
〈リンダは彼に目をつけているんです〉
　　☆ A　Linda's got her eye on him.
　　☆ B　Linda has her eye on him.
　　◎ C　Linda's got her eyes on him.
　　◎ D　Linda has her eyes on him.
　　○ E　Linda's got an eye on him.
　　○ F　Linda has an eye on him.
　　○ G　Linda has her sights set on him.
　　❖ A, B が「目をつけている」度合いは一番強い.

b) 強調して述べるとき
〈リンダは彼にすごく目をつけているんです〉
　　☆ A　Linda definitely's [really's] got her eye on him.
　　☆ B　Linda definitely [really] has her eye on him.
　　◎ C　Linda definitely's [really's] got her eyes on him.
　　◎ D　Linda definitely [really] has her eyes on him.
　　○ E　Linda really has an eye on him.
　　○ F　Linda really's got an eye on him.

2 《土地・家・店などを買おうとしているとき》
〈彼はこの土地に目をつけているんです〉
　　☆ A　He's got his eye on this land.
　　☆ B　He has his eye on this land.
　　◎ C　He's got his eyes [an eye] on this land.
　　◎ D　He has his eyes [an eye] on this land.

3 《警察が見張っているという意味での「目をつけている」とき》
〈刑事が彼に目をつけているんです〉
　　☆ A　The police detective's got an eye on him.
　　☆ B　The police detective has an eye on him.
　　◎ C　The police detective's watching him.
　　○ D　The police detective's got his eyes [eye] on him.
　　○ E　The police detective has his eyes [eye] on him.

目を離さない
〈子供たちから目を離さないで下さい〉
　　◎ A　Keep an [your] eye on my children.
　　◎ B　Watch my children closely [carefully].

面している
1 《湖・山などに面している場合》
〈ホテルは湖に面している〉
　　◎　　The hotel faces the lake.

2 《方角に面している場合》
〈ホテルは南に面しています〉
　　◎ A　The hotel faces south.
　　△ B　The hotel faces the south.

3 《「眺めがよい」ことに焦点がある場合》

〈ホテルは湖に面しています〉
- ◎ A The hotel looks out over [onto] the lake.
- ◎ B The hotel has a nice view of the lake.
- ◎ C The hotel overlooks the lake.
- ◎ D You can get a nice view of the lake from the hotel.
- ○ E The hotel looks out on the lake.
    - ❖ face と look out onto, look out over との比較：face を使った場合，眺めはよいかも知れないが特にその点に言及するニュアンスはなく，方角が湖に面しているということにすぎない．したがって，距離の遠近にかかわらず使える．look out onto, look out over は方角が面しているのみならず，湖の美しい眺めが見える，すなわち湖から近いというニュアンスがある．

4 《隣接していて，直接その場所へ出ていける場合》
〈私の部屋は前庭に面しています〉
- ◎ A My room faces the front yard.
- ◎ B My room opens (out) onto the front yard.
- ○ C My room opens up onto the front yard.
- ○ D My room looks out onto the front yard.
- △ E My room opens out on the front yard.
- ▽ F My room looks out into the front yard.
- ▽ G My room opens (out) into the front yard.
    - ❖ F, G が辞典に出ているがほとんど使われていない．

5 《通りに面している場合》
〈私の家は通りに面しています〉
- ◎ A My house faces the street.
- △ B My house looks onto the street.
- ▽ C My house fronts on the street.
    - ❖ C が辞典に出ているがまれにしか使われていない．

[も]

…も →…も(また), …も(また…でない)
もう
1 《動作動詞とともに》
〈彼はもう仕事を終えたはずです〉
- ◎　　He must have finished his work by now [already].
    - ❖ by now は「もういい加減に終わっているはずだ」といういらつきのニュアンスを含む．

2 《状態動詞とともに》
〈彼はもう出勤しているはずです〉
- ◎　　He should be in by now [already].
    - ❖ どちらもいらつきのニュアンスはない．

3 《疑問文》
〈彼はもう退社[帰宅]したのですか〉
- ◎ A Has he left the office yet?
- ◎ B Has he left the office already?
- ○ C Has he left the office this early?
    - ❖ A は「すでに退社した」という客観的事実のみを伝えるのに対して，B, C

は驚きの気持ちを表している.

もう一度
1 《「もう一度…したい」の意味のとき》
〈私はもう一度アメリカへ行きたいと思っています〉
- ☆ A I want to go to America again.
- ☆ B I want to go to America one more time.
- ◯ C I want to go to America once more.
- ◯ D I want to go to America a second time.
- △ E I want to go to America once again.

2 《実行可能なことを述べるとき》
〈あなたはそれをもう一度読んだほうがいいですよ〉
- ◎ A You'd better read it (all) over again.
- ◎ B You'd better read it over.
- ◎ C You'd better read it once more.
- ◎ D You'd better read it (once) again.

3 《実行不可能なことを述べるとき》
〈もう一度人生をやり直せたらいいんだけどなあ〉
- ◎ A I really wish I could start my life all over again.
- ◎ B I really wish I could start my life over.
- ◎ C I really wish I could start my life (once) again.
- ◎ D I really wish I could start my life all over.
- ◎ E I really wish I could start my life one more [another] time.

❖Aが一番強い響きがある.

4 《「試みる」というニュアンスがあるとき》
〈私はもう一度それをやってみたいんです〉
- ◎ A I want to try it one more time.
- ◎ B I want to try it again.
- ◎ C I want to have another try at it.
- ◎ D I want to give it another try.
- ◯ E I want to try it once again [more].

5 《相手が言ったことが聞き取れなかったとき》
〈もう一度言ってくれますか〉
- ◎ A Come again?
- ◎ B Once again?
- ◎ C Again?
- ◎ D Sorry?

❖詳細は「何ですって」の項を参照のこと.

もうおしまいだ
〈昨日私はもう少しでトラックと衝突するところだったんです.「もうおしまいだ」と本当に思いました〉
- ◎ A Yesterday I almost crashed into a truck. I really thought, "That's it."
- ◎ B Yesterday I almost crashed into a truck. I really thought, "That was it."
- ◎ C Yesterday I almost crashed into a truck. I really thought, "That was it for me."
- ◎ D Yesterday I almost crashed into a truck. I really thought, "It was over."

申し込む
1 《旅行》

〈私はカナダへの7日間の旅行に申し込むつもりです〉
- ◎ A I'm going to sign up for a seven-day trip to Canada.
- ○ B I'm going to join a seven-day trip to Canada.
- × C I'm going to sign on for a seven-day trip to Canada.
- ❖(1) C は辞典に出ているが使われていない．
- ❖(2) A は 1 人で行く場合と団体旅行に参加する場合の両方に使える．B は団体旅行にしか使えない．

2 《学校など》
a) 学校に
〈私はボストンアカデミーに申し込むつもりです〉
- ◎ A I'm going to enroll [register] at Boston Academy.
- ○ B I'm going to be enrolled at Boston Academy.

b) 講座に
〈私はボストンアカデミーの英語コースに申し込むつもりです〉
- ◎ A I'm going to sign up for [register for, enroll in] an English course at Boston Academy.
- △ B I'm going to join [be enrolled in] an English course at Boston Academy.
- × C I'm going to sign on for an English course at Boston Academy.
- ❖ C が辞典に出ているが使われていない．

もう少し

1 《売上げのノルマ・目標達成に近い人，数学などを解こうとしている人を励ますとき》
〈支配人：もう少しだね〉
Manager:
- ☆ A You're almost there.
- ◎ B You're just about there.
- ○ C You're on the right track.
- ○ D You're nearly [practically] there.
- × E You're virtually there.
- × F You're all but there.

2 《車などでどこかに到着できるとき》
〈サンフランシスコまでもう少しだね〉
- ☆ A We're almost in San Francisco.
- ◎ B We're almost [very close] to San Francisco.
- ◎ C We're nearly [just about] in San Francisco.
- ○ D We're nearly to San Francisco.
- ○ E We're practically in San Francisco.
- × F We're very close in San Francisco.

3 《仕事が終了したか否かの質問に対して》
〈もう少しです〉
- ☆ A Almost.
- ◎ B Just about.
- ◎ C I'm just about done [through, finished].
- ◎ D I'm almost done [there, finished].
- ○ E I'm just about wrapped up [there].
- ○ F I'm nearly there [done, wrapped up, through, finished].
- ○ G I'm almost through.

4 《形容詞を従えるとき》

〈彼はビルよりもう少し魅力的です〉
- ◎ A He's a little (bit) more attractive than Bill.
- △ B He's a bit more attractive than Bill.

5 《名詞を従えるとき》

〈彼は私よりもう少し稼ぎます〉
- ◎ He makes some [a little] more money than me.

6 《何かを「もう少しでしそこなってしまった」と述べたいとき》

〈私は今朝もう少しで電車に乗りそこなうところだった〉
- ◎ A I almost [just about] missed the train this morning.
- ○ B I nearly [practically] missed the train this morning.
- ○ C I came close [near] to missing the train this morning.

7 《「もう少しでするところだった」と述べたいとき》

〈私はもう少しで彼に電話するのを忘れるところだった〉
- ◎ A I almost forgot to call him.
- ○ B I just about forgot to call him.
- ○ C I nearly [practically] forgot to call him.
- ○ D I came close to forgetting to call him.
- △ E I came near to forgetting to call him.

もうたくさんだ

1 《文句など「もう言うのをやめて」という気持ちのとき》

〈もうたくさんだよ。あなたいつから私に文句を言っているか分かっているの〉
- ◎ A Give me [Gimme] a break. Do you know how long you've been complaining to me?
- ◎ B Stop bugging [bothering] me. Do you know how long you've been complaining to me?

2 《「文句を十分うかがいました」という気持ちで述べるとき》

〈あなたの文句はもうたくさんです〉
- ☆ A I've had enough of your complaints.
- ◎ B I've had enough of your complaining.
- ◎ C I've had it with your complaining [complaints].
- ◎ D I'm sick and tired of your complaining.
- ○ E I'm sick and tired of your complaints.
- △ F I'm fed up with your complaining [complaints].

3 《食事中にもっと食べることを勧められたとき》

〈夫：デザートを食べるかい〉

Husband: Would you like some dessert?

〈妻：もうたくさんだわ〉

Wife:
- ◎ A I've had enough.
- ◎ B I'm full.
- ○ C I've eaten enough.
- ○ D My stomach's full.

もうろくする

〈彼はもうろくしてきた〉
- ◎ A He's getting senile [old].
- ◎ B His memory's getting bad.
- × C He's falling into dotage.

❖ A の get old は単に「彼は年をとった」という意味にもなる．

黙秘権を行使する
〈彼女は多分そのことについては黙秘権を行使するでしょう〉
☆ A She'll probably take the Fifth on that.
◎ B She'll probably take the Fifth Amendment on that.
△ C She'll probably exercise her right to keep silence on that.
▽ D She'll probably invoke the Fifth on that.
❖ D が辞典に出ているがほとんど使われていない．

文字通り
1 《文字通り受け入れる》
〈彼が言ったことを文字通り取るな〉
◎ A Don't take what he said literally.
× B Don't take what he said to the letter.
2 《文字通り法律が施行される》
〈法令は文字通り施行されました〉
◎ A The law was enforced to the letter.
○ B The law was enforced literally.

持ち帰り
〈(ファーストフード店で) これはお持ち帰りですか〉
☆ A Is this to go?
◎ B Is this order to go?
◎ C Is this take-out?
○ D Is this carry-out?
△ E Is this a take-out [carry-out] order?

持ち出す
1 《話題》
〈二度とこの問題を持ち出さないで下さい〉
◎ A Don't bring this issue up again.
◎ B Don't bring up this issue [problem] again.
◎ C Don't raise this issue again.
◎ D Don't talk about this issue [problem] again.
◎ E Don't discuss this issue [problem] again.
× F Don't raise this problem again.
2 《イスなどを外に》
〈このイスを庭に持ち出していいですか〉
◎ A Can I take [bring] this chair out into the yard?
○ B Can I carry this chair out into the yard?
3 《本を図書館の外に》
〈この百科辞典は図書館外へは持ち出せません〉
◎ A You can't take this encyclopedia out of the library.
△ B You can't bring this encyclopedia out of the library.

持ち直す
1 《株式市場》
〈株式市場はまもなく持ち直すだろう〉
☆ A The stock market'll recover soon.
◎ B The stock market'll improve [go back up, bounce back, rebound] soon.
○ C The stock market'll pick up [come back, rally, jump back] soon.
△ D The stock market'll rise back soon.
❖(1) A と，C の come back, jump back は話し手が喜んでいるニュアンスが

他の表現より強い．
* (2) C の rally は株式市場の人の間では非常によく使われている．

2 《売上げ》
〈4月のうちの売上げは持ち直しました〉
- ◎ A Our sales bounced back in April.
- ◎ B Our sales jumped back up in April.
- ○ C Our sales recovered in April.
- ○ D Our sales went [rose, came] back up in April.
- ○ E Our sales rebounded [picked back up] in April.
  * A, B が一番強い響きがある．E が2番，C が3番，D が4番．

3 《患者》
〈患者はまもなく持ち直すでしょう〉
- ☆ A The patient'll recover soon.
- ◎ B The patient'll improve soon.
- ○ C The patient'll get well again soon.
- △ D The patient'll get his health back soon.
- △ E The patient'll rebound soon.
  * A, C, D は完全に回復するという響きがある．

もちろん

1 《丁寧に言う場合》
〈面接官：明日最終面接に来ることが出来ますか〉
Interviewer: Can you come for a final interview tomorrow?
〈応募者：もちろんです〉
Applicant:
- ☆ A Certainly.
- ◎ B Of course.
- ◎ C Definitely.
- ◎ D I certainly can.
- ○ E Sure.
- ○ F Sure I can.
- ○ G I sure can.
- ▽ H Certainly I can.
  * 大企業の面接など，丁寧さが求められているときは，Certainly. は Sure. よりよく使われている．

2 《少しくだけて言う場合》
〈面接官：月曜から働けますか〉
Interviewer: Can you start working Monday?
〈応募者：もちろんです〉
Applicant:
- ◎ A Sure.
- ◎ B Sure I can.
- ◎ C I sure can.
- ◎ D Definitely.
- ◎ E You bet.
  * コーヒーショップのアルバイトの面接など．

3 《親しい友人同士の場合》
〈ビル：僕たちが校庭で野球をした昔の日々を覚えているかい〉
Bill: Do you remember the old days when we played baseball in the schoolyard?

〈ジム：もちろんさ〉
- ◎ A Of course.
- ◎ B You bet.
- ◎ C You betcha.
- ◎ D Sure.
- ◎ E Sure I do.
- ◎ F I sure do.
- ▽ G You bet your boots [life].
  - ❖(1) G が辞典に出ているが，まれにしか使われていない．
  - ❖(2) C は中年以上の人の間では非常によく使われているが，年代が若くなるにつれて使用頻度は下がる．

持つ　→長持ちする
持っていく
 1 《誰かに持っていかせる》
〈彼にコーヒーを持っていってください〉
- ☆ A Please take him a cup of coffee.
- ◎ B Please bring him a cup of coffee.
- ○ C Please take a cup of coffee to him.
- ○ D Please bring a cup of coffee to him.
  - ❖どの辞典も B, D を紹介していないが，俗語ではなく，以前からよく使われ定着している．
 2 《話し手が聞き手の所へ電話などで尋ねている》
 a) 両者が対等の立場のとき
〈あなたの事務所へ行くとき何を持っていきましょうか〉
- ☆ A When I come to your office, what should I bring?
- ◎ B When I come to your office, what should I take?
- ◎ C When I come to your office, what should I bring [take] with me?
- ○ D When I come to your office, what should I take [bring] along?
 b) 聞き手に敬意を表す必要があるとき
〈あなたの事務所へ行くとき何をお持ちいたしましょうか〉
- ☆ A When I come to your office, what should I bring [take]?
- ◎ B When I come to your office, what should I bring [take] with me?
- △ C When I come to your office, what should I take [bring] along with me?

持ってくる
 1 《別の部屋にあるものを》
〈私に辞書を持ってきてくれますか〉
- ◎ A Will you go get the dictionary (for me)?
- ◎ B Will you get the dictionary for me?
- ◎ C Will you get [bring] me the dictionary?
- ○ D Will you bring the dictionary to me?
 2 《同じ部屋にあるものを》
〈私に辞書を持ってきてくれますか〉
- ◎ A Will you get the dictionary for me?
- ◎ B Will you get [bring] me the dictionary?
- ○ C Will you bring the dictionary to me?
- △ D Will you bring the dictionary for me?
- △ E Will you go get the dictionary (for me)?

戻る

1 《前いた場所へ》
〈三越へ戻りましょう〉
- ◎ A Let's go back to Mitsukoshi.
- △ B Let's return to Mitsukoshi.

2 《話が脱線したとき》
〈話していたことに戻りましょう〉
- ◎ A Let's get [go] back to what we were talking about.
- △ B Let's return to what we were talking about.

3 《盗まれたものが》
〈私の盗まれた車は戻りました〉
- ◎ My stolen car's been recovered [found].

…も (また)

1 《かしこまった話し方をするとき》
〈私は弁護士です．妻も(また)弁護士です〉
- ☆ A I'm a lawyer. My wife is as well.
- ◎ B I'm a lawyer. My wife is too [also].
- ◎ C I'm a lawyer. Same with my wife.
- ◎ D I'm a lawyer. My wife too.
- ◎ E I'm a lawyer. So is my wife.
- ◎ F I'm a lawyer. My wife is an attorney as well [too].

2 《くだけた話し方をするとき》
〈スミス氏：私はサンフランシスコから来ました〉
Mr. Smith: I come from San Francisco.
〈ブラウン氏：私もそうなんです〉
Mr. Brown:
- ☆ A Me too.
- ☆ B I do too.
- ◎ C Same with me.
- ◎ D Same here.
- ◎ E So do I.
- ○ F That makes two of us.
- △ G I do as well.

…も (また…でない)

〈リンダ：私はビルが好きじゃないの〉
Linda: I don't like Bill.
〈ジェーン：私もよ〉
Jane:
- ◎ A Me either.
- ◎ B Same here.
- ◎ C I don't (like him) either.
- ◎ D Me neither.
- ◎ E Neither do I.
- ○ F Same with me.
- △ G Me too.
- ▽ H Nor do I.

催す

〈ヒルトンでファッションショーを催す予定です〉
- ◎ A We're going to put on [have] a fashion show at the Hilton.

○　B　We're going to hold a fashion show at the Hilton.
　　△　C　We're going to give a fashion show at the Hilton.
　❖「開く」の項も参照のこと．

問題
1　《一般に》
a）解決が難しい問題
〈日本が直面している問題はたくさんあります〉
　　◎　　There are a lot of problems [troubles, issues] Japan's confronted with.
b）議論の的となる問題
〈これは日本で一番議論の余地がある問題です〉
　　◎　A　This is the most controversial issue in Japan.
　　×　B　This is the most controversial problem [trouble] in Japan.
c）経済的な問題
〈彼らは経済的な問題のために一家心中したんです〉
　　☆　A　They committed a family suicide because of their financial problems.
　　◎　B　They committed a family suicide because of their financial trouble(s).
　　○　C　They committed a family suicide because of their financial situations [circumstances].
d）社会問題
・会社の倒産などの経済問題
〈多くの会社が次々に倒産しているのは大きな社会問題だ〉
　　◎　　The way many companies are going bankrupt one after another is a big economic problem.
・小児の肥満などの健康問題
〈肥満児の数が増えているのは大きな社会問題だ〉
　　◎　　It's a big health problem that obese children are increasing in number.
　❖日本語で「社会問題」という場合に，アメリカ人は必ずしもIt's a social problem. とは言わない．マクロ的視野から「社会問題」という大きなくくりでとらえるのではなく，「経済問題」「健康問題」「環境問題」など，個々の問題の特質を具体的に指し示して表現することの方が多い．
e）「話題」「議題」の意味で
〈あなたの言っていることはこの問題に関係ありません〉
　　◎　A　What you're saying has nothing to do with this subject.
　　○　B　What you're saying has nothing to do with this topic.
　　△　C　What you're saying has nothing to do with this theme.
2　《テストの問題》
a）文科系科目の場合
〈歴史のテストの問題を全部答えることができましたか〉
　　◎　A　Were you able to answer all the questions on the history test?
　　×　B　Were you able to answer all the problems on the history test?
b）理数科系科目の場合
〈数学の問題を全部解くことができましたか〉
　　◎　A　Were you able to solve all the math problems?
　　×　B　Were you able to solve all the math questions?
3　《「…の［…という］問題」というとき》
a）of＋名詞の形で
〈それは時間の問題だ〉

- ◎ A It's a matter of time.
- ○ B It's a question of time.
- × C It's a case of time.
  - ❖ C は辞典に出ているが使われていない．

b）of＋疑問詞節の形で

〈それは私があなたに同意するかどうかの問題ではない〉

- ◎ A It's not a question of whether I agree with you or not.
- ○ B It's not a matter of whether I agree with you or not.

4 《「問題は…である」というとき》

a）疑問詞を伴って

〈私はハーバードとイエールの両方に合格したんです．問題はどちらへ私が行くべきかなんです〉

- ◎ A I've been accepted by both Harvard and Yale. The question is which I should go to.
- × B I've been accepted by both Harvard and Yale. The problem is which I should go to.

b）that 節を伴って

〈私はハーバードとイエールの両方に合格したんです．問題は両親がどちらも好きでないんです〉

- ◎ A I've been accepted by both Harvard and Yale. The thing is that my parents don't like either of them.
- ○ B I've been accepted by both Harvard and Yale. The problem [trouble] is that my parents don't like either of them.

5 《「問題は終わっている」と述べるとき》

〈デイヴィッド：僕は君が理解できないね．その問題は終わっているよ〉

David:
- ◎ A I don't understand you. The case's closed.
- ○ B I don't understand you. The matter's taken care of [closed].
- △ C I don't understand you. The matter's finished.
- × D I don't understand you. The case's taken care of [finished].
- × E I don't understand you. The problem's closed [finished].

問題外

〈火曜日は問題外だ〉

- ◎ A Tuesday's out.
- ◎ B Tuesday's out of the question.

〔や〕

八百長の
〈昨夜のボクシングの試合は八百長だったようだ〉
- ◎ A The boxing match last night seems to have been fixed.
- ○ B The boxing match last night seems to have been rigged.
- △ C The boxing match last night seems to have been staged [set up, thrown].

やかましい　→口やかましい

薬剤師　→職業 30

役所
1 《市役所》
〈市役所はどこにありますか〉
- ◎ A Where's (the) City Hall?
- ◎ B Where's the City Office?
- △ C Where's the municipal office?
  - ❖(1) A の(the) City Hall はいくつかの行政部門 (city office) が集合して成り立っている．したがって，厳密には同意語ではないが，一般には City Hall＝the City Office として使われている．

2 《役場》
〈役場はどこにあるのですか〉
- ◎ A Where's town hall?
- ○ B Where's the municipal office?
- △ C Where's the town office?

約束
1 《人と会う約束》
a） ビジネス上の約束
・一般的約束のとき
〈私は今日5つ約束があるんです〉
- ◎　　I have five appointments today.

・重要な地位についている人が主語のとき
〈上司は今週はずっと約束があるんです〉
- ◎　　My boss has engagements all this week.

b） 社交上の約束
・上品・高級な所へ行くとき
〈私たちは今週の金曜日先約があるんです．ブラウン夫妻とコンサートで会うんです〉
- ◎　　We have a prior engagement this Friday. We're meeting the Browns at the concert.

・ピクニック・映画・ドライブなど高級でない所へ行くとき
〈今週の金曜日はもう約束があるんです〉
- ◎　　We already have plans this Friday.

c） デートの約束
〈私は4時にロンと約束してるんです〉
- ◎ A I'm going to see Ron at 4:00.
- ◎ B I have a date with Ron at 4:00.

2 《約束の時間に》

〈私は約束の時間にそこへ行けなかったんです〉
- ◎ A I couldn't get there on time.
- △ B I couldn't get there by the appointed [designated] time.
- × C I couldn't get there on the due time.
- × D I couldn't get there by the promised time.

3 《約束を守る》

〈彼は約束を守るだろう〉
- ☆ A He'll keep his promise [word].
- ◎ B He'll make good on his promise [word].
- ○ C He'll be true to his promise [word].
- ○ D He'll stay by his promise [word].
- ○ E He'll fulfill his promise [word].
- ○ F He'll honor his promise [word].
- △ G He'll carry out his promise [word].
- △ H He'll abide by his promise [word].
- △ I He'll be as good as his promise [word].
- × J He'll meet his promise [word].
- × K He'll perform his promise [word].
- ❖J, K が辞典に出ているが使われていない.

4 《人に…することを約束する》

〈私は会議でビルを支持することを約束しました〉
- ◎ A I promised to support Bill at the meeting.
- ◎ B I promised Bill I'd support him at the meeting.
- ○ C I promised that I'd support Bill at the meeting.
- × D I promised Bill to support him at the meeting.
- ❖辞典に D を紹介しているが使われていない.ただし,子供の会話では時々使われている.

役人

1 《一般的に述べる場合》

〈彼は役人なんです〉
- ◎ A He's a bureaucrat.
- × B He's a government official [officer].
- × C He's a public servant [official, officer].
- ❖(1) 日本語の「役人」には下記の理由で bureaucrat が一番ぴったりする.
  ①日本語の「役人」は政府,県庁,市役所,町・村役場,区役所,つまり公務員を否定的ニュアンスで述べるときに使われているからである.
  ②英和辞典・和英辞典のどれを引いても bureaucrat に「官僚」という訳語を紹介している.しかし,日本語の「官僚」とは政府に勤めている地位が高い人たちを指していて,否定的ニュアンスは普通ない.したがって,「息子は官僚です」と親が述べているときは誇りを持って述べている.一方,英語の bureaucrat は政府,州庁,県庁,市役所,町・村役場の幹部を否定的に述べるときに使われているからである.
- ❖(2) B が辞典で「役人」の意味として出ているが次の理由で全く異なる.B の government official と government officer は, Federal Government (連邦政府) の「官僚」, state government (州政府), county government (県庁), city hall (市役所), town hall (町役場) の「幹部」に言及するときに使われているが, bureaucrat と違って否定的ニュアンスは全くない.したがって,B は「官僚」とか「幹部」の日本語には相当するが,「役人」のニュアンスとは大きく異なる.

❖(3) Cも辞典に「役人」の英語として出ているが次の理由で全然違う．public servantとpublic officialは選挙で選ばれた「国会議員」「知事」「市長」「町長」などの政治家に言及するときに使われている．日本語の「役人」は政治家ではなく公僕を揶揄して述べるときにのみ使われている．したがって，「役人」の英訳にはならない．public officerはまれにしか使われず，また意味もあいまいである．
2 《「小役人」と述べるとき》
〈彼はただの小役人です〉
- ◎ A He's just [only] a bureaucrat.
- ○ B He's just [only] a paper-pusher.
- × C He's just a petty official [civil servant, bureaucrat].
  - ❖(1) 辞典にCが出ているが使われていない．
  - ❖(2) Aは官僚，政治家の両方に使われているが，Bは官僚にしか使えない．

野菜
1 《緑黄色野菜》
〈あなたはもっと緑黄色野菜を食べるべきです〉
- ◎ A You should eat more (green) vegetables.
- ○ B You should eat more greens.
- × C You should eat more green and yellow vegetables.

2 《繊維質の多い野菜》
〈繊維質の多い野菜を食べるようにしています〉
- ◎ A I try to eat vegetables with high [a lot of] fiber.
- ○ B I try to eat vegetables with high in fiber.
- △ C I try to eat fibrous vegetables.

3 《無農薬野菜》
〈私は無農薬野菜しか食べません〉
- ☆ A I only eat organic vegetables.
- ◎ B I only eat organically-grown vegetables.
- ○ C I only eat pesticide-free [chemical-free] vegetables.

4 《根菜類》
〈私は根菜類をたくさん食べるようにしています〉
- ○ A I try to eat a lot of root vegetables.
- × B I try to eat a lot of rooted vegetables.
- × C I try to eat a lot of vegetables with roots.
  - ❖アメリカ人は日本人のように「根菜類」という概念がない．

5 《自家栽培野菜》
〈私は自家栽培野菜しか食べません〉
- ◎ A I only eat home-grown vegetables.
- ◎ B I only eat vegetables from our garden.
- ○ C I only eat our garden-grown vegetables.

6 《葉の多い野菜》
〈私は葉の多い野菜をたくさん食べるようにしています〉
- ◎ I try to eat a lot of leafy vegetables.

7 《温室野菜》
〈私は温室野菜しか食べません〉
- ◎ A I only eat greenhouse-grown vegetables.
- ○ B I only eat greenhouse vegetables.

8 《青果物》
〈日本の青果物はとても高い〉

◎ A The produce in Japan's very expensive.
　　◎ B The vegetables and fruit in Japan are very expensive.
　　❖ produce を英和辞典で引くと，チーズ，バターなどの乳製品が含まれていると紹介されているが，これは事実に反する．produce が名詞で使われるのは野菜と果物，つまり「青果物」である．

屋敷 →家 10

養う

1 《子供・妻》

〈私は家族を養わなければならないんです〉

　　☆ A I have to feed my family.
　　◎ B I have to support [take care of] my family.
　　○ C I have to provide for my family.
　　× D I have to keep [maintain] my family.
　　❖ D は辞典に出ているが会話では使われていない．しかし，堅い文章では時々使われている．

2 《親・祖父母》

〈私は親を養わなければならないんです〉

　　☆ A I have to take care of my parents.
　　◎ B I have to support my parents.
　　○ C I have to provide for my parents.
　　× D I have to feed [keep, maintain] my parents.

やじる

〈観客は選手たちをやじった〉

　　☆ A The crowd booed at the players.
　　◎ B The crowd booed the players.
　　○ C The crowd jeered at the players.
　　△ D The crowd scoffed at the players.
　　❖やじの強さの点では C が一番強く，A, B, D の順で下がる．

安い

1 《品物が主語の場合》

〈あのブルーのセーターはどうですか．あれは安いです〉

　　◎ A How about that blue sweater? That's not expensive.
　　◎ B How about that blue sweater? That's inexpensive.
　　◎ C How about that blue sweater? That's cheap.
　　❖ C の cheap は「安い」だけでなく「安っぽい」という意味もある．したがって店員は使わない．しかし，お客は非常によく使う．

2 《料金などが主語の場合》

〈授業料は安い〉

　　◎ A The fee is low.
　　△ B The fee is inexpensive [cheap].

3 《比較級・最上級の場合》

〈これはあれより安いです〉

　　◎ A This is less expensive than that.
　　◎ B This is cheaper than that.
　　× C This is more inexpensive than that.
　　❖(1) 1 と同様に，B は店員などには使われていない．
　　❖(2) inexpensive を比較級として more inexpensive とはしない．A のように less expensive とする．

安い買物 →いい買物

安くなる
1 《通貨のレートを述べるとき》
〈円はまもなく安くなると私は思います〉
- ☆ A I think the yen'll go up soon.
- ◎ B I think the yen'll climb soon.
- ◎ C I think the yen'll get [be] weaker soon.
- ○ D I think the yen'll come up soon.
    - ❖円が¥130から¥150に近づくことは日本人にとっては値下がりすることになる．しかし，一般のアメリカ人は次の2つの理由で「値上がりする」と言う．
    - ①円とドルの交換ルートが¥130から¥150になることは数字が上がるから．
    - ②アメリカのドルは1971年8月15日に金との兌換性を国際条約を破って一方的に停止したままにしてあるにもかかわらず，世界の基軸通貨，つまりドルを世界の中心通貨と考えているから．

2 《通貨のレートが安くなる数字を言及するとき》
〈円は近い将来安くなって200円になるでしょう〉
- ☆ A The yen'll go up to 200 in the near future.
- ◎ B The yen'll climb to 200 in the near future.
- △ C The yen'll climb up to 200 in the near future.

3 《主語に値段を示す語があるとき》
〈今年は天気がいいので米価は安くなるでしょう〉
- ◎ A Rice prices'll be less expensive this year because of this good weather.
- ◎ B Rice prices'll be lower this year because of this good weather.
- ◎ C Rice prices'll go down [fall, drop, come down, be down] this year because of this good weather.
    - ❖主語が tax（税金），rent（家賃），fare（運賃），personnel expenses（人件費）のようなその語に値段の意味があるときは上記の表現が使われる．

4 《物品を主語にして述べるとき》
〈お米は今年は安くなるでしょう〉
- ☆ A Rice'll be less expensive this year.
- ◎ B Rice'll be cheaper this year.
- ◎ C Rice'll become less expensive this year.
- ○ D Rice'll become cheaper this year.
- ○ E Rice'll get less expensive this year.
- △ F Rice'll get cheaper this year.

安普請の
〈私は安普請の家を買いたくないんです〉
- ◎ A I don't want to buy a cheaply-built [flimsy, shoddy] house.
- × B I don't want to buy a jerry-built house.
    - ❖Bが辞典に出ているが使われていない．

休み
1 《休憩》
a) 肉体労働・運動をしているとき
〈休憩しよう〉
- ☆ A Let's take a break.
- ◎ B Let's take a rest.
- ○ C Let's have a break.
- ○ D Let's rest.

△ E Let's have a rest.
b）肉体労働でない場合
〈休憩しよう〉
　　◎ A Let's take a break.
　　○ B Let's have a break.
　　△ C Let's take [have] a rest.
　　△ D Let's rest.
c）休憩を取っている
〈彼は休憩を取っています〉
　　◎ A He's on break.
　　◎ B He's taking a break.
d）昼休み
〈昼休みにしましょう〉
　　◎ A Let's have time off for lunch.
　　◎ B Let's take [have] a break for lunch.
　　× C Let's take [have] a rest for lunch.
2　《休日》
a）1日の仕事上の休日
〈火曜日が私の休日です〉
　　◎　　Tuesday's my day-off.
b）休む時間・曜日・日・週を明示するとき
〈あなたは　A午後　B明日　C月曜日　D来週　休みを取っていいですよ〉
　　◎ A You can take the afternoon off.
　　◎ B You can take tomorrow off.
　　◎ C You can take Monday off.
　　◎ D You can take next week off.
3　《祭日》
〈明日は祭日です〉
　　◎ A Tomorrow's a holiday.
　　◎ B Tomorrow's a Bank Holiday.
　　△ C Tomorrow's a Federal [legal, national] holiday.
　　× D Tomorrow's a public holiday.
　　❖(1) D が多くの辞典に出ているが使われていない．
　　❖(2) B はイギリスで非常によく使われている．
4　《休暇》
a）一般の人
〈彼は休暇を取っています〉
　　◎ A He's on vacation.
　　◎ B He's taking a vacation.
　　○ C He's taking his vacation.
　　○ D He's vacationing.
b）軍人・公務員・医師・看護婦
〈彼は休暇を取っています〉
　　◎ A He's on leave.
　　◎ B He's taking leave.
　　◎ C He's on vacation.
　　○ D He's taking a vacation.
　　❖(1) A, B は数日間の休暇，数時間の休憩にも使われている．
　　❖(2) A, B は「許可を取った休暇」というときに使われるのに対して，C, D

には「許可」というニュアンスがない．したがって，C，D は職業に関係なく広く使われている．
 c) 大学教授
〈彼は休暇を取っています〉
    ◎ A He's on sabbatical.
    ○ B He's taking a sabbatical.
        ❖ sabbatical は 7 年ごとに教授に与えられる 1 年，または半年の有給休暇．
 5 《有給休暇》
〈1 年にあなたには何日有給休暇があるのですか〉
    ◎ A How many paid-days-off a year do you have?
    × B How many paid-holidays a year do you have?
        ❖ B はアメリカ南部では時々使われている．
 6 《週休 2 日制》
〈日本のほとんどの小企業は週休 2 日制を採用していません〉
    ☆ A Most small businesses in Japan aren't adopting the five-day week.
    ◎ B Most small businesses in Japan aren't adopting the five-day work week.
    ○ C Most small businesses in Japan aren't adopting the five-day week system.
    ○ D Most small businesses in Japan aren't adopting the traditional work week.
    △ E Most small businesses in Japan aren't adopting the traditional work week system.
 7 《代休》
〈日曜日働いたから，明日は私の代休なんです〉
    ◎ A Tomorrow's my day-off because I worked Sunday.
    ○ B Tomorrow's my comp day because I worked Sunday.
    × C Tomorrow's my compensatory day-off [time-off] because I worked Sunday.
        ❖ C が辞典に出ているが使われていない．

やせこけている
 1 《一般的に述べる場合》
〈彼はやせこけている〉
    ◎ A He's all [just] skin and bones.
    ◎ B He's skinny [scrawny].
    △ C He's a walking [living] skeleton.
    △ D He's a bag of bones.
    × E He's worn to skeleton [a shadow].
    × F He's cadaverous.
    × G He's a rackabones [a rack of bones].
    × H He's an anatomy.
        ❖ E〜H が辞典に出ているが使われていない．
 2 《背が高くてやせていることを強調するとき》
〈彼はやせています〉
    ◎ A He's a bean pole.
    ◎ B He's lanky.
    ○ C He's a string bean.
    ○ D He's gangly.
        ❖ 背の高い順は A, B, C, D.

やせている
  1 《人が》
  〈彼はやせている〉
    ◎　　He's thin [lean].
    ❖ thin は普通, 病気などでやせているときに使われている. lean は thin ほどやせていない. 体質的に皮下脂肪が少なくやせているときに使われている.
  2 《土地が》
  〈この土地はやせすぎていて(作物の)栽培には向きません〉
    ◎ A This land's too barren [poor] to cultivate.
    △ B This land's too infertile to cultivate.
    × C This land's too impoverished [sterile] to cultivate.
    ❖ C が辞典に出ているが使われていない.

薬局 →店 37

やつれた
  1 《病気の場合》
  〈彼女は病気でやつれた顔をしている〉
    ☆ A She looks tired [worn-out] from her illness.
    ◎ B She looks haggard from her illness.
    ○ C She looks gaunt [worn] from her illness.
    △ D She looks wasted [emaciated] from her illness.
  2 《寝不足の場合》
  〈彼女は寝不足でやつれた顔をしている〉
    ☆ A She looks worn-out [tired] from lack of sleep.
    ◎ B She looks haggard from lack of sleep.
    △ C She looks gaunt [worn] from lack of sleep.
    × D She looks wasted [emaciated] from lack of sleep.
    ❖ D は辞典に出ているが, 寝不足によるやつれには使われていない.

やぶ医者 →医者 16

山の手
  〈彼は東京の山の手に住んでいます〉
    ◎ A He lives in uptown Tokyo.
    ◎ B He lives uptown in Tokyo.
    △ C He lives in the uptown area of Tokyo.
    × D He lives in the uptown of Tokyo.
    ❖「山の手」という表現に一番近いのは uptown だが, この語には形容詞, または副詞の働きしかない. 辞典には名詞の訳語が出ているが, 次の文でしか使われていない. This train'll get you to uptown.(この電車は山の手へ行きます). ただし使用頻度は高くない. downtown も同様.

山ほど →たくさん 4

やめる
  1 《飲酒を》
  a) 急にやめたとき
  〈リンダ：彼はまだお酒を飲むの〉
  Linda: Does he still drink?
  〈ジェーン：いいえ. 数ヵ月前にきっぱりやめたの〉
  Jane:
    ◎ A No, he gave it up cold turkey a couple of months ago.
    ◎ B No, he quit [stopped, went] cold turkey a couple of months ago.

× C No, he cold-turkeyed a couple of months ago.
　　× D No, he kicked cold turkey a couple of months ago.
　　❖ C, Dは辞典に出ているが使われていない.
b）徐々にやめたとき
〈リンダ：彼はまだお酒を飲むの〉
Linda: Does he still drink?
〈ジェーン：いいえ．数ヵ月前にきっぱりやめたの〉
Jane:
　　◎ A No, he gave it up completely [entirely, totally, all together] several months ago.
　　◎ B No, he stopped completely [entirely] several months ago.
　　◎ C No, he quit completely [entirely, totally, all together] several months ago.
　　○ D No, he stopped totally [all together] several months ago.

2 《雑誌などの購読を》
〈私は購読をやめたいのです〉
　　☆ A I want to stop the subscription.
　　◎ B I want to drop the subscription.
　　○ C I want to discontinue the subscription.
　　　❖ Cは購読を「更新しない」という意味で普通使われている．A, Bは「更新しない」と「中止する」，つまり cancel の両方の意味で使われている．

辞める
1 《普通の人》
〈私は月末に仕事を辞めます〉
　　◎ A I'm going to quit my job.
　　△ B I'm going to leave work.
　　△ C I'm going to leave my job.
　　× D I'm going to leave my work [place].
　　× E I'm going to quit my place.
　　❖辞典に D, E が出ているが使われていない.

2 《社長・専務など高い地位の人》
〈社長はたぶん辞めるでしょう〉
　　◎ A The CEO'll probably quit his job.
　　◎ B The CEO'll probably resign.
　　◎ C The CEO'll probably step down.
　　◎ D The CEO'll probably resign (from) his position.
　　○ E The CEO'll probably step down from his position.
　　○ F The CEO'll probably leave his job.
　　○ G The CEO'll probably quit.
　　△ H The CEO'll probably leave his position.

3 《首相など高い地位の公職の人》
〈首相はたぶん辞めるでしょう〉
　　☆ A The prime minister'll probably resign [step down].
　　◎ B The prime minister'll probably resign his post [position].
　　◎ C The prime minister'll probably step down from his post [position].
　　○ D The prime minister'll probably resign from his office.
　　○ E The prime minister'll probably leave his post.
　　○ F The prime minister'll probably step down from his office [job].
　　○ G The prime minister'll probably quit his job.

やり遂げる
〈私たちはこのプロジェクトをやり遂げられるかどうか分かりません〉
- ☆ A We don't know if we can carry through with this project.
- ☆ B We don't know if we can finish this project.
- ◎ C We don't know if we can complete this project.
- ◎ D We don't know if we can carry this project through [out].
- ◎ E We don't know if we can wrap up this project [wrap this project up].
- ○ F We don't know if we can accomplish this project.

やるべきことは何でもやった
〈ジム：課長に昇進したそうですね〉
Jim: I hear you've been promoted to manager.
〈ビル：ええ．でもやるべきことは何でもやったんです〉
Bill:
- ◎ A Yes, but I paid my dues.
- ◎ B Yes, but I worked my ass off getting it.
- ◎ C Yes, but I broke my back [neck] getting it.
- ◎ D Yes, but I worked my ass for it.
- ◎ E Yes, but I broke my back [neck] for it.
- ◎ F Yes, but I put a lot of time and effort into it.
    - ❖ Aは「(その地位を手に入れるために)ある程度犠牲をはらってまで，それだけの苦労をして」，B〜Eは「汗水たらして，大変な努力をして」というニュアンスがある．

和らげる
1 《痛みを》
a） 医者が患者に話している
〈この薬はあなたの痛みを和らげますよ〉
- ☆ A This medecine'll alleviate your pain.
- ◎ B This medecine'll relieve your pain.
- ○ C This medecine'll ease [sooth, mitigate, help (with)] your pain.

b） 家庭で話している
〈この薬はあなたの痛みを和らげますよ〉
- ◎ A This medecine'll help (with) your pain.
- ○ B This medecine'll relieve your pain.
- △ C This medecine'll alleviate [sooth, ease] your pain.
- × D This medecine'll mitigate your pain.

2 《心配を》
〈彼女は私の心配を和らげてくれました〉
- ◎ A She helped me with my problems.
- ○ B She helped with my problems.
- ○ C She helped me with my troubles.
- ○ D She alleviated my problems [troubles].

病んだ
1 《比喩的に述べるとき》
〈アメリカは以前は病める社会であった〉
- ◎ A America used to be a sick society.
- × B America used to be an ill society.
    - ❖ J.F.ケネディー大統領および弟のロバート・ケネディー，マーチン・ルーサー・キングといった人物が暗殺された時代のアメリカ，また犯罪率の高い

アメリカ社会を指して sick society と言うことが多い．
2 《実際に病気のとき》
〈彼は病んでいるんです〉
- ◎ A He's a sick man.
- × B He's an ill man.
    - ❖A は身体的な病気だけでなく心の病についても用いられる．「病気」の項も参照のこと．

〔ゆ〕

湯
1 《一般に》
〈(レストランで) 少しお湯をいただけますか〉
- ◎ A Can I have some hot water?
- × B Can I have some heated water?

2 《文中・前後に「熱い」「ぬるい」などの語があるとき》
〈お湯はとても熱いようだね〉
- ◎ A The water seems to be very hot.
- × B The hot water seems to be very hot.
    - ❖文中，または前後に hot (熱い)，warm (あったかい)，lukewarm (なまぬるい) があるときは，hot water (湯) は使えない．単に water とする．

優越感
〈彼は私に優越感を持っているんです〉
- ☆ A He thinks he's better than me.
- ◎ B He thinks he's superior to me.
- ○ C He has a superiority complex towards [to] me.
- △ D He has a sense of superiority towards [to] me.
- ▽ E He has a superiority complex with regard to me.
    - ❖(1) 辞典に A，B が出ていないが非常によく使われている．
    - ❖(2) 「劣等感」の項も参照のこと．

誘拐する
〈銀行家は家から誘拐されたんです〉
- ☆ A The banker was kidnapped from his house.
- ◎ B The banker was kidnapped out of his house.
- ○ C The banker was abducted from his house.
- ○ D The banker was abducted out of his house.
- × E The banker was spirited out of his house.
    - ❖(1) E が辞典に出ているが使われていない．
    - ❖(2) B，D は辞典に出ていないがよく使われている．

夕方
〈私に夕方電話しないで下さい〉
- ◎ A Please don't call me late in the afternoon.
- △ B Please don't call me in (the) late afternoon.
- × C Please don't call me in the evening.
    - ❖辞典に C が出ているが使われていない．

勇気
1 《告白する勇気》

〈ジムはゲイであることを妻に話す勇気を奮い起こすことができなかった〉
- ◎ A Jim couldn't summon the courage to tell his wife that he was gay.
- ▽ B Jim couldn't summon the guts to tell his wife that he was gay.

2 《達成しようという勇気》
〈私は山を見上げたとき，勇気がなくなってしまったんです〉
- ◎ A My courage left me when I looked up at the mountain.
- × B My guts left me when I looked up at the mountain.

3 《「勇気を尊敬する」と言うとき》
〈私はあなたの勇気を尊敬します〉
- ◎ A I respect your courage.
- △ B I respect your guts.

4 《デートに誘う勇気》
〈私は彼女をデートに誘う勇気がないんです〉
- ◎ A I don't have the guts to ask her out for a date.
- ○ B I don't have the courage to ask her out for a date.

5 《リスクを冒す勇気》
〈私はこの株にすべてのお金を投資する勇気はないんです〉
- ◎ A I don't have the guts to invest all the money in this stock.
- ○ B I don't have the courage to invest all the money in this stock.

有給休暇 →休み 5

融資

1 《融資を受ける》
〈問題はどこで融資をしてもらうかです〉
- ☆ A The question is where to get (the) financing.
- ◎ B The question is where to get a [the] loan.

2 《融資する》
a） 利息のレートに言及しないで述べるとき
〈銀行はうちの会社に融資するでしょう〉
- ☆ A The bank'll finance our company.
- ◎ B The bank'll help our company with the money.
- ◎ C The bank'll lend [loan] our company the money.
- ◎ D The bank'll loan the money to our company.
- ○ E The bank'll provide the money for our company.
- ○ F The bank'll provide our company with the money.
- ○ G The bank'll supply the money for [to] our company.
- △ H The bank'll supply our company with the money.
- × I The bank'll furnish [accommodate] the money to our company.
- × J The bank'll accommodate our company with the money.
  ❖ I, J が辞典に出ているが使われていない.

b） 利息のレートに言及するとき
〈アリゾナ銀行がテキサス銀行よりずっと低い利息で融資してくれます〉
- ☆ A Arizona Bank'll finance us at a much lower interest rate than Texas Bank.
- ◎ B Arizona Bank'll help us with the money at a much lower interest rate than Texas Bank.
- ◎ C Arizona Bank'll lend [loan] us the money at a much lower interest rate than Texas Bank.
- ◎ D Arizona Bank'll loan the money to us at a much lower interest rate than Texas Bank.

- ○ E　Arizona Bank'll provide the money for us at a much lower interest rate than Texas Bank.
- ○ F　Arizona Bank'll provide us with the money at a much lower interest rate than Texas Bank.
- ○ G　Arizona Bank'll supply the money for [to] us at a much lower interest rate than Texas Bank.

優柔不断
〈彼は優柔不断だ〉
- ◎ A　He can't decide.
- ○ B　He can't make up his mind.
- ○ C　He's indecisive.
- △ D　He's wishy-washy.
- × E　He's shilly-shally [irresolute].
- × F　He's a waverer [a man of indecision].
- × G　He lacks decision.

❖ E, F, G が辞典に出ているが使われていない.

優先する
〈人質の命が何よりも優先します〉
- ◎ A　The hostages' lives outweigh [override, take precedence over, come before] anything else.
- ◎ B　The hostages' lives are more important than anything else.

有能な
1 《秘書》
〈彼女は有能な秘書です〉
- ◎ A　She's a good secretary.
- ○ B　She's a capable secretary.
- ○ C　She's a competent secretary.
- ○ D　She's an efficient secretary.
- × E　She's an able secretary.

❖(1) E が辞典に出ているが使われていない.
❖(2) 有能である響きが一番強いのは A, 以下 B, D, C の順で弱くなる.
❖(3) A の good はすべての点で有能であることを言っている. B の capable は経験を積んでいるというニュアンス. C の competent は秘書としての「資格を持っている」が原義. それから一般的に「有能な」の意味でも使われるようになった. D の efficient は仕事を能率的にやるというニュアンスがある.

2 《弁護士》
〈彼女は有能な弁護士です〉
- ◎　She's a competent [capable, good] lawyer.

3 《セールスマン》
〈彼は有能なセールスマンです〉
- ◎　He's a good [capable] salesman.

裕福な
1 《一般的に言う場合》
〈彼らは裕福なんです〉
- ◎ A　They're wealthy.
- ○ B　They're well-to-do.
- ○ C　They're well-off.

❖(1) 裕福さの程度は A が一番高く, B, C の順で下がる.

❖(2) B, C は 40 歳以上の人の間ではよく使われているが，若年層になるほど使用頻度は下がる．
  2 《「出身」の意味で言う場合》
〈彼は裕福な家庭の出なんです〉
    ◎ A He comes from money.
    ◎ B He comes from a family with (a lot of) money.
    ◎ C He comes from a wealthy [well-to-do, good] family.
    ○ D He comes from a rich family.
    ○ E He comes from a lot of money.
    △ F He comes from the upper-class.
    △ G He comes from an upper-class family.

有名な
  1 《一般的に述べるとき》
〈ニューヨークは自由の女神で有名です〉
    ◎   New York's famous [well-known] for its Statue of Liberty.
  2 《悪評として述べるとき》
〈彼は人使いが荒いことで有名なんです〉
    ◎ A He's notorious [famous, well-known] for being a slave driver.
    × B He's infamous for being a slave driver.
      ❖ B の infamous は，日常的な文脈でも，特に皮肉をこめて言う場合には用いられる．Steve's infamous for spaghetti. (スティーブはスパゲッティ（の料理が下手なこと，まずいこと）で有名なのよ)．
  3 《犯罪として述べるとき》
〈KKK はアメリカの黒人に残酷なことをするので有名です〉
    ◎ A The KKK is infamous for displaying cruelty to American black people.
    × B The KKK is notorious for displaying cruelty to American black people.
    × C The KKK is well-known [famous] for displaying cruelty to American black people.
      ❖ A は the KKK の行為を犯罪だという視点から，B は悪評があるという点から，C は客観的によく知られているという意味でそれぞれ述べられている．したがって，犯罪という視点からでない場合には，B, C も非常によく使われている．
  4 《「高名な」「著名な」というニュアンスのとき》
〈彼は有名な経済学者です〉
    ◎ A He's a distinguished economist.
    ○ B He's an eminent [a noted, a renowned, a prominent, a celebrated] economist.
      ❖(1) A, B は堅い文章．ただし，教育レベルの高い人の間では日常会話でも非常によく使われている．
      ❖(2) A, B いずれもノーベル賞受賞者のようなニュアンスがある．

優良株 →株 4
雪がすごく降る
〈雪がすごく降っている〉
    ☆ A It's really snowing.
    ☆ B It's snowing really hard.
    ☆ C It's really coming down.
    ◎ D It's snowing really heavy [fast].

- ◎ E The snow's really coming down.
- ◎ F The snow's really falling hard.
- ◎ G The snow's falling really fast.
- ◎ H It's snowing very hard.
- ○ I It's snowing really [very] heavily.
- ○ J The snow's really falling fast.
- ○ K It's really snowing fast.
- ○ L It's snowing very heavy [fast, bad].
- ○ M It's snowing really bad.
- △ N It's snowing thick and fast.
- △ O The snow's really falling heavy.
- ▽ P The snow's really falling bad [heavily].

雪だるま式に増える
〈うちの会社の借金は雪だるま式に増えている〉
- ◎ A Our company's debt is growing [multiplying, increasing].
- ○ B Our company's debt is accumulating [escalating].
- △ C Our company's debt is snowballing.

輸血
1 《輸血をする場合》
〈私たちは彼に輸血をしなければなりません〉
- ◎ A We've got to give him a (blood) transfusion.
- ○ B We've got to give a (blood) transfusion to him.
- ▽ C We've got to transfuse (blood to) him.
  - ❖ C が辞典に出ているが使われてもまれ．

2 《輸血を受ける場合》
〈彼は輸血を受けなければなりません〉
- ☆ A He's got to get a (blood) transfusion.
- ◎ B He's got to be given a (blood) transfusion.
- ○ C He's got to receive a (blood) transfusion.

輸入品
〈これはイタリアからの輸入品です〉
- ☆ A This is from Italy.
- ◎ B This is imported from Italy.
- ◎ C This is an imported item [product] from Italy.
- ○ D This is imported merchandise from Italy.
- △ E This is an import from Italy.
- ▽ F This is an import item [product] from Italy.

夢にも思わなかった
〈ここであなたに会うとは夢にも思いませんでした〉
- ◎ A This is the last place I'd have expected to see you.
- ○ B This is the last place I expected to see you.
- △ C Fancy seeing [meeting] you here.
- × D Little did I dream of seeing you here.
- × E I little dreamed of seeing you here.
  - ❖(1) D, E は辞典に出ているが使われていない．
  - ❖(2) C はやや古い言いまわし．D, E は文学書では多少用いられている．

夢を実現する →実現する

揺れる
1 《建物が》

⟨ビルは地震の間激しく揺れました⟩
- ◎ A The building rocked violently during the earthquake.
- ◎ B The building shook violently during the earthquake.
- △ C The building jolted violently during the earthquake.
- ▽ D The building pitched [jerked, quaked, vibrated] violently during the earthquake.
- ▽ E The building tossed [bobbed] violently during the earthquake.
  - ❖(1) D, E が辞典に出ているがまれにしか使われていない．
  - ❖(2) B は横揺れだけでなく縦の揺れにも非常によく使われている．
  - ❖(3) 揺れは A が一番強い．2番目は C，3番目は B，4番目は D，5番目は E．

2 《吊り下げたものが》
⟨シャンデリアは地震の間揺れていました⟩
- ◎ A The chandelier was swinging during the earthquake.
- ○ B The chandelier was swaying during the earthquake.

3 《飛行機が》
⟨飛行機は激しく揺れました⟩
- ◎ The plane tossed [rocked, jerked, shook, jolted] the passengers violently.
  - ❖揺れは jerk, shake が一番強い．2番目は jolt，3番目は rock，4番目は toss．

〔よ〕

用件

1 《社内の人間が訪問者に事務所の入り口で》
⟨ご用件は何でしょうか⟩
- ◎ A May I [Can I] help you?
- ◎ B What can I do for you?

2 《面会を求められて用件を聞く際に》
⟨秘書：ご用件は何ですか⟩
Secretary:
- ◎ A May I ask you what it is regarding?
- ◎ B May I ask you what your business is regarding?
- ○ C May I ask you what's the nature of your business?
- △ D May I ask you what it is about?
- △ E May I ask you what your business is about?

3 《「やるべき用件」を済ませたか否かを尋ねるとき》
⟨市役所での用件を済ませたのかい⟩
- ◎ A Did you do [finish] your business at the City Hall?
- ◎ B Did you get business done at the City Hall?

4 《店でお客に用件をうかがっているか否かを尋ねるとき》
⟨誰かご用件をうかがっておりますか⟩
- ☆ A Is someone taking care of [helping] you?
- ◎ B Has someone taken care of [helped] you?
- ◎ C Are you being taken care of [helped]?
- ◎ D Have you been taken care of [helped]?

- ○ E Have you been waited on?
- ○ F Has someone waited on you?
- ○ G Is someone waiting on you?
- ○ H Are you being waited on?
- × I Has [Is] someone attended to you?
  - ❖ I が辞典に出ているが使われていない．ただし，超高級な宝石店などでは使われている．

(…の)ようだ

1 《相手が目前にいないとき》

a) 名詞を従えるとき

〈彼はいい人のようです〉
- ☆ A He seems like [to be] a nice guy.
- ◎ B It seems (like) he's a nice guy.
- ○ C It seems that he's a nice guy.

b) 形容詞を従えるとき

〈彼は給料に満足しているようです〉
- ☆ A He seems happy with his pay.
- ◎ B He seems to be happy with his pay.
- ◎ C It seems (like) he's happy with his pay.
- ○ D It seems that he's happy with his pay.

c) 現在分詞を従えるとき

〈あなたの提案は面白いようですね〉
- ☆ A Your proposal seems exciting.
- ◎ B Your proposal seems to be exciting.
- ◎ C It seems (like) your proposal's exciting.
- ○ D It seems that your proposal's exciting.

d) 過去分詞を従えるとき

〈彼は心配しているようですね〉
- ☆ A He seems worried.
- ◎ B He seems to be worried.
- ◎ C It seems (like) he's worried.
- ◎ D It seems that he's worried.

2 《相手が目前，または見えるところにいるとき》

〈彼はいい人のようです〉
- ☆ A He looks like a nice guy.
- ◎ B It looks like he's a nice guy.
- ○ C He appears to be a nice guy.
- ○ D It appears (that) he's a nice guy.
- ▽ E It appears like he's a nice guy.
- ▽ F He looks to be a nice guy.
- ▽ G He appears like a nice guy.
- × H It looks (that) he's a nice guy.

3 《現在の習慣的行為について言うとき》

〈彼は夜，働いているようだ〉
- ☆ A It looks (like) he's working at night.
- ◎ B It seems (like) he works at night.
- ◎ C It seems (like) he's working at night.
- ◎ D It appears he works at night.
- ◎ E It appears he's working at night.

- ○ F He seems [appears] to be working at night.
- △ G He seems [appears] to work at night.
  - ❖ look, seem, appear には前述の「現在の状態」の項で説明した違いがあるが,「現在の習慣的行為」について言及するときには,話題になっている人が話者の見えるところにいても,いなくても違いはない. ただし look を使うと,話者が話していることに一番確信を持っているとの響きがあり, appear, seem の順で弱くなる.

預金

1 《定期預金》

〈私は2年の定期預金をするつもりです〉

- ◎ A I'm going to buy a two-year CD.
- ○ B I'm going to buy a two-year certificate of deposit.
- × C I'm going to buy a two-year term [time, fixed] deposit.
  - ❖ C が辞典に出ているが使われていない. ただし, イギリスでは使われている.

2 《普通預金》

〈私はシカゴ銀行に普通預金口座を持っています〉

- ◎ A I have a savings account at Chicago Bank.
- × B I have an ordinary [a general] account at Chicago Bank.
  - ❖ B が辞典に出ているが使われていない.

3 《当座預金》

〈私はシカゴ銀行に当座預金口座を持っています〉

- ◎ A I have a checking account at Chicago Bank.
- × B I have a check [current] account at Chicago Bank.
- × C I have a current deposit at Chicago Bank.
  - ❖ B, C が辞典に出ているが使われていない.

よくあることだ

〈離婚のことを気にしては駄目ですよ. よくあることです〉

- ◎ A Don't let the divorce bother you. It's just one of those things.
- ◎ B Don't let the divorce bother you. Stuff happens.
- ○ C Don't let the divorce bother you. It could happen to anybody.

よく知っている

1 《一般的に》

a) 住んだのでよく知っている

〈私はニューヨークをよく知っています〉

- ◎ A I know New York well.
- ◎ B I know a lot about New York.
- ○ C I know lots about New York.
- ○ D I know a lot of stuff [things] about New York.
- ○ E I know a great deal about New York.

b) 住んでいないがよく知っている

〈私はニューヨークをよく知っています〉

- ◎ A I know a lot about New York.
- ○ B I know lots about New York.
- ○ C I know a lot of stuff [things] about New York.
- ○ D I know a great deal about New York.
- × E I know New York well.
  - ❖ A～D は本で調べたりした場合と, 実際に住んだ場合の両方に使えるが, E は実際に住んだ場合しか使えない.

2 《地理的な意味に限定して言う場合》
a）肯定文
〈私はニューヨークをよく知っています〉
   ◎ A I know New York like the back of my hand.
   ◎ B I know New York like a book.
   ◎ C I know New York very well.
   ○ D I know New York like the palm of my hand.
b）否定文
〈私はニューヨークをよく知りません〉
   ◎ A I don't know New York very well.
   × B I don't know New York like the back [palm] of my hand.
   × C I don't know New York like a book.
c）疑問文
〈あなたはニューヨークをよく知っていますか〉
   ◎ A Do you know New York very well?
   × B Do you know New York like the back [palm] of your hand?
   × C Do you know New York like a book?

予習する
〈8課を予習しておきなさい〉
   ☆ A Look over Lesson 8.
   ◎ B Go over Lesson 8.
   ◎ C Get ready for Lesson 8.
   ○ D Prepare for Lesson 8.
   × E Do the preparations for Lesson 8.
   ❖(1) E は辞典に出ているが使われていない．
   ❖(2) 予習の程度の深さは C, D が一番深い．2番目は B, A は一番浅い．

余剰
1 《人》
〈うちは余剰人員を削減しなければならないんだ〉
   ◎ A We have to fire the extra personnel [employees, staff].
   ◎ B We have to fire the excess personnel [employees].
   ○ C We have to fire the excess staff [workforce].
   ○ D We have to fire the extra workforce.
   △ E We have to fire the surplus personnel [employees, staff].
   ▽ F We have to fire the surplus workforce.
   ❖ workforce は大会社の人員を意味することがはっきりしている．

2 《物》
〈私たちは飢えている国に余剰農産物を寄付すべきだ〉
   ☆ A We should donate extra farm products to starving countries.
   ◎ B We should donate extra farm produce to starving countries.
   ◎ C We should donate surplus farm [agricultural] products to starving countries.
   ○ D We should donate extra agricultural products [produce] to starving countries.
   ○ E We should donate farm surpluses to starving countries.
   △ F We should donate excess [surplus] farm produce to starving countries.

(…に)よって
〈金持ちか貧乏かによって物の見方は違ってくる〉

- ◎ A We have different views of a thing depending on whether rich or poor.
- ◎ B We have different views of a thing according to whether rich or poor.
- × C We have different views of a thing according as whether rich or poor.
  - ❖(1) C が辞典に紹介されているが，現代英語では英米を問わず全く使われていない．
  - ❖(2) 日本のみならず，多くの英米の辞典，慣用辞典に according as+節，according to+句として紹介されているが，現代英語ではイギリスでもアメリカでも会話はもちろん，文章英語でも全く使われていない．現代英語では後に節が来るときは，according to+（how, what, whether, who）の型で表現する．なお，A のように depending on で書きかえられる場合には，B より A の方が少し使用頻度が高い．したがって，according to を使わなければならないとき以外は depending on を使うことを勧める．

酔っ払っている

1 《話し手・聞き手の間柄に気を使わずに述べるとき》

〈彼は酔っ払っているんです〉
- ◎　He's drunk.

2 《うちとけた話し方で述べるとき》

〈彼は酔っ払っているんです〉
- ○ A He's loaded.
- ○ B He's trashed.
- ○ C He's smashed.
- ○ D He's bombed.
- ○ E He's sloshed.
- ○ F He's plastered.
- ○ G He's inebriated.
- ○ H He's intoxicated.
- ○ I He's hammered.
  - ❖(1) G, H はブルーカラーの間ではあまり使われていない．
  - ❖(2) B～G, I は A および H より酔っているというニュアンスがある．

3 《ぐでんぐでんに酔っ払っているとき》

〈彼はぐでんぐでんに酔っ払っているんです〉
- ◎ A He's totally [really, completely] drunk.
- ◎ B He's totally [really] loaded.
- ◎ C He's totally [really, completely] trashed.
- ◎ D He's totally bombed.
- ◎ E He's really [completely] smashed.
- ◎ F He's really [completely] plastered.
- ◎ G He's completely wasted.

4 《ほろ酔い》

〈彼はほろ酔いなんです〉
- ☆ A He's a little drunk.
- ◎ B He's tipsy.
- ○ C He's slightly [a bit] drunk.
- ○ D He's lit.

5 《二日酔い》

a）今，二日酔いのとき

〈私は二日酔いなんです〉
- ☆ A I have a hangover.
- ◎ B I had one too many.
- ○ C I had too much of a good thing.
- △ D I had too much of a good time.
- × E I have the morning after the night before.
- × F I have a morning [next-morning] head.
- × G I have a hold over.
  - ❖ E, F, G が辞典に出ているが使われていない．

b）未来の二日酔いを言うとき

〈あまりたくさん飲んでは駄目ですよ．明朝二日酔いになりますよ〉
- ◎ A Don't drink too much, or you'll be hurting tomorrow morning.
- ○ B Don't drink too much, or your head'll hurt tomorrow morning.
- × C Don't drink too much, or you'll have [get] a morning after head tomorrow morning.
  - ❖ C を紹介している辞典があるが使われていない．

6 《酔っ払い運転》

〈彼は酔っ払い運転で捕まったんです〉
- ◎ A He was caught driving drunk.
- ◎ B He was caught for drunk driving.
- ○ C He was caught under the influence.
- △ D He was caught under the influence of alcohol.
- △ E He was caught for drunken driving.

7 《比喩的に「酔っている」と言うとき》

〈彼はマルキシズムに酔っている〉
- ◎ A He's obsessed with Marxism.
- △ B He's hooked on Marxism.
- × C He's intoxicated [drunk, loaded, infatuated] with Marxism.
  - ❖ C が辞典に紹介されているが使われていない．

(…する) 予定だ

1 《人》

a）一般の人

・差し迫った予定

〈私は次の駅で下車する予定です〉
- ◎ A I'm getting off at the next station.
- ○ B I'm going to get off at the next station.

・1ヶ月以上先の予定

〈私は今年の夏ヨーロッパを訪ねる予定です〉
- ◎ A I'm going [planning] to visit Europe this summer.
- ◎ B I plan to visit Europe this summer.

b）公の地位にある人

〈社長は来月辞任する予定です〉
- ☆ A The CEO's going to resign next month.
- ◎ B The CEO's supposed to resign next month.
- ◎ C The CEO's planning to resign next month.
- ◎ D The CEO plans to resign next month.
- ○ E The CEO's to resign next month.
- △ F The CEO's due to resign next month.
- △ G The CEO's scheduled to resign next month.

         ▽ H The CEO's slated to resign next month.
         ❖ 「確実に」というニュアンスは E, H が一番強い．2 番目は A, 3 番目は G.
  2 《(飛行機など) 公共の輸送機関》
  〈飛行機は 5 時に着く予定です〉
         ☆ A The plane's going to arrive at 5:00.
         ☆ B The plane's supposed to arrive at 5:00.
         ◎ C The plane's scheduled to arrive at 5:00.
         ◎ D The plane's due to arrive at 5:00.
         ○ E The plane's to arrive at 5:00.
         △ F The plane's expected [slated] to arrive at 5:00.
         × G The plane plans to arrive at 5:00.
  3 《会議・行事など》
  〈会合は 10 時に始まる予定です〉
         ◎ A The meeting's supposed [scheduled] to start at 10:00.
         ◎ B The meeting's going to start at 10:00.
         △ C The meeting's due to start at 10:00.
         △ D The meeting's to start at 10:00.

世慣れた
  〈彼は世慣れています〉
         ◎ A He's street-wise.
         ◎ B He's street-savvy.
         ○ C He's street-smart.

(…と)呼ばれる →レッテルをはられる

予防薬
  〈これは結核の予防薬です〉
         ◎ A This is a preventive [preventative] medicine against tuberculosis.
         ◎ B This is a preventative against tuberculosis.
         × C This is a preventive against tuberculosis.
         ❖ C が辞典に出ているが使われていない．

予約
  1 《ホテル》
  a) 一般に
  〈私はホテルの予約をしてあります〉
         ☆ A I have a hotel reservation.
         ◎ B I have a reservation for a hotel.
         ○ C I have a hotel room reserved [booked].
  b) ホテルの名を明示するとき
  〈私はヒルトンに部屋を予約しています〉
         ◎ A I have a reservation for [at] the Hilton.
         ◎ B I have a room reserved at the Hilton.
         ○ C I have a room booked at the Hilton.
  2 《歯医者》
  〈私は歯医者に予約をしてあるんです〉
         ◎ A I have a dental [dentist] appointment.
         ◎ B I have an appointment with my dentist.
  3 《医者》
  〈私は医者に予約をしてあるんです〉
         ◎ A I have a doctor's appointment.

○ B I have an appointment with my doctor.
  4 《弁護士》
〈私は弁護士に会う予約をしてあるんです〉
    ◎ A I have an appointment with my lawyer.
    × B I have a lawyer's appointment.
    ❖ Bの型は歯科医と医師以外には使えない．→2, 3
予約する
  1 《動作の場合》
〈ヒルトンに部屋を予約しよう〉
    ◎ A Let's reserve a room at the Hilton.
    ◎ B Let's make a reservation [make reservations] for a room at the Hilton.
    ○ C Let's book a room at the Hilton.
    △ D Let's have a room reserved at the Hilton.
    △ E Let's make a booking for a room at the Hilton.
    △ F Let's secure a room in advance at the Hilton.
    × G Let's engage [bespeak] a room in advance at the Hilton.
    ❖(1) Gは和英辞典に出ているが全く使われていない．
    ❖(2) 1部屋を予約する場合でも，単数，複数ともによく使われている．
  2 《状態の場合》
〈テーブルは全部予約されています〉
    ◎ A We're all booked up.
    ◎ B We're full.
    ◎ C All the tables're reserved.
    △ D All the tables're booked (up).
寄りかかる
  1 《壁に》
〈壁に寄りかからないで下さい〉
    ◎ A Don't lean against [on] the wall.
    ◎ B Don't stand against the wall.
  2 《人に》
〈私に寄りかからないで下さい〉
    ◎   Don't lean against [on, over] me.
  3 《車に》
〈私の車に寄りかからないで下さい〉
    ◎ A Please don't lean on [over, against] my car.
    ◎ B Please don't stand against my car.
    × C Please don't lean yourself on my car.
    ❖ Cが辞典に出ているが使われていない．
夜
  1 《夜》
  a) 日没時（6時頃〜就寝時）
〈夜，電話を下さい〉
    ◎ A Please call me in the evening.
    × B Please call me at night.
  b) 9時頃〜10時頃
〈夜遅く私に電話しないで下さい〉
    ◎ A Please don't call me late at night.
    △ B Please don't call me late in the evening.

❖何時までが早い夜か遅いかは個人差があるので9時～10時は人により違う。したがって，a），c）と重複する。

c) 9時頃～12時前

〈夜電話しないで下さい〉

◎ A Please don't call me at night.
× B Please don't call me in the evening.

d) 昼を念頭において述べるとき

〈ニューヨークの夜というツアーに参加しよう〉

◎ A Let's join a tour called "New York by night".
○ B Let's join a tour called "New York at night".
▽ C Let's join a tour called "New York in the night".
▽ D Let's join a tour called "New York during the night".

e) 昼と対照して述べるとき

〈夜の新宿は昼とは完全に違います〉

◎ A Shinjuku at night's [during the night's, in the evening's] completely different than in the daytime [in the day, during the day].
○ B Shinjuku by night's completely different from by day.

2 《「夜中」(12時過ぎから2時くらいまで)》

a) 習慣的なことを述べるとき

〈私の頭は夜中が一番調子がいいんです〉

☆ A I do my best thinking late at night.
○ B I do my best thinking in the wee hours of the morning.
△ C I do my best thinking in the small hours of the morning.
△ D I do my best thinking during [in] the night.

b) 非習慣的内容を述べるとき

〈夜中に大きな地震がありました〉

◎ A There was a major earthquake during [in] the night.
○ B There was a major earthquake at night.

(…に)よると

1 《公の機関・政府が主語のとき》

〈CIAによるとイラクはすでに大量の核兵器を持っているそうである〉

◎ A According to the CIA, Iraq already has a lot of nuclear weapons.
◎ B The CIA says, Iraq already has a lot of nuclear weapons.
○ C The CIA's saying, Iraq already has a lot of nuclear weapons.

2 《私人が主語のとき》

〈父によるとイラクはすでに大量の核兵器を持っているそうである〉

◎ A My father says Iraq already has a lot of nuclear weapons.
○ B My father's saying Iraq already has a lot of nuclear weapons.
○ C In my father's opinion Iraq already has a lot of nuclear weapons.
△ D According to my father Iraq already has a lot of nuclear weapons.

喜んで

1 《パーティーにビジネス上の知人から招待されたとき》

a) 女性の場合

・強く応答するとき

〈ブラウン氏：今度の金曜日にパーティーをやるんです。ご主人とご一緒にいらっしゃいませんか〉

Mr. Brown: We're going to have a party this Friday. Would you like to come with your husband?

〈喜んで〉

- ◎ A That'd [That'll] be fantastic.
- ◎ B Sure, I'd love to.
- ◎ C I'd love to.
- ◎ D That sounds fantastic.
- ◎ E Sounds terrific.
- ◎ F That'd [That'll] be terrific.
- ◎ G That sounds terrific [great].
- ◎ H Sounds great.
- ◎ I That'd be great.
- ○ J That'll be great.
- △ K That's terrific [fantastic. great].

・控え目に応答するとき
〈喜んで〉
- ◎ A That'd [That'll] be nice.
- ◎ B Sounds nice.
- ◎ C That sounds nice.
- ○ D I'd [I'll] be glad to.
- ○ E I'd [I'll] be happy to.
  - ❖(1) D, E は義務で招待を受けるという響きがある．
  - ❖(2) 控え目に応答するときは男女で表現の違いはない．

b) 男性の場合
・強く反応するとき
〈喜んで〉
- ◎ A That'd [That'll] be great.
- ◎ B That sounds great.
- ◎ C Sounds great.
- ○ D That'd [That'll] be terrific.
- ○ E That sounds terrific.
- ○ F Sounds terrific.
- ○ G I'd love to.
- △ H That'd [That'll] be fantastic.
- △ I Sure, I'd love to.
- △ J Sounds fantastic.

2 《初めてのデートに誘われたとき》
a) 女性の場合
・喜びを強く出して誘いを受けるとき
〈ビル：私と一緒に映画に行きませんか〉
Bill: Would you like to go to the movies with me?
〈喜んで〉
- ◎ A That sounds great.
- ◎ B That'd [That'll] be great.
- ◎ C Sounds great.
- ◎ D I'd love to.
- ○ E That'd [That'll] be terrific.
- ○ F That'd [That'll] be fantastic.
- ○ G That sounds terrific [fantastic].
- ○ H Sounds terrific [fantastic].
- ○ I Sounds like a great [good] idea.
- △ J I'd [I'll] be happy to.

- ❖(1) E〜H は他の表現より強い．
- ❖(2) That'd be のほうが That'll be より強い響きがある．

・控え目に応答するとき
〈喜んで〉
- ☆ A That'd [That'll] be nice.
- ◎ B That sounds nice [good].
- ◎ C Sounds nice [good].
- ○ D That'd [That'll] be good.
- △ E That'd [That'll] be O.K.
    - ❖(1) E が一番弱い．
    - ❖(2) 控え目に応答するときは男女で表現の違いはない．

b) 男性の場合
・喜びを強く出して誘いを受けるとき
〈ジェーン：私と一緒に映画に行きませんか〉
Jane: Would you like to go to the movies with me?
〈喜んで〉
- ◎ A That sounds great.
- ◎ B That'd [That'll] be great.
- ◎ C Sounds great.
- ◎ D Sounds like a good [great] idea.
- △ E That'd [That'll] be terrific.
- △ F I'd love to.
- ▽ G That'd [That'll] be fantastic.

3 《頼みごとに応じるとき》

a) 無条件に応じる場合
〈ジェーン：今度の土曜日引っ越すのを手伝っていただけますか〉
Jane: Could you help me move out this Saturday?
〈ビル：もちろん，喜んでお手伝いしますよ〉
Bill:
- ◎ A Sure, I'd be happy to (help).
- ◎ B Sure, I'd be glad to (help).
- ◎ C Sure, I'd be willing to help.
- × D Sure, I'd be willing to (do).
    - ❖A, B の方が C よりも喜んで手伝うという響きがある．

b) 条件付きで応じる場合
〈ジェーン：今度の土曜日引っ越すのを手伝っていただけますか〉
Jane: Could you help me move out this Saturday?
〈ビル：土曜日は手伝えないけど日曜日にしてくれれば喜んでお手伝いしますよ〉
Bill:
- ◎ A I can't help you on Saturday but I'll be willing to if you can make it Sunday.
- ◎ B I can't help you on Saturday but I'd be happy to do if you can make it Sunday.
- ◎ C I can't help you on Saturday but I'd be glad to (do it) if you can make it Sunday.
- ○ D I can't help you on Saturday but I'll be willing to do it if you can make it Sunday.
- ○ E I can't help you on Saturday but I'd be happy to if you can make it Sunday.

世論
1 《ある国の世論》
〈アメリカの世論は外国の製品に対して輸入課徴金をかけることに賛成のようだ〉
- ◎ A American opinion seems to favor a surcharge tax on foreign goods.
- × B American public opinion seems to favor a surcharge tax on foreign goods.
  - ❖国名を明示しない場合は，Public opinion is against the new policy.（世論は新しい政策に反対している）などのように言う。

2 《国際世論》
〈朴政権は国際世論の圧力のためにほとんどの政治犯の釈放を余儀なくされた〉
- ◎ A The Park regime was forced to set most political prisoners free because of pressure from international opinion.
- × B The Park regime was forced to set most political prisoners free because of pressure from international public opinion.

弱い
1 《暖房器具などの設定について言う場合》
a）普通に述べるとき
〈暖房を弱くしておいて下さい〉
- ◎ A Keep the heat (set) on low.
- ◎ B Keep the heat turned down low.
- ◎ C Keep the heat turned down.
- ◎ D Keep the heat down.

b）「最も」の意味で述べるとき
〈暖房を一番弱くしておいてください〉
- ☆ A Keep the heat all the way down.
- ☆ B Keep the heat down all the way.
- ◎ C Keep the heat turned down all the way.
- ◎ D Keep the heat turned all the way down.
- ◎ E Keep the heat on low.
- ◎ F Keep the heat turned [running] on low.
- ○ G Keep the heat going on low.
- ○ H Keep the heat going all the way down.
- ○ I Keep the heat going down all the way.
  - ❖E〜Gは「今より弱くしておいて下さい」に意味でも使われている。どちらであるかは話の前後で分かる。

2 《音量について言う場合》
〈テレビの音を弱くしておいて下さい〉
- ◎ A Keep the TV turned down.
- ◎ B Keep the TV turned down low.
- ◎ C Keep the TV volume set on low.
- ◎ D Keep the TV volume turned down low.
- ◎ E Keep the TV down.

呼んでくる
1 《タクシーを》
〈タクシーを呼んできてくれますか〉
- ◎ A Will you get a cab for me?
- ◎ B Will you get me a cab?
- ◎ C Will you go get a cab for me?
- ◎ D Will you call a cab?

- ○ E Will you get a cab?
- ○ F Will you go get a cab?
- × G Will you bring a cab for me?
  - ❖(1) A～F は「通りへ出ていって呼んでくる」の意味だけでなく「通りにいるとき手をあげてタクシーを呼ぶ」という意味でも非常によく使われている.
  - ❖(2) C は「電話をかけてタクシーを呼ぶ」の意味でも非常によく使われている. A, B, E もこの意味で C ほどではないがよく使われている.

2 《人を》

〈ジムを呼んできてくれますか〉

- ◎ A Will you go get Jim (for me)?
- ◎ B Will you get Jim (for me)?
- ○ C Will you get me Jim?
- △ D Will you bring Jim to me?
- × E Will you go bring Jim (for [to] me)?
- × F Will you go bring me Jim?
- × G Will you bring Jim?
  - ❖ B の get Jim for me は「電話口に出す」という意味で,「ジムに連絡してくれますか」の意味でもよく使われている.

〔ら〕

ライバル
1 《会社》
〈うちは売上高の点で、ライバル会社に追い越されたくないんです〉
　☆ A We don't want to fall behind the competition sales-wise.
　◎ B We don't want to fall behind the competitors sales-wise.
　○ C We don't want to fall behind the rivals [the rival companies] sales-wise.
　❖ Aの the competition は集合名詞．したがって，1つの会社については使えない．
2 《個人》
〈彼は私のライバルです〉
　◎ A He's my rival.
　◎ B I'm competing with him.
　○ C He's my competitor.
　○ D He and I're competing.

楽天的な
〈彼は将来のことを心配していません．楽天的なんです〉
　◎ He isn't worried about his future. He's happy-go-lucky [easy-going].

楽観的な
1 《特定のことを楽観的に見る場合》
〈彼はガンの回復の見通しについて楽観視しています〉
　◎ A He's optimistic [upbeat] about the prospect of his recovery from cancer.
　◎ B He's very hopeful about the prospect of his recovery from cancer.
　❖ Aの方がBより楽観視している度合いが強い．
2 《根拠もなく楽観的に考える場合》
〈新しいビジネスを始めるときに，先行きを楽観的に考えすぎてはいけない〉
　◎ Don't look at your future through rose-colored glasses when you start a new business.

ラリる →マリファナ 3

乱用する
〈彼は権力を乱用したために批判されたんです〉
　◎ A He was criticized for abusing his power.
　○ B He was criticized for misusing his power.
　× C He was criticized for shafting [wronging, misemploying, misappropriating] his power.
　❖ BはAより意味が弱い．

〔り〕

利益

1 《投資・株などが主語のとき》
〈これに投資すればうんと利益が出るでしょう〉
- ◎ A This investment'll give you a good return.
- ◎ B This investment'll bring you a good return [profit].
- ◎ C This investment'll bring a good return.
- ◎ D This investment'll make you good money.
- ◎ E This investment'll make good money for you.
- ◎ F This investment'll make a good return.
- ◎ G This investment'll bring you in a good return.
- ○ H This investment'll give [make] you a good profit.
- △ I This investment'll make a good return for you.
- × J This investment'll give you a good gain.

2 《ビジネス・商品が主語のとき》
〈このビジネスはうんと利益が出るでしょう〉
- ◎ A This business'll make you a good profit.
- ◎ B This business'll make you good money.
- ◎ C This business'll make good money [a good profit] for you.
- ◎ D This business'll bring you good money [a good profit].
- ○ E This business'll bring you in good money [a good profit].
- ○ F This business'll bring good money [a good profit] for you.

3 《利益の合計がある額に達することをいう場合》
〈今年うちの会社の利益は約30億ドルに達するでしょう〉
- ◎ A Our company's profits will run to about 3 billion dollars this year.
- △ B Our company's returns [gains] will run to about 3 billion dollars this year.
- × C Our company's proceeds [gaining] will run to about 3 billion dollars this year.
  - ❖(1) C が辞典に出ているが使われていない.
  - ❖(2) B の gains には金銭だけでなくビル，土地，特許，プロジェクトなど多くのものが意味される.

4 《チャリティなどの収益についていう場合》
〈私たちは資金集めの催しの利益の1/10を孤児たちに寄付する予定です〉
- ☆ A We're going to donate one-tenth of the proceeds from the fund-raiser to orphans.
- ◎ B We're going to donate one-tenth of the profits from the fund-raiser to orphans.
- △ C We're going to donate one-tenth of the gains from the fund-raiser to orphans.
- ▽ D We're going to donate one-tenth of the returns from the fund-raiser to orphans.

5 《ひと儲けする》
〈彼は最近取引でひと儲けしたんです〉
- ◎ A He made a killing [an easy money] on a deal recently.

○　B　He made a quick money on a deal recently.
6　《ボロ儲けする》
〈彼は最近取引でボロ儲けしたんです〉
◎　A　He made a killing on [from] a deal recently.
◎　B　He made a ton of money on [from] a deal recently.
◎　C　He made tons of money on [from] a deal recently.
◎　D　He made big bucks [a bundle] on a deal recently.
○　E　He made big bucks [a bundle] from a deal recently.
△　F　He made money hand over first on a deal recently.
❖(1) F は He's making money hand over first. (彼は一儲けしているんです) のように進行形ではよく使われている．
❖(2) A, B, C は他より強いニュアンスがある．

陸軍　→軍隊 2
履行する
〈あなたは契約を履行しなければならない〉
☆　A　You have to honor [fulfill] the contract.
◎　B　You have to stick with [to, by] the contract.
◎　C　You have to follow [live up to, abide by] the contract.
○　D　You have to make good on the contract.
○　E　You have to go by [carry out, adhere to, keep, hold to] the contract.
▽　F　You have to be faithful to the contract.
❖辞典に F が出ているがまれ．

離婚する
1　《夫婦が離婚した事実のみ述べる場合》
〈メアリーとビルは先月離婚したんです〉
◎　A　Mary and Bill (got) divorced last month.
◎　B　Mary and Bill got a divorce last month.
◎　C　Mary and Bill have (gotten) divorced last month.
◎　D　Mary and Bill have gotten a divorce last month.
2　《一方が望んだことを明示する場合》
〈メアリーはビルと先月離婚したんです〉
◎　A　Mary got a divorce from Bill last month.
◎　B　Mary divorced Bill last month.
◎　C　Mary got divorced from Bill last month.
◎　D　Mary has gotten a divorce from Bill last month.
◎　E　Mary has divorced Bill last month.
◎　F　Mary has gotten divorced from Bill last month.

リサイクルショップ　→店 17
リストラする
1　《人員削減を意味する場合》
a）大企業
〈うちはリストラしなければならないんです〉
☆　A　We have to downsize.
◎　B　We have to cut back on staff [the workforce].
◎　C　We have to cut down on staff [the workforce].
◎　D　We have to cut the staff [the workforce, the personnel].
○　E　We have to cut back on personnel [the staff, the personnel].
○　F　We have to cut down on personnel [the staff, the personnel].

- ○ G　We have to cut personnel [staff].
- △ H　We have to decrease (the) staff [personnel].
- △ I　We have to reduce (the) staff [personnel].
  - ❖ the workforce は会社全体, staff, personnel は全体にも使えるが会社のある部門のニュアンスが強い.

b）中企業

〈うちはリストラしなければならないんです〉

- ☆ A　We have to downsize.
- ◎ B　We have to cut back on staff.
- ◎ C　We have to cut down on staff.
- ◎ D　We have to cut the staff [the personnel].
- ○ E　We have to cut back on personnel [the staff, the personnel].
- ○ F　We have to cut down on personnel [the staff, the personnel].
- △ G　We have to decrease (the) staff [personnel].
- △ H　We have to reduce (the) staff [personnel].

c）小企業

〈うちはリストラしなければならないんです〉

- ◎ A　We have to let some people go.
- ◎ B　We have to let go of some people.
- ○ C　We have to let some employees go.
- ○ D　We have to let go of some employees.
- ○ E　We have to cut back [down] on the number of employees.

2　《規模縮小を意味する場合》

〈うちはリストラしなければならないんです〉

- ◎ A　We have to restructure.
- ◎ B　We have to restructure [reorganize] our company.
- △ C　We have to reorganize.

理想の

1　《結婚相手としての男性》

〈私は理想の男性が現れるのを待っています〉

- ☆ A　I'm waiting for Mr. Right.
- ◎ B　I'm waiting for the perfect man [guy] for me.
- ◎ C　I'm waiting for the right man [guy] (for me).
- ◎ D　I'm waiting for the perfect guy.
- ◎ E　I'm waiting for the ideal man [guy] for me.
- ○ F　I'm waiting for the perfect [right, ideal] husband for me.
- ○ G　I'm waiting for the ideal man.
- △ H　I'm waiting for the perfect man.
- △ I　I'm waiting for the ideal guy.
- △ J　I'm waiting for the perfect [right, ideal, model] husband.

2　《結婚相手としての女性》

〈私は理想の女性を探しているんです〉

- ◎ A　I'm looking for the right woman [girl, person, one] for me.
- ◎ B　I'm looking for the perfect woman [one] for me.
- ○ C　I'm looking for the perfect wife [person] for me.
- ○ D　I'm looking for the right wife for me.
- △ E　I'm looking for the ideal woman [person, one] for me.
- △ F　I'm looking for the model woman [wife] for me.
- △ G　I'm looking for Miss Right for me.

3 《理想の妻》
〈彼女は私にとって理想の妻です〉
- ☆ A She's the perfect woman for me.
- ◎ B She's the right woman [girl] for me.
- ◎ C She's the perfect girl [wife] for me.
- ○ D She's the right wife for me.
- △ E She's the ideal wife for me.
- △ F She's the [a] model wife for me.
- △ G She's an ideal woman for me.

4 《ビジネスの理想の場所》
〈新宿はこの仕事には理想の場所です〉
- ☆ A Shinjuku's the perfect location for this business.
- ◎ B Shinjuku's the right location [place] for this business.
- ◎ C Shinjuku's the ideal area for this business.
- ○ D Shinjuku's the right area for this business.
- ○ E Shinjuku's the perfect place [area] for this business.
- ○ F Shinjuku's the ideal location [place] for this business.

5 《住宅街として理想の場所》
〈原宿は住むには理想の所です〉
- ☆ A Harajuku's the perfect neighborhood [location] to live in.
- ◎ B Harajuku's the perfect area to live in.
- ◎ C Harajuku's the right location [neighborhood, area] to live in.
- ◎ D Harajuku's the ideal neighborhood [location, place, area] to live in.
- ○ E Harajuku's the perfect place to live in.
- △ F Harajuku's the model place to live in.
- ▽ G Harajuku's the model neighborhood [location, area] to live in.

6 《理想の大学》
〈ハーバードは私には理想の大学です〉
- ◎ A Harvard's the perfect [ideal, right] college for me.
- ▽ B Harvard's the model college for me.

7 《理想の子供》
〈日本での理想の子供はアメリカの理想の子供とは違います〉
- ☆ A Being the perfect child in Japan's different from in America.
- ◎ B Being the ideal child in Japan's different from in America.
- ○ C Being the model child in Japan's different from in America.
- × D Being the right child in Japan's different from in America.

離党する

1 《単に事実のみを述べるとき》
〈彼らは共和党を離党したんです〉
- ◎ A They left the Republican Party.
- ○ B They withdrew from [bolted] the Republican Party.
  - ❖ B の bolt には「素早く脱党する」というニュアンスがある．

2 《大きな影響があると述べるとき》
〈彼らは共和党を離党した〉
- ◎ A They deserted the Republican Party.
- ◎ B They walked out on the Republican Party.
- ○ C They abandoned the Republican Party.
  - ❖(1) A，B，C は集団で，または大物が 1 人で離党するときにも使える．

❖(2) A, C には「不忠実にも」というニュアンスがある．
3 《政策の不一致が原因というニュアンスのとき》
〈彼らは共和党を離党した〉
◎ A They broke away from the Republican Party.
△ B They broke with the Republican Party.
❖ともに政策をめぐって対立し，感情的に離党したという響きがある．また，離党を思いとどまらせたのを振り切ったというニュアンスもある．

リバウンドする
1 《リバウンドした程度に言及しないとき》
〈私は体重がリバウンドしてしまったんです〉
◎ A I've gained the weight back.
◎ B I've put the weight back on.
△ C I've regained the weight.
× D I've rebounded the weight.
❖rebound は体重には使えない．失意，失敗，病気などから「立ち直る」の意味ではよく使われている．詳細は「立ち直る」の項を参照のこと．

2 《少し体重が増えたとき》
〈私は少しリバウンドしてしまったんです〉
◎ A I've gained some [a little] weight back.
○ B I've put a little weight back.
△ C I've put back on a little weight.

3 《完全に元に戻ってしまったとき》
〈私は体重がリバウンドしてしまったんです〉
◎ A I've gained all the weight back.
◎ B I've put all the weight back on.
○ C I've gained the weight completely.
○ D I've regained all the weight back.

リベート
〈彼は建築会社からリベートを取った疑いで逮捕された〉
◎ A He was arrested on suspicion of getting a bribe from the construction company.
○ B He was arrested on suspicion of a kickback from the construction company.

理由
1 《…する理由》
〈私は彼女と離婚する理由がいくつもあるのです〉
◎ A I have several reasons to divorce her.
◎ B I have several reasons for divorcing her.
◎ C I have several reasons (why) I have to divorce her.
◎ D There are several reasons (why) I have to divorce her.
◎ E There are several reasons for me to divorce her.

2 《That（それが）が主語のとき》
〈それが私が彼女と離婚する理由なのです〉
☆ A That's why I have to divorce her.
◎ B That's the reason I have to divorce her.
○ C That's the reason why I have to divorce her.

3 《…できない理由》
〈クリス：どうしてパーティーに来なかったの〉
Chris: Why didn't you come to the party?

〈リンダ：行きたかったのよ．行けなかった理由は頭痛がひどかったからよ〉
- ☆ A I wanted to. The thing was, I had a terrible headache.
- ◎ B I wanted to. The trouble was, I had a terrible headache.
- ○ C I wanted to. The problem was, I had a terrible headache.
- ▽ D I wanted to. The reason why I didn't go was, I had a terrible headache.

流感　→病気 25

流行を追う

〈私は流行の先端を追うことには興味はありません〉
- ◎ A I'm not interested in keeping up with the latest style [fashion, fashion trends, trends].
- ○ B I'm not interested in being stylish [in style].

流暢に　→上手です 1 b)

流通している

1 《貨幣》

〈アメリカのドルは世界中に流通しています〉
- ◎ A The American dollar is circulated [used] all over the world.
- ◎ B The American dollar is in circulation all over the world.
- ◎ C The American dollar is being used [circulated] all over the world.

2 《商品》

〈アメリカではこういうふうに商品が流通しています〉
- ◎ A This is how merchandise is distributed in America.
- △ B This is how merchandise is circulated in America.
- ▽ C This is how merchandise is in distribution [circulation] in America.

3 《新聞・雑誌》

〈多くのアメリカの新聞と雑誌は日本で流通しています〉
- ◎ A A lot of American newspapers and magazines are (being) circulated in Japan.
- ◎ B A lot of American newspapers and magazines are in circulation in Japan.
- △ C A lot of American newspapers and magazines are distributed in Japan.
- × D A lot of American newspapers and magazines are in distribution in Japan.

流派

1 《芸術》

〈彼は絵の新しい流派を起こしました〉
- ◎　He created a new school [style] of painting.

2 《学派》

〈彼は経済学の新しい流派をつくりました〉
- ◎ A He created a new school of economics.
- × B He created a new style of economics.

両側に

1 《道などの両脇の場合》

〈通りの両側に美しいお屋敷がたくさんあります〉
- ◎ A There are a lot of beautiful mansions on either [each] side of the street.
- ◎ B There are a lot of beautiful mansions on both sides of the street.

2 《廊下などの両端の場合》
〈廊下の両端に非常口があります〉
- ◎ A There's an emergency exit at either end of the hallway.
- × B There's an emergency exit at both ends of the hallway.
- × C There's an emergency exit at each end of the hallway.

良心の呵責
〈彼を首にした後，良心の呵責を感じてならなかった〉
- ◎ A I felt guilty [bad] after I fired him.
- ◎ B I felt sorry for him after I fired him.
- × C I had a pang [twinge] of conscience after firing him.
- × D I had a qualms [compunction] after firing him.
  - ❖(1) C, D が辞典に出ているが使われていない．
  - ❖(2)「良心の呵責」という日本語のニュアンスに一番近いのは A．

利用する
1 《チャンス》
〈このチャンスを利用しなさい〉
- ☆ A Use this chance.
- ◎ B Take advantage of this chance.
- ○ C Make use of this chance.
- △ D Utilize this chance.
- × E Avail yourself of this chance.
- × F Turn this chance to good account.
  - ❖ E, F が辞典に出ているが使われていない．堅い文章でもまれ．

2 《最大限に》
a) チャンス
〈このチャンスを最大限に利用しなさい〉
- ◎ A Make the best [the most] of this chance.
- ○ B Use this chance to your best advantage.

b) 失敗
〈この失敗を最大限に利用しなさい〉
- ◎ A Make the most of this failure.
- ○ B Make the best of this failure.
- ○ C Use this failure to your best advantage.
  - ❖ 多くの辞典，慣用辞典に逆境・不利などのときは B を使い，その他は A を使うと解説しているが，英語の慣用事実を歪曲している．

3 《交通機関》
〈私は職場へオックスフォード線を利用しています〉
- ◎ A I take the Oxford Line to work.
- ○ B I use the Oxford Line to work.
- △ C I go [get] to work on the Oxford Line.

4 《皇族など特別高い地位を持っている人との関係》
〈彼は皇族との関係を利用している〉
- ◎ A He's putting [He puts] his relationship with the royal family to good use.
- ◎ B He's using [He uses] his relationship with the royal family to his advantage.
- × C He's using [He uses] his relationship with the royal family to good use.
- × D He turns his relationship with the royal family to good use.

料理
〈私はフランス料理が好きなんです〉
- ◎ A I like French food.
- ○ B I like French cuisine.
- △ C I like French dishes.
    - ❖(1) dishes は「料理」の訳語が辞典に出ているが，あまり使われていない．「～料理」の food が繰り返されるとき，繰り返しを避けるために使われる程度．
    - ❖(2) B の cuisine は French cuisine, Italian cuisine, Japanese cuisine のようにデリカシーな料理に使われている．

緑黄色野菜 →野菜 1
旅行する
1 《ツアーによる団体旅行の場合》
〈彼らはヨーロッパを旅行しています〉
- ◎ A They're on a tour of Europe.
- ◎ B They're touring Europe.
- ◎ C They're taking a tour of Europe.
- ○ D They're touring [traveling] around Europe.
- ○ E They're making [taking] a trip around Europe.

2 《個人でルートを決める旅行の場合》
〈彼らはヨーロッパを旅行しています〉
- ☆ A They're taking [making] a trip around Europe.
- ☆ B They're traveling around Europe.
- ◎ C They're touring (around) Europe.
- △ D They're taking a tour of Europe.
- ❖「ツアー」の項も参照のこと．

旅行代理店 →店 23
臨機応変に
〈彼はその種の問題なら何でも臨機応変に処理できる〉
- ◎ A He's capable of handling [dealing with] all such problems as the situation demands.
- ◎ B He's capable of handling all such problems as the occasion demands.
- × C He's capable of handling all such problems on an ad hoc basis.
- ❖ C が辞典に出ているが使われていない．

隣接している
1 《一般的に言うとき》
〈彼らの別荘は湖に隣接しています〉
- ◎ A Their vacation home borders (on) [sits on] the lake.
- ◎ B Their vacation home is on the lake.
- △ C Their vacation home is adjacent to the lake.
- ▽ D Their vacation home touches on [abuts on, adjoins, neighbors on] the lake.

2 《隣接していることを強調して言うとき》
〈彼らの別荘は湖にすぐ隣接しています〉
- ◎ A Their vacation home's right [directly] on the lake.
- ◎ B Their vacation home sits right on the lake.
- ○ C Their vacation home's immediately on the lake.
- △ D Their vacation home's just on the lake.

3 《国と国が隣接しているとき》
〈カナダはアメリカの北で隣接しています〉
- ☆ A Canada borders America to the north.
- ◎ B Canada borders America in the north.
- ○ C Canada borders America on the north.

淋病 →病気 26

〔る〕

類似点

1 《歴史上のつながりがあるとき》
〈日本と中国の間には多くの類似点がある〉
- ◎ A There are a lot of parallels between Japan and China.
- × B There are a lot of similarities between Japan and China.
  - ❖ A は日本と中国の過去の歴史から現在までを念頭において述べるときに使われる。B は現在のことだけを念頭において述べるときであれば、非常によく使われている。

2 《歴史上のつながりがないとき》
〈英語と日本語の間よりも、英語と中国語の間の方が、構造上類似点がたくさんある〉
- ◎ A There are more similarities between English and Chinese structure-wise than between English and Japanese.
- × B There are more parallels between English and Chinese structure-wise than between English and Japanese.

3 《2つの学問を対比させるとき》
〈ケインズは物理学と経済学の類似点を対比させるのが好きだった〉
- ◎ A Keynes liked to make analogies [parallels] between physics and economics.
- ○ B Keynes liked to make similarities between physics and economics.

〔れ〕

礼儀

1 《「礼儀を知らない」と言うとき》
〈彼は礼儀を知らない〉
- ◎ A He has bad [no] manners.
- ◎ B He's impolite.
- ○ C He's bad-mannered [ill-mannered, discourteous].
  - ❖ B は中の上、または上流階級の間で広く使われている。

2 《「礼儀正しい」と言うとき》
〈彼は礼儀正しいです〉
- ◎ A He's well-mannered.
- ◎ B He has good manners.
- ◎ C He's polite.
- ○ D He's courteous.
  - ❖ A は中の上、または上流階級の成人の間で非常に広く使われている。

3 《「礼儀上…する」という意味のとき》
〈私は礼儀上そう言ったんです〉
- ◎ A I said it out of courtesy.
- ◎ B I said it to be polite.
- ○ C I said it out of politeness.
- △ D I said it to be courteous.

礼拝する
1 《旧教・新教・ユダヤ教》
〈私は少なくとも1ヶ月に1度礼拝します〉
- ◎ I go to service(s) at least once a month.

2 《旧教・新教》
〈私は少なくとも1ヶ月に1度礼拝します〉
- ◎ A I go to church at least once a month.
- ◎ B I attend worship (service) at least once a month.
- △ C I go to [attend] the chapel at least once a month.

3 《旧教のみ》
〈私は少なくとも1ヶ月に1度礼拝します〉
- ◎ I go to [attend] mass at least once a month.

4 《新教のみ》
〈私は少なくとも1ヶ月に1度礼拝します〉
- ◎ I attend service at least once a month.

5 《新教・ユダヤ教》
〈私は少なくとも1ヶ月に1度礼拝します〉
- ◎ I attend services at least once a month.

6 《ユダヤ教のみ》
〈私は少なくとも1ヶ月に1度礼拝します〉
- ◎ I go to the synagogue at least once a month.

7 《イスラム教》
〈私は少なくとも1ヶ月に1度礼拝します〉
- ◎ I go to the mosque at least once a month.

8 《モルモン教・仏教・ユダヤ教》
〈私は少なくとも1ヶ月に1度礼拝します〉
- ◎ A I go to the temple at least once a month.
- × B I go to [attend] divine service(s) at least once a month.
   - ❖ B は辞典に出ているが使われていない．

歴史的に重要な
〈これはわが国の最も歴史的に重要な場所のひとつです〉
- ◎ A This is one of the most historic places in this country.
- ◎ B This is one of the most important places in this country's history.

レッテルをはられる
〈彼は女たらしのレッテルをはられている〉
- ☆ A They say he's a womanizer.
- ◎ B He's branded as a womanizer.
- ○ C He's labeled as a womanizer.
   - ❖(1) 意味としては B が一番強い．C，A の順で弱くなる．
   - ❖(2) C は改まった響きがあるので，会話では A，B ほど使われていない．しかし，堅い文章では非常によく使われている．

劣等感
〈彼はあなたに劣等感を持っているんです〉

◎ A He thinks he isn't as good as you.
◎ B He thinks he's worse than you.
◎ C He thinks he's inferior to you.
◎ D He thinks you're better than him.
○ E He's intimidated by you.
○ F He has an inferiority complex towards [to] you.
△ G He has a sense of inferiority towards [to] you.

レポート
〈私はレポートを書くのに忙しいんです〉
　　◎　I'm busy writing a paper [a report].
　　❖ paper は学生の課題のレポート，report は社会人の報告書などについて使われている．

連想する
1 《聞き手に尋ねるとき》
〈シカゴと聞くと何を連想しますか〉
　　◎ A What do you associate Chicago with?
　　◎ B What do you think of when you hear about Chicago?
　　◎ C What does Chicago remind you of?
2 《広く一般の人に尋ねるとき》
〈人はシカゴと聞いたら何を連想するのですか〉
　　◎ A What's Chicago associated with?
　　◎ B What do people think of when you hear about Chicago?

連帯保証人
1 《一般に》
〈彼が私の家の連帯保証人なんです〉
　　◎ A He's the cosigner for my house.
　　○ B He's the cosigner on my house.
2 《親子など親密な間柄の場合》
〈お父さん，銀行ローンを申し込むんですけど，連帯保証人になってくれますか〉
Son:
　　◎ A I'm going to apply for a bank loan. Would you cosign for me, Dad?
　　○ B I'm going to apply for a bank loan. Would you be my cosigner, Dad?
　　× C I'm going to apply for a bank loan. Would you be my guarantor, Dad?
　　× D I'm going to apply for a bank loan. Would you guarantee my loan, Dad?
　　❖ D は他人同士，特にビジネスピープルの間ではよく使われている．

連帯保証をする
〈父が私の車のローンの連帯保証をするんです〉
　　◎ A My father'll cosign for [on] my car loan.
　　○ B My father'll cosign my car loan.
　　○ C My father'll be the cosigner for my car loan.
　　× D My father'll be the guarantor [guarantee] for my car loan.
　　❖ D の guarantee は親子ではなくビジネスの世界ではよく使われている．

レンタカー屋　→店 20
連中　→悪い連中
レントゲン検査　→検査 5

連絡する
  1 《人の場合》
  a) 電話口へ呼び出すとき
  〈弁護士に連絡を取ってくれますか〉
    ◎ A Will you get my lawyer for me?
    ○ B Will you try to reach [get through to] my lawyer for me?
  b) 伝言するだけのとき
  〈弁護士に連絡を取ってくれますか〉
    ◎ A Will you get in touch with my lawyer?
    ◎ B Will you get a hold [ahold] of my lawyer?
    ○ C Will you contact my lawyer?
    ❖ C は少し改まった響きがある．
  2 《電車・飛行機などの交通機関》
  〈この電車は中野で東西線と連絡していますか〉
    ◎ A Does this train connect with the Tozai Line at Nakano?
    ○ B Does this train connect to the Tozai Line at Nakano?
    × C Does this train get a connection with the Tozai Line at Nakano?
    ❖ C が辞典に出ているが使われていない．

〔ろ〕

廊下
  1 《品物の所在地を言及するとき》
  〈ダニエル：自動販売機はどこにありますか〉
  Daniel: Where's the vending machine?
  〈マーク：廊下にあります〉
  Mark:
    ☆ A It's in the hallway.
    ◎ B It's in the hall.
    △ C It's in the corridor.
    × D It's in the passageway [passage].
    ❖ D が辞典に出ているが「廊下」の意味では使われていない．
  2 《通行が言及されているとき》
  〈ダニエル：ブラウンさんの事務所はどこですか〉
  Daniel: Where's Mr. Brown's office?
  〈マーク：この先です〉
  Mark:
    ◎ A It's down the hall.
    ○ B It's down the hallway.
    △ C It's down the corridor.
    × D It's down the passageway [passage].
    ❖ D が辞典に出ているが使われていない．

ろう学校 →各種学校 13
老後の備え
  〈私は老後に備えて貯金しなければならない〉
    ◎ A I have to save money for retirement.
    ○ B I have to save money for my retirement.

- △ C I have to save money for my old age.
- ▽ D I have to save money for my old years.
  - ❖これらは仕事をしている人が退職した後のことを述べるときの表現.

老人ホーム

1 《医療施設が特にないもの》
〈両親は老人ホームに住んでいます〉
- ◎ A My parents're living in a senior citizens' home.
- ◎ B My parents're living in a retirement home.
- ○ C My parents're living in an old age home.
- ○ D My parents're living in an adult community.
- ○ E My parents're living in a home for elderly people.
- △ F My parents're living in a home for old people [old folks, the aged].

2 《医療施設があるもの》
〈両親は老人ホームに住んでいます〉
- ◎ A My parents're living in a nursing home.
- △ B My parents're living in an assisted living facility.
- △ C My parents're living in a home for assisted living.

老婆心
〈老婆心から忠告するんだが,君はその取引から手を引いた方がいいよ〉
- ◎ A As a friend let me advise you to get out of the deal.
- ◎ B As one friend to another let me advise you to get out of the deal.
- × C Out of friendship let me advise you to get out of the deal.
  - ❖(1) C が辞典に出ているが使われていない.
  - ❖(2) 日本語の「老婆心から」にあたる英語の表現はないが, A, B がそれに近い.

〔わ〕

ワープロを打つ
　1　《打てるかどうかを尋ねるとき》
　〈あなたはワープロを打てますか〉
　　　◎　A　Can you use a word processor?
　　　○　B　Can you type on a word processor?
　2　《打つ技能について尋ねるとき》
　〈どのくらいの速度でワープロを打てますか〉
　　　◎　　　How fast can you type on [use] a word processor?

歪曲する
　〈事実を歪曲するな〉
　　　◎　A　Don't distort [twist] the facts.
　　　×　B　Don't pervert [contort] the facts.

わいせつな
　1　《写真・記事》
　〈この種の雑誌はわいせつな写真がいっぱいだから読みません〉
　　　☆　A　I don't read this kind of magazines because they're full of dirty [X-rated] pictures.
　　　◎　B　I don't read this kind of magazines because they're full of pornographic pictures.
　　　○　C　I don't read this kind of magazines because they're full of indecent [obscene, filthy, nasty, raunchy] pictures.
　　　○　D　I don't read this kind of magazines because they're full of porn [porno].
　　　△　E　I don't read this kind of magazines because they're full of lewd [smutty] pictures.
　2　《映画のわいせつな所》
　〈わいせつな所はすべて映画からカットされた〉
　　　☆　A　All the dirty [X-rated] parts were cut out of the film.
　　　◎　B　All the obscene [nasty, porn, pornographic, filthy, raunchy] parts were cut out of the film.
　　　○　C　All the indecent [lewd, porno] parts were cut out of the film.
　　　△　D　All the smutty parts were cut out of the film.

分かる
　1　《言っていること》
　〈私はあなたが言っていることは分かります〉
　　　☆　A　I understand you.
　　　◎　B　I get [got, follow] you.
　　　○　C　I understand [get, got, follow] what you're saying.
　2　《言わんとしていること》
　〈彼が言わんとしていることが分かりますか〉
　　　◎　A　Can you figure out [understand] what he's driving at?
　　　○　B　Can you see [get] what he's driving at?
　　　△　C　Can you make out what he's driving at?
　　　△　D　Can you get the picture of what he's driving at?

3 《友人・同僚・家族など気を使う必要のない人にだけ使える「分かった」》
〈分かった〉
- ☆ A Gothcha.
- ☆ B Got you.
- ◎ C I hear that.
- ○ D I hear you.

4 《「見分ける」という意味の「分かる」》
〈どうして彼が中国人だと分かるのですか〉
- ◎ A How can you tell that he's Chinese?
- ○ B How do you know that he's Chinese?
- ▽ C How can you distinguish [discern] that he's Chinese?

5 《「覚えている」という意味の「分かる」》
〈私たちは長年お互いに会っていなかったので私は彼が分からなかったんです〉
- ◎ A We didn't see each other for many years, so I couldn't recognize [remember] him.
- ○ B We didn't see each other for many years, so I couldn't place him.
- ○ C We didn't see each other for many years, so I couldn't figure out who he was.

6 《「認知する」という意味の「分かる」》
〈彼は背が高いから人込みの中でもすぐ分かりますよ〉
- ☆ A You can spot him easily even among the crowd because he's tall.
- ◎ B You can see [find] him easily even among the crowd because he's tall.
- ◎ C You can pick him out easily even among the crowd because he's tall.
- ○ D You can recognize [locate] him easily even among the crowd because he's tall.

7 《「予測する」という意味の「分かる」》
〈明日何が起こるか誰にも分かりません〉
- ☆ A You can't tell what's going to happen tomorrow.
- ◎ B You don't know what's going to happen tomorrow.
- ◎ C Nobody knows what's going to happen tomorrow.
- ◎ D Nobody can tell what's going to happen tomorrow.
- ○ E It's impossible to tell what's going to happen tomorrow.
- ○ F You can't say what's going to happen tomorrow.
- △ G There is no telling [knowing] what's going to happen tomorrow.
  ❖英文法書ではGだけを出しているが使用頻度は高くない.

8 《「鑑賞できる」という意味の「分かる」》
〈私はクラシック音楽が分かります〉
- ◎ A I enjoy classical music.
- ◎ B I can appreciate classical music.
- ○ C I have an ear for classical music.
- △ D I can understand classical music.

9 《説明されたときまたは質問文にexplanationがあったときの「分かる」》
〈ビル:彼の説明は分かりましたか〉
Bill: Was his explanation clear to you?
〈トム:はい, 分かりました〉
Tom:
- ☆ A Yes, I get the picture.
- ◎ B Yes, I got the picture.

◎ C Yes, I understand [get] it.
○ D Yes, I got it.
△ E Yes, I see it.

10 《教授・牧師・上司など敬意を表することが求められている人に「お分かりいただけますか」と尋ねるとき》
〈お分かりいただけますか〉

◎ A Am I making myself clear?
◎ B Am I expressing my answer clearly?
○ C Is my answer clear?
○ D Am I making my point clear?

11 《ぶっきら棒に「分からない」と答えるとき》
〈リンダ：世界で一番大きい銀行はどこなの〉
Linda: What's the world's largest bank?
〈ビル：分からないよ〉
Bill:

◎ A I don't know.
◎ B I have no idea.
◎ C Beats me.
◎ D You got me.
○ E You've got me.
△ F Search me.
△ G I'm in a fog.
❖ F は50歳以上の人の間で非常によく使われている．

12 《「全く分からない」と述べたいとき》
〈彼の講演はチンプンカンプンで全く分からなかった〉

◎ A His lecture was Greek to me.
○ B His lecture was all Greek to me.
△ C His lecture was over my head.
△ D His lecture was beyond me.
△ E His lecture was Hebrew to me.

13 《「悟る」という意味の「分かる」》
〈彼と話して私はその点で全く間違っていることが分かりました〉

☆ A After talking to him, I realized that I was wrong on that point.
◎ B After talking to him, I figured out [found out, saw, found] that I was wrong on that point.
○ C After talking to him, I noticed [sensed] that I was wrong on that point.
△ D After talking to him, I felt that I was wrong on that point.

14 《「明らかになる」という意味での「分かる」》
〈彼が脱税していたことが分かったんです〉

☆ A They found out he was cheating on his taxes.
◎ B They discovered he was cheating on his taxes.
○ C His tax evasion's been found out.
○ D It's come out that he was cheating on his taxes.
△ E His tax evasion's come out.
△ F His tax evasion's been brought to light.
△ G His tax evasion's come to light.

15 《「判明する」という意味の「分かる」》
〈彼が容疑者であることが分かった〉

☆ A He turned out to be the suspect.
◎ B It turned out he was the suspect.
○ C He proved to be the suspect.
○ D It turned out that he was the suspect.
× E It proved that he was the suspect.

16 《分からせる》
〈私は自分の論点を彼らに分からせることができませんでした〉
◎ A I couldn't get my point across [through] to them.
◎ B I couldn't make them understand my point.
○ C My point didn't get across [through] to them.

17 《読めば分かる》
〈ロン：契約書に書いてあることを説明してくれますか〉
Ron: Would you explain to me what the lease says?
〈不動産屋：読めば分かりますよ．自分で読んで下さい〉
Realtor:
◎ It's self-explanatory. Read it yourself.

別れる

1 《日常的に人と》
〈彼らと昨夜どこで別れたのですか〉
◎ A Where did you leave them last night?
△ B Where did you split up [part company] with them last night?

2 《恋人と》
a) 別れたことを述べるとき
〈2人は別れたんです〉
◎ A They've broken up.
○ B They've split up.
× C They've parted company.
❖ C は辞典に出ているが使われていない．

b) 別れたいと言うとき
〈私はあなたと別れたいんです〉
◎ A I'm breaking up with you.
◎ B I don't want to see you anymore.
○ C I want to break up with you.
× D I'm leaving you.
× E I'm separating from you.
× F I want to leave you.
❖ D, F の leave は恋人のときは使えない．E の separate は結婚している2人が「別居する」の意味．

3 《配偶者・同棲相手と》→離婚する
〈私はあなたと別れます〉
◎ A I'm leaving you.
× B I'm breaking [splitting] up with you.

若々しい

1 《外見》
〈私の祖母は75歳なのですけれど，外見が若々しいんです〉
◎ A Even though she's seventy-five years old, my grandmother has a youthful appearance.
○ B Even though she's seventy-five years old, my grandmother has a young appearance.

2 《態度・考え方》
〈彼女の気持ちは若い〉
    ◎ A She has a young mind.
    ○ B She has a youthful mind.
脇役にまわる
〈社長と一緒にいるときは脇役にまわったほうがいいよ〉
    ☆ A You'd better take a backseat when you're with the boss.
    ◎ B You'd better play a supporting role when you're with the boss.
    ○ C You'd better play a secondary [subordinate, supportive] role when you're with the boss.
    △ D You'd better play second fiddle when you're with the boss.
わざわざ…する
〈あなたはわざわざ彼らを空港へ車で送る必要はありません〉
    ☆ A You don't need to bother driving them to the airport.
    ◎ B You don't need to go through [go to] the trouble of driving them to the airport.
    ○ C You don't need to take the trouble to drive them to the airport.
    × D You don't need to trouble yourself to drive them to the airport.
      ❖ Dが辞典に出ているが使われていない．
忘れ物はないですか
〈忘れ物はないですか〉
    ☆ A Do you have everything?
    ◎ B Do you have all your stuff?
    ○ C Do you have everything with you?
    ○ D Don't forget your stuff.
    △ E Do you have all your stuff with you?
忘れる
  1 《…するのを忘れる》
〈私は昨夜彼に電話するのを忘れたんです〉
    ☆ A I forgot to call him last night.
    ◎ B I forgot I was going to call him last night.
    ○ C I forgot about calling him last night.
    △ D I forgot that I'd call him last night.
    × E I forgot that I should call him last night.
  2 《…したことを忘れる》
〈私はあの本を彼に貸したのを忘れていたんです〉
    ◎ A I forgot I lent him that book.
    ○ B I forgot I'd lent him that book.
    ○ C I forgot that I lent him that book.
    ○ D I forgot about lending him that book.
  3 《…したことを忘れない》
 a）ロマンチックな内容
〈私は今日ここであなたとお話ししたことを決して忘れません〉
    ◎ A I'll never forget talking to you here today.
    ◎ B I'll always remember talking to you here today.
    ◎ C I'll never forget I talked to you here today.
      ❖(1) Bが一番ロマンチックな響きが強い．Aが2番，Cはロマンチックな意味にもそうでないときにも使われる．
      ❖(2) Aのforget+〜ingの型はforgetより時間的に前の経験を述べるときに

使われ，普通，否定未来形で使う．
b）仕事上の内容
〈私はあなたとお話ししたことを決して忘れません〉
- ◎ A I'll never forget about talking to you.
- ◎ B I'll never forget that I talked to you.
- ◎ C I'll never forget I've talked to you.

4 《物を忘れてくる》
a）場所に言及しないとき
〈私は傘を忘れてきたんです〉
- ◎ A I forgot [left] my umbrella.
- ○ B I left my umbrella behind.
- × C I left my umbrella back.

b）場所に言及するとき
〈私は傘を電車に忘れてきたんです〉
- ◎ A I left [forgot] my umbrella (back) on the train.
- ○ B I left my umbrella behind on the train.

私が言いたいことは
〈私が言いたいことはあなたは彼らに妥協しないほうがいいということです〉
- ◎ A My point [The point, The bottom line] is you'd better not compromise with them.
- ◎ B What I'm trying to say [get at] is you'd better not compromise with them.

私が知っている限りでは（…ない）
〈外国人：東京にはスペインレストランがありますか〉
Foreigner: Are there any Spanish restaurants in Tokyo?
〈日本人：私の知っている限りではありません〉
Japanese:
- ☆ A Not that I know of.
- ◎ B Not as far as I know.
- ○ C As far as I know, there aren't.
- ○ D To the best of my knowledge, there aren't.

❖ A, B, C, D はニュアンス上の違いはない．

私には
1 《自分用にはという意味の場合》
〈そのドレスは私には（私が着るには）派手すぎます〉
- ☆ A That dress's too flashy for me.
- ◎ B That dress's too flashy for my taste.
- ◎ C That dress's too flashy for me to wear.
- ○ D For me that dress's too flashy.

2 《自分の目にはという意味の場合》
〈そのドレスは私には（私に言わせれば）派手すぎます〉
- ☆ A That dress's too flashy to me.
- ◎ B That dress's too flashy in my opinion.
- ◎ C In my opinion that dress's too flashy.
- ○ D To me that dress's too flashy.

割り引いて聞く
〈彼の言うことは割り引いて聞かなければ駄目です〉
- ◎ A You have to take what he says with a grain of salt.
- ◎ B Don't take what he says at face value.

悪い連中
〈彼らは悪い連中だ〉
- ◎ A They're bad people.
- ◎ B They're a bad group [crowd].
- ○ C They're a bad bunch.
- ○ D They're bad guys.
- △ E They're a bad lot.
- △ F They're bad company.

悪気はなかった
〈私には悪気はなかったんです〉
- ◎ A My intensions were good.
- ◎ B I didn't mean [intend] any harm.
- ◎ C I meant no harm.
- ◎ D No offense (was meant).
- ○ E My intentions were honorable.
- ○ F I didn't mean [intend] any offense.

悪口を言う
〈彼女はあなたの悪口を言っていましたよ〉
- ☆ A She said bad things about you.
- ☆ B She bad-mouthed you.
- ◎ C She said horrible [terrible] things about you.
- ◎ D She spoke [talked] bad about you.
- ◎ E She talked about you behind your back.
- ○ F She spoke [talked] badly about you.
- ○ G She said bad [horrible, terrible] stuff about you.
- △ H She said awful things about you.
- △ I She spoke horribly [terribly] about you.
- △ J She talked horribly [terribly] about you.
- △ K She talked shit about you.
- × L She spoke ill of you.
- ❖ L は辞典に出ているが使われていない.

我を忘れる
〈私はうれしくて我を忘れてしまいました〉
- ◎ A I was beside myself with joy.
- ◎ B I was so excited I couldn't contain myself.

ワンマン
〈彼は会社でワンマンだ〉
- ◎ A He's a tyrant at the office.
- △ B He's a dictator at the office.
- × C He's an autocrat.
- × D He's a one man at the office.
- × E He's a strong man.
- ❖(1) C, D, E が辞典に出ているが使われていない.
- ❖(2) E は「実力者」の意味ではよく使われている.

ワンルームマンション →マンション 3

英語語句索引

・主に注で説明・言及がある英語の語句の索引である.
・「air 放送する 1」は, air という語についての注・説明が見出し「放送する」の1の項にあることを示す.

a few いく人かの 1
according as (…に) よって
according to (…に) よって
acquaint 〈get acquainted〉 知り合う 1
after …後に 1
air 放送する 1
all or nothing 〈It's all or nothing.〉 一か八か 1
alumni association 同窓会 1 c)
analyst 評論家
appear ようだ 3
around まわり 1
associate 地位 6 a)
at that time その頃は 1
at the front of 前に 1 i)
back then その頃は 1
be なる 2 b)
be damaged 傷つく 7 b)
be delighted うれしい 4 a)
be delighted 知り合う 7 a)
be hurt けがをする 2
be injured けがをする 2
be running 経営者 2
be wounded けがをする 2
beach 海岸
beauty 美人 2
become なる 2 b)
begin 始める 1
big 大きい 2
bill 支払う 1 a)
Blackout! 停電 3
board 〈the board of directors〉 取締役 4
bomb 〈the bomb〉 すばらしい
bound 必ず…する 1
breach of contract 違反 1
bring 連れて行く 4
broadcast 放送する 1
bureaucrat 官僚 2 a)
bureaucrat 役人 1
care for 好きです 6
CEO 取締役 4
certain 必ず…する 1
certainly 必ず…する 1
chairman 取締役 4
chairman 地位 9 a)
change 換える
Chapter 11 破産する 2
Chapter 13 破産する 2
charming 感じのいい 2
cheap 安い 1
check 支払う 1 a)
Chief Executive Officer 取締役 4
city hall 公務員 3
city hall 役所 1
civil servant 公務員 1 a)
cleaners 店 12
close down 閉鎖する 1
college 大学 1
commentator 評論家
company 会社 2, 4
company 客 1 a), b)
competent きれる 1
confirm 確認する 4 a), b)
Congratulations! おめでとう 1, 2
contagious 伝染する 2
convenient 便利な 1
convince 説得する 1
cook 支度する 1 b)
Could you ...? …していただけますか 2
country 国家 3
county 公務員 2

critic　評論家
crop(s)　収穫物
cuisine　料理
damage 〈be damaged〉　傷つく　7 b)
dating service　結婚紹介所
day 〈in those days〉　その頃は　1
delight 〈be delighted〉　うれしい　4 a)
delight 〈be delighted〉　知り合う　7 a)
depending on　（…に）よって
diet　体重を減らす　1
director　地位　13
director 〈the board of directors〉　取締役　4
dirt　泥　1
dishes　料理
distributor　卸売り
downtown　…街　6
downtown　中心　1 a)
drug store　店　37
dump　振られる　1
elope　駆け落ちする　2
employee　地位　7 b)
enterprise　企業　2
equipment　器具　1
ethics　プライド　2
evidence　証拠
executive　取締役　4
face　面している　3
factory　工場　1
faculty　教えている
faculty　地位　20 b
faith　信念　2
female　女性…
fever　病気　19
few 〈a few〉　いく人かの　1
finish　卒業する［させる］　1 b)
firm　会社　3
forest　道　5 b)
forget　＋〜ing　忘れる　3 a)
fraud　詐欺（師）　3 b),4
front 〈at the front of〉　前に　1 i)
front 〈in front of〉　前に　1 a)
front 〈in front of〉　前に　1 i)
front 〈in the front of.　前に　1 i)
gain　利益　3
game　試合　1 b)

garage　店　19 b)
garden　庭　2
general practitioner　医者　10
get　なる　1 b),2 b)
get　急ぐ　8
get　支度する　1 b)
get　連れて行く　6
get acquainted　知り合う　1
get in　着く　2
get to know　知り合う　2,4
get to know you　知り合う　7 b)
get to work　始める　2
gift　プレゼント　1
go　なる　3
good　難しい　5
government employee　公務員　1 a)
government officer　公務員　1 a)
government officer　役人　1
government official　公務員　1 a)
government official　役人　1
government worker　公務員　1 a)
graduate　卒業する［させる］　1 b)
hand in　提出する　1
harvest　収穫物
health spa　スポーツクラブ　3
hot water　湯　2
housing project　公営住宅
How late ...?　何…　1 c)
hurry up to　急ぐ　1
hurt 〈be hurt〉　けがをする　2
ill　病気　1
in　…後に　1
in front of　前に　1 a)
in front of　前に　1 i)
in the front of　前に　1 i)
in those days　その頃は　1
inexpensive　安い　3
infamous　有名な　2
infectious　伝染する　2
injure 〈be injured〉　けがをする　2
instrument　器具　1
intern　医者　10
internist　医者　10
It's all or nothing.　一か八か　1
just　まだ　1 a)
kindergarten　…学生　5
know 〈get to know you〉　知り合う　7 b)
know 〈get to know〉　知り合う　2,4

large　大きい　2
laundry　店　12
lawful　法律で認められた　1
lean　やせている　1
lease　賃貸する　2 b)
leave　卒業する［させる］　1 b)
leave　別れる　2 b)
let　賃貸する　2 b)
light　信号　2
look　ようだ　3
look out onto　面している　3
look out over　面している　3
major　専攻する　2
make　なる　1 b)
make sure　確認する　4 a),b)
manager　地位　13
market　市場　1
match　試合　1 b)
meet　偶然　1
most　ほとんどの②　2 b)
most of　ほとんどの②　2 b)
most of　ほとんどの②　3
mud　泥　1
municipal government　公務員　3
nation　国家　1,3
national　国立の　1,2
neighborhood　近所　1
only　まだ　1 a)
over　…しながら　1 a),b)
over　(…と) 比較して　1,2
overwhelm　呆然とする　2
parking　駐車場　1
payroll　社員　1
personnel　リストラする　1 a)
personnel　社員　1
persuade　説得する　1
pharmacy　店　37
plant　工場　1
practicable　実行可能な
practical　実行可能な
prefecture　公務員　2
prepare　支度する　2
present　プレゼント　1
present　プレゼントする
president　取締役　4
pride　プライド　1
produce　野菜　8
project　公営住宅
proof　証拠

property　地価
propose　提案する　1
public official　役人　1
public servant　公務員　1 a)
public servant　役人　1
purse　財布
rationalize　合理化する　1
rationalize　正当化する　1
rebound　リバウンドする　1
rent　賃貸する　2 b)
return　帰る　12 b)
right away　すぐ　3
right now　すぐ　3
right off　すぐ　3
route　道　1 a)
run 〈be running〉　経営者　2
scenery　景色　1
secretary　職業　13 c)
see　偶然　1
see　見る・診る　10 b)
see　送る　1 f)
seem　ようだ　3
send in　提出する　1
separate　別れる　2 b)
several　いく人かの　1
ship　送る　2 b)
shore　海岸
shut down　閉鎖する　1
sick　病気　1
sick society　病んだ　1
slam　衝突する　1
smash　衝突する　1
some　いく人かの　1
spa　スポーツクラブ　3
staff　リストラする　1 a)
staff　社員　1
start　始める　1
state　国家　1
state　国立の　1
stomach　痛い　6 a)
stoplight　信号　2
streamline　合理化する　1
strike　殴る　1
suggest　提案する　1
supplier　卸売り
supplies　器具　1
supply　器具　1
tab　支払う　1 a)
temperature　病気　19 b)

the board of directors　取締役　4
the bomb　すばらしい
then　その頃は　1
thin　やせている　1
time ⟨at that time⟩　その頃は　1
tooth　痛い　3 a)
translator　職業　1 a)
turn　なる　3
turn in　提出する　1
university　大学　1
uptown　山の手
version　意見　2
villa　別荘　5
walk　送る　1 f)
wedding party　結婚式　2
what　どこの　2 c)
which　どこの　2 c)

wholesale company　卸売り
wholesale store　卸売り
Will you ...?　…していただけますか　2
within　…後に　1
woman　女性…
woods　道　5 b)
work force　リストラする　1 a)
work force　社員　1
working staff　社員　1
wound ⟨be wounded⟩　けがをする　2
yard　庭　2
You may as well.　…するといいでしょう　6
You name it.　何から何まで
your wife　奥様　1 a), b)

[著者略歴]

市橋敬三（いちはし けいぞう）
米国オハイオ州マウントユニオン大学を優等（cum laude）で卒業。アメリカ英語およびアメリカ学の研究を行った後，ニューヨークのビジネス界で過ごした。
日本でボストンアカデミーを開校，英会話上達には文法の知識が不可欠であることを説いてきた。現在，同校校長。
著書は，『必ずものになる話すための英文法』シリーズ4冊（研究社），『TOEIC Test』シリーズ6冊（ビジネス社），『魔法の英文法』シリーズ5冊（南雲堂），『TOEICテスト速習本』シリーズ5冊（南雲堂）など，約50点ある。

さいしん えい ご ひょうげん じ てん
最新アメリカ英語表現辞典

Ⓒ ICHIHASHI Keizo 2003

NDC 837　706p　天地20cm

初版第1刷発行	2003年4月30日
第2刷発行	2003年10月10日

著者	いちはしけいぞう　市橋敬三
発行者	鈴木一行
発行所	株式会社大修館書店

〒101-8466 東京都千代田区神田錦町3-24
電話 03-3295-6231 販売部/03-3294-2355 編集部
振替 00190-7-40504
[出版情報] http://www.taishukan.co.jp

装丁者	岡崎健二
印刷所	壮光舎印刷
製本所	牧製本

ISBN4-469-04163-7　　　　　　　Printed in Japan

Ⓡ本書の全部または一部を無断で複写複製（コピー）することは，著作権法上での例外を除き，禁じられています。